Synchronization Patterns

The *Scoped Locking* C++ idiom (325) ensures that a lock is acquired when control enters a scope and released automatically when control leaves the scope, regardless of the return path from the scope.

The *Strategized Locking* design pattern (333) parameterizes synchronization mechanisms that protect a component's critical sections from concurrent access.

The *Thread-Safe Interface* design pattern (345) minimizes locking overhead and ensures that intra-component method calls do not incur 'self-deadlock' by trying to reacquire a lock that is held by the component already.

The *Double-Checked Locking Optimization* design pattern (353) reduces contention and synchronization overhead whenever critical sections of code must acquire locks in a thread-safe manner just once during program execution.

Concurrency Patterns

The *Active Object* design pattern (369) decouples method execution from method invocation to enhance concurrency and simplify synchronized access to objects that reside in their own threads of control.

The *Monitor Object* design pattern (399) synchronizes concurrent method execution to ensure that only one method at a time runs within an object. It also allows an object's methods to cooperatively schedule their execution sequences.

The *Half-Sync/Half-Async* architectural pattern (423) decouples asynchronous and synchronous service processing in concurrent systems, to simplify programming without unduly reducing performance. The pattern introduces two intercommunicating layers, one for asynchronous and one for synchronous service processing.

The *Leader/Followers* architectural pattern (447) provides an efficient concurrency model where multiple threads take turns sharing a set of event sources in order to detect, demultiplex, dispatch, and process service requests that occur on the event sources.

The *Thread-Specific Storage* design pattern (475) allows multiple threads to use one 'logically global' access point to retrieve an object that is local to a thread, without incurring locking overhead on each object access.

PATTERN-ORIENTED SOFTWARE ARCHITECTURE

PATTERN-ORIENTED SOFTWARE ARCHITECTURE

Patterns for Concurrent and Networked Objects

Volume 2

Douglas Schmidt
University of California, Irvine

Michael Stal
Siemens AG, Corporate Technology

Hans Rohnert
Siemens AG, Germany

Frank Buschmann
Siemens AG, Corporate Technology

John Wiley & Sons, Ltd
Chichester · New York · Weinheim · Brisbane · Singapore · Toronto

Copyright © 2000 by John Wiley & Sons, Ltd, The Atrium, Southern Gate,
Chichester, West Sussex PO19 8SQ, England

Telephone (+44) 1243 779777

Email (for orders and customer service enquiries): cs-books@wiley.co.uk
Visit our Home Page www.wileyeurope.com or www.wiley.com

Reprinted with corrections April 2001 and April 2004, August 2005, January 2006

Other Wiley Editorial Offices

John Wiley & Sons Inc., 111 River Street, Hoboken, NJ 07030, USA

Jossey-Bass, 989 Market Street, San Francisco, CA 94103-1741, USA

Wiley-VCH Verlag GmbH, Boschstr. 12, D-69469 Weinheim, Germany

John Wiley & Sons Australia Ltd, 33 Park Road, Milton, Queensland 4064, Australia

John Wiley & Sons (Asia) Pte Ltd, 2 Clementi Loop #02-01, Jin Xing Distripark,
Singapore 129809

John Wiley & Sons (Canada) Ltd, 22 Worcester Road, Etobicoke, Ontario M9W 1L1

Wiley also publishes its books in a variety of electronic formats. Some content that appears
in print may not be available in electronic books.

British Library Cataloguing in Publication Data

A catalogue record for this book is available from the British Library

ISBN-10: 0–471–60695–2 (hbk)
ISBN-13: 978–0471–60695–6 (hbk)

Typeset in 9/13pt Palatino.
Printed and bound in Great Britain by Biddles Ltd, King's Lynn, Norfolk
This book is printed on acid-free paper responsibly manufactured from sustainable
forestation, for which at least two trees are planted for each one used for paper
production.

For Sonja, Mom, and Dad

Douglas C. Schmidt

For Gisela

Michael Stal

For Regine, Anja, Sandro, and Nicolas

Hans Rohnert

For Bebé[†] and Martina

Frank Buschmann

† Bebé, July 3, 1999

Table of Contents

Foreword

Middleware is the set of services, protocols, and support utilities providing the 'plumbing' that makes modern distributed systems and applications possible—the infrastructure that underlies web services, distributed objects, collaborative applications, e-commerce systems, and other important platforms. Not long ago, the term middleware was rarely heard, and middleware developers were rarer still. But over the past decade, the term, the research and practice, and its impact have become ubiquitous. Yet, until now, there has not been a book describing how to construct networked and concurrent object-oriented (OO) middleware, so its design has remained something of a black art. This book demystifies middleware construction, replacing the need to have an expert looking over your shoulder with well-reasoned, empirically-guided accounts of common design problems, forces, successful solutions, and consequences.

As is true for most concepts, nailing down the boundaries of middleware is hard. Conventionally, it consists of the software needed to build systems and applications, yet is not otherwise an intrinsic part of an operating system kernel. But it is not always possible to find middleware where you first look for it: middleware can appear in libraries and frameworks, operating systems and their add-ons, Java virtual machines and other run-time systems, large-grained software components, and in portions of end-products such as web services themselves.

This book is not a textbook surveying middleware or the types of applications and distributed system architectures you can devise using middleware. It instead presents a pattern language that captures the design steps leading to the construction of the OO communication support involved in most middleware. Many of the patterns described in this book also have utility in both higher-level and lower-level systems and applications that are not based directly upon middleware.

This book emphasizes practical solutions over theoretical formalisms. The basic ideas behind many presented patterns are well-known to experienced system developers—for example, dispatching, demultiplexing, callbacks, and configuration—and are sometimes variants of more general OO patterns—for example, proxies, adapters, and facades. This book's main contribution centers on in-depth engineering solutions based upon these ideas. Middleware developers must resolve a wide range of forces including throughput, responsiveness, dependability, interoperability, portability, extensibility, and accommodating legacy software. The diversity and severity of these forces accounts for the complexity of middleware patterns, as opposed to those seen in smaller-scale OO applications and concurrent programming.

The multitude of such forces, combined with years of engineering experience, often lead to a multitude of design considerations and engineering trade-offs separating an idea from its expression in middleware frameworks. The pattern description format used in this book helps to simplify this process by presenting solutions as series of concrete design steps. Many of these steps in turn invoke additional patterns. Together they form a pattern language, enabling developers to traverse from pattern to pattern while designing services and applications.

As mentioned by the authors, some of the ideas and techniques discussed in this book are complementary to those seen for example in W. Richard Stevens's pioneering books (e.g., [Ste98]) on network programming. The main point of departure is the unrelenting focus on higher-level design issues. Rather than, for example, discussing the ins and outs of the Unix select() call, this book explains how to build a composable and flexible framework—a Reactor—based on select() and other operating system calls.

One of the implicit themes of this book is how to apply the bits and pieces of functionality dealing with I/O, threading, synchronization, and event demultiplexing offered by contemporary platforms as the foundation for constructing higher-level frameworks and components. The primary emphasis on C/C++ on Unix and Microsoft operating systems does not detract from this theme. For example, Java programmers will find a few minor disconnects in cases where Java already directly implements some of the patterns discussed in this book, for example, Scoped Locking, or provides frameworks structured in accord with particular implementations of patterns, such as the JavaBeans framework's support of configurable components, as well as a few where Java lacks access to underlying system mechanisms, such as synchronous event demultiplexing.

However, readers most familiar with Java, Smalltalk, and other OO programming languages will still profit from the central ideas conveyed by the patterns, can better appreciate how and why some became directly supported in language features and libraries, and will be able to construct useful components based upon other patterns. As an example, until the advent of `java.nio`, Java did not provide access to system constructs useful for asynchronous I/O. However, after referring to a description of the Proactor pattern described in this book, I once put together a Java version that simulated the demultiplexing step via a simple spin-loop thread that checked for I/O availability across multiple channels. This was less efficient, but was perfectly adequate within its intended usage context.

Over the years, some of the accounts in this book, such as Reactor, have evolved from descriptions of design inventions to design patterns. Everyone constructing portable OO middleware has written or used at least one Wrapper Facade. But early presentations of several other patterns now contained in this book also discussed novel contributions about their design. It was at first a bit uncertain whether such descriptions should be considered as patterns, which must be time-proven, independently (re)discovered solutions. However, over time, the authors and the OO middleware community have become more and more confident that the patterns in this book do indeed capture the essence of key forces and design issues, and have witnessed the described solutions being used over and over again across diverse usage contexts.

I invite you to share in this phenomenon. By reading—and especially, using—the material in this book, you'll see why pattern names such as Reactor and Proactor have become as common among OO middleware developers as have Decorator and Observer among OO GUI developers.

Doug Lea

State University of New York at Oswego

About This Book

Patterns have taken the software development community by storm. Software developers have been enthusiastic about patterns ever since the seminal work *Design Patterns – Elements of Reusable Object-Oriented Software* [GoF95]. Its successors, such as the Pattern Languages of Programming Design (PLoPD) series [PLoPD1] [PLoPD2] [PLoPD3] [PLoPD4] and *A System of Patterns* [POSA1][1] have further fanned the burning interest in patterns kindled originally by earlier work on software idioms [Cope92], patterns for building architectures [Ale79] [AIS77], and patterns for cultural anthropology [Bat97].

This book, *Patterns for Concurrent and Networked Objects*, is the second volume in the *Pattern-Oriented Software Architecture* (POSA) series. Like its predecessor, *A System of Patterns* [POSA1], it documents patterns and best practices that represent concrete, well-proven and useful techniques for building industrial-strength software systems. These patterns and best practices can and have been applied to applications in a wide range of domains, including telecommunications and data communications, financial services, medical engineering, aerospace, manufacturing process control, and scientific computing. They also form the basis of popular distributed object computing middleware, such as CORBA [OMG98c], COM+ [Box97], Java RMI [WRW96], and Jini [Sun99a].

Moreover, all the patterns in this book build on the same solid conceptual foundation as those in the first POSA volume. For example, we use the same pattern categorization schema, the same pattern description format, and present examples and known uses in multiple programming languages, including C++, Java, and C.

---

1. We reference *A System of Patterns* as [POSA1] rather than by author. The same is true for this book, which we reference as [POSA2]. We use this convention to avoid a particular POSA volume being associated with a single author in reader's minds, in particular the first name on the book's cover.

Patterns for Concurrent and Networked Objects thus follows the same philosophy and path as *A System of Patterns* and has the same 'look and feel'.

In contrast to *A System of Patterns*, however, which covered a broad spectrum of general-purpose patterns, this book has a more specific focus: *concurrency* and *networking*. All the patterns in this book center on these two areas, allowing us to discuss many topics related to concurrency and networking in more depth than would be possible if the book contained patterns from many unrelated domains. The patterns in this book therefore complement the general-purpose patterns from *A System of Patterns* in these increasingly important areas of software development.

Yet we focus on *general, domain-independent* patterns for concurrent and networked applications and middleware. Our goal is to increase the likelihood that the patterns in this book will help projects in your daily work. Therefore, we do not cover patterns in this book that are *specific* to a particular application domain, such as those in [DeBr95] [Mes96] [ACGH+96], which address networking aspects that pertain to the telecommunication domain.

By focusing on general domain-independent patterns for concurrency and networking, this book also complements existing literature in concurrent network programming and object-oriented design:

- Literature on concurrent network programming generally focuses on the *syntax* and *semantics* of operating system APIs, such as Sockets [Ste98], POSIX Pthreads [Lew95], or Win32 threads [Ric97], that mediate access to kernel-level communication frameworks, such as System V STREAMS [Ris98] [Rago93], available on popular operating systems. In contrast, this book describes how to *use* these APIs effectively in the design and programming of high-quality concurrent and networked systems.

- Literature that addresses higher-level software design and quality factors [Boo94] [Mey97] [DLF93] generally has not focused on the development of concurrent and networked applications. Bridging this gap is the topic of this book.

Another way in which *Patterns for Concurrent and Distributed Objects* differs from *A System of Patterns* is that its patterns constitute more than just a catalog or system of patterns. Instead, they augment each other synergistically, providing the foundation of a *pattern language* for concurrent and networked software. When combined with patterns from other patterns literature, we describe how this pattern language can and has been used to build sophisticated concurrent and networked software systems and applications, web services, and distributed object computing middleware, as well as the underlying operating system networking protocols and mechanisms.

Yet we separate the description of the individual patterns from the discussion of how they form a pattern language. The patterns themselves are first described in a self-contained manner, so that they can be applied in the context that is most useful. A subsequent chapter then describes how the patterns interact and how they are complemented by other patterns.

It is important to note, however, that many patterns in this book can be applied outside the context of concurrency and networking. To illustrate the breadth of their applicability we present known uses from other domains, such as component-based or interactive software systems. In addition, we give examples of how these patterns apply to situations experienced in everyday life.

Some patterns may be familiar, because preliminary versions of them were published in the PLoP book series [PLoPD1] [PLoPD2] [PLoPD3] [PLoPD4], and the C++ Report magazine. In this book, however, we have improved upon the earlier versions considerably:

- This is the first time they have been woven into a single document, which helps to emphasize the pattern language they express.

- We have rewritten and revised these patterns substantially based on many suggestions for improvement we received at conferences and workshops, via e-mail, as well as from intensive internal reviewing and reviews provided by our shepherds.

- The patterns have been converted to the POSA pattern format and have a consistent writing style.

Intended Audience

Like our earlier book *A System of Patterns*, this volume is intended for professional software developers, particularly those who are building concurrent and networked systems. It helps these software professionals to think about software architecture in a new way and supports them in the design and programming of large-scale and complex middleware and applications.

This book is also suitable for advanced undergraduates or graduate students who have a solid grasp of networking and operating systems, and who want to learn the core principles, patterns, and techniques needed to design and implement such systems effectively.

Structure and Content

Patterns for Concurrent and Distributed Objects can be used as a text book and read from cover to cover, or used as a reference guide for exploring the nuances of specific patterns in detail.

The first chapter, *Concurrent and Networked Objects*, presents an overview of the challenges facing developers of concurrent and networked object-oriented applications and middleware. We use a real example, a concurrent Web server, to illustrate key aspects of these domains, including service access and configuration, event handling, synchronization, and concurrency.

Chapters 2 through 5 form the main part of the book. They contain patterns, the 'real things' [U2], that codify well-established principles and techniques for developing high-quality concurrent and networked systems. We hope these patterns will be useful role models for developing your own concurrent and networked applications, and for documenting patterns that you discover.

Chapter 6, *Weaving the Patterns Together*, discusses how the patterns in Chapters 2 through 5 are interconnected. We also show how they can be connected with other patterns in the literature to form a pattern language for concurrent networked systems and middleware. As mentioned earlier, some patterns are also applicable outside the context of concurrent and networked systems. For these patterns we summarize the scope of their applicability.

Chapter 7, *The Past, Present, and Future of Patterns*, revisits our 1996 forecast on 'where patterns will go', published in the first volume of the *Pattern-Oriented Software Architecture* series. We discuss the directions that patterns actually took during the past four years and analyze where patterns and the patterns community are now. Based on this retrospection, we revise our vision about future research and the application of patterns and pattern languages.

The book ends with a general reflection on the patterns we present, a glossary of frequently used terms, an appendix of notations, an extensive list of references to work in the field, a pattern index, a general subject index, and an index of names that lists all persons who helped us shaping this book

Supplementary material related to this book is available on-line at `http://www.posa.uci.edu/`. This URL also contains links to the ACE and TAO source code that contains C++ and some Java examples for all the patterns in this book.

There are undoubtedly aspects of concurrent and networked object systems that we have omitted, or which will emerge over time when applying and extending our pattern language in practice. If you have comments, constructive criticism, or suggestions for improving the style and content of this book, please send them to us via electronic mail to `patterns@mchp.siemens.de`. We also welcome public discussion of our entire work on patterns. Please use our mailing list, `siemens-patterns@cs.uiuc.edu`, to send us feedback, comments, and suggestions. Guidelines for subscription can be found on the patterns home page. Its URL is `http://hillside.net/patterns/`. This link also provides an important source of information on many aspects of patterns, such as available and forthcoming books, conferences on patterns, papers on patterns, and so on.

Acknowledgments

It is a pleasure for us to thank the many people who supported us in creating this book, either by sharing their knowledge with us or by reviewing earlier drafts of its parts and providing useful feedback.

Champion review honors go to Regine Meunier, Christa Schwanninger, Martin Botzler, Lutz Dominick, Prashant Jain, Michael Kircher, Karl Pröse, and Dietmar Schütz, our esteemed colleagues. They spent much of their valuable time helping to review the manuscript in the countless writer's workshops we ran, thus helping us to polish and shape the final content of this book. Similarly, we are grateful to members of the Distributed Object Computing (DOC) group—Tim Harrison, Prashant Jain, Carlos O'Ryan, and Irfan Pyarali—who co-authored initial versions of six patterns in this book. Together with the four lead authors, these researchers form the POSA team at Siemens in Munich, Washington University in St. Louis, and the University of California, Irvine.

We also owe most grateful thanks to Peter Sommerlad, Chris Cleeland, Kevlin Henney, and Paul McKenney. Peter, our shepherd, reviewed all our material in depth, focusing on its correctness, completeness, consistency, and quality. Chris, Kevlin, and Paul, our peer reviewers, provided us with additional detailed feedback. All four contributed significantly to improving *Patterns for Concurrent and Networked Objects*.

We are also grateful to the Software Architecture Group at University of Illinois at Urbana Champain, including Federico Balaguer, John Brant, Brian Foote, Alejandra Garrido, Peter Hatch, Ralph Johnson, Dragos Manolescu, Brian Marick, Hiroaki Nakamura, Reza Razavi, Don Roberts, Les Tyrrell, Joseph W. Yoder, Wanghong Yuan, Weerasak Witthawaskul, and Bosko Zivaljevic, who ran writer's workshops on many POSA2 patterns. They sent comments that helped us improve the correctness and comprehensibility of the book.

Many others from around the world provided feedback on earlier versions of the book, including Giorgio Angiolini, Brad Appleton, Paul Asman, David Barkken, John Basrai, Joe Bergin, Rainer Blome, Don Box, Martina Buschmann, Tom Cargill, Chuck and Lorrie Cranor, James O. Coplien, Ward Cunningham, Gisela Ebner, Ed Fernandez, Erich Gamma, Sonja Gary, Luciano Gerber, Bob Hanmer, Neil

Harrison, Michi Henning, David Holmes, Tom Jordan, Fabio Kon, Bob Laferriere, Greg Lavender, Doug Lea, John MacMillan, Mittal Monani, Duane Murphy, Jaco van der Merwe, Michael Ogg, Bill Pugh, Dirk Riehle, Linda Rising, Wolfgang Schroeder, Richard Toren, Siva Vaddepuri, John Vlissides, Roger Whitney, and Uwe Zdun. The *Credits* section of our patterns outline how their valuable contributions helped us polish this book.

We are also heavily indebted to all members, past and present, of the DOC group at Washington University in St. Louis, the University of California, Irvine, Object Computing Inc., and Riverace, who reified, refined, and optimized all the patterns presented in this book into components and frameworks in the ACE and TAO middleware projects. This inspirational group includes Everett Anderson, Alex Arulanthu, Shawn Atkins, Darrell Brunsch, Luther Baker, Matt Braun, Chris Cleeland, Angelo Corsaro, Sergio Flores-Gaitan, Chris Gill, Pradeep Gore, Andy Gokhale, Priyanka Gontla, Myrna Harbison, Tim Harrison, Shawn Hannan, John Heitmann, Joe Hoffert, James Hu, Steve Huston, Prashant Jain, Vishal Kachroo, Ray Klefstad, Yamuna Krishnamurthy, Michael Kircher, Fred Kuhns, David Levine, Ebrahim Moshiri, Michael Moran, Sumedh Mungee, Bala Natarjan, Ossama Othman, Jeff Parsons, Kirthika Parameswaran, Krish Pathayapura, Irfan Pyarali, Carlos O'Ryan, Malcolm Spence, Marina Spivak, Naga Surendran, Selcuk Uelker, Nanbor Wang, Seth Widoff, and Torben Worm. We would also like to acknowledge the substantial contribution of the thousands of ACE and TAO users around the world who have applied and enhanced the patterns and framework components described in this book over the past decade. Without their support, constant feedback, and encouragement we would never have written this book.

Special thanks go to Johannes Nierwetberg, Lothar Borrmann, and Monika Gonauser for their managerial support and backing at the software engineering labs of Corporate Technology of Siemens AG, Munich, Germany. We also thank Calinel Pasteanu at the Communication Devices business unit of Siemens AG in Munich for understanding the conflict between the chores of writing this book and the pressures of delivering products in 'Internet time'.

We are also grateful for the support from colleagues and sponsors of our research on patterns and the ACE and TAO middleware frameworks, notably the contributions of Ron Akers (Motorola), Al Aho (Lucent), Steve Bachinsky (SAIC), Detlef Becker (Siemens), Jim Blaine (Washington University), John Buttitto (Motorola), Becky Callison (Boeing), Wei Chiang (Nokia), Russ Claus (NASA), Joe Cross (Lockheed Martin), Bryan Doerr (Boeing), Karlheinz Dorn (Siemens), Sylvester Fernandez (Lockheed Martin), Andreas Geisler (Siemens), Helen Gill (DARPA), Trey Grubbs (Raytheon), Jody Hagins (ATD), Andy Harvey (Cisco), Thomas Heimke (Siemens), Kalai Kalaichelvan (Nortel), Arvind Kaushal (Motorola), Steve Kay (Tellabs), Chandra Kintala (Lucent), Gary Koob (DARPA), Sean Landis (Motorola), Rick Lett (Sprint), Joe Loyall (BBN), Mike Masters (NSWC), Ed Mays (US Marine Corps), John Mellby (Raytheon), Dave Meyer (Virtual Technology), Eileen Miller (Lucent), Stan Moyer (Telcordia), Russ Noseworthy (Object Sciences), Guru Parulkar (Cisco), Dan Paulish (Siemens), James Plamondon (Microsoft), Dieter Quehl (Siemens), Lucie Robillard (US Air Force), Allyn Romanow (Cisco), Rick Schantz (BBN), Steve Shaffer (Kodak), Dave Sharp (Boeing), Naval Sodha (Ericsson), Brian Stacey (Nortel), Paul Stephenson (Ericsson), Umar Syyid (Hughes), Dave Thomas (OTI), Lothar Werzinger (Krones), Shalini Yajnik (Lucent), and Tom Ziomek (Motorola).

Very special thanks go to Steve Rickaby, our copy editor, for enhancing our written material. In addition, we thank our editor, Gaynor Redvers-Mutton, and everyone else at John Wiley & Sons who made it possible to publish this book. This is the second book fostered by Gaynor and Steve. Their support has been superb and we look forward to working with them on forthcoming POSA volumes.

Finally, we would like to express our deepest gratitude to the late Richard Stevens, whose seminal books inspired us to explore the wonders of network programming so many years ago. His spirit pervades this book.

About The Authors

Douglas C. Schmidt

Dr. Douglas Schmidt is an Associate Professor in the Electrical and Computer Engineering department at the University of California, Irvine, USA. He is also serving as a Program Manager in the Information Technology Office (ITO) at DARPA, leading the national research effort on middleware. Before this he was an Associate Professor and Director of the Center for Distributed Object Computing in the Department of Computer Science at Washington University in St. Louis, Missouri. His research focuses on design patterns, optimization principles, and empirical analyses of object-oriented techniques that facilitate the development of high-performance and real-time distributed object computing middleware running over high-speed networks and embedded system interconnects.

Doug is an internationally-recognized expert on distributed object computing patterns, middleware frameworks, real-time CORBA, and open-source development. He has published widely in top technical journals, conferences, and books. He was editor of the *C++ Report* magazine for several years and has co-edited several popular books on patterns [PLoPD1] and frameworks [FJS99a] [FJS99b]. In addition to his academic research, Doug has led the development of ACE and TAO, which are widely-used open-source middleware frameworks that contain a rich set of reusable components implemented using the patterns presented in this book.

In his 'spare' time, he enjoys ballroom dancing with his wife Sonja, weight-lifting, guitar playing, world history, and Chevrolet Corvettes.

Michael Stal

Michael Stal joined the Corporate Technology department of Siemens AG in Munich, Germany in 1991. In his previous work he gained extensive experience developing software for compilers and computer graphics. He worked on runtime type information for C++ and served on the C++ standardization group X3J16. Since 1992 Michael's work has focused on the development of concurrent and distributed object-oriented systems using Sockets, CORBA, COM, and Java. Michael is Siemens' primary contact on CORBA at the OMG and is head of the Distributed Object Computing Group at Siemens's Corporate Technology department. He co-authored the first POSA volume *A System of Patterns*.

Michael's main research interests focus on methods for developing distributed systems efficiently and on patterns for describing the architecture of middleware platforms. In this context he has published articles in many magazines and given talks at many conferences. In addition, he is Editor-in-Chief of Java Spektrum, the major German magazine on the Java platform, as well as a columnist and member of the advisory board for Objektspektrum, the major German magazine on object technology.

In his spare time Michael attends soccer matches, supports his favorite team Bayern München, visits Munich beer gardens, tries to prevent his cats from destroying his apartment, watches movies, and reads books on physics, philosophy and humor. He is fan of Douglas Adams, Scott Adams, and Terry Pratchett.

Hans Rohnert

Dr. Hans Rohnert is a Senior Software Engineer at the Communication Devices business unit of Siemens AG in Munich, Germany. His primary aims are exploiting promising software technologies and introducing them into new products, such as next-generation mobile phones. His professional interests are software architecture, design patterns, and real-world programming. He has presented numerous talks on subjects ranging from dynamic graph algorithms to embedded Java virtual machines.

Hans is currently a member of the expert groups defining the small footprint KVM Java virtual machine and its libraries for use in small devices. His programming projects have included server-side modules for embedded servers, work flow in C++, base support for ATM switching, Java GUI front-ends for CORBA clients, and HTTP clients. He is also a co-author of the first POSA volume *A System of Patterns* and a co-editor of the fourth book in the PLoPD series [PLoPD4]. As a graduate student he performed original research on combinatorial algorithms, publishing and lecturing on them early in his career.

Hans is an ambitious tennis player, with more matches lost than won. He also enjoys exploring the nearby mountains, rock-climbing, and cross-country skiing. His most important 'hobby', however, is his family, most notably a new baby born during the hectic final phase of writing this book.

Frank Buschmann

Frank Buschmann is Principal Senior Software Engineer at Siemens Corporate Technology in Munich, Germany. His research interests include object technology, software architecture, frameworks, and patterns. He has published widely in all these areas, most visibly in his co-authorship of the first POSA volume *A System of Patterns*. Frank was a member of the ANSI C++ standardization committee X3J16 from 1992 to 1996. Frank initiated and organized the first conference on patterns held in Europe, EuroPLoP 1996, and is also a co-editor of the third book in the PLoPD series [PLoPD3]. In his development work Frank has led design and implementation efforts for several large-scale industrial software projects, including business information, industrial automation, and telecommunication systems.

When not at work Frank spends most of his time enjoying life with his wife Martina, watching the time go by in Munich beer gardens, having fun biking, skiing, and horse-riding, getting excited when watching his favorite soccer team Borussia Dortmund, dreaming when listening to a performance at the Munich opera, and relaxing with rare Scotch single malts before bedtime.

Guide To The Reader

*"Cheshire-Puss will you tell me, please,
which way I ought to go from here?"*

*"That depends a good deal on
where you want to get to," said the Cat.*

"I don't much care where—," said Alice.

*"Then it doesn't matter which way you go,"
said that cat.*

*"—so long as I get somewhere"
Alice added as an explanation.*

*"Oh, you're sure to do that," said the Cat,
"if you only walk long enough."*

Louis Carroll, "Alice in Wonderland"

This book is structured so you can read it cover-to-cover. If you know where you want to get to, however, you may want to choose your own route through the book. In this case, the following hints can help you decide which topics to focus upon and the order in which to read them.

Introduction to Patterns

If this book is your initial exposure to patterns, we suggest you first read the introduction to patterns in [POSA1] and [GoF95], which explore the concepts and terminology related to patterns for software architectures and designs. In particular, all the patterns presented in this book build upon the conceptual foundation for patterns specified in [POSA1]:

- The definition of patterns for software architectures

- The categorization of these patterns into architectural patterns, design patterns, and idioms[1] and

- The pattern description format

Moreover, the implementations of many patterns in this book are enhanced by using patterns from [POSA1] and [GoF95]. To guide the application of the patterns in production software development projects we therefore suggest you keep all three books handy.

Structure and Content

The first chapter in this book, *Concurrent and Networked Objects*, describes the key challenges of designing concurrent and networked systems. It also outlines the scope and context for the patterns we present. Finally, it presents a case study that applies eight patterns in this book to develop a concurrent Web server.

Sixteen pattern descriptions and one idiom form the main part of this book. We group them into four chapters, corresponding to key problem areas—*service access and configuration*, *event handling*, *synchronization* and *concurrency*—in the development of concurrent and networked middleware and applications. The order in which you read this material is up to you. One approach is to read important core patterns first:

- The Wrapper Facade design pattern (47)[2]

- The Reactor architectural pattern (179)

---

1. See the *Glossary* for a definition of these pattern categories.

2. We adopt the page number notation introduced by [GoF95]. (47) means that the corresponding pattern description starts on page 47.

- The Acceptor-Connector design pattern (285)

- The Active Object design pattern (369)

The other twelve patterns and one idiom in the book are arranged to minimize forward references. You can read them in any order of course, and we provide page numbers for following references to other patterns within the book. This material completes and complements the concepts defined by the four patterns listed above and covers a range of issues relevant to designing and implementing concurrent and networked objects effectively.

You can also use this book to find solutions to problems you encounter in your projects. Use the overview of our patterns in Chapter 6, *Weaving the Patterns Together*, to guide your search, then locate in Chapters 2 through 5 the detailed descriptions of the patterns you select as potential solutions.

No pattern is an island, completely separated from other patterns. Therefore, Chapter 6, *Weaving the Patterns Together*, also describes how all the patterns in this book can be woven together to form a pattern language for building networked applications and middleware. If you want an overall perspective of the patterns in this book *before* delving into the individual patterns, we recommend you skim the pattern language presentation in Chapter 6 before reading the patterns in Chapters 2 through 5 in depth.

Chapter 7, *The Past, Present, and Future of Patterns* and Chapter 8, *Concluding Remarks* complete the main content of this book. The remainder of the book consists of a glossary of technical terms, an overview of the notations used in the figures, references to related work, and an index of patterns, topics, and names.

Pattern Form

All patterns presented in this book are self-contained, following the [POSA1] pattern form. This form allows us to present both the essence and the key details of a pattern. Our goal is to serve readers who simply want an overview of the pattern's fundamental ideas, as well as those who want to know how the patterns work in depth.

Each section in our pattern form sets the stage for the subsequent section. For instance, the *Example* section introduces the *Context*,

Problem, and *Solution* sections, which summarize a pattern's essence. The *Solution* section foreshadows the *Structure* and *Dynamics* section, which then present more detailed information about how a pattern works, preparing readers for the *Implementation* section.

The *Example Resolved, Variants, Known Uses, Consequences* and *See Also* sections complete each pattern description. We include extensive cross-references to help you to understand the relationships between the patterns in this book and other published patterns.

To anchor the presentation of a pattern's implementation activities to production software systems, much of the sample code is influenced by components provided in the ACE framework [Sch97]. If you first want to get an overview of all the patterns you may therefore want to skip over the *Implementation* sections on your initial pass through the book and come back to them when you need to know a particular pattern's implementation details.

Although the pattern form we use in this book incurs some repetition within the pattern descriptions, we have found that this repetition helps readers navigate through the descriptions more effectively by minimizing 'back-tracking'.

In the diagrams that explain the structure and behavior of our patterns we tried to follow standard UML whenever possible. In few cases, however, UML did not allow us to express ourselves precisely enough. Thus we 'extended' the standard notation slightly, as specified in the *Notations* chapter.

Background Reading

Many patterns, particularly Reactor (179), Proactor (215), Half-Sync/ Half-Async (423), and Leader/Followers (447), assume you are familiar with the following topics:

- *Object-oriented design techniques*, such as patterns [GoF95] [POSA1] and idioms [Cope92], UML notation [BRJ98], and the principles of structured programming, specifically encapsulation and modularity [Mey97].

- *Object-oriented programming language features*, such as classes [Str97], inheritance and polymorphism [AG98], and parameterized types [Aus98]. Many examples in this book are written in C++, though we present Java known uses for most of the patterns.

- *Systems programming concepts and mechanisms*, such as process and thread management [Lew95] [Lea99a] [Ric97], synchronization [Ste98], and interprocess communication [Ste99].

- *Network services and protocols*, such as client-server computing [CoSte92] and the Internet protocols [Ste93] [SW94].

This book contains an extensive glossary and bibliography to clarify unfamiliar terminology, and suggest sources for information on topics you may want to learn more about. It is not, however, an introductory tutorial on concurrency and network programming. Thus, if you are not familiar with certain topics listed above, we encourage you to do some background reading on the material we recommend in conjunction with reading this book.

1 Concurrent and Networked Objects

"With the exception of music, we have been trained to think of patterns as fixed affairs. It's easier and lazier that way, but, of course, all nonsense. The right way to begin to think of the pattern which connects is to think of a dance of interacting parts, pegged down by various sorts of limits."

Gregory Bateson — Cultural Anthropologist

This chapter introduces topics related to concurrent and networked objects. We first motivate the need for advanced software development techniques in this area. Next, we present an overview of key design challenges faced by developers of concurrent and networked object-oriented applications and middleware. To illustrate how patterns can be applied to resolve these problems, we examine a case study of an object-oriented framework and a high-performance Web server implemented using this framework. In the case study we focus on key patterns presented in this book that help to simplify four important aspects of concurrent and networked applications:

- Service access and configuration
- Event handling
- Synchronization and
- Concurrency

1.1   Motivation

During the past decade advances in VLSI technology and fiber-optics have increased computer processing power by 3–4 orders of magnitude and network link speeds by 6–7 orders of magnitude. Assuming that these trends continue, by the end of this decade

- Desktop computer clock speeds will run at ~100 Gigahertz
- Local area network link speeds will run at ~100 Gigabits/second
- Wireless link speeds will run at ~100 Megabits/second and
- The Internet backbone link speeds will run at ~10 Terabits/second

Moreover, there will be billions of interactive and embedded computing and communication devices in operation throughout the world. These powerful computers and networks will be available largely at commodity prices, built mostly with robust common-off-the-shelf (COTS) components, and will inter-operate over an increasingly convergent and pervasive Internet infrastructure.

To maximize the benefit from these advances in hardware technology, the quality and productivity of technologies for developing concurrent and networked middleware and application software must also increase. Historically, hardware has tended to become smaller, faster, and more reliable. It has also become cheaper and more predictable to develop and innovate, as evidenced by 'Moore's Law'. In contrast, concurrent and networked software has often grown larger, slower, and more error-prone. It has also become very expensive and time-consuming to develop, validate, maintain, and enhance.

Although hardware improvements have alleviated the need for some low-level software optimizations, the lifecycle cost [Boe81] and effort required to develop software—particularly mission-critical concurrent and networked applications—continues to rise. The disparity between the rapid rate of hardware advances versus the slower software progress stems from a number of factors, including:

- *Inherent and accidental complexities*. There are vexing problems with concurrent and networked software that result from inherent and accidental complexities. *Inherent* complexities arise from fundamental domain challenges, such as dealing with partial failures, distributed deadlock, and end-to-end quality of service (QoS) requirements. As networked systems have grown in scale and functionality they must now cope with a much broader and harder set of these complexities.

Accidental complexities arise from limitations with software tools and development techniques, such as non-portable programming APIs and poor distributed debuggers. Ironically, many accidental complexities stem from deliberate choices made by developers who favor low-level languages and tools that scale up poorly when applied to complex concurrent and networked software.

- *Inadequate methods and techniques.* Popular software analysis methods [SM88] [CY91] [RBPEL91] and design techniques [Boo94] [BRJ98] have focused on constructing single-process, single-threaded applications with 'best-effort' QoS requirements. The development of high-quality concurrent and networked systems—particularly those with stringent QoS requirements, such as video-conferencing—has been left to the intuition and expertise of skilled software architects and engineers. Moreover, it has been hard to gain experience with concurrent and networked software techniques without spending considerable time learning via trial and error, and wrestling with platform-specific details.

- *Continuous re-invention and re-discovery* of core concepts and techniques. The software industry has a long history of recreating incompatible solutions to problems that are already solved. For example, there are dozens of non-standard general-purpose and real-time operating systems that manage the same hardware resources. Similarly, there are dozens of incompatible operating system encapsulation libraries that provide slightly different APIs that implement essentially the same features and services.

If effort had instead been focused on enhancing and optimizing a small number of solutions, developers of concurrent and networked software would be reaping the benefits available to developers of hardware. These developers innovate rapidly by using and applying common CAD tools and standard instruction sets, buses, and network protocols.

No single silver bullet can slay all the demons plaguing concurrent and networked software [Broo87]. Over the past decade, however, it has become clear that *patterns* and *pattern languages* help to alleviate many inherent and accidental software complexities.

A pattern is a recurring solution schema to a standard problem in a particular context [POSA1]. Patterns help to capture and reuse the static and dynamic structure and collaboration of key participants in software designs. They are useful for documenting recurring micro-architectures, which are abstractions of software components that experienced developers apply to resolve common design and implementation problems [GoF95].

When related patterns are woven together, they form a 'language' that helps to both

- Define a vocabulary for talking about software development problems [SFJ96] and

- Provide a process for the orderly resolution of these problems [Ale79] [AIS77]

By studying and applying patterns and pattern languages, developers can often escape traps and pitfalls that have been avoided traditionally only via long and costly apprenticeship [PLoPD1].

Until recently [Lea99a] patterns for developing concurrent and networked software existed only in programming folklore, the heads of expert researchers and developers, or were buried deep in complex source code. These locations are not ideal, for three reasons:

- Re-discovering patterns opportunistically from source code is expensive and time-consuming, because it is hard to separate the essential design decisions from the implementation details.

- If the insights and rationale of experienced designers are not documented, they will be lost over time and thus cannot help guide subsequent software maintenance and enhancement activities.

- Without guidance from earlier work, developers of concurrent and networked software face the Herculean task [SeSch70] of engineering complex systems from the ground up, rather than reusing proven solutions.

As a result many concurrent and networked software systems are developed from scratch. In today's competitive, time-to-market-driven environments, however, this often yields non-optimal *ad hoc* solutions. These solutions are hard to customize and tune, because so much effort is spent just trying to make the software operational. Moreover, as requirements change over time, evolving *ad hoc* software solutions becomes prohibitively expensive. Yet, end-users expect—or at least desire—software to be affordable, robust, efficient, and agile, which is hard to achieve without solid architectural underpinnings.

To help rectify these problems, this book documents key architectural and design patterns for concurrent and networked software. These patterns can and have been applied to solve many common problems that arise when developing object-oriented middleware frameworks and applications. When used as a documentation aid, these patterns preserve vital design information that helps developers evolve *existing* software more robustly. When used as a design aid, the patterns help guide developers to create *new* software more effectively.

Of course, patterns, objects, components, and frameworks are no panacea. They cannot, for example, absolve developers from responsibility for solving all complex concurrent and networked software analysis, design, implementation, validation, and optimization problems. Ultimately there is no substitute for human creativity, experience, discipline, diligence, and judgement.

When used properly, however, the patterns described in this book help alleviate many of the complexities enumerated earlier. In particular, the patterns

- *Direct* developer focus towards higher-level software application architecture and design concerns, such as the specification of suitable service access and configuration, event processing, and threading models. These are some of the key *strategic* aspects of concurrent and networked software. If they are addressed properly, the impact of many vexing complexities can be alleviated greatly.

- *Redirect* developer focus away from a preoccupation with low-level operating system and networking protocols and mechanisms. While having a solid grasp of these topics is important, they are *tactical* in scope and must be placed in the proper context within the overall software architecture and development effort.

1.2   Challenges of Concurrent and Networked Software

In theory, developing software applications that use concurrent and networked services can improve system performance, reliability, scalability, and cost-effectiveness. In practice, however, developing efficient, robust, extensible, and affordable concurrent and networked applications is hard, due to key differences between stand-alone and networked application architectures.

In stand-alone application architectures, user interface, application service processing, and persistent data resources reside within one computer, with the peripherals attached directly to it. In contrast, in networked application architectures, interactive presentation, application service processing, and data resources may reside in multiple loosely-coupled host computers and service tiers connected together by local area or wide area networks.

A network of X-terminals and 'thin client NetPCs' is an example of a networked system architecture. In this environment, user interface presentation is handled by a display service on end-user hosts. The processing capabilities are provided by host computer(s) on which all or part of application services run. Access to persistent resources is mediated by one or more network file servers. Other services, such as naming and directory services, time services, HTTP servers, and caches and network management services, can run in the network and provide additional capabilities to applications.

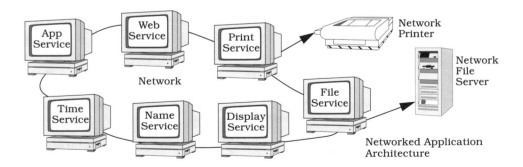

There are three common reasons to adopt a networked architecture:

- *Collaboration and connectivity*. The explosive growth of the Web and e-commerce exemplify one of the most common reasons for networking: the ability to connect to and access vast quantities of geographically-distributed information and services. The popularity of the instant messaging and 'chat rooms' available on the Internet underscores another common networking motivation: staying connected to family, friends, collaborators, and customers.

- *Enhanced performance, scalability, and fault tolerance*. The performance and scalability of a networked architecture may be enhanced by taking advantage of the parallel processing capabilities that are available in a network. For example, multiple computation and communication service processing tasks can be run in parallel on different hosts. Similarly, various application services can be replicated across multiple hosts. Replication can minimize single points of failure, thereby improving the system's reliability in the face of partial failures.

- *Cost effectiveness*. Networked architectures yield decentralized and modular applications that can share expensive peripherals, such as high-capacity file servers and high-resolution printers. Similarly, selected application components and services can be delegated to run on hosts with specialized processing attributes, such as high-performance disk controllers, large amounts of memory, or enhanced floating-point performance.

Although networked applications offer many potential benefits, they are harder to design, implement, debug, optimize, and manage than stand-alone applications. For example, developers must address topics that are either not relevant or are less problematic for stand-alone applications in order to handle the requirements of networked applications. These topics include:

- Connection establishment and service initialization
- Event demultiplexing and event handler dispatching
- Interprocess communication (IPC) and network protocols
- Primary and secondary storage management and caching

- Static and dynamic component configuration

- Concurrency and synchronization

These topics are generally independent of specific application requirements, so learning to master them helps to address a wide range of software development problems. Moreover, in the context of these topics many design and programming challenges arise due to several *inherent* and *accidental* complexities associated with concurrent and networked systems:

- Common *inherent* complexities associated with concurrent and networked systems include managing bandwidth [ZBS97], minimizing delays (latency) [SC99] and delay variation (jitter) [PRS+99], detecting and recovering from partial failures [CRSS+98], determining appropriate service partitioning and load balancing strategies [IEEE95], and ensuring causal ordering of events [BR94]. Similarly, common inherent complexities found in concurrent programming include eliminating race conditions and avoiding deadlocks [Lea99a], determining suitable thread scheduling strategies [SKT96], and optimizing end-system protocol processing performance [SchSu95].

- Common *accidental* complexities associated with concurrent and networked systems include lack of portable operating system APIs [Sch97], inadequate debugging support and lack of tools for analyzing concurrent and networked applications [LT93], widespread use of algorithmic—rather than object-oriented—decomposition [Boo94], and continual rediscovery and reinvention of core concepts and common components [Kar95].

In this section, we therefore discuss many of the design and programming challenges associated with building concurrent and networked systems. Yet the patterns in this book do not address all the aspects associated with concurrency and networking. Therefore, Chapter 6, *Weaving the Patterns Together*, relates the patterns in this book with others from the literature that handle many of these aspects. The remaining challenges constitute open issues for future patterns research, as described in Chapter 7, *The Past, Present, and Future of Patterns*.

Challenge 1: Service Access and Configuration

Components in a stand-alone application can collaborate within a single address space by passing parameters via function calls and by accessing global variables. In contrast, components in networked applications can collaborate using:

- Interprocess communication (IPC) mechanisms, for example shared memory, pipes, and Sockets [Ste98],[1] which are based on network protocols like TCP, UDP and IP [Ste93], or ATM [CFFT97].

- Communication protocols [Ste93], such as TELNET, FTP, SMTP, HTTP, and LDAP, which are used by many types of services, for example remote log-in, file transfer, email, Web content delivery, and distributed directories, to export cohesive software components and functionality to applications.

- Remote operations on application-level service components using high-level communication middleware, such as COM+ [Box97] and CORBA [OMG98c].

Applications and software components can access these communication mechanisms via programming APIs defined at all levels of abstraction in a networked system:

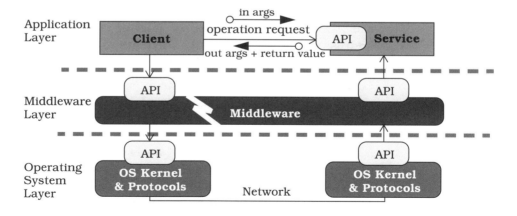

1. In the remainder of this chapter we refer to and use concrete UNIX and Win32 operating system APIs in our discussion. You may want to keep copies of references such as [Ste99] [Ste98] [Lew95] [Ric97] handy to clarify some topics or terms if they are unfamiliar.

Designing effective APIs for accessing these communication mechanisms is important, because these are the interfaces programmed directly by application, component, and service developers.

For infrastructure networking or systems programs, such as TELNET or FTP, service access traditionally involved calling

- Concurrency service access APIs, such as UNIX processes [Ste99], POSIX Pthreads [IEEE96], or Win32 threads [Sol98], to manage concurrency and

- IPC service access APIs, such as UNIX- and Internet-domain Sockets [Ste98], to configure connections and communicate between processes co-located on a single host and on different hosts, respectively.

Several accidental complexities arise, however, when accessing networking and host services via low-level operating system C APIs:

- *Excessive low-level details*. Building networked applications using operating system APIs requires developers to have intimate knowledge of many low-level details. For instance, developers must carefully track which error codes are returned by each system call and handle these problems in the application code itself. UNIX server developers, for example, who use the wait() system call must distinguish between return errors due to no child processes being present and errors from signal interrupts. In the latter case, the wait() must be reissued. Forcing *application* developers to address these details diverts their attention from more strategic issues, such as a server's semantics and its software architecture.

- *Continuous rediscovery and reinvention of incompatible higher-level programming abstractions*. A common remedy for the excessive level of detail with operating system APIs is to define higher-level programming abstractions. For example, many Web servers create a file cache component to avoid accessing the file system for each client request [HPS99]. However, these types of abstractions are often re-discovered and re-invented independently by each developer or team. This *ad hoc* software programming process can actually hamper productivity if it diverts application developers from meeting their customer's requirements. It can also create a plethora of incompatible components that are inadequately documented and debugged, and therefore not readily reusable within and across projects.

- *High potential for errors*. Programming to operating system APIs is tedious and error-prone due to their lack of type-safety and their subtlety. For example, many networked applications are programmed with the Socket API [MBKQ96], which is defined in C. However, socket endpoints are represented as untyped handles. These handles increase the potential for subtle programming mistakes and run-time errors [Sch92]. In particular, operations can be applied incorrectly, such as invoking a data transfer operation on a passive-mode handle that is only supposed to establish connections.

- *Lack of portability*. Operating system APIs are notoriously non-portable, even across releases of the same platform. Implementations of the Socket API on Win32 platforms (WinSock), for example, are subtly different than on UNIX platforms. Advanced Socket operations, such as multicast and broadcast, are not portable across these platforms as a result. Even WinSock implementations on different versions of Windows possess incompatible timing-related bugs that cause sporadic failures when performing non-blocking connections.

- *Steep learning curve*. Due to the excessive level of detail, the effort required to master operating system APIs can be very high. For example, it is hard to learn how to program with POSIX asynchronous I/O [POSIX95] correctly. It is even harder to learn how to write a *portable* application using asynchronous I/O mechanisms, because they differ so widely across operating system platforms.

- *Inability to scale up to handle increasing complexity*. Operating system APIs define basic interfaces to mechanisms, such as process and thread management, interprocess communication, file systems, and memory management. However, these basic interfaces do not scale up gracefully as applications grow in size and complexity. For example, a typical UNIX process allows a backlog of only ~7 pending connections [Ste98]. This number is completely inadequate for heavily accessed e-commerce servers that must handle hundreds or thousands of simultaneous clients.

Key design challenges for infrastructure networking or system programs thus center on minimizing the accidental complexities outlined above without sacrificing performance.

For higher-level distributed object computing applications, service access often involves invoking remote operations on reusable components that define common services, such as naming [OMG97a], trading [OMG98b], and event notification [OMG99c]. Many component models, such as Enterprise JavaBeans [MaHa99], COM+ [Box97], and the CORBA component model [OMG99a], allow components to export different service roles to different clients, depending on factors, such as the version expected by the client or the authorization level of the client. A key design challenge at this level therefore centers on ensuring that clients do not access invalid or unauthorized component service roles.

Resolving this challenge is important: networked applications are more vulnerable to security breaches than stand-alone applications, because there are more access points for an intruder to attack [YB99]. For example, many shared-media networks, such as Ethernet, Token Ring, and FDDI, provide limited built-in protection against cable tapping and 'packet snooping' tools [Ste93]. Similarly, networked applications must guard against one host masquerading as another to access unauthorized information. Although some network software libraries, such as OpenSSL [OSSL00], support authentication, authorization, and data encryption, a single API to access these security services has not been adopted universally.

Supporting the static and dynamic evolution of services and applications is another key challenge in networked software systems. Evolution can occur in two ways:

- Interfaces to and connectivity between component service roles can change, often at run-time, and new service roles can be implemented and installed into existing components.

- Distributed system performance can be improved by reconfiguring service load to harness the processing power of multiple hosts.

Ideally these component configuration and reconfiguration changes should be transparent to client applications that access the various services. Another design challenge therefore is to ensure that an entire system need not be shut down, recompiled, relinked, and restarted simply because a particular service role in a component is reconfigured or its load is redistributed.

It is even more challenging to determine how to access services that are configured into a system 'on-demand' and whose implementations are unknown when the system was designed originally.

Many modern operating systems and run-time environments provide explicit dynamic linking APIs [WHO91] that enable the configuration of applications on-demand:

- UNIX defines the `dlopen()`, `dlsym()`, and `dlclose()` API that can be used to load a designated dynamically linked library (DLL) into an application process explicitly, extract a designated factory function from the DLL, and unlink/unload the DLL, respectively [Ste98].

- Win32 provides the `LoadLibrary()`, `GetProcAddr()`, and `CloseHandle()` API that perform the same functionality as the UNIX DLL API [Sol98].

- Java's `java.applet.Applet` class defines `init()`, `start()`, `stop()`, and `destroy()` hook methods that support the initializing, starting, stopping, and terminating of applets loaded dynamically.

However, configuring services into applications on-demand requires more than dynamic linking *mechanisms*—it requires patterns for coordinating (re)configuration *policies*. Here the design challenges are two-fold. First, an application must export new services, even though it may not know their detailed interfaces. Second, an application must integrate these services into its own control flow and processing sequence transparently and robustly, even at run-time.

Chapter 2, *Service Access and Configuration Patterns*, presents four patterns for designing effective programming APIs to access and configure services and components in stand-alone and networked software systems and applications. These patterns are *Wrapper Facade* (47), *Component Configurator* (75), *Interceptor* (109), and *Extension Interface* (141).

Challenge 2: Event Handling

As systems become increasingly networked, software development techniques that support event-driven applications have become increasingly pervasive. Three characteristics differentiate event-driven applications from those with the traditional 'self-directed' flow of control [PLoPD1]:

- Application behavior is triggered by external or internal events that occur asynchronously. Common sources of events include device drivers, I/O ports, sensors, keyboards or mice, signals, timers, or other asynchronous software components.

- Most events must be handled promptly to prevent CPU starvation, improve perceived response time, and keep hardware devices with real-time constraints from failing or corrupting data.

- Finite state machines [SGWSM94] may be needed to control event processing and detect illegal transitions, because event-driven applications generally have little or no control over the order in which events arrive.

Therefore, event-driven applications are often structured as layered architectures [POSA1] with so-called 'inversion of control' [John97]:

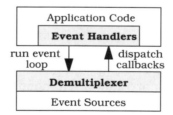

- At the bottom layer are *event sources*, which detect and retrieve events from various hardware devices or low-level software device drivers that reside within an operating system.

- At the next layer is an *event demultiplexer*, such as select() [Ste98], which waits for events to arrive on the various event sources and then dispatches events to their corresponding *event handler* callbacks.

- The *event handlers*, together with the application code, form yet another layer that performs application-specific processing in response to callbacks—hence the term 'inversion of control'.

The separation of concerns in this event-driven architecture allows developers to concentrate on application layer functionality, rather than rewriting the event source and demultiplexer layers repeatedly for each new system or application.

In many networked systems, applications communicate via peer-to-peer protocols, such as TCP/IP [Ste93], and are implemented using the layered event-driven architecture outlined above. The events that are exchanged between peers in this architecture play four different roles [Bl91]:

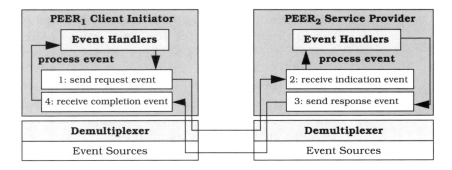

- $PEER_1$, the client initiator application, invokes a send operation to pass a *request event* to $PEER_2$, the service provider application. The event can contain data necessary for $PEER_1$ and $PEER_2$ to collaborate. For example, a $PEER_1$ request may contain a CONNECT event to initiate a bidirectional connection, or a DATA event to pass an operation and its parameters to be executed remotely at $PEER_2$.

- The $PEER_2$ service provider application is notified of the request event arrival via an *indication event*. $PEER_2$ can then invoke a receive operation to obtain and use the indication event data to perform its processing. The demultiplexing layer of $PEER_2$ often waits for a set of indication events to arrive from multiple peers.

- After the $PEER_2$ service provider application finishes processing the indication event, it invokes a send operation to pass a *response event* to $PEER_1$, acknowledging the original event and returning any results. For example, $PEER_2$ could acknowledge the CONNECT event as part of an initialization 'handshake', or it could acknowledge the DATA event in a reliable two-way remote method invocation.

- The PEER$_1$ client initiator application is notified of a response event arrival via a *completion event*. At this point it can use a receive operation to obtain the results of the request event it sent to the PEER$_2$ service provider earlier.

If after sending a request event the PEER$_1$ application blocks to receive the completion event containing PEER$_2$'s response, it is termed a *synchronous* client.[2] In contrast, if PEER$_1$ does not block after sending a request it is termed an *asynchronous* client. Asynchronous clients can receive completion events via asynchrony mechanisms, such as UNIX signal handlers [Ste99] or Win32 I/O completion ports [Sol98].

Traditional networked applications detect, demultiplex, and dispatch various types of control and data events using low-level operating system APIs, such as Sockets [Ste98], select() [Ste98], poll() [Rago93], WaitForMultipleObjects(), and I/O completion ports [Sol98]. However, using these low-level APIs increases the accidental complexity of event-driven programming. Programming with these low-level APIs also increases code duplication and maintenance effort by coupling the I/O and demultiplexing aspects of an application with its connection and concurrency mechanisms.

Chapter 3, *Event Handling Patterns*, presents four patterns that describe how to initiate, receive, demultiplex, dispatch, and process various types of events effectively in networked software frameworks. The patterns are *Reactor* (179), *Proactor* (215), *Asynchronous Completion Token* (261), and *Acceptor-Connector* (285).

Challenge 3: Concurrency

Concurrency is a term that refers to a family of policies and mechanisms that enable one or more threads or processes to execute their service processing tasks simultaneously [Ben90]. Many networked applications, particularly servers, must handle requests from multiple clients concurrently. Therefore, developers of

---

2. While reading the patterns in this book it is important to recognize that the terms 'client' and 'service' are not immutable properties of particular software or hardware components. Instead, they are *roles* [RG98] played during a particular request/ response interaction. For example, in a symmetric peer-to-peer system PEER$_1$ and PEER$_2$ could play both the roles of client initiator and service provider at various times during their interactions.

concurrent networked software often need to become proficient with various process and thread management mechanisms.

A *process* is a collection of resources, such as virtual memory, I/O handles, and signal handlers, that provide the context for executing program instructions. In earlier-generation operating systems, for example BSD UNIX [MBKQ96], processes had a single thread of control.

A *thread* is a single sequence of instruction steps executed in the context of a process [Lew95]. In addition to an instruction pointer, a thread consists of resources, such as a run-time stack of function activation records, a set of registers, and thread-specific data.

The use of single-threaded processes simplified certain types of concurrent applications, such as remote logins, because separate processes could not interfere with each other without explicit programmer intervention. It is hard, however, to use single-threaded processes to develop networked applications. For example, single-threaded BSD UNIX servers cannot block for extended periods while handling one client request without degrading their responsiveness to other clients. Although it is possible to use techniques like signal-driven Socket I/O or forking multiple processes to work around these limitations, the resulting programs are complex and inefficient.

Modern operating systems overcome the limitations of single-threaded processes by providing *multi-threaded* concurrency mechanisms that support the creation of multiple processes, each of which may contain multiple concurrent threads. In these operating systems the processes serve as *units of protection and resource allocation* within hardware-protected address spaces. Similarly, the threads serve as *units of execution* that run within a process address space shared by other threads:

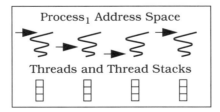
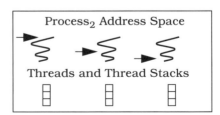

Popular thread programming models, such as POSIX Pthreads [IEEE96] and Win32 threads [Sol98], offer four benefits:

- They *improve performance transparently* by using the parallel processing capabilities of hardware and software platforms.

- They *improve performance explicitly* by allowing programmers to overlap computation and communication service processing.

- They *improve perceived response time* for interactive applications, such as graphical user interfaces, by associating separate threads with different service processing tasks in an application.

- They *simplify application design* by allowing multiple service processing tasks to run independently using synchronous programming abstractions, for example two-way method invocations.

It is remarkably hard, however, to develop efficient, predictable, scalable, and robust concurrent applications [Lea99a]. One source of complexity arises from common multi-threading hazards, for example race conditions and deadlocks [Lea99a]. Another source of complexity arises from limitations with existing development methods, tools, and operating system platforms. In particular, the heterogeneity of contemporary hardware and software platforms complicates the development of concurrent applications and tools that must run on multiple operating systems.

For example, shutting down multi-threaded programs gracefully and portably is hard. The problem stems from inconsistent thread cancellation semantics [Lew95] across operating systems, such as POSIX/UNIX, Win32, and real-time embedded systems like VxWorks or LynxOS. Similarly, support for advanced threading features, for example thread-specific storage (475), 'detached' threads [Lew95], real-time scheduling [Kan92], and scheduler activations [ABLL92] varies widely across operating systems. It is therefore infeasible to write portable concurrent applications by programming directly to the operating system APIs.

General-purpose design patterns, such as Adapter [GoF95] and Wrapper Facade (47), can be applied to shield concurrent software from the accidental complexities of the APIs outlined above. In addition, off-the-shelf 'infrastructure' middleware [SFJ96], such as ACE [Sch97] and JVMs, is now widely available and has reified these patterns into efficient and reusable object-oriented operating system encapsulation layers. However, even after adopting this level of middleware many challenges remain, due to inherent complexities associated with concurrent application development, including:

- Determining an efficient application concurrency architecture that minimizes context switching, synchronization, and data copying/movement overhead in concurrent applications [SchSu95] [SKT96].

- Designing complex concurrent systems containing synchronous and asynchronous service processing tasks to simplify programming without degrading execution efficiency [Sch96].

- Selecting appropriate synchronization primitives to increase performance, prevent race conditions, and reduce the maintenance costs of concurrent applications on multi-processors [McK95].

- Eliminating unnecessary threads and locks in concurrent [HPS99] or real-time [HLS97] applications to enhance performance or simplify resource management without compromising correctness, incurring deadlocks, or blocking application progress unduly.

Resolving these inherent complexities requires more than general-purpose design patterns and portable infrastructure middleware threading APIs. Instead, it requires developers to learn and internalize the successful patterns for developing concurrent applications, components, frameworks, and system architectures.

Chapter 5, *Concurrency Patterns*, includes five patterns that define various types of concurrency architectures for components, subsystems, and entire applications. These are *Active Object* (369), *Monitor Object* (399), *Half-Sync/Half-Async* (423), *Leader/Followers* (447), and *Thread-Specific Storage* (475).

Challenge 4: Synchronization

The efficiency, responsiveness, and design of many networked applications can benefit from the use of the concurrency mechanisms and patterns outlined above. For example, objects in an application can run concurrently in different threads to simplify program structure. If multiple processors are available, threads can be programmed to exploit true hardware parallelism and thus improve performance.

In addition to the complexities outlined in *Challenge 3: Concurrency*, concurrent programming is also harder than sequential programming due to the need to synchronize access to shared resources. For example, threads that run concurrently can access the same objects or variables simultaneously, and potentially corrupt their internal states. To prevent this problem, code that should not execute concurrently in objects or functions can be synchronized within a *critical section*. A critical section is a sequence of instructions that obeys the following invariant: while one thread or process is executing in the critical section, no other thread or process can execute in the same critical section [Tan95]:

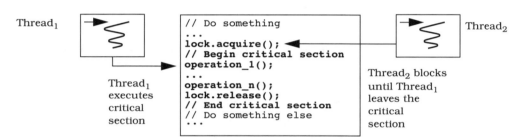

A common way to implement a critical section in object-oriented programs is to hard-code some type of lock object into a class or component. For example, a mutual exclusion (mutex) object is a type of lock that must be acquired and released *serially*. If multiple threads attempt to acquire the mutex simultaneously, only one thread will succeed. The others must wait until the mutex is released, after which all waiting threads will compete again for the lock [Tan92]. Other types of locks, such as semaphores and readers/writer locks, use a similar acquire/release protocol [McK95].

Unfortunately, programming these locking techniques using low-level operating system APIs yields two drawbacks:

- *Error-prone*. Explicitly acquiring a lock before entering a critical section and explicitly releasing it when exiting a critical section is surprisingly hard. In particular, if a critical section has multiple return paths, the lock must be released explicitly in all of them. This usage is a common source of subtle programming errors, because it is easy to forget to release a lock in one of the return paths, particularly if exceptions are thrown in the block. If the lock is not released, deadlock will occur when subsequent threads enter the critical section and they will then block indefinitely.

- *Inflexible and inefficient.* Depending on the context where an application runs, performance requirements may necessitate that different lock types be used to implement critical sections. For example, if an application that used a mutex originally is run on a large-scale multi-processor platform, performance may be improved by changing the locking mechanism to a readers/writer lock. This type of lock allows multiple reader threads to access a shared resource in parallel [McK95]. If the locking primitives are hard-coded into the software at every point of use, however, changing the primitives becomes unnecessarily hard and time-consuming.

Chapter 4, *Synchronization Patterns*, describes four patterns that alleviate the problems described above to simplify serialization and locking in concurrent systems. These patterns are *Scoped Locking* (325), *Strategized Locking* (333), *Thread-Safe Interface* (345), and *Double-Checked Locking Optimization* (353).

Other Challenges for Networked Software

The four topic areas covered above—service access and configuration, event handling, concurrency, and synchronization—represent the core networked software development challenges addressed by the patterns in this book. However, developers of networked application software must address issues in other topic areas, such as dependability, service naming, and location selection. Although these topics are beyond the scope of this book, we outline the important challenges below to illustrate the scope of the field.

Dependability. One of the reasons for adopting a networked architecture is to improve reliability and prevent single points of failure. Ironically, networked applications often require substantial effort to achieve levels of dependability equivalent to those provided by stand-alone applications. Detecting service failures in a stand-alone application is relatively easy, because the operating system has global knowledge of the health and status of system services and peripheral devices. Thus if a resource is unavailable the operating system can notify the application quickly. Similarly, if a service or device fails, the operating system can terminate an application, leaving no doubt about its exit status.

In contrast, detecting errors in networked applications is harder, due to incomplete knowledge of global system state. For example, networked applications are designed to tolerate some amount of latency jitter and non-determinism. As a result, a client may not detect an abnormal server termination until after valuable information has been lost. Similarly, server responses may get lost in the network, causing clients to retransmit duplicate requests.

There are several techniques for improving application dependability:

- *Reactivation*. Applications and services can be run under control of a *monitor daemon* that detects and automatically restarts servers if they terminate unexpectedly [HK93]. Servers report their current status to their associated monitor daemon periodically via 'heart-beat' messages. If a message does not arrive within a designated interval, the monitor daemon assumes that the server has terminated abnormally and reactivates it.

- *Replication*. Applications and services can be run under control of a *replica manager* at multiple locations throughout a network [GS97]. Replica managers can update service replicas continuously using 'active replication', or just when a primary service fails using 'passive replication'. Replication frameworks [FGS98] provide various monitoring, membership, consensus, and messaging mechanisms to help enhance application dependability.

A large body of research literature and tools focuses on improving the dependability of processes [GS97] [BR94] [HK93] or distributed objects [CRSS+98] [FGS98]. Some work has been documented in pattern form [IM96] [Maf96] [SPM98] [ACGH+96] [Stal00], though much research remains to be done. With the adoption of the Fault Tolerant CORBA specification [OMG99g] and ORBs that implement it, more application developers will be able to document their experience with the patterns of fault-tolerant distributed object computing.

Service Naming and Location Selection. Stand-alone applications generally identify their constituent services via object and function memory addresses. In contrast, networked applications require more elaborate mechanisms to name, locate, and select their remote services. IP host addresses and TCP port numbers are a common remote service addressing scheme used by CORBA, DCOM, Java RMI, DCE, and SunRPC. These low-level mechanisms are often inadequate for large-scale networked systems, however, because they are hard to administer in a portable and unambiguous manner. For example, TCP port 5000 need not refer to the same service on host machines configured by different vendors or network administrators.

Distributed object computing and RPC middleware therefore provide *location brokers* that allow clients to access services via higher-level names rather than by their low-level IP addresses and TCP port numbers. Location brokers simplify networked system administration and promote more flexible and dynamic placement of services throughout a network by automating the following tasks:

- *Name binding.* This task binds service names onto their current host/process locations. For example, the SunRPC rpcbind facility performs the port mapping task on a single end-system [Sun88]. More general name binding mechanisms, such as the DCE Cell Directory Service (CDS) [RKF92], LDAP [HSGH99], X.500 [SS99], and the CORBA Naming Service [OMG97a], are also available. These services implement a global name-space within an administrative domain, such as a local area network or intranet.

- *Service location.* A service or resource may often run at several locations throughout a network to improve reliability via replication. In this case applications may use a location broker to determine which service provider is most appropriate. For example, the CORBA Trading Service allows clients to select remote objects via a set of *properties* associated with services [OMG98b]. A client can select an appropriate resource by using these properties, such as choosing a printer by determining which printers in a building have Postscript support, color printing, 1200 dpi resolution, and sufficient paper.

Patterns related to name binding and service location have appeared in [POSA1] [Doble96] [JK00].

1.3   A Case Study: Designing a Concurrent Web Server

The volume of Web traffic is growing rapidly due to the proliferation of Web browsers that allow end-users easy access to a wide range of content [PQ00]. Similarly, Web technology is being increasingly applied to computationally-expensive tasks, such as medical image processing servers [PHS96] and database search engines. To keep pace with increasing demand, it is essential to develop concurrent Web servers that can provide efficient caching and content delivery services to Internet and intranet users.

The figure below presents an overview of a typical Web system and its components:

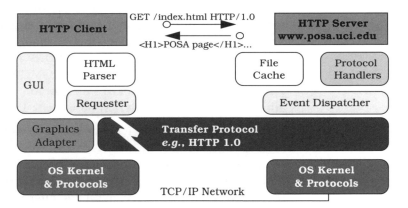

These Web system components interact as follows when an *HTTP client* retrieves an HTML file from an *HTTP server*:

1 Through *GUI* interactions via a Web browser, an end-user instructs the HTTP client to download a particular file.

2 The *requester* is the active component of the HTTP client that communicates over a *TCP/IP network*. It uses the appropriate *transfer protocol* syntax, such as HTTP 1.0 [Ste96], to send TCP connection events and HTTP GET request events, which are strings that inform the server to download a particular file.

3 Events arriving at an HTTP server are received by the *event dispatcher*. This is the server's demultiplexing engine that accepts

TCP connection events and coordinates the socket handles and threads used to receive and process HTTP GET request events.

4 Each HTTP GET request event is processed by a *protocol handler*, which parses and logs the request, fetches file status information, updates the *file cache*, transmits the file back to the HTTP client, and cleans up any resources it allocated.

5 When a requested file is returned to the client it is parsed by an *HTML parser*, which interprets and renders the file. At this point, the *requester* may issue other requests on behalf of the client, such as updating a client-side cache or downloading embedded images.

Developers must avoid common problems when creating and optimizing Web servers. These problems include wrestling with low-level programming details and portability constraints, committing to a particular server configuration prematurely, and being overwhelmed by the breadth of design alternatives, including:

• *Concurrency models*, such as thread-per-request or thread pool variants

• *Event demultiplexing models*, such as synchronous or asynchronous event demultiplexing

• *File caching models*, such as least-recently used (LRU) or least-frequently used (LFU)

• *Content delivery protocols*, such as HTTP/1.0 [BFF96], HTTP/1.1 [FGMFB97], or HTTP-NG [W3C98]

The reason there are so many alternatives is to help ensure that Web servers can be tailored to different end-user needs and traffic workloads. However, no single set of configuration choices is optimal for all hardware/software platforms and workloads [HPS99][HMS98]. Moreover, without proper guidance it is time-consuming and error-prone to navigate through all these design alternatives.

The remainder of this section illustrates how eight patterns in this book have been applied to produce a flexible and efficient Web server called JAWS [HPS99]. JAWS is both a Web server and a framework from which other types of servers can be built [HS98].

We selected JAWS as our example application for four reasons:

- It is a production-quality Web server [ENTERA00] that is representative of challenges that arise when developing concurrent and networked software.

- JAWS' throughput and scalability are high and its latency and jitter are low [HPS99] [HMS98], demonstrating that pattern- and framework-oriented software architectures can be efficient.

- The JAWS framework itself is developed using the ACE framework [Sch97], which provides object-oriented implementations of most patterns in this book.

- ACE and JAWS are open-source,[3] so you can see first-hand how patterns are applied to avoid rediscovering and reinventing solutions to concurrent and networked software design problems.

Overview of the JAWS Framework

There are three main framework components in JAWS:

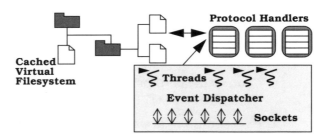

- *Event Dispatcher*. This accepts client connection request events, receives HTTP GET requests, and coordinates JAWS' event demultiplexing strategy with its concurrency strategy. As events are processed they are dispatched to the appropriate Protocol Handler.

- *Protocol Handler*. This implements the parsing and protocol processing of HTTP request events. JAWS Protocol Handler design allows multiple Web protocols, such as HTTP/1.0, HTTP/1.1, and HTTP-NG, to be incorporated into a Web server. To add a new

---

3. The source for JAWS and ACE can be downloaded at http://www.posa.uci.edu/.

protocol, developers just have to write a new Protocol Handler component and configure it into the JAWS framework.

- *Cached Virtual Filesystem.* This improves Web server performance by reducing the overhead of file system accesses when processing HTTP GET requests. Various caching strategies, such as least-recently used (LRU) or least-frequently used (LFU), can be selected according to the actual or anticipated workload and configured statically or dynamically.

Applying Patterns to Resolve Common Design Challenges in JAWS

The overview of the JAWS framework architecture above describes how JAWS is structured, but does not explain *why* it is structured in this way. Understanding why the JAWS framework contains these particular components—and why the components are designed the way they are—requires a deeper knowledge of the patterns underlying the domain of concurrent and networked software in general, and concurrent Web servers in particular.

Eight patterns are used to implement the main components in JAWS:

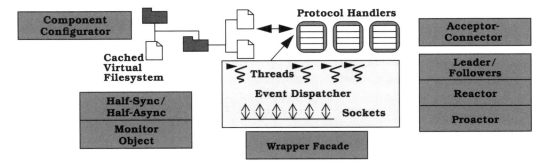

These patterns help resolve the following seven common challenges that arise when developing concurrent servers:

- Encapsulating low-level operating system APIs
- Decoupling event demultiplexing and connection management from protocol processing
- Scaling up server performance via multi-threading
- Implementing a synchronized request queue

- Minimizing server threading overhead

- Using asynchronous I/O effectively

- Enhancing server configurability

In addition to describing the patterns using a minimal 'context/ problem/solution' form, we note the trade-offs between certain patterns and show how these patterns are applied to develop the concurrent JAWS Web server. Chapters 2 through 5 describe these patterns both more generally and in more detail.

Encapsulating Low-level Operating System APIs

Context   A Web server must manage a variety of operating system services, including processes, threads, Socket connections, virtual memory, and files. Most operating systems, such as Win32 or POSIX, provide low-level APIs written in C to access these services.

Problem   The diversity of hardware and operating systems makes it hard to build portable and robust Web server software by programming to low-level operating system APIs directly. These APIs are tedious, error-prone, and non-portable, which makes them an ineffective way to develop Web servers or other networked applications.

Solution   *Apply the Wrapper Facade pattern (47) to avoid accessing low-level operating system APIs directly.* This design pattern encapsulates the functions and data provided by existing non-object-oriented APIs, for example low-level operating system APIs, within more concise, robust, portable, maintainable, and cohesive object-oriented class interfaces.

Use in JAWS   JAWS uses the wrapper facades defined by ACE to ensure its framework components can run on many operating systems, including Windows, UNIX, and many real-time operating systems.

For example, JAWS uses the ACE `Thread_Mutex` wrapper facade to provide a portable interface to operating system mutual exclusion mechanisms.

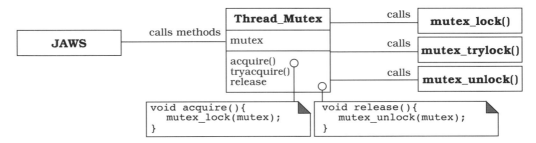

The `Thread_Mutex` wrapper shown in the diagram is implemented using the Solaris threading API [EKBF+92]. However, the ACE `Thread_Mutex` wrapper facade is also available for other threading APIs, for example Win32 threads or POSIX Pthreads. Other ACE wrapper facades used in JAWS encapsulate Sockets, process and thread management, memory-mapped files, explicit dynamic linking, and time operations [Sch97].

Decoupling Event Demultiplexing and Connection Management from Protocol Processing

Context   A Web server can be accessed simultaneously by multiple clients, each of which has its own connection to the server. A Web server must therefore be able to demultiplex and process multiple types of indication events that can arrive from different clients concurrently:

- A connection request, which the server receives via a CONNECT indication event that instructs it to accept the client connection

- An HTTP GET request to download a file, which the server receives via a READ indication event that instructs it to receive a request from one of its client connections

A common way to demultiplex events in a Web server is to use `select()` [Ste98]. This function reports which socket handles have indication events pending so that Socket operations, such as `accept()` for accepting a client connection request or `recv()` for receiving a client request, can be invoked without blocking the server.

Problem   Developers often tightly couple a Web server's event-demultiplexing and connection-management code with its protocol-handling code that performs HTTP 1.0 processing. In such a design, however, the demultiplexing and connection-management code cannot be reused as black-box components by other HTTP protocols, or by other middleware and applications, such as ORBs [SC99] and imaging servers [PHS96]. Moreover, changes to the event-demultiplexing and connection-management code, such as porting it to use TLI [Rago93] or `WaitForMultipleObjects()` [Sol98], will affect the Web server protocol code directly and may introduce subtle bugs.

Solution   *Apply the Reactor pattern (179) and the Acceptor-Connector pattern (285) to separate the generic event-demultiplexing and connection-management code from the HTTP protocol code.* The Reactor architectural pattern decouples the synchronous event demultiplexing and dispatching logic of server applications from the service(s), such as HTTP protocol processing, performed in response to events. The Acceptor-Connector design pattern can build on the Reactor pattern to decouple the connection and initialization of co-operating peer services, for example an HTTP client and server, from the processing activities performed by these peer services once they are connected and initialized.

Use in JAWS   JAWS uses the Reactor pattern to process multiple synchronous events from multiple sources of events *without* polling all its event sources or blocking indefinitely on any single source of events. Similarly, it uses the Acceptor-Connector pattern to vary its protocol-processing code independently from its connection-management code.

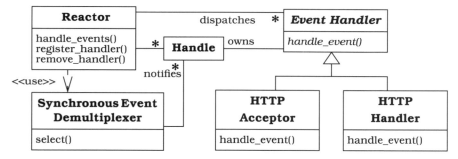

In this design, the `select()` synchronous event demultiplexer waits for events to occur on a set of handles. When an event arrives, `select()` notifies a reactor, which then demultiplexes and dispatches this event to a designated event handler for further processing.

There are two types of event handlers in JAWS:

- The `HTTP_Acceptor` registers itself with the `Reactor` for `CONNECT` events. When these events occur the `Reactor` invokes the `handle_event()` hook method of the `HTTP_Acceptor`, which then creates, connects, and activates an `HTTP_Handler`.

- Each `HTTP_Handler` is a Protocol Handler whose `handle_event()` hook method is responsible for receiving and processing the HTTP `GET` request sent by its connected client.

By using the Reactor and Acceptor-Connector patterns, the protocol-specific processing code in the `HTTP_Handler` is decoupled from the protocol-independent event demultiplexing and connection-management code in the Event Dispatcher. This design makes it easier to maintain and reuse the various components in JAWS.

Scaling Up Server Performance via Multi-threading

Context   HTTP runs over TCP, which uses flow control to ensure that senders do not produce data more rapidly than slow receivers or congested networks can buffer and process [Ste93]. Achieving efficient end-to-end *quality of service* (QoS) is important to handle heavy Web traffic loads [PQ00]. A Web server must therefore scale up efficiently as its number of clients increases.

Problem   Processing all HTTP `GET` requests reactively within a single-threaded process does not scale up efficiently, because each Web server CPU time-slice spends much of its time blocked waiting for I/O operations to complete. Similarly, to improve QoS for all its connected clients, an entire Web server process must not block while waiting for connection flow control to abate so it can finish sending a file to a client.

Solution   *Apply the Half-Sync/Half-Async pattern (423) to scale up server performance by processing different HTTP requests concurrently in multiple threads.* This architectural pattern defines two service processing layers—one asynchronous and one synchronous—along with a queueing layer that allows services to exchange messages between the two layers. The pattern allows synchronous services, such as HTTP protocol processing, to run concurrently, relative both to each other and to asynchronous services, such as event demultiplexing.

This solution yields two benefits:

- Threads can be mapped to separate CPUs to scale up server performance via multi-processing.

- Each thread blocks independently, which prevents one flow-controlled connection from degrading the QoS other clients receive.

Use in JAWS   JAWS can use the Half-Sync/Half-Async pattern to process HTTP GET requests synchronously from multiple clients, but concurrently in separate threads of control:

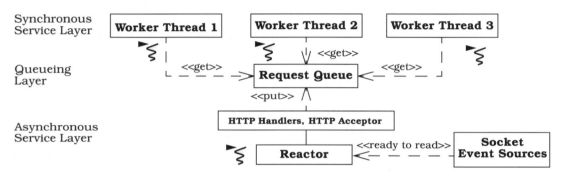

Synchronous
Service Layer

Queueing
Layer

Asynchronous
Service Layer

The Reactor's HTTP_Handlers constitute the services in JAWS' 'asynchronous' layer. Although the Reactor is not truly asynchronous, it shares key properties with asynchronous services. For example, an HTTP_Handler dispatched by the Reactor cannot block for long without starving other clients. Therefore, in this design an HTTP_Handler just reads an incoming HTTP GET request and inserts it into a request queue serviced by a pool of worker threads.

The worker thread that removes the request performs HTTP protocol processing synchronously. It then transfers the file back to the client. If flow control occurs on its client connection this thread can block without degrading the QoS experienced by clients serviced by other worker threads in the pool.

Implementing a Synchronized Request Queue

Context   At the center of the Half-Sync/Half-Async pattern is a queueing layer. In JAWS, the Reactor thread is a 'producer' that inserts HTTP GET requests into a queue. The worker threads in the pool are 'consumers' that remove and process requests from the queue.

Problem   A naive implementation of a request queue will incur race conditions or 'busy waiting' when multiple threads insert and remove requests. For example, multiple concurrent producer and consumer threads can corrupt the queue's internal state if it is not synchronized properly. Similarly, these threads will 'busy wait' when the queue is empty or full, which wastes CPU cycles unnecessarily.

Solution   *Apply the Monitor Object pattern (399) to implement a synchronized request queue.* This design pattern synchronizes method execution to ensure only one method at a time runs within an object, such as the Web server's request queue. In addition, it allows an object's methods to schedule their execution sequences co-operatively. For example, a monitor object can be used to prevent threads from 'busy waiting' when the request queue is empty or full.

Use in JAWS   The JAWS synchronized request queue uses a pair of POSIX condition variables to implement the queue's *not-empty* and *not-full* monitor conditions. This synchronized request queue can be integrated into the Half-Sync/Half-Async thread pool implementation in JAWS' Event Dispatcher:

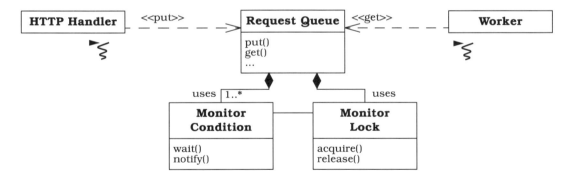

When a worker thread attempts to dequeue an HTTP GET request from an empty queue, the request queue's get() method atomically releases the monitor lock and the worker thread suspends itself on the *not-empty* monitor condition. It remains suspended until the queue is no longer empty, which happens when an HTTP_Handler running in the Reactor thread inserts a request into the queue.

Minimizing Server Threading Overhead

Context   Socket implementations in certain multi-threaded operating systems, such as Windows NT and Solaris, provide a concurrent `accept()` optimization [Ste98] to accept client connection requests. This optimization improves the performance of Web servers that implement the HTTP 1.0 protocol in three ways:

- The operating system allows a pool of threads in a Web server to call `accept()` on the same passive-mode socket handle.

- When a connection request arrives, the operating system's transport layer creates a new connected transport endpoint, encapsulates this new endpoint with a data-mode socket handle and passes the handle as the return value from `accept()`.

- The operating system then schedules one of the threads in the pool to receive this data-mode handle, which it uses to communicate with its connected client.

Problem   The Half-Sync/Half-Async threading model described in the discussion on *Scaling Up Server Performance via Multi-threading* (31) is more scalable than the purely reactive model described in the sub-section on *Decoupling Event Demultiplexing and Connection Management from Protocol Processing* (29). It is not necessarily the most efficient design, however. For example, it incurs a dynamic memory allocation, multiple synchronization operations, a context switch, and cache updates to pass a request between the `Reactor` thread and a worker thread. This overhead makes JAWS' latency unnecessarily high, particularly on operating systems that support the concurrent `accept()` optimization outlined in the *Context* discussion.

Solution   *Apply the Leader/Followers pattern (447) to minimize server threading overhead.* This architectural pattern provides an efficient concurrency model where multiple threads take turns to share event sources, such as a passive-mode socket handle, in order to detect, demultiplex, dispatch, and process service requests that occur on the event sources. This pattern eliminates the need for—and the overhead of— a separate `Reactor` thread and synchronized request queue.

Use in JAWS JAWS' Event Dispatcher and Protocol Handler can be implemented via a Leader/Followers thread pool design, as follows:

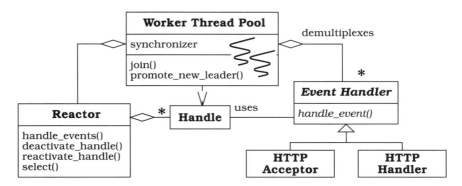

In this design, multiple worker threads in a pool share the same passive-mode socket handle. There are two variants to consider:

- If the operating system supports the concurrent `accept()` optimization described in the *Context* paragraph, all worker threads can simply call `accept()`. The operating system thread scheduler then determines the order in which client HTTP GET requests are dispatched to `HTTP_Handlers` by applying the steps outlined above. Each `HTTP_Handler` now runs in its own thread of control, so it can perform its I/O operations synchronously without blocking other threads that are processing their client requests.

- If the operating system does not support the `accept()` optimization a different Leader/Followers implementation can be used to share the passive-mode socket handle. In this design, one thread at a time—the *leader* thread—calls the `Reactor's` `handle_events()` method to wait for a connection to arrive on the passive-mode socket handle. The other threads—the *followers*—queue waiting their turn to become the leader.

After the current leader thread receives a newly-connected socket handle, it promotes a follower thread to become the new leader. It then plays the role of a *processing* thread, using the `Reactor` to demultiplex and dispatch the event to an `HTTP_Handler` that performs all HTTP protocol processing for that client's request. Multiple processing threads can run concurrently while the new leader thread waits for new connections to arrive via the `Reactor`.

After handling its HTTP GET request, a processing thread reverts to a follower role and waits to become the leader thread again.

The Leader/Followers thread pool design is highly efficient [SMFG00]. If there are requirements besides just raw performance, however, the Half-Sync/Half-Async (423) design may still be a more appropriate concurrency model for a Web server:

- The Half-Sync/Half-Async design can reorder and prioritize client requests more flexibly, because it has a synchronized request queue implemented using the Monitor Object pattern (399).

- It may be more scalable, because it queues requests in Web server virtual memory, rather than the operating system kernel [Sch97].

We cover both thread pool alternatives here to illustrate how the use of patterns helps to make these design trade-offs explicit.

Leveraging Asynchronous I/O Effectively

Context   Synchronous multi-threading may not be the most scalable way to implement a Web server on operating system platforms that support asynchronous I/O more efficiently than synchronous multi-threading. For example, highly-efficient Web servers can be implemented on Windows NT [Sol98] by invoking asynchronous Win32 operations that perform the following activities:

- Processing indication events, such as TCP CONNECT and HTTP GET requests, via `AcceptEx()` and `ReadFile()`, respectively

- Transmitting requested files to clients asynchronously via `Write-File()` or `TransmitFile()` [HPS99]

When these asynchronous operations complete, the operating system delivers the associated completion events containing their results to the Web server. It then processes these events and performs the appropriate actions before returning to its event loop.

Problem   Developing software that achieves the potential efficiency and scalability of asynchronous I/O is hard. The challenge is due largely to the separation in time and space of asynchronous operation invocations and their subsequent completion events.

Solution   *Apply the Proactor pattern (215) to make efficient use of asynchronous I/O.* This architectural pattern structures event-driven concurrent server applications that receive and process requests from multiple clients asynchronously. Application services are split into two parts:

- Operations that execute asynchronously, for example to accept connections and receive client HTTP GET requests

- The corresponding completion handlers that process the asynchronous operation results, for example to transmit a file back to a client after an asynchronous connection operation completes

As with the Reactor pattern, the Proactor pattern decouples the event demultiplexing and event-handler dispatching logic of server applications from the service(s) performed in response to events. The primary difference is that the Proactor handles *completion* events resulting from *asynchronous* operations, whereas the Reactor handles *indication* events that trigger *synchronous* operations.

Use in JAWS   JAWS can use the Proactor pattern to perform its Protocol Handler processing, such as parsing the headers of an HTTP GET request, while processing other connection- and I/O-related events asynchronously. JAWS can thus implement its Event Dispatcher and Protocol Handler components efficiently on Windows NT:

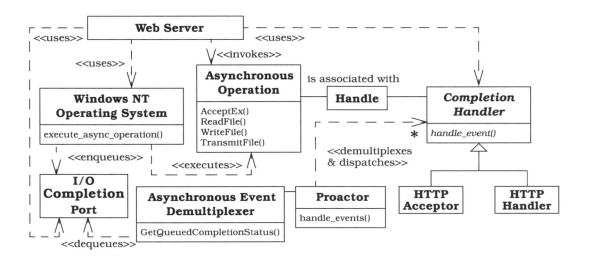

In this design, JAWS initiates asynchronous Win32 operations via socket handles to process service requests 'proactively'. For example, `AcceptEx()` can accept incoming connection requests from clients and `TransmitFile()` can send a file back to the client. These operations are executed asynchronously by the Windows NT kernel.

When an asynchronous operation finishes, the kernel inserts a completion event containing that operation's results into an I/O completion port, which queues the completion events. Completion events are removed from this port via the `GetQueuedCompletionStatus()` Win32 function, which is called by the `Proactor` that runs JAWS' event loop. The `Proactor` demultiplexes and dispatches completion events to the appropriate `HTTP_Acceptor` or `HTTP_Handler` that is associated with the asynchronous operation.

Completion handlers process the results of asynchronous operations, potentially invoking additional asynchronous operations. For example, the completion handler for an asynchronous `AcceptEx()` operation typically initiates an asynchronous `WriteFile()` or `TransmitFile()` operation to download a requested file to the client.

On platforms that support asynchronous I/O efficiently, Proactor pattern implementations of Web servers are often substantially more efficient than Half-Sync/Half-Async (423) and Leader/Followers (447) pattern implementations [HPS99]. However, the Proactor pattern can be more complex to implement than the other two concurrency architectures:

- It has more participants than the other two patterns, which requires more effort to understand and implement.

- The combination of 'inversion of control' and asynchrony in Proactor requires a great deal of experience to program and debug.

As discussed in the section *Minimizing Server Threading Overhead*, (34) the use of patterns enables us to evaluate the pros and cons of various Web server architectures without being distracted by non-essential implementation details, such as the syntax of a platform's threading, demultiplexing, or connection-management APIs.

Enhancing Server Configurability

Context The implementation of certain Web server strategies depends on a variety of factors. Certain factors are *static*, such as the number of available CPUs and operating system support for asynchronous I/O. Other factors are *dynamic*, such as Web workload characteristics.

Problem No single Web server configuration is optimal for all use cases. In addition, some design decisions cannot be made efficiently until run-time. Prematurely committing to a particular Web server configuration is therefore inflexible and inefficient. For example, it is undesirable to include unused Protocol Handler or Cached Virtual Filesystem components in a Web server, because this increases its memory footprint and can degrade its performance.

Solution *Apply the Component Configurator pattern (75) to enhance the configurability of a Web server.* This design pattern allows an application to link and unlink its component implementations at run-time. New and enhanced services can therefore be added without having to modify, recompile, statically relink, or shut down and restart a running application.

Use in JAWS JAWS uses the Component Configurator pattern to dynamically optimize, control, and reconfigure the behavior of its Web server strategies at installation-time or during run-time. For example, JAWS applies the Component Configurator pattern to configure its various Cached Virtual Filesystem strategies, such as least-recently used (LRU) or least-frequently used (LFU):

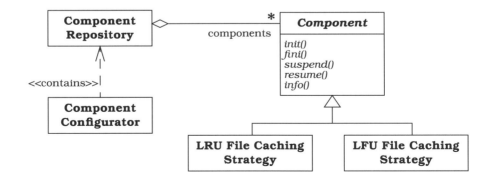

The Component class defines a uniform interface for configuring and controlling a particular application service that it provides. Concrete components, which include the LRU_File_Caching_Strategy class and the LFU_File_Caching_Strategy class, then implement this interface. Web server administrators can use the Component interface to initiate, suspend, resume, and terminate the concrete components dynamically, depending on anticipated or actual workload.

Concrete components can be packaged into a suitable unit of configuration, such as a dynamically linked library (DLL). Only the components that are currently in use need to be configured into the Web server. These components can be linked/unlinked into and out of an application dynamically under the control of a Component Configurator. In turn, this object uses a Component Repository, which is a memory-resident database that manages all concrete components configured into the Web server.

Other Patterns Used to Implement JAWS

The implementation of JAWS applies other design patterns to improve its flexibility and modularity. For example, two other design patterns and an idiom in this book are used in JAWS:

- The *Thread-Safe Interface* (345) and *Strategized Locking* (333) patterns help minimize locking overhead in the JAWS' Cached Virtual Filesystem file cache strategies. They also ensure that intra-component method calls do not incur 'self-deadlock' by trying to reacquire a lock that a file cache already holds.

- The *Scoped Locking* C++ idiom (325) is used throughout JAWS to ensure that a lock is acquired when control enters a scope and the lock is released automatically when control leaves the scope, regardless of the path out of the scope.

Three patterns from [GoF95] are also used in JAWS:

- The *Singleton* pattern ensures that a class has only one instance and provides a global point of access to it. JAWS uses a Singleton to ensure that only one instance of its Cached Virtual Filesystem exists in a Web server process.

- The *State* pattern defines a composite object whose behavior depends upon its state. The Event Dispatcher in JAWS uses the

State pattern to support both different concurrency strategies and synchronous and asynchronous I/O seamlessly [HPS99].

- The *Strategy* pattern defines a family of algorithms, encapsulates each one, and makes them interchangeable. JAWS uses this pattern extensively, for example to select different HTTP protocols without affecting its Protocol Handler software architecture.

Other design patterns from [GoF95], such as Adapter, Bridge, Factory Method, Iterator and Template Method, and from [POSA1], such as Proxy, are used in JAWS to implement the eight patterns we presented above. The pattern descriptions presented in Chapters 2 through 5 describe the relationships between all these patterns in full detail.

In contrast to the four architectural patterns—Reactor, Proactor, Half-Sync/Half-Async, and Leader/Followers—described in section *Applying Patterns to Resolve Common Design Challenges in JAWS*, these design patterns have a relatively localized impact on JAWS. For example, although the Strategized Locking pattern is domain-independent and widely applicable, the problem it addresses does not impact JAWS' Web server software architecture as pervasively as the Proactor or Leader/Followers patterns. A thorough understanding of design patterns is essential, however, to implement highly-flexible software that is resilient to changes in application requirements and platform characteristics.

1.4   Wrapping Up

Computing power and network bandwidth will continue to increase dramatically during this decade. However, the requirements, scale, and complexity of the concurrent and networked application software that builds on these hardware advances will also increase at a similar pace. Without corresponding advances in software techniques, it will be hard to manage lifecycle costs and develop quality software within a reasonable time and level of effort.

Much of the cost and effort of concurrent and networked software stems from the continual rediscovery and reinvention of fundamental patterns and framework components that reify these patterns. Patterns and pattern languages help reduce this cost and improve the quality of software by using proven architectures and designs to produce applications and application frameworks. These frameworks can be customized to meet existing application requirements, as well as extended to meet future requirements.

The JAWS example presented in this chapter demonstrates how the effort required to develop concurrent and networked software can be reduced significantly by applying patterns and framework components judiciously. Rather than rediscovering solutions to complex concurrent and networked software problems and reinventing the corresponding software from scratch, developers can instead focus on achieving their strategic technical and business objectives. Even when changes to technologies or tools preclude the direct use of existing components, algorithms, detailed designs, and implementations, the core architectural and design patterns that underlie these artifacts often can still be reused.

The JAWS example also illustrates the importance of understanding how groups of patterns collaborate to help resolve complex concurrent and networked application design problems. Problems and forces are often inter-related, and these relationships should be considered when addressing key design issues and implementation trade-offs. Regardless of their individual utility, therefore, no single pattern is an island. Instead, patterns must be understood in the larger software architecture context in which they apply.

2 Service Access and Configuration Patterns

There once was a man who went to a computer trade show. Each day as he entered, the man told the guard at the door: "I am a great thief, renowned for my feats of shoplifting. Be forewarned, for this trade show shall not escape unplundered."

This speech disturbed the guard greatly, because there were millions of dollars of computer equipment inside, so he watched the man carefully. But the man merely wandered from booth to booth, asking questions and humming quietly to himself.

When the man left, the guard took him aside and searched his clothes, but nothing was to be found. On the next day of the trade show, the man returned and chided the guard saying: "I escaped with a vast booty yesterday, but today will be even better." So the guard watched him ever more closely, but to no avail.

On the final day of the trade show, the guard could restrain his curiosity no longer. "Sir Thief", he said, "I am so perplexed, I cannot live in peace. Please enlighten me. What is it that you are stealing?"

The man smiled. "I am stealing patterns", he said.

*Adapted from "The TAO Of Programming" [JH98]
by Geoffrey James and Duke Hillard*

This chapter presents four patterns for designing effective application programming interfaces (APIs) to access and configure services and components in stand-alone and networked systems: Wrapper Facade, Component Configurator, Interceptor, and Extension Interface.

Networked systems are inherently heterogeneous [HV99]. Therefore, a key challenge confronting researchers and developers is how to effectively design and configure application access to the interfaces and implementations of evolving service components. This chapter presents four patterns that address various aspects of service access and configuration:

- The *Wrapper Facade* design pattern (47) encapsulates the functions and data provided by existing non-object-oriented APIs within more concise, robust, portable, maintainable, and cohesive object-oriented class interfaces. Wrapper Facade is often applied to improve application portability by 'wrapping' lower-level operating system APIs. It can also alleviate the accidental complexity associated with programming using low-level APIs.

  To minimize redundancy in other patterns in the book, the *Implementation* section of the Wrapper Facade pattern contains detailed coverage of wrapper facades for threads, mutex locks, condition variables, and Sockets. Subsequent patterns, such as Reactor (179), Proactor (215), Acceptor-Connector (285), Strategized Locking (333), Active Object (369), and Monitor Object (399), use these wrapper facades in their own implementations. Therefore, we recommend you read Wrapper Facade first.

- The *Component Configurator* design pattern (75) allows an application to link and unlink its component implementations at run-time without having to modify, recompile, or relink the application statically. Applications with high availability requirements, such as mission-critical systems that perform on-line transaction processing or real-time industrial process automation, often require such flexible configuration capabilities. Component Configurator therefore addresses aspects of service configuration and service evolution.

  Other patterns in this section, particularly Extension Interface (141) and Interceptor (109), can use the Component Configurator pattern to (re)configure various service roles into components in application processes without having to shut down and restart running application processes.

- The *Interceptor* architectural pattern (109) allows services to be added to a framework transparently and to be triggered automatically when certain events occur. Interceptor therefore prepares a framework for its own evolution to accommodate services that are not configured or not even known during the framework's original development. Interceptor also allows other applications to integrate components and services with instances of the framework. Such services are often 'out-of-band' or application-specific from the perspective of the framework instance, but are important for the productive and proper operation of applications that use the framework.

- The *Extension Interface* design pattern (141) prevents the 'bloating' of interfaces and breakage of client code when developers extend or modify the service functionality of existing components. Multiple extension interfaces can be attached to the same component. Extension Interface addresses both the challenge of component and service evolution and the provision of clients with an authorized and role-specific access to a component's functionality.

The topics of service access and configuration involve more challenges than are addressed by the patterns in this section. These challenges include:

- Mediating access to remote services via local proxies

- Managing the lifecycle of services, locating services in a distributed system and

- Controlling the operating system and computing resources a server can provide to the service implementations it hosts

Other patterns in the literature address these issues, such as Activator [Stal00], Evictor [HV99], Half Object plus Protocol [Mes95], Locator [JK00], Object Lifetime Manager [LGS99], and Proxy [POSA1] [GoF95]. These patterns complement those presented in this section and together describe key principles that well-structured distributed systems should apply to configure and provide access to the services they offer.

Wrapper Facade

The *Wrapper Facade* design pattern encapsulates the functions and data provided by existing non-object-oriented APIs within more concise, robust, portable, maintainable, and cohesive object-oriented class interfaces.

Example   Consider a server for a distributed logging service that handles multiple clients concurrently using the connection-oriented TCP protocol [Ste98]. To log data a client must send a connection request to a server transport address, which consists of a TCP port number and IP address. In the logging server, a passive-mode *socket handle factory* listens on this address for connection requests. The socket handle factory accepts the connection request and creates a data-mode socket handle that identifies this client's transport address. This handle is passed to the server, which spawns a *logging handler* thread that processes client logging requests.

After a client is connected it sends logging requests to the server. The logging handler thread receives these requests via its connected socket handle. It then processes the requests in the logging handler thread and writes the requests to a log file.

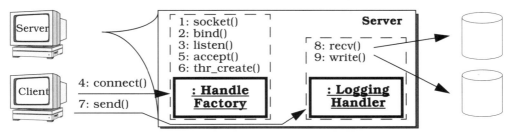

A common way to develop this logging server is to use low-level C language APIs, such as Solaris threads [EKBF+92] and Sockets [Ste98], to program the server's threading, synchronization, and network communication functionality. If the logging server runs on multiple platforms, however, there will be differences between functions and data in the low-level APIs, as well as different operating system and compiler features and defects. Developers commonly handle these differences by inserting conditional compilation directives, such as C/C++ #ifdefs, throughout their code. For instance, the following code illustrates a logging server that has been implemented using #ifdefs to run on Solaris and Windows NT:

```
#if defined (_WIN32)
    #include <windows.h>
    typedef int ssize_t;
#else
    typedef unsigned int UINT32;
    #include <thread.h>
    #include <unistd.h>
    #include <sys/socket.h>
    #include <netinet/in.h>
    #include <memory.h>
#endif /* _WIN32 */

// Keep track of number of logging requests.
static int request_count;

// Lock that serializes concurrent access to request_count.
#if defined (_WIN32)
    static CRITICAL_SECTION lock;
#else
    static mutex_t lock;
#endif /* _WIN32 */

// Maximum size of a logging record.
static const int LOG_RECORD_MAX = 1024;

// Port number to listen on for requests.
static const int LOGGING_PORT = 10000;

// Entry point that writes logging records.
int write_record (char log_record[], int len) {
    /* ... */
    return 0;
}

// Entry point that processes logging records for
// one client connection.
#if defined (_WIN32)
    u_long
#else
    void *
#endif /* _WIN32 */
logging_handler (void *arg) {
    // Handle UNIX/Win32 portability.
#if defined (_WIN32)
    SOCKET h = reinterpret_cast <SOCKET> (arg);
#else
    int h = reinterpret_cast <int> (arg);
#endif /* _WIN32 */

    for (;;) {
#if defined (_WIN32)
        ULONG len;
#else
        UINT32 len;
#endif /* _WIN32 */
        // Ensure a 32-bit quantity.
        char log_record[LOG_RECORD_MAX];
        // The first <recv> reads the length
        // (stored as a 32-bit integer) of
        // adjacent logging record. This code
        // does not handle "short-<recv>s".
        ssize_t n = recv (h,
                    reinterpret_cast <char *> (&len),
                    sizeof len, 0);
        // Bail out if we're shutdown or
        // errors occur unexpectedly.
        if (n <= sizeof len) break;
        len = ntohl (len);
        if (len > LOG_RECORD_MAX) break;

        // The second <recv> then reads <len>
        // bytes to obtain the actual record.
        // This code handles "short-<recv>s".
        for (size_t nread = 0; nread < len; nread += n) {
            n = recv (h, log_record + nread,
                        len - nread, 0);
            // Bail out if an error occurs.
            if (n <= 0) return 0;
        }
```

```
#if defined (_WIN32)
        EnterCriticalSection (&lock);
#else
        mutex_lock (&lock);
#endif /* _WIN32 */
        // Execute following two statements in a critical
        // section to avoid ace conditions and scrambled
        // output, respectively.
        ++request_count;
        // A return value of -1 signifies failure.
        if (write_record (log_record, len) == -1)
            break;
#if defined (_WIN32)
        LeaveCriticalSection (&lock);
#else
        mutex_unlock (&lock);
#endif /* _WIN32 */
    }
#if defined (_WIN32)
    closesocket (h);
#else
    close (h);
#endif /* _WIN32 */
    return 0;
}

// Main driver function for the server.
int main (int argc, char *argv[]) {
    struct sockaddr_in sock_addr;
    // Handle UNIX/Win32 portability.
#if defined (_WIN32)
    SOCKET acceptor;
    WORD version_requested = MAKEWORD(2, 0);
    WSADATA wsa_data;
    int error = WSAStartup(version_requested, &wsa_data);
    if (error != 0) return -1;
#else
    int acceptor;
#endif /* _WIN32 */
    // Create a local endpoint of communication.
    acceptor = socket (AF_INET, SOCK_STREAM, 0);
    // Set up the address to become a server.
    memset (&sock_addr, 0, sizeof sock_addr);
    sock_addr.sin_family = PF_INET;
    sock_addr.sin_port = htons (LOGGING_PORT);
    sock_addr.sin_addr.s_addr = htonl (INADDR_ANY);
    // Associate address with endpoint.
    bind (acceptor, reinterpret_cast<struct sockaddr *>
            (&sock_addr), sizeof sock_addr);
    // Make endpoint listen for connections.
    listen (acceptor, 5);

    // Main server event loop.
    for (;;) {
        // Handle UNIX/Win32 portability.
#if defined (_WIN32)
        SOCKET h;
        DWORD t_id;
#else
        int h;
        thread_t t_id;
#endif /* _WIN32 */
        // Block waiting for clients to connect.
        h = accept (acceptor, 0, 0);
        // Spawn a new thread that runs the <server>
        // entry point.
#if defined (_WIN32)
        CreateThread (0, 0,
                LPTHREAD_START_ROUTINE(&logging_handler),
                reinterpret_cast <void *> (h), 0, &t_id);
#else
        thr_create
                (0, 0, logging_handler,
                reinterpret_cast <void *> (h),
                THR_DETACHED, &t_id);
#endif /* _WIN32 */
    }
    return 0;
}
```

The design shown above may work for short-lived, 'throw-away' prototypes [FoYo99]. It is inadequate, however, for software that must be maintained and enhanced over time. The use of conditional compilation directives and direct programming of low-level APIs makes the code unnecessarily hard to understand, debug, port, maintain, and evolve.

Certain problems can be alleviated by moving platform-specific declarations, such as the mutex and socket types, into separate configuration header files. This solution is incomplete, however, because the #ifdefs that separate the *use* of platform-specific APIs, such as thread creation calls, will still pollute application code. Supporting new platforms will also require modifications to platform-specific declarations, irrespective of whether they are included directly into application code or separated into configuration files.

Several well-known patterns address similar problems, but unfortunately do not help to resolve the problems outlined above. For example, Facade [GoF95] encapsulates object-oriented subsystems rather than lower-level non-object-oriented APIs. Decorator [GoF95] extends an object *dynamically* by attaching additional responsibilities transparently, which incurs unnecessary performance overhead. Bridge and Adapter [GoF95] also introduce an additional layer of indirection that can incur overhead. In general, therefore, these patterns are not well suited to encapsulate existing lower-level non-object oriented APIs, where it may be more important that the solution be efficient than be dynamically extensible.

Context Maintainable and evolvable applications that access mechanisms or services provided by existing non-object-oriented APIs.

Problem Applications are often written using non-object-oriented operating system APIs or system libraries. These APIs access network and thread programming mechanisms, as well as user interface or database programming libraries. Although this design is common, it causes problems for application developers by not resolving the following *forces*:

- Concise code is often more robust than verbose code because it is easier to develop and maintain. Using object-oriented languages that support higher-level features, such as constructors, destructors, exceptions, and garbage collection, reduces the likelihood of common programming errors. However, developers who program using lower-level function-based APIs directly tend to rewrite a great deal of verbose and error-prone software repeatedly.

➥   The code for creating and initializing an acceptor socket in the `main()` function of our logging server example is error-prone. Moreover, these errors are subtle, such as failing to initialize the `sock_addr` to zero or not using the `htons()` macro to convert the `LOGGING_PORT` number into network byte order [Sch92]. The lack of constructors and destructors in C also makes it hard to ensure that resources are allocated and released properly. For example, note how the lock that serializes access to `request_count` will not be released correctly if the `write_record()` function returns −1.❏

- Software that is portable or can be ported easily to different operating systems, compilers, and hardware platforms helps increase product market-share. Although reusing existing lower-level APIs may reduce some of the software development effort, applications programmed directed with lower-level APIs are often non-portable. Programming using lower-level APIs across different versions of the *same* operating system or compiler also may be non-portable due to the lack of source-level or binary-level compatibility across software releases [Box97].

➥   Our logging server example has hard-coded dependencies on several non-portable operating system threading and network programming C APIs. For example, the Solaris `thr_create()`, `mutex_lock()`, and `mutex_unlock()` functions are not portable to Win32 platforms. Although the code is quasi-portable—it also compiles and runs on Win32 platforms—there are various subtle portability problems. In particular, there will be resource leaks on Win32 platforms because there is no equivalent to the Solaris `THR_DETACHED` feature, which spawns a 'detached' thread whose exit status is not retained by the threading library [Lew95].   ❏

- Improving software maintainability helps reduce lifecycle costs. Programs written directly to low-level non-object-oriented APIs are often hard to maintain, however. For example, C and C++ developers often address portability issues by embedding conditional compilation directives into their application source. Unfortunately, addressing platform-specific variations via conditional compilation at *all* points of use increases the software's physical design complexity [Lak95]. For instance, platform-specific details become scattered throughout the application source files.

➡ Maintenance of our logging server is impeded by the #ifdefs that handle Win32 and Solaris portability, for example the differences in the type of a socket on Win32 and Solaris. In general, developers who program to low-level C APIs like these must have intimate knowledge of many operating system idiosyncrasies to maintain and evolve their code.   ❏

- Cohesive components are easier to learn, maintain, and enhance. However, low-level APIs are rarely grouped into cohesive components because languages like C lack features such as classes, namespaces, or packages. It is hard, therefore, to recognize the extent of low-level APIs. Programming with non-cohesive stand-alone function APIs also scatters common code throughout an application, making it hard to 'plug in' new components that support different policies and mechanisms.

➡ The Socket API is particularly hard to learn because the several dozen C functions in the Socket library lack a uniform naming convention. For example, it is not obvious that socket(), bind(), listen(), connect(), and accept() are related. Other low-level network programming APIs, such as TLI, address this problem by prepending a common function prefix, such as the t_ prefixed before each function in the TLI API. However, the use of a common prefix does not by itself make the TLI API more 'pluggable' than Sockets. It remains a low-level function-based API rather than a more cohesive object-oriented class interface.   ❏

In general, developing applications by programming to non-object-oriented APIs directly is a poor design choice for software that must be maintained and evolved over time.

Solution   Avoid accessing non-object-oriented APIs directly. For each set of related functions and data in a non-object-oriented API, create one or more *wrapper facade* classes that encapsulate these functions and data within the more concise, robust, portable, and maintainable methods provided by the object-oriented wrapper facade(s).

Structure   There are two participants in the Wrapper Facade pattern:

Functions are the building blocks of existing non-object-oriented APIs. They provide a stand-alone service or mechanism and manipulate data passed as parameters or accessed through global variables.

A *wrapper facade* is a set of one or more object-oriented classes that encapsulate existing functions and their associated data. These class(es) export a cohesive abstraction that provides a specific type of functionality. Each class represents a specific role in this abstraction.

The methods in the wrapper facade class(es) generally forward application invocations to one or more of the functions, passing the data as parameters. The data is often hidden within the private portion of the wrapper facade and is not accessible to client applications. Compilers can then enforce type safety because primitive data types, such as pointers or integers, are encapsulated within strongly-typed wrapper facades.

Class	*Collaborator*
Wrapper Facade	• API Functions
Responsibility	
• Encapsulates non-object-oriented functions and data-structures with a cohesive object-oriented abstraction	

Class	*Collaborator*
API Function	
Responsibility	
• Provides a single service via a well-defined API	

The following class diagram illustrates the structure of Wrapper Facade:

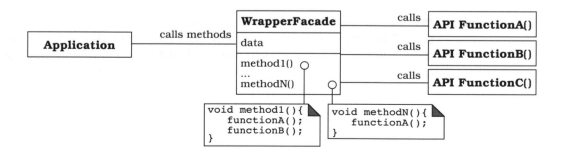

Dynamics Collaborations in the Wrapper Facade pattern are often straightforward:

- The application code invokes a method on an instance of the wrapper facade.

- The wrapper facade method forwards the request and its parameters to one or more of the lower-level API functions that it encapsulates, passing along any internal data needed by the underlying function(s).

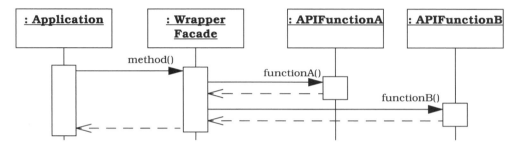

Implementation This section describes the activities involved in implementing the Wrapper Facade pattern. Certain activities may require multiple iterations to identify and implement suitable wrapper facade abstractions. To reduce repetition elsewhere in the book, we present an in-depth discussion of concrete wrapper facades for mutexes, condition variables, Sockets, and threads in this section. Although this lengthens the current section somewhat, the implementation examples of other patterns in this book, including Acceptor-Connector (285), Strategized Locking (333), Thread-Specific Storage (475), and Monitor Object (399), are simplified by using these wrapper facades.

1 *Identify the cohesive abstractions and relationships among existing low-level APIs*. Mature low-level APIs contain functions and data structures that define many cohesive abstractions and map cleanly onto object-oriented classes and methods. Common examples include the C APIs for Win32 synchronization and threading, POSIX network programming, and X Windows GUI event dispatching. Due to the lack of data abstraction in languages like C, however, it may not be clear how functions in these existing APIs relate to each other. The first activity in implementing the Wrapper Facade pattern is therefore to identify the cohesive abstractions and relations among existing APIs.

➡   The original implementation of our logging server carefully uses many low-level functions that provide several cohesive operating system mechanisms, such as synchronization and network communication. The Solaris `mutex_lock()` and `mutex_unlock()` functions, for example, are associated with a mutex synchronization abstraction. Similarly, the `socket()`, `bind()`, `listen()`, and `accept()` functions play various roles in a network programming abstraction.   ❏

If existing functions and data structures have been developed as throw-away code or via piecemeal growth [FoYo99], they may exhibit little or no cohesive abstractions. In this case the code should be refactored [Opd92] [FBBOR99], if possible, before proceeding with the implementation of the Wrapper Facade pattern.

2   *Cluster cohesive groups of functions into wrapper facade classes and methods*. This activity defines one or more class abstractions that shield applications from low-level data representations, arbitrary variations in function syntax, and other implementation details. It can be decomposed into five sub-activities:

2.1   *Create cohesive classes*. We start by defining one or more wrapper facade classes for each group of existing non-object-oriented APIs that are related to a particular abstraction. Common criteria used to create cohesive classes include the following:

- Coalesce functions and data with high *cohesion* into individual classes, while minimizing unnecessary *coupling* between classes. Examples of cohesive functions are those that manipulate common data structures, such as a Socket, a file, or a signal set [Ste98].

- Identify the *common* and *variable* aspects in the underlying functions and data [Cope98]. Common aspects include mechanisms for synchronization, threading, memory management, addressing, and operating system platform APIs. Variable aspects often include the implementations of these mechanisms. Whenever possible variation in functions and data should be factored into classes that isolate variation behind uniform interfaces to enhance extensibility.

In general, if the original API contains a wide range of related functions, it may be necessary to create several wrapper facade classes to separate concerns properly.

2.2 *Coalesce multiple individual functions into a single method.* In addition to grouping existing functions into classes, it may be useful to coalesce multiple individual functions into a smaller number of methods in each wrapper facade class. Coalescing can be used to ensure that a group of lower-level functions are called in the appropriate order, as with the Template Method pattern [GoF95].

2.3 *Automate creation and destruction operations, if possible.* Lower-level APIs often require programmers to call functions explicitly to create and destroy data structures that implement instances of the API. This procedure is error-prone, however, because developers may forget to call these functions in one or more paths through their code. A more robust approach therefore is to leverage the implicit creation and destruction operation capabilities provided by object-oriented languages, such as C++ and Java. In fact, the ability to create and destroy objects automatically often justifies the use of the Wrapper Facade pattern, even if the wrapper facade methods do nothing but forward control to the lower-level function calls.

2.4 *Select the level of indirection.* Most wrapper facade classes simply forward their method calls to the underlying low-level functions, as mentioned above. If wrapper facade methods can be inlined implicitly or explicitly, there need be no run-time indirection overhead when compared to invoking the low-level functions directly. It is also possible to add another level of indirection by dispatching wrapper facade implementations using dynamically bound methods or some other form of polymorphism. In this case the wrapper facade classes play the role of the *abstraction* class in the Bridge pattern [GoF95].

2.5 *Determine where to encapsulate any platform-specific variation.* A common use of the Wrapper Facade pattern is to minimize platform-specific variation in application code. Although wrapper facade method *implementations* may differ across different operating system platforms, they should provide uniform, platform-independent *interfaces*. Where platform-specific variation exists it can be encapsulated via *conditional compilation* or *separate directories*:

- *Conditional compilation* can be used to select among different wrapper facade class method implementations. The use of conditional compilation is inelegant and tedious when `#ifdefs` are scattered throughout application code. Conditional compilation may be acceptable, however, if it is localized in a few platform-specific wrapper facade classes or files that are not accessed directly by application developers. When conditional compilation is used in conjunction with auto-configuration tools, such as GNU `autoconf`, platform-independent wrapper facades can be created within a single source file. As long as the number of variations supported in this file is not unwieldy therefore, conditional compilation can help localize variation and simplify maintenance.

- *Separate directories* can be used to factor out different wrapper facade implementations, thereby minimizing conditional compilation or avoiding it altogether. For example, each operating system platform can have its own directory containing implementations of platform-specific wrapper facades. Language processing tools can be used to include the appropriate wrapper facade class from the relevant directory at compilation. To obtain a different implementation, a different include path could be provided to the compiler. This strategy avoids the problems with conditional compilation described above because it physically decouples the various alternative implementations into separate directories.

Choosing a strategy depends on how often wrapper facade interfaces and implementations change. If changes occur frequently it may be time-consuming to update the conditional compilation sections for each platform. Similarly, all files that depend on the affected files will be recompiled even if the change is only necessary for one platform. Therefore the use of condition compilation becomes increasingly complex as a larger number of different platforms are supported. Regardless of which strategy is selected, however, the burden of maintaining wrapper facade implementations should be the responsibility of wrapper facade developers rather than application developers.

➡ To simplify our logging server implementation, we define wrapper facades that encapsulate existing low-level C APIs for mutexes, Sockets, and threads. Each wrapper facade illustrates how various design issues outlined above can be addressed systematically. We focus on defining wrapper facades for C functions because C is used to define popular operating system APIs, such as POSIX or Win32. However, the same design principles and techniques can be applied to other non-object-oriented languages, such as

FORTRAN, Ada 83, Scheme, or Pascal, as well as to non-operating
system APIs, such as X Windows or ODBC database toolkits [San98].

Mutex wrapper facades. We first define a `Thread_Mutex` abstraction
that encapsulates the Solaris mutex functions with a uniform and
portable class interface:[1]

```
class Thread_Mutex {
public:
    Thread_Mutex ()
        { mutex_init (&mutex_, USYNC_THREAD, 0); }
    ~Thread_Mutex () { mutex_destroy (&mutex_); }

    void acquire () { mutex_lock (&mutex_); }
    void release () { mutex_unlock (&mutex_); }
private:
    // Solaris-specific Mutex mechanism.
    mutex_t mutex_;

    // Disallow copying and assignment.
    Thread_Mutex (const Thread_Mutex &);
    void operator= (const Thread_Mutex &);

    // Define a <Thread_Condition> as a friend so it can
    // access <mutex_>.
    friend class Thread_Condition;
};
```

Note how we define the copy constructor and assignment operator as
private methods in the `Thread_Mutex` class. This C++ idiom ensures
that application programmers cannot copy or assign one `Thread_`
`Mutex` to another accidentally [Mey98] [Str97]. Copying mutexes is a
semantically-invalid operation that is erroneously permitted by the
less strongly-typed C programming API. Our `Thread_Mutex` wrapper
facade therefore provides a mutex interface that is less error-prone
than programming directly to the lower-level Solaris synchronization
functions.

By defining a `Thread_Mutex` class interface and then writing applications to use it, rather than lower-level native operating system C APIs,
we can port our wrapper facade to other platforms more easily. For

---

1. To conserve space and focus on the essential design issues, many of our method
implementations in this book do not check for errors, nor do they always return values
from functions with non-void return types or throw exceptions. Naturally, production
software should always check for and propagate errors consistently and correctly.

example, the identical `Thread_Mutex` interface can be implemented to run on Win32:

```
class Thread_Mutex {
public:
    Thread_Mutex ()
        { InitializeCriticalSection (&mutex_); }
    ~Thread_Mutex ()
        { DeleteCriticalSection (&mutex_); }

    void acquire () { EnterCriticalSection (&mutex_); }
    void release () { LeaveCriticalSection (&mutex_); }
private:
    // Win32-specific Mutex mechanism.
    CRITICAL_SECTION mutex_;

    // Disallow copying and assignment.
    Thread_Mutex (const Thread_Mutex &);
    void operator= (const Thread_Mutex &);
};
```

Naturally, a complete implementation of `Thread_Mutex` would map the platform-specific error handling return values from the various `mutex_t` and `CRITICAL_SECTION` functions to portable C++ exceptions.

As described earlier, we can support multiple operating systems simultaneously by using conditional compilation and `#ifdef`'ing the `Thread_Mutex` method implementations. If conditional compilation is unwieldy due to the number of supported platforms, it is possible to factor out the different `Thread_Mutex` implementations into separate directories. In this case, language processing tools such as compilers and preprocessors can be instructed to include the appropriate platform-specific variant into the application during compilation.

Condition variable wrapper facade. A condition variable is a synchronization mechanism used by collaborating threads to suspend themselves temporarily until condition expressions involving data shared between the threads attain desired states [IEEE96]. We describe the wrapper facade for condition variables at this point because they are often used in conjunction with the `Thread_Mutex` wrapper facade described above. Although our logging server example does not use condition variables, they are used by other patterns throughout the book, such as Strategized Locking (333), Leader/Followers (447), and Monitor Object (399).

As mentioned above, a condition variable is always used in conjunction with a mutex that the client thread must acquire before evaluating the condition expression. If the condition expression is false the client suspends itself on the condition variable and releases the mutex atomically, so that other threads can change the shared data. When a cooperating thread changes this data it can notify the condition variable, which resumes a thread atomically that had suspended itself previously on the condition variable. The thread then re-acquires the mutex associated with the condition variable.

After re-acquiring its mutex a newly-resumed thread next re-evaluates its condition expression. If the shared data has attained the desired state, the thread continues. Otherwise it suspends itself on the condition variable again until it is resumed. This process can repeat until the condition expression becomes true.

In general, when complex condition expressions or scheduling behaviors are required, combining a mutex with a condition variable is more appropriate than just using a mutex. For example, condition variables can be used to implement synchronized message queues, as shown in the Monitor Object pattern example (399). In this situation a pair of condition variables are employed to block supplier threads cooperatively when a message queue is full, and to block consumer threads when the queue is empty.

The following `Thread_Condition` class is a wrapper facade that is implemented using the Solaris condition variable API:

```
class Thread_Condition {
public:
    // Initialize the condition variable and
    // associate it with the <mutex_>.
    Thread_Condition (const Thread_Mutex &m) : mutex_ (m)
        { cond_init (&cond_, USYNC_THREAD, 0); }

    // Destroy the condition variable.
    ~Thread_Condition () { cond_destroy (&cond_); }

    // Wait for the <Thread_Condition> to be notified
    // or until <timeout> has elapsed. If <timeout> == 0
    // then wait indefinitely.
    void wait (Time_Value *timeout = 0) {
        cond_timedwait (&cond_, &mutex_.mutex_,
                        timeout == 0
                            ? 0 : timeout->msec ());
    }
```

```
// Notify one thread waiting on <Thread_Condition>.
void notify () { cond_signal (&cond_); }

// Notify all threads waiting on <Thread_Condition>.
void notify_all () { cond_broadcast (&cond_); }
private:
// Solaris condition variable.
cond_t cond_;

// Reference to mutex lock.
const Thread_Mutex &mutex_;
};
```

The constructor initializes the condition variable and associates it with the Thread_Mutex passed as a parameter. The destructor destroys the condition variable, which releases allocated resources. Note that the mutex is not owned by the Thread_Condition so it is not destroyed in the destructor.

When called by a client thread the wait() method performs the following two steps atomically:

* It releases the associated mutex and

* It suspends itself atomically for up to a timeout amount of time, waiting for the Thread_Condition object to be notified by another thread.

The notify() method resumes one thread waiting on a Thread_ Condition. Similarly the notify_all() method notifies *all* threads that are currently waiting on a Thread_Condition. The mutex_ lock is reacquired by the wait() method before it returns to its client thread, either because the condition variable was notified or because its timeout expired.

Socket wrapper facades. Our next wrapper facade encapsulates the Socket API. This API is much larger and more expressive than the Solaris mutex API [Sch92]. We must therefore define a *group* of related wrapper facade classes to encapsulate Sockets. We start by defining a typedef and a macro that hide some of the UNIX/POSIX and Win32 portability differences:

```
typedef int SOCKET;
const int INVALID_HANDLE_VALUE = -1;
```

Both SOCKET and INVALID_HANDLE_VALUE are defined in the Win32 API already. Therefore, we could either integrate them using #ifdefs or using separate platform-specific directories, as discussed earlier in implementation activity 2.5 (55).

Next, we define an INET_Addr class that encapsulates the internet domain address struct:

```
class INET_Addr {
public:
    INET_Addr (u_short port, u_long addr) {
        // Set up the address to become a server.
        memset (&addr_, 0, sizeof addr_);
        addr_.sin_family = AF_INET;
        addr_.sin_port = htons (port);
        addr_.sin_addr.s_addr = htonl (addr);
    }

    u_short get_port () const { return addr_.sin_port; }

    u_long get_ip_addr () const
        { return addr_.sin_addr.s_addr; }

    sockaddr *addr () const
        { return reinterpret_cast <sockaddr *> (&addr_);}

    size_t size () const { return sizeof (addr_); }

    // ...
private:
    sockaddr_in addr_;
};
```

Note how the INET_Addr constructor eliminates several common Socket programming errors. For example, it initializes the sockaddr_ in field to zero, and ensures the TCP port number and IP address are converted into network byte order by applying the ntons() and ntonl() macros automatically [Ste98].

The next wrapper facade class, SOCK_Stream, encapsulates the I/O operations, such as recv() and send(), that an application can invoke on a connected socket handle:

```
class SOCK_Stream {
public:
    // Default and copy constructor.
    SOCK_Stream () : handle_ (INVALID_HANDLE_VALUE) { }
    SOCK_Stream (SOCKET h): handle_ (h) { }

    // Automatically close the handle on destruction.
    ~SOCK_Stream () { close (handle_); }
```

```
    // Set/get the underlying SOCKET handle.
    void set_handle (SOCKET h) { handle_ = h; }
    SOCKET get_handle () const { return handle_; }

    // Regular I/O operations.
    ssize_t recv (void *buf, size_t len, int flags);
    ssize_t send (const char *buf, size_t len, int flags);

    // I/O operations for "short" receives and sends.
    ssize_t recv_n (char *buf, size_t len, int flags);
    ssize_t send_n (const char *buf, size_t len,
                    int flags);

    // ... other methods omitted.
private:
    // Socket handle for exchanging socket data.
    SOCKET handle_;
};
```

As discussed in implementation activity 2.3 (55), this class leverages the semantics of C++ destructors to ensure that a socket handle is closed automatically when a SOCK_Stream object goes out of scope. In addition, the send_n() and recv_n() methods can handle networking idiosyncrasies, for example 'short' send and receive operations.

SOCK_Stream objects can be created via a connection factory, called SOCK_Acceptor, which encapsulates *passive* establishment of Socket connections. The SOCK_Acceptor constructor initializes the passive-mode acceptor socket to listen at the sock_addr address. The SOCK_Acceptor's accept() method is a factory that initializes the SOCK_Stream parameter with a socket handle to a new connection:

```
class SOCK_Acceptor {
public:
    // Initialize a passive-mode acceptor socket.
    SOCK_Acceptor (const INET_Addr &addr) {
        // Create a local endpoint of communication.
        handle_ = socket (PF_INET, SOCK_STREAM, 0);
        // Associate address with endpoint.
        bind (handle_, addr.addr (), addr.size ());
        // Make endpoint listen for connections.
        listen (handle_, 5);
    };

    // A second method to initialize a passive-mode
    // acceptor socket, analogously to the constructor.
    void open (const INET_Addr &sock_addr) { /* ... */ };
```

```
    // Accept a connection and initialize the <stream>.
    void accept (SOCK_Stream &s) {
        s.set_handle (accept (handle_, 0, 0));
    }
private:
    SOCKET handle_; // Socket handle factory.
};
```

Note how the constructor for the SOCK_Acceptor applies the strategy discussed in implementation activity 2.2 (55) to ensure that the low-level socket(), bind(), and listen() functions are always called together and in the correct order.

A complete set of Socket [Sch97] wrapper facades would also include a SOCK_Connector that encapsulates the logic for establishing connections actively. The SOCK_Acceptor and SOCK_Connector classes are *concrete IPC mechanisms* that can be used to instantiate the generic acceptor and connector classes described in the Acceptor-Connector pattern (285) to perform connection establishment.

Thread wrapper facade. Our final wrapper facade encapsulates operating system threading APIs that are available on different operating system platforms, including Solaris threads, POSIX Pthreads, and Win32 threads. These APIs exhibit subtle syntactic and semantic differences. For example, Solaris and POSIX threads can be spawned in 'detached' mode, whereas Win32 threads cannot. It is possible, however, to provide a Thread_Manager wrapper facade that encapsulates these differences in a uniform manner. The Thread_Manager wrapper facade below, which is a Singleton [GoF95], illustrates the spawn method implemented for Solaris threads:

```
class Thread_Manager {
public:
    // Singleton access point.
    Thread_Manager *instance ();

    // Spawn a thread.
    void spawn (void *(*entry_point_function) (void *),
                void *arg = 0, long flags = 0,
                long stack_size = 0,
                void *stack_pointer = 0,
                thread_t *t_id = 0) {
        thread_t t;
        if (t_id == 0)
            t_id = &t;
```

```
                        thr_create
                            (stack_size, stack_pointer,
                             entry_point_function, arg, flags, t_id);
                    }

                    // ... Other methods omitted.
            };
```

The `Thread_Manager` class also provides methods for joining and canceling threads that can be ported to other operating systems. ❑

3 *Consider allowing applications controlled access to implementation details.* One benefit of defining a wrapper facade is to make it hard to write incorrect or non-portable applications. For example, wrapper facades can shield applications from error-prone or platform-specific implementation details, such as whether a socket is represented as a pointer or an integer. Cases may arise, however, where the extra abstraction and type safety actually prevent programmers from using a wrapper facade in useful ways not anticipated by its designer. This experience can be frustrating and may discourage programmers from leveraging other benefits of wrapper facades.

A common solution to the problem of 'too much' abstraction is to provide an 'escape hatch' mechanism or open implementation technique, such as AOP [KLM+97]. This design allows applications to access implementation details in a controlled manner.

➥   The `SOCK_Stream` class defines a pair of methods that set and get the underlying `SOCKET` handle:

```
class SOCK_Stream {
public:
    // Set/get the underlying SOCKET handle.
    void set_handle (SOCKET h) { handle_ = h; }
    SOCKET get_handle () const { return handle_; }
```

These methods can be used to set and get certain Socket options, such as support for 'out-of-band' data [Ste98], that were not defined by the original Socket wrapper facades. ❑

Escape-hatch mechanisms should be used sparingly of course, because they decrease portability and increase the potential for errors, thereby nullifying key benefits of the Wrapper Facade pattern. If applications use certain escape hatches repeatedly in similar situations, it may indicate that explicit methods should be added to the public interface of the wrapper facade. The Extension Interface pattern (141) defines techniques for adding these new methods without disrupting existing clients.

4   *Develop an error-handling mechanism.* Low-level C operating system function APIs often use return values and integer codes, such as errno, to return errors to their calling code. This technique can be error-prone, however, if callers do not check the return status of their function calls.

A more elegant way of reporting errors is to use exception handling. Many programming languages, such as C++ and Java, support exception handling as a fundamental error-reporting mechanism. It is also used in some operating systems, for example Win32 [Sol98]. There are several benefits of using exception handling as the error-handling mechanism for wrapper facade classes:

- *It is extensible*, for example by defining hierarchies of exception classes in C++ and Java.

- *It cleanly decouples error handling from normal processing.* Error handling information is neither passed to an operation explicitly, nor can an application accidentally ignore an exception by failing to check function return values.

- *It can be type-safe.* In languages like C++ and Java, exceptions can be thrown and caught in a strongly-typed manner.

➡   We can define the following exception class to keep track of which operating system error or condition has occurred:

```
class System_Ex : public exception {
public:
    // Map <os_status> into a platform-independent error
    // or condition status and store it into <error_>.
    System_Ex (int os_status) { /* ... */ }

    // Platform-independent error or condition status.
    int status () const { return status_; }
    // ...
private:
    // Store platform-independent error/condition status.
    int status_;
};
```

Platform-independent errors and conditions could be defined via macros or constants that map onto unique values across all operating systems. For instance, the Solaris implementation of the Thread_

`Mutex::acquire()` method shown on page 57 could be written as follows:

```
void Thread_Mutex::acquire () {
    int result = mutex_lock (&mutex);
    if (result != 0) { throw System_Ex (result); }
}                                                              ❏
```

Unfortunately, there are several drawbacks to the use of exception handling for wrapper facade classes:

* *Not all languages or implementations provide exception handling.* For example, C does not define an exception model and some C++ compilers do not implement exceptions.

* *Languages implement exceptions in different ways.* It can thus be hard to integrate components written in different languages when they throw exceptions. Using proprietary exception handling mechanisms, such as Windows NT's structured exception handling [Sol98], can also reduce the portability of applications that use these mechanisms.

* *Resource management can be complicated* if there are multiple exit paths from a block of C++ or Java code [Mue96]. If garbage collection is not supported by the language or programming environment, care must be taken to ensure that dynamically-allocated objects are deleted when an exception is thrown.

* *Poor exception handling implementations incur time or space overheads* even when exceptions are not thrown [Mue96]. This overhead is problematic for embedded systems that must be efficient and have small memory footprints [GS98].

The drawbacks of exception handling are particularly problematic for wrapper facades that encapsulate kernel-level device drivers or low-level operating system APIs that must run on many platforms [Sch92], such as the mutex, Socket and thread wrapper facades described above. A common error handling mechanism for system-level wrapper facades [Sch97] is based on the Thread-Specific Storage pattern (475) in conjunction with errno. This solution is efficient, portable, and thread-safe, though more obtrusive and potentially error-prone than using C++ exceptions.

5   *Define related helper classes (optional).* After lower-level APIs are encapsulated within wrapper facade classes it often becomes possible to
create other helper classes that further simplify application development. The benefits of these helper classes are often apparent only
after the Wrapper Facade pattern has been applied to cluster lower-
level functions and their associated data into classes.

➥   In our logging example we can leverage the Guard template class
defined in the Strategized Locking pattern (333) [Str97]. This class
ensures that a Thread_Mutex is acquired and released properly
within a scope regardless of how the method's flow of control leaves
the scope. The Guard class constructor acquires the mutex and the
destructor releases it within a scope automatically:

```
{
    // Constructor of <guard> automatically
    // acquires the <mutex> lock.
    Guard<Thread_Mutex> guard (mutex);
    // ... operations that must be serialized.

    // Destructor of <guard> automatically
    // releases the <mutex> lock.
}
```

We can easily substitute a different type of locking mechanism while
still using the Guard's automatic locking and unlocking protocol
because we used a *class* as the Thread_Mutex wrapper facade. For
example, we can replace the Thread_Mutex class with a Process_
Mutex class:

```
// Acquire a process-wide mutex.
Guard<Process_Mutex> guard (mutex);
```

It is much harder to achieve this degree of 'pluggability' using lower-
level C functions and data structures instead of C++ classes. The
main problem is that the functions and data lack language support
for cohesion, whereas the C++ classes provide this support naturally.❏

Example   The code below illustrates the logging_handler() function of our
Resolved   logging server after it has been rewritten to use the wrapper facades
for mutexes, Sockets, and threads described in the *Implementation*
section. To ease comparison with the original code, we present it in a
two-column table with the original code from the example section in
the left-hand column and the new code in the right-hand column

```cpp
#if defined (_WIN32)
    #include <windows.h>
    typedef int ssize_t;
#else
    typedef unsigned int UINT32;
    #include <thread.h>
    #include <unistd.h>
    #include <sys/socket.h>
    #include <netinet/in.h>
    #include <memory.h>
#endif /* _WIN32 */

// Keep track of number of logging requests.
static int request_count;

// Lock to protect request_count.
#if defined (_WIN32)
    static CRITICAL_SECTION lock;
#else
    static mutex_t lock;
#endif /* _WIN32 */

// Maximum size of a logging record.
static const int LOG_RECORD_MAX = 1024;

// Port number to listen on for requests.
static const int LOGGING_PORT = 10000;

// Entry point that writes logging records.
int write_record (const char log_record[], size_t len) {
    /* ... */ return 0;
}

// Entry point that processes logging records for
// one client connection.
#if defined (_WIN32)
    u_long
#else
    void *
#endif /* _WIN32 */
logging_handler (void *arg) {
#if defined (_WIN32)
    SOCKET h = reinterpret_cast <SOCKET> (arg);
#else
    int h = reinterpret_cast <int> (arg);
#endif /* _WIN32 */

    for (;;) {
        // Ensure a 32-bit quantify;
#if defined (_WIN32)
        ULONG len;
#else
        UINT32 len;
#endif /* _WIN32 */
        char log_record[LOG_RECORD_MAX];

        // The first <recv> reads the length
        // (stored as a 32-bit integer) of
        // adjacent logging record.
        ssize_t n = recv (h, &len, sizeof len, 0);

        if (n <= sizeof len) break; // Bailout on error.
        len = ntohl (len);
        if (len > LOG_RECORD_MAX) break;
        // Loop to <recv> the data.
        for (size_t nread = 0; nread < len; nread += n) {
            n = recv (h, log_record + nread,
                      len - nread, 0);
            if (n <= 0) return 0;
        }
#if defined (_WIN32)
        EnterCriticalSection (&lock);
#else
        mutex_lock (&lock);
#endif /* _WIN32 */
        ++request_count;
        // A -1 return value signifies failure.
        if (write_record (log_record, len) == -1)
            break;
#if defined (_WIN32)
        LeaveCriticalSection (&lock);
#else
        mutex_unlock (&lock);
#endif /* _WIN32 */
    }
#if defined (_WIN32)
    closesocket (h);
#else
    close (h);
#endif /* _WIN32 */
    return 0;
}
```

```cpp
#include "ThreadManager.h"
#include "ThreadMutex.h"
#include "Guard.h"
#include "INET_Addr.h"
#include "SOCKET.h"
#include "SOCK_Acceptor.h"
#include "SOCK_Stream.h"


// Keep track of number of logging requests.
static int request_count;




// Maximum size of a logging record.
static const int LOG_RECORD_MAX = 1024;

// Port number to listen on for requests.
static const int LOGGING_PORT = 10000;

// Entry point that writes logging records.
int write_record (const char log_record[], size_t len) {
    /* ... */ return 0;
}

// Entry point that processes logging records for
// one client connection.



void *logging_handler (void *arg) {

    SOCKET h = reinterpret_cast <SOCKET> (arg);

    // Create a <SOCK_Stream> object.
    SOCK_Stream stream (h);
    for (;;) {
        // Ensure a 32-bit quantity.
        UINT_32 len;



        char log_record[LOG_RECORD_MAX];

        // The first <recv_n> reads the length
        // (stored as a 32-bit integer) of
        // adjacent logging record.
        ssize_t n = stream.recv_n (&len, sizeof len);

        if (n <= 0) break; // Bailout on error.
        len = ntohl (len);
        if (len > LOG_RECORD_MAX) break;
        // Second <recv_n> reads the data.
        n = stream.recv_n (log_record, len);

        if (n <= 0) break;
        {
            // Constructor acquires the lock.
            Guard<Thread_Mutex> mon (lock);


            ++request_count;
            // A -1 return value signifies failure.
            if (write_record (log_record, len) == -1)
                break;

            // Destructor releases the lock.
        }
    }



    return 0;
    // Destructor of <stream> closes down <h>.
}
```

The code in the right-hand column addresses the problems with the code shown in the left-hand column. For example, the destructors of SOCK_Stream and Guard will close the socket handle and release the Thread_Mutex, respectively, regardless of how the code blocks are exited. This code is also easier to understand, maintain, and port because it is more concise and uses no platform-specific APIs.

Analogously to the logging_handler() function, we present a two-column table below that compares the original code for the main() function with the new code using wrapper facades:

```
// Main driver function for the server.
int main (int argc, char *argv[]) {
    struct sockaddr_in sock_addr;
    // Handle UNIX/Win32 portability.
#if defined (_WIN32)
    SOCKET acceptor;
    WORD version_requested = MAKEWORD(2, 0);
    WSADATA wsa_data;
    int error = WSAStartup(version_requested, &wsa_data);
    if (error != 0) return -1;
#else
    int acceptor;
#endif /* _WIN32 */
    // Create a local endpoint of communication.
    acceptor = socket (AF_INET, SOCK_STREAM, 0);
    // Set up the address to become a server.
    memset (reinterpret_cast<void *> (&sock_addr),
            0, sizeof sock_addr);
    sock_addr.sin_family = PF_INET;
    sock_addr.sin_port = htons (LOGGING_PORT);
    sock_addr.sin_addr.s_addr = htonl (INADDR_ANY);
    // Associate address with endpoint.
    bind (acceptor, reinterpret_cast<struct sockaddr *>
          (&sock_addr), sizeof sock_addr);
    // Make endpoint listen for connections.
    listen (acceptor, 5);
    // Main server event loop.
    for (;;) {
        // Handle UNIX/Win32 portability.
#if defined (_WIN32)
        SOCKET h;
        DWORD t_id;
#else
        int h;
        thread_t t_id;
#endif /* _WIN32 */
        // Block waiting for clients to connect.
        h = accept (acceptor, 0, 0);



        // Spawn a new thread that runs the <server>
        // entry point.
#if defined (_WIN32)
        CreateThread (0, 0,
            LPTHREAD_START_ROUTINE(&logging_handler),
            reinterpret_cast <void *> (h), 0, &t_id);
#else
        thr_create
            (0, 0, logging_handler,
            reinterpret_cast <void *> (h),
            THR_DETACHED, &t_id);
#endif /* _WIN32 */
    }
    return 0;
}
```

```
// Main driver function for the server.
int main (int argc, char *argv[]) {
    INET_Addr addr (port);

    // Passive-mode acceptor object.
    SOCK_Acceptor server (addr);
    SOCK_Stream new_stream;
    // Main server event loop.


    for (;;) {




        // Accept a connection from a client.
        server.accept (new_stream);

        // Get the underlying handle.
        SOCKET h = new_stream.get_handle ();

        // Spawn off a thread-per-connection.

        thr_mgr.spawn
            (logging_handler
            reinterpret_cast <void *> (h),
            THR_DETACHED);
    }


    return 0;
}
```

Note how literally dozens of lines of low-level, conditionally compiled code disappear in the right-hand column version that uses the Wrapper Facade pattern.

Known Uses   **Microsoft Foundation Classes (MFC)**. MFC [Pro99] provides a set of wrapper facades that encapsulate many lower-level C Win32 APIs. It focuses largely on providing GUI components that implement the Microsoft Document-View architecture, which is a variant of the Document-View architecture described in [POSA1].

ACE. The Socket, thread, and mutex wrapper facades described in the *Implementation* section are abstractions of ACE framework [Sch97] components, such as the ACE_SOCK*, ACE_Thread_Manager and ACE_ Thread_Mutex classes, respectively.

Rogue Wave. Rogue Wave's Net.h++ and Threads.h++ class libraries implement wrapper facades for Sockets, threads, and synchronization mechanisms on a number of operating system platforms.

ObjectSpace. The ObjectSpace System<Toolkit> also implements platform-independent wrapper facades for Sockets, threads, and synchronization mechanisms.

Java Virtual Machine and Java class libraries. The Java Virtual Machine (JVM) and various Java class libraries, such as AWT and Swing [RBV99], provide a set of wrapper facades that encapsulate many low-level native operating system calls and GUI APIs.

Siemens REFORM. The REFORM framework [BGHS98] for hot rolling mill process automation uses the Wrapper Facade pattern to shield the object-oriented parts of the system, such as material tracking and setpoint transmission, from a neural network for the actual process control. This neural network is programmed in C due to its algorithmic nature and contains mathematical models that characterize the physics of the automation process.

The wrapper facades defined in the REFORM framework differ from wrapper facades for operating system mechanisms because the process-control APIs they encapsulate are at a higher level of abstraction. In fact the neural network is part of the REFORM system itself. However, its function-based C APIs are lower-level compared to the complex object-oriented high-level structure and logic of the hot rolling mill framework. The REFORM wrapper facades therefore have similar goals and properties as the lower-level operating system wrapper facades:

• They provide the views and abstractions that the object-oriented parts of the framework need of the process control neural network.

There is a separate wrapper facade for every component using the neural network.

- They hide API variations. For different customer-specific instances of the framework there may be (slightly) different implementations of the neural network. As a result, semantically identical functions in these neural network implementations may have different signatures. These differences do not affect the framework implementation, however.

- They ensure lower-level C functions are invoked in the right order.

Books consisting of edited collections of papers. A real-life example of the Wrapper Facade pattern are books consisting of edited collections of papers that are organized into one or more 'themes'. For example, the PLoPD series [PLoPD1] [PLoPD2] [PLoPD3] [PLoPD4] consist of individual papers that are organized into cohesive sections, such as event handling, fault tolerance, application framework design, or concurrency. Thus, readers who are interested in a particular topic area or domain can focus their attention on these sections, rather than having to locate each paper individually.

Consequences   The Wrapper Facade pattern provides the following **benefits**:

Concise, cohesive and robust higher-level object-oriented programming interfaces. The Wrapper Facade pattern can be used to encapsulate lower-level APIs within a more concise and cohesive set of higher-level object-oriented classes. These abstractions reduce the tedium of developing applications, thereby decreasing the potential for certain types of programming error. In addition, the use of encapsulation eliminates programming errors that occur when using untyped data structures incorrectly, such as socket or file handles. Application code can therefore use wrapper facades to access lower-level APIs correctly and uniformly.

Portability and maintainability. Wrapper facades can be implemented to shield application developers from non-portable aspects of lower-level APIs. The Wrapper Facade pattern also improves software structure by replacing an application configuration strategy based on *physical design* entities, such as files and #ifdefs, with *logical design* entities, such as base classes, subclasses, and their relationships. It is often much easier to understand, maintain, and enhance applications in terms of their logical design rather than their physical design [Lak95].

Modularity, reusability and configurability. The Wrapper Facade pattern creates cohesive and reusable class components that can be 'plugged' into other components in a wholesale fashion, using object-oriented language features like inheritance and parameterized types. In contrast, it is harder to replace groups of functions without resorting to coarse-grained operating system tools such as linkers or file systems.

The Wrapper Facade pattern incurs several **liabilities**:

Loss of functionality. Whenever an abstraction is layered on top of an existing abstraction it is possible to lose functionality. In particular, situations can occur in which the new abstraction prevents developers from accessing certain capabilities of the underlying abstraction. It is hard to define a suitable high-level abstraction that covers all these use cases without becoming bloated. One useful heuristic to follow is to design wrapper facades so that they are easy to use correctly, hard to use incorrectly, but not impossible to use in ways that the original designers did not anticipate. An 'escape-hatch' mechanism or open implementation [KLM+97] technique can often help reconcile these design forces cleanly.

Performance degradation. The Wrapper Facade pattern can degrade performance. For example, if wrapper facade classes are implemented with the Bridge pattern [GoF95], or if they make several forwarding function calls per method, the additional indirection may be more costly than programming to the lower-level APIs directly. However, languages that support inlining, such as C++ or certain C compilers, can implement the Wrapper Facade pattern with no significant overhead, because compilers can inline the method calls used to implement the wrapper facades. The overhead is therefore the same as calling lower-level functions directly.

Programming language and compiler limitations. Defining C++ wrapper facades for well-designed C APIs is relatively straightforward, because the C++ language and C++ compilers define features that facilitate cross-language integration. It may be hard to define wrapper facades for other languages, however, due to a lack of language support or limitations with compilers. For example, there is no universally accepted standard for integrating C functions into languages like Ada, Smalltalk, and Java. Programmers may therefore need to use to non-portable mechanisms to develop wrapper facades.

See Also   The Wrapper Facade pattern is related to several of the structural patterns in [GoF95], including Facade, Bridge, Adapter, and Decorator.

Facade. The intent of Facade is to provide a unified interface that simplifies client access to subsystem interfaces. The intent of Wrapper Facade is more specific: it provides concise, robust, portable, maintainable, and cohesive class interfaces that encapsulate lower-level APIs such as operating system mutex, Socket, thread, and GUI C APIs. In general, facades hide complex class relationships behind a simpler API, whereas wrapper facades hide complex function and data structure API relationships behind richer object-oriented classes. Wrapper facades also provide building-block components that can be 'plugged' into higher-level objects or components.

Bridge. The intent of Bridge is to decouple an abstraction from its implementation, so the two can vary independently and dynamically via polymorphism. Wrapper Facade has a similar intent: minimizing the overhead of indirection and polymorphism. Wrapper Facade implementations rarely vary dynamically, however, due to the nature of the systems programming mechanisms that they encapsulate.

Adapter. The intent of Adapter is to convert the interface of a class into another interface that is expected by a client. A common application of Wrapper Facade is to create a set of classes that 'adapt' low-level operating system APIs to create a portable set of wrapper facades that appear the same for all applications. Although the structure of this solution is not identical to either the object or class form of Adapter in [GoF95], the wrapper facades play a similar role as an adapter by exporting an object-oriented interface that is common across platforms.

Decorator. The intent of Decorator is to extend an object *dynamically* by attaching responsibilities transparently. In contrast, Wrapper Facade *statically* encapsulates lower-level functions and data with object-oriented class interfaces.

In general, Wrapper Facade should be applied in lieu of these other patterns when there are existing lower-level, non-object-oriented APIs to encapsulate, and when it is more important that the solution be efficient than be dynamically extensible.

The Layers pattern [POSA1] helps organize multiple wrapper facades into a separate component layer. This layer resides directly on top of the operating system and shields applications from all the low-level APIs they use.

Credits   Thanks to Brad Appleton, Luciano Gerber, Ralph Johnson, Bob Hanmer, Roger Whitney, and Joe Yoder for extensive comments that improved the form and content of the Wrapper Facade pattern description substantially.

During the public review of Wrapper Facade we debated the best name for this pattern. Several reviewers suggested to call it *Wrapper* because the Wrapper Facade pattern describes what is often referred to as a 'wrapper' by software developers. Unfortunately the term 'wrapper' is already overloaded in the patterns community. For example, Wrapper is listed in the *Also Known As* sections of the Adapter and Decorator patterns [GoF95]. However, the pattern in this book differs from these patterns. We therefore decided to use a non-overloaded name for the pattern we present here.

Component Configurator

The *Component Configurator* design pattern allows an application to link and unlink its component implementations at run-time without having to modify, recompile, or statically relink the application. Component Configurator further supports the reconfiguration of components into different application processes without having to shut down and re-start running processes.

Also Known As   Service Configurator [JS97b]

Example   A distributed time service [Mil88] [OMG97c] provides accurate clock synchronization for computers that collaborate in local-area or wide-area networks. Its architecture contains three types of components:

- *Time server* components answer queries about the current time.

- *Clerk* components query one or more time servers to sample their notion of the current time, calculate the 'approximate' correct time, and update their own local system time accordingly.

- *Client* application components use the globally-consistent time information maintained by their clerks to synchronize their behavior with clients on other hosts.

The conventional way to implement this distributed time service is to configure the functionality of the time server, clerk, and client components statically at compile-time into separate processes running on hosts in the network:

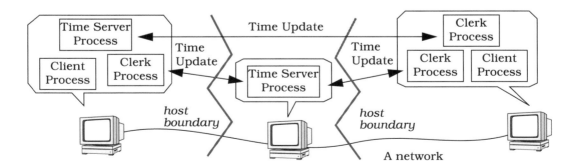

In such a configuration, one or more hosts run processes containing time service components that handle requests for time updates. A clerk component runs in a process on each host on which applications require global time synchronization. Client components in application processes perform computations using the synchronized time reported by their local clerk component.

Although a distributed time service design can be implemented in this way, two general types of problems arise:

- The choice of component implementation can depend on the environment in which applications run. For example, if a WWV receiver is available,[2] the Cristian time service algorithm [Cris89] is most appropriate. Otherwise the Berkeley algorithm [GZ89] is the better choice.

  Changing the environment in which applications run may therefore also require a change to the implementation of time service components. A design in which the implementation of a particular component is fixed statically within a process at compile-time, however, makes it hard to exchange this component's implementation. In addition, as each component is coupled statically with a process, existing applications must be modified, recompiled, and statically relinked when changes occur.

- Components may also need to be *reconfigured* to enhance key quality-of-service (QoS) properties, such as latency and throughput. For example, we can reconfigure the clerk and the time server components in our distributed time service so they are collocated [WSV99] on the same host. In this case, communication overhead can be minimized by allowing the clerk to access the time server's notion of time via shared memory, rather than exchanging data through a pipe or 'loopback' Socket connection.

  However, if components are configured statically into processes, making the changes outlined above requires terminating, reconfiguring, and restarting running time service processes. These activities are not only inefficient, they are potentially infeasible for systems with high availability requirements.

---

2. A WWV receiver intercepts the short pulses broadcast by the US National Institute of Standard Time (NIST) to provide Universal Coordinated Time (UTC) to the public.

Unfortunately patterns such as Bridge and Strategy [GoF95] are not sufficient by themselves to solve these types of problems. For example, Bridge and Strategy are often used to alleviate unnecessary coupling between components. When these patterns are applied to our example application in isolation, however, all possible implementations of time service components must be configured at compile-time in order to support the selection of different strategies at run-time. This constraint may be excessively inflexible or costly for certain applications.

For example, if a time service runs on a personal computing device with stringent memory and power limitations, components that are not currently in use should be unlinked to minimize resource consumption. This 'dynamic reconfiguration' aspect is not addressed directly by patterns such as Bridge and Strategy.

Context   An application or system in which components must be initiated, suspended, resumed, and terminated as flexibly and transparently as possible.

Problem   Applications that are composed of components must provide a mechanism to configure these components into one or more processes. The solution to this problem is influenced by three *forces*:

- Changes to component functionality or implementation details are common in many systems and applications. For example, better algorithms or architectures may be discovered as an application matures. It should be possible therefore to modify component implementations at any point during an application's development and deployment lifecycle.

  Modifications to one component should have minimal impact on the implementation of other components that use it. Similarly, it should be possible to initiate, suspend, resume, terminate, or exchange a component dynamically within an application at run-time. These activities should have minimal impact on other components that are configured into the application.

- Developers often may not know the most effective way to collocate or distribute multiple component components into processes and hosts at the time an application is developed. If developers commit prematurely to a particular configuration of components it may impede flexibility, reduce overall system performance and functionality, and unnecessarily increase resource utilization.

In addition, initial component configuration decisions may prove to be sub-optimal over time. For example, platform upgrades or increased workloads may require the redistribution of certain components to other processes and hosts. In such cases, it may be helpful to make these component configuration decisions as late as possible in an application's development or deployment cycle, without having to modify or shut down an application obtrusively.

• Performing common administrative tasks such as configuring, initializing, and controlling components should be straightforward and component-independent. These tasks can often be managed most effectively by a central administrator rather than being distributed throughout an application or system. They should be automated whenever possible, for example by using some type of scripting mechanism [MGG00].

Solution   Decouple component interfaces from their implementations and make applications independent of the point(s) in time at which component implementations are configured into application processes.

In detail: a *component* defines a uniform interface for configuring and controlling a particular type of application service or functionality that it provides. *Concrete components* implement this interface in an application-specific manner. Applications or administrators can use component interfaces to initiate, suspend, resume, and terminate their concrete components dynamically, as well as to obtain run-time information about each configured concrete component. Concrete components are packaged into a suitable unit of configuration, such as a dynamically linked library (DLL). This DLL can be dynamically linked and unlinked into and out of an application under the control of a *component configurator*, which uses a *component repository* to manage all concrete components configured into an application.

Structure The Component Configurator pattern includes four participants:

A *component* defines a uniform interface that can be used to configure and control the type of application service or functionality provided by a component implementation. Common control operations include initializing, suspending, resuming, and terminating a component.

Concrete components implement the component control interface to provide a specific type of component. A concrete component also implements methods to provide application-specific functionality, such as processing data exchanged with other connected peer components. Concrete components are packaged in a form that can be dynamically linked and unlinked into or out of an application at run-time, such as a DLL.

Class	*Collaborator*
Component	
Responsibility	
• Defines an interface for configuring and controlling a component implementation	

Class	*Collaborator*
Concrete Component	• Concrete Component
Responsibility	
• Implements an application component that can be configured dynamically	

➡ Two types of concrete components are used in our distributed time service: *time server* and *clerk*. Each of these concrete components provides specific functionality to the distributed time service. The time server component receives and processes requests for time updates from clerks. The clerk component queries one or more time servers to determine the 'approximate' correct time and uses this value to update its own local system time. Two time server implementations are available in our example, one for the Cristian algorithm and one for the Berkeley algorithm. ❑

A *component repository* manages all concrete components that are configured currently into an application. This repository allows system management applications or administrators to control the behavior of configured concrete components via a central administrative mechanism.

A *component configurator* uses the component repository to coordinate the (re)configuration of concrete components. It implements a mechanism that interprets and executes a script specifying which of the available concrete components to (re)configure into the application via dynamic linking and unlinking from DLLs.

Class	Collaborator	Class	Collaborator
Component Repository	• Concrete Component	Component Configurator	• Concrete Component • Service Repository
Responsibility		**Responsibility**	
• Maintains the Components configured into an application		• Configures Components into an application process	

The class diagram for the Component Configurator pattern is as follows:

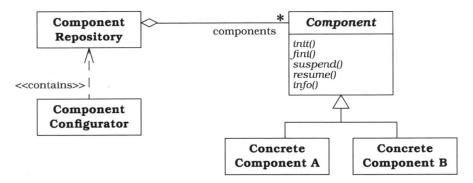

Dynamics   The behavior of the Component Configurator pattern can be characterized by three phases:

- *Component initialization.* The component configurator dynamically links a component into an application and initializes it.[3] After a component has been initialized successfully the component configurator adds it to its component repository. This repository manages all configured components at run-time.

---

3. The *Implementation* section describes how parameters can be passed into the component, as well as different options for activating the component.

- *Component processing.* After being configured into an application, a component performs its processing tasks, such as exchanging messages with peer components and performing service requests. The component configurator can suspend and resume existing components temporarily, for example when (re)configuring other components.

- *Component termination.* The component configurator shuts down components after they are no longer needed, allowing them the opportunity to clean up their resources before terminating. When terminating a component, the component configurator removes it from the component repository and unlinks it from the application's address space.

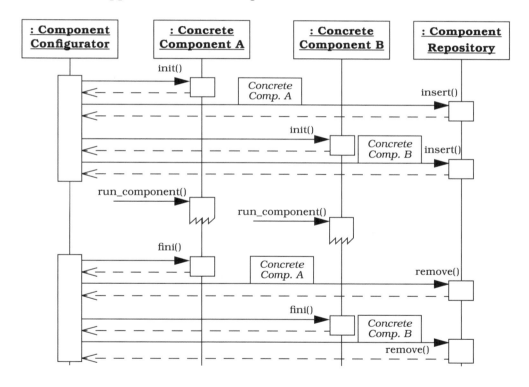

The following state chart diagram illustrates how a component configurator controls the lifecycle of a single concrete component:

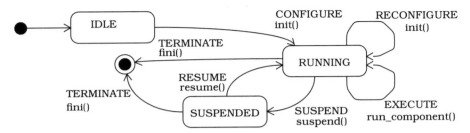

This diagram illustrates the event-driven 'inversion of control' [Vlis98a] behavior of a component configurator. For example, in response to the occurrence of events like CONFIGURE and TERMINATE, the component configurator invokes the component's corresponding method, in this case init() and fini(), respectively.

Implementation   The participants in the Component Configurator pattern can be decomposed into two layers:

- *Configuration management layer components.* This layer performs general-purpose, application-independent strategies that install, initialize, control, and terminate components.

- *Application layer components.* This layer implements the concrete components that perform application-specific processing.

The implementation activities in this section start at the 'bottom' with the configuration management layer and work upwards to components in the application layer.

1   *Define the component configuration and control interface.* Components should support the following operations so that they can be configured and controlled by a component configurator:

- *Component initialization.* Initialize or re-initialize a component.

- *Component finalization.* Shut down a component and clean up its resources.

- *Component suspension.* Suspend component execution temporarily.

- *Component resumption.* Resume execution of a suspended component.

- *Component information.* Report information describing the static or dynamic directives of a component.

The interface used to configure and control a component can be based on either an *inheritance* or a *message passing* strategy:

- *Inheritance-based interface.* In this strategy, each component inherits from a common base class that contains pure virtual hook methods [Pree95] for each component configuration and control operation.

  ➥ The following abstract Component class is based on the ACE framework [SchSu94]:

  ```
  class Component : public Event_Handler {
  public:
      // Initialization and termination hooks.
      virtual void init (int argc, const char *argv[]) = 0;
      virtual void fini () = 0;

      // Scheduling hooks.
      virtual void suspend ();
      virtual void resume ();

      // Status information hook.
      virtual void info (string &status) const = 0;
  };
  ```

  The component execution mechanism for our time service example is based on a reactive event handling model within a single thread of control, as described by the Reactor pattern (179). By inheriting from the Reactor pattern's Event_Handler participant, a Component implementation can register itself with a reactor, which then demultiplexes and dispatches events to the component. ❑

- *Message-based interface.* Another strategy for configuring and controlling components is to program them to respond to a set of messages, such as INIT, SUSPEND, RESUME, and FINI, sent to the component from the component configurator. Component developers must write code to process these messages, in this case to initialize, suspend, resume, and terminate a component, respectively. Using messages rather than inheritance makes it possible to implement the Component Configurator pattern in non-object-oriented programming languages that lack inheritance, such as C or Ada 83.

2   *Implement a component repository.* All concrete component implemen-
    tations that are linked into an application via DLLs are managed by a
    component repository. A component configurator uses this repository
    to control a component when it is configured into or out of an appli-
    cation. Each component's current status, such as whether it is active
    or suspended, can be maintained in the repository.

    A component repository can be a reusable container, for example a
    Java `java.util.Hashtable` [Sun00a] or a C++ standard template li-
    brary map [Aus98]. Conversely it can be implemented as a container
    in accordance with the Manager pattern [Som97]. This container can
    be stored in main memory, a file system, or shared memory. Depend-
    ing on where it resides, a component repository can be managed
    within the application or by a separate process.

➡   The interface of our `Component_Repository` class is also based
on the ACE framework [SchSu94]:

```
class Component_Repository {
public:
    // Initialize and close down the repository.
    Component_Repository ();
    ~Component_Repository ();

    // Insert a new <Component> with <component_name>.
    void insert (const string &component_name,
                 Component *);

    // Find <Component> associated with <component_name>.
    Component *find (const string &component_name);

    // Remove <Component> associated with
    // <component_name>.
    void remove (const string &component_name);

    // Suspend/resume <Component> associated with
    // <component_name>.
    void suspend (const string &component_name);
    void resume (const string &component_name);
private:
    // ...
};
```
❏

3 *Implement the component (re)configuration mechanism.* A component must be configured into an application's address space before it can be executed. The component configurator defines a mechanism to control the static and/or dynamic (re)configuration of components into application processes. The implementation of a component configurator involves five sub-activities:

3.1 *Define the component configurator interface.* The component configurator is often implemented as a singleton facade [GoF95]. This can mediate access to other Component Configurator pattern components, such as the component repository described in implementation activity 2 (84) and the mechanism for interpreting the component configuration directives described in implementation activity 3.3 (88).

➥ The following C++ interface, which is also based on ACE, is the singleton facade used for our distributed time server example:

```cpp
class Component_Configurator {
public:
    // Initialize the component configurator.
    Component_Configurator ();

    // Close down the component configurator and free up
    // dynamically allocated resources.
    ~Component_Configurator ();

    // Process the directives specified in the
    // <script_name>.
    void process_directives (const string &script_name);

    // Process a single directive specified as a string.
    void process_directive
        (const string &directive_string);

    // Accessor to the <Component_Repository>.
    Component_Repository *component_repository ();

    // Singleton accessor.
    static Component_Configurator *instance ();
private:
    // ...
};                                                        ❑
```

3.2   *Define a language for specifying component configuration directives.*
These directives supply the component configurator with the
information it needs to locate and initialize a component's
implementation at run-time, as well as to suspend, resume, re-
initialize, and/or terminate a component after it has been initialized.
Component configuration directives can be specified in various ways,
such as via the command line, environment variables, a graphical
user interface, or a configuration script.

➥   To simplify installation and administration, the component
configurator in our distributed time server example uses a component
scripting mechanism similar to the one provided by ACE [SchSu94].
A script file, which we call `comp.conf`, consolidates component
configuration directives into a single location that can be managed
centrally by applications, developers, or administrators. Every
component to be (re)configured into an application is specified by a
directive in the `comp.conf` script.

The following `comp.conf` script illustrates how a time server can be
configured dynamically into an application:

```
# Configure a Time Server.
dynamic Time_Server Component *
    cristian.dll:make_Time_Server()
            "-p $TIME_SERVER_PORT"
```

The directive in this `comp.conf` script contains a `dynamic` command,
which instructs the interpreter to perform two actions:

• Dynamically link the `cristian.dll` DLL into the application's
  address space and

• Invoke the `make_Time_Server()` factory function automatically.
  This function allocates a new time server instance dynamically:

```
// Keep C++ compiler from non-portably mangling name!
extern "C"
Component *make_Time_Server () {
    // <Time_Server> inherits from the <Component>
    // class.
    return new Time_Server;
}
```

The string parameter `"-p $TIME_SERVER_PORT"` at the end of the
directive contains an environment variable that specifies the port
number on which the time server component listens to receive
connections from clerks. The component configurator converts this

string into an 'argc/argv'-style array and passes it to the init() hook method of the time server component. If the init() method initializes the component successfully, a pointer to the component is stored in the component repository under the name 'Time_Server'. This name identifies the newly-configured component so that it can be controlled dynamically by the component configurator on behalf of an application or an administrator.

The directives in a comp.conf script are processed by the component configurator's directive interpreter, as described in implementation activity 3.3 (88). Each directive begins with a command that instructs the interpreter how to configure, reconfigure, or control a component:

Command	Description
dynamic	Dynamically link and initialize a component
static	Initialize a statically linked component
remove	Remove a component from the component repository and unlink it
suspend	Suspend a component temporarily without removing it
resume	Resume a previously suspended component

Directives can be written using a simple configuration scripting language defined by the following BNF grammar:

```
<directive>::= <dynamic> | <static> | <suspend>
                     | <resume> | <remove>
<dynamic> ::= dynamic <comp-location> <parameters-opt>
<static> ::= static <comp-name> <parameters-opt>
<suspend> ::= suspend <comp-name>
<resume> ::= resume <comp-name>
<remove> ::= remove <comp-name>
<comp-location> ::= <comp-name> <type> <function-name>
<type> ::= Component '*' | NULL
<function-name> ::= STRING ':' STRING '(' ')'
<parameters-opt> ::= '"' STRING '"'| NULL
<comp-name> ::= STRING
```
❑

3.3 *Implement a mechanism for parsing and processing component configuration directives.* This mechanism is often implemented as a *directive interpreter* that decouples the configuration-related aspects of a component from its run-time aspects. A directive interpreter can be implemented using the Interpreter pattern [GoF95], or standard parser-generator tools, such as `lex` and `yacc` [SchSu94].

➡   The `Component_Configurator` facade class defines two methods that allow applications to invoke a component configurator's directive interpreter. The `process_directives()` method can process a sequence of (re)configuration and control directives that are stored in a designated script file. This method allows multiple directives to be stored persistently and processed iteratively. Conversely, the `process_directive()` method can process a single directive passed as a `string` parameter. This method allows directives to be created dynamically and/or processed interactively.   ❏

A simple directive interpreter executes each component configuration directive in the order in which they are specified. In this case, application developers are responsible for ensuring this execution sequence satisfies any ordering dependencies among components being configured. A more complex interpreter and scripting language could of course be devised to allow the directive interpreter to handle ordering dependencies automatically, for example by using topological sorting.

3.4 *Implement the dynamic configuration mechanism.* A component configurator uses this mechanism to link and unlink components into and out of an application process dynamically. Modern operating systems, such as System V Release 4 (SVR4) UNIX and Win32, support this feature via explicit dynamic linking mechanisms [WHO91].

SVR4 UNIX, for example, defines the `dlopen()`, `dlsym()`, and `dlclose()` API to link a designated DLL dynamically into an application process explicitly, extract a designated factory function from the DLL, and unlink the DLL, respectively. Microsoft's Win32 operating systems support the `LoadLibrary()`, `GetProcAddr()`, and `CloseHandle()` APIs to perform the same functionality. As the component configurator's directive interpreter parses and processes directives, it uses these APIs to link and unlink DLLs dynamically into the application's address space.

➥ Our Component_Configurator implementation uses the following explicit dynamic linking API, based on the wrapper facade (47) defined in ACE [Sch97]:

```
class DLL {
    // This wrapper facade defines a portable interface to
    // program various DLL operations. The <OS::*>
    // methods are lower-level wrapper facades that
    // encapsulate the variation among explicit dynamic
    // linking APIs defined on different operating
    // systems.
public:
    // Opens and dynamically links the DLL <dll_name>.
    DLL (const string &dll_name) {
        handle_ = OS::dlopen (dll_name.c_str ());
    }

    // Unlinks the DLL opened in the constructor.
    ~DLL () { OS::dlclose (handle_); }

    // If <symbol_name> is in the symbol table of the DLL
    // return a pointer to it, else return 0.
    void *symbol (const string &symbol_name) {
        return OS::dlsym (handle_, symbol_name.c_str ();
    }
private:
    // Handle to the dynamically linked DLL.
    HANDLE handle_;
};
```

To illustrate how a component configurator can use this API, consider the directive used to configure a Time_Server component shown in implementation activity 3.2 (86). In this example the component configurator performs seven steps:

1 It creates a DLL object and passes the 'cristian.dll' string to its constructor.

2 The cristian.dll DLL is then linked into the application's address space dynamically via the OS::dlopen() method called in the DLL class constructor.

3 The component configurator next passes the string 'make_Time_ Server()' to the symbol() method of the DLL object.

4 This method uses the OS::dlsym() method to locate the make_ Time_Server entry in the symbol table of the cristian.dll DLL and returns a pointer to this factory function.

5 Assuming the first four steps succeed, the component configurator invokes the factory function, which returns a pointer to a `Time_ Server` component.

6 The component configurator then calls the `init()` method of this component, passing the string '`-p $TIME_SERVER_PORT`' as an '`argc/argv`'-style array. The `init()` method is a hook that the `Time_Server` component uses to initialize itself.

7 Finally, the component configurator stores the initialized `Time_ Server` component into its component repository.

3.5 *Implement the dynamic reconfiguration mechanism.* This mechanism builds on the dynamic configuration mechanism described above to trigger dynamic *reconfiguration* of component implementations. Component reconfiguration should have minimal impact on the execution of other components in an application process. The following two aspects should therefore be addressed when implementing a dynamic reconfiguration mechanism:

Define the reconfiguration triggering strategy. There are two strategies for triggering component reconfiguration, *in-band* and *out-of-band*:

• An in-band strategy initiates reconfigurations synchronously by using an IPC mechanism, such as a Socket connection or a CORBA operation. The application and/or component configurator is responsible for checking for such a reconfiguration event at designated 'reconfiguration points'.

• An out-of-band strategy generates an asynchronous event, such as a UNIX SIGHUP signal, that can interrupt a running application process or thread to initiate reconfiguration. In either case, on receiving a reconfiguration event the component configurator will interpret a new set of component configuration directives.

An in-band strategy for triggering reconfiguration is generally easier to implement, because there is less potential for race conditions. In-band triggering may, however, be less responsive, because reconfiguration can only occur at designated reconfiguration points. In contrast, out-of-band reconfiguration triggering is more responsive. However, it is harder to use out-of-band reconfiguration to implement robust protocols for determining when configuration can occur.

Define protocols for ensuring robust reconfiguration. Another important aspect to consider when implementing a reconfiguration mechanism is *robustness*. For example, if other components in an application are using a component that is being reconfigured, a component configurator may not be able to execute requests to remove or suspend this component immediately. Instead, certain components must be allowed to finish their computation before reconfiguration can be performed.

If a new component is configured into an application, other components may want to be notified, so that they can interact with the new component. Similarly, when a suspended component is resumed, other components may want to be notified so that they can resume their computations.

The Component Configurator pattern focuses on (re)configuration *mechanisms*, such as how to interpret a script containing component configuration directives to link and unlink components dynamically. It is therefore beyond the scope of Component Configurator to ensure robust dynamic component reconfiguration unilaterally. Supporting robust reconfiguration requires collaboration between a component configurator and component/configuration-specific *protocols*. These protocols determine when to trigger a reconfiguration and which components to link and interact with to configure particular application processes.

One way to implement a robust reconfiguration mechanism is to apply the Observer pattern [GoF95]. Client components that want to access a particular component are *observers*. These observers register with the component configurator, which contains a notifier that plays the role of the Observer pattern's *subject* participant.

When a component is scheduled for termination, the component configurator implements a two-phase protocol. The first phase notifies its registered client component 'observers' to finish their computations. In the second phase, the component configurator removes the component after all client components acknowledge this notification. When a new component is initialized, the component configurator re-notifies its registered client components to indicate that they can connect to the new component.

Similarly, client components can register with the component configurator and be notified when a particular component's execution is suspended and resumed.

➡ For example, the following changes could be made to the `Component` and `Component_Configurator` classes to support the Observer-based reconfiguration mechanism:

```
class Component : public Event_Handler {
public:
    // Hook method called back when <observed_component>
    // receives a configuration-related event.
    virtual void handle_update
               (Component *observed_component,
                Configuration_Event_Type event);
    // ...
};

class Component_Configurator {
public:
    // Type of configuration-related events.
    enum Event_Type { INIT, SUSPEND, RESUME, FINI };

    // Register <notified_component> to receive
    // notifications when <observed_component> is
    // reconfigured or suspended/resumed.
    void register_observer
               (Component *notified_component,
                Component *observed_component);
    // ...
};
```
❑

4   *Implement the concrete components.* Concrete component classes can be derived from a common base class such as the `Component` class specified in implementation activity 1 (82). They can also be implemented via a message-passing mechanism that allows them to receive and process component control messages. Components often implement other methods, such as establishing connections with remote peer components and processing service requests received from clients. Component implementations typically reside in DLLs, though they can also be linked statically with the application.

Implementing concrete components involves three sub-activities:

4.1 *Implement the concrete component concurrency model.* An important aspect of implementing a concrete component involves selecting the component's concurrency strategy. For example, a component configured into an application by a component configurator can be executed using event demultiplexing patterns such as Reactor (179) or Proactor (215), or concurrency patterns, such as Active Object (369), Monitor Object (399), Half-Sync/Half-Async (423), or Leader/Followers (447):

- *Reactive/proactive execution.* Using these strategies, one thread of control can be used to process all components reactively or proactively. Components implemented using the Reactor pattern are relatively straightforward to (re)configure and control, because race conditions are minimized or eliminated. However, reactive components may not scale as well as other strategies because they are single-threaded.

  Conversely, components using the Proactor pattern may be more efficient than reactive implementations on platforms that support asynchronous I/O efficiently. However, it may be more complicated to reconfigure and control proactive components, due to the subtleties of canceling asynchronous operations. See the Proactor pattern's liability discussion on page 258 for more details.

- *Multi-threaded or multi-process concurrent execution.* Using these strategies, the configured components execute in their own threads or processes after being initialized by a component configurator. For instance, components can run concurrently using the Active Object pattern (369), or execute within a pre-spawned pool of threads or processes in accordance with the Leader/Followers (447) or Half-Sync/Half-Async (423) patterns.

  In general, executing components in one or more threads within the same process as the component configurator may be more efficient than running the components in separate processes. Conversely, configuring components into separate processes may be more robust and secure, because each component can be isolated from accidental corruption via operating system and hardware protection mechanisms [Sch94].

4.2 *Implement a mechanism for inter-component communication.* Some components run in complete isolation, whereas other components must communicate with one another. In the latter case, component developers must select a mechanism for inter-component communication.

The choice of mechanism is often guided by whether the communicating components will be collocated or distributed:

- When components are collocated, the choice is typically between hard-coding pointer relationships between components, which is inflexible and can defeat the benefits of dynamic component configuration, versus accessing components 'by name' using a component repository.

  ➥ Applications in our time service example use a template to retrieve concrete components from a singleton Component_Configurator's Component_Repository in a type-safe manner:

```
template <class COMPONENT>
class Concrete_Component {
public:
    // Return a pointer to the <COMPONENT> instance
    // in the singleton <Component_Configurator>'s
    // <Component_Repository> associated with <name>.
    static COMPONENT *instance (const string &name);
};
```

  The instance() method is implemented as follows:

```
template <class COMPONENT>
COMPONENT *Concrete_Component<COMPONENT>::instance
    (const string &name) {
    // Find the <Component> associated with <name>,
    // and downcast to ensure type-safety.
    Component *comp = Component_Configurator::
        instance ()->component_repository ()->find(name);
    return dynamic_cast<COMPONENT *> (comp);
}
```

  This template is used to retrieve components from the component repository:

```
Time_Server *time_server =
    Concrete_Component<Time_Server>::instance
        ("Time_Server");
// Invoke methods on the <time_server> component...    ❑
```

- When components are distributed, the typical choice is between low-level IPC mechanisms, such as TCP/IP connections programmed using Sockets [Ste98] or TLI [Rago93], and higher-level mechanisms, such as CORBA [OMG98a]. One of the benefits of using CORBA is that the ORB can transparently optimize for the fastest IPC mechanism, by determining automatically whether the component is collocated or distributed [WSV99].

4.3 *Implement a mechanism to re-establish component relationships.* As outlined in implementation activity 4.2 (93), components can use other components, or even other objects in an application, to perform the services they offer. Replacing one component implementation with another at run-time therefore requires the component configurator to reconnect the new component automatically with components used by the removed component.

One strategy for implementing this mechanism is to checkpoint a component's references to its related components and store it in a Memento [GoF95]. This memento can be passed to the component configurator before shutting down the component. Similarly, the memento may contain additional state information passed from the old to the new component. After the new component is installed, the component configurator can pass the memento to the new component. This component then re-installs the connections and state information that were saved in the memento.

➥   Implementing a mechanism to save and re-establish component relationships would require three changes to our `Component_ Configurator` and `Component` classes:

- *Define a Memento hierarchy.* For every concrete component type, define a memento that saves the references that the component type can maintain to other components. A reference can be denoted either by a component's name or by a pointer, as outlined in implementation activity 4.2 (93). All mementos derive from an abstract memento. This allows the `Component_Configurator` to handle arbitrary mementos using polymorphism.

- *Implement a mechanism for maintaining mementos in the component configurator.* During a component's reconfiguration, the memento containing references to other components is stored in the `Component_Configurator`. The corresponding infrastructure for handling this memento within the `Component_Configurator` can contain a reference to the memento, as well as the component type whose references the memento stores.

- *Change the component interface and implementation.* To pass a memento from a component to the `Component_Configurator` and vice versa, we must change the `Component` interface. For example, the memento can be passed to a `Component` as a parameter to its init() method, and back to the Component_Configurator via a parameter in the Component's fini() method. Within the init() and fini() method implementations of concrete components, the memento is then used to retrieve and save the component's relationships to other components and objects.

In addition to component references, the memento could maintain other state information that is passed to the new component. For example, Clerk components could pass the frequency at which they poll time servers, so that new Clerk components can update their local system time at the same frequency.   ❏

In the remainder of this section, we show how the implementation activity 4 (92) and its sub-activities can be applied to guide the implementation of concrete component participants in our distributed time service example.

➥   There are two types of concrete components in a distributed time service: Time_Server and Clerk. The Time_Server component receives and processes requests for time updates from Clerks. Both Time_Server and Clerk components are designed using the Acceptor-Connector pattern (285). As outlined in implementation activity 1 (82), the component execution mechanism for the Time_Server and Clerk is based on a reactive event-handling model within a single thread of control, in accordance with the Reactor pattern (179).

The Time_Server inherits from the Component class:

```
class Time_Server : public Component {
public:
    // Initialize and terminate a <Time_Server>.
    virtual void init (int argc, const char *argv[]);
    virtual void fini ();

    // Other methods (e.g., <info>, <suspend>, and
    // <resume>) omitted.
private:
    // The <Time_Server_Acceptor> that creates, accepts,
    // and initializes <Time_Server_Handler>s.
    Time_Server_Acceptor acceptor_;

    // A C++ standard library <list> of
    // <Time_Server_Handler>s.
    list<Time_Server_Handler *> handler_list_;
};
```

By inheriting from Component, Time_Server objects can be linked and unlinked by the Component_Configurator dynamically. This design decouples the implementation of the Time_Server from the time or context when it is configured, allowing developers to switch readily between different Time_Server algorithms.

Before storing the Time_Server component in its component repository, the application's component configurator singleton invokes the component's init() hook method. This allows the Time_Server component to initialize itself.

Internally, the Time_Server contains a Time_Server_Acceptor that listens for connection requests to arrive from Clerks. It also contains a C++ standard template library [Aus98] list of Time_Server_ Handlers that process time update requests. The Time_Server_ Acceptor is created and registered with a reactor when the Time_ Server's init() method is called.

When a new connection request arrives from a Clerk, the acceptor creates a new Time_Server_Handler, which processes subsequent time update requests from the Clerk. When its init() method is invoked by the Time_Server_Acceptor, each handler registers itself with the singleton reactor, which subsequently dispatches the handler's handle_event() method when time update requests arrive.

When a component configurator terminates a Time_Server, it calls the Time_Server's fini() method. This method unregisters the Time_Server_Acceptor and all of its associated Time_Server_ Handlers from the reactor and destroys them.

We provide two Time_Server component implementations:

- The first component implements Cristian's algorithm [Cris89]. In this algorithm each Time_Server is a passive entity that responds to queries made by Clerks. In particular, a Time_Server does not query other machines actively to determine its own notion of time.

- The second component implements the Berkeley algorithm [GZ89]. In this algorithm, the Time_Server is an active component that polls every machine in the network periodically to determine its local time. Based on the responses it receives, the Time_Server computes an aggregate notion of the correct time.

As with the Time_Server above, the Clerk inherits from the Component class:

```
class Clerk : public Component {
public:
    // Initialize and terminate a <Clerk>.
    virtual void init (int argc, const char *argv[]);
    virtual void fini ();

    // <info>, <suspend>, and <resume> methods omitted.

    // Hook method invoked by a <Reactor> when a timeout
    // occurs periodically. This method contacts several
    // <Time_Server>s to compute its local notion of time.
    virtual void handle_event (HANDLE, Event_Type);
private:
    // The <Clerk_Connector> that connects and
    // initializes <Clerk_Handler>s.
    Clerk_Connector connector_;

    // A C++ standard library <list> of <Clerk_Handler>s.
    list<Clerk_Handler *> handler_list_;
};
```

By inheriting from Component, the Clerk can be linked and unlinked dynamically by a component configurator. Similarly, a component configurator can configure, control and reconfigure the Clerk it manages by calling its init(), suspend(), resume(), and fini() hook methods.

Our Clerk component establishes and maintains connections with Time_Servers and queries them to calculate the current time. The Clerk's init() method dynamically allocates Clerk_Handlers that send time update requests to Time_Servers connected via a Clerk_Connector. It also registers the Clerk with a reactor to receive timeout events periodically, such as every five minutes.

When the timeout period elapses, the reactor notifies the Clerk's handle_event() hook method. This method instructs the Clerk's Clerk_Handlers to request the current time at the time servers to which they are connected. The Clerk receives and processes these server replies, then updates its local system time accordingly. When Clients ask the Clerk component for the current time, they receive a locally-cached time value that has been synchronized with the global notion of time. The Clerk's fini() method shuts down and cleans up its connector and handlers.

The two alternative implementations of the time services are provided within two DLLs. The `cristian.dll` contains a factory that creates components that run the Cristian algorithm. Likewise, the `berkeley.dll` contains a factory that creates components that run the Berkeley algorithm.   ❏

Example Resolved

In this section, we show how our example distributed time server implementation applies the Component Configurator pattern using a configuration mechanism based on explicit dynamic linking [SchSu94] and a `comp.conf` configuration script. The example is presented as follows:

- We first show how the configuration mechanism supports the dynamic configuration of `Clerk` and `Time_Server` components into application processes via scripting.

- We then show how these features allow `Clerk` components to change the algorithms used to compute local system time. In particular, after a new algorithm has been selected, a singleton `Component_Configurator` can reconfigure the `Clerk` component dynamically without affecting the execution of other types of components controlled by the component configurator.

There are two general strategies for configuring a distributed time component application: *collocated* and *distributed*. We outline each strategy to illustrate how a component configurator-enabled application can be dynamically (re)configured and run.

Collocated configuration. This configuration uses a `comp.conf` script to collocate the `Time_Server` and the `Clerk` within the same process.

A generic `main()` program configures components dynamically using the `process_directives()` method of the `Component_Configura-tor` object and then runs the application's event loop. This event loop is based on the Reactor pattern (179):

```
int main (int argc, char *argv[]) {
    Component_Configurator server;

    // Interpret the comp.conf file specified in argv[1].
    server.process_directives (argv[1]);

    // Reactor singleton perform component processing and
    // any reconfiguration updates.
    for (;;)
        Reactor::instance ()->handle_events ();
    /* NOTREACHED */
}
```

The `process_directives()` method configures components into the server process dynamically as it interprets the following `comp.conf` configuration script:

```
# Configure a Time Server.
dynamic Time_Server Component *
    cristian.dll:make_Time_Server()
        "-p $TIME_SERVER_PORT"

# Configure a Clerk.
dynamic Clerk Component *
    cristian.dll:make_Clerk()
        "-h tango.cs:$TIME_SERVER_PORT"
        "-h perdita.wuerl:$TIME_SERVER_PORT"
        "-h atomic-clock.lanl.gov:$TIME_SERVER_PORT"
        "-P 10" # polling frequency
```

The directives in `comp.conf` specify to the `Component_Configurator` how to configure a collocated `Time_Server` and `Clerk` dynamically in the same application process using the Cristian algorithm. The `Component_Configurator` links the `cristian.dll` DLL into the application's address space dynamically and invokes the appropriate factory function to create new component instances. In our example, these factory functions are called `make_Time_Server()` and `make_Clerk()`, which are defined as follows:

```
Component *make_Time_Server () { return new Time_Server; }
Component *make_Clerk () { return new Clerk; }
```

After each factory function returns its new allocated component, the designated initialization parameters in the `comp.conf` script are passed to the respective init() hook methods. These perform the corresponding component-specific initialization, as illustrated in implementation activity 4 (92).

Distributed configuration. To reduce the memory footprint of an application, we may want to collocate the Time_Server and the Clerk in different processes. Due to the flexibility of the Component Configurator pattern, all that is required to distribute these components is to split the comp.conf script into two parts and run them in separate processes or hosts. One process contains the Time_ Server component and the other process contains the Clerk component.

The figure below shows what the configuration looks like with the Time_Server and Clerk collocated in the same process, as well as the new configuration after the reconfiguration split. Note that the components themselves need not change, because the Component Configurator pattern decouples their processing behavior from the point in time when they are configured.

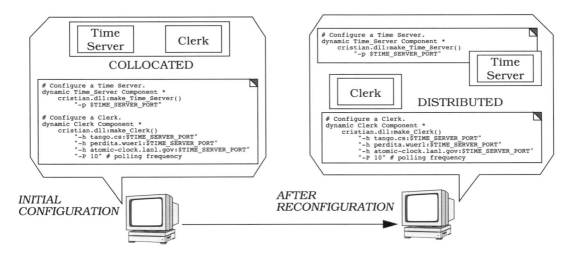

Reconfiguring an application's components. Now consider what happens if we decide to change the algorithms that implement components in the distributed time service. For example, we may need to switch from Cristian's algorithm to the Berkeley algorithm to take advantage of new features in the environment. For example, if the machine on which the Time_Server resides has a WWV receiver, the Time_Server can act as a passive entity and the Cristian algorithm may be appropriate. Conversely, if the machine on which the `Time_Server` resides does not have a WWV receiver, an implementation of the Berkeley algorithm may be more appropriate.

Ideally, we should be able to change `Time_Server` algorithm implementations without affecting the execution of other components of the distributed time service. Accomplishing this using the Component Configurator pattern simply requires minor modifications to our distributed time service configuration activities:

1 *Modify the existing comp.conf script.* We start by making the following change to the `comp.conf` script:

```
# Shut down <Time_Server>.
remove Time_Server
```

This directive instructs the `Component_Configurator` to shut down the `Time_Server` component, remove it from the `Component_Repository`, and unlink the `cristian.dll` if there are no more references to it.

2 *Notify the component configurator to reinterpret the comp.conf script.* Next we must instruct the `Component_Configurator` to process the updated `comp.conf` script. This can be triggered either *in-band*, such as via a Socket connection or a CORBA operation, or *out-of-band*, such as via a UNIX `SIGHUP` signal. Regardless of which triggering strategy is used, after the `Component_Configurator` receives a reconfiguration event, it consults its `comp.conf` script again and shuts down the `Time_Server` component by calling its `fini()` method. During this step the execution of other components should be unaffected.

3 *Initiate reconfiguration.* We can now repeat steps 1 and 2 to reconfigure the Berkeley `Time_Server` component implementation into an application. The `comp.conf` script must be modified with a new directive to specify that the Berkeley `Time_Server` component be linked dynamically from the `berkeley.dll` DLL:

```
# Configure a Time Server.
dynamic Time_Server Component *
    berkeley.dll:make_Time_Server()
        "-p $TIME_SERVER_PORT"
```

Finally, an event is generated to trigger the `Component_Config-urator` in the process to reread its `comp.conf` script and add the updated `Time_Server` component to the `Component_Repository`.

This component starts executing immediately after its init() method is invoked successfully.

The ease with which new component implementations can be replaced dynamically exemplifies the flexibility and extensibility provided by the Component Configurator pattern. In particular, no other configured components in an application should be affected when the Component_Configurator removes or reconfigures the Time_Server component.

Known Uses   **The Windows NT Service Control Manager** (SCM). The SCM allows a master SCM process to initiate and control administrator-installed service components automatically using the message-based strategy described in the *Implementation* section. The master SCM process initiates and manages system service components by passing them various control messages, such as PAUSE, RESUME, and TERMINATE, that must be handled by each service component. SCM-based service components run as separate threads within either a single-service or a multi-service server process. Each installed service component is responsible for configuring itself and monitoring any communication endpoints, which can be more general than socket ports. For instance, the SCM can control named pipes and shared memory.

Modern operating system **device drivers**. Most modern operating systems, such as Solaris, Linux, and Windows NT, provide support for dynamically-configured kernel-level device drivers. These drivers can be linked into and unlinked out of the system dynamically via hooks, such as the init(), fini(), and info() functions defined in SVR4 UNIX [Rago93]. These operating systems apply the Component Configurator pattern to allow administrators to reconfigure the operating system kernel without having to shut it down, recompile, and statically relink new drivers and restart it.

Java applets. The applet mechanism in Java supports dynamic downloading, initializing, starting, stopping, and terminating of Java applets. Web browsers implement the infrastructure software to actually download applets and prepare them for execution. The class java.applet.Applet provides empty methods init(), start(), stop(), and destroy(), to be overridden in application-specific subclasses. Java therefore uses the inheritance-based strategy described in the *Implementation* section. The four life-cycle hook methods mentioned above are called by the browser at the correct time. They give the applet a chance to provide custom behavior that will be called at appropriate times.

For example, the `init()` hook will be called by the browser once the applet is loaded. The `start()` hook will be called once set-up is complete and the applet should start its application logic. The `stop()` hook will be called when the user leaves the Web site. Note that `start()` and `stop()` can be called repeatedly, for example when the user visits and leaves a Web site multiple times. The `destroy()` hook is called once the applet is reclaimed and should free all resources. Finer-grained life-cycle behavior inside an applet can be achieved by creating multiple threads inside the applet and having them scheduled as in ordinary Java applications. Additional examples of how the Component Configurator pattern is used for Java applets are presented in [JS97b].

The **dynamicTAO reflective ORB** [KRL+00] implements a collection of component configurators that allow the transfer of components across a distributed system, loading and unloading modules into the ORB run-time system, and inspecting and modifying the ORB configuration state. Each component configurator is responsible for handling the (re)configuration of a particular aspect of dynamicTAO. For example, its `TAOConfigurator` component configurator contains hooks to which implementations of concurrency and scheduling strategies, as well as security and monitoring interceptors (109), can be attached. In addition, a `DomainConfigurator` provides common services for loading and unloading components into dynamicTAO. It is the base class from which all other component configurators derive, such as `TAOConfigurator`.

ACE [Sch97]. The ADAPTIVE Communication Environment (ACE) framework provides a set of C++ mechanisms for configuring and controlling components dynamically using the inheritance-based strategy described in the *Implementation* section. The ACE Service Configurator framework [SchSu94] extends the mechanisms provided by `Inetd`, `Listen`, and `SCM` to support automatic dynamic linking and unlinking of communication service components.

The Service Configurator framework provided by ACE was influenced by the mechanisms and patterns used to configure and control device drivers in modern operating systems. Rather than targeting kernel-level device drivers, however, ACE focuses on dynamic configuration and control of application-level components. These ACE components are often used in conjunction with the Reactor (179), Acceptor-Connector (285), and Active Object (369) patterns to implement communication services.

In **football**, which Americans call soccer, each team's coach can substitute a limited number of players during a match. The coach is the component configurator who decides which players to substitute, and the players embody the role of components. All players obey the same protocol with respect to substitution, which occurs dynamically, that is, the game does not stop during the substitutions. When players see a sign waved with their numbers, they leave the field and new players join the game immediately. The coach's list of the current 11 players corresponds to the Component Repository. Just as the reconfiguration script is not always written by the coach: some home crowds are renowned for asking and shouting for specific players to be put into the game—and for firing the coach.

Consequences The Component Configurator pattern offers the following **benefits**:

Uniformity. The Component Configurator pattern imposes a uniform configuration and control interface for managing components. This uniformity allows components to be treated as building blocks that can be integrated as components into a larger application. Enforcing a common interface across all components makes them 'look and feel' the same with respect to their configuration activities, which simplifies application development by promoting the 'principle of least surprise'.

Centralized administration. The Component Configurator pattern groups one or more components into a single administrative unit. This consolidation simplifies development by enabling common component initialization and termination activities, such as opening/closing files and acquiring/releasing locks, to be performed automatically. In addition, the pattern centralizes the administration of components by ensuring that each component supports the same configuration management operations, such as init(), suspend(), resume(), and fini().

Modularity, testability, and reusability. The Component Configurator pattern improves application modularity and reusability by decoupling the implementation of components from the manner in which the components are configured into processes. Because all components have a uniform configuration and control interface, monolithic applications can be decomposed more easily into reusable components that can be developed and tested independently. This separation of concerns encourages greater reuse and simplifies development of subsequent components.

Configuration dynamism and control. The Component Configurator pattern enables a component to be dynamically reconfigured without modifying, recompiling, or statically relinking existing code. In addition, (re)configuration of a component can often be performed without restarting the component or other active components with which it is collocated. These features help create an infrastructure for application-defined component configuration frameworks.

Tuning and optimization. The Component Configurator pattern increases the range of component configuration alternatives available to developers by decoupling component functionality from component execution mechanisms. For instance, developers can tune server concurrency strategies adaptively to match client demands and available operating system processing resources. Common execution alternatives include spawning a thread or process upon the arrival of a client request or pre-spawning a thread or process at component creation time.

The Component Configurator pattern has several **liabilities**:

Lack of determinism and ordering dependencies. The Component Configurator pattern makes it hard to determine or analyze the behavior of an application until its components are configured at run-time. This can be problematic for certain types of system, particularly real-time systems, because a dynamically-configured component may not behave predictably when run with certain other components. For example, a newly configured component may consume excessive CPU cycles, thereby starving other components of processing time and causing them to miss deadlines.

Reduced security or reliability. An application that uses the Component Configurator pattern may be less secure or reliable than an equivalent statically-configured application. It may be less secure because impostors can masquerade as components in DLLs. It may be less reliable because a particular component configuration may adversely affect component execution. A faulty component may crash, for example, corrupting state information it shares with other components configured into the same process.

Increased run-time overhead and infrastructure complexity. The Component Configurator pattern adds levels of abstraction and indirection when executing components. For example, the component configurator first initializes components and then links them into the component repository, which may incur excessive overhead in time-critical applications. In addition, when dynamic linking is used to implement components many compilers add extra levels of indirection to invoke methods and access global variables [GLDW87].

Overly narrow common interfaces. The initialization or termination of a component may be too complicated or too tightly coupled with its context to be performed in a uniform manner via common component control interfaces, such as init() and fini().

See Also The intent of the Component Configurator pattern is similar to the Configuration pattern [CMP95]. The Configuration pattern decouples structural issues related to configuring protocols and services in distributed applications from the execution of the protocols and services themselves. The Configuration pattern has been used in frameworks that support the construction of distributed systems out of building-block components.

In a similar way, the Component Configurator pattern decouples component initialization from component processing. The primary difference is that the Configuration pattern focuses on the active composition of chains of related protocols and services. In contrast, the Component Configurator pattern focuses on the dynamic initialization of components that process requests exchanged between transport endpoints.

Credit Thanks to Giorgio Angiolini, who provided us with feedback on an earlier version of this pattern. In addition, thanks to Prashant Jain, who was the co-author of the original version of the Service Configurator pattern, which formed the basis for the Component Configurator pattern described here. Fabio Kon contributed the description of the dynamicTAO known use.

Interceptor

The *Interceptor* architectural pattern allows services to be added transparently to a framework and triggered automatically when certain events occur.

Example   MiddleSoft Inc. is developing an object request broker (ORB) middleware framework called MiddleORB, which is an implementation of the Broker pattern [POSA1]. MiddleORB provides communication services that simplify the development of distributed applications. In addition to core communication services, such as connection management and transport protocols, applications using MiddleORB may require other services, such as transactions and security, load balancing and fault tolerance, auditing, and logging, non-standard communication mechanisms like shared memory, and monitoring and debugging tools.

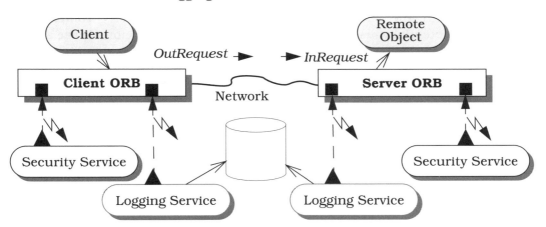

To satisfy a wide-range of application demands, the MiddleORB architecture must support the integration of these extended services. One strategy for coping [Cope98] with this requirement is to integrate as many services as possible into the default MiddleORB configuration. This strategy is often infeasible, however, because not all ORB services can be anticipated at its development time. As distributed applications evolved, the ORB framework would inevitably expand to include new features. Such piecemeal growth can complicate ORB design and maintenance, as well as increase its memory footprint, even though many of these features are not used by all applications all the time.

An alternative strategy is to keep the MiddleORB framework as simple and concise as possible. In this model, if application developers require services not available in the framework, they would implement them along with their own client and server code. However, this strategy would require developers to implement much code that was unrelated to their application logic.

In addition, certain services cannot be implemented solely at the application client and object level, because they must interact intimately with core ORB features. For example, a security service should be integrated with the ORB infrastructure. Otherwise, applications can masquerade as privileged users and gain unauthorized access to protected system resources.

Clearly, neither strategy outlined above is entirely satisfactory. With the first strategy MiddleORB will be too large and inflexible, whereas with the second, applications will become overly complex and potentially insecure or error-prone. We must therefore devise a better strategy for integrating application-specific services into MiddleORB.

Context   Developing frameworks that can be extended transparently.

Problem   Frameworks, such as ORBs, application servers, and domain-specific software architectures [SG96], cannot anticipate all the services they must offer to users. It may also not be feasible to extend certain types of frameworks, particularly black-box frameworks [HJE95], with new services that they were not originally designed to support. Similarly, it is often undesirable to rely upon applications to implement all the necessary services themselves, because this defeats many benefits of reuse. Framework developers must therefore address the following three *forces*:

- A framework should allow integration of additional services without requiring modifications to its core architecture.

  ➡   For example, it should be possible to extend MiddleORB to support security services, such as Kerberos or SSL [OSSL00], without modifying the structure of its internal design [OMG98d].❏

- The integration of application-specific services into a framework should not affect existing framework components, nor should it require changes to the design or implementation of existing applications that use the framework.

  ➡ For instance, adding load balancing to MiddleORB should be unobtrusive to existing MiddleORB client and server applications.❏

- Applications using a framework may need to monitor and control its behavior.

  ➡ For example, some applications may want to control MiddleORB's fault tolerance strategies [OMG99g] via the Reflection pattern [POSA1] to direct its responses to failure conditions.   ❏

Solution   Allow applications to extend a framework transparently by registering 'out-of-band' services with the framework via predefined interfaces, then let the framework trigger these services automatically when certain events occur.[4] In addition, open the framework's implementation [Kic92] so that the out-of-band services can access and control certain aspects of the framework's behavior.

In detail: for a designated set of events processed by a framework, specify and expose an *interceptor* callback interface. *Applications* can derive *concrete interceptors* from this interface to implement out-of-band services that process occurrences of these events in an application-specific manner. Provide a *dispatcher* for each interceptor that allows applications to register their concrete interceptors with the framework. When the designated events occur, the framework notifies the appropriate dispatchers to invoke the callbacks of the registered concrete interceptors.

Define *context objects* to allow a concrete interceptor to introspect and control certain aspects of the framework's internal state and behavior in response to events. Context objects provide methods to access and modify a framework's internal state, thus opening its implementation. Context objects can be passed to concrete interceptors when they are dispatched by the framework.

---

4. In this context, *events* denotes application-level events such as the delivery of requests and responses within an ORB framework. These events are often visible only within the framework implementation.

Structure   A *concrete framework* instantiates a generic and extensible architecture to define the services provided by a particular system, such as an ORB, a Web server, or an application server.

Class	*Collaborator*
Concrete Framework	• Dispatcher
Responsibility	
• Defines application-services	
• Integrates dispatchers that allow applications to intercept events	
• Delegates events to associated dispatchers	

➡   Two types of concrete frameworks are available in MiddleORB, one for the client and one for the server:[5]

• Client applications use the client concrete ORB framework's programming interface to access remote objects. This concrete framework provides common services, such as binding to a remote object, sending requests to the object, waiting for replies, and returning them to the client.

• The server concrete ORB framework provides complementary services, including registering and managing object implementations, listening on transport endpoints, receiving requests, dispatching these requests to object implementations, and returning replies to clients.❏

Interceptors are associated with a particular event or set of events exposed by a concrete framework. An interceptor defines the signatures of hook methods [Pree95] [GHJV95] that the concrete framework will invoke automatically via a designated dispatching mechanism when the corresponding events occur. *Concrete interceptors* specialize interceptor interfaces and implement their hook methods to handle these events in an application-specific manner.

---

5. ORBs support peer-to-peer communication. Thus 'client' and 'server' are relative terms corresponding to roles played during a particular request/response interaction, rather than being fundamental properties of particular system components.

➥   In our MiddleORB example, we specify an interceptor interface containing several hook methods that the client and server concrete ORB frameworks dispatch automatically when a client application invokes a remote operation and the corresponding server receives the new request, respectively.   ❑

Class Interceptor	*Collaborator*	*Class* Concrete Interceptor	*Collaborator* • Context Object
Responsibility • Defines an interface for integrating out-of-band services		*Responsibility* • Implements a specific out-of-band service • Uses context object to control the concrete framework	

To allow interceptors to handle the occurrence of particular events, a concrete framework defines *dispatchers* for configuring and triggering concrete interceptors. Typically there is a dispatcher for each interceptor. A dispatcher defines registration and removal methods that applications use to subscribe and un-subscribe concrete interceptors with the concrete framework.

A dispatcher also defines another interface that the concrete framework calls when specific events occur for which concrete interceptors have registered. When the concrete framework notifies a dispatcher that such an event has occurred, the dispatcher invokes all the concrete interceptor callbacks that have registered for it. A dispatcher maintains all its registered interceptors in a container.

➥   In our MiddleORB example, the client concrete ORB framework implements a dispatcher that allows client applications to intercept certain events, such as outgoing requests to remote objects and incoming object replies. Servers use a corresponding dispatcher in the server concrete ORB framework to intercept related events, such as incoming client requests and outgoing object replies. Other dispatchers can be defined at different layers in the ORB to intercept other types of events such as connection and message transport events. ❑

Concrete interceptors can use *context objects* to access and control certain aspects of a concrete framework. Context objects can provide *accessor methods* to obtain information from the concrete framework and *mutator methods* to control the behavior of the concrete framework. A context object can be instantiated by a concrete framework and passed to a concrete interceptor with each callback invocation. In this case the context object can contain information related to the event that triggered its creation.

Conversely, a context object can be passed to an interceptor when it registers with a dispatcher. This design provides less information but also incurs less overhead.

Class	Collaborator	Class	Collaborator
Dispatcher	• Interceptor • Application	Context Object	• Concrete Framework
Responsibility		**Responsibility**	
• Allows applications to register and remove concrete interceptors • Dispatches registered concrete interceptor callbacks when events occur		• Allows services to obtain information from the concrete framework • Allows services to control certain behavior of the concrete framework	

➥   In our MiddleORB example, the interceptor interface defines methods that the client concrete ORB framework dispatches automatically when it processes an outgoing request. These methods are passed a context object parameter containing information about the current request. Each context object defines accessor and mutator methods that allow a concrete interceptor to query and change ORB state and behavior, respectively.

For example, an accessor method in a context object can return the arguments for a remote operation. Using the context object's mutator methods, a client application's concrete interceptor can redirect an operation to a different object. This feature can be used to implement custom load balancing and fault tolerance services [ZBS97].   ❏

An *application* runs on top of a concrete framework and reuses the services it provides. An application can also implement concrete interceptors and register them with the concrete framework to handle certain events. When these events occur, they trigger the concrete framework and its dispatchers to invoke concrete interceptor callbacks that perform application-specific event processing.

Class	Collaborator
Application	• Dispatcher • Concrete Interceptor
Responsibility	
• Runs atop the concrete framework • Implements concrete interceptors and registers them with dispatchers	

The class diagram below illustrates the structure of participants in the Interceptor pattern.

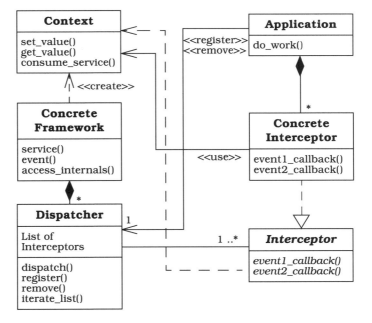

Dynamics A typical scenario for the Interceptor pattern illustrates how an application implements a concrete interceptor and registers it with the corresponding dispatcher. The dispatcher then invokes the interceptor callback when the concrete framework notifies it that an event of interest has occurred:

• An application instantiates a concrete interceptor that implements a specific interceptor interface. The application registers this concrete interceptor with the appropriate dispatcher.

- The concrete framework subsequently receives an event that is subject to interception. In this scenario a special context object is available for each kind of event. The concrete framework therefore instantiates an event-specific context object that contains information related to the event, as well as functionality to access and potentially control the concrete framework.

- The concrete framework notifies the appropriate dispatcher about the occurrence of the event, passing the context object as a parameter.

- The dispatcher iterates through its container of registered concrete interceptors and invokes their callback hook methods, passing the context object as an argument.

- Each concrete interceptor can use its context object to retrieve information about the event or the concrete framework. After processing this information, a concrete interceptor can optionally call method(s) on the context object to control the behavior of the concrete framework and its subsequent event processing.

- After all concrete interceptor callback methods have returned, the concrete framework continues with its normal operation.

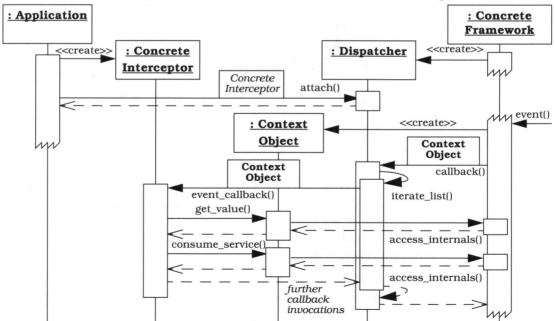

Implementation Seven implementation activities describe a common approach for implementing the Interceptor pattern.

1 *Model the internal behavior of the concrete framework* using a state machine or an equivalent notation, if such a model is not available already. This modeling need not capture all abstractions of the concrete framework, but should document the aspects that are related to interception. To minimize the complexity of any given state machine, the modeled parts of the concrete framework can be composed from smaller state machines that together form a composite state machine.[6]

Each smaller state machine represents a particular aspect of the concrete framework. Once the dynamic aspects of the concrete framework are modeled as a state machine, use this model to determine where and when certain events can be intercepted.

In ORB middleware and many other component-based systems at least two types of concrete frameworks exist, one for the role of client and one for the role of server. In this case the concrete frameworks should be modeled as separate state machines. In general, state machine modeling helps identify where to place interceptors and how to define their behavior in a concrete framework.

➥ Consider the client concrete ORB framework defined by MiddleORB. During ORB start-up this framework is initialized to continue processing client requests until it is shut down. The client concrete ORB framework provides two types of service to clients:

• When a client binds to a new remote object, the concrete framework creates a proxy that connects to the object.

• If the bind operation is successful the client can send requests to the remote object. Each request is marshaled and delivered to the remote object using a pre-established connection. After successful delivery, the concrete framework waits for the object's response message, demarshals it upon arrival, returns the result to the client, and transitions to the idle state.

Additional error states denote situations in which problems are encountered, such as communication errors or marshaling errors,

---

6. More details on composite state machines is available in the UML User Guide [BRJ98].

are shown in the following figure. Note that this figure illustrates only a portion of the client concrete ORB framework's internal composite state machine.

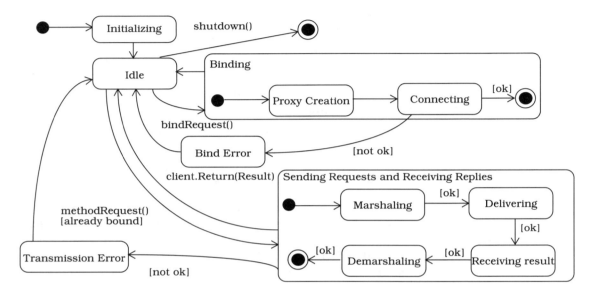

2 *Identify and model interception points.* This implementation activity can be divided into four sub-activities:

2.1 *Identify concrete framework state transitions* that may not be visible to external applications, but are subject to interception. For example, a client may want to intercept outgoing requests so it can add functionality, such as logging or changing certain request parameters, dynamically. We call these state transitions 'interception points'.

2.2 *Partition interception points into reader and writer sets.* The *reader set* includes all state transitions in which applications only access information from the concrete framework. Conversely the *writer set* includes all state transitions in which applications can modify the behavior of the concrete framework.

2.3 *Integrate interception points into the state machine model.* Interception points can be modeled in the state machine by introducing intermediary states. If a state transition is subject to interception, place a new interception state between the source state and the sink state of the original transition. This interception state triggers the corresponding interceptors. For interception points that belong to the writer set, introduce additional state transitions in which the following properties apply:

- The interception state is the start node and

- The target nodes are states that represent the subsequent behavior of the concrete framework after the interception.

Many component-based distributed systems define peer concrete frameworks, such as client and server ORBs, that are organized in accordance with the Layers pattern [POSA1]. When identifying interception points in one of these concrete frameworks, introduce a related interception point in the other peer concrete framework at the same logical layer. For example, if a client ORB intercepts outgoing requests, it is likely that the server ORB should also intercept incoming requests. When integrating layered services, such as adding security tokens on the client-side and encrypting outgoing request data, a corresponding interceptor is therefore required on the server to extract the security token and decrypt the incoming data.

➡   By applying the state machine model of the client concrete ORB framework shown above, we can identify the potential interception points shown in the following table:

Interception Point	Description	Reader / Writer
Shut-down	The concrete framework is shutting down its operation. Clients may need to perform certain cleanup work, such as freeing resources they have allocated previously.	Reader
Binding	The client application is binding to a remote object. The concrete framework instantiates a new proxy and establishes a communication channel. A monitoring service might intercept this event to visualize new client/object relationships.	Reader
PreMarshalOutRequest	The client application sends a request to the remote object. Interceptors might be used to change the target object or the parameter values to support load balancing, validate certain preconditions, or encrypt parameters.	Reader + Writer

Interception Point	Description	Reader / Writer
PostMarshalOutRequest	The client concrete ORB framework has marshaled the data but not yet delivered it. A client may be interested in monitoring activities, such as starting a timer to measure the round-trip latency.	Reader
PreMarshalInReply	The reply just arrived and the concrete framework has not yet demarshaled the data. A client may be interested in monitoring this event or stopping a round-trip latency timer.	Reader
PostMarshalInReply	The client concrete ORB framework has marshaled the reply. An interceptor might evaluate post-conditions or change the result. For example, it could decrypt the result if it was encrypted by a server-side interceptor.	Reader + Writer

Additional interception points may be required if a client intercepts exceptions, such as failed connection events. The server concrete ORB framework can also define peer interception points. ❏

2.4 *Partition interception points into disjoint interception groups.* To process events, concrete frameworks often perform a series of related activities, each of which may be associated with an interception point. To emphasize the relationship between each activity, it may be useful to coalesce a series of semantically-related interception points into an *interception group.*

For example, all interception points associated with sending a request can form one interception group, whereas all interception points associated with receiving a request can form another group. These interception groups help to minimize the number of necessary interceptors and dispatchers as shown in implementation activity 4 (123).

To identify interception groups, analyze the state machine for interception points that are located in the same area of the state machine and participate in the same activity. For example, interception points that are triggered by transitions originating from a particular state, ending in a particular state, or ending in a particular set of neighbor states may be candidates for consideration as part of the same interception group.

➡ In MiddleORB, both the *PreMarshalOutRequest* and *Post–MarshalOutRequest* interception points participate in sending a request. These interception points can therefore constitute the *OutRequest* interception group. This interception group coalesces all events related to the activities of sending a request in order to differentiate these events from other interception groups, such as *InRequest*, *OutReply*, or *InReply*. ❏

3 *Specify the context objects.* Context objects allow interceptors to access and control aspects of the framework's internal state and behavior in response to certain events. Three sub-activities can be applied to specify context objects:

3.1 *Determine the context object semantics.* Context objects provide information about an interception point and may also define services to control the framework's subsequent behavior. Concrete interceptors use the information and services to handle interception points in an application-specific manner. The accessor and mutator methods defined for context objects can be based on information that a concrete framework provides to interceptors, as well as the degree to which a framework is 'open':

- If an interception point belongs to the reader set, determine what information the concrete framework should provide the interceptor for each event it handles. For example, if a context object provides information about a particular remote operation invocation, it may contain the reference of the target object being called as well as the operation's name and parameter values.

- If the interception point belongs to the writer set, determine how to 'open' the concrete framework's implementation so that concrete interceptors can control selected aspects of its behavior [Kic92]. For example, if a context object provides information about a particular remote operation invocation, it may contain methods that can modify the operation's parameter values. The design force to balance here, of course, is 'open extensibility' versus 'error-prone interception code'.

Although concrete frameworks with open implementations can have powerful interceptors, they are also more vulnerable to interceptors that maliciously or accidentally corrupt the concrete framework's robustness and security. Some interception designs therefore disallow mutator functionality within context objects.

3.2 *Determine the number of context object types*. Here are two strategies for selecting the number and types of context objects:

- *Multiple interfaces*. If the interception points in a concrete framework cover a diverse set of requirements, different types of context objects can be defined for different interception points. This strategy is flexible, because it allows fine-grained control of particular interception points. However it increases the number of interfaces that developers of concrete interceptors must understand.

- *Single interface*. It is possible to specify a generic context object with a single interface. Using a single interface reduces the number of context object interfaces, but may yield a bloated and complex context object interface.

In general, multiple interfaces are useful when client applications intercept a wide variety of different framework events. In other cases, however, the single interface strategy may be preferable due to its simplicity.

➡   When the MiddleORB client ORB framework intercepts outgoing client requests, applications may want to access and/or control the following aspects:

- Reading and changing the target object reference to implement fault tolerance or load balancing.

- Reading and modifying parameter values to encrypt data, validate selected arguments, or change behavior reflectively [POSA1].

- Adding new data to the request to send out-of-band information, such as security tokens or transaction contexts.

- Integrating custom parameter marshalers and demarshalers.

These activities correspond to those specified by the *PreMarshalOut-Request* and *PostMarshalOutRequest* interception points outlined in the table in implementation activity 2.3 (118). We therefore introduce two corresponding context object types, `UnmarshaledRequest` and `MarshaledRequest`. The interface `UnmarshaledRequest` is structured as follows:

```
public interface UnmarshaledRequest {
    public String getHost (); // get host
    public void setHost (String host); // set host
    public long getPort (); // get server port
    public void setPort (long newPort); // set new port
    public String getObjName (); // get object name
    public void setObjName (String newName); // set name
    public String getMethod (); // get method name
    public void setMethod (String name); // set method
    public Enumeration getParameters ();// get parameters
    public Object getArg (long i); // get i_th arg
    public void setArg (long i, Object o); // set i_th arg
    public void addInfo (Object info); // add extra info.
    // ...
}                                                              ❏
```

3.3   *Define how to pass context objects to concrete interceptors.* Context objects are instantiated by the concrete framework. They are passed to a concrete interceptor using one of the following two strategies:

- *Per-registration.* In this strategy a context object is passed to an interceptor once when it registers with a dispatcher.

- *Per-event.* In this strategy a context object is passed to a concrete interceptor with every callback invocation.

The per-event strategy allows a concrete framework to provide fine-grained information about the occurrence of a particular event. In contrast, the per-registration strategy only provides general information common to all occurrences of a particular event type. The per-event strategy may incur higher overhead, however, due to repeated creation and deletion of context objects.

4   *Specify the interceptors.* An interceptor defines a generic interface that a concrete framework uses to invoke concrete interceptors, via dispatchers, when interception points are triggered. An interceptor is defined for each interception group identified in implementation activity 2.4 (120). Consequently each concrete interceptor that derives from a particular interceptor is responsible for handling all the interception points of a specific interception group.

For each interception point in an interception group, an interceptor defines a designated callback hook method. There is thus a one-to-one relationship between an interception point and an interceptor hook method. In general the interceptor corresponds to the *observer* participant in the Observer pattern [GoF95], where its callback hook methods play the role of event-specific *update methods*. If the 'per-event' context object strategy described in implementation activity 3 (121) is applied, context objects can be passed as parameters to the concrete interceptor callback hook methods. These methods can return results or raise exceptions, in accordance with the policies described in implementation activity 6 (126).

➡   In implementation activity 2.4 (120) we identified the interception group *OutRequest*. Below we illustrate a common interceptor interface for this interception group:

```
public interface ClientRequestInterceptor {
    public void onPreMarshalRequest
        (UnmarshaledRequest context);
    public void onPostMarshalRequest
        (MarshaledRequest context);
}
```

For each interception point associated with the *OutRequest* interception group, the ClientRequestInterceptor defines a separate hook method that is called back by the dispatcher at the appropriate interception point.   ❏

5   *Specify the dispatchers.* For each interceptor, define a *dispatcher* interface that applications can use to register and remove concrete interceptors with the concrete framework. In addition, this interface is used by the framework to dispatch concrete interceptors registered at interception points. Two sub-activities are involved:

5.1   *Specify the interceptor registration interface.* A dispatcher corresponds to the Observer pattern's [GoF95] *subject* role. It implements a registration interface for interceptors, which correspond to the *observer* role. Applications pass a reference to a concrete interceptor to the registration method, which stores the reference in a container in accordance with the Manager pattern [Som97].

To implement different callback policies, an application can pass a dispatcher additional parameters. For example, it can pass a priority value that determines the invocation order when multiple interceptors are registered for the same interception point, as described in implementation activity 6 (126). The dispatcher returns a key to the application that identifies the registered interceptor uniquely. An application passes this key to the dispatcher when it removes an interceptor it registered previously.

To automate interceptor registration, and to hide its implementation, a concrete framework can implement helper classes that provide 'no-op' implementations of interceptor interfaces. The constructors of these classes register instances automatically with the concrete framework. Applications derive their concrete interceptor implementations from the appropriate helper class, override its methods and call the base class constructor to register their interceptors implicitly.

In general, a specific dispatcher can forward every occurrence of its corresponding event types from the concrete framework to the concrete interceptors that registered for these events. Dispatchers are therefore often implemented using the Singleton pattern [GoF95].

➥   The methods defined in the following `ClientRequestDispatcher` class allow applications to register and remove `ClientRequestInterceptor` instances with the MiddleORB concrete framework:

```
public class ClientRequestDispatcher {
    // Interceptors are stored in a Java vector and called
    // in FIFO order.
    Vector interceptors_;

    synchronized public void
    registerClientRequestInterceptor
        (ClientRequestInterceptor i) {
        interceptors_.addElement (i); // Add interceptor.
    }

    synchronized public void
    removeClientRequestInterceptor
        (ClientRequestInterceptor i) {
        // Remove interceptor.
        interceptors_.removeElement (i);
    }
    // ...
}
```
❏

5.2 *Specify the dispatcher callback interface.* When an interception event occurs the concrete framework notifies its dispatcher. When notified, a dispatcher invokes the corresponding hook methods of its registered concrete interceptors. A dispatcher often provides the same interface to the concrete framework that its associated interceptor provides to the dispatcher.

There are two reasons for this similarity:

- It streamlines performance, by allowing a dispatcher to delegate event notifications to its registered interceptors efficiently, without transforming any parameters.

- It localizes and minimizes the modifications required if the public interface of the dispatcher changes. An example of such a modification might be the addition of a new interception point to the interception group associated with the dispatcher callback interface. In this case an additional hook method would be added to the callback interface.

➥ In MiddleORB the internal dispatcher ClientRequestDispatcher also implements the interface ClientRequestInterceptor:

```
public class ClientRequestDispatcher
      implements ClientRequestInterceptor { /* ... */ }
```

The MiddleORB client concrete ORB framework can thus use the callback hook methods in this interface to notify the dispatcher about all events related to client requests.   ❑

6   *Implement the callback mechanisms in the concrete framework.* When an interception event occurs the concrete framework notifies the corresponding dispatcher. The dispatcher then invokes the hook methods of all registered concrete interceptor callbacks in turn. A mechanism is therefore needed to propagate events from the concrete framework to its dispatchers and from the dispatchers to the registered interceptors. This mechanism can be implemented by applying the Observer pattern [GoF95] twice.

The first application of the Observer pattern occurs whenever the concrete framework reaches an interception point. At this point it creates the appropriate context object and notifies the dispatcher about the occurrence of the event. In terms of the Observer pattern, the concrete framework is a *subject* that is *observed* by a dispatcher.

When the concrete framework notifies the dispatcher, it can either pass the context object as a parameter, or it can use a pre-allocated singleton context object that acts as an interface to the concrete framework. In the first strategy, all event-related information is encapsulated in the context object, while the second strategy requires the concrete framework to store all of the necessary information. The choice of strategy depends on the design of the concrete framework, as described in implementation activity 3.3 (123).

The second application of the Observer pattern occurs after the dispatcher is notified. At this point it iterates over all interceptors that have registered at this interception point and invokes the appropriate callback method in their interface, passing the context object as a parameter. The dispatcher is thus also a *subject* that is *observed* by concrete interceptors.

The dispatcher's internal callback mechanism can be implemented with the Iterator pattern [GoF95]. Similarly, a dispatcher can apply the Strategy pattern [GoF95] to allow applications to select from among several interceptor callback orderings:

- Simple invocation strategies include 'first-in first-out' (FIFO) or 'last-in first-out' (LIFO) ordering strategies, where interceptors are invoked in the order they were registered or vice-versa. When using the Interceptor pattern to implement a particular 'interceptor stack', a combined FIFO/LIFO approach can be used to process messages traversing the stack. On the client a FIFO strategy can be used to pass messages down the stack. On the server a LIFO strategy can be used to pass messages up the stack.

- A more sophisticated ordering callback strategy dispatches concrete interceptors in priority order. In this strategy an application passes a priority parameter when registering a concrete interceptor with a dispatcher. When propagating an event, the dispatcher invokes interceptors with higher priorities first.

- Another sophisticated callback strategy is based on the Chain of Responsibility pattern [GoF95]. If a concrete interceptor can handle the event that its dispatcher delivers, it returns the corresponding result. Otherwise it can return a special value or raise an exception to indicate it is not interested in intercepting the event. In this case the callback dispatching mechanism asks the next interceptor in the chain to handle the event. This progression stops after one of the interceptors handles the event.

If an interceptor encounters error conditions that prevent it from completing its work successfully, it can invoke exceptions or return failure values to propagate these errors to handlers. In this case the concrete framework must be prepared to handle these errors.

➡ When a client concrete ORB framework processes a request it instantiates a context object, and notifies the corresponding dispatcher to iterate through the registered interceptors to call their appropriate event handling hook methods, such as `onPreMarshal-Request()`:

```
public class ClientRequestDispatcher {
    // ...
    public void
    dispatchClientRequestInterceptorPreMarshal
        (UnmarshaledRequest context) {
        Vector interceptors;
        synchronized (this) { // Clone vector.
            interceptors = (Vector)
                interceptors.clone ();
        }
        for (int i = 0; i < interceptors.size (); ++i) {
            ClientRequestInterceptor ic =
            (ClientRequestInterceptor)
                interceptors.elementAt (i);
            // Dispatch callback hook method.
            ic.onPreMarshalRequest (context);
        }
    }
    // ...
}                                                              ❑
```

7   *Implement the concrete interceptors.* Concrete interceptors can derive from and implement the corresponding interceptor interface in application-specific ways. A concrete interceptor can use the context object it receives as a parameter to either:

- Obtain additional information about the event that occurred or

- Control the subsequent behavior of the concrete framework, as described in implementation activity 3 (121)

The Extension Interface pattern (141) can be applied to minimize the number of different interceptor types in an application. Each interception interface becomes an extension interface of a single interceptor object. The same 'physical' object can thus be used to implement different 'logical' interceptors.

➥   A client application can provide its own ClientRequest-Interceptor class:

```
public class Client {
    static final void main (String args[]) {
        ClientRequestInterceptor myInterceptor =
            // Use an anonymous inner class.
            new ClientRequestInterceptor () {
            public void onPreMarshalRequest
                (UnmarshaledRequest context) {
                System.out.println
                    (context.getObj () + " called");
                // ...
            }
            public void onPostMarshalRequest
                (MarshaledRequest context) { /* ... */ }
        };
        ClientRequestDispatcher.theInstance ().
            registerClientRequestInterceptor
                (myInterceptor);
        // Do normal work.
    }
}
```

In this implementation the client's main() method creates an instance of an anonymous ClientRequestInterceptor inner class and registers it with the singleton instance of the ClientRequest-Dispatcher class. Whenever the client concrete ORB framework encounters a client request event it notifies the dispatcher, which then calls back the appropriate hook method of the registered interceptor. In this example the interceptor just prints a message on the screen after a method is invoked but before it is marshaled.   ❑

Example Resolved   Applications can use the Interceptor pattern to integrate a customized load-balancing mechanism into MiddleORB. By using interceptors, this mechanism is transparent to the client application, the server application, and the ORB infrastructure itself. In this example a pair of concrete interceptors are interposed by the client application:

• *Bind interceptor.* When a client binds to a remote object, the bind interceptor determines whether subsequent invocations on the CORBA object should be load balanced. All such 'load balancing' objects can be replicated [GS97] automatically on predefined server machines. Information on load balancing, servers, and available replicated objects can be maintained in the ORB's Implementation

Repository [Hen98] and cached within memory-resident tables. Information on the current system load can reside in separate tables.

- *Client request interceptor.* When a client invokes an operation on a remote object, the client request concrete interceptor is dispatched. This interceptor checks whether the object is replicated. If it is, the interceptor finds a server machine with a light load and forwards the request to the appropriate target object. The algorithm for measuring the current load can be configured using the Strategy pattern [GoF95]. Client developers can thus substitute their own algorithms transparently without affecting the ORB infrastructure or the client/server application logic.

The following diagram illustrates the scenario executed by the client request interceptor after the bind interceptor has replicated an object that is load balanced on multiple servers:

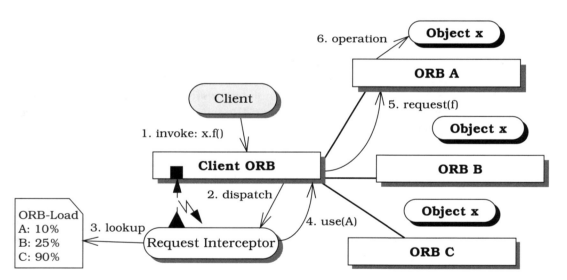

This scenario involves three steps:

- A client invokes an operation on a replicated object (1).

- The client request interceptor intercepts this request (2). It then consults a table containing the object's replicas to identify a server with a lightest load (3). The bind interceptor created this table earlier when the object was replicated.

- The client ORB forwards the request to the server with a light load (4). The server's ORB then delivers it to the object implementation residing on this server (5) and dispatches its operation (6).

Variants *Interceptor Proxy* variant (also known as *Delegator*). This variant is often used on the server-side of a distributed system to intercept remote operations. The server concrete framework automatically instantiates a proxy [POSA1] to a local object implementation residing on the server. This proxy implements the same interfaces as the object. When the proxy is instantiated it receives a reference to the actual server object.

When a client issues a request, the server's proxy intercepts the incoming request and performs certain pre-processing functionality, such as starting a new transaction or validating a security tokens. The proxy then forwards the request to the local server object, which performs its process operations in the context established by the proxy:

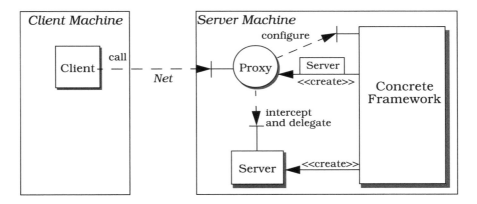

After the object processing is finished, the proxy performs any post-processing that is needed and returns the result, if any, to the client. Both the client and the server object are oblivious to the existence of the interceptor proxy.

Single Interceptor-per-Dispatcher. This variant allows only one interceptor to register with a specific dispatcher. This restriction can simplify the pattern's implementation when it makes no sense to have more than one interceptor, in which case there is no need for the concrete framework to retain a whole collection of interceptors.

➥ In MiddleORB there could be an interceptor interface for changing the concrete framework's transport protocol dynamically [Naka00]. At most there should be one interceptor that changes the default behavior of the concrete framework. Thus, there is no reason to register a chain of different interceptors that are each responsible for changing the transport protocol.   ❏

Interceptor Factory. This variant is applicable when the concrete framework instantiates the same class multiple times and each instance of the class is subject to interception. Instead of registering an interceptor for each object with the dispatcher explicitly, applications register interceptor factories with the concrete framework. Thus, for every object the concrete framework instantiates, it also instantiates a concrete interceptor using the supplied factory.

➥ In MiddleORB there could be a different interceptor for each object implementation created by the server concrete ORB framework. In addition the client concrete ORB framework could use a factory to instantiate a separate client interceptor for each proxy. ❏

Implicit Interceptor Registration. Rather than registering interceptors via dispatchers explicitly, a concrete framework can load interceptors dynamically. There are two ways to implement this strategy:

- The concrete framework searches for interceptor libraries in predefined locations. It then loads these libraries into the concrete framework and ensures that they support the required interceptor interfaces before installing and dispatching events to them.

- The concrete framework can link interceptors dynamically using a run-time configuration mechanism, such as the one defined by the Component Configurator pattern (75). In this design a component configurator component within the concrete framework interprets a script that specifies which interceptors to link, where to find the dynamically linked libraries (DLLs) that contain these interceptors, and how to initialize them. The component configurator then links the specified DLLs and registers the interceptors contained within them with the concrete framework.

Known Uses   **Component-based application servers** for server-side components, such as EJB [MaHa99], CORBA Components [OMG99a], or COM+ [Box97], implement the Interceptor Proxy variant. To help developers focus on their application-specific business logic, special concrete frameworks—often denoted as 'containers' in this context—are introduced to shield components from the system-specific run-time environment. Components need not implement all their infrastructural services, such as transactions, security, or persistence, but instead declare their requirements using configuration-specific attributes. The diagram below illustrates this container architecture:

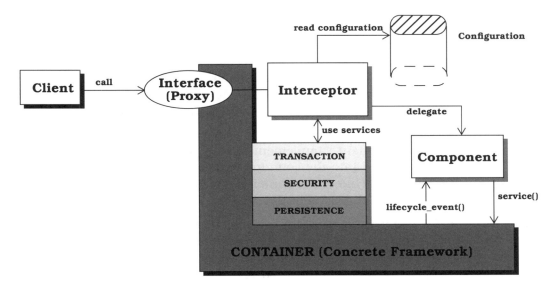

After a new component is instantiated, the concrete framework also instantiates an interceptor proxy and associates it with that particular component, for example, by providing the proxy with a component reference during its initialization. After any client request arrives the proxy checks the configuration-specific attributes of the component and performs the services it expects, such as initiating new transactions.

Application servers often provide an instantiation of the standard Interceptor pattern to notify components about lifecycle events, such as connection initiation and termination, component activation and passivation, or transaction-specific events.

CORBA implementations [OMG98c] such as TAO [SLM98] and Orbix [Bak97] apply the Interceptor pattern so that application developers can integrate additional services to handle specific types of events. Interceptors enhance ORB flexibility by separating request processing from the traditional ORB communication mechanisms required to send and receive requests and replies.

For example, Orbix defines the concept of filters that are based on the concept of 'flexible bindings' [Shap93]. By deriving from a predefined base class, developers can intercept events. Common events include client-initiated transmission and arrival of remote operations, as well as the object implementation-initiated transmission and arrival of replies. Developers can choose whether to intercept the request or result before or after marshaling. Orbix programmers can leverage the same filtering mechanism to build multi-threaded servers [SV96a] [SV96b] [SV96c]. Other ORBs, such as Visibroker, implement the Interceptor Factory variant of the Interceptor pattern.

The OMG has introduced a **CORBA Portable Interceptor** specification [OMG99f] to standardize the use of interceptors for CORBA-compliant implementations. Portable Interceptors are intimately tied into the communication between a client and server. They can thus affect the contents of CORBA requests and replies as they are exchanged, as outlined in the following two examples:

- A client-side security interceptor can add authorization information to a request transparently before it leaves the client process. The matching server-side security interceptor in the receiving server could then verify that the client is authorized to invoke requests on the target object before the request is dispatched. If authorization fails the request should be rejected.

- A transaction interceptor is another example of a Portable Interceptor. This interceptor adds a transaction ID to a request before it leaves the client. The corresponding server-side transaction interceptor then ensures the request is dispatched to the target object within the context of that particular transaction.

Fault-tolerant ORB frameworks. The Interceptor pattern has been applied in a number of fault-tolerant ORB frameworks, such as the Eternal system [NMM99] [MMN99] and the CORBA Fault-Tolerance specification [OMG99g]. Eternal intercepts system calls made by clients through the lower-level I/O subsystem and maps these system calls to a reliable multicast subsystem. Eternal does not modify the ORB or the CORBA language mapping, thereby ensuring the transparency of fault tolerance from applications.

The AQuA framework [CRSS+98] also provides a variant of the Interceptor pattern. The AQuA gateway acts as an intermediary between the CORBA objects and the Ensemble group communication subsystem, and translates GIOP messages to group communication primitives. AQuA uses the Quality Objects (QuO) [ZBS97] framework to allow applications to specify their dependability requirements.

COM [Box97] [HS99a] programmers can use the Interceptor pattern to implement the standard interface IMarshal in their components. IMarshal provides custom marshaling functionality rather than standard marshaling, which is useful for several reasons. For example, custom marshaling can be used to send complex data such as graph structures across a network efficiently.

When the COM run-time system transfers an interface pointer from a component to a client residing in another execution environment, it queries the corresponding component for an implementation of the interceptor interface IMarshal. If the component actually implements IMarshal, the COM run-time uses the methods of this interceptor interface to ask the component for specific information to allow it to externalize the data to a stream object.

Web browsers. Web browsers implement the Interceptor pattern to help third-party vendors and users integrate their own tools and plug-ins. For example, Netscape Communicator and Internet Explorer allow browsers to register plug-ins for handling specific media types. When a media stream arrives from a Web server the browser extracts the content type. If the browser does not support the content type natively, it checks whether a plug-in has registered for it. The browser then invokes the appropriate plug-in automatically to handle the data.

The **dynamicTAO reflective ORB** [KRL+00] supports interceptors for monitoring and security. Particular interceptor implementations are loaded into dynamicTAO using component configurators (75). Using component configurators to install interceptors in dynamicTAO allows applications to exchange monitoring and security strategies at run-time.

Change of address surface mail forwarding. A real-life example of the Interceptor pattern arises when people move from one house to another. The post office can be instructed to intercept surface mail addressed to the original house and have it transparently forwarded to the new house. In this case, the contents of the mail is not modified and only the destination address is changed.

Consequences   The Interceptor pattern offers the following **benefits**:

Extensibility and flexibility. By customizing and configuring interceptor and dispatcher interfaces, users of a concrete framework can add, change, and remove services without changing the concrete framework architecture or implementation.

Separation of concerns. Interceptors can be added transparently without affecting existing application code because interceptors are decoupled from application behavior. Interceptors can be viewed as *aspects* [KLM+97] that are woven into an application, so that programmers can focus on application logic rather than on infrastructure services. The Interceptor pattern also helps to decouple programmers who write interceptor code from programmers who are responsible for developing and deploying application logic.

Support for monitoring and control of frameworks. Interceptors and context objects help to obtain information from the concrete framework dynamically, as well as to control its behavior. These capabilities help developers build administration tools, debuggers, and other advanced services, such as load balancing and fault tolerance.

When a client invokes a remote operation, an interceptor can be notified automatically. By using the context object the interceptor can change the target object specified in the method invocation from the original destination to another server that provides the requested service. The choice of server can depend on various dynamic factors, such as current server load or availability. If a framework cannot complete a request successfully, another interceptor can be activated to re-send the request to a replicated server that provides the same service, thereby enhancing fault tolerance via replication [OMG99a].

Layer symmetry. To implement layered services, developers can introduce symmetrical interceptors for related events exposed by the concrete framework. For example, in a CORBA environment developers could write a client-side interceptor that creates security tokens and automatically adds these tokens to outgoing requests. Similarly, they could write a symmetrical server-side interceptor that extracts these tokens before the incoming request is forwarded to the actual object implementation.

Reusability. By separating interceptor code from other application code, interceptors can be reused across applications. For example, an interceptor used to write information into a log file may be reused in other applications that require the same type of logging functionality.

The Interceptor pattern also incurs the following **liabilities**:

Complex design issues. Anticipating the requirements of applications that use a specific concrete framework is non-trivial, which makes it hard to decide which interceptor dispatchers to provide. In general, providing insufficient dispatchers reduces the flexibility and extensibility of the concrete framework. Conversely, providing too many dispatchers can yield large, inefficient systems that are complex to implement, use and optimize.

A similar problem arises when a concrete framework defines many different interceptor interfaces and dispatchers. In this case interceptor implementors must address all these heterogeneous extensibility mechanisms. If there are too many different mechanisms it is hard to learn and use them. In contrast, providing only one generic interceptor and one generic dispatcher can lead to bloated interfaces or complex method signatures. In general, it is hard to find the right balance without knowledge of common application usages.

Malicious or erroneous interceptors. If a concrete framework invokes an interceptor that fails to return, the entire application may block. To prevent blocking, concrete frameworks can use configurable time-out values. If the interceptor does not return control after a specified time, a separate thread can interrupt the execution of the interceptor. This approach can complicate concrete framework design, however.

For example, complex functionality may be required to help concrete frameworks recover from time-outs without leaking resources or corrupting important data structures. Interceptors can also perform unanticipated activities or cause run-time errors. It is hard to prevent these problems because concrete frameworks and interceptors generally execute in the same address space.

Potential interception cascades. If an interceptor leverages a context object to change the behavior of the concrete framework it may trigger new events, thereby initiating state transitions in the underlying state machine. These state transitions may cause the concrete framework to invoke a cascade of interceptors that trigger new events, and so on. Interception cascades can lead to severe performance bottlenecks or deadlocks. The more interceptor dispatchers that a concrete framework provides, the greater the risk of interception cascades.

See Also   The Template Method pattern [GoF95] specifies a skeleton for an algorithm—called the 'template method'—where different steps in the algorithm can vary. The execution of these variants is delegated to hook methods, which can be overridden in subclasses provided by clients. The template method can therefore be viewed as a lightweight concrete framework, and the hook methods as lightweight interceptors. The Template Method pattern can be used to leverage interception locally at a particular level of abstraction, whereas the Interceptor pattern promotes interception as a fundamental design aspect that cuts across multiple layers in a framework architecture.

The Chain-of-Responsibility pattern [GoF95] defines different handlers that can be interposed between the sender and the receiver of a request. As with the Interceptor pattern, these handlers can be used to integrate additional services between senders and receivers. In the Chain-of-Responsibility pattern, however, requests are forwarded until one of the intermediary handlers processes the request. In contrast, a dispatcher in the Interceptor pattern usually forwards events to all concrete interceptors that have registered for it.

To emulate the Interceptor pattern, each intermediary handler in a chain of responsibility must therefore both handle *and* forward the request. Interceptor and Chain of Responsibility differ in two other aspects, however. Event handlers in a chain of responsibility are chained together, as the name of the pattern implies. In contrast, concrete interceptors in a framework need not be chained together, but can instead be associated at various levels of abstraction in a layered architecture [POSA1]. Event handlers in a chain of responsibility also cannot control the subsequent behavior of other event handlers or application components. Conversely, a key aspect of the Interceptor pattern is its ability to control a concrete framework's subsequent behavior when a specific event occurs.

The Pipes and Filters pattern [POSA1] defines an architecture for processing a stream of data in which each processing step is encapsulated in a filter component. Data is passed through pipes between adjacent filters. If a concrete framework is structured as a Pipes and Filters architecture with clients and objects being the endpoints, each pipe in the Pipes and Filter chain defines a potential location at which interceptors can be interposed between adjacent filters. In this case, registration of interceptors consists of re-configuring the Pipes and Filters chain.

The context object is the information passed from the source filter to the interceptor. The interceptor is responsible for sending information to the sink filter in the appropriate format. However, in the Pipes and Filters pattern, filters are chained via pipes, whereas in the Interceptor pattern concrete interceptors at different layers are often independent. In addition, Pipes and Filters defines a fundamental computational model for a complete application 'pipeline', whereas interceptors are used to implement 'out-of-band' services in any type of concrete framework.

The Proxy pattern [GoF95] [POSA1] provides a surrogate or placeholder for an object to control access to itself. Although proxies can be used to integrate additional functionality to a system, their use is restricted to objects that are already visible in a system. In contrast, interceptors allow external components to access and control internal and otherwise 'invisible' components. As described in the *Variants* section, to instantiate the Interceptor Proxy variant, we can instantiate the Proxy pattern with enhancements such as context objects.

The Observer [GoF95] and Publisher-Subscriber [POSA1] patterns help synchronize the state of cooperating components. These patterns perform a one-way propagation of changes in which a publisher can notify one or more observers/subscribers when the state of a subject changes. In contrast to the Interceptor pattern, the Observer and Publisher-Subscriber patterns do not specify how observers/subscribers should access the functionality of publishers because they define only one-way communication from the publishers to the subscribers. These patterns also emphasize event notifications, whereas the Interceptor pattern focuses on the integration of services into a framework.

These differences are also illustrated by the difference between event objects and context objects. While event objects often contain values related to the current event, context objects provide an additional programming interface to access and control concrete frameworks. The Observer and Publisher-Subscriber patterns can therefore be viewed as variants of the Interceptor pattern, in which context objects correspond to event types that are transferred from concrete frameworks playing the subject role to interceptors playing the observer/subscribe roles.

The Reflection pattern [POSA1] provides a mechanism for changing structure and behavior of software systems. A layer of *base-level* objects includes the application logic. An additional layer, the *meta-level*, provides information about system properties and allows developers to control the semantics of the base level. The relationship between the Reflection pattern and the Interceptor pattern is twofold:

- *Interception provides a means to implement reflective mechanisms.* For example, to instantiate the Reflection pattern we can introduce dispatchers that help developers introduce new behavior by registering interceptors with the meta-level. Interception can thus be viewed as a lightweight reflective approach that is easier to implement and less consumptive of CPU and memory. Moreover, interception only exposes certain of the internals of the underlying system, whereas reflection often covers a broader scope.

- *Reflection can define a type of interception mechanism.* The main intent of reflection is to allow applications to observe their own state so that they can change their own behavior dynamically. In contrast, the main intent of Interceptor is to allow other applications to extend and control the behavior of a concrete framework.

The Reactor pattern (179) demultiplexes and dispatches service requests that are delivered concurrently to an application from one or more clients. While the Reactor pattern focuses on handling system-specific events, the Interceptor pattern helps to intercept application-specific events. The Reactor pattern is often instantiated to handle system events occurring in the lower layers of a communication framework, whereas the Interceptor pattern is used in multiple layers between the framework and the application.

Credits   Thanks to Fabio Kon who contributed the dynamicTAO known use.

Extension Interface

The *Extension Interface* design pattern allows multiple interfaces to be exported by a component, to prevent bloating of interfaces and breaking of client code when developers extend or modify the functionality of the component.

Example   Consider a telecommunication management network (TMN) [ITUT92] framework that can be customized to monitor and control remote network elements such as IP routers and ATM switches. Each type of network element is modeled as a multi-part framework component in accordance with the Model-View-Controller pattern [POSA1]. A view and a controller are located on a management application console. The view renders the current state of a network element on the console and the controller allows network administrators to manage the network element.

A model resides on the network element and communicates with the view and controller to receive and process commands, such as commands to send state information about the network element to the management application console. All components in the TMN framework are organized in a hierarchy. The `UniversalComponent` interface shown in the following figure provides the common functionality needed by every component, such as displaying key properties of a network element and accessing its neighbors.

```
public interface UniversalComponent {
    public void render () { ... }
    public int getState (){ ... }
    public long getPermissions (){ ... }
    public Enumeration getNeighbors (){ ... }
    public void lock (){ ... }
    public void unlock (){ ... }
    public Object getData (String key) { ... }
    public void setData (String key, Object v) { ... }
    // ... many other methods ...
}
```

In theory, this design might be appropriate if the `UniversalComponent` interface shown above is never changed, because it would allow client applications to access a wide range of network elements via a uniform interface. In practice, however, as the TMN framework becomes increasingly popular, management application developers will request that new functionality and new methods, such as `dump()` and `persist()`, be added to the `UniversalComponent` interface.

Over time the addition of these requests can bloat the interface with functionality not anticipated in the initial framework design. If new methods are added to the `UniversalComponent` interface directly, all client code must be updated and recompiled. This is tedious and error-prone. A key design challenge is therefore to ensure that evolutionary extensions to the TMN framework do not bloat its interfaces or break its client code.

Context   An application environment in which component interfaces may evolve over time.

Problem   Coping with changing application requirements often necessitates modifications and extensions to component functionality. Sometimes all interface changes can be anticipated before components are released to application developers. In this case it may be possible to apply the 'Liskov Substitution Principle' [Mar95]. This principle defines stable base interfaces whose methods can be extended solely via subclassing and polymorphism.

In other cases, however, it is hard to design stable interfaces, because requirements can change in unanticipated ways after components have been delivered and integrated into applications. When not handled carefully, these changes can break existing client code that uses the components. In addition, if the new functionality is used by only few applications, all other applications must incur unnecessary time and space overhead to support component services they do not need.

To avoid these problems, it may be necessary to design components to support evolution, both anticipated and unanticipated. This requires the resolution of four *forces*:

• When component interfaces do not change, modifications to component implementations should not break existing client code.

➡   If implementations of our `UniversalComponent` interface store their state persistently in external storage, clients should not be affected if this functionality is re-implemented differently, as long as the component's interface is unchanged.   ❏

- Existing client code should not break when developers extend a component with new services that are visible externally. Ideally it should not be necessary to re-compile client code.

➡   It may be necessary to add a logging service to the `Universal-Component` interface so that management applications and network elements can log information to a central repository. Existing clients that are aware of the original version of `UniversalComponent` should not be affected by this change, whereas new clients should be able to take advantage of the new logging functionality.   ❏

- Changing or extending a component's functionality should be relatively straightforward, neither bloating existing component interfaces nor destabilizing the internal architecture of existing components.

➡   When adding the logging service outlined above, we should minimize changes to existing implementations of the `Universal Component` interface.   ❏

- It should be possible to access components remotely or locally using the same interface. If components and their clients are distributed across network nodes, the interfaces and implementations of a component should be decoupled.

➡   Management applications can benefit from location-transparent access to remote network elements in our TMN system. It should therefore be possible to separate the interfaces of network element management components from their physical implementations. These can be distributed throughout the network.   ❏

Solution Program clients to access components via separate interfaces, one for each role a component plays, rather than programming clients to use a single component that merges all its roles into a single interface or implementation.

In detail: export *component* functionality via *extension interfaces*, one for each semantically-related set of operations. A component must implement at least one extension interface. To add new functionality to a component, or to modify existing component functionality, export new extension interfaces rather than modify existing ones. Moreover, program clients to access a component via its extension interfaces instead of its implementation. Hence, clients only have dependencies on the different roles of a component, each of which is represented by a separate extension interface.

To enable clients to create component instances and retrieve component extension interfaces, introduce additional indirection. For example, introduce an associated *component factory* for each component type that creates component instances. Ensure that it returns an initial interface reference that clients can use to retrieve other component extension interfaces. Similarly, ensure that each interface inherits from a *root interface* that defines functionality common to all components, such as the mechanism for retrieving a particular extension interface. All other extension interfaces derive from the root interface. This ensures that at minimum they offer the functionality it exports.

Structure   The structure of the Extension interface pattern includes four participants:

Components aggregate and implement various types of service-specific functionality. This functionality can often be partitioned into several independent roles, each of which defines a set of semantically-related operations.

Class Component	*Collaborator*
Responsibility • Plays different roles • Implements extension interfaces • Returns initial interface to component factory	

➡ Components in our TMN framework play various roles, such as storing and retrieving the state of a network element or managing the persistence of a component's internal state. ❑

Extension interfaces export selected facets of a component's implementation. There is one extension interface for each role [RG98] that a component implements. In addition, an extension interface implicitly specifies a contract that describes how clients should use the component's functionality. This contract defines the protocol for invoking the methods of the extension interface, such as the acceptable parameter types and the order in which methods must be called.

➡ The components in the TMN framework can implement the IStateMemory interface, which allows them to maintain their state in memory. A persistence manager, such as the CORBA Persistent State Service [OMG99e] can use the IStateMemory interface to manage component persistence without requiring components to expose their representational details.

If new network element components are added that also implement IStateMemory, the persistence manager can manage their persistence without requiring any changes. The IStateMemory interface contains methods to prepare the component for reading and writing its state, as well as its read and write operations. The implicit contract between the interface and its users therefore prescribes that the prepare() method must be called before either readState() or writeState(). ❑

The *root interface* is a special extension interface that provides three types of functionality:

- *Core functionality* that all extension interfaces must support, for example functionality that allows clients to retrieve the interfaces they request. This functionality defines the basic mechanisms a component must implement to allow clients to retrieve and navigate among its interfaces.

- *Domain-independent functionality,* such as methods that manage component life-cycles.

- *Domain-specific functionality* that should be provided by all components within a particular domain.

Although the root interface must implement core functionality, it need not support domain-independent or domain-specific functionality. However, all extension interfaces must support the functionality defined by the root interface. Each extension interface can thus play the role of the root interface, which guarantees that every extension interface can return any other extension interface on behalf of a client request.

Class Root Interface	*Collaborator* • Component	*Class* Extension Interface	*Collaborator* • Component
Responsibility • Defines the functionality that each extension interface must provide		*Responsibility* • Defines a role-specific interface offered by a component	

➥   A `UniversalComponent` interface can be defined as the root interface in our TMN framework. Unlike the multi-faceted—and increasingly bloated—`UniversalComponent` interface outlined in the *Example* section, however, this root interface only defines the minimum set of methods that are common to all components in the TMN framework.   ❏

Clients access the functionality provided by components only via extension interfaces. After a client retrieves a reference to an initial extension interface, it can use this reference to retrieve any other extension interface supported by a component.

➥   A management application console client can use components in the TMN framework to render the state of network elements and their relations visually on the screen, as well as to store and retrieve their state using persistent storage.   ❏

To retrieve an initial reference, clients interact with a *component factory* associated with a particular component type. This component factory separates the creation and initialization aspects of a component from its processing aspects. When a client creates a new component instance, it delegates this task to the appropriate component factory.

After a component is created successfully, the component factory returns a reference to an extension interface to the client. A component factory may allow clients to request a specific type of initial extension interface. Factories may also provide functionality to locate and return references to existing component instances.

Class	*Collaborator*	*Class*	*Collaborator*
Client	• Extension Interface(s)	Component Factory	• Component
Responsibility	• Root Interface	*Responsibility*	
• Implements application-specific functionality • Accesses factories to create new components • Uses extension interfaces to access component functionality	• Factory	• Defines functionality for creating components • (Optionally) contains functionality for locating existing components	

The class diagram below illustrates the participants in the Extension Interface pattern. This diagram emphasizes logical rather than physical relationships between components. For example, extension interfaces could be implemented using multiple inheritance or nested classes, as described in implementation activity 6.1 (155). Such implementation details are transparent to clients.

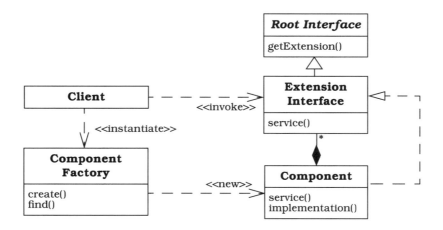

Dynamics   We illustrate the key collaborations in the Extension Interface pattern using two scenarios. **Scenario I** depicts how clients create new components and retrieve an initial extension interface:

- The client requests a component factory to create a new component and return a reference to a particular extension interface.

- The component factory creates a new component and retrieves a reference to its root interface.

- The component factory asks the root interface for the requested extension interface, then returns a reference to the extension interface to the client.

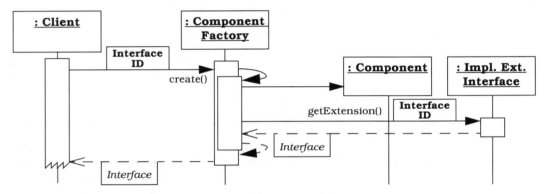

Note that the factory could return any interface to the client, instead of retrieving a specific extension one. Such a design can incur additional round-trips in a distributed system, however, which increases the overhead of accessing the required interface.

Scenario II depicts the collaboration between clients and extension interfaces. Note that the component implementation itself is not visible to the client, because it only deals with extension interfaces:

- The client invokes a method on extension interface A, which can either be the root interface or an extension interface.

- The implementation of extension interface A within the component executes the requested method and returns the results, if any, to the client.

- The client calls the getExtension() method on extension interface A and passes it a parameter that specifies the extension interface in which the client is interested. The getExtension()

method is defined in the root interface, so it is supported by all extension interfaces. The implementation of extension interface A within the component locates the requested extension interface B and returns the client a reference to it.

- The client invokes a method on extension interface B, which is then executed within the component implementation.

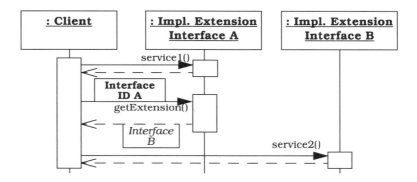

Implementation   This section describes the activities associated with implementing the Extension Interface pattern. This pattern should be familiar to anyone who has programmed with Microsoft's Component Object Model (COM) [Box97], Enterprise JavaBeans (EJB) [MaHa99], or the CORBA Component Model (CCM) [OMG99a], because it captures and generalizes the core concepts underlying these component technologies.

1   *Determine the stability of the design and the long-term application requirements.* Before applying the Extension Interface pattern, it is important to determine whether it is really needed. Although this pattern is a powerful solution to a particular set of forces, it is non-trivial to implement. It can also complicate a software design significantly if applied unnecessarily.

We therefore recommend that the forces outlined in the *Problem* section are considered carefully. You should ensure that these issues are faced in your software system before applying this pattern. For example, it may turn out that the *complete* set of methods an interface requires can be determined during system development, and that the interface will not change over time as application requirements evolve. In this case, it may be simpler to use the Liskov

Substitution Principle [Mar95] rather than the Extension Interface pattern.

2 *Analyze the domain and specify a domain-specific component model.* Assuming that the Extension Interface pattern is necessary, the next activity involves analyzing domain-specific application requirements. In particular, this activity focuses on identifying application-specific entities, such as the network elements in our TMN example, the roles a particular entity provides to the system, and the functionality that supports the different roles. The result is a domain model that identifies which components to implement, as well as the functionality they must provide.

➡   For the management application console, every type of entity to be controlled is implemented as a separate *managed object* [ITUT92], which is an abstraction used to represent hardware units, such as routers, computers, bridges, or switches. Managed objects can also represent software elements, such as applications, ports, or connections. Management applications use managed objects to control and monitor the state of network elements, display debugging information, or visualize system behavior on a management console.   ❏

After devising a domain model, it is necessary to specify a component model to implement the identified components:

- If the components are restricted to a single application domain or a small set of related domains, consider specifying a domain-specific component model that is tailored for the application or family of applications being developed.

- Conversely, if the components must be applied to a wide range of applications, or even across multiple domains, consider using an existing component technology, such as Microsoft COM [Box97], EJB [MaHa99], or the CORBA Component Model [OMG99a].

In the latter case, the next implementation activity can be skipped, because these component models define the infrastructure it specifies.

3 *Specify the root interface.* Determine if each type of functionality identified in implementation activity 2 above should form part of the root interface, or be separated into an extension interface.

With this criteria in mind, iterate through three sub-activities:

3.1   *Specify core functionality.* Several issues must be addressed when defining the core functionality of the root interface:

- *Extension interface retrieval.* At minimum, the root interface must include a method that returns extension interface references to clients. The type of information returned from this method depends largely on the programming language. For example, Java clients expect to retrieve an object reference, whereas pointers are an appropriate choice for C++.

- *Unique naming.* Extension interfaces must be named using integer values or strings. Strings can be read more easily by programmers and simple management tools, but integer values can be smaller and processed more efficiently. To prevent name clashes, interface identifiers can be generated algorithmically. For instance, Microsoft COM uses 128 bit globally unique identifiers (GUIDs) based on the address of the network interface, the date, and the time.

- *Error handling.* Component developers must determine what a component should do when a client requests an extension interface that is not supported. For example, a component could either return an error value or raise an exception. The *Implementation* section of the Wrapper Facade pattern (47) discusses several strategies for implementing an error-handling mechanism and evaluates their trade-offs.

3.2   *Specify domain-independent services.* In addition to defining a method for retrieving extension interfaces, the root interface can provide methods for various domain-independent services. Here are two possibilities:

- *Reference counting.* In programming languages that do not provide automatic garbage collection, such as C or C++, clients are responsible for deleting extension interfaces they no longer need. However, multiple clients may share the same extension interface. Components can thus provide a reference counting mechanism to prevent the accidental deletion of resources used to implement extension interfaces.

  Reference counting enables components to track the number of clients accessing specific extension interfaces. After an extension interface is no longer referenced by any clients, the resources used by the component's implementation of the interface can be released automatically. The Counted Pointer idiom [POSA1] [Cope92] presents several options for implementing a reference counting mechanism.

- *Run-time reflection.* Another example of a domain-independent service is a run-time reflection mechanism. This mechanism allows components to publish information about the specific roles, extension interfaces, and methods they support. Using this knowledge, clients can construct and send method invocations dynamically [GS96]. This enables scripting languages to integrate components into existing client applications at run-time. Reflection mechanisms can be instantiated using the Reflection architectural pattern [POSA1].

3.3 *Specify domain-specific functionality.* The root interface can also export domain-specific functionality if all components implementing the root interface provide this functionality.

➡ In our management application console, the drawing functionality could be moved to the root interface.   ❏

The decision about which domain-specific services to specify in the root interface should normally be deferred until after implementation activity 4 (153). Ideally, all domain-specific functionality should reside in separate extension interfaces. If all components end up implementing a particular extension interface, refactor the current solution [Opd92] [FBBOR99] and move the methods of that particular extension interface to the root interface.

➡ In our TMN framework example, extension interfaces are identified by unique integer constants. We use Java as the implementation language because it provides automatic garbage collection, which simplifies memory management. The only common functionality therefore required in the root interface—which we call IRoot—is a method that allows client to retrieve any interface they need.

```
// Definition of IRoot:
public interface IRoot {
    IRoot getExtension (int ID) throws UnknownEx;
}
```

IRoot serves as a generic base interface for all extension interfaces. If a component does not support a particular interface, it throws an UnknownEx exception:

```
// Definition of UnknownEx:
public class UnknownEx extends Exception {
    protected int ID;
    public UnknownEx (int ID) { this.ID = ID; }
    public int getID () { return ID; }
}
```

The unique identifier of the requested interface is passed as an argument to the UnknownEx constructor. This allows a client to determine which interface caused the exception.   ❏

Another potential candidate for inclusion in the root interface is a persistence mechanism. However, there are many different strategies and policies for handling persistence, such as managing component state in databases or flat files, which makes it hard to anticipate all possible use cases. Therefore, components can choose to support whatever persistence mechanism they consider appropriate by implementing specific extension interfaces.

4   *Introduce general-purpose extension interfaces.* General-purpose extension interfaces contain functional roles that must be provided by more than one component and that are not included in the root interface. A separate extension interface should be defined for each role. For example, extension interfaces can be defined to handle persistence aspects of components, as discussed at the end of implementation activity 3 (150).

➥   Our management application console helps to control and monitor remote network entities via managed objects. Managed objects are implemented as components that send information to the management application console and receive commands from it.

Every managed object therefore implements the following interface,
IManagedObject:[7]

```
// Definition of IManagedObject:
import java.util.*;

public interface IManagedObject extends IRoot {
    public void setValue (String key, Object value);
    public Object getValue (String key) throws
            WrongKeyEx;
    public void setMultipleValues
        (Vector keys, Vector values);
    public Vector getMultipleValues
        (Vector keys) throws WrongKeyEx;
    public long addNotificationListener
        (INotificationSink sink);
    public void removeNotificationListener (long handle);
    public void setFilter (String expr);
}
```

This example illustrates managed objects that are visualized on a
management console. We therefore introduce two additional
extension interfaces, IDump and IRender, which are implemented by
all components that print debug information on the console or draw
themselves.

```
// Definition of IDump:
public interface IDump extends IRoot {
    public String dump ();
}

// File IDraw.java.
public interface IRender extends IRoot {
    public void render ();
}
```
❏

If a particular general-purpose extension interface must be supported
by all components, it may be feasible to refactor the root interface
specified in implementation activity 3 (150) and integrate this
functionality there. Note, however, that refactoring the root interface
may bloat it with functionality or break existing applications, thereby
defeating the benefits of the Extension Interface pattern.

---

7. Note that a component may provide interfaces, such as IManagedObject, that are
accessed locally by the client, while their actual implementation resides on a remote
network node. By using the Proxy pattern [POSA1] [GoF95], distribution can be
transparent to clients. For clarity we assume that all interfaces have local
implementations in this example. For information on how proxies can be introduced to
support distributed environments, refer to the *Distributed Extension Interface* variant.

5 *Define component-specific extension interfaces.* The extension interfaces needed to export generic component functionality were specified in implementation activities 3 (150) and 4 (153). This implementation activity defines additional interfaces that are specific to a particular component or that are applicable to a limited range of components.

➡ For our TMN framework, we specify the extension interfaces IPort and IConnection. Managed objects that represent ports on a particular host implement IPort:

```
// Definition of IPort:
public interface IPort extends IRoot {
    public void setHost (String host);
    public String getHost ();
    public void setPort (long port);
    public long getPort ();
}
```

Likewise, objects that represent the connection between two ports implement IConnection:

```
// Definition of IConnection:
public interface IConnection extends IRoot {
    public void setPort1 (IPort p1);
    public IPort getPort1 ();
    public void setPort2 (IPort p2);
    public IPort getPort2 ();
    public void openConnection () throws CommErrorEx;
    public void closeConnection () throws CommErrorEx;
}
```
❑

6 *Implement the components.* The implementation of components involves five sub-activities:

6.1 *Specify the component implementation strategy.* This activity determines how extension interface implementations should be linked, in accordance with the following three strategies:

- *Multiple inheritance.* In this strategy a component class inherits from all of its extension interfaces.

- *Nested classes.* In this strategy extension interfaces can be implemented as nested classes within the component class. The component class instantiates a singleton instance [GoF95] of each nested class. Whenever the client asks for a particular extension interface, the getExtension() method implementation returns the appropriate nested class object.

- *Separate interface classes*. Extension interfaces can use the Bridge or Adapter patterns [GoF95] to implement separate classes that are independent of the component itself. This strategy is particularly useful when applying the Extension Interface pattern to refactor an existing component that does not implement the pattern.

  The 'tie' adapter [SV98a] defined in the CORBA IDL mappings for Java and C++ is an example of this component implementation strategy. In CORBA a tie adapter inherits from an automatically-generated servant class, overrides all its pure virtual methods, and delegates these methods to another C++ object, the so-called 'tied object'. A server application developer defines the tied object.

Regardless of which component implementation strategy is selected, the client is unaffected, because it only accesses the component via references to extension interfaces.

6.2 *Implement the mechanism to retrieve extension interfaces.* When implementing the generic method that retrieves extension interfaces on behalf of clients, ensure that the method implementation conforms to three conventions:

- *Reflexivity*. When clients query extension interface A for the same extension interface A, they must always receive the same reference A.

- *Symmetry*. If a client can retrieve extension interface B from extension interface A, it also must be able to retrieve extension interface A from extension interface B.

- *Transitivity*. If a client can retrieve extension interface B from extension interface A and extension interface C from extension interface B, it must be possible to retrieve extension interface C directly from extension interface A.

Following the conventions above ensures that a client can always navigate from a specific extension interface of a component to any other extension interface of the same component. In other words, each extension interface can be connected with every other extension interface via navigation.

6.3 *Implement a reference counting mechanism (optional).* If the root interface requires the reference counting mechanism discussed in implementation activity 3.2 (151), specify the resources in the component implementation that must be managed by this mechanism. There are two common options for implementing a reference counting mechanism:

- If each interface implementation requires or uses separate resources, or if there are separate implementations for each interface, introduce a separate reference counter for each extension interface. If a particular reference counter drops to zero, release all resources used by the corresponding extension interface. After the last reference counter has fallen to zero, all resources associated with the component can be released.

- If all interface implementations share the same resources, introduce a global reference counter for the entire component. After this global reference counter reaches zero, release the component's resources.

The first option can optimize resource management more effectively than the second option, because in the second option all resources must always be available. In the first option, in contrast, extension interfaces and their required resources may be activated and deactivated on demand. Only those extension interfaces and resources actually used by clients are activated. The disadvantage of maintaining extension interface-specific reference counters, however, is their complex implementation within the component.

➡ We can apply reference counting to activate and deactivate extension interface implementations on-demand in our TMN framework. This avoids the unnecessary commitment of resources such as memory or socket handles. For example, when a management application client accesses an extension interface whose reference counter is zero, the component can activate the interface implementation and its resources transparently. When no clients access the extension interface, the corresponding implementation and resources can be deactivated and released selectively. The COM [Box97] component model implements this strategy. ❑

6.4   *Select a concurrency strategy.* In concurrent or networked systems, multiple clients can access a particular extension interface simultaneously. Implementations of different extension interfaces may share state and resources within the component. Critical sections and state within the component's implementation must be serialized therefore to provide corruption from concurrent access by clients.

The Active Object (369) and Monitor Object (399) concurrency patterns, as well as the Scoped Locking (325), Strategized Locking (333), and Thread-Safe Interface (345) synchronization patterns, define various strategies and mechanisms for protecting critical sections and state within components.

6.5   *Implement the extension interface functionality* using the selected component implementation strategy. This implementation activity is largely domain- or application-specific, so there are no general issues to address.

➥   In our TMN framework example we implement components using multiple interface inheritance. Our components do not require explicit reference counting, because Java provides automatic garbage collection.

For simplicity, we do not illustrate the component concurrency strategy. To identify different extension interfaces uniquely, we define an `InterfaceID` class that enumerates all interface identifiers. These are defined to be integers via the following types:

```
// Definition of InterfaceID:
public class InterfaceID {
    public final static int ID_ROOT  = 0;
    public final static int ID_MANOBJ= 1;
    public final static int ID_DUMP  = 2;
    public final static int ID_RENDER= 3;
    public final static int ID_PORT  = 4;
    public final static int ID_CONN  = 5;
}
```

A more sophisticated implementation could use a repository of interface identifiers. In this case, unique identifiers could be generated automatically by tools to prevent name clashes when different component providers define different interfaces. We could also use a `String` as the identifier type rather than an `int`. This might improve the readability and debuggability of the component system, but at the expense of larger memory footprint and slower lookup time.

One of the component types in the management application console represents a connection between two ports. This component supports the extension interfaces IManagedObject, IRender, IConnection, and IDump. We implement all extension interfaces using Java interface inheritance:

```
// Definition of ConnectionComponent:
public class ConnectionComponent implements
IManagedObject, IRender, IDump, IConnection {
    // <table> contains all properties.
    private Hashtable table = new Hashtable ();

    // <listener> contains event sinks.
    private Hashtable listeners = new Hashtable ();
    private long nListeners = 0;

    private IPort port1, port2;
    private String filterExpression;

    // <IRoot> method.
    public IRoot getExtension (int ID)
        throws UnknownEx {
        switch(ID) {
            case InterfaceID.ID_ROOT:
            case InterfaceID.ID_MANOBJ:
            case InterfaceID.ID_DUMP:
            case InterfaceID.ID_RENDER:
            case InterfaceID.ID_CONNECT:
                return this;
            default:
                throw new UnknownEx (ID);
        }
    }
```

Note how the getExtension() interface uses a switch statement to determine which interface is supported by the component. Had the identifier type been defined as a String rather than an int, we would have used a different type of lookup strategy such as linear search, dynamic hashing, or perfect hashing [Sch98a].

```
// Definition of IManagedObject:
public void setValue (String key, Object value) {
    table.put (key, value);
}
```

```
        public Object getValue (String key)
            throws WrongKeyEx {
            WrongKeyEx wkEx = new WrongKeyEx ();
            if (!table.containsKey (key)) {
                wkEx.addKey (key); throw wkEx;
            }
            return table.get (key);
        }

        // Additional methods from <IManagedObject>.
        public void setMultipleValues
            (Vector keys, Vector values) { /* ... */ }
        public Vector getMultipleValues
            (Vector keys) throws WrongKeyEx { /* ... */ }
        public long addNotificationListener
                (INotificationSink sink) { /* ... */ }
        public void removeNotificationListener
                (long handle) { /* ... */ }
        public void setFilter (String expr) { /* ... */ }

        // <IDump> and <IRender> methods.
        public String dump () { /* ... */ }
        public void render () { /* ... */ }

        // <IConnection> methods.
        public void setPort1 (IPort p1) { port1 = p1; }
        public IPort getPort1 () { return port1; }
        public void setPort2 (IPort p2) { port2 = p2; }
        public IPort getPort2 () { return port2; }
        public void openConnection () throws CommErrorEx { }
        public void closeConnection () throws CommErrorEx { }
    }
```

7   *Implement component factories.* Every component type must implement a factory that clients can use to obtain instances of the component type. This involves three sub-activities:

7.1 *Define the association between component factories and components.* For every component type, a singleton [GoF95] component factory can be defined to create instances of this component type. Two strategies can be applied to implement this association:

   • *One component factory interface per component type.* In this strategy a separate factory interface is defined for every component type and used to instantiate the component type. One component type could offer a component factory interface with a single method create(). Another component type could offer a selection of different methods for creating components. The Factory Method pattern [GoF95] can be used to implement this strategy. It requires clients to handle many different component factory interfaces, however.

- *One component factory interface for all component types.* In this strategy there is only one component factory interface that all concrete component factories must implement. This design enables clients to create different components in a uniform manner. For example, when a client creates a new component, it only must know how to invoke the generic component factory interface. The Abstract Factory design pattern [GoF95] can be used to implement this strategy.

7.2 *Decide which functionality the factory will export.* Regardless of the strategy selected in implementation activity 7.1 (160), the following issues must be addressed when specifying the interface of a particular component factory:

- There could be one or more different methods for creating new components. These creation methods are similar to constructors in object-oriented programming languages, such as C++ or Java, in that they instantiate and initialize component types. Different types of initialization information might be necessary to construct a new component instance. For each of these alternatives, a separate create method is introduced with its own, possibly empty, set of initialization parameters.

- Methods could be available for finding existing components rather than creating them for each invocation. If component instances are already available and if they can be identified uniquely, a factory can be implemented using the Manager pattern [Som97]. In this case, its find() methods are passed a set of conditions as arguments, such as the primary key associated with each component. It then retrieves one or more components that adhere to the condition arguments.

- Clients can specify component usage policies. For example, one policy could provide a singleton implementation for a particular component type. Another policy could determine whether a specific component is expected to maintain its state persistently.

- Life-cycle management support for components is another candidate for the component factory interface. For example, methods to release existing components might be included in the component factory.

➥   For every managed object in our TMN framework, we provide a separate component factory, implemented as a singleton. The interface `IFactory` is generic and is supported by all concrete component factory implementations. It contains the `create()` method that clients use to instantiate a new component and to return the `IRoot` interface to the caller:

```
// Definition of Factory:
public interface Factory {
    IRoot create ();
}
```

Every concrete component factory must implement this factory interface:

```
// Definition of ConnectionFactory:
public class ConnectionFactory implements Factory {
    // Implement the Singleton pattern.
    private static ConnectionFactory theInstance;

    private ConnectionFactory () { }

    public static ConnectionFactory getInstance () {
        if (theInstance == null)
            theInstance = new ConnectionFactory ();
        return theInstance;
    }

    // Component creation method.
    public IRoot create () {
        return new ConnectionComponent ();
    }
}
```
                                                                                      ❑

7.3   *Introduce a component factory finder.* As the number of component types increases, the problem of how to find the associated component factories arises. One way to resolve this is to define a global component factory finder. This finder could maintain the associations between component types and their component factories, as specified in implementation activity 7.1 (160).

To obtain the component factory for a particular component type, clients must indicate to the component factory finder which component type they require. Component types must therefore be identified uniquely. A common way to implement this identification mechanism is to introduce a *primary key* type for every component type. This key type helps to associate component instances with instances of the primary key type uniquely.

For example, each component instance might be associated uniquely with an integer value. This integer value might be passed as an argument to a particular find() method of the component factory, which uses the primary key to obtain the associated component instance. For this purpose, the component factory can apply the Manager pattern [Som97] and map from primary key values to component instances. To simplify client programming, the same primary key type can be used to identify both component instances and extension interfaces, as shown in implementation activity 3.1 (151). In Microsoft COM, for example, globally-unique identifiers (GUIDs) identify both extension interfaces and component types.

When clients request a specific component factory from the component factory finder, the factory finder returns the interface of the component factory. By using this interface, clients can instantiate the components they need. If there is only one global component factory finder in the system, use the Singleton pattern [GoF95] to implement it.

The component factory finder can optionally provide a trading mechanism [OMG98b]. In this case, clients do not pass a concrete component type to the component factory finder. Instead, they specify properties that can be used by the component factory finder to retrieve an appropriate component factory. For example, a client might specify certain properties of extension interfaces in which it is interested to a component factory finder. The component factory finder then locates a component type that implements all the requested interfaces.

➼   Management application clients in our TMN system need not know all component factories. We therefore introduce a component factory finder that is responsible for managing a hash table with component-to-factory associations. Clients need only know where the single component factory finder is located. To identify components uniquely, we apply the same strategy used for interfaces in implementation activity 6.5 (158).

A class `ComponentID` is introduced that contains integer values, each associated with a single component factory:

```
// Definition of ComponentID:
public class ComponentID {
    public final static int CID_PORT = 0;
    public final static int CID_CONN = 1;
}
```

The component factory finder is implemented as a singleton. It contains two methods that are publicly accessible. The `registerFactory()` method must be called—either by clients or by components—to register component factories with the component factory finder. The `findFactory()` method is used to search for existing component factories.

```
// Definition of FactoryFinder:
import java.util.*;

public class FactoryFinder {
    // ID/factory associations are stored in a hash table.
    Hashtable table = null;
    // Implement the Singleton pattern.
    private static FactoryFinder theInstance;

    public static FactoryFinder getInstance () {
        if (theInstance == null) {
            theInstance = new FactoryFinder ();
        }
        return theInstance;
    }

    private FactoryFinder () {
        table = new Hashtable ();
    }

    // Component factory is registered with the finder.
    public void registerFactory (int ID, Factory f) {
        table.put (new Integer (ID), f);
    }

    // Finder is asked for a specific component factory.
    public Factory findFactory (int ID)
        throws UnknownEx {
        Factory f = (Factory) table.get
            (new Integer (ID));
        if (f == null) throw new UnknownEx (ID);
        else return f;
    }
}
```

8 *Implement the clients.* Clients use functionality provided by components. They may also act as containers[8] for these components. To implement clients apply the following steps:

- First determine which component functionality they require. For example, determine if there are existing components that cover some or all of the functionality the clients are expected to provide.

- Identify which components should be composed together and determine which components can use other components.

- Determine if there are any subsystems within the client application that might be used in other applications and separate these into new component types.

After evaluating these issues, integrate the client application using the components identified via the analysis outlined in the implementation activities above.

➥ In our example, to localize the initialization of our TMN system we provide a class ComponentInstaller within a client that creates all the necessary component factories and registers them with the component factory finder:

```
class ComponentInstaller {
    static public void install () {
        // First, get the global factory finder instance.
        FactoryFinder finder =
            FactoryFinder.getInstance ();
        // Ask the factory finder for the comp. factories
        PortFactory pFactory =
            PortFactory.getInstance ();
        ConnectionFactory cFactory =
            ConnectionFactory.getInstance ();

        // Register both component factories.
        finder.registerFactory
            (componentID.CID_PORT, pFactory);
        finder.registerFactory
            (componentID.CID_CONN, cFactory);
    }
}
```

---

8. Typically a component is loaded into the address space of a run-time environment that provides resources such as CPU time and memory to its components. This run-time environment is often called a *container*, because it shields components from the details of their underlying infrastructure, such as an operating system. In non-distributed use cases, clients can contain components and therefore act as containers.

The main class of the client application defines the methods
dumpAll() and drawAll(). Both methods are passed an array of
components as a parameter. They then iterate through the array
querying each component for the extension interface IDump and
IRender, respectively, calling the methods dump() and render() if
the query succeeds. This example shows that polymorphism can be
supported by using interface inheritance rather than implementation
inheritance.

```
// This client instantiates three components: two ports
// and a connection between them.
public class Client {
    private static void dumpAll (IRoot components[])
        throws UnknownEx {
        for (int i = 0; i < components.length; ++i) {
            IDump d = (IDump)
                components[i].getExtension
                    (InterfaceID.ID_DUMP);
            System.out.println (d.dump ());
        }
    }

    private static void drawAll (IRoot components[])
        throws UnknownEx {
        for (int i = 0; i < components.length; ++i) {
            IRender r = (IRender)
                components[i].getExtension
                    (InterfaceID.ID_RENDER);
            r.render ();
        }
    }
```

The main() method is the entry point into the client application. It
first initializes the TMN system using the initialization component
introduced above, then it retrieves the required component factories
representing ports and connections between ports:

```
public static void main (String args[]) {
    Factory pFactory = null;
    Factory cFactory = null;

    // Register components with the factory finder.
    ComponentInstaller.install ();

    // access factory finder.
    FactoryFinder finder =
        FactoryFinder.getInstance ();
```

```
                    try {
                        // Get factories.
                        pFactory = finder.findFactory
                                    (componentID.CID_PORT);
                        cFactory = finder.findFactory
                                    (componentID.CID_CONN);
                    }
                    catch (UnknownEx ex) {
                        System.out.println (ex.getID () +
                                            "not found!");
                        System.exit (1);
                    }

                    // Create two ports and a connection.
                    IRoot port1Root = pFactory.create ();
                    IRoot port2Root = pFactory.create ();
                    IRoot connectionRoot = cFactory.create ();
```

Note that a client could type cast port1Root and port2Root below instead of calling the getExtension() method, because the components use interface inheritance to implement the extension interfaces. However, this design would tightly couple the client implementation and the component implementation. If we later restructured the components to use Java inner classes rather than multiple interface inheritance, for example, all the client code would break.

```
                    try {
                        // Initialize port 1.
                        IPort p1 = (IPort) port1Root.getExtension
                                    (InterfaceID.ID_PORT);
                        p1.setHost ("Machine A");
                        p1.setPort (PORT_NUMBER);
                        // ...Initialize port 2 and connection...

                        // Build array of components.
                        IRoot components[] = { c, p1, p2 };
                        // Dump all components.
                        dumpAll (components);
                        // Draw all components.
                        drawAll (components);
                    } catch (UnknownEx error) {
                        System.out.println ("Interface "
                            +error.getID () + " not supported!");
                    } catch (CommErrorEx commError) {
                        System.out.println ("Connection problem");
                    }
                }
            }
```

❏

Example Resolved Shortly after delivering the component-based management application console to their customers, the TMN framework developers receive two change requests. The first request requires each component in the TMN framework to load and store its state from a persistent database. The second request requires a new component with a star connection topology. This topology denotes a set of network elements that are all connected to a central element, yielding a star-like shape.

To satisfy these change requests, the TMN framework developers can apply the Extension Interface pattern:

- To support loading and storing component state from a persistent database, a new extension interface called IPersistence is defined:

```
public interface IPersistence extends IRoot {
    public PersistenceId store ();
    public load (PersistenceId persistenceId);
}
```

Every existing component is then enhanced to implement this interface. In detail, a component implementor must add all methods defined in the new interface to the component implementation. The amount of work necessary to extend a component with a new extension interface directly depends on the particular extension interface added to the component. The persistence example requires just a few database calls to implement the new interface.

- To support star connection topologies, we define an IConnectionStar interface:

```
public interface IConnectionStar extends IRoot {
    public void setAllPorts (IPort ports[]);
    public void setPort (long whichPort, IPort port);
    public IPort getPort (long whichPort);
}
```

All TMN framework components must then implement the IRender, IDump, IConnectionStar, IManagedObject and IPersistence interfaces.

The InterfaceID class defined in implementation activity 6.5 (158) is extended with identifiers for the new interfaces.

If a client needs to access the new functionality, it can retrieve any extension interface from the component, query the component for a new extension interface and use the new service:

```
IRoot iRoot = /* ... */; // use any component interface
try {
    PersistenceId storage = /* ... */;
    IPersistence iPersistence =
        iRoot.getExtension (InterfaceID.ID_PERSISTENCE);
    PersistenceId id = iPersistence.load (storage);
} catch (UnknownEx ue) {
    // Provide exception handling code here when
    // <getExtension> fails to return <IPersistence>.
}
```

Variants   *Extension Object* [PLoPD3]. In this variant there is no need for a component factory because each component is responsible for returning interface references to clients. Extension objects are well-suited for components that are built using a single object-oriented programming language, such as C++ or Java, where components derive from all interfaces they implement. Type-safe downcasting can be used to retrieve component interfaces. In these language-specific implementations component factories are not needed because component classes map directly to language classes, which are themselves responsible for instance creation.

Distributed Extension Interface. This variant features an additional type of participant, *servers*, which host the implementations of components. Each server contains the factory as well as the implementation of all supported extension interfaces. A single server can host more than one component type. In distributed systems, clients and servers do not share the same address space. It is the task of the server to register and unregister its components with a locator service, so that clients or factory finders can retrieve remote components.

In distributed systems there is a physical separation of interfaces and implementations. Client proxies can be introduced to attach clients to remote extension interfaces transparently [POSA1] [GoF95]. Client-side proxies implement the same extension interfaces as the components they represent. They also shield clients from tedious and error-prone communication mechanisms by forwarding method invocations over the network to remote components. Proxies can be defined so that clients can leverage the *Extension Object* variant outlined above. To enhance performance, client proxies can provide co-located [WSV99] local implementations of general-purpose extension interfaces to reduce network traffic, in accordance with the Half Object plus Protocol pattern [Mes95].

In distributed object computing middleware [OMG98c], proxies can be implemented automatically via an interface definition language (IDL) compiler. An IDL compiler parses files containing interface definitions and generates source code that performs various network programming tasks, such as marshaling, demarshaling, and error-checking [GS98]. The use of interface definition languages simplifies the connection of components and clients written in different programming languages. To ensure this degree of distribution and location transparency, the underlying component infrastructure can instantiate the Broker architectural pattern [POSA1].

Extension Interface with Access Control. In this variant the client must authenticate itself to the extension interface. Client access to an extension interface can be restricted by this method. For example, an administrator might be granted access to all interfaces of a component, whereas another client would be allowed to invoke methods on a subset of interfaces that provided specific functionality.

Asymmetric Extension Interface. This variant specifies one distinguished interface that is responsible for providing access to all other interfaces. In contrast to the symmetric case, clients are not capable of navigating from an extension interface to any other extension interface. They must instead use the distinguished extension interface to navigate to any other extension interface. This interface may be provided by the component itself, as defined by the Extension Object variant.

Known Uses   **Microsoft's COM/COM+** technology is based upon extension interfaces [Box97]. Each COM class implementation must provide a factory interface called `IClassFactory` that defines the functionality to instantiate new instances of the class. When the COM run-time activates the component implementation, it receives a pointer to the associated factory interface. Using this interface, clients can to create new component instances.

Each COM class implements one or more interfaces that are derived from a common root interface called `IUnknown`. The `IUnknown` interface contains the method `QueryInterface(REFIID, void**)`, which allows clients to retrieve particular extension interfaces exported by a component. The first parameter to QueryInterface() is a unique identifier that determines which extension interface to return to a client. If the component implements the interface requested by a client, it returns an interface pointer in the second parameter, otherwise an error is returned.

This activity is called *interface negotiation*, because clients can interrogate components to determine whether they support particular extension interfaces. COM/COM+ implements the Distributed Extension Interface variant and allows clients and components to be developed in any programming language supported by Microsoft, including Visual Basic, C, C++ and Java.

CORBA 3 [Vin98] introduces a CORBA Component Model (CCM) [OMG99a] in which each component may provide more than one interface. Clients first retrieve a distinguished interface, the component's so-called 'equivalent' interface. They then use specific 'provide' methods to navigate to one of the extension interfaces, called 'facets' in CCM. Every CCM interface must implement the method get_component(), which is similar to COM's QueryInterface() method described above. It is therefore always possible to navigate from a facet back to the component's equivalent interface.

To obtain a reference to an existing component, or to create a new component, clients access a so-called 'home' interface, which is associated with a single component type. This interface represents the component factory interface, as defined by CORBA components and Enterprise JavaBeans. The factory finder within CCM is implemented by the ComponentHomeFinder, whereas EJB relies on the Java Naming and Directory Interface (JNDI) for the same purpose. CORBA components and the Java-centric subset Enterprise JavaBeans (EJB) [MaHa99] use the Asymmetric Extension Interface variant.

OpenDoc [OHE96] introduces the concept of adding functionality to objects using extensions. Functionality is provided to retrieve extensions in the root interface, as well as for reference counting. OpenDoc implements the Extension Object variant of Extension Interface.

Consequences The Extension Interface pattern offers the following **benefits**:

Extensibility. Extending the functionality of a component should only require adding new extension interfaces. Existing interfaces remain unchanged, so existing clients should not be affected adversely. Developers can prevent *interface bloating* by using multiple extension interfaces rather than merging all methods into a single base interface.

Separation of concerns. Semantically-related functionality can be grouped together into separate extension interfaces. A component can play different roles for the same or different clients by defining a separate extension interface for each role.

Polymorphism is supported without requiring inheritance from a common interface. If two components implement the same extension interface, a client of that particular extension interface need not know which component actually provides the functionality. Similarly, multiple components can implement the same set of interfaces, thereby allowing them to exchange component implementations transparent.

Decoupling of components and their clients. Clients access extension interfaces rather than component implementations. There is therefore no (tight) coupling between a component implementation and its clients. New implementations of extension interfaces can thus be provided without breaking existing client code. It is even possible to separate the implementation of a component from its interfaces by using proxies [POSA1] [GoF95].

Support for interface aggregation and delegation. Components can aggregate other components and offer the aggregated interfaces as their own. The aggregate interfaces delegate all client requests to the aggregated component that implements the interface. This allows the aggregate interfaces to assume the identity of every aggregated component and to reuse their code. However, a pre-condition for this design is that the aggregate interface component and its constituent aggregated components collaborate via the getExtension() method.

However, the Extension Interface pattern also can incur the following **liabilities**:

Increased component design and implementation effort. The effort required to develop and deploy components can be non-trivial. The component programming effort is particularly tedious when the Extension Interface pattern is not integrated transparently in a particular programming language. For example, it is relatively straightforward to instantiate the pattern using Java or C++. Implementing it in C is extremely complex, however, due to the lack of key language features such as inheritance or polymorphism.

Increased client programming complexity. The Extension Interface pattern makes clients responsible for determining which interfaces are suitable for their particular use case. Clients must therefore perform a multi-step protocol to obtain a reference to an extension interface before using it. A client must also keep track of a variety of bookkeeping details, such as interface or instance identifiers and reference counts, that can obscure the client's core application logic.

Additional indirection and run-time overhead. Clients never access components directly, which may reduce run-time efficiency slightly. Similarly, run-time reference counting of initialized components is complex and potentially inefficient in multi-threaded or distributed environments. In certain cases, however, this additional indirection is negligible, particularly when accessing components across high-latency networks.

See Also Components and clients may not reside in the same address space, be written in the same programming language or be deployed in binary form, but it still may be necessary to interconnect them. The Proxy pattern [POSA1] [GoF95] can be applied in this context to decouple a component's interface from its implementation. For a more sophisticated and flexible solution, the Broker pattern [POSA1] can be applied. In this pattern components act as servers and the broker, among its other responsibilities, provides a globally-available factory finder service.

The *Extension Object* variant of the Extension Interface pattern is introduced in [PLoPD3]. This variant is applicable whenever the object model of the underlying programming language can be used to implement a non-distributed component extension mechanism. In this case,

- Components and component factories map directly to programming language classes

- Component interfaces map to programming language interfaces and

- The retrieval of component interfaces is implemented using type-safe downcasting

Credits   We were pleased to co-operate with Erich Gamma on this pattern description. Erich published the *Extension Object* variant in [PLoPD3] and provided our inspiration for documenting the more general Extension Interface pattern described here. We would also like to thank Don Box, *aka* the 'COM guy' [Box97], for providing many insights into the Microsoft COM paradigm, and for identifying the fiduciary benefits of networking and distributed object computing in the days when he was Doug Schmidt's office-mate in graduate school at the University of California, Irvine.

3 Event Handling Patterns

*"The power to guess the unseen from the seen,
to trace the implications of things,
to judge the whole piece by the pattern . . .
this cluster of gifts may almost be said
to constitute experience."*

Henry James, Jr. (1843-1916) — English Author

This chapter presents four patterns that describe how to initiate, receive, demultiplex, dispatch, and process events in networked systems: Reactor, Proactor, Asynchronous Completion Token, and Acceptor-Connector.

Event-driven architectures are becoming pervasive in networked software applications. The four patterns in this chapter help to simplify the development of flexible and efficient event-driven applications. The first pattern can be applied to develop synchronous service providers:

- The *Reactor* architectural pattern (179) allows event-driven applications to demultiplex and dispatch service requests that are delivered to an application from one or more clients. The structure introduced by the Reactor pattern 'inverts' the flow of control within an application, which is known as the *Hollywood Principle*— 'Don't call us, we'll call you' [Vlis98a].

  It is the responsibility of a designated component, called reactor, *not* an application, to wait for indication events synchronously, demultiplex them to associated event handlers that are responsible for processing these events, and then dispatch the appropriate hook method on the event handler. In particular, a reactor dispatches event handlers that *react* to the occurrence of a specific event. Application developers are therefore only responsible for implementing concrete event handlers and can reuse the reactor's demultiplexing and dispatching mechanisms.

Although the Reactor pattern is relatively straightforward to program and use, it has several constraints that can limit its applicability. In particular it does not scale to support a large number of simultaneous clients and/or long-duration client requests well, because it serializes all event handler processing at the event demultiplexing layer. The second pattern in this chapter can help alleviate these limitations for event-driven applications that run on platforms that support asynchronous I/O efficiently:

- The *Proactor* architectural pattern (215) allows event-driven applications to efficiently demultiplex and dispatch service requests triggered by the completion of asynchronous operations. It offers the performance benefits of concurrency without incurring some of its liabilities.

  In the Proactor pattern, application components—represented by clients and completion handlers—are *proactive* entities. Unlike the Reactor pattern (179), which waits passively for indication events to arrive and then *reacts*, clients and completion handlers in the

Proactor pattern instigate the control and data flow within an application by initiating one or more asynchronous operation requests *proactively* on an asynchronous operation processor.

When these asynchronous operations complete, the asynchronous operation processor and and a designated proactor component collaborate to demultiplex the resulting completion events to their associated completion handlers and dispatch these handlers' hook methods. After processing a completion event, a completion handler may initiate new asynchronous operation requests proactively.

The remaining two design patterns in this chapter can be applied in conjunction with the first two architectural patterns to cover a broader range of event-driven application concerns.

The next pattern is particularly useful for optimizing the demultiplexing tasks of a Proactor (215) implementation, because it addresses an important aspect of asynchronous application design:

- The *Asynchronous Completion Token* design pattern (261) allows an application to demultiplex and process efficiently the responses of asynchronous operations it invokes on services.

The final pattern in this chapter is often used in conjunction with the Reactor (179) pattern for networking applications:

- The *Acceptor-Connector* design pattern (285) decouples the connection and initialization of cooperating peer services in a networked system from the processing they perform once connected and initialized. Acceptor-Connector allows applications to configure their connection topologies in a manner largely independent of the services they provide. The pattern can be layered on top of Reactor to handle events associated with establishing connectivity between services.

All four patterns presented in this chapter are often applied in conjunction with the patterns presented in Chapter 5, *Concurrency Patterns*. Other patterns in the literature that address event handling include Event Notification [Rie96], Observer [GoF95], and Publisher-Subscriber [POSA1].

Reactor

The *Reactor* architectural pattern allows event-driven applications to demultiplex and dispatch service requests that are delivered to an application from one or more clients.

Also known as   Dispatcher, Notifier

Example   Consider an event-driven server for a distributed logging service. Remote client applications use this logging service to record information about their status within a distributed system. This status information commonly includes error notifications, debugging traces, and performance diagnostics. Logging records are sent to a central logging server, which can write the records to various output devices, such as a console, a printer, a file, or a network management database.

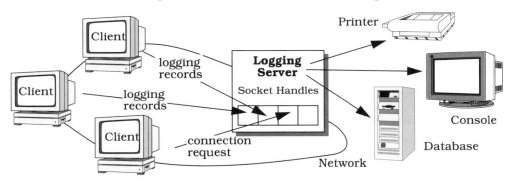

Clients communicate with the logging server using a connection-oriented protocol, such as TCP [Ste98]. Clients and the logging service are thus bound to transport endpoints designated by *full associations* consisting of the IP addresses and TCP port numbers that uniquely identify clients and the logging service.

The logging service can be accessed simultaneously by multiple clients, each of which maintains its own connection with the logging server. A new client connection request is indicated to the server by a CONNECT event. A request to process logging records within the logging service is indicated by a READ event, which instructs the logging service to read new input from one of its client connections. The logging records and connection requests issued by clients can arrive *concurrently* at the logging server.

One way to implement a logging server is to use some type of multi-threading model. For example, the server could use a 'thread-per-connection' model that allocates a dedicated thread of control for each connection and processes logging records as they arrive from clients. Using multi-threading can incur the following liabilities, however:

- Threading may be inefficient and non-scalable due to context switching, synchronization, and data movement among CPUs.

- Threading may require the use of complex concurrency control schemes throughout server code.

- Threading is not available on all operating systems, nor do all operating systems provide portable threading semantics.

- A concurrent server may be better optimized by aligning its threading strategy to available resources, such as the number of CPUs, rather than to the number of clients is services concurrently.

These drawbacks can make multi-threading an inefficient and overly-complex solution for developing a logging server. To ensure adequate quality of service for all connected clients, however, a logging server must handle requests efficiently and fairly. In particular, it should not service just one client and starve the others.

Context   An event-driven application that receives multiple service requests simultaneously, but processes them synchronously and serially.

Problem   Event-driven applications in a distributed system, particularly servers,[1] must be prepared to handle multiple service requests simultaneously, even if those requests are ultimately processed serially within the application. The arrival of each request is identified by a specific *indication* event, such as the CONNECT and READ events in our logging example. Before executing specific services serially, therefore, an event-driven application must demultiplex and dispatch the concurrently-arriving indication events to the corresponding service implementations.

---

1. The *Known Uses* section lists examples in which the Reactor pattern is used to implement event handling for applications that play both client *and* server roles.

Resolving this problem effectively requires the resolution of four *forces*:

- To improve scalability and latency, an application should not block on any single source of indication events and exclude other event sources, because blocking on one event source can degrade the server's responsiveness to clients.

- To maximize throughput, any unnecessary context switching, synchronization, and data movement among CPUs should be avoided, as outlined in the *Example* section.

- Integrating new or improved services with existing indication event demultiplexing and dispatching mechanisms should require minimal effort.

- Application code should largely be shielded from the complexity of multi-threading and synchronization mechanisms.

Solution   Synchronously wait for the arrival of indication events on one or more event sources, such as connected socket handles. Integrate the mechanisms that demultiplex and dispatch the events to services that process them. Decouple these event demultiplexing and dispatching mechanisms from the application-specific processing of indication events within the services.

In detail: for each service an application offers, introduce a separate *event handler* that processes certain types of events from certain event sources. Event handlers register with a *reactor*, which uses a *synchronous event demultiplexer* to wait for indication events to occur on one or more event sources. When indication events occur, the synchronous event demultiplexer notifies the reactor, which then synchronously dispatches the event handler associated with the event so that it can perform the requested service.

Structure   There are five key participants in the Reactor pattern:

Handles are provided by operating systems to identify event sources, such as network connections or open files, that can generate and queue indication events. Indication events can originate from external sources, such as CONNECT events or READ events sent to a service from clients, or internal sources, such as time-outs. When an indication event occurs on an event source, the event is queued on its associated handle and the handle is marked as 'ready'. At this point, an operation, such as an `accept()` or `read()`, can be performed on the handle without blocking the calling thread.

➥   Socket handles are used in the logging server to identify transport endpoints that receive CONNECT and READ indication events. A passive-mode transport endpoint and its associated socket handle listen for CONNECT indications events. The logging server then maintains a separate connection, and thus a separate socket handle, for each connected client.   ❑

A *synchronous event demultiplexer* is a function called to wait for one or more indication events to occur on a set of handles—a *handle set*. This call blocks until indication events on its handle set inform the synchronous event demultiplexer that one or more handles in the set have become 'ready', meaning that an operation can be initiated on them without blocking.

➥   `select()` is a common synchronous event demultiplexer function for I/O events [Ste98] supported by many operating systems, including UNIX and Win32 platforms. The `select()` call indicates which handles in its handle set have indication events pending. Operations can be invoked on these handles synchronously without blocking the calling thread.   ❑

Class	*Collaborator*	*Class*	*Collaborator*
Handle and Handle Set		Synchronous Event Demultiplexer	• Handle • Handle Set
Responsibility • A handle identifies a source of indication events in an operating system • A handle can queue up indication events • A handle set is a collection of handles		*Responsibility* • Can block waiting for indication events to occur on a handle set • Indicates an operation can be initiated on a handle without blocking	

An *event handler* specifies an interface consisting of one or more hook methods [Pree95] [GoF95]. These methods represent the set of operations available to process application-specific indication events that occur on handle(s) associated with an event handler.

Concrete event handlers specialize the event handler and implement a specific service that the application offers. Each concrete event handler is associated with a handle that identifies this service within the application. In particular, concrete event handlers implement the hook method(s) responsible for processing indication events received through their associated handle. Any results of the service can be returned to its caller by writing output to the handle.

➥ The logging server contains two types of concrete event handlers: logging acceptor and logging handler. The logging acceptor uses the Acceptor-Connector pattern (285) to create and connect logging handlers. Each logging handler is responsible for receiving and processing logging records sent from its connected client. ❏

Class	*Collaborator*
Event Handler	• Handle
Responsibility	
• Defines an interface for processing indication events that occur on a handle	

Class	*Collaborator*
Concrete Event Handler	• Handle
Responsibility	
• Processes indication events on a handle in an application-specific manner • Defines an application service	

A *reactor* defines an interface that allows applications to register or remove event handlers and their associated handles, and run the application's event loop. A reactor uses its synchronous event demultiplexer to wait for indication events to occur on its handle set. When this occurs, the reactor first *demultiplexes* each indication event from the handle on which it occurs to its associated event handler, then it *dispatches* the appropriate hook method on the handler to process the event.

Class	*Collaborator*
Reactor	• Handle Set • Event Handlers
Responsibility	• Synchronous Event Demultiplexer
• Registers and removes event handlers and their associated handles • Manages a handle set • Runs the application's event loop	

Note how the structure introduced by the Reactor pattern 'inverts' the flow of control within an application. It is the responsibility of a reactor, *not* an application, to wait for indication events, demultiplex these events to their concrete event handlers, and dispatch the appropriate hook method on the concrete event handler. In particular, a reactor is not called by a concrete event handler, but instead a reactor dispatches concrete event handlers, which *react* to the occurrence of a specific event. This 'inversion of control' is known as the *Hollywood* principle [Vlis98a].

Application developers are thus only responsible for implementing the concrete event handlers and registering them with the reactor. Applications can simply reuse the reactor's demultiplexing and dispatching mechanisms.

The structure of the participants in the Reactor pattern is illustrated in the following class diagram:

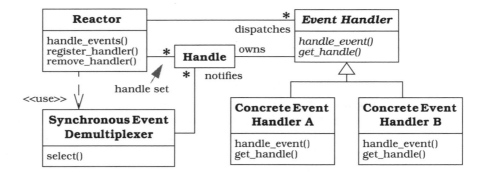

Dynamics   The collaborations in the Reactor pattern illustrate how the flow of control oscillates between the reactor and event handler components:

- An application registers a concrete event handler with the reactor. At this point, the application also indicates the type of indication event(s) the event handler wants the reactor to notify it about, when such event(s) occur on the associated handle.

- The reactor instructs each event handler to provide its internal handle, in our example by invoking their get_handle() method. This handle identifies the source of indication events to the synchronous event demultiplexer and the operating system.

- After all event handlers are registered, the application starts the reactor's event loop, which we call `handle_events()`. At this point the reactor combines the handles from each registered event handler into a handle set. It then calls the synchronous event demultiplexer to wait for indication events to occur on the handle set.

- The synchronous event demultiplexer function returns to the reactor when one or more handles corresponding to event sources becomes 'ready', for example when a Socket becomes 'ready to read'.

- The reactor then uses the ready handles as 'keys' to locate the appropriate event handler(s) and dispatch the corresponding hook method(s). The type of indication event that occurred can be passed as a parameter to the hook method. This method can use this type information to perform any additional application-specific demultiplexing and dispatching operations.[2]

- After the appropriate hook method within the event handler is dispatched, it processes the invoked service. This service can write the results of its processing, if any, to the handle associated with the event handler so that they can be returned to the client that originally requested the service.

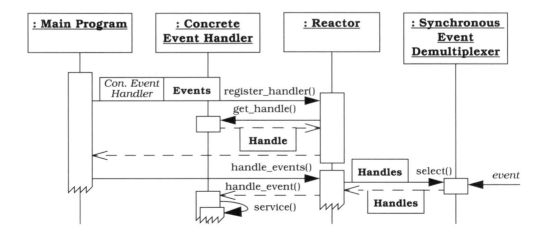

---

2. An alternative dispatching approach is described in the *Implementation* section.

Implementation The participants in the Reactor pattern decompose into two layers:

- *Demultiplexing/dispatching infrastructure layer components.* This layer performs generic, application-independent strategies for demultiplexing indication events to event handlers and then dispatching the associated event handler hook methods.

- *Application layer components.* This layer defines concrete event handlers that perform application-specific processing in their hook methods.

The implementation activities in this section start with the generic demultiplexing/dispatching infrastructure components and then cover the application components. We focus on a reactor implementation that is designed to demultiplex handle sets and dispatch hook methods on event handlers within a single thread of control. The *Variants* section describes the activities associated with developing concurrent reactor implementations.

1 *Define the event handler interface.* Event handlers specify an interface consisting of one or more hook methods [Pree95]. These hook methods represent the set of services that are available to process indication events received and dispatched by the reactor. As described in implementation activity 5 (196), concrete event handlers are created by application developers to perform specific services in response to particular indication events. Defining an event handler interface consists two sub-activities:

1.1 *Determine the type of the dispatching target.* Two types of event handlers can be associated with a handle to serve as the target of a reactor's dispatching strategy:

- *Event handler objects.* In object-oriented applications a common way to associate an event handler with a handle is to create an event handler object. For example, the Reactor pattern implementation shown in the *Structure* section dispatches concrete event handler objects. Using an object as the dispatching target makes it convenient to subclass event handlers to reuse and extend existing components. Similarly, objects make it easy to integrate the state and methods of a service into a single component.

- *Event handler functions.* Another strategy for associating an event handler with a handle is to register a pointer to a function with a reactor rather than an object. Using a pointer to a function as the dispatching target makes it convenient to register callbacks without having to define a new subclass that inherits from an event handler base class.

The Adapter pattern [GoF95] can be employed to support both objects and pointers to functions simultaneously. For example, an adapter could be defined using an event handler object that holds a pointer to an event handler function. When the hook method was invoked on the event handler adapter object it could automatically forward the call to the event handler function that it encapsulates.

1.2 *Determine the event handling dispatch interface strategy.* We must next define the type of interface supported by the event handlers for processing events. Assuming that we use event handler objects rather than pointers to functions, there are two general strategies:

- *Single-method dispatch interface strategy.* The class diagram in the *Structure* section illustrates an implementation of the Event_ Handler base class interface that contains a single event handling method, which is used by a reactor to dispatch events. In this case, the type of the event that has occurred is passed as a parameter to the method.

  ➡   We specify a C++ abstract base class that illustrates the single-method interface. We start by defining a useful type definition and enumeration literals that can be used by both the single-method and multi-method dispatch interface strategies:

  ```
  typedef unsigned int Event_Type;
  enum {
      // Types of indication events.
      READ_EVENT = 01,    // ACCEPT_EVENT aliases READ_EVENT
      ACCEPT_EVENT = 01, // due to <select> semantics.
      WRITE_EVENT = 02, TIMEOUT_EVENT = 04,
      SIGNAL_EVENT = 010, CLOSE_EVENT = 020
      // These values are powers of two so
      // their bits can be "or'd" together efficiently.
  };
  ```

  Next, we implement the Event_Handler class:

  ```
  class Event_Handler { // Single-method interface.
  public:
      // Hook method dispatched by <Reactor> to handle
      // events of a particular type.
      virtual void handle_event (HANDLE handle,
                                 Event_Type et) = 0;
  ```

```
        // Hook method that returns the I/O <HANDLE>.
        virtual HANDLE get_handle () const = 0;
protected:
        // Virtual destructor is protected to ensure
        // dynamic allocation.
        virtual ~Event_Handler ();
    };                                                    ❏
```

The single-method dispatch interface strategy makes it possible to support new types of indication events without changing the class interface. However, this strategy encourages the use of C++ switch and if statements in the concrete event handler's handle_ event() method implementation to handle a specific event, which degrades its extensibility.

- *Multi-method dispatch interface strategy.* A different strategy for defining the Event_Handler dispatch interface is to create separate hook methods for handling each type of event, such as input events, output events, or time-out events. This strategy can be more extensible than the single-method dispatch interface because the demultiplexing is performed by a reactor implementation, rather than by a concrete event handler's handle_event() method implementation.

➡ The following C++ abstract base class illustrates the multi-method interface:

```
class Event_Handler {
public:
        // Hook methods dispatched by a <Reactor> to handle
        // particular types of events.
        virtual void handle_input (HANDLE handle) = 0;
        virtual void handle_output (HANDLE handle) = 0;
        virtual void handle_timeout (const Time_Value &) = 0;
        virtual void handle_close (HANDLE handle,
                                   Event_Type et) = 0;
        // Hook method that returns the I/O <HANDLE>.
        virtual HANDLE get_handle () const = 0;
    };                                                    ❏
```

The multi-method dispatch interface strategy makes it easy to override methods in the base class selectively, which avoids additional demultiplexing via switch or if statements in the hook method implementation. However, this strategy requires pattern implementors to anticipate the event handler methods in advance. The various handle_*() methods in the Event_Handler dispatch interface above are tailored for I/O and time-out indication events supported by the select() function. This function does not encompass all the types of indication events, such as synchronization events that can be handled via the Win32 WaitForMultipleObjects() function [SchSt95].

Both the single-method and multi-method dispatch interface strategies are implementations of the Hook Method [Pree95] and Template Method [GoF95] patterns. Their intent is to provide well-defined hooks that can be specialized by applications and called back by lower-level dispatching code. This allows application programmers to define concrete event handlers using inheritance and polymorphism.

2 *Define the reactor interface.* The reactor's interface is used by applications to register or remove event handlers and their associated handles, as well as to invoke the application's event loop. The reactor interface is often accessed via a Singleton [GoF95] because a single reactor is often sufficient for each application process.

To shield applications from complex and non-portable demultiplexing and dispatching operating system platform mechanisms, the Reactor pattern can use the Bridge pattern [GoF95]. The reactor interface corresponds to the abstraction participant in the Bridge pattern, whereas a platform-specific reactor instance is accessed internally via a pointer, in accordance with the implementation hierarchy in the Bridge pattern.

➡ The reactor interface in our logging server defines an abstraction for registering and removing event handlers, and running the application's event loop reactively:

```
class Reactor {
public:
    // Methods that register and remove <Event_Handler>s
    // of particular <Event_Type>s on a <HANDLE>.
    virtual void register_handler
        (Event_Handler *eh, Event_Type et) = 0;
    virtual void register_handler
        (HANDLE h, Event_Handler *eh, Event_Type et) = 0;
    virtual void remove_handler
        (Event_Handler *eh, Event_Type et) = 0;
    virtual void remove_handler
        (HANDLE h, Event_Type et) = 0;

    // Entry point into the reactive event loop. The
    // <timeout> can bound time waiting for events.
    void handle_events (Time_Value *timeout = 0);
```

```
      // Define a singleton access point.
      static Reactor *instance ();
private:
      // Use the Bridge pattern to hold a pointer to
      // the <Reactor_Implementation>.
      Reactor_Implementation *reactor_impl_;
};                                                              ❏
```

A typical reactor interface also defines a pair of overloaded methods, which we call register_handler(), that allow applications to register handles and event handlers at run-time with the reactor's internal demultiplexing table described in implementation activity 3.3 (193). In general, the method for registering event handlers can be defined using either or both of the following signatures:

• *Two parameters.* In this design, one parameter identifies the event handler and another that indicates the type of indication event(s) the event handler has registered to process. The method's implementation uses 'double-dispatching' [GoF95] to obtain a handle by calling back to an event handler method get_handle(). The advantage of this design is that the 'wrong' handle cannot be associated with an event handler accidentally.

➠ The following code fragment illustrates how double-dispatching is used in the register_handler() implementation:

```
      void Select_Reactor_Implementation::register_handler
             (Event_Handler *event_handler,
              Event_Type event_type) {
      // Double-dispatch to obtain the <HANDLE>.
      HANDLE handle = event_handler->get_handle ();
      // ...
      }                                                         ❏
```

• *Three parameters.* In this design a third parameter is used to pass the handle explicitly. Although this design can be more error-prone than the two-parameter signature, it allows an application to register the same event handler for multiple handles, which may help to conserve memory.

Both types of registration methods store their parameters into the appropriate demultiplexing table, as indicated by the handle.

The reactor interface also defines two other overloaded methods, which we call remove_handler(), that can be used to remove an event handler from a reactor. For example, an application may no longer want to process one or more types of indication events on a particular handle. These methods remove the event handler from a reactor's internal demultiplexing table so that it is no longer registered for any types of indication events. The signatures of the methods that remove an event handler can be passed either a handle or an event handler in the same way as the event handler registration methods.

The reactor interface also defines its main entry point method, which we call `handle_events()`, that applications can use to run their reactive event loop. This method calls the synchronous event demultiplexer to wait for indication events to occur on its handle set. An application can use the `timeout` parameter to bound the time it spends waiting for indication events, so that the application will not block indefinitely if events never arrive.

When one or more indication events occur on the handle set, the synchronous event demultiplexer function returns. At this point the `handle_events()` method 'reacts' by demultiplexing to the event handler associated with each handle that is now ready. It then dispatches the handler's hook method to process the event.

3   *Implement the reactor interface.* Four sub-activities help implement the reactor interface defined in implementation activity 2 (189):

3.1   *Develop a reactor implementation hierarchy.* The reactor interface abstraction illustrated in implementation activity 2 (189) delegates all its demultiplexing and dispatching processing to a reactor implementation, which plays the role of the implementation hierarchy in the Bridge pattern [GoF95]. This design makes it possible to implement and configure multiple types of reactors transparently. For example, a concrete reactor implementation can be created using different types of synchronous event demultiplexers, such as `select()` [Ste98], `poll()` [Rago93], or `WaitForMultipleObjects()` [Sol98], each of which provides the features and limitations described in implementation activity 3.2 (192).

➥   In our example the base class of the reactor implementation hierarchy is defined by the class `Reactor_Implementation`. We omit its declaration here because this class has essentially the same interface as the `Reactor` interface in implementation activity 2 (189). The primary difference is that its methods are pure virtual, because it forms the base of a hierarchy of concrete reactor implementations.❑

3.2   *Choose a synchronous event demultiplexer mechanism.* The reactor implementation calls a synchronous event demultiplexer to wait for one or more indication events to occur on the reactor's handle set. This call returns when any handle(s) in the set are 'ready', meaning that operations can be invoked on the handles without blocking the application process. The synchronous event demultiplexer, as well as the handles and handle sets, are often existing operating system mechanisms, so they need not be developed by reactor implementors.

➡   For our logging server, we choose the `select()` function, which is a synchronous event demultiplexer that allows event-driven reactive applications to wait for an application-specified amount of time for various types of I/O events to occur on multiple I/O handles:

```
int select (u_int max_handle_plus_1,
            fd_set *read_fds, fd_set *write_fds,
            fd_set *except_fds,timeval *timeout);
```

The `select()` function examines the three 'file descriptor set' (`fd_set`) parameters whose addresses are passed in `read_fds`, `write_fds`, and `except_fds` to see if any of their handles are 'ready for reading', 'reading for writing', or have an 'exceptional condition', respectively. Collectively, the handle values in these three file descriptor set parameters constitute the handle set participant in the Reactor pattern.

The `select()` function can return multiple 'ready' handles to its caller in a single invocation. It cannot be called concurrently on the same handle set by multiple threads of control, however, because the operating system will erroneously notify more than one thread calling `select()` when I/O events are pending on the same subset of handles [Ste98]. In addition, `select()` does not scale up well when used with a large set of handles [BaMo98].   ❑

Two other synchronous event demultiplexers that are available on some operating systems are the `poll()` and `WaitForMultiple-Objects()` functions. These two functions have similar scalability problems as `select()`. They are also less portable, because they are only available on platforms compatible with Win32 and System V Release 4 UNIX, respectively. The *Variants* section describes a unique feature of `WaitForMultipleObjects()` that allows it to be called concurrently on the same handle set by multiple threads of control.

3.3 *Implement a demultiplexing table.* In addition to calling the synchronous event demultiplexer to wait for indication events to occur on its handle set, a reactor implementation maintains a demultiplexing table. This table is a manager [Som97] that contain a set of *<handle, event handler, indication event types>* tuples. Each handle serves as a 'key' that the reactor implementation uses to associate handles with event handlers in its demultiplexing table. This table also stores the type of indication event(s), such as CONNECT and READ, that each event handler has registered on its handle.

The demultiplexing table can be implemented using various search strategies, such as direct indexing, linear search, or dynamic hashing. If handles are represented as a continuous range of integers, as they are on UNIX platforms, direct indexing is most efficient, because demultiplexing table tuple entries can be located in constant $O(1)$ time.

On platforms like Win32 where handles are non-contiguous pointers, direct indexing is infeasible. Some type of linear search or hashing must therefore be used to implement a demultiplexing table.

➥ I/O handles in UNIX are contiguous integer values, which allows our demultiplexing table to be implemented as a fixed-size array of structs. In this design, the handle values themselves index directly into the demultiplexing table's array to locate event handlers or event registration types in constant time. The following class illustrates such an implementation that maps HANDLEs to Event_Handlers and Event_Types:

```
class Demux_Table {
public:
    // Convert <Tuple> array to <fd_set>s.
    void convert_to_fd_sets (fd_set &read_fds,
                             fd_set &write_fds,
                             fd_set &except_fds);

    struct Tuple {
        // Pointer to <Event_Handler> that processes
        // the indication events arriving on the handle.
        Event_Handler *event_handler_;

        // Bit-mask that tracks which types of indication
        // events <Event_Handler> is registered for.
        Event_Type event_type_;
    };
```

```
        // Table of <Tuple>s indexed by Handle values. The
        // macro FD_SETSIZE is typically defined in the
        // <sys/socket.h> system header file.
        Tuple table_[FD_SETSIZE];
    };
```

In this simple implementation, the Demux_Table's table_ array is indexed by UNIX I/O handle values, which are unsigned integers ranging from 0 to FD_SETSIZE-1. Naturally, a more portable solution should encapsulate the UNIX-specific implementation details with a wrapper facade (47). ❏

3.4   *Define the concrete reactor implementation.* As shown in implementation activity 2 (189), the reactor interface holds a pointer to a concrete reactor implementation and forwards all method calls to it.

➥   Our concrete reactor implementation uses select() as its synchronous event demultiplexer and the Demux_Table class as its demultiplexing table. It inherits from the Reactor_Implementation class and overrides its pure virtual methods:

```
    class Select_Reactor_Implementation :
        public Reactor_Implementation {
    public:
```

The handle_events() method defines the entry point into the reactive event loop of our Select_Reactor_Implementation:

```
        void Select_Reactor_Implementation::handle_events
            (Time_Value *timeout = 0) {
```

This method first converts the Demux_Table tuples into fd_set handle sets that can be passed to select():

```
        fd_set read_fds, write_fds, except_fds;

        demux_table.convert_to_fd_sets
            (read_fds,write_fds,except_fds);
```

Next, select() is called to wait for up to timeout amount of time for indication events to occur on the handle sets:

```
            HANDLE max_handle = // Max value in <fd_set>s.
            int result = select
                (max_handle + 1,
                 &read_fds, &write_fds, &except_fds,
                 timeout);

            if (result <= 0)
                throw /* handle error or timeout cases */;
```

Finally, we iterate over the handle sets and dispatch the hook method(s) on event handlers whose handles have become 'ready' due to the occurrence of indication events:

```
for (HANDLE h = 0; h <= max_handle; ++h) {
    // This check covers READ_ + ACCEPT_EVENTs
    // because they have the same enum value.
    if (FD_ISSET (&read_fds, h))
        demux_table.table_[h].event_handler_->
            handle_event (h, READ_EVENT);

    // ... perform the same dispatching logic for
    // WRITE_EVENTs and EXCEPT_EVENTs ...
}
```

For brevity, we omit implementations of other methods in our reactor, for example those for registering and unregistering event handlers.

The private portion of our reactor class maintains the event handler demultiplexing table:

```
private:
    // Demultiplexing table that maps <HANDLE>s to
    // <Event_Handler>s and <Event_Type>s.
    Demux_Table demux_table_;
};
```

Note that this implementation only works on operating system platforms where I/O handles are implemented as contiguous unsigned integers, such as UNIX. Implementing this pattern on platforms where handles are non-contiguous pointers, such as Win32, therefore requires an additional data structure to keep track of which handles are in use. ❏

4 *Determine the number of reactors needed in an application.* Many applications can be structured using a single instance of the Reactor pattern. In this case the reactor can be implemented using the Singleton pattern [GoF95], as shown in implementation activity 2 (189). This pattern is useful for centralizing event demultiplexing and dispatching in one reactor instance within an application.

However, some operating systems limit the number of handles that it is possible to wait for within a single thread of control. Win32, for example, allows WaitForMultipleObjects() to wait for a maximum of 64 handles in a single thread. To develop a scalable application in this case, it may be necessary to create multiple threads, each of which runs its own instance of the Reactor pattern.

Allocating a separate reactor to each of the multiple threads can also be useful for certain types of real-time applications [SMFG00]. For example, different reactors can be associated with threads running at different priorities. This design provides different quality of service levels to process indication events for different types of synchronous operations.

Note that event handlers are only serialized within an instance of the Reactor pattern. Multiple event handlers in multiple threads can therefore run in parallel. This configuration may necessitate the use of additional synchronization mechanisms if event handlers in different threads access shared state concurrently. The *Variants* section describes techniques for adding concurrency control to reactor and event handler implementations.

5   *Implement the concrete event handlers.* Concrete event handlers derive from the event handler interface described in implementation activity 1 (186) to define application-specific functionality. Three sub-activities must be addressed when implementing concrete event handlers.

5.1   *Determine policies for maintaining state in concrete event handlers.* An event handler may need to maintain state information associated with a particular request. In our example, this could occur when an operating system notifies the logging server that only part of a logging record was read from a Socket, due to the occurrence of transport-level flow control. As a result, a concrete event handler may need to buffer the logging record fragment and return to the reactor's event loop to await notification that the remainder of the record has arrived. The concrete event handler must therefore keep track of the number of bytes read so that it can append subsequent data correctly.

5.2   *Implement a strategy to configure each concrete event handler with a handle.* A concrete event handler performs operations on a handle. The two general strategies for configuring handles with event handlers are:

- *Hard-coded.* This strategy hard-codes handles, or wrapper facades (47) for handles, into the concrete event handler. This strategy is straightforward to implement, but is less reusable if different types of handles or IPC mechanisms must be configured into an event handler for different use cases.

➡ The *Example Resolved* section illustrates the SOCK_Acceptor and SOCK_Stream classes, which are hard-coded into the logging server components. These two classes are wrapper facades that are defined in the *Implementation* section of the Wrapper Facade pattern (47). They encapsulate the stream Socket semantics of socket handles within a portable and type-secure object-oriented interface. In the Internet domain, stream Sockets are implemented using TCP.   ❏

- *Generic*. A more generic strategy is to instantiate wrapper facades (47) via parameterized types in a templatized event handler class. This strategy creates more flexible and reusable event handlers, although it may be unnecessarily general if a single type of handle or IPC mechanism is always used.

  ➡ The Acceptor, Connector, and Service_Handler classes shown in the *Implementation* section of the Acceptor-Connector pattern (285) are templates instantiated with wrapper facades. ❏

5.3 *Implement concrete event handler functionality.* Application developers must decide the processing actions to be performed to implement a service when its corresponding hook method is invoked by a reactor implementation. To separate connection-establishment functionality from subsequent service processing, concrete event handlers can be divided into several categories in accordance with the Acceptor-Connector pattern (285). In particular, service handlers implement application-specific services, whereas the reusable acceptors and connectors establish connections on behalf of these service handlers passively and actively, respectively.

Example Resolved Our logging server uses a singleton reactor implemented via the select() synchronous event demultiplexer along with two concrete event handlers—logging acceptor and logging handler—that accept connections and handle logging requests from clients, respectively. Before we discuss the implementation of the two concrete event handlers, which are based on the single-method dispatch interface strategy, we first illustrate the general behavior of the logging server using two scenarios.

The first scenario depicts the sequence of steps performed when a client connects to the logging server:

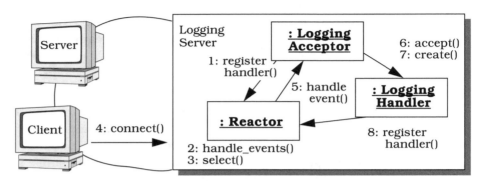

- The logging server first registers the logging acceptor with the reactor (1) to handle indication events corresponding to client connection requests. The logging server next invokes the event loop method of the reactor singleton (2).

- The reactor singleton invokes the synchronous event demultiplexing select() operation to wait for connection indication events or logging data indication events to arrive (3). At this point, all further processing on the server is driven by the *reactive* demultiplexing and dispatching of event handlers.

- A client sends a connection request to the logging server (4), which causes the reactor singleton to dispatch the logging acceptor's handle_event() hook method (5) to notify it that a new connection indication event has arrived.

- The logging acceptor accepts the new connection (6) and creates a logging handler to service the new client (7).

- The logging handler registers its socket handle with the reactor singleton (8) and instructs the reactor to notify it when the reactor receives an indication event signaling that the Socket is now 'ready for reading'.

After the client is connected, it can send logging records to the server using the socket handle that was connected in step 6.

The second scenario therefore depicts the sequence of steps performed by the reactive logging server to service a logging record:

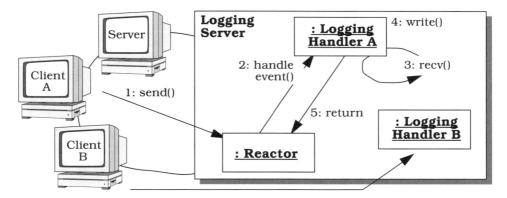

- A client sends a logging record request (1), which causes the server's operating system to notify the reactor singleton that an indication event is pending on a handle it is select()'ing on.

- The reactor singleton dispatches the handle_event() method of the logging handler associated with this handle (2), to notify it that the new indication event is intended for it.

- The logging handler reads the record from the Socket in a non-blocking manner (3). Steps 2 and 3 are repeated until the logging record has been completely received from the socket handle.

- The logging handler processes the logging record and writes it to the standard output of the logging server (4), from which it can be redirected to the appropriate output device.

- The logging handler returns control back to the reactor's event loop (5), which continues to wait for subsequent indication events.

The following code implements the concrete event handlers for our logging server example. A Logging_Acceptor class provides *passive connection establishment* and a Logging_Handler class provides application-specific *data reception and processing*.

The Logging_Acceptor class is an example of the acceptor component in the Acceptor-Connector pattern (285). It decouples the task of connection establishment and service initialization from the tasks performed after a connection is established and a service is initialized. The pattern enables the application-specific portion of a service, such as the `Logging_Handler`, to vary independently of the mechanism used to establish the connection and initialize the handler.

A `Logging_Acceptor` object accepts connection requests from client applications passively and creates client-specific `Logging_Handler` objects, which receive and process logging records from clients. Note that `Logging_Handler` objects maintain sessions with their connected clients. A new connection is therefore not established for every logging record.

The `Logging_Acceptor` class inherits from the 'single-method' dispatch interface variant of the `Event_Handler` base class that was defined in implementation activity 1.2 (187). The `Logging_Acceptor` constructor registers itself with a reactor for ACCEPT events:

```
class Logging_Acceptor : public Event_Handler {
public:
    Logging_Acceptor (const INET_Addr &addr,
                      Reactor *reactor):
        acceptor_ (addr), reactor_ (reactor) {
        reactor_->register_handler (this, ACCEPT_EVENT);
    }
```

Note that the `register_handler()` method 'double dispatches' to the `Logging_Acceptor`'s `get_handle()` method to obtain its passive-mode socket handle. From this point, whenever a connection indication arrives the reactor dispatches the `Logging_Acceptor`'s `handle_event()` method, which is a factory method [GoF95]:

```
virtual void handle_event
    (HANDLE, Event_Type event_type) {
    // Can only be called for an ACCEPT event.
    if (event_type == ACCEPT_EVENT) {
        SOCK_Stream client_connection;

        // Accept the connection.
        acceptor_.accept (client_connection);

        // Create a new <Logging_Handler>.
        Logging_Handler *handler = new
            Logging_Handler (client_connection,
                             reactor_);
    }
}
```

The `handle_event()` hook method invokes the `accept()` method of the `SOCK_Acceptor`, which initializes a `SOCK_Stream`. After the

SOCK_Stream is connected with the new client passively, a Logging_ Handler object is allocated dynamically in the logging server to process the logging requests.

The final method in this class returns the I/O handle of the underlying passive-mode socket:

```
virtual HANDLE get_handle () const {
    return acceptor_.get_handle ();
}
```

This method is called by the reactor singleton when the Logging_ Acceptor is registered. The private portion of the Logging_Acceptor class is hard-coded to contain a SOCK_Acceptor wrapper facade (47):

```
private:
    // Socket factory that accepts client connections.
    SOCK_Acceptor acceptor_;

    // Cached <Reactor>.
    Reactor *reactor_;
};
```

The SOCK_Acceptor handle factory enables a Logging_Acceptor object to accept connection indications on a passive-mode socket handle that is listening on a transport endpoint. When a connection arrives from a client, the SOCK_Acceptor accepts the connection passively and produces an initialized SOCK_Stream. The SOCK_ Stream is then uses TCP to transfer data reliably between the client and the logging server.

The Logging_Handler class receives and processes logging records sent by a client application. As with the Logging_Acceptor class shown above, the Logging_Handler inherits from Event_Handler so that its constructor can register itself with a reactor to be dispatched when READ events occur:

```
class Logging_Handler : public Event_Handler {
public:
    Logging_Handler (const SOCK_Stream &stream,
                     Reactor *reactor):
        peer_stream_ (stream) {
        reactor->register_handler (this, READ_EVENT);
}
```

Subsequently, when a logging record arrives at a connected Socket and the operating system generates a corresponding READ indication event, the reactor dispatches the handle_event() method of the associated Logging_Handler automatically:

```
virtual void handle_event (HANDLE,
                           Event_Type event_type) {
    if (event_type == READ_EVENT) {
        Log_Record log_record;

        // Code to handle "short-reads" omitted.
        peer_stream_.recv (&log_record,
                           sizeof log_record);

        // Write logging record to standard output.
        log_record.write (STDOUT);
    }
    else if (event_type == CLOSE_EVENT) {
        peer_stream_.close ();

        // Deallocate ourselves.
        delete this;
    }
}
```

The handle_event() method receives, processes, and writes the logging record[3] to the standard output (STDOUT). Similarly, when the client closes down the connection, the reactor passes the CLOSE event flag, which informs the Logging_Handler to shut down its SOCK_Stream and delete itself. The final method in this class returns the handle of the underlying data-mode stream socket:

```
virtual HANDLE get_handle () const {
    return peer_stream_.get_handle ();
}
```

This method is called by the reactor when the Logging_Handler is registered. The private portion of the Logging_Handler class is hard-coded to contain a SOCK_Stream wrapper facade (47):

```
private:
    // Receives logging records from a connected client.
    SOCK_Stream peer_stream_;
};
```

---

3. Log_Record's memory layout is identical to a conventional C-style struct. Thus, there are no virtual functions, pointers, or references, and all its values are stored contiguously.

The logging server contains a single main() function that implements a single-threaded logging server that waits in the reactor singleton's handle_events() event loop:

```
// Logging server port number.
const u_short PORT = 10000;

int main () {
    // Logging server address.
    INET_Addr addr (PORT);

    // Initialize logging server endpoint and register
    // with reactor singleton.
    Logging_Acceptor la (addr, Reactor::instance ());

    // Event loop that processes client connection
    // requests and log records reactively.
    for (;;)
        Reactor::instance ()->handle_events ();
    /* NOTREACHED */
}
```

As requests arrive from clients and are converted into indication events by the operating system, the reactor singleton invokes the hook methods on the Logging_Acceptor and Logging_Handler concrete event handlers to accept connections, and receive and process logging records, respectively.

The sequence diagram below illustrates the behavior in the logging server:

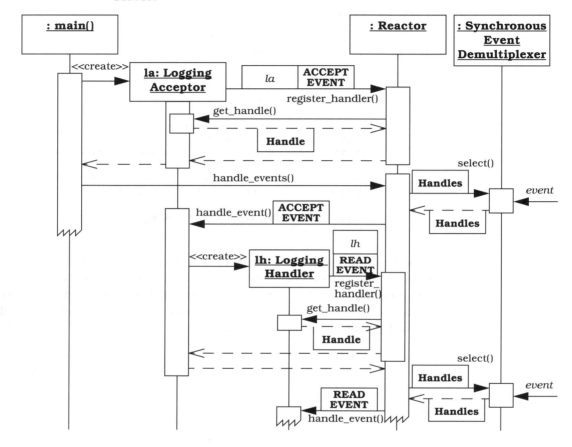

Variants   The *Implementation* section described the activities involved in implementing a reactor that demultiplexes indication events from a set of I/O handles within a *single* thread of control. The following are variations of the Reactor pattern that are needed to support concurrency, re-entrancy, or timer-based events.

Thread-safe Reactor. A reactor that drives the main event loop of a single-threaded application requires no locks, because it serializes the dispatching of event handler `handle_event()` hook methods implicitly within its application process.

However, a reactor also can serve as a single-threaded demultiplexer/dispatcher in *multi-threaded* applications. In this case, although only one thread runs the reactor's handle_events() event loop method, multiple application threads may register and remove event handlers from the reactor. In addition, an event handler called by the reactor may share state with other threads and work on that state concurrently with them. Three issues must be addressed when designing a thread-safe reactor:

- *Preventing race conditions.* Critical sections within a reactor must be serialized to prevent race conditions from occurring when multiple application threads modify the reactor's internal shared state. A common technique for preventing race conditions is to use mutual exclusion mechanisms, such as semaphores or mutexes, to protect internal state shared by multiple threads.

  For example, a mutex can be added to the reactor's demultiplexing table, and the Scoped Locking idiom (325) can be used in the reactor's methods for registering and removing event handlers to acquire and release this lock automatically. This enhancement helps ensure that multiple threads cannot corrupt the reactor's demultiplexing table by registering or removing handles and event handlers simultaneously.

  To ensure the reactor implementation is not penalized when used in single-threaded applications, the Strategized Locking pattern (333) can be applied to parameterize the locking mechanism.

- *Preventing self-deadlock.* In multi-threaded reactors, the reactor implementation described in implementation activity 3.4 (194) must be serialized, to prevent race conditions when registering, removing, and demultiplexing event handlers. However, if this serialization is not added carefully, self-deadlock can occur when the reactor's handle_events() method calls back on application-specific concrete event handlers that then subsequently re-enter the reactor via its event handler registration and removal methods.

  To prevent self-deadlock, mutual exclusion mechanisms can use *recursive locks* [Sch95], which can be re-acquired by the thread that owns the lock without incurring self-deadlock on the thread. In the Reactor pattern, recursive locks help prevent deadlock when locks are held by the same thread across event handler hook methods dispatched by a reactor.

• *Explicitly notify a waiting reactor event loop thread.* The thread running a reactor's event loop often spends much of its time waiting on its synchronous event demultiplexer for indication events to occur on its handle set. The reactor event loop thread may therefore need to be notified explicitly when other threads change the contents of its demultiplexing table by calling its methods for registering and removing event handlers. It may not otherwise find out about these changes until much later, which may impede its responsiveness to important events.

   An efficient way for an application thread to notify the reactor thread is to pre-establish a pair of 'writer/reader' IPC handles when a reactor is initialized, such as a UNIX pipe or a 'loopback' TCP Socket connection. The reader handle is registered with the reactor along with a special 'notification event handler', whose purpose is simply to wake up the reactor whenever a byte is sent to it via its connected writer handle.

   When any application thread calls the reactor's methods for registering and removing event handlers, they update the demultiplexing table and then send a byte to the writer handle. This wakes up the reactor's event loop thread and allows it to reconstruct its updated handle set before waiting on its synchronous event demultiplexer again.

Concurrent Event Handlers. The *Implementation* section described a single-threaded reactive dispatching design in which event handlers borrow the thread of control of a reactor. Event handlers can also run in their own thread of control. This allows a reactor to demultiplex and dispatch new indication events concurrently with the processing of hook methods dispatched previously to its event handlers. The Active Object (369), Leader/Followers (447), and Half-Sync/Half-Async (423) patterns can be used to implement concurrent concrete event handlers.

Concurrent Synchronous Event Demultiplexer. The synchronous event demultiplexer described in the *Implementation* section is called *serially* by a reactor in a single thread of control. However, other types of synchronous event demultiplexers, such as the WaitForMultiple-

`Objects()` function, can be called *concurrently* on the same handle set by multiple threads.

When it is possible to initiate an operation on one handle without the operation blocking, the concurrent synchronous event demultiplexer returns a handle to one of its calling threads. This can then dispatch the appropriate hook method on the associated event handler.

Calling the synchronous event demultiplexer concurrently can improve application throughput, by allowing multiple threads to simultaneously demultiplex and dispatch events to their event handlers. However, the reactor implementation can become much more complex and much less portable.

For example, it may be necessary to perform a reference count of the dispatching of event handler hook methods. It may also be necessary to queue calls to the reactor's methods for registering and removing event handlers, by using the Command pattern [GoF95] to defer changes until no threads are dispatching hook methods on an event handler. Applications may also become more complex if concrete event handlers must be made thread-safe.

Re-entrant Reactors. In general, concrete event handlers just *react* when called by a reactor and do not invoke the reactor's event loop themselves. However, certain situations may require concrete event handlers to retrieve specific events by invoking a reactor's `handle_events()` method to run its event loop. For example, the CORBA asynchronous method invocation (AMI) feature [ARSK00] requires an ORB Core to support nested `work_pending()`/`perform_work()` ORB event loops. If the ORB Core uses the Reactor pattern [SC99], therefore, its reactor implementation must be re-entrant.

A common strategy for making a reactor re-entrant is to copy the handle set state information residing in its demultiplexing table to the run-time stack before calling the synchronous event demultiplexer. This strategy ensures that any changes to the handle set will be local to that particular nesting level of the reactor.

Integrated Demultiplexing of Timer and I/O Events. The reactor described in the *Implementation* section focuses primarily on demultiplexing and dispatching features necessary to support our logging server example. It therefore only demultiplexes indication events on handle sets. A more general reactor implementation can integrate the demultiplexing of timer events *and* I/O events.

A reactor's timer mechanism should allow applications to register time-based concrete event handlers. This mechanism then invokes the handle_timeout() methods of the event handlers at an application-specified future time. The timer mechanism in a reactor can be implemented using various strategies, including heaps [BaLee98], delta-lists [CoSte91], or timing wheels [VaLa97]:

- A heap is a 'partially-ordered, almost-complete binary tree' that ensures the average- and worst-case time complexity for inserting or deleting a concrete event handler is *O(log n)*.

- Delta-lists store time in 'relative' units represented as offsets or 'deltas' from the earliest timer value at the front of the list.

- Timing wheels use a circular buffer that makes it possible to start, stop, and maintain timers within the range of the wheel in constant *O(1)* time.

➥   Several changes are required to the Reactor interface defined in implementation activity 2 (189) to enable applications to schedule, cancel, and invoke timer-based event handlers:

```
class Reactor {
public:
    // ... same as in implementation activity 2 ...

    // Schedule a <handler> to be dispatched at
    // the <future_time>.  Returns a timer id that can
    // be used to cancel the timer.
    timer_id schedule (Event_Handler *handler,
                       const void *act,
                       const Time_Value &future_time);

    // Cancel the <Event_Handler> matching the <timer_id>
    // value returned from <schedule>.
    void cancel (timer_id id, const void **act = 0);

    // Expire all timers <= <expire_time>.  This
    // method must be called manually since it
    // is not invoked asynchronously.
    void expire (const Time_Value &expire_time);
private:
    // ...
};
```

An application uses the schedule() method to schedule a concrete event handler to expire after future_time. An asynchronous completion token (ACT) (261) can be passed to schedule(). If the timer expires the ACT is passed as the value to the event handler's handle_timeout() hook method. The schedule() method returns a timer id value that identifies each event handler's registration in the reactor's timer queue uniquely. This timer id can be passed to the cancel() method to remove an event handler before it expires. If a non-NULL act parameter is passed to cancel(), it will be assigned the ACT passed by the application when the timer was scheduled originally, which makes it possible to delete dynamically-allocated ACTs to avoid memory leaks.

To complete the integration of timer and I/O event demultiplexing, the reactor implementation must be enhanced to allow for both the timer queue's scheduled event handler deadlines and the timeout parameter passed to the handle_events() method. This method is typically generalized to wait for the closest deadline, which is either the timeout parameter or the earliest deadline in the timer queue. ❏

Known uses **InterViews** [LC87]. The Reactor pattern is implemented by the InterViews windowing system, where it is known as the Dispatcher. The InterViews Dispatcher is used to define an application's main event loop and to manage connections to one or more physical GUI displays. InterViews therefore illustrates how the Reactor pattern can be used to implement reactive event handling for graphical user interface systems that play the role of both client and server.

The **Xt toolkit** from the X Windows distribution uses the Reactor pattern to implement its main event loop. Unlike the Reactor pattern implementation described in the *Implementation* section, callbacks in the Xt toolkit use C function pointers rather than event handler objects. The Xt toolkit is another example of how the Reactor pattern can be used to implement reactive event handling for graphical user interface systems that play the role of both client and server.

ACE Reactor Framework [Sch97]. The ACE framework uses an object-oriented framework implementation of the Reactor pattern as its core event demultiplexer and dispatcher. ACE provides a class, called ACE_Reactor, that defines a common interface to a variety of reactor implementations, such as the ACE_Select_Reactor and the

ACE_WFMO_Reactor. These two reactor implementations can be created using different synchronous event demultiplexers, such as WaitForMultipleObjects() and select(), respectively.

The **ORB Core** component in many implementations of CORBA [OMG98a], such as TAO [SC99] and ORBacus, use the Reactor pattern to demultiplex and dispatch client requests to servants that process the requests.

Call Center Management System. The Reactor pattern has been used to manage events routed by Event Servers [SchSu94] between PBXs and supervisors in a Call Center Management system.

Project Spectrum. The high-speed I/O transfer subsystem of Project Spectrum [PHS96] uses the Reactor pattern to demultiplex and dispatch events in an electronic medical imaging system.

Receiving phone calls. The Reactor pattern occurs frequently in everyday life, for example in telephony. Consider yourself as an event handler that registers with a reactor—a telecommunication network—to 'handle' calls received on a particular phone number—the handle. When somebody calls your phone number, the network notifies you that a 'call request' event is pending by ringing your phone. After you pick up the phone, you react to this request and 'process' it by carrying out a conversation with the connected party.

Consequences   The Reactor pattern offers the following **benefits**:

Separation of concerns. The Reactor pattern decouples application-independent demultiplexing and dispatching mechanisms from application-specific hook method functionality. The application-independent mechanisms can be designed as reusable components that know how to demultiplex indication events and dispatch the appropriate hook methods defined by event handlers. Conversely, the application-specific functionality in a hook method knows how to perform a particular type of service.

Modularity, reusability, and configurability. The pattern decouples event-driven application functionality into several components. For example, connection-oriented services can be decomposed into two components: one for establishing connections and another for receiving and processing data.

This decoupling enables the development and configuration of generic event handler components, such as acceptors, connectors, and service handlers, that are loosely integrated together through a reactor. This modularity helps promote greater software component reuse, because modifying or extending the functionality of the service handlers need not affect the implementation of the acceptor and connector components.

➡ In our logging server, the `Logging_Acceptor` class can easily be generalized to create the acceptor component described in the Acceptor-Connector pattern (285). This generic acceptor can be reused for many different connection-oriented services, such as file transfer, remote log-in, and video-on-demand. It is thus straightforward to add new functionality to the `Logging_Handler` class without affecting the reusable acceptor component. ❑

Portability. UNIX platforms offer two synchronous event demultiplexing functions, `select()` [Ste98] and `poll()` [Rago93], whereas on Win32 platforms the `WaitForMultipleObjects()` [Sol98] or `select()` functions can be used to demultiplex events synchronously. Although these demultiplexing calls all detect and report the occurrence of one or more indication events that may occur simultaneously on multiple event sources, their APIs are subtly different. By decoupling the reactor's interface from the lower-level operating system synchronous event demultiplexing functions used in its implementation, the Reactor pattern therefore enables applications to be ported more readily across platforms.

Coarse-grained concurrency control. Reactor pattern implementations serialize the invocation of event handlers at the level of event demultiplexing and dispatching within an application process or thread. This coarse-grained concurrency control can eliminate the need for more complicated synchronization within an application process.

The Reactor pattern can also incur the following **liabilities**:

Restricted applicability. The Reactor pattern can be applied most efficiently if the operating system supports synchronous event demultiplexing on handle sets. If the operating system does not provide this support, however, it is possible to emulate the semantics of the Reactor pattern using multiple threads within the reactor implementation. This is possible, for example, by associating one thread to process each handle.

Whenever events are available on a handle, its associated thread reads the event and places it on a queue that is processed sequentially by the reactor implementation. This design can be inefficient, however, because it serializes all the event handler threads. Thus, synchronization and context switching overhead increases without enhancing application-level parallelism.

Non-pre-emptive. In a single-threaded application, concrete event handlers that borrow the thread of their reactor can run to completion and prevent the reactor from dispatching other event handlers. In general, therefore, an event handler should not perform long duration operations, such as blocking I/O on an individual handle, because this can block the entire process and impede the reactor's responsiveness to clients connected to other handles.

To handle long-duration operations, such as transferring multi-megabyte images [PHS96], it may be more effective to process event handlers in separate threads. This design can be achieved via an Active Object (369) or Half-Sync/Half-Async (423) pattern variant that performs services concurrently to the reactor's main event loop.

Complexity of debugging and testing. It can be hard to debug applications structured using the Reactor pattern due to its inverted flow of control. In this pattern control oscillates between the framework infrastructure and the method call-backs on application-specific event handlers. The Reactor's inversion of control increases the difficulty of 'single-stepping' through the run-time behavior of a reactive framework within a debugger, because application developers may not understand or have access to the framework code.

These challenges are similar to the problems encountered trying to debug a compiler's lexical analyzer and parser written with lex and yacc. In such applications, debugging is straightforward when the thread of control is within user-defined semantic action routines. After the thread of control returns to the generated Deterministic Finite Automata (DFA) skeleton, however, it is hard to follow the program's logic.

See Also   The Reactor pattern is related to the Observer [GoF95] and Publisher-Subscriber [POSA1] patterns, where all dependents are informed when a single subject changes. In the Reactor pattern, however, a single handler is informed when an event of interest to the handler occurs on a source of events. In general, the Reactor pattern is used to demultiplex indication events from multiple event sources to their associated event handlers. In contrast, an observer or subscriber is often associated with only a single source of events.

The Reactor pattern is related to the Chain of Responsibility pattern [GoF95], where a request is delegated to the responsible service handler. The Reactor pattern differs from the Chain of Responsibility because the Reactor associates a specific event handler with a particular source of events. In contrast, the Chain of Responsibility pattern searches the chain to locate the first matching event handler.

The Reactor pattern can be considered a *synchronous* variant of the asynchronous Proactor pattern (215). The Proactor supports the demultiplexing and dispatching of multiple event handlers that are triggered by the *completion* of *asynchronous* operations. In contrast, the Reactor pattern is responsible for demultiplexing and dispatching multiple event handlers that are triggered when indication events signal that it is possible to *initiate* an operation *synchronously* without blocking.

The Active Object pattern (369) decouples method execution from method invocation to simplify synchronized access to shared state by methods invoked in different threads. The Reactor pattern is often used in lieu of the Active Object pattern when threads are unavailable or the overhead and complexity of threading is undesirable.

The Reactor pattern can be used as the underlying synchronous event demultiplexer for the Leader/Followers (447) and Half-Sync/Half-Async (423) pattern implementations. Moreover, if the events processed by a reactor's event handlers are all short-lived, it may be possible to use the Reactor pattern in lieu of these other two patterns. This simplification can reduce application programming effort significantly and potentially improve performance, as well.

Java does not offer a synchronous demultiplexer for network events. In particular, it does not encapsulate `select()` due to the challenges of supporting synchronous demultiplexing in a portable way. It is therefore hard to implement the Reactor pattern directly in Java. However, Java's event handling in AWT, particularly the listener or delegation-based model, resembles the Reactor pattern in the following way:

- Typically, application developers reuse prefabricated graphical components, such as different kinds of buttons. Developers typically write event handlers that encode the application-specific logic to process certain events, such as a mouse-click on a button. Before receiving button-related events on a button, an event handler must register itself with this button for all events of this type, which are called `ActionEvents`.

- When the underlying native code is called by the Java virtual machine (JVM), it notifies the button's peer, which is the first Java layer on top of the native code. The button peer is platform-specific and posts a new `ActionEvent` to be executed in the event handler thread, which is a specific-purpose thread created by the JVM.

- Events are then entered into a queue and an `EventDispatch-Thread` object runs a loop to 'pump' events further up the AWT widget hierarchy, which ultimately dispatches the event to all registered listeners stored in a recursive data structure called `AWT-EventMulticaster`.

All pumping, dispatching, and subsequent event processing runs synchronously in the same thread, which resembles the synchronous processing of events by a reactor.

Credits   John Vlissides, the shepherd of the [PLoPD1] version of Reactor, Ralph Johnson, Doug Lea, Roger Whitney, and Uwe Zdun provided many useful suggestions for documenting the original Reactor concept in pattern form.

Proactor

The *Proactor* architectural pattern allows event-driven applications to efficiently demultiplex and dispatch service requests triggered by the completion of asynchronous operations, to achieve the performance benefits of concurrency without incurring certain of its liabilities.

Example Consider a networking application that must perform multiple operations simultaneously, such as a high-performance Web server that processes HTTP requests sent from multiple remote Web browsers [HPS99]. When a user wants to download content from a URL four steps occur:

1 The browser establishes a connection to the Web server designated in the URL and then sends it an HTTP GET request.

2 The Web server receives the browser's CONNECT indication event, accepts the connection, reads and then parses the request.

3 The server opens and reads the specified file.

4 Finally, the server sends the contents of the file back to the Web browser and closes the connection.

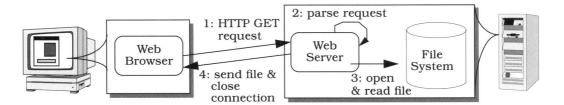

One way to implement a Web server is to use a reactive event demultiplexing model in accordance with the Reactor pattern (179). In this design, whenever a Web browser connects to a Web server, a new event handler is created to read, parse, and process the request and transfer the contents of the file back to the browser. This handler is registered with a reactor that coordinates the synchronous demultiplexing and dispatching of each indication event to its associated event handler.

Although a reactive Web server design is straightforward to program, it does not scale up to support many simultaneous users and/or long-duration user requests, because it serializes all HTTP processing at the event demultiplexing layer. As a result, only one GET request can be dispatched and processed iteratively at any given time.

A potentially more scalable way to implement a Web server is to use some form of *synchronous multi-threading*. In this model a separate server thread processes each browser's HTTP GET request [HS98]. For example, a new thread can be spawned dynamically for each request, or a pool of threads can be pre-spawned and managed using the Leader/Followers (447) or Half-Sync/Half-Async (423) patterns. In either case each thread performs connection establishment, HTTP request reading, request parsing, and file transfer operations *synchronously*—that is, server processing operations block until they complete.

Synchronous multi-threading is a common concurrency model. However, problems with efficiency, scalability, programming complexity, and portability may occur, as discussed in the *Example* section of the Reactor pattern (179).

On operating systems that support asynchronous I/O efficiently, our Web server can therefore invoke operations asynchronously to improve its scalability further. For example, on Windows NT the Web server can be implemented to invoke asynchronous Win32 operations that process externally-generated indication events, such as TCP CONNECT and HTTP GET requests, and transmit requested files to Web browsers asynchronously.

When these asynchronous operations complete, the operating system returns the associated completion events containing their results to the Web server, which processes these events and performs the appropriate actions before returning to its event loop. Building software that achieves the potential performance of this asynchronous event processing model is hard due to the separation in time and space of asynchronous invocations and their subsequent completion events. Thus, asynchronous programming requires a sophisticated yet comprehensible event demultiplexing and dispatching mechanism.

Context An event-driven application that receives and processes multiple service requests asynchronously.

Problem   The performance of event-driven applications, particularly servers, in a distributed system can often be improved by processing multiple service requests asynchronously. When asynchronous service processing completes, the application must handle the corresponding completion events delivered by the operating system to indicate the end of the asynchronous computations.

For example, an application must demultiplex and dispatch each completion event to an internal component that processes the results of an asynchronous operation. This component can reply to external clients, such as a Web browser client, or to internal clients, such as the Web server component that initiated the asynchronous operation originally. To support this asynchronous computation model effectively requires the resolution of four *forces*:

- To improve scalability and latency, an application should process multiple completion events simultaneously without allowing long-duration operations to delay other operation processing unduly.

- To maximize throughput, any unnecessary context switching, synchronization, and data movement among CPUs should be avoided, as outlined in the *Example* section.

- Integrating new or improved services with existing completion event demultiplexing and dispatching mechanisms should require minimal effort.

- Application code should largely be shielded from the complexity of multi-threading and synchronization mechanisms.

Solution   Split application services into two parts: long-duration operations that execute asynchronously and completion handlers that process the results of these operations when they finish. Integrate the demultiplexing of completion events, which are delivered when asynchronous operations finish, with their dispatch to the completion handlers that process them. Decouple these completion event demultiplexing and dispatching mechanisms from the application-specific processing of completion events within completion handlers.

In detail: for every service offered by an application, introduce *asynchronous operations* that initiate the processing of service requests 'proactively' via a *handle*, together with *completion handlers* that process completion events containing the results of these asynchronous operations. An asynchronous operation is invoked within an application by an *initiator*, for example, to accept incoming connection requests from remote applications. It is executed by an *asynchronous operation processor*. When an operation finishes executing, the asynchronous operation processor inserts a completion event containing that operation's results into a *completion event queue*.

This queue is waited on by an *asynchronous event demultiplexer* called by a *proactor*. When the asynchronous event demultiplexer removes a completion event from its queue, the proactor demultiplexes and dispatches this event to the application-specific *completion handler* associated with the asynchronous operation. This completion handler then processes the results of the asynchronous operation, potentially invoking additional asynchronous operations that follow the same chain of activities outlined above.

Structure   The Proactor pattern includes nine participants:

Handles are provided by operating systems to identify entities, such as network connections or open files, that can generate completion events. Completion events are generated either in response to external service requests, such as connection or data requests arriving from remote applications, or in response to operations an application generates internally, such as time-outs or asynchronous I/O system calls.

➡   Our Web server creates a separate socket handle for each Web browser connection. In Win32 each socket handle is created in 'overlapped I/O' mode, which means that operations invoked on the handles run asynchronously. The Windows NT I/O subsystem also generates completion events when asynchronously-executed operations complete.   ❑

Asynchronous operations represent potentially long-duration operations that are used in the implementation of services, such as reading and writing data asynchronously via a socket handle. After an asynchronous operation is invoked, it executes without blocking its caller's thread of control. Thus, the caller can perform other operations. If an operation must wait for the occurrence of an event, such as a connection request generated by a remote application, its execution will be deferred until the event arrives.

➥ Our proactive Web server invokes the Win32 `AcceptEx()` operation to accept connections from Web browsers asynchronously. After accepting connections the Web server invokes the Win32 asynchronous `ReadFile()` and `WriteFile()` operations to communicate with its connected browsers. ❑

Class	*Collaborator*	*Class*	*Collaborator*
Handle		Asynchronous Operation	• Handle • Asynchronous Operation Processor
Responsibility • A handle identifies an operating system resource that can be the target of asynchronous operation invocations or a source of completion events in an operation system		*Responsibility* • Defines an operation that can be executed asynchronously • Used to implement a service	

A *completion handler* specifies an interface that consists of one or more hook methods [Pree95] [GHJV95]. These methods represent the set of operations available for processing information returned in the application-specific completion events that are generated when asynchronous operations finish executing.

Concrete completion handlers specialize the completion handler to define a particular application service by implementing the inherited hook method(s). These hook methods process the results contained in the completion events they receive when the asynchronous operations associated with the completion handler finish executing. A concrete completion handler is associated with a handle that it can use to invoke asynchronous operations itself.

For example, a concrete completion handler can itself receive data from an asynchronous read operation it invoked on a handle earlier. When this occurs, the concrete completion handler can process the data it received and then invoke an asynchronous write operation to return the results to its connected remote peer application.

➥ Our Web server's two concrete completion handlers—HTTP acceptor and HTTP handler—perform completion processing on the results of asynchronous `AcceptEx()`, `ReadFile()`, and Write-

File() operations. The HTTP acceptor is the completion handler for the asynchronous `AcceptEx()` operation—it creates and connects HTTP handlers in response to connection request events from remote Web browsers. The HTTP handlers then use asynchronous `Read-File()` and `WriteFile()` operations to process subsequent requests from remote Web browsers.   ❑

Class	Collaborator	Class	Collaborator
Completion Handler		Concrete Completion Handler	• Handle
Responsibility		**Responsibility**	
• Defines an interface for processing results of asynchronous operations		• Processes results of asynchronous operations in an application-specific manner	

Asynchronous operations are invoked on a particular handle and run to completion by an *asynchronous operation processor*, which is often implemented by an operating system kernel. When an asynchronous operation finishes executing the asynchronous operation processor generates the corresponding completion event. It inserts this event into the *completion event queue* associated with the handle upon which the operation was invoked. This queue buffers completion events while they wait to be demultiplexed to their associated completion handler.

Class	Collaborator	Class	Collaborator
Asynchronous Operation Processor	• Asynchronous Operation • Completion Event Queue	Completion Event Queue	• Handle
Responsibility		**Responsibility**	
• Executes asynchronous operations • Queues completion events on a completion event queue when asynchronous operations complete		• Buffers completion events while they are waiting to be removed by an asynchronous event demultiplexer	

➡   In our Web server example, the Windows NT operating system is the asynchronous operation processor. Similarly, the completion event queue is a Win32 *completion port* [Sol98], which is a queue of completion events maintained by the Windows NT kernel on behalf of an application. When an asynchronous operation finishes the Windows NT kernel queues the completion event on the completion port associated with the handle on which the asynchronous operation was originally invoked.   ❏

An *asynchronous event demultiplexer* is a function that waits for completion events to be inserted into a *completion event queue* when an asynchronous operation has finished executing. The asynchronous event demultiplexer function then removes one or more completion event results from the queue and returns to its caller.

➡   One asynchronous event demultiplexer in Windows NT is Get-QueuedCompletionStatus(). This Win32 function allows event-driven proactive applications to wait up to an application-specified amount of time to retrieve the next available completion event.   ❏

A *proactor* provides an event loop for an application process or thread. In this event loop, a proactor calls an asynchronous event demultiplexer to wait for completion events to occur. When an event arrives the asynchronous event demultiplexer returns. The proactor then demultiplexes the event to its associated completion handler and dispatches the appropriate hook method on the handler to process the results of the completion event.

Class	*Collaborator*	*Class*	*Collaborator*
Asynchronous Event Demultiplexer	• Completion Event Queue	Proactor	• Completion Handler • Asynchronous Event Demultiplexer • Completion Event Queue
Responsibility • Can block waiting for completion events to occur on a completion event queue • Removes a completion event and returns it to its caller		*Responsibility* • Calls the asynchronous event demultiplexer to dequeue a completion event • Demultiplexes and dispatches completion events to completion handler hook methods	

➡   Our Web server application calls the proactor's event loop method. This method calls the GetQueuedCompletionStatus() Win32 function, which is an asynchronous event demultiplexer that waits until it can dequeue the next available completion event from the proactor's completion port. The proactor's event loop method uses information in the completion event to demultiplex the next event to the appropriate concrete completion handler and dispatch its hook method.   ❏

An *initiator* is an entity *local* to an application that invokes asynchronous operations on an asynchronous operation processor. The initiator often processes the results of the asynchronous operations it invokes, in which case it also plays the role of a concrete completion handler.

➡   In our example HTTP acceptors and HTTP handlers play the role of both initiators *and* concrete completion handlers within the Web server's internal thread of control. For example, an HTTP acceptor invokes `AcceptEx()` operations that accept connection indication events asynchronously from remote Web browsers. When a connection indication event occurs, an HTTP acceptor creates an HTTP handler, which then invokes an asynchronous `ReadFile()` operation to retrieve and process HTTP `GET` requests from a connected Web browser.   ❏

Class	Collaborator
Initiator	• Asynchronous Operation Processor
Responsibility	• Asynchronous Operation
• Invokes asynchronous operations	• Concrete Completion Handler
• May optionally serve as a concrete completion handler	• Proactor

Note how in the Proactor pattern the application components, represented by initiators and concrete completion handlers, are *proactive* entities. They instigate the control and data flow within an application by invoking asynchronous operations *proactively* on an asynchronous operation processor.

When these asynchronous operations complete, the asynchronous operation processor and proactor collaborate via a completion event queue. They use this queue to demultiplex the resulting completion events back to their associated concrete completion handlers and dispatch these handlers' hook methods. After processing a completion event, a completion handler may invoke new asynchronous operations proactively.

The structure of the participants in the Proactor pattern is illustrated in the following class diagram:

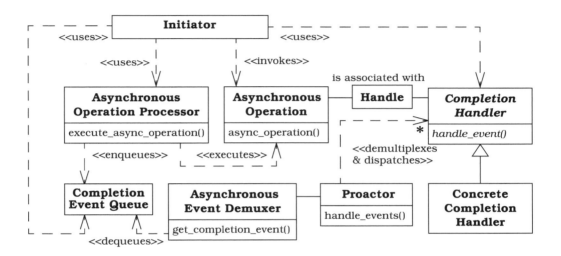

Dynamics The following collaborations occur in the Proactor pattern:

- An application component playing the role of an initiator invokes an asynchronous operation on an asynchronous operation processor via a particular handle. In addition to passing data parameters to the asynchronous operation, the initiator also passes certain completion processing parameters, such as the completion handler or a handle to the completion event queue. The asynchronous operation processor stores these parameters internally for later use.

  ➥ The HTTP handler in our Web server can instruct the operating system to read a new HTTP GET request by invoking the Read-File() operation asynchronously on a particular socket handle. When initiating this operation on the handle, the HTTP handler passes itself as the completion handler so that it can process the results of an asynchronous operation. ❏

- After an initiator invokes an operation on the asynchronous operation processor, the operation and initiator can run independently. In particular, the initiator can invoke new asynchronous operations while others continue to execute concurrently.[4] If the asynchronous operation is intended to receive a service request from a remote application, the asynchronous operation processor defers the operation until this request arrives. When the event corresponding to the expected request arrives, the asynchronous operation will finish executing.

   ➥   The Windows NT operating system defers the asynchronous `ReadFile()` operation used to read an HTTP `GET` request until this request arrives from a remote Web browser.   ❏

- When an asynchronous operation finishes executing, the asynchronous operation processor generates a completion event. This event contains the results of the asynchronous operation. The asynchronous operation processor then inserts this event into the completion event queue associated with the handle upon with the asynchronous operation was originally invoked.

   ➥   If an HTTP handler invoked an asynchronous `ReadFile()` operation to read an HTTP `GET` request, the Windows NT operating system will report the completion status in the completion event, such as its success or failure and the number of bytes read.   ❏

- When an application is ready to process the completion events resulting from its asynchronous operations, it invokes the proactor's event loop entry-point method, which we call `handle_ events()`. This method calls an asynchronous event demultiplexer[5] to wait on its completion event queue for completion events to be inserted by the asynchronous operation processor. After removing a completion event from the queue the proactor's `handle_events()` method demultiplexes the event to its associated completion handler. It then dispatches the appropriate hook method on the completion handler, passing it the results of the asynchronous operation.

---

4. For simplicity this case is not illustrated in the sequence diagram on page 226.

5. Due to space limitations in the sequence diagram shown on page 226 we assume that the asynchronous event demultiplexer is integrated with the proactor component.

➥   The proactor in our Web server example uses a Win32 completion port as its completion event queue. Similarly, it uses the Win32 GetQueuedCompletionStatus() function [Sol98] as its asynchronous event demultiplexer to remove completion events from a completion port.   ❑

- The concrete completion handler then processes the completion results it receives. If the completion handler returns a result to its caller, two situations are possible. First, the completion handler that processes the results of the asynchronous operations also can be the initiator that invoked the operation originally. In this case the completion handler need not perform additional work to return the result to its caller, because it *is* the caller.

  Second, a remote application or an application internal component may have requested the asynchronous operation. In this case, the completion handler can invoke an asynchronous write operation on its transport handle to return results to the remote application.

  ➥   In response to an HTTP GET request from a remote Web browser, an HTTP handler might instruct the Windows NT operating system to transmit a large file across a network by calling WriteFile() asynchronously. After the operating system completes the asynchronous operation successfully the resulting completion event indicates the number of bytes transferred to the HTTP handler. The entire file may not be transferred in one Write-File() operation due to transport-layer flow control. In this case the HTTP handler can invoke another asynchronous WriteFile() operation at the appropriate file offset.   ❑

- After the completion handler finishes its processing it can invoke other asynchronous operations, in which case the whole cycle outlined in this section begins again.

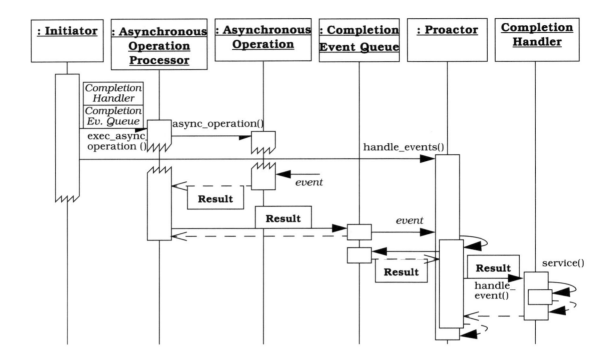

Implementation   The participants in the Proactor pattern can be decomposed into two
layers:

- *Demultiplexing/dispatching infrastructure layer components.* This
  layer performs generic, application-independent strategies for
  executing asynchronous operations. It also demultiplexes and
  dispatches completion events from these asynchronous operations
  to their associated completion handlers.

- *Application layer components.* This layer defines asynchronous
  operations and concrete completion handlers that perform
  application-specific service processing.

The implementation activities in this section start with the generic
demultiplexing/dispatching infrastructure components and then
cover the application components. We focus on a proactor
implementation that is designed to invoke asynchronous operations
and dispatch hook methods on their associated completion handlers
using a single thread of control. The *Variants* section describes the

activities associated with developing multi-threaded proactor implementations.

1 *Separate application services into asynchronous operations and completion handlers.* To implement the Proactor pattern, application services must be designed to separate the initiation of asynchronous operations via a handle from the processing of these operations' results. *Asynchronous operations* are often long-duration and/or concerned with I/O, such as reading and writing data via a socket handle or communicating with a database. The results of asynchronous operations are processed by *completion handlers*. In addition to processing results, completion handlers can play the role of initiators, that is, they invoke asynchronous operations themselves.

The products of this activity are a set of asynchronous operations, a set of completion handlers, and a set of associations between each asynchronous operation and its completion handler.

2 *Define the completion handler interface.* Completion handlers specify an interface consisting of one or more hook methods [Pree95]. These hook methods represent the completion handling for application-specific completion events generated when asynchronous operations finish executing. The implementation of completion handlers consists of three sub-activities:

2.1 *Define a type to convey the results of asynchronous operation.* When an asynchronous operation completes or is canceled its completion event results must be conveyed to its completion handler. These results indicate its success or failure and the number of bytes that were transmitted successfully. The Adapter pattern [GoF95] is often used to convert information stored in a completion event into a form used to dispatch to its associated concrete completion handler.

➧ The following C++ class conveys the results of an asynchronous Win32 operation back to a concrete completion handler:

```
class Async_Result : public OVERLAPPED {
    // The Win32 OVERLAPPED struct stores the file offset
    // returned when an asynchronous operation completes.
public:
    // Dispatch to completion handler hook method.
    virtual void complete () = 0;
```

```
        // Set/get number of bytes transferred by an
        // asynchronous operation.
        void bytes_transferred (u_long);
        u_long bytes_transferred () const;

        // Set/get the status of the asynchronous operation,
        // i.e., whether it succeeded or failed.
        void status (u_long);
        u_long status () const;

        // Set/get error value if the asynchronous operation
        // failed or was canceled by the initiator.
        void error (u_long);
        u_long error () const;
private:
        // ... data members omitted for brevity ...
    };
```

Deriving `Async_Result` from the `OVERLAPPED` struct allows
applications to add custom state and methods to the results of
asynchronous operations. C++ inheritance is used because the
Win32 API does not provide a more direct way to pass a per-operation
result object to the operating system when an asynchronous
operation is invoked.   ❑

2.2   *Determine the type of the dispatching target.* Two types of completion
      handlers can be associated with a handle to serve as the target of a
      proactor's dispatching mechanism, objects and pointers to functions.
      Implementations of the Proactor pattern can choose the type of
      dispatching target based on the same criteria described in
      implementation activity 1.1 of the Reactor (179) pattern.

2.3   *Define the completion handler dispatch interface strategy.* We next
      define the type of interface supported by the completion handler to
      process completion events. As with the Reactor pattern (179),
      assuming that we use completion handler objects rather than
      pointers to functions, two general strategies exist:

      • *Single-method dispatch interface strategy.* The class diagram in the
        Structure section illustrates an implementation of the
        `Completion_Handler` interface that contains a single event han-
        dling method, which we call `handle_event()`. A proactor uses this
        method to dispatch completion events to their associated comple-
        tion handlers. In this case the type of completion event that has
        occurred is passed as a parameter to the method. The second pa-
        rameter is the base class for all asynchronous results, which,

depending on the completion event, can be further downcast to the correct type.

➡ The following C++ abstract base class illustrates the single-method dispatch interface strategy. We start by defining useful type definitions and enumeration literals that can be used by both the single-method and multi-method dispatch interface strategies:

```
typedef unsigned int Event_Type;
enum {
    // Types of indication events.
    READ_EVENT = 01,
    ACCEPT_EVENT = 01, // An "alias" for READ_EVENT.
    WRITE_EVENT = 02, TIMEOUT_EVENT = 04,
    SIGNAL_EVENT = 010, CLOSE_EVENT = 020
    // These values are powers of two so
    // their bits can be "or'd" together efficiently.
};
```

Next, we implement the Completion_Handler class:

```
class Completion_Handler {
public:
    // Cache the <proactor> so that hook methods can
    // invoke asynchronous operations on <proactor>.
    Completion_Handler (Proactor *proactor):
        proactor_ (proactor) { }

    // Virtual destruction.
    virtual ~Completion_Handler ();

    // Hook method dispatched by cached <proactor_> to
    // handle completion events of a particular type that
    // occur on the <handle>. <Async_Result> reports the
    // results of the completed asynchronous operation.
    virtual void handle_event
        (HANDLE handle, Event_Type et,
         const Async_Result &result) = 0;

    // Returns underlying I/O <HANDLE>.
    virtual HANDLE get_handle () const = 0;
private:
    // Cached <Proactor>.
    Proactor *proactor_;
};                                                                    ❏
```

The single-method dispatch interface strategy makes it possible to add new types of events without changing the class interface. However, to handle a specific event, this strategy encourages the use of C++ switch and if statements in the concrete event handler's handle_event() method implementation, which degrades its internal extensibility.

- *Multi-method dispatch interface strategy.* A different strategy for implementing the Completion_Handler interface is to define separate hook methods for handling each type of event, such as handle_read(), handle_write(), or handle_accept(). This strategy can be more extensible than the single-method dispatch interface because the demultiplexing is performed by a proactor implementation, rather than by a concrete event handler's handle_event() method implementation.

➥ The following C++ abstract base class illustrates a multi-method interface used by a proactor for network events in our Windows NT-based Web server example:

```
class Completion_Handler {
public:
    // The <proactor> is cached to allow hook methods to
    // invoke asynchronous operations on <proactor>.
    Completion_Handler (Proactor *proactor):
        proactor_ (proactor) { }

    // Virtual destruction.
    virtual ~Completion_Handler ();

    // The next 3 methods use <Async_Result> to report
    // results of completed asynchronous operation.
    // Dispatched by <proactor_> when an asynchronous
    // read operation completes.
    virtual void handle_read
        (HANDLE handle, const Async_Result &result) = 0;
    // Dispatched by <proactor_> when an asynchronous
    // write operation completes.
    virtual void handle_write
        (HANDLE handle, const Async_Result &result) = 0;
    // Dispached by <proactor_> when an asynchronous
    // <accept> operation completes.
    virtual void handle_accept
        (HANDLE handle, const Async_Result &result) = 0;

    // Dispatched by <proactor_> when a timeout expires.
    virtual void handle_timeout
        (const Time_Value &tv, const void *act) = 0;

    // Returns underlying I/O <HANDLE>.
    virtual HANDLE get_handle () const = 0;
```

```
private:
    // Cached <Proactor>.
    Proactor *proactor_;
};                                                                    ❏
```

The multi-method dispatch interface strategy makes it easy to override methods in the base class selectively, which avoids further demultiplexing via `switch` or `if` statements in the hook method implementation. However, this strategy requires pattern implementors to anticipate the hook methods in advance. The various `handle_*()` hook methods in the `Completion_Handler` interface above are tailored for networking events. However, these methods do not encompass all the types of events handled via the Win32 `WaitForMultipleObjects()` mechanism, such as synchronization object events [SchSt95].

Both the single-method and multiple-method dispatch interface strategies are implementations of the Hook Method [Pree95] and Template Method [GoF95] patterns. The intent of these patterns is to provide well-defined hooks that can be specialized by applications and called back by lower-level dispatching code.

Completion handlers are often designed to act both as a target of a proactor's completion dispatching *and* an initiator that invokes asynchronous operations, as shown by the `HTTP_Handler` class in the *Example Resolved* section. Therefore, the constructor of class `Completion_Handler` associates a `Completion_Handler` object with a pointer to a proactor. This design allows a `Completion_Handler`'s hook methods to invoke new asynchronous operations whose completion processing will be dispatched ultimately by the same proactor.

3   *Implement the asynchronous operation processor.* An asynchronous operation processor executes operations asynchronously on behalf of initiators. Its primary responsibilities therefore include:

- Defining the asynchronous operation interface

- Implementing a mechanism to execute operations asynchronously and generating and

- Queueing completion events when an operation finishes

3.1   *Define the asynchronous operation interface.* Asynchronous opera-
      tions can be passed various parameters, such as a handle,[6] data
      buffers, buffer lengths, and information used to perform completion
      processing when the operation finishes. Two issues must be ad-
      dressed when designing a programming interface that initiators use
      to invoke asynchronous operations on an asynchronous operation
      processor:

- *Maximizing portability and flexibility.* Asynchronous operations can
  be used to read and write data on multiple types of I/O devices,
  such as networks and files, and on multiple operating systems,
  such as Windows NT, VMS, Solaris, and Linux. The Wrapper
  Facade (47) and Bridge [GoF95] patterns can be applied to
  decouple the asynchronous operation interface from underlying
  operating system dependencies and ensure the interface works for
  multiple types of I/O devices.

- *Handling multiple completion handlers, proactors, and completion
  event queues efficiently and concisely.* More than one completion
  handler, proactor, and completion event queue can be used
  simultaneously within an application. For example, different
  proactors can be associated with threads running at different
  priorities, to provide different quality of service levels for processing
  different completion handlers. In addition to its data parameters,
  an asynchronous operation must then indicate which handle,
  concrete completion handler, proactor, and completion event
  queue to use when processing the completion of asynchronous
  operations.

  A common strategy to consolidate all this completion processing
  information efficiently is to apply the Asynchronous Completion
  Token pattern (261). When an initiator invokes an asynchronous
  operation on a handle, an asynchronous completion token (ACT)
  can then be passed to the asynchronous operation processor,
  which can store this ACT for later use. Each ACT contains
  information that identifies a particular operation and guides its
  subsequent completion processing.

---

6. The handles themselves are often provided by the operating system and need not be
implemented.

When an asynchronous operation finishes executing, the asynchronous operation processor locates the operation's ACT it stored earlier and associates it with the completion event it generates. It then inserts this updated completion event into the appropriate completion event queue. Ultimately, the proactor that runs the application's event loop will use an asynchronous event demultiplexer to remove the completion event results and ACT from its completion event queue. The proactor will then use this ACT to complete its demultiplexing and dispatching of the completion event results to the completion handler designated by the ACT.

➥ Although our Web server is implemented using Win32 asynchronous Socket operations, we apply the Wrapper Facade pattern (47) to generalize this class and make it platform-independent. It can therefore be used for other types of I/O devices supported by an asynchronous operation processor.

The following `Async_Stream` class interface is used by HTTP handlers in our Web server example to invoke asynchronous operations:

```cpp
class Async_Stream {
public:
    // Constructor 'zeros out' the data members.
    Async_Stream ();

    // Initialization method.
    void open (Completion_Handler *handler,
               HANDLE handle, Proactor *proactor);

    // Invoke an asynchronous read operation.
    void async_read (void *buf, u_long n_bytes);

    // Invoke an asynchronous write operation.
    void async_write (const void *buf, u_long n_bytes);
private:
    // Cache parameters passed in <open>.
    Completion_Handler *completion_handler_;
    HANDLE handle_;
    Proactor *proactor_;
};
```

A concrete completion handler, such as an HTTP handler, can pass itself to open(), together with the handle on which the Async_ Stream's async_read() and async_write() methods are invoked:

```
void Async_Stream::open (Completion_Handler *handler,
                         HANDLE handle,
                         Proactor *proactor) {
    completion_handler_ = handler;
    handle_ = handle;
    proactor_ = proactor;

    // Associate handle with <proactor>'s completion
    // port, as shown in implementation activity 4.
    proactor->register_handle (handle);
}
```

To illustrate the use of asynchronous completion tokens (ACTs), consider the following implementation of the Async_Stream:: async_read() method. It uses the Win32 ReadFile() function to read up to n_bytes asynchronously and store them in its buf parameter:

```
void Async_Stream::read (void *buf, u_long n_bytes) {
    u_long bytes_read;

    OVERLAPPED *act = new // Create the ACT.
        Async_Stream_Read_Result (completion_handler_);

    ReadFile (handle_, buf, n_bytes, &bytes_read, act);
}
```

The ACT passed as a pointer to ReadFile() is a dynamically allocated instance of the Async_Stream_Read_Result class below:

```
class Async_Stream_Read_Result : public Async_Result {
public:
    // Constructor caches the completion handler.
    Async_Stream_Read_Result
        (Completion_Handler *completion_handler):
         completion_handler_ (completion_handler) { }

    // Adapter that dispatches the <handle_event>
    // hook method on cached completion handler.
    virtual void complete ();
private:
    // Cache a pointer to a completion handler.
    Completion_Handler *completion_handler_;
};
```

This class plays the role of an ACT and an adapter [GoF95]. It inherits from Async_Result, which itself inherits from the Win32

OVERLAPPED struct, as shown in implementation activity 2.1 (227). The ACT can be passed as the lpOverlapped parameter to the ReadFile() asynchronous function. ReadFile() forwards the ACT to the Windows NT operating system, which stores it for later use.

When the asynchronous ReadFile() operation finishes it generates a completion event that contains the ACT it received when this operation was invoked. When the proactor's handle_events() method removes this event from its completion event queue, it invokes the complete() method on the Async_Stream_Read_Result. This adapter method then dispatches the completion handler's handle_event() hook method to pass the event, as shown in implementation activity 5.4 (240). ❑

3.2 *Choose the asynchronous operation processing mechanism.* When an initiator invokes an asynchronous operation, an asynchronous operation processor executes the operation without blocking the initiator's thread of control. An asynchronous operation processor provides mechanisms for managing ACTs and executing operations asynchronously. It also generates completion events when operations finish and queues the events into the appropriate completion event queue.

Some asynchronous operation processors allow initiators to cancel asynchronous operations. However, completion events are still generated. Thus, ACTs and other resources can be reclaimed properly by completion handlers.

Certain operating environments provide these asynchronous operation execution and completion event generation mechanisms, such as Real-time POSIX [POSIX95] and Windows NT [Sol98]. In this case implementing the asynchronous completion processor participant simply requires mapping existing operating system APIs onto the asynchronous operation wrapper facade (47) interfaces described in implementation activity 3.1 (232). The *Variants* section describes techniques for emulating an asynchronous operation processor on operating system platforms that do not support this feature natively.

4 *Define the proactor interface.* The proactor's interface is used by applications to invoke an event loop that removes completion events from a completion event queue, demultiplexes them to their designated completion handlers, and dispatches their associated

hook method. The proactor interface is often accessed via a singleton [GoF95] because a single proactor is often sufficient for each application process.

The Proactor pattern can use the Bridge pattern [GoF95] to shield applications from complex and non-portable completion event demultiplexing and dispatching mechanisms. The proactor interface corresponds to the abstraction participant in the Bridge pattern, whereas a platform-specific proactor instance is accessed internally via a pointer, in accordance with the implementation hierarchy in the Bridge pattern.

➥   The proactor interface in our Web server defines an abstraction for associating handles with completion ports and running the application's event loop proactively:

```
class Proactor {
public:
    // Associate <handle> with the <Proactor>'s
    // completion event queue.
    void register_handle (HANDLE handle);

    // Entry point into the proactive event loop. The
    // <timeout> can bound time waiting for events.
    void handle_events (Time_Value *wait_time = 0);

    // Define a singleton access point.
    static Proactor *instance ();
private:
    // Use the Bridge pattern to hold a pointer to
    // the <Proactor_Implementation>.
    Proactor_Implementation *proactor_impl_;
};                                                              ❑
```

A proactor interface also defines a method, which we call `register_handle()`, that associates a handle with the proactors completion event queue, as described in implementation activity 5.5 (240). This association ensures that the completion events generated when asynchronous operations finish executing will be inserted into a particular proactor's completion event queue.

The proactor interface also defines the main entry point method, we call it `handle_events()`, that applications use to run their proactive event loop.[7] This method calls the asynchronous event demultiplexer, which waits for completion events to arrive on its completion event queue, as discussed in implementation activity 3.1 (232). An application can use the timeout parameter to bound the time it spends waiting for completion events. Thus, the application need not block indefinitely if events never arrive.

After the asynchronous operation processor inserts a completion event into the proactor's completion event queue, the asynchronous event demultiplexer function returns. At this point the proactor's handle_events() method dequeues the completion event and uses its associated ACT to demultiplex to the asynchronous operation's completion handler and dispatch the handler's hook method.

5   *Implement the proactor interface.* Five sub-activities can be used to implement the proactor interface:

5.1   *Develop a proactor implementation hierarchy.* The proactor interface abstraction illustrated in implementation activity 4 (235) delegates all its demultiplexing and dispatching processing to a proactor implementation. This plays the role of the implementation hierarchy in the Bridge pattern [GoF95]. This design allows multiple types of proactors to be implemented and configured transparently. For example, a concrete proactor implementation can be created using different types of asynchronous event demultiplexers, such as POSIX aio_suspend() [POSIX95], or the Win32 GetQueuedCompletionStatus() or Wait-ForMultipleObjects() functions [Sol98].

➡   In our example the base class of the proactor implementation hierarchy is defined by the class Proactor_Implementation. We omit its declaration here because this class has essentially the same interface as the Proactor interface in implementation activity 4 (235). The primary difference is that its methods are purely virtual, because it forms the base of a hierarchy of concrete proactor implementations.   ❏

5.2   *Choose the completion event queue and asynchronous event demultiplexer mechanisms.* The handle_events() method of the proactor implementation calls an asynchronous event demultiplexer function, which waits on the completion event queue for the asynchronous operation processor to insert completion events. This function returns whenever there is a completion event in the queue. Asynchronous

---

7. Multiple threads can call handle_events() on the same proactor simultaneously, as described in the *Variants* section. This design is well-suited for I/O bound applications [HPS99].

event demultiplexers can be distinguished by the types of semantics they support, which include one of the following:

- *FIFO demultiplexing.* This type of asynchronous event demultiplexer function waits for completion events corresponding to any asynchronous operations that are associated with its completion event queue. The events are removed from the queue in the order in which they are inserted.

  ➥ The Win32 `GetQueuedCompletionStatus()` function allows event-driven proactive applications to wait up to an application-specified amount of time for any completion events to occur on a completion port. Events are removed in FIFO order [Sol98]. ❑

- *Selective demultiplexing.* This type of asynchronous event demultiplexer function waits selectively for a particular subset of completion events that must be passed explicitly when the function is called.

  ➥ The POSIX `aio_suspend()` function [POSIX95] and the Win32 `WaitForMultipleObjects()` function [Sol98] are passed an array parameter designating asynchronous operations explicitly. They suspend their callers for an application-specified amount of time until at least one of these asynchronous operations has completed. ❑

The completion event queue and asynchronous event demultiplexer are often existing operating system mechanisms that need not be developed by Proactor pattern implementors.

The primary difference between `GetQueuedCompletionStatus()`, `aio_suspend()`, and `WaitForMultipleObjects()` is that the latter two functions can wait selectively for completion events specified via an array parameter. Conversely, `GetQueuedCompletionStatus()` just waits for the next completion event enqueued on its completion port. Moreover, the POSIX `aio_*()` functions can only demultiplex asynchronous I/O operations, such as `aio_read()` or `aio_write()`, whereas `GetQueuedCompletionStatus()` and `WaitForMultiple-Objects()` can demultiplex other Win32 asynchronous operations, such as timers and synchronization objects.

➥ Our Web server uses a Win32 completion port as the completion event queue and the `GetQueuedCompletionStatus()` function as its asynchronous event demultiplexer:

```
BOOL GetQueuedCompletionStatus
     (HANDLE CompletionPort,
     LPDWORD lpNumberOfBytesTransferred,
     LPDWORD lpCompletionKey,
     LPOVERLAPPED *lpOverlapped,
     DWORD dwMilliseconds);
```

As shown in implementation activity 5.5 (240), our proactor implementation's `handle_events()` method uses this function to dequeue a completion event from the specified `CompletionPort`. The number of bytes transferred is returned as an 'out' parameter. The `lpOverlapped` parameter points to the ACT passed by the original asynchronous operation, such as the `ReadFile()` call in the `Async_Stream::async_read()` method shown in implementation activity 3.1 (232).

If there are no completion event results queued on the port, the function blocks the calling thread, waiting for asynchronous operations associated with the completion port to finish. The `GetQueuedCompletionStatus()` function returns when it is able to dequeue a completion event result or when the `dwMilliseconds` timeout expires. ❏

5.3 *Determine how to demultiplex completion events to completion handlers.* An efficient and concise strategy for demultiplexing completion events to completion handlers is to use the Asynchronous Completion Token pattern (261), as described in implementation activity 3.1 (232). In this strategy, when an asynchronous operation is invoked by an initiator the asynchronous operation processor is passed information used to guide subsequent completion processing. For example, a handle can be passed to identify a particular socket endpoint and completion event queue, and an ACT can be passed to identify a particular completion handler.

When the asynchronous operation completes, the asynchronous operation processor generates the corresponding completion event, associates it with its ACT and inserts the updated completion event into the appropriate completion event queue. After an asynchronous event demultiplexer removes the completion event from its completion event queue, the proactor implementation can use the completion event's ACT to demultiplex to the designated completion handler in constant *O(1)* time.

➡   As shown in implementation activity 3.1 (232), when an `async_read()` or `async_write()` method is invoked on an `Async_Stream`, they create a new `Async_Stream_Read_Result` or `Async_Stream_Write_Result` ACT, respectively and pass it to the corresponding Win32 asynchronous operation. When this asynchronous operation finishes, the Windows NT kernel queues the completion event on the completion port designated by the handle that was passed during the original asynchronous operation invocation. The ACT is used by the proactor to demultiplex the completion event to the completion handler designated in the original call.   ❏

5.4   *Determine how to dispatch the hook method on the designated completion handler.* After the proactor's `handle_events()` method demultiplexes to the completion handler it must dispatch the appropriate hook method on the completion handler. An efficient strategy for performing this dispatching operation is to combine the Adapter pattern [GoF95] with the Asynchronous Completion Token pattern (261), as shown at the end of implementation activity 3.1 (232).

➡   An `Async_Stream_Read_Result` is an adapter, whose `complete()` method can dispatch the appropriate hook method on the completion handler that it has cached in the state of its ACT:

```
void Async_Stream_Read_Result::complete () {
    completion_handler_->handle_event
        (completion_handler_->get_handle (),
        READ_EVENT, *this);
}
```

Note how the `handle_event()` dispatch hook method is passed a reference to the `Async_Stream_Read_Result` object that invoked it. This double-dispatching interaction [GoF95] allows the completion handler to access the asynchronous operation results, such as the number of bytes transferred and its success or failure status.   ❏

5.5   *Define the concrete proactor implementation.* The proactor interface holds a pointer to a concrete proactor implementation and forwards all method calls to it, as shown in implementation activity 4 (235).

➥   Our concrete proactor implementation overrides the pure virtual methods it inherits from class `Proactor_Implementation`:

```
class Win32_Proactor_Implementation :
    public Proactor_Implementation {
public:
```

The `Win32_Proactor_Implementation` constructor creates the completion port and caches it in the `completion_port_` data member:

```
Win32_Proactor_Implementation::
    Win32_Proactor_Implementation () {
        completion_port_ = CreateIoCompletionPort
            (INVALID_HANDLE, 0, 0, 0);
}
```

The `register_handle()` method associates a `HANDLE` with the completion port:

```
void Win32_Proactor_Implementation::register_handle
    (HANDLE h) {
    CreateIoCompletionPort (h, completion_port_,0,0);
}
```

All subsequent completion events hat result from asynchronous operations invoked via the `HANDLE` will be inserted into this proactor's completion port by the Windows NT operating system.

The next code fragment shows how to implement the `handle_events()` method:

```
void Win32_Proactor_Implementation::handle_events
    (Time_Value *wait_time = 0) {
    u_long num_bytes;
    OVERLAPPED *act;
```

This method first calls the `GetQueuedCompletionStatus()` asynchronous event demultiplexing function to dequeue the next completion event from the completion port:

```
BOOL status = GetQueuedCompletionStatus
    (completion_port_, &num_bytes,
     0, &act,
     wait_time == 0 ? 0 : wait_time->msec ());
```

When this function returns, the ACT received from the Windows NT operating system is downcast to become an `Async_Result *`:

```
Async_Result *async_result =
    static_cast <Async_Result *> (act);
```

The completion event that `GetQueuedCompletionStatus()` returned updates the completion result data members in `async_result`:

```
async_result->status (status);
if (!status)
    async_result->error (GetLastError ());
else
    async_result->bytes_transferred(num_bytes);
```

The proactor implementation's `handle_events()` method then invokes the `complete()` method on the `async_result` adapter:

```
async_result->complete ();
```

Implementation activity 5.4 (240) illustrates how the `complete()` method in the `Async_Stream_Read_Result` adapter dispatches to the concrete completion handler's `handle_event()` hook method.

Finally, the proactor deletes the `async_result` pointer, which was allocated dynamically by an asynchronous operation interface method, as shown in implementation activity 3.1 (232).

```
        delete async_result;
    }
```

The private portion of our proactor implementation caches the handle to its Windows NT completion port:

```
private:
    // Store a HANDLE to a Windows NT completion port.
    HANDLE completion_port_;
};                                                              ❑
```

6   *Determine the number of proactors in an application.* Many applications can be structured using just one instance of the Proactor pattern. In this case the proactor can be implemented using the Singleton pattern [GoF95], as shown in implementation activity 4 (235). This design is useful for centralizing event demultiplexing and dispatching of completion events to a single location in an application.

It can be useful to run multiple proactors simultaneously within the same application process, however. For example, different proactors can be associated with threads running at different priorities. This design provides different quality of service levels to process completion handlers for asynchronous operations.

Note that completion handlers are only serialized per thread within an instance of the proactor. Multiple completion handlers in multiple threads can therefore run in parallel. This configuration may necessitate the use of additional synchronization mechanisms if completion handlers in different threads access shared state concurrently. Mutexes and synchronization idioms such as Scoped Locking (325) are suitable.

7   *Implement the concrete completion handlers.* Concrete completion handlers specialize the completion handler interface described in implementation activity 2.3 (228) to define application-specific functionality. Three sub-activities must be addressed when implementing concrete completion handlers:

7.1 *Determine policies for maintaining state in concrete completion handlers.* A concrete completion handler may need to maintain state information associated with a particular request. For example, an operating system may notify a server that only part of a file was written to a Socket asynchronously, due to the occurrence of transport-level flow control. A concrete completion handler must then send the remaining data, until the file is fully transferred or the connection becomes invalid. It must therefore know which file was originally specified, how many bytes remain to be sent, and the position of the file at the start of the previous request.

7.2 *Select a mechanism to configure concrete completion handlers with a handle.* Concrete completion handlers perform operations on handles. The same two strategies described in implementation activity 6.2 of the Reactor (179) pattern—*hard-coded* and *generic*—can be applied to configure handles with event handlers in the Proactor pattern. In both strategies wrapper facades (47) can encapsulate handles used by completion handler classes.

7.3 *Implement completion handler functionality.* Application developers must decide the processing actions that should be performed to implement a service when its corresponding hook method is invoked by a proactor. To separate connection establishment functionality from subsequent service processing, concrete completion handlers can be divided into several categories in accordance with the Acceptor-Connector pattern (285). In particular, service handlers implement application-specific services. In contrast, acceptors and connectors establish connections passively and actively, respectively, on behalf of these service handlers.

8   *Implement the initiators.* In many proactive applications, such as our Web server example, the concrete completion handlers *are* the initiators. In this case this implementation activity can be skipped. Initiators that are not completion handlers, however, are often used to initiate asynchronous service processing during an application's start-up phase.

Example Resolved   Our Web server uses Windows NT features, such as overlapped I/O, completion ports, and GetQueuedCompletionStatus(), to implement proactive event demultiplexing. It employs a single-method completion handler dispatch interface strategy that can process multiple Web browser service requests asynchronously. HTTP acceptors asynchronously connect and create HTTP handlers using a variant of the Acceptor-Connector pattern (285). Each HTTP handler is responsible for asynchronously receiving, processing, and replying to a Web browser GET request delivered to the Web server's proactor via a completion event. The example shown here uses a single thread to invoke asynchronous operations and handle completion event processing. It is straightforward to enhance this example to take advantage of multiple threads, however, as described in the *Variants* section.

The Web server's main() function starts by performing its initialization activities, such as creating a proactor singleton, a Windows NT completion port, and an HTTP acceptor. This acceptor associates its passive-mode acceptor handle with the proactor singleton's completion port. The Web server next performs the following scenario during its connection processing:

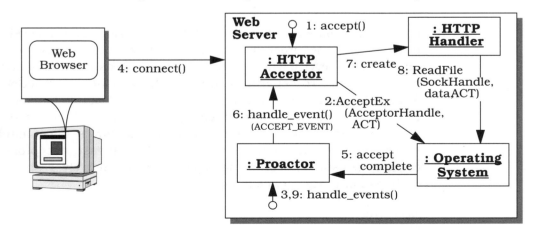

- The Web server invokes the HTTP acceptor's `accept()` method (1). This method creates an ACT containing itself as the concrete completion handler.

- Acting in the role of an initiator, the HTTP acceptor's `accept()` method then invokes the Win32 `AcceptEx()` operation asynchronously. It passes the ACT to `AcceptEx()`, together with a `HANDLE` that identifies both the passive-mode socket endpoint to accept connections and the completion port that Windows NT[8] should use to queue the completion event when `AcceptEx()` finishes accepting a connection.

- The Web server's `main()` function then invokes the proactor's (3) `handle_events()` method. This method runs the proactor's event loop, which calls the `GetQueuedCompletionStatus()` asynchronous event demultiplexer. This function waits on its completion port for the operating system to queue completion events when asynchronous operations finish executing.

- A remote Web browser subsequently connects to the Web server (4), which causes the asynchronous `AcceptEx()` operation to accept the connection and generate an *accept* completion event. The operating system then locates this operation's ACT and associates it with the completion event. At this point it queues the updated completion event on the appropriate completion port (5).

- The `GetQueuedCompletionStatus()` function running in the application's event loop thread then dequeues the completion event from the completion port. The proactor uses the ACT associated with this completion event to dispatch the `handle_event()` hook method on the HTTP acceptor completion handler (6), passing it the `ACCEPT_EVENT` event type.

- To process the completion event, the HTTP acceptor creates an HTTP handler (7) that associates its I/O handle with the proactor's completion port. This HTTP handler then immediately invokes an asynchronous `ReadFile()` operation (8) to obtain the `GET` request data sent by the Web browser. The HTTP handler passes itself as the completion handler in the ACT to `ReadFile()` together with the I/O handle. The operating system uses the completion port associ-

---

8. For conciseness we refer to 'Windows NT' or simply 'the operating system' rather than 'asynchronous operation processor' in the remainder of this section.

ated with this handle to notify the proactor's `handle_events()` method when the asynchronous `ReadFile()` operation finishes executing.

- Control of the Web server then returns to the proactor's event loop (9), which calls the `GetQueuedCompletionStatus()` function to continue waiting for completion events.

After the connection is established and the HTTP handler is created, the following diagram illustrates the subsequent scenario used by a proactive Web server to service an HTTP GET request:

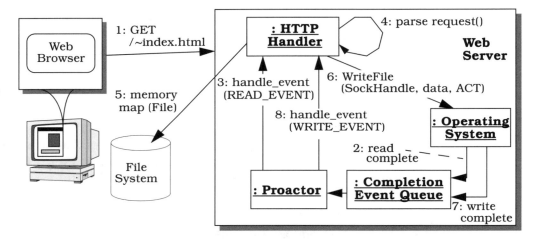

- The Web browser sends an HTTP GET request (1).

- The asynchronous `ReadFile()` operation invoked in the previous scenario then finishes executing and the operating system queues the *read* completion event onto the completion port (2). This event is then dequeued by `GetQueuedCompletionStatus()`, which returns to the proactor's `handle_events()` method. This method demultiplexes the completion event's ACT to the designated HTTP handler and dispatches the handler's `handle_event()` hook method, passing the READ_EVENT event type (3).

- The HTTP handler parses the request (4). Steps (2) through (4) then repeat as necessary until the entire GET request has been received asynchronously.

- After the GET request has been completely received and validated, the HTTP handler memory-maps the requested file (5) and invokes an asynchronous `WriteFile()` operation to transfer the file data via the connection (6). The HTTP handler passes an ACT that identifies itself as a completion handler to `WriteFile()`, so that the proactor can notify it after the asynchronous `WriteFile()` operation finishes.

● After the asynchronous `WriteFile()` operation finishes the operating system inserts a *write* completion event into the completion port. The proactor uses `GetQueuedCompletionStatus()` again to dequeue the completion event (7). It uses its associated ACT to demultiplex to the HTTP handler, then dispatches its `handle_event()` hook method (8) to process the write completion event results. Steps (6) through (8) continue asynchronously until the entire file has been delivered to the Web browser.

Below we illustrate how the HTTP handler in our Web server can be written using the `Completion_Handler` class defined in the *Implementation* section.

```
class HTTP_Handler : public Completion_Handler  {
    // Implements HTTP using asynchronous operations.
```

`HTTP_Handler` inherits from the 'single-method' dispatch interface variant of the `Completion_Handler` base class defined in implementation activity 2.3 (228). This design enables the proactor singleton to dispatch its `handle_events()` hook method when asynchronous `ReadFile()` and `WriteFile()` operations finish. The following data members are contained in each `HTTP_Handler` object:

```
private:
    // Cached <Proactor>.
    Proactor *proactor_;
    // Memory-mapped file_;
    Mem_Map file_;
    // Socket endpoint, initialized into "async-mode."
    SOCK_Stream *sock_;
    // Hold the HTTP Request while its being processed.
    HTTP_Request request_;
    // Read/write asynchronous socket I/O.
    Async_Stream stream_;
```

The constructor caches a pointer to the proactor used by the `HTTP_Handler`:

```
public:
    HTTP_Handler (Proactor *proactor):
        proactor_ (proactor) { }
```

When a Web browser connects to the Web server the following open()
method of the HTTP handler is called by the HTTP acceptor:

```
virtual void open (SOCK_Stream *sock) {
    // Initialize state for request.
    request_.state_ = INCOMPLETE;

    // Store pointer to the socket.
    sock_ = sock;

    // Initialize <Async_Stream>.
    stream_.open
        (this, // This completion handler.
         sock_->handle (), proactor_);

    // Start asynchronous read operation on socket.
    stream_.async_read
     (request_.buffer (), request_.buffer_size ());
}
```

In open(), the Async_Stream is initialized with the completion
handler, handle, and proactor to use when asynchronous Read–
File() and WriteFile() operations finish. It then invokes an
async_read() operation and returns to the proactor that dispatched
it. When the call stack unwinds the Web server will continue running
its handle_events() event loop method on its proactor singleton.

After the asynchronous ReadFile() operation completes, the
proactor singleton demultiplexes to the HTTP_Handler completion
handler and dispatches its subsequent handle_event() method:

```
virtual void handle_event
    (HANDLE,
     Event_Type event_type,
     const Async_Result &async_result) {
    if (event_type == READ_EVENT) {
        if (!request_.done
            (async_result.bytes_transferred ()))
            // Didn't get entire request, so start a
            // new asynchronous read operation.
            stream_.async_read (request_.buffer (),
                            request_.buffer_size ());
        else
            parse_request ();
    }
    // ...
}
```

If the entire request has not arrived, another asynchronous Read–
File() operation is invoked and the Web server returns once again

to its event loop. After a complete GET request has been received from a Web browser, however, the following parse_request() method maps the requested file into memory and writes the file data to the Web browser asynchronously:

```
void parse_request () {
    // Switch on the HTTP command type.
    switch (request_.command ()) {

    // Web browser is requesting a file.
    case HTTP_Request::GET:
        // Memory map the requested file.
        file_.map (request_.filename ());
        // Invoke asynchronous write operation.
        stream_.async_write (file_.buffer (),
                             file_.buffer_size ());
        break;
    // Web browser is storing file at the Web server.
    case HTTP_Request::PUT:
        // ...
    }
}
```

This sample implementation of parse_request() uses a C++ switch statement for simplicity and clarity. A more extensible implementation could apply the Command pattern [GoF95] or Command Processor pattern [POSA1] instead.

When the asynchronous WriteFile() operation completes, the proactor singleton dispatches the handle_event() hook method of the HTTP_Handler:

```
virtual void handle_event
    (HANDLE, Event_Type event_type,
     const Async_Result &async_result) {
    // ... see READ_EVENT case above ...
    else if (event_type == WRITE_EVENT) {
        if (!file_.done
            (async_result.bytes_transferred ()))
            // Didn't send entire data, so start
            // another asynchronous write.
            stream_.async_write
             (file_.buffer (),file_.buffer_size ());
        else
            // Success, so free up resources...
    }
}
```

After all the data has been received the HTTP handler frees resources that were allocated dynamically.

The Web server contains a `main()` function that implements a single-threaded server. This server first calls an asynchronous accept operation and the waits in the proactor singleton's `handle_events()` event loop:

```
// HTTP server port number.
const u_short PORT = 80;

int main () {
    // HTTP server address.
    INET_Addr addr (PORT);

    // Initialize HTTP server endpoint, which associates
    // the <HTTP_Acceptor>'s passive-mode socket handle
    // with the <Proactor> singleton's completion port.
    HTTP_Acceptor acceptor (addr, Proactor::instance ());

    // Invoke an asynchronous <accept> operation to
    // Invoke the Web server processing.
    acceptor.accept ();

    // Event loop processes client connection requests
    // and HTTP requests proactively.
    for (;;)
        Proactor::instance ()->handle_events ();
    /* NOTREACHED */
}
```

As service requests arrive from Web browsers and are converted into indication events by the operating system, the proactor singleton invokes the event handling hook methods on the `HTTP_Acceptor` and `HTTP_Handler` concrete event handlers to accept connections and receive and process logging records asynchronously. The sequence diagram below illustrates the behavior in the proactive Web server.

The proactive processing model shown in this diagram can scale when multiple HTTP handlers and HTTP acceptors process requests from remote Web browsers simultaneously. For example, each handler/acceptor can invoke asynchronous `ReadFile()`, `Write-File()`, and `AcceptEx()` operations that run concurrently. If the underlying asynchronous operation processor supports asynchronous I/O operations efficiently the overall performance of the Web server will scale accordingly.

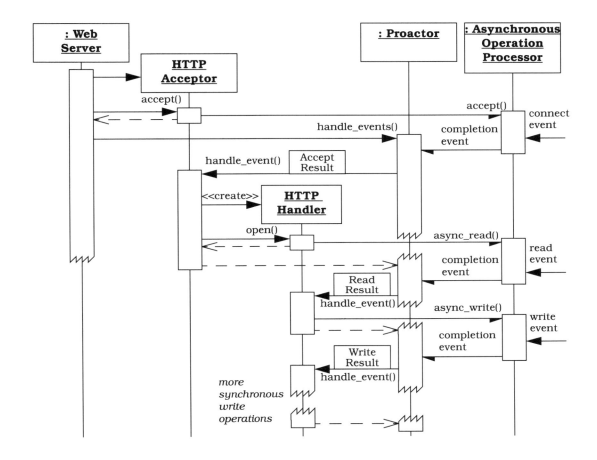

Variants   *Asynchronous Completion Handlers.* The *Implementation* section describes activities used to implement a proactor that dispatches completion events to completion handlers within a single proactor event
loop thread. When a concrete completion handler is dispatched, it
borrows the proactor's thread to perform its completion processing.
However, this design may restrict the concrete completion handler to
perform short-duration synchronous processing to avoid decreasing
the overall responsiveness of the application significantly.

To resolve this restriction, all completion handlers could be required
to act as initiators and invoke long-duration asynchronous
operations immediately, rather than performing the completion
processing synchronously. Some operating systems, such as

Windows NT, explicitly support asynchronous procedure calls (APCs). An APC is a function that executes asynchronously in the context of its calling thread. When an APC is invoked the operating system queues it within the thread context. The next time the thread is idle, such as when it blocks on an I/O operation, it can run the queued APCs.

Concurrent Asynchronous Event Demultiplexer. One downside to using APCs is that they may not use multiple CPUs effectively. This is because each APC runs in a single thread context. A more scalable strategy therefore may be to create a pool of threads that share an asynchronous event demultiplexer, so that a proactor can demultiplex and dispatch completion handlers concurrently. This strategy is particularly scalable on operating system platforms that implement asynchronous I/O efficiently.

For example, a Windows NT completion port [Sol98] is optimized to run efficiently when accessed by `GetQueuedCompletionStatus()` from multiple threads simultaneously [HPS99]. In particular, the Windows NT kernel schedules threads waiting on a completion port in 'last-in first-out' (LIFO) order. This LIFO protocol maximizes CPU cache affinity [Mog95] by ensuring that the thread waiting the shortest time is scheduled first, which is an example of the Fresh Work Before Stale pattern [Mes96].

Shared Completion Handlers. Iinitiators can invoke multiple asynchronous operations simultaneously, all of which share the same concrete completion handler [ARSK00]. To behave correctly, however, each shared handler may need to determine unambiguously which asynchronous operation has completed. In this case, the initiator and proactor must collaborate to shepherd operation-specific state information throughout the entire asynchronous processing life-cycle.

As with implementation activity 3.1 (232), the Asynchronous Completion Token pattern (261) can be re-applied to disambiguate each asynchronous operation—an initiator can create an asynchronous completion token (ACT) that identifies each asynchronous operation uniquely. It then 'piggy-backs' this initiator-ACT onto the ACT passed when an asynchronous operation is invoked on an asynchronous operation processor. When the operation finishes executing and is being processed by the proactor,

the 'initiator-ACT' can be passed unchanged to the shared concrete
completion handler's hook method. This initiator-ACT allows the
concrete completion handler to control its subsequent processing
after it receives an asynchronous operation's completion results.

➡ To share a concrete completion handler we first add an initiator-
ACT data member and a pair of set/get methods to the Async_Result
class:

```
class Async_Result : public OVERLAPPED {
private:
    const void *initiator_act_;
    // ....
public:
    // Set/get initiator's ACT.
    void initiator_act (const void *);
    const void *initiator_act ();
    // ...
```

We next modify the Async_Stream I/O methods to 'piggy-back' the
initiator-ACT with its existing ACT:

```
int Async_Stream::async_read (void *buf,
                              u_long n_bytes,
                              const void *initiator_act)
{
    u_long bytes_read;
    OVERLAPPED *act = new // Create the ACT.
        Async_Stream_Read_Result (completion_handler_);

    // Set <initiator_act> in existing ACT.
    act->initiator_act (initiator_act);

    ReadFile (handle_, buf, n_bytes, &bytes_read, act);
}
```

Finally, we can retrieve this initiator-ACT in a concrete event
handler's handle_event() method via the Async_Result parameter:

```
virtual void handle_event
            (HANDLE, Event_Type event_type,
             const Async_Result &async_result) {
    const void *initiator_act =
        async_result.initiator_act ();
    // ...
}
```

The handle_event() method can use this initiator_act to
disambiguate its subsequent processing.   ❏

Asynchronous Operation Processor Emulation. Many operating system platforms, including the traditional versions of UNIX [MBKQ96] and the Java Virtual Machine (JVM), do not export asynchronous operations to applications. There are several techniques that can be used to emulate an asynchronous operation processor on such platforms, however. A common solution is to employ a concurrency mechanism to execute operations without blocking initiators, such as the Active Object pattern (369) or some type of threading model. Three activities must be addressed when implementing a multi-threaded asynchronous operation processor:

- *Operation invocation.* When an operation is invoked the asynchronous operation processor must first store its associated ACT in an internal table. This can be implemented using the Manager pattern [Som97].

- *Asynchronous operation execution.* The operation will next be executed in a different thread of control than the invoking initiator thread. One strategy is to spawn a thread for each operation. A more scalable strategy is for the asynchronous operation processor to maintain a pool of threads using the Active Object pattern (369) Thread Pool variant. This strategy requires the initiator thread to queue the operation request before continuing with its other computations.

  Each operation will subsequently be dequeued and executed in a thread internal to the asynchronous operation processor. For example, to implement asynchronous read operations an internal thread can block while reading from socket or file handles. Operations thus appear to execute asynchronously to initiators that invoke them, even though the operations block internally within the asynchronous operation processor in their own thread of control.

- *Operation completion handling.* When an asynchronous operation completes the asynchronous operation processor generates a completion event and associates it with the appropriate ACT it had cached during the original invocation. It then queues the updated completion event into the appropriate completion event queue.

Other variants. Several variants of the Proactor pattern are similar to variants in the Reactor pattern (179), such as integrating the demultiplexing of timer and I/O events, and supporting concurrent concrete completion handlers.

Known uses **Completion ports in Windows NT**. The Windows NT operating system provides the mechanisms to implement the Proactor pattern efficiently [Sol98]. Various asynchronous operations are supported by Windows NT, such as time-outs, accepting new network connections, reading and writing to files and Sockets, and transmitting entire files across a Socket connection. The operating system itself is thus the asynchronous operation processor. Results of the operations are queued as completion events on Windows NT completion ports, which are then dequeued and dispatched by an application-provided proactor.

The POSIX AIO family of asynchronous I/O operations. On some real-time POSIX platforms the Proactor pattern is implemented by the aio_*() family of APIs [POSIX95]. These operating system features are similar to those described above for Windows NT. One difference is that UNIX signals can be used to implement a pre-emptively asynchronous proactor in which a signal handler can interrupt an application's thread of control. In contrast, the Windows NT API is not pre-emptively asynchronous, because application threads are not interrupted. Instead, the asynchronous completion routines are called back at well-defined Win32 function points.

ACE Proactor Framework. The ADAPTIVE Communication Environment (ACE) [Sch97] provides a portable object-oriented Proactor framework that encapsulates the overlapped I/O and completion port mechanisms on Windows NT and the aio_*() family of asynchronous I/O APIs on POSIX platforms. ACE provides an abstraction class, ACE_Proactor, that defines a common interface to a variety of proactor implementations, such as ACE_Win32_Proactor and ACE_POSIX_Proactor. These proactor implementations can be created using different asynchronous event demultiplexers, such as GetQueuedCompletionStatus() and aio_suspend(), respectively.

Operating system device driver interrupt-handling mechanisms. The Proactor pattern is often used to enhance the structure of operating system kernels that invoke I/O operations on hardware devices driven by asynchronous interrupts. For example, a packet of data can be written from an application to a kernel-resident device driver, which then passes it to the hardware device that transmits the data asynchronously. When the device finishes its transmission it generates a hardware interrupt that notifies the appropriate handler in the device driver. The device driver then processes the interrupt to completion, potentially initiating another asynchronous transfer if more data is available from the application.

Phone call initiation via voice mail. A real-life application of the Proactor pattern is the scenario in which you telephone a friend, who is currently away from her phone, but who returns calls reliably when she comes home. You therefore leave a message on her voice mail to ask her to call you back. In terms of the Proactor pattern, you are a initiator who invokes an asynchronous operation on an asynchronous operation processor—your friend's voice mail—to inform your friend that you called. While waiting for your friend's 'call-back' you can do other things, such as re-read chapters in POSA2. After your friend has listened to her voice mail, which corresponds to the completion of the asynchronous operation, she plays the proactor role and calls you back. While talking with her, you are the completion handler that 'processes' her 'callback'.

Consequences   The Proactor pattern offers a variety of **benefits**:

Separation of concerns. The Proactor pattern decouples application-independent asynchronous mechanisms from application-specific functionality. The application-independent mechanisms become reusable components that know how to demultiplex the completion events associated with asynchronous operations and dispatch the appropriate callback methods defined by concrete completion handlers. Similarly, the application-specific functionality in concrete completion handlers know how to perform particular types of service, such as HTTP processing.

Portability. The Proactor pattern improves application portability by allowing its interface to be reused independently of the underlying operating system calls that perform event demultiplexing. These system calls detect and report the events that may occur simultaneously on multiple event sources. Event sources may include I/O ports, timers, synchronization objects, signals, and so on. For example, on real-time POSIX platforms the asynchronous I/O functions are provided by the `aio_*()` family of APIs [POSIX95].

Similarly, on Windows NT, completion ports and overlapped I/O are used to implement asynchronous I/O [MDS96].

Encapsulation of concurrency mechanisms. A benefit of decoupling the proactor from the asynchronous operation processor is that applications can configure proactors with various concurrency strategies without affecting other application components and services.

Decoupling of threading from concurrency. The asynchronous operation processor executes potentially long-duration operations on behalf of initiators. Applications therefore do not need to spawn many threads to increase concurrency. This allows an application to vary its concurrency policy independently of its threading policy. For instance, a Web server may only want to allot one thread per CPU, but may want to service a higher number of clients simultaneously via asynchronous I/O.

Performance. Multi-threaded operating systems use context switching to cycle through multiple threads of control. While the time to perform a context switch remains fairly constant, the total time to cycle through a large number of threads can degrade application performance significantly if the operating system switches context to an idle thread.[9] For example, threads may poll the operating system for completion status, which is inefficient. The Proactor pattern can avoid the cost of context switching by activating only those logical threads of control that have events to process. If no GET request is pending, for example, a Web server need not activate an HTTP Handler.

Simplification of application synchronization. As long as concrete completion handlers do not spawn additional threads of control, application logic can be written with little or no concern for synchronization issues. Concrete completion handlers can be written as if they existed in a conventional single-threaded environment. For example, a Web server's HTTP handler can access the disk through an asynchronous operation, such as the Windows NT TransmitFile() function [HPS99], hence no additional threads need to be spawned.

---

9. Some older operating system exhibit this behavior, though most modern operating systems do not.

The Proactor pattern has the following **liabilities**:

Restricted applicability. The Proactor pattern can be applied most efficiently if the operating system supports asynchronous operations natively. If the operating system does not provide this support, however, it is possible to emulate the semantics of the Proactor pattern using multiple threads within the proactor implementation. This can be achieved, for example, by allocating a pool of threads to process asynchronous operations. This design is not as efficient as native operating system support, however, because it increases synchronization and context switching overhead without necessarily enhancing application-level parallelism.

Complexity of programming, debugging and testing. It is hard to program applications and higher-level system services using asynchrony mechanisms, due to the separation in time and space between operation invocation and completion. Similarly, operations are not necessarily constrained to run at well-defined points in the processing sequence—they may execute in non-deterministic orderings that are hard for many developers to understand.

Applications written with the Proactor pattern can also be hard to debug and test because the inverted flow of control oscillates between the proactive framework infrastructure and the method callbacks on application-specific handlers. This increases the difficulty of 'single-stepping' through the run-time behavior of a framework within a debugger, because application developers may not understand or have access to the proactive framework code.

Scheduling, controlling, and canceling asynchronously running operations. Initiators may be unable to control the scheduling order in which asynchronous operations are executed by an asynchronous operation processor. If possible, therefore, an asynchronous operation processor should employ the Strategy pattern [GoF95] to allow initiators to prioritize and cancel asynchronous operations. Devising a completely reliable and efficient means of canceling all asynchronous operations is hard, however, because asynchronous operations may complete before they can be cancelled.

See Also The Proactor pattern is related to the Observer [GoF95] and Publisher-Subscriber [POSA1] patterns, in which all dependents are informed when a single subject changes. In the Proactor pattern, however, completion handlers are informed automatically when completion events from multiple sources occur. In general, the Proactor pattern is used to demultiplex multiple sources of asynchronously delivered completion events to their associated completion handlers, whereas an observer or subscriber is usually associated with a single source of events.

The Proactor pattern can be considered an *asynchronous* variant of the synchronous Reactor pattern (179). The Reactor pattern is responsible for demultiplexing and dispatching multiple event handlers that are triggered when it is possible to *invoke* an operation *synchronously* without blocking. In contrast, the Proactor pattern supports the demultiplexing and dispatching of multiple completion handlers that are triggered by the *completion* of operations that execute *asynchronously*.

Leader/Followers (447) and Half-Sync/Half-Async (423) are two other patterns that demultiplex and process various types of events synchronously. On platforms that support asynchronous I/O efficiently, the Proactor pattern can often be implemented more efficiently than these patterns. However, the Proactor pattern may be harder to implement because it has more participants, which require more effort to understand. The Proactor's combination of 'inversion of control' and asynchrony may also require application developers to have more experience to use and debug it effectively.

The Active Object pattern (369) decouples method execution from method invocation. The Proactor pattern is similar, because an asynchronous operation processor performs operations asynchronously on behalf of initiators. Both patterns can therefore be used to implement asynchronous operations. The Proactor pattern is often used instead of the Active Object pattern on operating systems that support asynchronous I/O efficiently.

The Chain of Responsibility [GoF95] pattern decouples event handlers from event sources. The Proactor pattern is similar in its segregation of initiators and completion handlers. In the Chain of Responsibility pattern, however, the event source has no prior knowledge of which handler will be executed, if any. In Proactor, initiators have full control over the target completion handler. The two patterns can be combined by establishing a completion handler that is the entry point into a responsibility chain dynamically configured by an external factory.

Current Java implementations do not support Proactor-like event processing schemes, because `java.io` does not support asynchronous I/O. In basic Java implementations blocking I/O operations can even block the whole Java Virtual Machine (JVM)—the I/O operation blocks the current thread and, as multi-threading may be implemented in user space, the operating system considers the task running the JVM as blocked and schedules other operating system processes instead of other JVM threads.

More sophisticated Java implementations work around this problem by implementing asynchronous I/O internally on the native code level—the thread doing the blocking call is blocked, but other threads are able to run. The blocked thread is subsequently called back, or may explicitly wait for the blocking call to return. Applications cannot make use of this directly, however, because current JDK libraries do not expose asynchronous I/O. This will change with the next generation of the Java I/O system, which is under development and will appear as a package called `java.nio` or something similar [JSR51].

Certain programming languages, such as Scheme, support *continuations*. Continuations can be used in single-threaded programs to enable a sequence of function calls to relinquish its run-time call stack when blocked without losing the execution history of the call stack. In the context of the Proactor pattern, the indirect transfer of control from an asynchronous operation invocation to the subsequent processing by its completion handler can be modeled as a continuation.

Credits   Tim Harrison, Thomas D. Jordan, and Irfan Pyarali are co-authors of the original version of the Proactor pattern. Irfan also provided helpful comments on this version. Thanks to Ralph Johnson for suggestions that helped improve this pattern and for pointing out how this pattern relates to the programming language feature *continuations*.

Asynchronous Completion Token

The *Asynchronous Completion Token* design pattern allows an application to demultiplex and process efficiently the responses of asynchronous operations it invokes on services.

Also Known As   Active Demultiplexing [PRS+99], 'Magic Cookie'

Example   Consider a large-scale distributed e-commerce system consisting of clusters of *Web servers*. These servers store and retrieve various types of content in response to requests from Web browsers. The performance and reliability of such e-commerce systems has become increasingly crucial to many businesses.

For example, in a web-based stock trading system, it is important that the current stock quotes, as well as subsequent buy and sell orders, are transmitted efficiently and reliably. The Web servers in the e-commerce system must therefore be monitored carefully to ensure they are providing the necessary quality of service to users. Autonomous *management agents* can address this need by propagating management events from e-commerce system Web servers back to *management applications*:

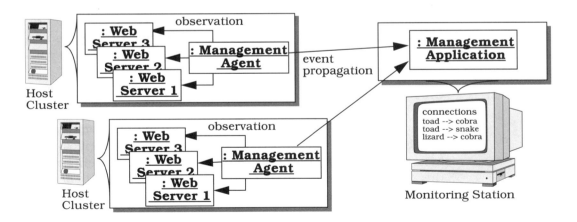

System administrators can use these management agents, applications, and events to monitor, visualize, and control the status and performance of Web servers in the e-commerce system [PSK+97].

Typically, a management application uses the Publisher-Subscriber pattern [POSA1] to subscribe with one or more management agents to receive various types of events, such as events that report when Web browsers establish new connections with Web servers. When a management agent detects activities of interest to a management application, it sends *completion events* to the management application, which then processes these events.

In large-scale e-commerce systems, however, management applications may invoke subscription operations on many management agents, requesting notification of the occurrence of many different types of events. Moreover, each type of event may be processed differently in a management application using specialized *completion handlers*. These handlers determine the application's response to events, such as updating a display, logging events to a database, or automatically detecting performance bottlenecks and system failures.

One way in which a management application could match its subscription operations to their subsequent completion events would be to spawn a separate thread for each event subscription operation it invoked on a management agent. Each thread would then block synchronously, waiting for completion event(s) from its agent to arrive in response to its original subscription operation. In this synchronous design, a completion handler that processed management agent event responses could be stored implicitly in each thread's run-time stack.

Unfortunately this synchronous multi-threaded design incurs the same context-switching, synchronization, and data-movement performance overhead drawbacks described in the *Example* section of the Reactor pattern (179). Therefore, management applications may instead opt to initiate subscription operations asynchronously. In this case, management applications must be designed to demultiplex management agent completion events to their associate completion handlers efficiently and scalably, thereby allowing management applications to react promptly when notified by their agents.

Context An event-driven system in which applications invoke operations asynchronously on services and subsequently process the associated service completion event responses.

Problem When a client application invokes an operation request on one or more services asynchronously, each service returns its response to the application via a completion event. The application must then *demultiplex* this event to the appropriate handler, such as a function or object, that it uses to process the asynchronous operation response contained in the completion event. To address this problem effectively, we must resolve three *forces*:

- A service may not know the original context in which a client application invoked its operations asynchronously. For example, one client might dedicate a separate thread for each operation, whereas another might handle all operations in a single thread. This lack of context makes it hard for a service to know what information its clients need in order to demultiplex and process completion events. Therefore the client application, not the service, should be responsible for determining how completion events are demultiplexed to the handler designated to process them.

  ➥ Management agent services in our e-commerce system example do not, and should not, know how a management application will demultiplex and process the various completion events it receives from the agents in response to its asynchronous subscription operations. ❑

- As little communication overhead as possible should be incurred between a client application and a service to determine how the client will demultiplex and process completion events after asynchronous operations finish executing. Minimizing communication overhead is important for client applications that are latency-constrained and those that interact with services over bandwidth-limited communication links.

  ➥ In our e-commerce system a management application and an agent service should have a minimal number of interactions, such as one to invoke the asynchronous subscription operation and one for each completion event response. Moreover, the data transferred to help demultiplex completion events to their handlers should add

minimal extra bytes beyond an operation's input parameters and
return values.   ❏

- When a service response arrives at a client application, the
  application should spend as little time as possible demultiplexing
  the completion event to the handler that will process the
  asynchronous operation's response.

  ➨ A large-scale e-commerce application may have hundreds of
  Web servers and management agents, millions of simultaneous
  Web browser connections and a correspondingly large number of
  asynchronous subscription operations and completion events.
  Searching a large table to associate a completion event response
  with its original asynchronous operation request could thus degrade the performance of management applications significantly.❏

Solution   Together with each asynchronous operation that a client *initiator*
invokes on a *service*, transmit information that identifies how the
initiator should process the service's response. Return this
information to the initiator when the operation finishes, so that it can
be used to demultiplex the response efficiently, allowing the initiator
to process it accordingly.

In detail: for every asynchronous operation that a client initiator
invokes on a service, create an *asynchronous completion token* (ACT).
An ACT contains information that uniquely identifies the *completion
handler*, which is the function or object responsible for processing the
operation's response. Pass this ACT to the service together with the
operation, which holds but does not modify the ACT. When the service
replies to the initiator, its response includes the ACT that was sent
originally. The initiator can then use the ACT to identify the
completion handler that will process the response from the original
asynchronous operation.

Structure   Four participants form the structure of the Asynchronous
Completion Token pattern:

A *service* provides some type of functionality that can be accessed
asynchronously.

➨ Management agents provide a distributed management and
monitoring service to our e-commerce system.   ❏

A client *initiator* invokes operations on a service asynchronously. It also demultiplexes the response returned by these operations to a designated *completion handler*, which is a function or object within an application that is responsible for processing service responses.

➨ In our e-commerce system management applications invoke asynchronous operations on management agents to subscribe to various types of events. The management agents then send completion event responses to the management applications asynchronously when events for which they have registered occur. Completion handlers in management applications process these completion events to update their GUI display and perform other actions. ❑

Class	Collaborator
Initiator	• Service
	• ACT
Responsibility	
• Invokes operations on a service asynchronously	
• Defines completion handlers	

Class	Collaborator
Service	
Responsibility	
• Provides application functionality	

An *asynchronous completion token* (ACT) contains information that identifies a particular initiator's completion handler. The initiator passes the ACT to the service when it invokes an operation; the service returns the ACT to the initiator unchanged when the asynchronous operation completes. The initiator then uses this ACT to efficiently demultiplex to the completion handler that processes the response from the original asynchronous operation. Services can hold a collection of ACTs to handle multiple asynchronous operations invoked by initiators simultaneously.

Class	Collaborator
Completion Handler	
Responsibility	
• Defines an interface for processing results of asynchronous operations	

Class	Collaborator
ACT	• Completion Handler
Responsibility	
• Identifies the completion handler that an initiator uses to process the response from an asynchronous operation invoked on a service	

➡   In our e-commerce system a management application initiator can create ACTs that are indices into a table of completion handlers, or are simply direct pointers to completion handlers. To a management agent service, however, the ACT is simply an opaque value that it returns unchanged to the management application initiator.   ❏

The following class diagram illustrates the participants of the Asynchronous Completion Token pattern and the relationships between these participants:

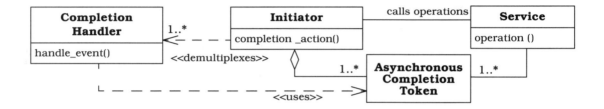

Dynamics   The following interactions occur in the Asynchronous Completion Token pattern:

- Before invoking an asynchronous operation on a service, the initiator creates the ACT that identifies the completion handler it associates with the operation.

- When invoking an operation on the service, the initiator passes the ACT to the service.

- The initiator can continue invoking other operations or processing responses while the service executes its asynchronous operation.

- When the asynchronous operation completes, the service sends a response to the initiator that contains the original ACT. The initiator uses the ACT to demultiplex to a completion handler that performs application-specific processing upon the response of the asynchronous operation.

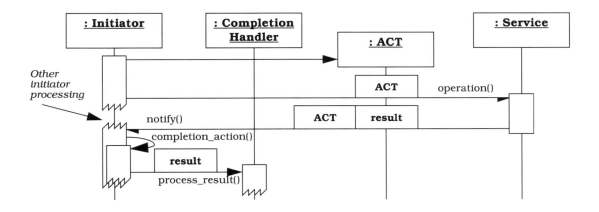

Implementation There are six activities involved in implementing the Asynchronous Completion Token pattern. These activities are largely orthogonal to the implementations of initiators, services, and completion handlers, which are covered by other patterns, such as Proxy [GoF95] [POSA1], Proactor, or Reactor (179). This section therefore focuses mainly on implementing ACTs, the protocol for exchanging ACTs between initiators and services, and the steps used to demultiplex ACTs efficiently to their associated completion handlers.

1 *Define the ACT representation.* The representation of an ACT should be meaningful for an initiator and its completion handler, but opaque to a service. Three common ACT representations:

  • *Pointer ACTs.* ACTs are often represented as pointers to programming language constructs, such as pointers to completion handler objects in C++ or references to completion handler objects in Java. In C++, for example, when an initiator initiates an operation on a service, it can create a completion handler ACT object and cast its address to a void pointer. This pointer is then passed to the service via the asynchronous operation call. Pointer ACTs are used primarily to pass ACTs among initiators and services running on relatively homogeneous platforms, such as those on which pointers have the same number of bytes. It may be necessary therefore to use portability features, such as typedefs or macros, to ensure a uniform representation of pointers throughout heterogeneous distributed systems.

- *Object reference ACTs.* To simplify the use of ACTs in heterogeneous systems, ACTs can be represented as object references defined in distributed object computing middleware, such as CORBA [OMG98c]. CORBA object references provide a standard, portable, and inter-operable means to communicate ACTs between distributed initiators and services. Upon receiving an object reference ACT from a service, an initiator can use the CORBA _narrow() operation to downcast the ACT to a completion handler type that is meaningful to it. Naturally, object references may not be a feasible ACT representation if middleware is not used.

- *Index ACTs.* ACTs also can be represented as indices into a table of completion handlers accessible to the initiator. When a response arrives from the service, the initiator simply uses the ACT to index into the table and access the corresponding completion handler. This representation is particularly useful for languages, such as FORTRAN, that do not support object references or pointers. Database identifiers or offsets into memory-mapped files are useful to associate ACTs with persistent completion handlers whose life-cycle extends beyond the life-time of a particular process. Index ACTs are also useful for improving initiator robustness, as described in implementation activity 2 (269).

Another aspect to consider when defining an ACT representation is the support it offers the initiator for demultiplexing to the appropriate completion handlers. By using common patterns such as Command or Adapter [GoF95], ACTs can provide a uniform interface to initiators. Concrete ACT implementations then map this interface to the specific interface of a particular completion handler, as described in implementation activity 6 (271).

➥   The following abstract class defines a C++ interface that can be used as the base for a wide range of pointer ACTs. It defines a pure virtual handle_event() method, which an initiator can use to dispatch a specific completion handler that processes the response from an asynchronous operation:

```
class Completion_Handler_ACT {
public:
    virtual void handle_event
        (const Completion_Event &event) = 0;
};
```

Application developers can define new types of completion handlers by subclassing from `Completion_Handler_ACT` and overriding its `handle_event()` hook method to call a specific completion handler. The e-commerce system presented in the *Example Resolved* section illustrates this implementation strategy.   ❑

2 *Select a strategy for holding the ACT at the initiator.* An initiator can invoke more than one service asynchronously. Supporting this behavior requires initiators to select one of the following strategies for holding the ACT:

- *Implicit ACTs.* In this strategy the ACT is held 'implicitly' by simply defining it to be the address of an initiator completion handler object. This strategy is often used with pointer or object reference ACTs. The *Example Resolved* section illustrates the use of implicit ACTs. The benefits of implicit ACTs are their *efficient time and space utilization* because they are simply memory addresses that point directly to the associated completion handler. However, implicit ACTs may not be as robust or secure as the explicit ACT strategy described next.

- *Explicit ACTs.* In this strategy the initiator holds its ACTs in an explicit data structure, for example a table of completion handlers organized using the Manager pattern [Som97] or an active demultiplexing table [PRS+99]. This strategy is well suited for index ACTs. Two benefits of using an explicit data structure to maintain ACTs in the initiator are increased *robustness* and *authenticity*. For example, if services do not return responses due to crash or hang failures, the corresponding ACTs can be located in the table and released wholesale.

  In addition, if the initiator cannot trust the service to return the original ACT unchanged, the explicit data structure can store additional information to authenticate whether the returned ACT really exists within the initiator. This authentication check, however, can increase the overhead of locating the ACT and demultiplexing it to the completion handler within the initiator.

Regardless of which strategy is used, initiators are responsible for freeing any resources associated with ACTs after they are no longer needed. The Object Lifetime Manager pattern [LGS99] is a useful way to manage the deletion of ACT resources robustly.

3 *Determine how to pass the ACT from the initiator to the service.* Initiators can use two strategies to pass ACTs along with asynchronous service operation requests:

- *Implicit parameters* are often stored in a context or environment that is passed to the service transparently. The CORBA context parameters and GIOP service context fields [OMG98c] are examples of implicit parameters.

- *Explicit parameters* are defined in the signature of the asynchronous operations. The *Example Resolved* section illustrates how an ACT can be passed as an explicit parameter to service operations.

4 *Determine a strategy for holding the ACT in the service.* After an ACT is received by a service it must hold the ACT while performing the operation invoked by the initiator. There are the two general strategies for holding ACTs in a service:

- If a service executes *synchronously*, the ACT can simply reside in the service's run-time stack while the service processes the operation. If a service runs in a different thread or process than its initiator, its operations can execute synchronously while still providing an asynchronous programming model to initiators [SV98b].

- If a service processes initiator operations *asynchronously*, it may need to handle multiple requests simultaneously. In this case the service must maintain the ACTs in a data structure that resides outside the scope of any service's run-time stack. The Manager pattern [Som97] can be used to organize this collection of ACTs.

5 *Determine the number of times an ACT can be used.* Both an initiator and a service can use the same ACT multiple times:

- Typically, an *initiator* passes a separate ACT for each asynchronous invocation. However, an initiator can invoke a particular asynchronous operation on a service multiple times. For each invocation, it can designate the same completion handler to process the operation's responses, thereby minimizing the cost of ACT creation and destruction. Similarly, an initiator can invoke the same operation on multiple service instances and designate the same completion handler to process the responses returned from all instances.

- A *service* may return an ACT just once along with the response from an asynchronous operation. However, a service can also issue a series of responses using the same ACT whenever a particular event occurs. In this case an ACT from a single asynchronous operation invocation can be returned to the initiator multiple times.

➥   In our e-commerce system example the management application initiator can subscribe the same ACT with multiple agent services and use it to demultiplex and dispatch these management agents' responses, such as 'connection established' completion events. Moreover, each agent can return this ACT multiple times, for example whenever it detects the establishment of a new connection.   ❏

6 *Determine the initiator strategy for demultiplexing ACTs to completion handler hook methods.* Initiators are responsible for demultiplexing asynchronous operation completion events to their completion handlers efficiently. Two strategies can be used to demultiplex an ACT to its associated completion handler when an asynchronous operation finishes:

- *Queued completion events.* In this strategy, ACTs can be placed in a completion event queue by a service, or by a local service proxy if the service is remote. An initiator can remove the ACT from a completion event queue at its discretion and then use the information encapsulated in the ACT to control its subsequent processing. Windows NT features, such as overlapped I/O, completion ports, and the `GetQueuedCompletionStatus()` function, use this strategy, as described in the *Known Uses* section [Sol98].

  After a completion event and its corresponding ACT are retrieved from the completion event queue, the initiator can use the ACT to demultiplex to the appropriate completion handler. At this point, it can dispatch the ACT's hook method, such as the `handle_event()` method illustrated in implementation activity 1 (267). This hook method processes the completion event containing the asynchronous operation's response. Implementation activity 5.2 in the Proactor pattern (215) illustrates this strategy.

- *Callbacks.* In this strategy an initiator passes a callback function or object[10] to the service. When an asynchronous operation completes, the callback can be invoked by the service or by a local service proxy. The ACT can be returned as a parameter to the callback function or object and downcast to identify the completion handler used for subsequent processing efficiently. For example, the ACT's handle_event() method can be called and passed the completion event, as described above.

In general, a single callback handler object can be used to demultiplex and process different types of completion events efficiently. A callback handler can therefore be implemented using the Singleton pattern [GoF95] within the initiator application.

Callbacks can be delivered to an initiator *asynchronously* or *synchronously*. In the asynchronous strategy the callback is invoked via an interrupt or signal handler [POSIX95]. Initiators need not therefore explicitly wait for notifications by blocking in an event loop. In the synchronous strategy, the application that hosts the initiator often waits in a reactive or proactive event loop. When the response returns from the service, it is dispatched to the appropriate callback.

➥ Our e-commerce system example illustrates how the synchronous callback object strategy can be implemented using pointer ACTs. We define a generic callback handler class that uses the Callback_Handler_ACT defined in implementation activity 1 (267).

The completion_event() method of this class initiates the appropriate management application completion handler processing when completion events are returned from management agents:

```
class Callback_Handler {
public:
    // Callback method.
    virtual void completion_event
        (const Completion_Event &event,
         Completion_Handler_ACT *act) {
        act->handle_event (event);
    };
};
```

When invoking an asynchronous operation on a service, the initiator passes a reference to the callback handler instance as a parameter to the service in addition to the ACT. When an

---

10. Implementation activity 1.1 in the Reactor pattern (179) outlines the pros and cons of callback functions versus callback objects.

asynchronous operation finishes, the service or its local service proxy dispatches the callback handler's `completion_event()` method synchronously to pass the completion event and ACT from the management agent service to the management application.

The `completion_event()` method then demultiplexes to the `handle_event()` hook method on the ACT it receives. In turn this method performs the completion handler processing on the asynchronous operation's response.   ❏

Note how both demultiplexing strategies described above allow initiators to process many different types of completion events efficiently. In particular the ACT demultiplexing step requires constant *O(1)* time, regardless of the number of completion handlers represented by subclasses of `Completion_Handler_ACT`.

Example Resolved In our example scenario, system administrators employ the management application in conjunction with management agents to display and log all connections established between Web browsers and Web servers. In addition, the management application displays and logs each file transfer, because the HTTP 1.1 protocol can multiplex multiple GET requests over a single connection [Mog95].

We first define a management agent proxy that management applications can use to subscribe asynchronously for completion events. We next illustrate how to define a concrete ACT that is tailored to the types of completion events that occur in our e-commerce system. Finally we implement the `main()` function that combines all these components to create the management application.

The management agent proxy [GoF95]. This class defines the types of events that management applications can subscribe to, as well as a method that allows management applications to subscribe a callback with a management agent asynchronously:

```
class Management_Agent_Proxy {
public:
    enum Event_Type { NEW_CONNECTIONS, FILE_TRANSFERS };

    void subscribe (Callback_Handler *handler,
                    Event_Type type,
                    Completion_Handler_ACT *act);
    // ...
};
```

This proxy class is implemented using the Half-Object plus Protocol [PLoPD1] pattern, which defines an object interface that encapsulates the protocol between the proxy and a management agent. When an event of a particular Event_Type occurs, the management agent returns the corresponding completion event to the Management_ Agent_Proxy. This proxy then invokes the method completion_ event() on the Callback_Handler. This method returns a pointer to the Completion_Handler_ACT that the management application passed to subscribe() originally, as shown in implementation activity 6 (271).

The concrete ACT. Management applications playing the role of initiators and management agent services in our e-commerce system exchange pointers to Completion_Handler_ACT subclass objects, such as the following Management_Completion_Handler:

```
class Management_Completion_Handler :
    public Completion_Handler_ACT {
private:
    Window *window_; // Used to display and
    Logger *logger_; // to log completion events.
public:
    Management_Completion_Handler (Window *w, Logger *l):
        window_ (w), logger_ (l) { }

    virtual void handle_event
        (const Completion_Event &event) {
        window_->update (event);
        logger_->update (event);
    }
};
```

The parameters passed to the Management_Completion_Handler constructor identify the concrete completion handler state used by the management application to process completion events. These two parameters are cached in internal data members in the class, which point to the database logger and the GUI window that will be updated when completion events arrive from management agents via the handle_event() hook method. This hook method is dispatched by the Callback_Hander's completion_event() method, as shown in implementation activity 6 (271).

The main() function. The following main() function shows how a management application invokes asynchronous subscription operations on a management agent proxy and then processes the subsequent connection and file transfer completion event responses. To simplify and optimize the demultiplexing and processing of completion handlers, the management application passes a pointer ACT to a `Management_Completion_Handler` when it subscribes to a management agent proxy. Generalizing this example to work with multiple management agents and other types of completion events is straightforward.

```
int main () {
```

The application starts by creating a single instance of the `Callback_Handler` class defined in implementation activity 6 (271):

```
Callback_Handler callback_handler;
```

This `Callback_Handler` is shared by all asynchronous subscription operations and is used to demultiplex all types of incoming completion events.

The application next creates an instance of the `Management_Agent` proxy described above:

```
Management_Agent_Proxy agent_proxy = // ...
```

This `agent` will call back to the `callback_handler` when connection and file transfer completion events occur.

The application then creates several objects to handle logging and display completion processing:

```
Logger database_logger (DATABASE);
Logger console_logger (CONSOLE);
Window main_window (200, 200);
Window topology_window (100, 20);
```

Some completion events will be logged to a database, whereas others will be written to a console window. Depending on the event type, different graphical displays may need to be updated. For example, a topology window might show an iconic view of the system.

The `main()` function creates two `Management_Completion_Handler` objects that uniquely identify the concrete completion handlers that process connection establishment and file transfer completion events, respectively:

```
Management_Completion_Handler connection_act
    (&topology_window, &database_logger);
Management_Completion_Handler file_transfer_act
    (&main_window, &console_logger);
```

The `Management_Completion_Handler` objects are initialized with pointers to the appropriate `Window` and `Logger` objects. Pointer ACTs to these two `Management_Completion_Handler` objects are passed explicitly when the management application asynchronously subscribes the `callback_handler` with `Management_Agent_Proxy` for each type of event:

```
agent_proxy.subscribe
    (&callback_handler,
     Management_Agent_Proxy::NEW_CONNECTIONS,
     &connection_act);

agent_proxy.subscribe
    (&callback_handler,
     Management_Agent_Proxy::FILE_TRANSFERS,
     &file_transfer_act);
```

Note that the `Management_Completion_Handlers` are held 'implicitly' in the address space of the initiator, as described in implementation activity 2 (269).

Once these subscriptions are complete the application enters its event loop, in which all subsequent processing is driven by callbacks from completion events.

```
    run_event_loop ();
}
```

Whenever a management agent detects a new connection or file transfer, it sends the associated completion event to the `Management_Agent_Proxy`. This proxy then extracts the `Management_Completion_Handler` ACT from the completion event and uses the `Callback_Handler`'s `completion_event()` method to dispatch the `Management_Completion_Handler`'s `handle_events()` hook method, which processes each completion event. For example, file transfer events can be displayed on a GUI window and logged to the console, whereas new connection establishment events could be displayed on a system topology window and logged to a database.

The following sequence diagram illustrates the key collaborations between components in the management application. For simplicity we omit the creation of the agent, callback handler, window, and logging handlers, and focus on using only one window and one logging handler.

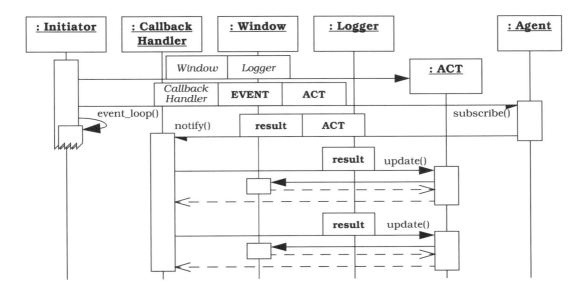

Variations   *Chain of Service ACTs.* A chain of services can occur when intermediate services also play the role of initiators that invoke asynchronous operations on other services to process the original initiator's operation.

➥   For example, consider a management application that invokes operation requests on an agent, which in turn invokes other requests on a timer mechanism. In this scenario the management application initiator uses a chain of services. All intermediate services in the chain—except the two ends—are both initiators *and* services, because they both receive and initiate asynchronous operations.   ❏

A chain of services must decide which service ultimately responds to the initiator. Moreover, if each service in a chain uses the Asynchronous Completion Token pattern, four issues related to passing, storing, and returning ACTs must be considered:

• If no service in the chain created new ACTs, then the last service in the chain can simply notify the initiator. This design can optimize ACT processing because it makes it unnecessary to 'unwind' the chain of services.

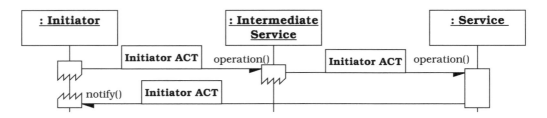

- If an intermediate service does not associate any completion processing with the asynchronous operation(s) it initiates, it can simply forward the original ACT it received from its previous initiator.

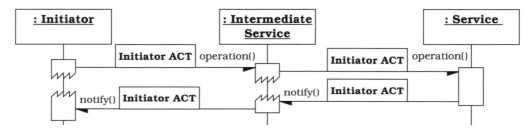

- When completion processing must be associated with an asynchronous operation and an intermediate service can be sure that its initiators' ACT values are unique, the service can use initiator ACT values to index into a data structure that maps each ACT to completion processing actions and state:

Intermediate Service	maintains	Initiator ACT1	**Initiator ACT2**	...	Index
		state1	state2	...	Entries
		actions1	...	...	

- If an intermediate service cannot assume uniqueness of initiator ACTs, the original ACT cannot be reused to reference intermediate completion actions and state. In this case an intermediate service must create a new ACT and maintain a table that stores these ACTs so they can be mapped back to their original ACTs when the chain 'unwinds'.

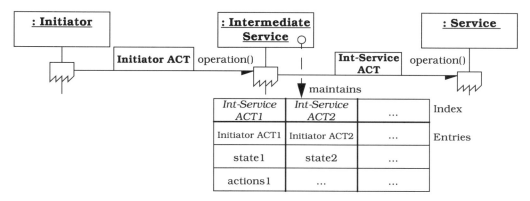

Non-opaque ACTs. In some implementations of the Asynchronous Completion Token pattern, services do not treat the ACT as purely opaque. For example, Win32 OVERLAPPED structures are non-opaque ACTs, because certain fields can be modified by the operating system kernel. One solution to this problem is to pass subclasses of the OVERLAPPED structure that contain additional ACT state, as shown in implementation activity 1.1 in the Proactor pattern (215).

Synchronous ACTs. ACTs can also be used for operations that result in synchronous callbacks. In this case the ACT is not really an *asynchronous* completion token but rather a *synchronous* one. Using ACTs for synchronous callback operations provides a well-structured means of passing state related to an operation through to a service. In addition this approach decouples concurrency policies, so that the code receiving an ACT can be used for either synchronous or asynchronous operations.

Known Uses   **HTTP-Cookies**. Web servers can use the Asynchronous Completion Token pattern if they expect responses from Web browsers. For example, a Web server may expect a user to transmit data they filled into a form that was downloaded from the server to the browser in response to a previous HTTP GET request. Due to the 'sessionless' design of the HTTP protocol, and because users need not complete forms immediately, the Web server, acting in the role of a 'initiator', transmits a cookie (the ACT) to the Web browser along with the form. This cookie allows the server to associate the user's response with his or her original request for the form. Web browsers need not interpret the cookie, but simply return it unchanged to the Web server along with the completed form.

Operating system **asynchronous I/O mechanisms**. The Asynchronous Completion Token pattern is used by operating systems that support asynchronous I/O. For instance, the following techniques are used by Windows NT and POSIX:

- **Windows NT**. ACTs are used in conjunction with handles, Overlapped I/O, Win32 I/O completion ports on Windows NT [Sol98]. When Win32 handles[11] are created they can be associated with completion ports using the `CreateIoCompletionPort()` function. Completion ports provide a location for kernel-level services to queue completion events. These events can be dequeued and processed subsequently by initiators that invoked the asynchronous operations originally.

  For example, when initiators initiate asynchronous reads and writes via `ReadFile()` or `WriteFile()`, they can specify `OVERLAPPED` struct ACTs that will be queued at a completion port when the operations finish. Initiators can then use the `GetQueued-CompletionStatus()` function to dequeue completion events that return the original `OVERLAPPED` struct as an ACT. Implementation activity 5.5 in the Proactor pattern (215) illustrates this design in more detail.

- **POSIX**. The POSIX Asynchronous I/O API [POSIX95] can be programmed to pass ACTs to its asynchronous I/O operations. This can be accomplished by subclassing the ACT from the `aiocb` struct, which then can be passed to `aio_read()` or `aio_write()`. These ACTs can be retrieved subsequently via the `aio_suspend()` asynchronous event demultiplexing function and downcast to the appropriate completion handlers. In addition, initiators can specify that completion events for asynchronous I/O operations be returned via asynchronous UNIX 'real-time' signals or synchronously via the `sigtimedwait()` or `sigwaitinfo()` functions.

CORBA demultiplexing. The TAO CORBA Object Request Broker [SC99] uses the Asynchronous Completion Token pattern to demultiplex various types of GIOP requests and responses efficiently, scalably, and predictably in both the client initiator and server.

---

11. Win32 handles are similar to UNIX file descriptors. For Win32 overlapped I/O, handles are used to identify network transport endpoints or open files.

In a multi-threaded client initiator, for example, TAO uses ACTs to associate GIOP responses from a server with the appropriate client thread that initiated the request over a single multiplexed TCP/IP connection to the server process. Each TAO client request carries a unique opaque sequence number, the ACT, represented as a 32-bit integer. When an operation is invoked the client-side TAO ORB assigns its sequence number to be an index into an internal connection table managed using the Leader/Followers pattern (447).

Each table entry keeps track of a client thread that is waiting for a response from its server over the multiplexed connection. When the server replies, it returns the sequence number ACT sent by the client. TAO's client-side ORB uses the ACT to index into its connection table to determine which client thread to awaken and pass the reply.

In the server, TAO uses the Asynchronous Completion Token pattern to provide low-overhead demultiplexing throughout the various layers of features in an Object Adapter [SC99]. For example, when a server creates an object reference, TAO Object Adapter stores special object ID and POA ID values in its object key, which is ultimately passed to clients as an ACT contained in an object reference.

When the client passes back the object key with its request, TAO's Object Adapter extracts the special values from the ACT and uses them to index directly into tables it manages. This so-called 'active demultiplexing' scheme [PRS+99] uses an ACT to ensure constant-time $O(1)$ lookup regardless of the number of objects in a POA or the number of nested POAs in an Object Adapter.

Electronic medical imaging system management. The management example described in this pattern is derived from a distributed electronic medical imaging system developed at Washington University for Project Spectrum [BBC94]. In this system, management applications monitor the performance and status of multiple distributed components in the medical imaging system, including image servers, modalities, hierarchical storage management systems, and radiologist diagnostic workstations. Management agents provide an asynchronous service that notifies management application of events, such as *connection establishment events* and *image transfer events*. This system uses the Asynchronous Completion Token pattern so that management applications can associate state efficiently with the arrival of events from management agents received asynchronous subscription operations earlier.

Jini. The handback object in Jini [Sun99a] distributed event specification [Sun99b] is a Java-based example of the Asynchronous Completion Token pattern. When a consumer registers with an event source to receive notifications, it can pass a handback object to this event source. This object is a `java.rmi.MarshalledObject`, which is therefore not demarshaled at the event source, but is simply 'handed back' to the consumer as part of the event notification.

The consumer can then use the `getRegistrationObject()` method of the event notification to retrieve the handback object that was passed to the event source when the consumer registered with it. Thus, consumers can recover the context rapidly in which to process the event notification. This design is particularly useful when a third party registered the consumer to receive event notifications.

FedEx inventory tracking. An intriguing real-life example of the Asynchronous Completion Token pattern is implemented by the inventory tracking mechanism used by the US Federal Express postal services. A FedEx Airbill contains a section labeled: 'Your Internal Billing Reference Information (Optional: First 24 characters will appear on invoice).'

The sender of a package uses this field as an ACT. This ACT is returned by FedEx (the service) to you (the initiator) with the invoice that notifies the sender that the transaction has completed. FedEx deliberately defines this field very loosely: it is a maximum of 24 characters, which are otherwise 'untyped.' Therefore, senders can use the field in a variety of ways. For example, a sender can populate this field with the index of a record for an internal database or with a name of a file containing a 'to-do list' to be performed after the acknowledgment of the FedEx package delivery has been received.

Consequences   There are several **benefits** to using the Asynchronous Completion Token pattern:

Simplified initiator data structures. Initiators need not maintain complex data structures to associate service responses with completion handlers. The ACT returned by the service can be downcast or reinterpreted to convey all the information the initiator needs to demultiplex to its appropriate completion action.

Efficient state acquisition. ACTs are time efficient because they need not require complex parsing of data returned with the service response. All relevant information necessary to associate the response with the original request can be stored either in the ACT or in an object referenced by the ACT. Alternatively, ACTs can be used as indices or pointers to operation state for highly efficient access, thereby eliminating costly table searches.

Space efficiency. ACTs can consume minimal data space yet can still provide applications with sufficient information to associate large amounts of state to process asynchronous operation completion actions. For example, in C and C++, void pointer ACTs can reference arbitrarily large objects held in the initiator application.

Flexibility. User-defined ACTs are not forced to inherit from an interface to use the service's ACTs. This allows applications to pass as ACTs objects for which a change of type is undesirable or even impossible. The generic nature of ACTs can be used to associate an object of any type with an asynchronous operation. For example, when ACTs are implemented as CORBA object references they can be narrowed to the appropriate concrete interface.

Non-dictatorial concurrency policies. Long duration operations can be executed asynchronously because operation state can be recovered from an ACT efficiently. Initiators can therefore be single-threaded or multi-threaded depending on application requirements. In contrast, a service that does not provide ACTs may force delay-sensitive initiators to perform operations synchronously within threads to handle operation completions properly.

There are several **liabilities** to avoid when using the Asynchronous Completion Token pattern.

Memory leaks. Memory leaks can result if initiators use ACTs as pointers to dynamically allocated memory and services fail to return the ACTs, for example if the service crashes. As described in implementation activity 2 (269), initiators wary of this possibility should maintain separate ACT repositories or tables. These can be used for explicit garbage collection if services fail or if they corrupt the ACT.

Authentication. When an ACT is returned to an initiator on completion of an asynchronous event, the initiator may need to authenticate the

ACT before using it. This is necessary if the server cannot be trusted to have treated the ACT opaquely and may have changed its value. Implementation activity 2 (269) describes a strategy for addressing this liability.

Application re-mapping. If ACTs are used as direct pointers to memory, errors can occur if part of the application is re-mapped in virtual memory. This situation can occur in persistent applications that are restarted after crashes, as well as for objects allocated from a memory-mapped address space. To protect against these errors, indices to a repository can be used as ACTs, as described in implementation activities 1 (267) and 2 (269). The extra level of indirection provided by these 'index ACTs' protects against re-mappings, because indices can remain valid across re-mappings, whereas pointers to direct memory may not.

See Also   The Asynchronous Completion Token and Memento patterns [GoF95] are similar with respect to their participants. In the Memento pattern, originators give mementos to caretakers who treat the Memento as 'opaque' objects. In the Asynchronous Completion Token pattern, initiators give ACTs to services that treat the ACTs as 'opaque' objects.

These patterns differ in motivation and applicability however. The Memento pattern takes 'snapshots' of object states, whereas the Asynchronous Completion Token pattern associates state with the completion of asynchronous operations. Another difference is in their dynamics. In the Asynchronous Completion Token pattern, the initiator—which corresponds to the originator in Memento—*creates* the ACT proactively and passes it to the service. In Memento, the caretaker—which is the initiator in terms of Asynchronous Completion Token pattern—*requests* the creation of a memento from an originator, which is reactive.

Credits   Irfan Pyarali and Timothy Harrison were co-authors on the original version of the Asynchronous Completion Token pattern. Thanks to Paul McKenney and Richard Toren for their insightful comments and contributions, and to Michael Ogg for supplying the Jini known use.

Acceptor-Connector

The *Acceptor-Connector* design pattern decouples the connection and initialization of cooperating peer services in a networked system from the processing performed by the peer services after they are connected and initialized.

Example Consider a large-scale distributed system management application consisting that monitors and controls a satellite constellation [Sch96]. Such a management application typically consists of a multi-service, application-level gateway that routes data between transport endpoints connecting remote peer hosts.

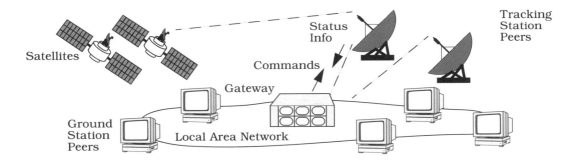

Each service in the peer hosts uses the gateway to send and receive several types of data, including status information, bulk data, and commands, that control the satellites. The peer hosts can be distributed throughout local area and wide-area networks.

The gateway transmits data between its peer hosts using the connection-oriented TCP/IP protocol [Ste93]. Each service in the system is bound to a particular transport address, which is designated by a tuple consisting of an IP host address and a TCP port number. Different port numbers uniquely identify different types of service.

Unlike the binding of services to specific TCP/IP host/port tuples, which can be selected early in the distributed system's lifecycle, it may be premature to designate the connection establishment and service initialization roles *a priori*. Instead, the services in the gateway and peer hosts should be able to change their connection roles flexibly to support the following run-time behavior:

- Services in a gateway may *actively* initiate connection requests to services located in remote peer hosts, then route data to them.

- Services in a gateway may *passively* accept connection requests from services within the peer hosts, which then route data through the gateway to a service on another peer host.

- Services residing in peer hosts may be active connection initiators in one situation and passive connection acceptors in another.

- Hybrid configurations that combine passive and active connection behavior in the same gateway or peer host may also occur.

In general, the inherent flexibility required to support such a run-time behavior demands communication software that allows the connection establishment, initialization, and processing of peer services to evolve gracefully and to vary independently.

Context A networked system or application in which connection-oriented protocols are used to communicate between peer services connected via transport endpoints.

Problem Applications in connection-oriented networked systems often contain a significant amount of configuration code that establishes connections and initializes services. This configuration code is largely independent of the processing that services perform on data exchanged between their connected transport endpoints. Tightly coupling the configuration code with the service processing code is therefore undesirable, because it fails to resolve four *forces*:

- It should be easy to change connection roles to support different application behavior, as discussed in the *Example* section. Connection roles determine whether an application actively initiates or passively accepts a connection. In contrast, communication roles determine whether an application plays the role of a client, a server, or both client and server in a peer-to-peer configuration.

- It should be easy to add new types of services, service implementations, and communication protocols without affecting existing connection establishment and service initialization configuration code.

➥   The gateway from our example may require integration with a directory service that runs over the TP4 or SPX transport protocols rather than TCP. Ideally, this integration should have little or no effect on the implementation of the gateway services themselves.❑

- In general, connection establishment and service initialization strategies change less frequently than the communication protocols and services implemented by an application.

    ➥   FTP, TELNET, HTTP and CORBA IIOP services all use different application-level communication protocols. However, they can all be configured using the same connection and initialization mechanisms.   ❑

- For large-scale networked systems it should be possible to reduce connection establishment latency by using advanced operating system features, such as asynchronous connection mechanisms.

    ➥   Applications with a large number of peers may need to establish many connections asynchronously and concurrently. Efficient and scalable connection establishment is particularly important for applications, such as our gateway example, that communicate over long-latency wide area networks.   ❑

Solution   Decouple the connection and initialization of peer services in a networked application from the processing these peer services perform after they are connected and initialized.

In detail: encapsulate application services within peer *service handlers*. Each service handler implements one half of an end-to-end service in a networked application. Connect and initialize peer service handlers using two factories: *acceptor* and *connector*. Both factories cooperate to create a *full association* [Ste93] between two peer service handlers and their two connected transport endpoints, each encapsulated by a transport handle.

The acceptor factory establishes connections passively on behalf of an associated peer service handler upon the arrival of connection request events[12] issued by remote peer service handlers. Likewise,

---

12. Henceforth, we refer to connection request events and data request events as simply *connection requests* and *data requests*.

the connector factory establishes connections actively to designated remote peer service handlers on behalf of peer service handlers.

After a connection is established, the acceptor and connector factories initialize their associated peer service handlers and pass them their respective transport handles. The peer service handlers then perform application-specific processing, using their transport handles to exchange data via their connected transport endpoints. In general, service handlers do not interact with the acceptor and connector factories after they are connected and initialized.

Structure   There are six key participants in the Acceptor-Connector pattern:

A *passive-mode transport endpoint* is a factory that listens for connection requests to arrive, accepts those connection requests, and creates *transport handles* that encapsulate the newly *connected transport endpoints*. Data can be exchanged via connected transport endpoints by reading and writing to their associated transport handles.

Class Transport Endpoint	*Collaborator*
Responsibility • Allows Service Handlers to exchange requests and data over a network	

Class Transport Handle	*Collaborator* • Transport Endpoint
Responsibility • Encapsulates a Transport Endpoint	

➡️   In the gateway example, we use socket handles to encapsulate transport endpoints. In this case, a passive-mode transport endpoint is a passive-mode socket handle [Ste98] that is bound to a TCP port number and IP address. It creates connected transport endpoints that are encapsulated by data-mode socket handles. Standard Socket API operations, such as `recv()` and `send()`, can use these connected data-mode socket handles to read and write data.   ❑

A *service handler* defines one half of an end-to-end service in a networked system. A concrete service handler often plays either the client role or server role in this end-to-end service. In peer-to-peer use cases it can even play both roles simultaneously. A service handler provides an activation hook method that is used to initialize it after it is connected to its peer service handler. In addition, the service handler contains a transport handle, such as a data-mode socket handle, that encapsulates a transport endpoint. Once connected, this transport handle can be used by a service handler to exchange data with its peer service handler via their connected transport endpoints.

Class	*Collaborator*
Service Handler	• Dispatcher
	• Transport Endpoint
Responsibility	
• Implements a half of an end-to-end service in a networked application	

➥ In our example the service handlers are both cooperating components within the gateway and peer hosts that communicate over TCP/IP via their connected socket handles. Service handlers are responsible for processing status information, bulk data, and commands that monitor and control a satellite constellation. ❑

An *acceptor* is a factory that implements a strategy for *passively* establishing a connected transport endpoint, and creating and initializing its associated transport handle and service handler. An acceptor provides two methods, *connection initialization* and *connection completion*, that perform these steps with the help of a passive-mode transport endpoint.

When its initialization method is called, an acceptor binds its passive-mode transport endpoint to a particular transport address, such as a TCP port number and IP host address, that listens passively for the arrival of connection requests.

When a connection request arrives, the acceptor's connection completion method performs three steps:

• Firstly, it uses its passive-mode transport endpoint to create a connected transport endpoint and encapsulate the endpoint with a transport handle.

• Secondly, it creates a service handler that will process data requests emanating from its peer service handler via their connected transport endpoints.

- Thirdly, it stores the transport handle in its associated service handler and invokes the service handler's activation hook method, which allows the service handler to finish initializing itself.

A *connector*[13] is a factory that implements the strategy for *actively* establishing a connected transport endpoint and initializing its associated transport handle and service handler. It provides two methods, *connection initiation* and *connection completion*, that perform these steps.

The connection initiation method is passed an existing service handler and establishes a connected transport endpoint for it with an acceptor. This acceptor must be listening for connection requests to arrive on a particular transport address, as described above.

Separating the connector's connection initiation method from its completion method allows a connector to support both synchronous and asynchronous connection establishment transparently:

- In the synchronous case, the connector initiating the connection request blocks its caller until the transport endpoints are connected. At this point, the connector calls the service handler's activation hook method directly.

- In the asynchronous case, the connection request runs asynchronously and the connector's initiation method returns immediately. The service handler is activated by the connection completion method only after the connector is notified that the transport endpoint has finished connecting asynchronously.

Class Acceptor	*Collaborator* • Service Handler • Dispatcher • Transport Endpoint	*Class* Connector	*Collaborator* • Service Handler • Dispatcher • Transport Endpoint
Responsibility • Passively connects and initializes an associated Service Handler		*Responsibility* • Actively connects and initializes an associated Service Handler	

Regardless of whether a transport endpoint is connected synchronously or asynchronously, both acceptors and connectors

---

13. Note that the notion of connector in the Acceptor-Connector pattern differs from the notion of connector in [SG96]. There, a connector is a software architecture specification concept that denotes the collaborations among components in a system.

initialize a service handler by calling its activation hook method after a transport endpoint is connected. From this point service handlers generally do not interact with their acceptor and connector factories.

A *dispatcher* is responsible for demultiplexing indication events that represent various types of service requests, such as connection requests and data requests.

Class	*Collaborator*
Dispatcher	• Acceptor
	• Connector
Responsibility	• Service Handler
• Registers Acceptors, Connectors, and Service Handlers	• Transport Endpoint
• Dispatches Acceptors, Connectors, and Service Handlers	

- For the acceptor, the dispatcher demultiplexes connection indication events received on one or more transport handles that encapsulate transport endpoints. Multiple acceptors can register with a dispatcher, which listens on their behalf for connection requests to arrive from peer connectors.

- For the connector, the dispatcher demultiplexes completion events that arrive in response to connections that were initiated asynchronously. To handle this situation, a connector registers itself with a dispatcher to receive these connection completion events. The dispatcher then runs its event loop. When a completion event arrives it notifies the corresponding connector. The connector can then invoke the designated service handler's activation hook method to allow the service handler to initialize itself. A single dispatcher and connector can therefore initiate and complete connections asynchronously on behalf of multiple service handlers.

Note that a dispatcher is not necessary for synchronous connection establishment, because the thread that initiates the connection will block awaiting the connection completion event. As a result this thread can activate the service handler directly.

- Service handlers can register their transport handles with a dispatcher, which will notify the service handlers when indication events occur on those handles.

Networked applications and services can be built by subclassing and instantiating the generic participants of the Acceptor-Connector pattern described above to create the following *concrete* components.

Concrete service handlers define the application-specific portions of end-to-end services. They are activated by *concrete acceptors* or *concrete connectors*. Concrete acceptors instantiate generic acceptors with concrete service handlers, transport endpoints, and transport handles used by these service handlers. Similarly, concrete connectors instantiate generic connectors.

Concrete service handlers, acceptors, and connectors are also instantiated with a specific type of interprocess communication (IPC) mechanism, such as Sockets [Ste98] or TLI [Rago93]. These IPC mechanisms are used to create the transport endpoints and transport handles that connected peer service handlers use to exchange data.

The class diagram of the Acceptor-Connector pattern is shown in the following figure:

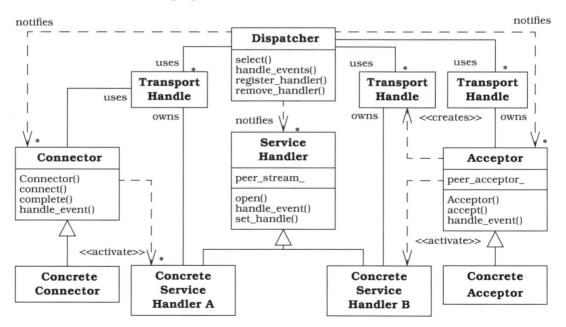

Dynamics To illustrate the collaborations performed by participants in the Acceptor-Connector pattern, we examine three canonical scenarios:

- Scenario I shows passive connection establishment

- Scenario II shows synchronous active connection establishment

- Scenario III shows asynchronous active connection establishment

Scenario I: This scenario illustrates the collaboration between acceptor and service handler participants and is divided into three phases:

- *Passive-mode transport endpoint initialization phase.* An application that plays a passive connection role first calls the acceptor's connection initialization method. This method initializes a passive-mode transport endpoint and binds it to a transport address, such as the local host's IP address and a TCP port number. The acceptor then listens on this transport address for connection requests initiated by peer connectors.[14]

  Next, the acceptor's initialization method registers itself with a dispatcher, which will notify the acceptor when connection indication events arrive from peer connectors. After the acceptor's initialization method returns, the application initiates the dispatcher's event loop. This loop waits for connection requests and other types of indication events to arrive from peer connectors.

- *Service handler initialization phase.* When a connection request arrives for a particular transport address, the dispatcher notifies the associated acceptor. This acceptor uses its passive-mode transport endpoint to create a new connected transport endpoint and encapsulate it with a transport handle. It next creates a new service handler, stores the transport handle into the service handler, and calls the service handler's activation hook method.

  This hook method performs service handler-specific initialization, for example allocating locks, spawning threads, or establishing a session with a logging service. A service handler may elect to register itself with a dispatcher, which will notify the handler automatically when indication events containing data requests arrive for it.

---

14. For simplicity we omit the creation and use of the passive-mode transport endpoint in the sequence diagram for this scenario.

- *Service processing phase.* After a transport endpoint has been connected and the associated service handler has been initialized, the service processing phase begins. In this phase an application-level communication protocol such as TELNET, FTP, HTTP or CORBA IIOP can be used to exchange data between the peer service handlers via their connected transport endpoints. When all exchanges are complete, the transport endpoints, transport handles, and service handlers can be shut down and their resources released.

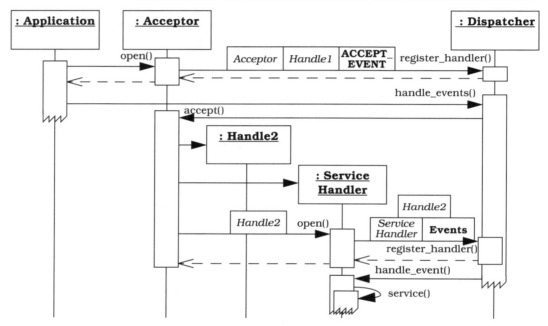

A connector can initialize its service handler using two general strategies: *synchronous* and *asynchronous*. Synchronous service initialization is useful:

- If connection establishment latency is very low, for example establishing a connection with a server on the same host via a 'loopback network' device

- If multiple threads of control are available and it is efficient to use a thread-per-connection model [Sch97] to connect each service handler synchronously or

- If the services must be initialized in a fixed order and the client cannot perform useful work until all connections are established.

Asynchronous service initialization is useful in different situations, such as establishing connections over high latency links, using single-threaded applications, or initializing a large number of peers that can be connected in an arbitrary order.

Scenario II: The collaborations among participants in the *synchronous* connector scenario can be divided into three phases:

- *Connection initiation phase.* To establish a connection synchronously between a service handler and its peer, an application can invoke the connector's connection initiation method. Using the transport handle associated with the service handler, this method actively establishes the connection by blocking the application's thread until the connection completes synchronously.

- *Service handler initialization phase.* After a connection completes synchronously, the connection initiation method calls the associated service handler's activation hook method directly. This hook method performs service handler-specific initializations.

- *Service processing phase.* After a service handler is initialized, it performs application-specific service processing using data exchanged with its connected peer service handler. This phase is similar to the service processing phase performed by service handlers that are created and initialized by acceptors.

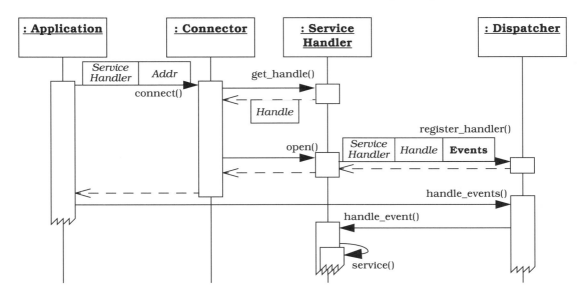

In the synchronous scenario, the connector combines the connection initiation and service initialization phases into a single blocking operation. Only one connection is established per thread for every invocation of a connector's connection initiation method.

Scenario III: The collaborations among participants in the *asynchronous* connector scenario are also divided into three phases:

* *Connection initiation phase.* To connect a service handler and its peer service handler *asynchronously*, an application invokes the connector's connection initiation method. As with the synchronous Scenario II, the connector initiates the connection actively.

  Unlike Scenario II, however, the connection initiation request executes asynchronously. The application thread therefore does not block while waiting for the connection to complete. To receive a notification when a connection completes, the connector registers itself and the service handler's transport handle with the dispatcher and returns control back to the application.

* *Service handler initialization phase.* After a connection completes asynchronously, the dispatcher notifies the connector's connection completion method. This method cleans up any resources allocated to manage the pending connection, then it calls the service handler's activation hook method to perform service-specific initialization.

* *Service processing phase.* After a service handler is activated, it performs application-specific service processing using data exchanged with its connected peer service handler. This phase is similar to the service processing phases described in Scenarios I and II.

Note in the following figure how the connection initiation phase in Scenario III is separated temporally from the service handler initialization phase. This decoupling enables multiple connection initiations and completions to proceed concurrently, thereby maximizing the parallelism inherent in networks and hosts.

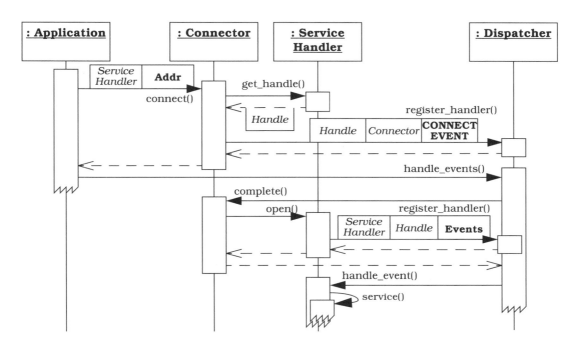

Implementation   The participants in the Acceptor-Connector pattern can be decomposed into three layers:

- *Demultiplexing/dispatching infrastructure layer components*. This layer performs generic, application-independent strategies for dispatching events.

- *Connection management layer components*. This layer performs generic, application-independent connection and initialization services.

- *Application layer components*. This layer then customizes the generic strategies performed by the other two layers via subclassing, object composition, and/or parameterized type instantiation, to create concrete components that establish connections, exchange data, and perform service-specific processing.

Our coverage of the Acceptor-Connector implementation starts with the demultiplexing/dispatching component layer and progresses upwards through the connection management and application component layers.

1   *Implement the demultiplexing/dispatching infrastructure component layer.* This layer handles events that occur on transport endpoints and consists of transport mechanisms and dispatching mechanisms. This implementation activity can be divided into two sub-activities:

1.1 *Select the transport mechanisms.* These mechanisms consist of:

- Passive-mode transport endpoint components
- Connected transport endpoint components
- Transport address components
- Transport handle components

A passive-mode transport endpoint is a factory that listens on an advertised transport address for connection requests to arrive. When such a request arrives, a passive-mode transport endpoint creates a connected transport endpoint and encapsulates this new endpoint with a transport handle. An application can use this transport handle to exchange data with its peer-connected transport endpoint. The transport mechanism components are often provided by the underlying operating system platform and may be accessed via wrapper facades (47), as shown in implementation activity 3 (311).

➥   For our gateway example we implement the transport mechanism components using the Sockets API [Ste98]. The passive-mode transport endpoints and connected transport endpoints are implemented by passive-mode and data-mode sockets, respectively. Transport handles are implemented by socket handles. Transport addresses are implemented using IP host addresses and TCP port numbers.   ❏

1.2 *Implement the dispatching mechanisms.* These mechanisms consist of dispatcher and event handler components. A dispatcher is responsible for associating requests to their corresponding acceptors, connectors, and service handlers. An event handler defines the event processing interface provided by a service of an event-driven application.

To implement the dispatching mechanisms, follow the guidelines described in the Reactor (179) or Proactor (215) event demultiplexing patterns. These patterns handle synchronous and asynchronous event demultiplexing, respectively. A dispatcher can also be implemented as a separate thread or process using the Active Object pattern (369) or Leader/Followers (447) thread pools.

➡ For our gateway example, we implement the dispatcher and event handler using components from the Reactor pattern (179). This enables efficient synchronous demultiplexing of multiple types of events from multiple sources within a single thread of control. The dispatcher, which we call 'reactor' in accordance with Reactor pattern terminology, uses a reactive model to demultiplex and dispatch concrete event handlers.

We use a reactor Singleton [GoF95] because only one instance of it is needed in the entire application process. The event handler class, which we call Event_Handler in our example, implements methods needed by the reactor to notify its service handlers, connectors, and acceptors when events they have registered for occur. To collaborate with the reactor, therefore, these components must subclass from class Event_Handler, as shown in implementation activity 2 (299).❏

2   *Implement the connection management component layer.* This layer creates service handlers, passively or actively connects service handlers to their remote peer service handlers, and activates service handlers after they are connected. All components in this layer are generic and delegate to concrete IPC mechanisms, concrete service handlers, concrete acceptors, and concrete connectors. These are instantiated by the application layer described in implementation activity 3 (311). There are three primary components in the connection management layer: *service handler, acceptor,* and *connector.*

2.1 *Define a generic service handler interface.* A service handler provides a generic interface for processing services defined by clients, servers, or both client and server roles in peer-to-peer services. This interface includes methods for initializing a service handler, executing the service it defines, and for maintaining the IPC mechanism it uses for communication. To create a concrete service handler, applications must customize this component using subclassing, object composition, or parameterized type instantiation.

Applications must also configure a service handler component with a concrete IPC mechanism that encapsulates a transport handle and its corresponding transport endpoint. These IPC mechanisms are often implemented as wrapper facades (47). Concrete service handlers can use these IPC mechanisms to communicate with their remote peer service handlers.

➥ In our gateway example we define a `Service_Handler` abstract base class that inherits from the `Event_Handler` class defined in implementation activity 1 of the Reactor pattern (179):

```
template <class IPC_STREAM>
    // <IPC_STREAM> is the type of concrete IPC data
    // transfer mechanism.
class Service_Handler : public Event_Handler {
public:
    typedef typename IPC_STREAM::PEER_ADDR Addr;

    // Pure virtual method (defined by a subclass).
    virtual void open () = 0;

    // Access method used by <Acceptor> and <Connector>.
    IPC_STREAM &peer () { return ipc_stream_; }

    // Return the address we are connected to.
    Addr &remote_addr () {
        return ipc_stream_.remote_addr ();
    }

    // Set the <handle> used by this <Service_Handler>.
    void set_handle (HANDLE handle){
        return ipc_stream_.set_handle (handle);
    }
private:
    // Template 'placeholder' for a concrete IPC
    // mechanism wrapper facade, which encapsulates a
    // data-mode transport endpoint and transport handle.
    IPC_STREAM ipc_stream_;
};
```

This design allows a `Reactor` to dispatch the service handler's event handling method it inherits from class `Event_Handler`. In addition, the `Service_Handler` class defines methods to access its IPC mechanism, which is configured into the class using parameterized types. Finally this class includes an activation hook that acceptors and connectors can use to initialize a `Service_Handler` object once a connection is established. This pure virtual method, which we call open(), must be overridden by a concrete service handler to perform service-specific initialization.   ❑

2.2 *Define the generic acceptor interface.* The acceptor component implements the generic strategy for establishing connections passively and creating and initializing the concrete service handlers that exchange data with peer service handlers over these connections. An acceptor also defines an initialization method that an application can call to advertise its passive-mode transport endpoint address to other applications on the network.

A generic acceptor is customized by the components in the application layer, as described in implementation activity 3 (311) to establish connections passively on behalf of a particular service handler using a designated IPC mechanism. To support this customization an acceptor implementation can use two general strategies, *polymorphism* or *parameterized types*:

- *Polymorphism*. In this strategy, illustrated in the *Structure* section, concrete acceptors are specified by subclassing from a generic acceptor. The acceptor method, which we call `accept()`, responsible for accepting connection requests from remote clients is a template method [GoF95]. It performs the generic processing that constitutes the acceptor's passive connection establishment and service initialization logic.

  The behavior of the individual steps in this process are delegated to hook methods [Pree95] that are also declared in the acceptor's interface. These hook methods can be overridden by concrete acceptors to perform application-specific strategies, for example to use a particular concrete IPC mechanism to establish connections passively. The concrete service handler created by a concrete acceptor can be manufactured via a factory method [GoF95] called as one of the steps in the acceptor's `accept()` template method.

- *Parameterized types*. This strategy encapsulates IPC mechanisms for passive connection establishment within wrapper facades (47) and configures them into an acceptor component via parameterized types. As with the polymorphic strategy outlined above, the acceptor's `accept()` method is a template method [GoF95] whose hook methods delegate to the particular IPC mechanism configured into the acceptor. The type of concrete service handler used to instantiate a concrete acceptor can also be supplied as a template parameter to the generic acceptor.

One advantage of using parameterized types is that they allow the IPC connection mechanisms and service handlers associated with an acceptor to be changed easily and efficiently. This flexibility simplifies porting an acceptor's connection establishment code to platforms with different IPC mechanisms. It also allows the same connection establishment and service initialization code to be reused for different types of concrete service handlers.

Inheritance and parameterized types have the following trade-offs:

- Parameterized types may incur additional compile and link-time overhead, but generally compile into faster code [CarEl95]

- Inheritance may incur additional run-time overhead due to the indirection of dynamic binding [HLS97], but is generally faster to compile and link

Different applications and application services have different needs that are best served by one or the other strategies.

➥   In our gateway example we use parameterized types to configure the acceptor with its designated service handler and a concrete IPC mechanism that establishes connections passively. The acceptor inherits from Event_Handler to receive events from a reactor singleton, which pays the role of the dispatcher in this example:

```
template <class SERVICE_HANDLER, class IPC_ACCEPTOR>
    // The <SERVICE_HANDLER> is the type of concrete
    // service handler created/accepted/activated when a
    // connection request arrives.
    // The <IPC_ACCEPTOR> provides the concrete IPC
    // passive connection mechanism.
class Acceptor : public Event_Handler {
public:
    typedef typename IPC_ACCEPTOR::PEER_ADDR Addr;

    // Constructor initializes <local_addr> transport
    // endpoint and register with the <Reactor>.
    Acceptor (const Addr &local_addr, Reactor *r);

    // Template method that creates, connects,
    // and activates <SERVICE_HANDLER>'s.
    virtual void accept ();
protected:
    // Factory method hook for creation strategy.
    virtual SERVICE_HANDLER *make_service_handler ();

    // Hook method for connection strategy.
    virtual void accept_service_handler
                (SERVICE_HANDLER *);

    // Hook method for activation strategy.
    virtual void activate_service_handler
                (SERVICE_HANDLER *);
```

```
                          // Hook method that returns the I/O <HANDLE>.
                          virtual HANDLE get_handle () const;

                          // Hook method invoked by <Reactor> when a
                          // connection request arrives.
                          virtual void handle_event (HANDLE, Event_Type);

                  private:
                          // Template 'placeholder' for a concrete IPC
                          // mechanism that establishes connections passively.
                          IPC_ACCEPTOR peer_acceptor_;
                  };
```

The Acceptor template is parameterized by concrete types of IPC_ACCEPTOR and SERVICE_HANDLER. The IPC_ACCEPTOR is a placeholder for the concrete IPC mechanism used by an acceptor to passively establish connections initiated by peer connectors. The SERVICE_HANDLER is a placeholder for the concrete service handler that processes data exchanged with its peer connected service handler. Both of these concrete types are provided by the components in the application layer.   ❏

2.3   *Implement the generic acceptor methods.* Applications initialize an acceptor by calling its initialization method with a parameter specifying a transport address, such as the local host's IP name and TCP port number. The acceptor uses this address to listen for connections initiated by peer connectors. It forwards this address to the concrete IPC connection mechanism configured into the generic acceptor, either by an acceptor's concrete acceptor subclasses or by a parameterized type. This IPC connection mechanism then initializes the acceptor's passive-mode transport endpoint, which advertises its address to remote applications who are interested in connecting to the acceptor.

The behavior of the acceptor's passive-mode transport endpoint is determined by the type of concrete IPC mechanism used to customize the generic acceptor. This IPC mechanism is often accessed via a wrapper facade (47), such as the ACE wrapper facades [Sch92] for Sockets [Ste98], TLI [Rago93], STREAM pipes [PR90], or Win32 Named Pipes [Ric97].

The acceptor's initialization method also registers itself with a dispatcher. This dispatcher then performs a 'double dispatch' [GoF95] back to the acceptor to obtain a handle to the passive-mode transport endpoint of its underlying concrete IPC mechanism. This handle allows the dispatcher to notify the acceptor when connection requests arrive from peer connectors.

➡   The Acceptor from our example implements its constructor initialization method as follows:

```
template <class SERVICE_HANDLER, class IPC_ACCEPTOR>
void Acceptor<SERVICE_HANDLER, IPC_ACCEPTOR>::Acceptor
    (const Addr &local_addr, Reactor *reactor) {
    // Initialize the IPC_ACCEPTOR.
    peer_acceptor_.open (local_addr);

    // Register with <reactor>, which uses <get_handle>
    // to get handle via 'double-dispatching.'
    reactor->register_handler (this, ACCEPT_MASK);
}                                                                     ❏
```

When a connection request arrives from a remote peer, the dispatcher automatically calls back to the acceptor's accept() template method [GoF95]. This template method implements the acceptor's strategies for creating a new concrete service handler, accepting a connection into it, and activating the handler. The details of the acceptor's implementation are delegated to hook methods. These hook methods represent the set of operations available to perform customized service handler connection and initialization strategies.

If polymorphism is used to specify concrete acceptors, the hook methods are dispatched to their corresponding implementations within the concrete acceptor subclass. When using parameterized types, the hook methods invoke corresponding methods on the template parameters used to instantiate the generic acceptor. In both cases, concrete acceptors can modify the generic acceptor's strategies transparently without changing its accept() method's interface. This flexibility makes it possible to design concrete service handlers whose behavior can be decoupled from their passive connection and initialization.

➡ The Acceptor class in our gateway example implements the following accept() method:

```
template <class SERVICE_HANDLER, class IPC_ACCEPTOR>
void Acceptor<SERVICE_HANDLER, IPC_ACCEPTOR>::accept () {
    // The following methods comprise the core
    // strategies of the <accept> template method.

    // Factory method creates a new <SERVICE_HANDLER>.
    SERVICE_HANDLER *service_handler =
        make_service_handler ();

    // Hook method that accepts a connection passively.
    accept_service_handler (service_handler);

    // Hook method that activates the <SERVICE_HANDLER>
    // by invoking its <open> activation hook method.
    activate_service_handler (service_handler);
}
```

The make_service_handler() factory method [GoF95] is a hook used by the generic acceptor template method to create new concrete service handlers. Its connection acceptance strategy is defined by the accept_service_handler() hook method. By default this method delegates connection establishment to the accept() method of the IPC_ACCEPTOR, which defines a concrete passive IPC connection mechanism. The acceptor's service handler activation strategy is defined by the activate_service_handler() method. This method can be used by a concrete service handler to initialize itself and to select its concurrency strategy.

In our gateway example the dispatcher is a reactor that notifies the acceptor's accept() method indirectly via the handle_event() method that the acceptor inherits from class Event_Handler. The handle_event() method is an adapter [GoF95] that transforms the general-purpose event handling interface of the reactor to notify the acceptor's accept() method. ❑

When an acceptor terminates, due to errors or due to its application process shutting down, the dispatcher notifies the acceptor to release any resources it acquired dynamically.

➡ In our gateway, the reactor calls the acceptor's handle_close() hook method, which closes its passive-mode socket. ❑

2.4   *Define the generic connector interface.* The connector component implements the generic strategy for actively establishing connections and initializing the associated service handlers that process request and response events on the connections.

A connector contains a map of concrete service handlers that manage the completion of pending asynchronous connections. Service handlers whose connections are initiated asynchronously are inserted into this map. This allows their dispatcher and connector to activate the handlers after the connections complete.

As with the generic acceptors described in implementation activity 2.2 (300), components in the application layer described in implementation activity 3 (311) customizes generic connectors with particular concrete service handlers and IPC mechanisms. We must therefore select the strategy—*polymorphism* or *parameterized types*—for customizing concrete connectors. Implementation activity 2.2 (300) discusses both strategies and their trade-offs.

As with the acceptor's `accept()` method, a connector's connection initiation and completion methods are template methods [GoF95], which we call `connect()` and `complete()`. These methods implement the generic strategy for establishing connections actively and initializing service handlers. Specific steps in these strategies are delegated to hook methods [Pree95].

➥   We define the following interface for the connector used to implement our gateway example. It uses C++ templates to configure the connector with a concrete service handler and the concrete IPC connection mechanism. It inherits from class `Event_Handler` to receive asynchronous completion event notifications from the reactor dispatcher:

```
template <class SERVICE_HANDLER, class IPC_CONNECTOR>
    // The <SERVICE_HANDLER> is the type of concrete
    // service handler activated when a connection
    // request completes. The <IPC_CONNECTOR> provides
    // the concrete IPC active connection mechanism.
class Connector : public Event_Handler {
public:
    enum Connection_Mode {
        SYNC, // Initiate connection synchronously.
        ASYNC // Initiate connection asynchronously.
    };
```

```
            typedef typename IPC_CONNECTOR::PEER_ADDR Addr;

            // Initialization method that caches a <Reactor> to
            // use for asynchronous notification.
            Connector (Reactor *reactor): reactor_ (reactor) { }

            // Template method that actively connects a service to
            // a <remote_addr>.
            void connect (SERVICE_HANDLER *sh,
                          const Addr &remote_addr,
                          Connection_Mode mode);
        protected:
            // Hook method for the active connection strategy.
            virtual void connect_service_handler
                (const Addr &addr, Connection_Mode mode);

            // Register the <SERVICE_HANDLER> so that it can be
            // activated when the connection completes.
            int register_handler (SERVICE_HANDLER *sh,
                                  Connection_Mode mode);

            // Hook method for the activation strategy.
            virtual void activate_service_handler
                (SERVICE_HANDLER *sh);

            // Template method that activates a <SERVICE_HANDLER>
            // whose non-blocking connection completed. This
            // method is called by <connect> in the synchronous
            // case or by <handle_event> in the asynchronous case.
            virtual void complete (HANDLE handle);
        private:
            // Template 'placeholder' for a concrete IPC
            // mechanism that establishes connections actively.
            IPC_CONNECTOR connector_;

            typedef map<HANDLE, SERVICE_HANDLER*> Connection_Map;

            // C++ standard library map that associates <HANDLE>s
            // with <SERVICE_HANDLER> *s for pending connections.
            Connection_Map connection_map_;

            // <Reactor> used for asynchronous connection
            // completion event notifications.
            Reactor *reactor_;

            // Inherited from <Event_Handler> to allow the
            // <Reactor> to notify the <Connector> when events
            // complete asynchronously.
            virtual void handle_event (HANDLE, Event_Type);
        };
```

The Connector template is parameterized by a concrete IPC_CON-NECTOR and SERVICE_HANDLER. The IPC_CONNECTOR is a concrete IPC mechanism used by a connector to synchronously or asynchronously establish connections actively to remote acceptors. The SERVICE_HANDLER template argument defines one-half of a service that processes data exchanged with its connected peer service handler. Both concrete types are provided by components in the application layer.❏

2.5   *Implement the generic connector methods*. The connector's connect() method is used by an application to initiate a connection. This template method [GoF95] allows concrete connectors to modify the active connection strategy transparently, *without* changing the connector's interface or implementation. Therefore, connect() delegates individual steps of its connection strategy to hook methods that concrete connectors can over-ride to perform custom operations.

When connect() establishes a connection asynchronously on behalf of a service handler, the connector inserts that handler into an internal container—in our example a C++ standard template library map [Aus98]—that keeps track of pending connections. When an asynchronously-initiated connection completes, its dispatcher notifies the connector. The connector uses the pending connection map to finish activating the service handler associated with the connection.

If connect() establishes a connection synchronously, the connector can call the concrete service handler's activation hook directly, without calling complete(). This short-cut reduces unnecessary dynamic resource management and processing for synchronous connection establishment and service handler initialization.

➥   The code fragment below shows the connect() method of our Connector. If a SYNC value of the Connection_Mode parameter is passed to this method, the concrete service handler will be activated *after* the connection completes synchronously. Conversely, connections can be initiated asynchronously by passing the Connection_Mode value ASYNC to the connect() method:

```
template <class SERVICE_HANDLER, class IPC_CONNECTOR>
void Connector<SERVICE_HANDLER,IPC_CONNECTOR>::connect
        (SERVICE_HANDLER *service_handler,
          const Addr &addr, Connection_Mode mode) {
    // Hook method delegates connection initiation.
    connect_service_handler (service_handler, addr,mode);
}
```

The template method connect() delegates the initiation of a connection to its connect_service_handler() hook method. This method defines a default implementation of the connector's connection strategy. This strategy uses the concrete IPC mechanism provided by the IPC_CONNECTOR template parameter to establish connections, either synchronously or asynchronously.

```
template <class SERVICE_HANDLER, class IPC_CONNECTOR>
void Connector<SERVICE_HANDLER,
          IPC_CONNECTOR>::connect_service_handler
      (SERVICE_HANDLER *svc_handler,
       const Addr &addr,
       Connection_Mode mode) {
    try {
        // Concrete IPC_CONNECTOR establishes connection.
        connector_.connect (*svc_handler, addr, mode);

        // Activate if we connect synchronously.
        activate_service_handler (svc_handler);
    } catch (System_Ex &ex) {
        if (ex.status () == EWOULDBLOCK && mode == ASYNC)
        {
            // Connection did not complete immediately,
            // so register with <reactor_>, which
            // notifies <Connector> when the connection
            // completes.
            reactor_ ()->register_handler (this,
                                    WRITE_MASK);

            // Store <SERVICE_HANDLER *> in map.
            connection_map_ [connector_.get_handle ()]
                = svc_handler;
        }
    }
}
```

Note how connect() will activate the concrete service handler directly if the connection happens to complete synchronously. This may occur, for example, if the peer acceptor is co-located in the same host or process.   ❑

The complete() method activates the concrete service handler after its initiated connection completes. For connections initiated synchronously, complete() need not be called if the connect() method activates the service handler directly. For connections initiated asynchronously, however, complete() is called by the dispatcher when the connection completes. The complete() method examines the map of concrete service handlers to find the service handler whose connection just completed. It removes this service handler from the map and invokes its activation hook method. In addition, complete() unregisters the connector from the dispatcher to prevent it from trying to notify the connector accidentally.

Note that the service handler's open() activation hook method is called regardless of whether connections are established synchronously or asynchronously, or even if they are connected actively or passively. This uniformity makes it possible to define concrete service handlers whose processing can be completely decoupled from the time and manner in which they are connected and initialized.

➡ When a connection is initiated synchronously in our gateway, the concrete service handler associated with it is activated by the Connector's connect_service_handler() method, rather than by its complete() method, as described above. For asynchronous connections, conversely, the reactor notifies the handle_event() method inherited by the Connector from the Event_Handler class.

We implement this method as an adapter [GoF95] that converts the reactor's event handling interface to forward the call to the connector's complete() method. The complete() method then invokes the activation hook of the concrete service handler whose asynchronously initiated connection completed successfully most recently.

The complete() method shown below finds and removes the connected service handler from its internal map of pending connections and transfers the socket handle to the service handler.

```
template <class SERVICE_HANDLER, class IPC_CONNECTOR>
void Connector<SERVICE_HANDLER,
            IPC_CONNECTOR>::complete(HANDLE handle) {
  // Find <service_handler> associated with <handle> in
  // the map of pending connections.
  Connection_Map::iterator i =
      connection_map_.find (handle);

  if (i == connection_map_.end ())
      throw /* ...some type of error... */;

  // We just want the value part of the <key, value>
  // pair in the map
  SERVICE_HANDLER *svc_handler = (*i).second;

  // Transfer I/O handle to <service_handler>.
  svc_handler->set_handle (handle);
```

```
                    // Remove handle from <Reactor> and .
                    // from the pending connection map.
                    reactor_->remove_handler (handle, WRITE_MASK);
                    connection_map_.erase (i);

                    // Connection is complete, so activate handler.
                    activate_service_handler (svc_handler);
            }
```

Note how the `complete()` method initializes the service handler by invoking its `activate_service_handler()` method. This method delegates to the initialization strategy designated in the concrete service handler's `open()` activation hook method.   ❏

3 *Implement the components in the application layer.* This layer defines the concrete service handlers, concrete acceptors, and concrete connectors that Acceptor-Connector pattern specifies in the *Structure* section. Components in the application layer instantiate the generic service handler, acceptor, and connector components described in implementation activity 2 (299) to create custom concrete components.

Concrete service handlers define the application's services. When implementing an end-to-end service in a networked system that consists of multiple peer service handlers, the Half Object plus Protocol pattern [Mes95] can help structure the implementation of these service handlers. In particular, Half Object plus Protocol helps decompose the responsibilities of an end-to-end service into service handler interfaces and the protocol used to collaborate between them.

Concrete service handlers can also define a service's concurrency strategy. For example, a service handler may inherit from the event handler and employ the Reactor pattern (179) to process data from peers in a single thread of control. Conversely, a service handler may use the Active Object (369) or Monitor Object (399) patterns to process incoming data in a different thread of control than the one used by the acceptor that connects it.

In the *Example Resolved* section, we illustrate how several different concurrency strategies can be configured flexibly into concrete service handlers for our gateway example without affecting the structure or behavior of the Acceptor-Connector pattern.

Concrete connectors and concrete acceptors are factories that create concrete service handlers. They generally derive from their corresponding generic classes and implement these in an application-specific manner, potentially overriding the various hook methods called by the `accept()` and `connect()` template methods [GoF95].

Another way to specify a concrete acceptor is to parameterize the generic acceptor with a concrete service handler and concrete IPC passive connection mechanism, as discussed in previous implementation activities and as outlined in the *Example Resolved* section. Similarly, we can specify concrete connectors by parameterizing the generic connector with a concrete service handler and concrete IPC active connection mechanism.

Components in the application layer can also provide custom IPC mechanisms for configuring concrete service handlers, concrete connectors, and concrete acceptors. IPC mechanisms can be encapsulated in separate classes according to the Wrapper Facade pattern (47). These wrapper facades create and use the transport endpoints and transport handles that exchange data with connected peer service handlers transparently.

The use of the Wrapper Facade pattern simplifies programming, enhances reuse, and enables wholesale replacement of concrete IPC mechanisms via generic programming techniques. For example, the `SOCK_Connector`, `SOCK_Acceptor`, and `SOCK_Stream` classes used in the *Example Resolved* section are provided by the ACE C++ Socket wrapper facade library [Sch92].

Example Resolved   Peer host and gateway components in our satellite constellation management example use the Acceptor-Connector pattern to simplify their connection establishment and service initialization tasks:

- First we illustrate how to implement the peer host components, which play a passive role in our example.

- Second we illustrate how to implement the gateway, which plays an active role in establishing connections with the passive peer hosts.

By using the Acceptor-Connector pattern, we can also reverse or combine these roles with minimal impact on the service handlers that implement the peer hosts and gateway services.

Implement the peer host application. Each peer host contains `Status_Handler`, `Bulk_Data_Handler`, and `Command_Handler` components, which are concrete service handlers that process routing messages exchanged with a gateway.

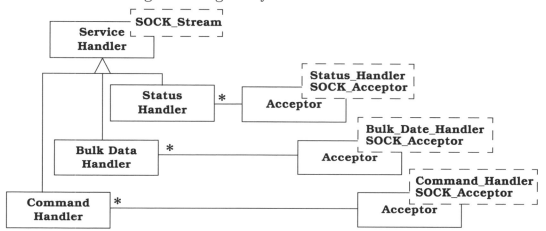

Each of these concrete service handlers inherit from the `Service_Handler` class defined in implementation activity 2.4 (306), enabling them to be initialized passively by an acceptor. For each type of concrete service handler, there is a corresponding concrete acceptor that creates, connects, and initializes instances of the concrete service handler.

To demonstrate the flexibility of the Acceptor-Connector pattern, each concrete service handler's `open()` hook method in our example implements a different concurrency strategy. For example, when a `Status_Handler` is activated it runs in a separate thread, a `Bulk_Data_Handler` runs as a separate process, and a `Command_Handler` runs in the same thread as the `Reactor` that demultiplexes connection requests to concrete acceptors. Note that changing these concurrency strategies does not affect the implementation of the `Acceptor` class.

We start by defining a type definition called `Peer_Handler`:

```
typedef Service_Handler <SOCK_Stream> Peer_Handler;
```

This type definition instantiates the `Service_Handler` generic template class with a `SOCK_Stream` wrapper facade (47). This wrapper facade[15] defines a concrete IPC mechanism for transmitting data

between connected transport endpoints using TCP. The PEER_
HANDLER type definition is the basis for all the subsequent concrete
service handlers used in our example. For example, the following
Status_Handler class inherits from Peer_Handler and processes
status data, such as telemetry streams, exchanged with a gateway:

```
class Status_Handler : public Peer_Handler {
public:
    // Performs handler activation.
    virtual void open () {
        // Make this handler run in separate thread (note
        // that <Thread::spawn> requires a pointer to
        // a static method as the thread entry point).
        Thread_Manager::instance ()->spawn
            (&Status_Handler::svc_run, this);
    }

    // Static entry point into thread. This method can
    // block on the handle_event() call because it
    // runs in its own thread.
    static void *svc_run (Status_Handler *this_obj) {
        for (;;)
            this_obj->run ();
    }

    // Receive and process status data from Gateway.
    virtual void run () {
        char buf[BUFSIZ];
        peer ().recv (buf, sizeof buf);
        // ...
    }
    // ...
};
```

The other concrete service handlers in our example, Bulk_Data_
Handler and Command_Handler, also subclass from Peer_Handler.
The primary differences between these classes are localized in the implementation of their open() and handle_event() methods, which
vary according to their selected concurrency mechanisms.

The Status_Acceptor, Bulk_Data_Acceptor, and Command_
Acceptor type definitions shown below are template instantiations of
concrete acceptor factories that create, connect, and activate the
Status_Handlers, Bulk_Data_Handlers, and Command_Handlers
concrete service handlers, respectively.

---

15. The complete SOCK_Stream interface is presented on page 61 in the
Implementation section of the Wrapper Facade (47) pattern.

```
// Accept connection requests from the gateway and
// activate a <Status_Handler> to process status data.
typedef Acceptor<Status_Handler, SOCK_Acceptor>
        Status_Acceptor;

// Accept connection requests from a gateway and activate
// a <Bulk_Data_Handler> to process bulk data requests.
typedef Acceptor<Bulk_Data_Handler, SOCK_Acceptor>
        Bulk_Data_Acceptor;

// Accept connection requests from a gateway and
// activate a <Command_Handler> to process commands.
typedef Acceptor<Command_Handler, SOCK_Acceptor>
        Command_Acceptor;
```

The type definitions above are defined by instantiating the generic Acceptor template class defined in implementation activity 2.2 (300) with a SOCK_Acceptor wrapper facade (47), which is a concrete IPC mechanism that establishes connections passively.[16]

Note how the use of C++ templates and dynamic binding permits specific details of concrete acceptors and concrete service handlers to change flexibly. In particular, no changes to the acceptor component are required if the concurrency strategies of Status_Handlers, Bulk_Data_Handlers, and/or Command_Handlers change. The flexibility of this design stems from the separation of concerns enforced by the Acceptor-Connector pattern. In particular, concurrency strategies have been factored out into concrete service handlers rather than being tightly coupled with the acceptors.

The main peer host application function initializes the concrete acceptors by passing their constructors the TCP ports used to advertise each service to peer connectors. Each concrete acceptor registers itself automatically with an instance of the Reactor passed as a parameter to its constructor, as shown in the implementation activity 2.3 (303).

```
// Main program run on a peer host.
int main () {
    // Initialize concrete acceptors to listen for
    // connections on their well-known ports.
    Status_Acceptor s_acceptor (STATUS_PORT,
                                Reactor::instance ());
```

16. The complete SOCK_Acceptor interface is presented on page 62 in the *Implementation* section of the Wrapper Facade (47) pattern.

```
Bulk_Data_Acceptor bd_acceptor (BULK_DATA_PORT,
                               Reactor::instance ());

Command_Acceptor c_acceptor (COMMAND_PORT,
                             Reactor::instance ());

// Event loop that accepts connection request
// events and processes data from a gateway.
for (;;)
    Reactor::instance ()->handle_events ();
/* NOTREACHED */
}
```

After all three concrete acceptors are initialized, the main peer host application enters an event loop that uses the reactor singleton to detect connection requests from the gateway. When such requests arrive, the reactor notifies the appropriate concrete acceptor. The acceptor then creates the appropriate concrete service handler, accepts the connection into the handler, and activates the handler so that it can exchange routing messages with the gateway.

Implement the gateway application. The `main()` function above illustrates how to define the concrete acceptors and their concrete service handlers for the peer host application in our satellite constellation management example. We now illustrate how to implement the concrete connectors and corresponding concrete service handlers used within a gateway application.

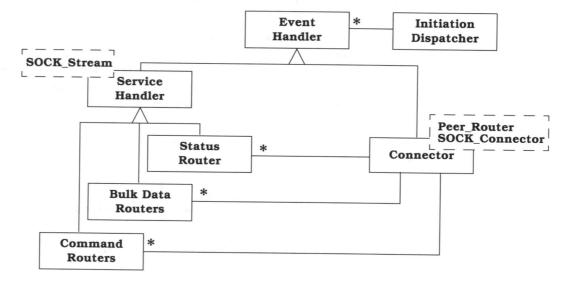

A gateway contains multiple instances of Status_Router, Bulk_
Data_Router, and Command_Router concrete service handlers,
which route data they receive from a peer host *source* to one or more
peer host *destinations*. These concrete service handlers inherit from
the Service_Handler class, which enables them to be connected
actively and initialized automatically by a connector.

Each open() hook method in a concrete service handler implements
a different concurrency strategy. This is analogous to the handlers
defined for the peer host application. As before, changes to these
concurrency strategies need not affect the Connector's
implementation, which is highly flexible and reusable.

We start by defining a concrete service handler that is specialized for
TCP/IP data transfer. We instantiate it with the appropriate IPC
mechanism encapsulated by the SOCK_Stream wrapper facade (47):

```
typedef Service_Handler <SOCK_Stream> Peer_Router;
```

This type definition is used as the base class for all other routing services in a gateway. For example, the Bulk_Data_Router exchanges
bulk data with peer hosts as follows:

```
class Bulk_Data_Router : public Peer_Router {
public:
    // Activates router in separate process.
    virtual void open () {
        if (fork () == 0) // In child process.
            // This method can block because it runs in
            // its own process.
            for (;;)
                run ();
        // ...
    }

    // Receive and route bulk data from/to Peers.
    virtual void run () {
        char buf[BUFSIZ];
        peer ().recv (buf, sizeof buf);
        // Routing takes place here...
    }
};
```

Unlike the Status_Handler defined in the peer host application,
which ran in its own thread, the Bulk_Data_Router runs in its own
process. We can define similar subclasses to form the
Status_Router and Command_Router. As before, all these subclasses differ primarily in their open() and handle_event() method

implementations, which vary according to the concurrency mechanisms they select.

The following type definition defines a connector specialized for Peer_ Routers:

```
typedef Connector<Peer_Router, SOCK_Connector>
        Peer_Connector;
```

This type definition instantiates the Connector class defined in implementation activity 2.4 (306) with a SOCK_Connector wrapper facade (47). This wrapper facade is a concrete IPC mechanism that establishes connections actively to remote peer transport endpoints. The gateway application requires just one concrete connector, because the concrete service handlers passed to its connect() method are created and initialized externally to the concrete connector. The gateway's concrete service handlers, such as its Bulk_Data_Routers or Command_Routers, can therefore be treated uniformly as Peer_ Routers.

In contrast, peer host applications require a concrete acceptor for *each* type of concrete service handler, such as a Bulk_Data_Handler or a Command_Handler, because the concrete type of service handler must be specified *a priori* in the signature of the concrete Acceptor's template instantiation.

In the main function of the gateway application, the concrete service handlers Status_Router, Bulk_Data_Router, and Command_Router are created by the function get_peer_addrs(). This function, whose implementation we omit, reads a list of peer addresses from a configuration file or naming service. Each peer address consists of an IP host address and a port number. Once these concrete service handlers are initialized, all connections are initiated asynchronously by passing the ASYNC flag to the concrete connector's connect() method.

```
// Obtain a C++ standary library vector of
// <Status_Router>s, <Bulk_Data_Router>s, and
// <Command_Router>s from a configuration file.
void get_peer_addrs (vector<Peer_Router> &peers);

// The gateway application's main entry point.
int main () {
    // Concrete connector that serves as a factory
    // for <Peer_Router>s.
    Peer_Connector peer_connector (Reactor::instance ());
```

```
                    // A vector of <Peer_Router>s that perform
                    // the gateway's routing services.
                    vector<Peer_Router> peers;

                    // Get vector of peers to connect with.
                    get_peer_addrs (peers);

                    // Iterate through all the <Peer_Router>s and
                    // initiate connections asynchronously.
                    typedef vector<Peer_Router>::iterator Peer_Iterator;
                    for (Peer_Iterator peer = peers.begin ();
                         peer != peers.end ();
                         ++peer) {
                        peer_connector.connect (*peer,
                                            peer->remote_addr (),
                                            Peer_Connector::ASYNC);
                    }

                    // Event loop that handles connection indication
                    // events and routes data from peer hosts.
                    for (;;)
                        Reactor::instance ()->handle_events ();
                    /* NOTREACHED */
                }
```

All connections are invoked asynchronously and complete concurrently via the peer_connector's complete() method, which the reactor notifies via a callback within the context of its event loop. The reactor's event loop also demultiplexes and dispatches routing events for Command_Router objects. These run in the same thread of control as the reactor. Conversely, instances of Status_Router and Bulk_Data_Router execute in separate threads and processes, respectively.

Known Uses   **UNIX network superservers**. Superserver implementations, for example Inetd [Ste98], Listen [Rago93], and the Service Configurator [JS97b] from the ACE framework, use a master acceptor process that listens for connections on a set of communication ports. In Inetd, for example, each port is associated with a service, such as the standard Internet services FTP, TELNET, DAYTIME, and ECHO. The acceptor process decouples the functionality of the Inetd superserver into two separate parts: one for establishing connections and another for receiving and processing requests from peers. When a service request arrives on a port monitored by Inetd, it accepts the request and dispatches an appropriate pre-registered handler to perform the service.

CORBA Object Request Brokers (ORB) [OMG98a]. The ORB Core layer in many implementations of CORBA uses the Acceptor-Connector pattern to passively and actively initialize connection handlers when clients request ORB services. [SC99] describes how the Acceptor-Connector pattern is used to implement the ORB Core portion in The ACE ORB (TAO), which is a real-time implementation of CORBA.

Web Browsers. The HTML parsing components in Web browsers, such as Netscape and Internet Explorer, use the asynchronous version of the connector component to establish connections with servers associated with images embedded in HTML pages. This pattern allows multiple HTTP connections to be initiated asynchronously. This avoids the possibility of the browser's main event loop blocking.

Ericsson EOS Call Center Management System. This system uses the Acceptor-Connector pattern to allow application-level Call Center Manager event servers [SchSu94] to establish connections actively with passive supervisors in a networked center management system.

Project Spectrum. The high-speed medical image transfer subsystem of project Spectrum [BBC94] uses the Acceptor-Connector pattern to establish connections passively and initialize application services for storing large medical images. Once connections are established, applications send and receive multi-megabyte medical images to and from the image stores.

ACE [Sch97]. Implementations of the generic `Service_Handler`, `Connector`, and `Acceptor` components described in the *Implementation* section are provided as reusable C++ classes in the ADAPTIVE Communication Environment (ACE) concurrent object-oriented network programming framework.

Java ACE [JACE99] is a version of ACE implemented in Java. It provides the `JACE.Connection.SvcHandler`, `JACE.Connection.Acceptor`, and `JACE.Connection.Connector` components. These correspond to the service handler, acceptor, and connector participants of the Acceptor-Connector pattern.

Managers and secretaries. A real-life implementation of the Acceptor-Connector pattern is often found in organizations that provide secretaries for their managers. A manager wishing to make a phone call to another manager asks her secretary to establish the call rather than doing it herself. However, the call is not received by the called manager directly, but by *his* secretary. Once the connection is established it is then passed to the managers. In terms of the Acceptor-Connector pattern, the secretary that initiates the phone call is the connector, the secretary that receives the call is the acceptor and the two managers are peer service handlers.

Consequences   The Acceptor-Connector pattern provides three **benefits**:

Reusability, portability, and extensibility. The Acceptor-Connector pattern decouples mechanisms for connecting and initializing service handlers from the service processing performed after service handlers are connected and initialized. Application-independent mechanisms in acceptors and connectors are reusable components that know how to establish connections and initialize the associated service handler when the connection is established. Similarly, service handlers know how to perform application-specific service processing.

This strict separation of concerns is achieved by decoupling the connection and initialization strategies from the service handling strategy. Each strategy can therefore evolve independently. The strategies for connection and initialization can be written once, placed in a class library or framework and reused via inheritance, object composition or template instantiation. The same connection and initialization code therefore need not be rewritten for each application.

Service handlers, in contrast, may vary according to different application requirements. By parameterizing the acceptor and connector components with a particular type of service handler, the impact of this variation is localized to a small number of components in the software.

Robustness. The Acceptor-Connector pattern strongly decouples the service handler from the acceptor. This decoupling ensures that a passive-mode transport endpoint—the PEER_ACCEPTOR in our gateway example—cannot be used to read or write data accidentally. This added degree of type-safety eliminates a class of errors that often arise when programming with weakly-typed network programming interfaces, such as Sockets or TLI [SHS95].

Efficiency. The Acceptor-Connector pattern can establish connections actively with a large number of hosts asynchronously and efficiently over long-latency wide area networks. Asynchrony is important in this situation because a large networked system may have hundreds or thousands of host that must be connected.

One way to connect all these peers to the gateway is to use the synchronous mechanisms described in the *Implementation* section. However, the round-trip delay for a 3-way TCP connection handshake over a long-latency wide area network, such as a geosynchronous satellite or trans-atlantic fiber cable, may be several seconds per handshake. In this case asynchronous connection mechanisms may perform better, because they can utilize the inherent parallelism of the network and hosts in the wide area network.

The Acceptor-Connector pattern has the following **liabilities**:

Additional indirection. The Acceptor-Connector pattern can incur additional indirection compared to using the underlying network programming interfaces directly. However, languages that support parameterized types, such as C++, Ada, or Eiffel, can implement these patterns with no significant overhead when compilers inline the method calls used to implement the patterns.

Additional complexity. The Acceptor-Connector pattern may add unnecessary complexity for simple client applications that connect with only one server and perform one service using a single network programming interface. However, the use of generic acceptor and connector wrapper facades may simplify even these applications by shielding developers from tedious, error-prone, and non-portable low-level network programming mechanisms.

See also   The intent of the Acceptor-Connector pattern is similar to that of the Client-Dispatcher-Server pattern [POSA1] in that both are concerned with the separation of active connection establishment from subsequent service processing. The primary difference is that the Acceptor-Connector pattern addresses passive *and* active connection establishment and initialization of both synchronous *and* asynchronous connections. In contrast, the Client-Dispatcher-Server pattern focuses on synchronous connection establishment.

4 Synchronization Patterns

> *"I will be the pattern of all patience."*
> *William Shakespeare*

This chapter describes three patterns and one idiom that simplify locking in concurrent systems: Scoped Locking, Strategized Locking, Thread-Safe Interface, and Double-Checked Locking Optimization.

Developing multi-threaded applications is harder than developing sequential programs because an object can be manipulated concurrently by multiple threads, which may corrupt its internal state. *Synchronization* mechanisms, such as mutexes or semaphores [McK95], can help ensure objects are serialized correctly. This chapter presents three patterns and an idiom that provide solutions to problems related to synchronizing concurrent objects.

The first idiom and pattern address lock acquisition/release and locking strategies:

- The *Scoped Locking* C++ idiom (325) ensures that a lock is acquired automatically when control enters a scope and released automatically when control leaves the scope, regardless of the return path from the scope.

- The *Strategized Locking* design pattern (333) is a specialization of the Strategy pattern [GoF95] that parameterizes the synchronization mechanisms used in a component that protect its critical sections from concurrent access.

When implemented in C++ the Strategized Locking pattern often applies the Scoped Locking idiom. The other two patterns help improve the robustness and efficiency of synchronization mechanisms:

- The *Thread-Safe Interface* design pattern (345) minimizes locking overhead and ensures that intra-component method calls do not incur 'self-deadlock' by trying to reacquire a lock that a component already holds.

- The *Double-Checked Locking Optimization* design pattern (353) reduces contention and synchronization overhead whenever critical sections of code must acquire locks in a thread-safe manner only once during program execution.

All four patterns and idioms can be used to enhance the implementations of the patterns presented in Chapter 5, *Concurrency Patterns*.

Other patterns related to synchronization include Code Locking and Data Locking [McK95], Reader/Writer Locking [McK95] [Lea99a], Object Synchronizer [SPM99], as well as Balking and Guarded Suspension [Lea99a].

Scoped Locking

The *Scoped Locking* C++ idiom ensures that a lock is acquired when control enters a scope and released automatically when control leaves the scope, regardless of the return path from the scope.

Also Known As Synchronized Block, Resource-Acquisition-is-Initialization [Str97],[1] Guard, Execute Around Object [Hen00]

Example Commercial Web servers often maintain a 'hit count' that records how many times each URL is accessed by clients over a period of time. To reduce latency a Web server process maintains the hit counts in a memory-resident component rather than in a disk file.

Web server processes are often multi-threaded [HS98] to increase throughput. Public methods in the hit-count component must therefore be serialized to prevent threads from corrupting its internal state when hit counts are updated concurrently.

One way to serialize access to a hit-count component is to acquire and release a lock explicitly in each public method. The following C++ example uses the `Thread_Mutex` defined in the Wrapper Facade pattern (47) to serialize access to critical sections:

```
class Hit_Counter {
public:
    // Increment the hit count for a URL <path> name.
    bool increment (const string &path) {
        // Acquire lock to enter critical section.
        lock_.acquire ();
        Table_Entry *entry = lookup_or_create (path);
        if (entry == 0) {
            // Something's gone wrong, so bail out.
            lock_.release ();
            return false; // Return a 'failure' value.
        }
```

---

1. The Scoped Locking idiom is a specialization of Stroustrup's 'Resource-Acquisition-is-Initialization' idiom [Str97]. We include this idiom here to make the book self-contained and to illustrate how Stroustrup's idiom can be applied to concurrent programs.

```
            else { // Increment hit count for <path> name.
                entry->increment_hit_count ();
                // Release lock to leave critical section.
                lock_.release ();
                return true;
            }
        }

        // Other public methods omitted...
    private:
        // Lookup the table entry that maintains the hit count
        // associated with <path> name, creating the entry if
        // it doesn't exist.
        Table_Entry *lookup_or_create (const string &path);

        // Serialize access to the critical section.
        Thread_Mutex lock_;
    };
```

Although this code works, the Hit_Counter implementation is unnecessarily hard to develop and maintain. For instance, maintenance programmers may forget to release the lock_ on some return paths out of the increment() method, such as when modifying its else branch to check for a new failure condition:

```
            else if (entry->increment_hit_count () == SOME_FAILURE)
                return false; // Return a 'failure' value.
```

In addition, the implementation is not exception-safe. Thus, lock_ will not be released if a later version of the increment() method throws an exception or calls a helper method that throws an exception [Mue96].

Both of these modifications will cause the increment() method to return *without* releasing the lock_. If the lock_ is not released, however, the Web server process will hang when other threads block indefinitely while trying to acquire the lock_. Moreover, if these error cases are rare, the problems with this code may not show up during system testing.

Context   A concurrent application containing shared resources that are manipulated by multiple threads concurrently.

Problem   Code that should not execute concurrently must be protected by some type of lock that is acquired and released when control enters and leaves a critical section, respectively. If programmers must acquire and release locks explicitly, however, it is hard to ensure that the locks are released in all paths through the code. For example, in C++ control can leave a scope due to a `return`, `break`, `continue`, or `goto` statement, as well as from an unhandled exception being propagated out of the scope.

Solution Define a guard class whose constructor automatically acquires a lock when control enters a scope and whose destructor automatically releases the lock when control leaves the scope. Instantiate instances of the guard class to acquire/release locks in method or block scopes that define critical sections.

Implementation The implementation of the Scoped Locking idiom is straightforward.

1 *Define a guard class that acquires and releases a particular type of lock* in its constructor and destructor, respectively. The constructor of the guard class stores a pointer or reference to the lock and then acquires the lock. The destructor of the guard class uses the pointer or reference stored by the constructor to release the lock.

➥ The following class illustrates a guard designed for the `Thread_Mutex` wrapper facade (47):

```
class Thread_Mutex_Guard {
public:
    // Store a pointer to the lock and acquire the lock.
    Thread_Mutex_Guard (Thread_Mutex &lock)
        : lock_ (&lock), owner_ (false) {
        lock_->acquire ();

        // Only set to true if <acquire> succeeds.
        owner_ = true;
    }

    // Release the lock when the guard goes out of scope.
    ~Thread_Mutex_Guard () {
        // Only release the lock if it was acquired
        // successfully, i.e., <false> indicates that
        // <acquire> failed..
        if (owner_) lock_->release ();
    }
private:
    Thread_Mutex *lock_; // Pointer to our lock.
    bool owner_; // Is <lock_> held by this object?

    // Disallow copying or assignment.
    Thread_Mutex_Guard (const Thread_Mutex_Guard &);
    void operator= (const Thread_Mutex_Guard &);
};
```

A pointer to a lock, rather than a lock object, should be used in a guard class implementation to prevent copying or assigning a lock, which is erroneous, as discussed in the Wrapper Facade pattern (47).

In addition, it is useful to add a flag, such as the owner_ flag in the Thread_Mutex_Guard example above, that indicates whether or not a guard acquired the lock successfully. The flag can also indicate failures that arise from 'order of initialization bugs' if static/global locks are used erroneously [LGS99]. By checking this flag in the guard's destructor, a subtle run-time error can be avoided that would otherwise occur if the lock was released when it was not held by the guard.

2 *Let critical sections correspond to the scope and lifetime of a guard object.* To protect a critical region from concurrent access, scope it— if this has not already been done—and create a guard object on the stack as the first statement within the scope. The constructor of the guard class acquires the lock automatically. When leaving the scope of the critical section, the guard's destructor is called automatically, which releases the lock. Due to the semantics of C++ destructors, guarded locks will be released even if C++ exceptions are thrown from within the critical section.

➡   The Scoped Locking idiom resolves the original problems with the Hit_Counter class in our multi-threaded Web server:

```
class Hit_Counter {
public:
    // Increment the hit count for a URL <path> name.
    bool increment (const string &path) {
        // Use Scoped Locking to acquire and release
        // the <lock_> automatically.
        Thread_Mutex_Guard guard (lock_);

        Table_Entry *entry = lookup_or_create (path);
        if (entry == 0)
            return false; // Destructor releases <lock_>
        else {
            // Increment hit count for this <path> name.
            entry->increment_hit_count ();
            return true; // Destructor releases <lock_>
    }

    // Other public methods omitted.
```

```
      private:
          // Serialize access to the critical section.
          Thread_Mutex lock_;
      };
```

In this solution the guard ensures that the `lock_` is acquired and released automatically as control enters and leaves the `increment()` method, respectively.   ❏

Variants   *Explicit Accessors.* One drawback with the `Thread_Mutex_Guard` interface described in the *Implementation* section is that it is not possible to release the lock explicitly without leaving the method or block scope.

➥   For example, the following code fragment illustrates a situation where the lock could be released twice, depending on whether or not the condition in the `if` statement evaluates to true:

```
      {
          Thread_Mutex_Guard guard (lock);
          // Do some work ...
          if (/* a certain condition holds */)
             lock->release ()
          // Do some more work ...
          // Leave the scope, which releases the lock again.
      }                                                                      ❏
```

To prevent this erroneous use, programmers should not access the lock directly. Instead, explicit accessor methods to the underlying lock can be defined in the in the lock's guard class:

➥   We revise the `Thread_Mutex_Guard` class as follows:

```
      class Thread_Mutex_Guard {
      public:
          // Store a pointer to the lock and acquire the lock.
          Thread_Mutex_Guard (Thread_Mutex &lock)
              : lock_ (&lock), owner_ (false) {
              acquire ();
          }

          void acquire () {
              lock_->acquire ();
              // Only set to <true> if <acquire> succeeds.
              owner_ = true;
          }
```

```
        void release () {
            // Only release <lock_> if it was acquired
            // successfully and we haven't released it yet!
            if (owner_) {
                owner_ = false;
                lock_->release ();
            }
        }

        // Release the lock when the guard goes out of scope.
        ~Thread_Mutex_Guard () { release (); }
private:
        Thread_Mutex *lock_; // Pointer to our lock.
        bool owner_; // Is <lock_> held by this object?

        // ... disallow copying and assignment ...
    };                                                                   ❏
```

The acquire() and release() accessor methods track whether the lock has been already released, and if so, the lock will not be released in the guard's destructor.

➡ Using the revised Thread_Mutex_Guard our code will work correctly:

```
    {
        Thread_Mutex_Guard guard (lock);
        // Do some work ...
        if (/* a certain condition holds */)
            guard.release ();
        // Do some more work ...
        // Leave the scope, lock is not released again.
    }                                                                    ❏
```

Strategized Scoped Locking. Defining a different guard for each type of lock is tedious, error-prone, and excessive, because it may increase the memory footprint of applications or components. Therefore, a common variant of the Scoped Locking idiom is to apply either the parameterized type or polymorphic version of the Strategized Locking pattern (333).

Known Uses   **Booch Components**. The Booch Components [BV93] were one of the first C++ class libraries to use the Scoped Locking idiom for multi-threaded C++ programs.

ACE [Sch97]. The Scoped Locking idiom is used extensively throughout the ADAPTIVE Communication Environment framework, which defines an ACE_Guard implementation similar to the Thread_

`Mutex_Guard` class described in the *Implementation* and *Variants* sections.

Threads.h++. The Rogue Wave Threads.h++ library defines a set of guard classes that are modeled after the ACE Scoped Locking designs.

Java defines a programming feature called a synchronized block that implements the Scoped Locking idiom in that language. Java compilers generate a corresponding block of bytecode instructions where a `monitorenter` and a `monitorexit` bracket this block. To ensure that the lock is always released, the compiler also generates an exception handler to catch all exceptions thrown in the synchronized block [Eng99].

Consequences The Scoped Locking idiom offers the following **benefit**:

Increased robustness. By applying this idiom, locks are acquired and released automatically when control enters and leaves critical sections defined by C++ method and block scopes. This idiom increases the robustness of concurrent applications by eliminating common programming errors related to synchronization and multi-threading.

There are two **liabilities** of applying the Scoped Locking idiom to concurrent applications and components:

Potential for deadlock when used recursively. If a method that uses the Scoped Locking idiom calls itself recursively, 'self-deadlock' will occur if the lock is not a 'recursive' mutex. The Thread-Safe Interface pattern (345) describes a technique that avoids this problem. This pattern ensures that only interface methods apply the Scoped Locking idiom, whereas implementation methods do not apply it.

Limitations with language-specific semantics. The Scoped Locking idiom is based on a C++ language feature and therefore will not be integrated with operating system-specific system calls. Thus, locks may not be released automatically when threads or processes abort or exit inside a guarded critical section. Likewise, they will not be released properly if the standard C `longjmp()` function is called because this function does not call the destructors of C++ objects as the run-time stack unwinds.

➡   The following modification to increment() will prevent the Scoped Locking idiom from working:

```
Thread_Mutex_Guard guard (&lock_);
Table_Entry *entry = lookup_or_create (path);
if (entry == 0)
    // Something's gone wrong, so exit the thread.
    thread_exit ();
    // Destructor will not be called so the
    // <lock_> will not be released!                    ❏
```

In general, therefore, it is inappropriate to abort or exit a thread or process within a component. Instead, an exception-handling mechanism or error-propagation pattern should be used [Mue96].

Excessive compiler warnings. The Scoped Locking idiom defines a guard object that is not used explicitly within the scope, because its destructor releases the lock implicitly. Unfortunately, some C++ compilers print 'statement has no effect' warnings when guards are defined but not used explicitly within a scope. At best these warnings are distracting—at worst, they encourage developers to disable certain compiler warnings, which may mask other warnings that indicate actual problems with the code. An effective way to handle this problem is to define a macro that eliminates the warnings without generating additional code.

➡   The following macro is defined in ACE [Sch97]:

```
#define UNUSED_ARG(arg) { if (&arg) /* null */; }
```

This macro can be placed after a guard to keep many C++ compilers from generating spurious warnings:

```
{ // New scope.
    Thread_Mutex_Guard guard (lock_);
    UNUSED_ARG (guard);
    // ...                                              ❏
```

See Also   The Scoped Locking idiom is a special case of a more general C++ idiom [Str97] and the Execute Around Object [Hen00] idiom, in which a constructor acquires a resource and a destructor releases the resource when a scope is entered and exited, respectively. When these idioms are applied to concurrent applications, the resource that is acquired and released is some type of lock.

Credits   Thanks to Brad Appleton for comments on the Scoped Locking idiom.

Strategized Locking

The *Strategized Locking* design pattern parameterizes synchronization mechanisms that protect a component's critical sections from concurrent access.

Example
A key component for implementing high-performance Web servers is a *file cache*, which maps URL path names to memory-mapped files or open file handles [HS98]. When a client requests a URL that is in the cache, the Web server can transfer the file contents to the client immediately without accessing slower secondary storage via multiple `read()` and `write()` operations.

A file cache implementation for a portable high-performance should run efficiently on a range of multi-threaded and single-threaded operating systems. One way to achieve this portability is to develop multiple file cache classes:

```
// A single-threaded file cache implementation.
class File_Cache_ST {
public:
    // Return a pointer to the memory-mapped file
    // associated with <path> name.
    const void *lookup (const string &path) const {
        // No locking required because we're
        // single-threaded.
        const void *file_pointer = 0;

        // ... look up the file in the cache, mapping it
        // into memory if it is not currently in the cache.
        return file_pointer;
    }
    // ...
private:
    //File cache implementation...

    // No lock required because we are
    // single-threaded.
};
```

```
// A multi-threaded file cache implementation.
class File_Cache_Thread_Mutex {
public:
    // Return a pointer to the memory-mapped file
    // associated with <path> name.
    const void *lookup (const string &path) const {
        // Use the Scoped Locking idiom to serialize
        // access to the file cache.
        Thread_Mutex_Guard guard (lock_);
        const void *file_pointer = 0;

        // ... look up the file in the cache, mapping it
        // into memory if it is not currently in the cache.
        return file_pointer;
    }
    // ...
private:
    //File cache implementation...

    // Synchronization strategy.
    mutable Thread_Mutex lock_;
};
```

These two implementations form part of a component family whose classes differ only in their synchronization strategy. One component in the family—class `File_Cache_ST`—implements a single-threaded file cache with no locking. The other component—class `File_Cache_Thread_Mutex`—implements a file cache that uses a mutex to serialize multiple threads that access the cache concurrently. Maintaining separate implementations of these file cache components can be tedious, however. In particular, future enhancements and fixes must be added consistently in each component's implementation.

Context   An application or system where components must run efficiently in a variety of different concurrency architectures.

Problem   Components that run in multi-threaded environments must protect their critical sections from concurrent client access. When integrating synchronization mechanisms with component functionality two *forces* must be resolved:

• Different applications may require different synchronization strategies, such as mutexes, readers/writer locks, or semaphores [McK95]. It should therefore be possible to customize a component's synchronization mechanisms according to the requirements of particular applications.

➥   In our example the synchronization strategy is hard-coded. To increase performance on large-scale multi-processor platforms, a new class must therefore be written to support a file cache implementation that uses a readers/writer lock instead of a thread mutex. It is time-consuming, however, to customize an existing file cache class to support new more efficient synchronization strategies.   ❏

• Adding new enhancements and bug fixes should be straightforward. In particular, to avoid 'version-skew', changes should apply consistently and automatically to all members in a component family.

➥   If there are multiple copies of the same basic file cache component, version-skew will likely to occur because changes to one component may be applied inconsistently to other component implementations. Applying each change manually is also error-prone and non-scalable.   ❏

Solution   Parameterize a component's synchronization aspects by making them 'pluggable' types. Each type objectifies a particular synchronization strategy, such as a mutex, readers/writer lock, semaphore, or 'null' lock. Define instances of these pluggable types as objects contained within a component that can use the objects to synchronize its method implementations efficiently.

Implementation The Strategized Locking pattern can be implemented via five activities.

1   *Define the component interface and implementation* without concern for the component's synchronization aspects.

➥   The following class defines the `File_Cache` interface and implementation:

```
class File_Cache {
public:
    const void *lookup (const string &path) const;
    // ...
private:
    // data members and private methods go here...
};
```                                                                            ❏

2   *Strategize the locking mechanisms.* Many components have relatively simple synchronization aspects that can be implemented using common locking strategies, such as mutexes and semaphores. These synchronization aspects can be strategized uniformly using either *polymorphism* or *parameterized types*. In general, polymorphism should be used when the locking strategy is not known until run-time. Conversely, parameterized types should be used when the locking strategy *is* known at compile-time. As usual the trade-off is between the efficient run-time performance of parameterized types versus the potential for run-time extensibility with polymorphism.

Assuming the Scoped Locking idiom (325) is applied, the strategization of locks involves two sub-activities:

2.1 *Define an abstract interface for the locking mechanisms.* To configure a component with alternative locking mechanisms, all concrete implementations of these mechanisms must employ an abstract interface with common signatures for acquiring and releasing locks based on either polymorphism or parameterized types.

   • *Polymorphism.* In this strategy, define a polymorphic lock object that contains dynamically-bound `acquire()` and `release()` methods. Derive all concrete locks from this base class and override its methods to define a concrete locking strategy, as outlined in implementation activity 5 (339).

➠   To implement a polymorphic lock object for our file cache example, we first define an abstract locking class with virtual acquire() and release() methods:

```
class Lock {
public:
    // Acquire and release the lock.
    virtual void acquire () = 0;
    virtual void release () = 0;

    // ...
};                                                                ❏
```

- *Parameterized types.* In this strategy, we must ensure that all concrete locks employ the same signature for acquiring and releasing locks. The usual way to ensure this is to implement concrete locks using the Wrapper Facade pattern (47).

2.2 *Use the Scoped Locking Idiom (325) to define a guard class that is strategized by its synchronization aspect.* This design follows the Strategy Pattern [GHJV95], in which the guard class serves as the context that holds a particular lock and the concrete locks provide the strategies. The Scoped Locking idiom can be implemented either with *polymorphism* or with *parameterized* types.

- *Polymorphism.* In this approach, pass a polymorphic lock object to the guard's constructor and define an instance of this lock object as a private data member. To acquire and release the lock with which it is configured, the implementation of the guard class can use the interface of the polymorphic Lock base class defined in implementation sub-activity 2.1 (335).

➠   A Guard class that controls a polymorphic lock can be defined as follows:

```
class Guard {
public:
    // Store a pointer to the lock and acquire the lock.
    Guard (Lock &lock)
        : lock_ (&lock), owner_ (false)
        { lock_->acquire (); owner_ = true; }

    // Release the lock when the guard goes out of scope.
    ~Guard () {
        // Only release lock if it <acquire> succeeded.
        if (owner_) lock_->release ();
    }
```

```
        private:
            // Pointer to the lock we're managing.
            Lock *lock_;
            // Records if the lock was acquired successfully.
            bool owner_;
        };                                                    ❏
```

- *Parameterized types*. In this approach, define a template guard class that is parameterized by the type of lock that will be acquired and released automatically.

➥ The following illustrates a Guard class that is strategized by a LOCK template parameter:

```
        template <class LOCK>
        class Guard {
        public:
            // Store a pointer to the lock and acquire the lock.
            Guard (LOCK &lock)
                : lock_ (&lock), owner_ (false)
                { lock_->acquire (); owner_ = true; }

            // Release the lock when the guard goes out of scope,
            // but only if <acquire> succeeded.
            ~Guard () { if (owner_) lock_->release (); }
        private:
            // Pointer to the lock we're managing.
            LOCK *lock_;

            // Records if the lock is held by this object.
            bool owner_;

            // ... disallow copying and assignment ...
        };                                                    ❏
```

3 *Update the component interface and implementation.* After synchronization mechanisms are strategized, components can use these mechanisms to protect their critical sections, either by acquiring or releasing a lock explicitly or by using the guard class defined in implementation activity 2.2 (336). The latter approach follows the Scoped Locking idiom (325). Depending on whether the polymorphic or parameterized type strategy is used, the lock can be passed to the component either as a parameter in its constructor or by adding a lock template parameter to the component declaration. In either case, the lock passed to a component must follow the signature expected by the guard class, as discussed in implementation activity 2.2 (336).

➥   This version of our file cache component is passed a polymorphic lock parameter:

```
class File_Cache {
public:
    // Constructor.
    File_Cache (Lock &l): lock_ (&l) { }

    // A method.
    const void *lookup (const string &path) const {
        // Use the Scoped Locking idiom to acquire
        // and release the <lock_> automatically.
        Guard guard (*lock_);
        // Implement the <lookup> method.
    }

    // ...
private:
    // The polymorphic strategized locking object.
    mutable Lock *lock_;
    // Other data members and methods go here...
};
```

Similarly, we can define a templatized version of the file cache:

```
template <class LOCK>
class File_Cache {
public:
    // A method.
    const void *lookup (const string &path) const {
        // Use the Scoped Locking idiom to acquire
        // and release the <lock_> automatically.
        Guard<LOCK> guard (lock_);
        // Implement the <lookup> method.
    }

    // ...
private:
    // The parameterized type strategized locking object.
    mutable LOCK lock_;

    // Other data members and methods go here...
};
```

If a C++ compiler supports default template arguments, it may be useful to add a default LOCK to handle the most common use case. For example, we can define the default LOCK as a readers/writer lock:

```
template <class LOCK = RW_Lock>
class File_Cache { /* ... */ }
```                                                                   ❑

4   *Revise the component implementation to avoid deadlock and remove unnecessary locking overhead.* If intra-component method invocations occur, developers must design their component implementation carefully to avoid self-deadlock and unnecessary synchronization overhead. The Thread-Safe Interface pattern (345) provides a straightforward technique that prevents these problems.

5   *Define a family of locking strategies with uniform interfaces* that can support various application-specific concurrency designs. Common locking strategies include recursive and non-recursive mutexes, readers/writer locks, semaphores, and file locks.

When applying the polymorphic approach, implement the locking strategies as subclasses of the abstract class Lock, as discussed in implementation activity 2 (335). If parameterized types are used, ensure that all concrete lock implementations follow the signature for locks defined in implementation activity 2 (335).

➡   In addition to the Thread_Mutex locking strategy defined in Wrapper Facade (47), the Null_Mutex is surprisingly useful. This class defines an efficient locking strategy for single-threaded applications and components:

```
class Null_Mutex {
public:
    Null_Mutex () { }
    ~Null_Mutex () { }
    void acquire () { }
    void release () { }
};
```

All methods in Null_Mutex are empty C++ inline functions that can be removed completely by optimizing compilers. This class is an example of the Null Object pattern [PLoPD3], which simplifies applications by defining a 'no-op' placeholder that removes conditional statements in the component's implementation. A use of Null_Mutex and other locking strategies appears in the *Example Resolved* section.   ❏

If existing locking mechanisms have incompatible interfaces, use the Wrapper Facade (47) or Adapter [GoF95] patterns to ensure the interfaces conform to the signatures expected by the component's synchronization aspects.

➥   The following class wraps the `Thread_Mutex` from the *Implemen-tation* section of the Wrapper Facade pattern (47), thereby connecting it to our polymorphic lock hierarchy:

```
class Thread_Mutex_Lock : public Lock {
public:
    // Acquire and release the lock.
    virtual void acquire () { lock_.acquire (); }
    virtual void release () { lock_.release (); }
private:
    // Concrete lock type.
    Thread_Mutex lock_;
};
```
❑

Example Resolved   We can apply the parameterized type form of the Strategized Locking pattern to implement a file cache for Web server content that is tuned for various single-threaded and multi-threaded concurrency models:

- *Single-threaded file cache.*

  ```
  typedef File_Cache<Null_Mutex> Content_Cache;
  ```

- *Multi-threaded file cache using a thread mutex.*

  ```
  typedef File_Cache<Thread_Mutex> Content_Cache;
  ```

- *Multi-threaded file cache using a readers/writer lock.*

  ```
  typedef File_Cache<RW_Lock> Content_Cache;
  ```

- *Multi-threaded file cache using a C++ compiler that supports default template parameters*, with the lock defaulting to a readers/writer lock, as declared in implementation activity 3 (337).

  ```
  typedef File_Cache<> Content_Cache;
  ```

Note how in each configuration the `Content_Cache` interface and implementation require no changes. This flexibility stems from the Strategized Locking pattern, which abstracts synchronization aspects into 'pluggable' parameterized types. Moreover, the details of locking have been strategized via a C++ `typedef`. It is therefore straightforward to define a `Content_Cache` object that does not expose synchronization aspects to applications:

```
Content_Cache cache;
```

Variants   *Bridge strategy.* Unfortunately, configuring the polymorphic file cache in implementation activity 3 (337) differs from configuring the templatized file cache, because a polymorphic lock implemented as a pointer cannot be passed as a parameter to the templatized File_Cache and Guard classes. Instead, we need a 'real' object, rather than a pointer to an object. Fortunately, the Bridge pattern [GoF95] can help us implement a family of locking strategies that is applicable to *both* polymorphic and parameterized type approaches. To apply this bridge strategy variant we simply define an additional abstraction class that encapsulates, and can be configured with, a polymorphic lock. An instance of this abstraction class then can be passed uniformly to both polymorphic and templatized components.

➥   Consider the hierarchy of polymorphic locks defined in implementation activity 2 (335) as being a Bridge implementation class hierarchy. The following abstraction class then can be used to encapsulate this hierarchy:

```
class Lock_Abstraction {
public:
    // Constructor stores a reference to the base class.
    Lock_Abstraction (Lock &l): lock_ (l) { };

    // Acquire the lock by forwarding to the
    // polymorphic acquire() method.
    void acquire () { lock_.acquire (); }

    // Release the lock by forwarding to the
    // polymorphic release() method.
    void release () { lock_.release (); }
private:
    // Maintain a reference to the polymorphic lock.
    Lock &lock_;
};
```

Note how this design allows us to initialize both our polymorphic and parameterized File_Cache and Guard classes with a single Lock_ Abstraction class that can be configured with a concrete lock from our hierarchy of locking mechanisms.   ❑

As a result of using this variation of Strategized Locking, the family of locking mechanisms becomes more reusable and easier to apply across applications. Be aware however that while this scheme is flexible, it is also more complicated to implement. It should therefore be used with care.

Known Uses   **ACE** [Sch97]. The Strategized Locking pattern is used extensively throughout the ADAPTIVE Communication Environment framework. Most synchronization aspects of ACE containers components, such as `ACE_Hash_Map_Manager`, can be strategized via parameterized types.

Booch Components. The Booch Components [BV93] were one of the first C++ class libraries to parameterize locking strategizes via templates.

The **Dynix/PTX** operating system applies the Strategized Locking pattern extensively throughout its kernel.

ATL Wizards. The Microsoft ATL Wizard in Visual Studio uses the parameterized type implementation of Strategized Locking, completed with default template parameters. In addition, it implements a class similar to the `Null_Mutex`. If a COM class is implemented as a single-threaded apartment a no-op lock class is used, whereas in multi-threaded apartments a 'real' recursive mutex is used.

Consequences   There are three **benefits** of applying the Strategized Locking pattern:

Enhanced flexibility and customization. It is straightforward to configure and customize a component for certain concurrency models because the synchronization aspects of components are strategized. If no suitable locking strategy is available for a new concurrency model, the family of locking strategies can be extended without affecting existing code.

Decreased maintenance effort for components. It is straightforward to add enhancements and bug fixes to a component because there is only one implementation, rather than a separate implementation for each concurrency model. This centralization of concerns helps minimize version-skew.

Improved reuse. Components implemented using this pattern become less dependent on specific synchronization mechanisms. They therefore become more reusable, because their locking strategies can be configured orthogonally to their behavior.

There are two **liabilities** of applying the Strategized Locking pattern:

Obtrusive locking. If templates are used to parameterize locking aspects this will expose the locking strategies to application code. Although this design is flexible, it also can be obtrusive, particularly for compilers that do not support templates efficiently or correctly. One way to avoid this problem is to apply the polymorphic strategy to vary component locking behavior.

Over-engineering. Externalizing a locking mechanism by placing it in a component's interface may actually provide *too much* flexibility in certain situations. For example, inexperienced developers may try to parameterize a component with the wrong type of lock, resulting in improper compile- or run-time behavior. Similarly, only a single type of synchronization mechanism may be needed for a particular type of component. In this case the flexibility of Strategized Locking is unnecessary. In general this pattern is most effective when practical experience reveals a component's behavior to be orthogonal to its locking strategy, and that locking strategies do indeed vary in semantically meaningful and efficient ways.

See Also   The main synchronization mechanism in Java is the monitor. The Java language does not provide 'conventional' concurrency control mechanisms, such as mutexes and semaphores, to application developers. The Strategized Locking pattern therefore need not be applied to Java directly.

It is possible, however, to implement different concurrency primitives, such as mutexes, semaphores, and readers/writer locks in Java. For example, the `util.concurrent` package in [Lea99a] defines various types of locks, such as readers/writer locks. The implementation of these primitives then can be used as locking strategies to support various application-specific concurrency use cases. Due to the lack of parameterized types in Java specifications to date, only the polymorphic approach of Strategized Locking pattern could be used to configure different synchronization strategies. In this case, Java implementations of this pattern will be similar to the C++ versions described in this pattern.

Credits   Thanks to Brad Appleton for comments on this pattern and Prashant Jain for his contribution explaining how this pattern applies to Java.

Thread-Safe Interface

The *Thread-Safe Interface* design pattern minimizes locking overhead and ensures that intra-component method calls do not incur 'self-deadlock' by trying to reacquire a lock that is held by the component already.

Example   When designing thread-safe components when intra-component method calls, developers must be careful to avoid self-deadlock and unnecessary locking overhead. For example, consider a more complete implementation of the `File_Cache` component outlined in the Strategized Locking pattern (333):

```cpp
template <class LOCK>
class File_Cache {
public:
    // Return a pointer to the memory-mapped file
    // associated with <path> name, adding
    // it to the cache if it doesn't exist.
    const void *lookup (const string &path) const {
        // Use the Scoped Locking idiom to acquire
        // and release the <lock_> automatically.
        Guard<LOCK> guard (lock_);
        const void *file_pointer = check_cache (path);
        if (file_pointer == 0) {
            // Insert the <path> name into the cache.
            // Note the intra-class <insert> call.
            insert (path);
            file_pointer = check_cache (path);
        }
        return file_pointer;
    }
    // Add <path> name to the cache.
    void insert (const string &path) {
        // Use the Scoped Locking idiom to acquire
        // and release the <lock_> automatically.
        Guard<LOCK> guard (lock_);
        // ... insert <path> into the cache...
    }
private:
    mutable LOCK lock_;
    const void *check_cache (const string &) const;
    // ... other private methods and data omitted...
};
```

This implementation of `File_Cache` works efficiently only when strategized by a 'null' lock such as the `Null_Mutex` described in the Strategized Locking pattern (333). If the `File_Cache` implementation is strategized with a recursive mutex, however, it will incur unnecessary overhead when it reacquires the mutex in the `insert()` method. Even worse, if it is strategized with a non-recursive mutex, the code will 'self-deadlock' when the `lookup()` method calls the `insert()` method. This self-deadlock occurs because `insert()` tries to reacquire the LOCK that has been acquired by `lookup()` already.

It is therefore counter-productive to apply the Strategized Locking pattern to the implementation of `File_Cache` shown above, because there are so many restrictions and subtle problems that can arise. Yet the `File_Cache` abstraction can still benefit from the flexibility and customization provided by Strategized Locking.

Context   Components in multi-threaded applications that contain intra-component method calls.

Problem   Multi-threaded components often contain multiple publicly-accessible interface methods and private implementation methods that can alter the component states. To prevent race conditions, a lock internal to the component can be used to serialize interface method invocations that access its state. Although this design works well if each method is self-contained, component methods may call each other to carry out their computations. If this occurs, the following *forces* will be unresolved in multi-threaded components that use improper intra-component method invocation designs:

- Thread-safe components should be designed to avoid 'self-deadlock'. Self-deadlock can occur if one component method acquires a non-recursive lock in the component and then calls another component method that tries to reacquire the same lock.

- Thread-safe components should be designed to incur only minimal locking overhead, for example to prevent race conditions on component state. If a recursive component lock is selected to avoid the self-deadlock problem outlined above, however, unnecessary overhead will be incurred to acquire and release the lock multiple times across intra-component method calls.

Solution   Structure all components that process intra-component method invocations according two design conventions:

- *Interface methods check.* All interface methods, such as C++ public methods, should only acquire/release component lock(s), thereby performing synchronization checks at the 'border' of the component. After the lock is acquired, the interface method should forward immediately to an implementation method, which performs the actual method functionality. After the implementation method returns, the interface method should release the lock(s) before returning control to the caller.

- *Implementation methods trust.* Implementation methods, such as C++ private and protected methods, should only perform work when called by interface methods. They therefore trust that they are called with the necessary lock(s) held and should never acquire or release lock(s). Implementation methods should also never call 'up' to interface methods, because these methods acquire lock(s).

Implementation   The Thread-Safe Interface pattern can be implemented using two activities:

1   *Determine the interface and corresponding implementation methods.* The interface methods define the public API of the component. For each interface method, define a corresponding implementation method.

➡   The interface and implementation methods for `File_Cache` can be defined as follows:

```
template <class LOCK>
class File_Cache {
public:
    // The following two interface methods just
    // acquire/release the <LOCK> and forward to
    // their corresponding implementation methods.
    const void *lookup (const string &path) const;
    void insert (const string &path);
private:
    // The following two implementation methods do not
    // acquire/release the <LOCK> and perform the actual
    // work associated with managing the <File_Cache>.
    const void *lookup_i (const string &path) const;
    void insert_i (const string &path);
    // ... Other implementation methods omitted ...
};
```

2   *Program the interface and implementation methods.* The bodies of the
    interface and implementation methods are programmed according to
    the design conventions described in the *Solution* section.

➥   Our `File_Cache` implementation applies Thread-Safe Interface
    to minimize locking overhead and prevent self-deadlock in class
    methods:

```
template <class LOCK>
class File_Cache {
public:
    // Return a pointer to the memory-mapped file
    // associated with <path> name, adding it to
    // the cache if it doesn't exist.
    const void *lookup (const string &path) const {
        // Use the Scoped Locking idiom to acquire
        // and release the <lock_> automatically.
        Guard<LOCK> guard (lock_);
        return lookup_i (path);
    }

    // Add <path> name to the file cache.
    void insert (const string &path) {
        // Use the Scoped Locking idiom to acquire
        // and release the <lock_> automatically.
        Guard<LOCK> guard (lock_);
        insert_i (path);
    }
private:
    mutable LOCK lock_; // The strategized locking object

    // The following implementation methods do not
    // acquire or release <lock_> and perform their
    // work without calling any interface methods.
    const void *lookup_i (const string &path) const {
        const void *file_pointer = check_cache_i (path);
        if (file_pointer == 0) {
            // If <path> name isn't in the cache then
            // insert it and look it up again.
            insert_i (path);
            file_pointer = check_cache_i (path);
            // The calls to implementation methods
            // <insert_i> and <check_cache_i> assume
            // that the lock is held and perform work.
        }
        return file_pointer;
    }
```

```
const void *check_cache_i (const string &) const
    { /* */ }

void insert_i (const string &) { /* ... */ }

// ... other private methods and data omitted ...
};
```

Variants   *Thread-Safe Facade.* This variant can be used if access to a whole subsystem or coarse-grained component must be synchronized. A facade [GoF95] can be introduced as the entry point for all client requests. The facade's methods correspond to the interface methods. The classes that belong to the subsystem or component provide the implementation methods. If these classes have their own internal concurrency strategies, refactoring may be needed to avoid *nested monitor lockout*[2] [JS97a].

Nested monitor lockup occurs when a thread acquires object X's monitor lock without relinquishing the lock already held on monitor Y, thereby preventing a second thread from acquiring the monitor lock for Y. This can lead to deadlock because, after acquiring monitor X, the first thread may wait for a condition to become true that can only change as a result of actions by the second thread after it has acquired monitor Y. It may not be possible to refactor the code properly to avoid nested monitor lockouts if the subsystem or component cannot be modified, for example if it is a third-party product or legacy system. In this case, Thread-Safe Facade should not be applied.

Thread-Safe Wrapper Facade. This variant helps synchronize access to a non-synchronized class or function API that cannot be modified. A wrapper facade (47) provides the interface methods, which encapsulate the corresponding implementation calls on the class or function API with actions that acquire and release a lock. The wrapper facade thus provides a synchronization proxy [POSA1] [GoF95] that serializes access to the methods of the class or function API.

Known Uses   **ACE** [Sch97]. The Thread-Safe Interface pattern is used throughout the ADAPTIVE Communication Environment framework, for example in its ACE_Message_Queue class.

---

2. See the Consequences Section of the Monitor Object pattern (399) for a more detailed discussion of the nested monitor lockout problem.

The **Dynix/PTX** operating system applies the Thread-Safe Interface pattern in portions of its kernel.

Java. The hash table implementation in java.util.Hashtable uses the Thread-Safe Interface design pattern. Hashtable's interface methods, such as put(Object key, Object value), acquire a lock before changing the underlying data structure, which consists of an array of linked lists. The implementation method rehash() is called when the load threshold is exceeded. A new larger hash table is created, all elements are moved from the old to the new hash table, and the old table is left to the garbage collector. Note that the rehash() method is not protected by a lock, in contrast to the publicly accessible methods such as put(Object key, Object value). Protecting rehash() by a lock would not deadlock the program due to Java's reentrant monitors. It would, however, diminish its performance due to the locking overhead.

A more sophisticated use case was introduced in JDK 1.2 with the Collection classes, which applies the Thread-Safe Wrapper Facade variant to make collection data structures thread-safe. The java.util.Collections takes any class implementing the Map interface and returns a SynchronizedMap, which is a different class implementing Map. The methods of SynchronizedMap do no more than synchronize on an internal monitor and then forward to the method of the original object. Developers can therefore choose between fast or thread-safe variants of data structures, which only need be implemented once.

Security checkpoints. You may encounter a real-life variation of the Thread-Safe Interface pattern when entering a country or commercial office building that has a security guard at the border or entrance. To be admitted, you must sign in. After being admitted, other people that you interact with typically trust that you are supposed to be there.

Consequences   There are three **benefits** of applying the Thread-Safe Interface pattern:

Increased robustness. This pattern ensures that self-deadlock does not occur due to intra-component method calls.

Enhanced performance. This pattern ensures that locks are not acquired or released unnecessarily.

Simplification of software. Separating the locking and functionality concerns can help to simplify both aspects.

However, there are also four **liabilities** when applying the Thread-Safe Interface pattern:

Additional indirection and extra methods. Each interface method requires at least one implementation method, which increases the footprint of the component and may also add an extra level of method-call indirection for each invocation. One way to minimize this overhead is to inline the interface and/or implementation methods.

Potential deadlock. By itself, the Thread-Safe Interface pattern does not resolve the problem of self-deadlock completely. For example, consider a client that calls an interface method on component A, which then delegates to an implementation method that calls an interface method on another component B. If the implementation of component B's method calls back on an interface method of component A, deadlock will occur when trying to reacquire the lock that was acquired by the first call in this chain.

Potential for misuse. Object-oriented programming languages, such as C++ and Java, support class-level rather than object-level access control. As a result, an object can bypass the public interface to call a private method on another object of the same class, thus bypassing that object's lock. Therefore, programmer's should be careful to avoid invoking private methods on any object of their class other than themselves.

Potential overhead. The Thread-Safe Interface pattern prevents multiple components from sharing the same lock. Therefore synchronization overhead may increase because multiple locks must be acquired, which also makes it harder to detect and avoid deadlocks. Moreover, the pattern prevents locking at a finer granularity than the component, which can increase lock contention, thereby reducing performance.

See Also   The Thread-Safe Interface pattern is related to the Decorator pattern [GoF95], which extends an object transparently by attaching additional responsibilities dynamically. The intention of the Thread-Safe Interface pattern is similar, in that it attaches robust and efficient locking strategies to make components thread-safe. The primary difference is that the Decorator pattern focuses on attaching additional responsibilities to objects dynamically, whereas the Thread-Safe Interface pattern focuses on the static partitioning of method responsibilities in component classes.

Components designed according to the Strategized Locking pattern (333) should employ the Thread-Safe Interface pattern to ensure that the component will function robustly and efficiently, regardless of the type of locking strategy that is selected.

Java implements locking at the method level via monitor objects (399) designated by the synchronized keyword. In Java, monitors are recursive. The problem of self-deadlock therefore cannot occur as long as developers reuse the same monitor, that is, synchronize on the same object. However, the problem of nested monitor lockout [JS97a] [Lea99a] can occur in Java if multiple nested monitors are used carelessly.

The problem of locking overhead depends on which Java Virtual Machine (JVM) is used. If a specific JVM implements monitors inefficiently and monitors are acquired recursively, the Thread-Safe Interface pattern may be able to help improve component run-time performance.

Credits   Thanks to Brad Appleton for comments on this pattern. Prashant Jain provided the Thread-Safe Interface variants and the Java nested monitor lockout discussion.

Double-Checked Locking Optimization

The *Double-Checked Locking Optimization* design pattern reduces contention and synchronization overhead whenever critical sections of code must acquire locks in a thread-safe manner just once during program execution.

Also Known As   Lock Hint [Bir91]

Example   The Singleton pattern ensures a class has only one instance and provides a global access point to that instance. The following C++ code shows the canonical implementation of Singleton from [GoF95]:

```
class Singleton {
public:
    static Singleton *instance () {
        if (instance_ == 0) {
            // Enter critical section.
            instance_ = new Singleton ();
            // Leave critical section.
        }
        return instance_;
    }
    void method_1 (); // Other methods omitted.
private:
    static Singleton *instance_;
    // Initialized to 0 by the compiler/linker.
};
```

Applications use the static instance() method to retrieve a pointer to the Singleton and then invoke public methods:

Singleton::instance ()->method_1 ();

Unfortunately the canonical implementation of the Singleton pattern shown above is problematic on platforms with preemptive multi-tasking or true hardware parallelism. In particular, the Singleton constructor can be called multiple times if

- Multiple pre-emptive threads invoke Singleton::instance() simultaneously *before* it is initialized and

- Multiple threads execute the dynamic initialization of the Singleton constructor within the critical section.

At best calling the `Singleton` constructor multiple times will cause a memory leak. At worst it can have disastrous consequences if singleton initialization is not idempotent.

To protect the critical section from concurrent access we could apply the Scoped Locking idiom (345) to acquire and release a mutex lock automatically:

```
class Singleton {
public:
    static Singleton *instance () {
        // Scoped Locking acquires <singleton_lock_>.
        Guard<Thread_Mutex> guard (singleton_lock_);
        if (instance_ == 0)
            instance_ = new Singleton;
        return instance_;
        // Destructor releases lock automatically.
    }
private:
    static Singleton *instance_;
    static Thread_Mutex singleton_lock_;
};
```

Assuming `singleton_lock_` is initialized correctly, `Singleton` is now thread-safe. The additional locking overhead may be excessive, however. In particular every call to `instance()` now acquires and releases the lock, even though the critical section should be executed just once. By placing the guard inside the conditional check, we can remove the locking overhead:

```
static Singleton *instance () {
    if (instance_ == 0) {
        Guard<Thread_Mutex> guard (singleton_lock_);
        // Only come here if <instance_>
        // has not been initialized yet.
        instance_ = new Singleton;
    }
    return instance_;
}
```

Unfortunately, this solution does not provide thread-safe initialization because a race condition in multi-threaded applications can cause multiple initializations of `Singleton`. For example, consider two threads that simultaneously check for `instance_ == 0`. Both will succeed, one will acquire the lock via the `guard` and the other will block. After the first thread initializes `Singleton` and releases the lock, the blocked thread will obtain the lock and erroneously initialize `Singleton` a second time.

Context A application containing shared resources accessed concurrently by multiple threads.

Problem Concurrent applications must ensure that certain portions of their code execute serially to avoid race conditions when accessing and modifying shared resources. A common way of avoiding race conditions is to serialize access to the shared resources' critical sections via locks, such as mutexes. Every thread that wants to enter a critical section must first acquire a lock. If this lock is already owned by another thread, the thread will block until the lock is released and the lock can be acquired.

The serialization approach outlined above can be inappropriate for objects or components that require 'just once' initialization. For example, the critical section code in our Singleton example must be executed just once during its initialization. However, every method call on the singleton acquires and releases the mutex lock, which can incur excessive overhead [PLoPD3]. To avoid this overhead, programmers of concurrent applications may revert to using global variables rather than applying the Singleton pattern. Unfortunately, this 'solution' has two drawbacks [LGS99]:

- It is *non-portable* because the order in which global objects defined in different files are constructed is often not specified.

- It is *overly resource consumptive* because global variables will be created even if they are not used.

Solution Introduce a flag that provides a 'hint' about whether it is necessary to execute a critical section *before* acquiring the lock that guards it. If this code need not be executed the critical section is skipped, thereby avoiding unnecessary locking overhead. The general pseudo-code design of this code is shown below:

```
// Perform first-check to evaluate 'hint'.
if (first_time_in_flag is FALSE) {
    acquire the mutex
    // Perform double-check to avoid race condition.
    if (first_time_in_flag is FALSE) {
        execute the critical section
        set first_time_in_flag to TRUE
    }
    release the mutex
}
```

Implementation   The   Double-Checked   Locking   Optimization   pattern   can   be
implemented via three activities:

1   *Identify the critical section to be executed just once.* This critical
    section performs operations, such as initialization logic, that are
    executed just once in a program.

    ➥   For example, a singleton is initialized just once in a program. The
    call to the singleton's constructor is thus executed only once in a
    critical section, regardless of the number of times the accessor
    method `Singleton::instance()` is called.   ❏

2   *Implement the locking logic.* The locking logic serializes access to the
    critical section of code that is executed just once. To implement this
    locking logic we can employ the Scoped Locking idiom (345) to ensure
    that the lock is acquired automatically when the appropriate scope is
    entered and released automatically when it goes out of scope.

    ➥   In accordance with the Scoped Locking idiom (345) a `Thread_`
    `Mutex singleton_lock_` is used to ensure that the singleton's
    constructor does not execute concurrently.   ❏

This lock must be initialized prior to the first call to the code that is
executed just once. In C++, one way to ensure that a lock is initialized
prior to its first use is to define it as a static object, as shown in the
Example section. Unfortunately the C++ language specification does
not guarantee the order of initialization of static objects that are
defined in separate compilation units. As a result, different C++
compiler and linker platforms may behave inconsistently and the lock
may not be initialized when it is first accessed.

A better way to avoid this problem is to use the Object Lifetime
Manager pattern [LGS99]. This pattern defines a portable object
manager component that governs the entire lifetime of global or static
objects as follows:

• The object manager creates these objects prior to their first use and

• It ensures they are destroyed properly at program termination

For example, the lock can be placed under the control of an object
manager that will ensure it is initialized before any singleton attempts
to use the lock to serialize its initialization. The object manager can
also delete the singleton when the program terminates, thereby

preventing the memory and resource leaks that can otherwise occur with the Singleton pattern [Vlis98a].

3   *Implement the first-time-in flag.* This flag indicates whether the critical section has been executed already.

➡   The `Singleton::instance_` pointer is used as the first-time-in flag. If the flag evaluates to true the critical section is skipped. If the flag also has a particular application-specific purpose, as our `Singleton::instance_` pointer is used, it must be an atomic type that can be set without a partial read or write. The following code for the `Singleton` example is thread-safe, but avoids unnecessary locking overhead by placing the call to new within another conditional test:

```
class Singleton {
public:
    static Singleton *instance () {
        // First check
        if (instance_ == 0) {
            // Use Scoped Locking to acquire and
            // release <singleton_lock_> automatically.
            Guard<Thread_Mutex> guard (singleton_lock_);
            // Double check.
            if (instance_ == 0)
                instance_ = new Singleton;
        }
        return instance_;
    }
private:
    static Singleton *instance_;
    static Thread_Mutex singleton_lock_;
};
```

The first thread that acquires the `singleton_lock_` will construct the `Singleton` object and assign the pointer to `instance_`, which serves as the first-time-in flag in this example. All threads that call `instance()` subsequently will find `instance_` is not equal to zero and will thus skip the initialization step.

The second check prevents a race condition if multiple threads try to initialize `Singleton` simultaneously. This handles the case in which multiple threads execute in parallel. In the code above these threads will queue up at the `singleton_lock_` mutex. When the queued threads finally obtain the mutex `singleton_lock_` they will find instance_ is not equal to zero and will then skip the Singleton initialization.

This implementation of the Singleton::instance() method only incurs locking overhead for threads that are active inside instance() when the Singleton is first initialized. In subsequent calls to instance() the instance_ pointer is not zero and thus singleton_ lock_ is neither acquired nor released.   ❑

Variants   *Volatile Data.* The Double-Checked Locking Optimization pattern implementation may require modifications if a compiler optimizes the first-time-in flag by caching it in some way, such as storing it in a CPU register. In this case, cache coherency may become a problem. For example, copies of the first-time-in flag held simultaneously in registers by multiple threads may become inconsistent if one thread's setting of the value is not reflected in other threads' copies.

A related problem is that a highly optimizing compiler may consider the second check of flag == 0 to be superfluous and optimize it away. A solution to both these problems is to declare the flag as volatile data, which ensures the compiler will not perform aggressive optimizations that change the program's semantics.

➥   For our Singleton example, this results in the following code:

```
class Singleton {
    // ...
private:
    static Singleton *volatile instance_;
    // instance_ is volatile.
};
```

The use of volatile ensures that a compiler will not place the instance_ pointer into a register, nor will it optimize away the second check in instance().   ❑

The downside of using volatile is that all access to will be through memory rather than through registers, which may degrade performance.

Template Adapter. Another variation for the Double-Checked Locking Optimization pattern is applicable when the pattern is implemented in C++. In this case, create a template adapter that transforms classes to have singleton-like behavior and performs the Double-Checked Locking Optimization pattern automatically.

➥ The following code illustrates how to write this template in C++:

```
template <class TYPE>
class Singleton {
public:
    static TYPE *instance () {
        // First check
        if (instance_ == 0) {
            // Scoped Locking acquires and release lock.
            Guard<Thread_Mutex> guard (singleton_lock_);
            // Double check instance_.
            if (instance_ == 0)
                instance_ = new TYPE;
        }
        return instance_;
    }
private:
    static TYPE *instance_;
    static Thread_Mutex singleton_lock_;
};
```

The Singleton template is parameterized by the TYPE that will be accessed as a singleton. The Double-Checked Locking Optimization pattern is applied automatically on the singleton_lock_ within the instance() method.

The Singleton template adapter can also be integrated with the Object Lifetime Manager pattern [LGS99], which ensures that dynamically allocated singletons are deallocated automatically when an application process exits. This pattern can also ensure that the static singleton_lock_ data member is initialized properly before its first use. ❑

Pre-initialization of Singletons. This variation is an alternative that may alleviate the need for Double-Checked Locking Optimization. It does this by initializing all objects explicitly at program start-up, for example in a program's main() function. Thus, there are no race conditions because the initialization is constrained to occur within a single thread.

This solution is inappropriate, however, when expensive calculations must be performed that may be unnecessary in certain situations. For instance, if a singleton is never actually created during program execution, initializing it during program start-up will simply waste resources. Pre-initialization can also break encapsulation by forcing application components with singletons in their implementation to expose this information so the singletons can be initialized explicitly. Likewise, pre-initialization makes it hard to compose applications using components that are configured dynamically using the Component Configurator pattern (75).

Known Uses   **ACE** [Sch97]. The Double-Checked Locking Optimization pattern is used extensively throughout the ACE framework. To reduce code duplication, ACE defines a reusable adapter template called `ACE_Singleton` that is similar to the one shown in the Variants section and is used to transform 'normal' classes into singletons. Although singletons are not the only use of the Double-Checked Locking Optimization pattern in the ACE framework, they are a common example that demonstrates the utility of the pattern.

Sequent Dynix/PTX. The Doubled-Checked Locking Optimization pattern is used in the Sequent Dynix/PTX operating system.

POSIX and **Linux.** The Double-Checked Locking Optimization pattern can be used to implement POSIX 'once' variables [IEEE96], which ensure that functions are invoked just once in a program. This pattern has been used in the LinuxThreads `pthread_once()` implementation to ensure its function-pointer parameter `init_routine()` is called only once—on its first call—and not subsequently.

Andrew Birrell describes the use of the Double-Checked Locking Optimization pattern in [Bir91]. Birrell refers to the first check of the flag as a 'lock hint'.

The **Solaris 2.x** documentation for `pthread_key_create(3T)`, which is shown in the Thread-Specific Storage pattern (475) *Known Uses* section, illustrates how to use the Double-Checked Locking Optimization to initialize thread-specific data.

Consequences   There are two **benefits** of using the Double-Checked Locking Optimization pattern:

Minimized locking overhead. By performing two first-time-in flag checks, the Double-Checked Locking Optimization pattern minimizes overhead for the common case. After the flag is set the first check ensures that subsequent accesses require no further locking.

Prevents race conditions. The second check of the first-time-in flag ensures that the critical section is executed just once.

However, there are three **liabilities** of using the Double-Checked Locking Optimization pattern that can arise if the pattern is used in software that is ported to certain types of operating system, hardware, or compiler/linker platforms. However, because this pattern is applicable to a large class of platforms, we outline techniques for overcoming these limitations.

Non-atomic pointer or integral assignment semantics. If an `instance_` pointer is used as the flag in a singleton implementation, all bits of the singleton `instance_` pointer must be read and written atomically in a single operation. If the write to memory after the call to new is not atomic, other threads may try to read an invalid pointer. This can result in sporadic illegal memory accesses.

These scenarios are possible on systems where memory addresses straddle word alignment boundaries, such as 32-bit pointers used on a computer with a 16 bit word bus, which requires two fetches from memory for each pointer access. In this case it may be necessary to use a separate, word-aligned integral flag—assuming that the hardware supports atomic word-based reads and writes—rather than using an `instance_` pointer.

Multi-processor cache coherency. Certain multi-processor platforms, such as the COMPAQ Alpha and Intel Itanium, perform aggressive memory caching optimizations in which read and write operations can execute 'out of order' across multiple CPU caches. On these platforms, it may not be possible to use the Double-Checked Locking Optimization pattern without further modifications because CPU cache lines will not be flushed properly if shared data is accessed without locks held.

To use the Double-Checked Locking Optimization pattern correctly on these types of hardware platforms, CPU-specific instructions, such as memory barriers to flush cache lines, must be inserted into the Double-Checked Locking Optimization implementation. Note that a serendipitous side-effect of using the template adapter variation of the Double-Checked Locking Optimization pattern is that it centralizes the placement of these CPU-specific cache instructions.

➡️   For example, a memory barrier instruction can be located within the `instance()` method of the `Singleton` template adapter class:

```
template <class TYPE>
TYPE *Singleton<TYPE>::instance () {
    TYPE *tmp = instance_;

#if defined (ALPHA_MP)
    // Insert the CPU-specific memory barrier instruction
    // to synchronize the cache lines on multi-processor.
    asm ("mb");
#endif /* ALPHA_MP */

    // First check
    if (tmp == 0) {
        // Scoped Locking acquires and releases lock.
        Guard<Thread_Mutex> guard (singleton_lock_);

        // Double check.
        if (tmp == 0) {
            tmp = new TYPE;

#if defined (ALPHA_MP)
            // Insert a second CPU-specific memory
            // barrier instruction.
            asm ("mb");
#endif /* ALPHA_MP */

            instance_ = tmp;
        }
    }
    return tmp;
}
```

As long as the `Singleton` template adapter is used uniformly, it is straightforward to localize the placement of CPU-specific code without affecting applications. Conversely, if the Double-Checked Locking Optimization pattern is hand-crafted into singletons at each point of use much more effort is required to add this CPU-specific code.   ❑

Unfortunately, the need for CPU-specific code in implementations of the Double-Checked Locking Optimization pattern makes this pattern inapplicable for Java applications. Java's bytecodes are designed to be cross-platform and therefore its JVMs lack a memory barrier instruction that can resolve the problem outlined in this liability.

Additional mutex usage. Regardless of whether a singleton is allocated on-demand, some type of lock, such as the `Thread_Mutex` used in our examples, is allocated and retained for the lifetime of the program. One technique for minimizing this overhead is to pre-allocate a singleton lock within an object manager [LGS99] and use this lock to serialize *all* singleton initialization. Although this may increase lock contention, it may not affect program performance because each singleton will most likely acquire and release the lock only once when its initialized.

See Also The Double-Checked Locking Optimization pattern is a thread-safe variant of the Lazy Evaluation pattern [Mey98] [Beck97]. This pattern is often used in programming languages such as C that lack constructors in order to ensure components are initialized before their state is accessed.

➡ For example the following C code initializes a stack:

```
static const int STACK_SIZE = 1000;
static Type *stack_;
static int top_;

void push (Type *item) {
    // First-time-in-check.
    if (stack_ == 0) {
        // Allocate the pointer, which implicitly
        // indicates that initialization was performed.
        stack_ = malloc (STACK_SIZE * sizeof Type);
        top_ = 0;
    }
    stack_[top_++] = item;
    // ...
}
```

The first time that push() is called, stack_ is 0, which triggers its implicit initialization via malloc(). ❑

Credits The co-author of the original version [PLoPD3] of this pattern was Tim Harrison. Thanks to John Basrai, James Coplien, Ralph Johnson, Jaco van der Merwe, Duane Murphy, Paul McKenney, Bill Pugh, and Siva Vaddepuri for their suggestions and comments on the Double-Checked Locking Optimization pattern.

5 Concurrency Patterns

*"You look at where you're going and where you are
and it never makes sense,
but then you look back at where you've been
and a pattern seems to emerge.
And if you project forward from that pattern,
then sometimes you can come up with something."*

Robert M. Pirsig

This chapter presents five patterns that address various types of concurrency architecture and design issues for components, subsystems, and applications: Active Object, Monitor Object, Half-Sync/Half-Async, Leader/Followers, and Thread-Specific Storage.

The choice of concurrency architecture has a significant impact on the design and performance of multi-threaded networking middleware and applications. No single concurrency architecture is suitable for all workload conditions and hardware and software platforms. The patterns in this chapter therefore collectively provide solutions to a variety of concurrency problems.

The first two patterns in this chapter specify designs for sharing resources among multiple threads or processes:

- The *Active Object* design pattern (369) decouples method execution from method invocation. Its purpose is to enhance concurrency and simplify synchronized access to objects that reside in their own threads of control

- The *Monitor Object* design pattern (399) synchronizes concurrent method execution to ensure that only one method at a time runs within an object. It also allows an object's methods to schedule their execution sequences cooperatively.

Both patterns can synchronize and schedule methods invoked concurrently on objects. The main difference is that an active object executes its methods in a different thread than its clients, whereas a monitor object executes its methods by borrowing the thread of its clients. As a result active objects can perform more sophisticated—albeit expensive—scheduling to determine the order in which their methods execute.

The next two patterns in this chapter define higher-level concurrency architectures:

- The *Half-Sync/Half-Async* architectural pattern (423) decouples asynchronous and synchronous processing in concurrent systems, to simplify programming without reducing performance unduldy. The pattern introduces two intercommunicating layers, one for asynchronous and one for synchronous service processing. A further queuing layer mediates communication between services in the asynchronous and synchronous layers.

- The *Leader/Followers* architectural pattern (447) provides an efficient concurrency model where multiple threads take turns to share a set of event sources to detect, demultiplex, dispatch, and process service requests that occur on the event sources. The Leader/Followers pattern can be used in lieu of the Half-Sync/

Half-Async and Active Object patterns to improve performance when there are no synchronization or ordering constraints on the processing of requests by pooled threads.

Implementors of the Half-Sync/Half-Async and Leader/Followers patterns can use the Active Object and Monitor Object patterns to co-ordinate access to shared objects efficiently.

The final pattern in this chapter offers a different strategy for addressing certain inherent complexities of concurrency:

- The *Thread-Specific Storage* design pattern (475) allows multiple threads to use one 'logically global' access point to retrieve an object that is local to a thread, without incurring locking overhead on each access to the object. To some extent this pattern can be viewed as the 'antithesis' of the other patterns in this section, because it addresses several inherent complexities of concurrency by preventing the sharing of resources among threads.

Implementations of all patterns in this chapter can use the patterns from Chapter 4, *Synchronization Patterns*, to protect critical regions from concurrent access.

Other patterns in the literature that address concurrency-related issues include Master-Slave [POSA1], Producer-Consumer [Grand98], Scheduler [Lea99a], and Two-phase Termination [Grand98].

Active Object

The *Active Object* design pattern decouples method execution from method invocation to enhance concurrency and simplify synchronized access to objects that reside in their own threads of control.

Also Known As   Concurrent Object

Example   Consider the design of a communication gateway,[1] which decouples cooperating components and allows them to interact without having direct dependencies on each other. As shown below, the gateway may route messages from one or more supplier processes to one or more consumer processes in a distributed system.

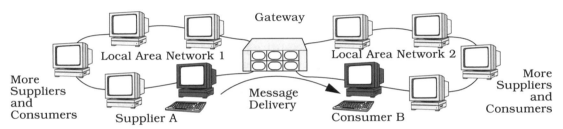

The suppliers, consumers, and gateway communicate using TCP [Ste93], which is a connection-oriented protocol. The gateway may therefore encounter flow control from the TCP transport layer when it tries to send data to a remote consumer. TCP uses flow control to ensure that fast suppliers or gateways do not produce data more rapidly than slow consumers or congested networks can buffer and process the data. To improve end-to-end *quality of service* (QoS) for all suppliers and consumers, the entire gateway process must not block while waiting for flow control to abate over any one connection to a consumer. In addition the gateway must scale up efficiently as the number of suppliers and consumers increase.

An effective way to prevent blocking and improve performance is to introduce *concurrency* into the gateway design, for example by associating a different thread of control for each TCP connection. This

---

1. See the Acceptor-Connector pattern (285) for further details of this example.

design enables threads whose TCP connections are flow controlled to block without impeding the progress of threads whose connections are not flow controlled. We thus need to determine how to program the gateway threads and how these threads interact with supplier and consumer handlers.

Context Clients that access objects running in separate threads of control.

Problem Many applications benefit from using concurrent objects to improve their quality of service, for example by allowing an application to handle multiple client requests simultaneously. Instead of using a single-threaded passive object, which executes its methods in the thread of control of the client that invoked the methods, a concurrent object resides in its own thread of control. If objects run concurrently, however, we must synchronize access to their methods and data if these objects are shared and modified by multiple client threads, in which case three *forces* arise:

- Processing-intensive methods invoked on an object concurrently should not block the entire process indefinitely, thereby degrading the quality of service of other concurrent objects.

  ➥ For example, if one outgoing TCP connection in our gateway example is blocked due to flow control, the gateway process still should be able to run other threads that can queue new messages while waiting for flow control to abate. Similarly, if other outgoing TCP connections are not flow controlled, it should be possible for other threads in the gateway to send messages to their consumers independently of any blocked connections.   ❏

- Synchronized access to shared objects should be straightforward to program. In particular, client method invocations on a shared object that are subject to synchronization constraints should be serialized and scheduled transparently.

  ➥ Applications like our gateway can be hard to program if developers use low-level synchronization mechanisms, such as acquiring and releasing mutual exclusion (mutex) locks explicitly. Methods that are subject to synchronization constraints, such as enqueueing and dequeueing messages from TCP connections, should be serialized transparently when objects are accessed by multiple threads.   ❏

- Applications should be designed to leverage the parallelism available on a hardware/software platform transparently.

    ➥ In our gateway example, messages destined for different consumers should be sent concurrently by a gateway over different TCP connections. If the entire gateway is programmed to only run in a single thread of control, however, performance bottlenecks cannot be alleviated transparently by running the gateway on a multi-processor platform.   ❏

Solution   For each object exposed to the forces above, decouple method invocation on the object from method execution. Method invocation should occur in the client's thread of control, whereas method execution should occur in a separate thread. Moreover, design the decoupling so the client thread appears to invoke an ordinary method.

In detail: A *proxy* [POSA1] [GoF95] represents the interface of an active object and a *servant* [OMG98a] provides the active object's implementation. Both the proxy and the servant run in separate threads so that method invocations and method executions can run concurrently. The proxy runs in the client thread, while the servant runs in a different thread.

At run-time the proxy transforms the client's method invocations into *method requests*, which are stored in an *activation list* by a *scheduler*. The scheduler's event loop runs continuously in the same thread as the servant, dequeueing method requests from the activation list and dispatching them on the servant. Clients can obtain the result of a method's execution via a *future* returned by the proxy.

Structure   An active object consists of six components:

A *proxy* [POSA1] [GoF95] provides an interface that allows clients to invoke publicly-accessible methods on an active object. The use of a proxy permits applications to program using standard strongly-typed language features, rather than passing loosely-typed messages between threads. The proxy resides in the client's thread.

When a client invokes a method defined by the proxy it triggers the construction of a method request object. A method request contains the context information, such as a method's parameters, necessary to execute a specific method invocation and return any result to the client. A *method request* class defines an interface for executing the methods of an active object. This interface also contains *guard* methods that can be used to determine when a method request can be executed. For every public method offered by a proxy that requires synchronized access in the active object, the method request class is subclassed to create a *concrete method request* class.

Class	*Collaborator*
Proxy	• Method Request
	• Scheduler
Responsibility	• Future
• Defines the active object's interface to clients	
• Creates Method Requests	
• Runs in the client's thread	

Class	*Collaborator*	*Class*	*Collaborator*
Method Request	• Servant	Concrete Method Request	• Servant
	• Future		• Future
Responsibility		*Responsibility*	
• Represents a method call on the active object		• Implements the representation of a specific method call	
• Provides guards to check when the method request becomes runnable		• Implements guards	

A proxy inserts the concrete method request it creates into an *activation list*. This list maintains a bounded buffer of pending method requests created by the proxy and keeps track of which method requests can execute. The activation list decouples the client thread where the proxy resides from the thread where the servant method is executed, so the two threads can run concurrently. The internal state of the activation list must therefore be serialized to protect it from concurrent access.

A *scheduler* runs in a different thread than its client proxies, namely in the active object's thread. It decides which method request to execute next on an active object. This scheduling decision is based on various criteria, such as *ordering*—the order in which methods are called on the active object—or certain *properties* of an active object, such as its state. A scheduler can evaluate these properties using the method requests' guards, which determine when it is possible to execute the method request [Lea99a]. A scheduler uses an activation list to manage method requests that are pending execution. Method requests are inserted in an activation list by a proxy when clients invoke one of its methods.

Class	Collaborator
Activation List	
Responsibility	
• Maintains Method Requests pending for execution • Method Requests are inserted by the proxy and removed by the scheduler	

Class	Collaborator
Scheduler	• Activation List • Method Request
Responsibility	
• Inserts Method Requests into the Activation List • Runs in the active object's thread	

A *servant* defines the behavior and state that is modeled as an active object. The methods a servant implements correspond to the interface of the proxy and method requests the proxy creates. It may also contain other *predicate* methods that method requests can use to implement their guards. A servant method is invoked when its associated method request is executed by a scheduler. Thus, it executes in its scheduler's thread.

When a client invokes a method on a proxy it receives a *future* [Hal85] [LS88]. This future allows the client to obtain the result of the method invocation after the servant finishes executing the method. Each future reserves space for the invoked method to store its result. When a client wants to obtain this result, it can *rendezvous* with the future, either blocking or polling until the result is computed and stored into the future.

Class	Collaborator
Servant	
Responsibility	
• Implements the active object • Runs in the active object thread	

Class	Collaborator
Future	
Responsibility	
• Stores the result of a method call on an active object • Provides a rendezvous point for a client	

The class diagram for the Active Object pattern is shown below:

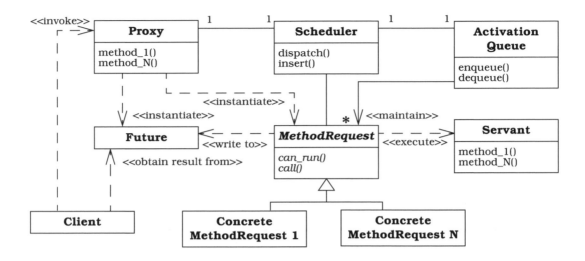

Dynamic   The behavior of the Active Object pattern can be divided into three phases:

- *Method request construction and scheduling.* A client invokes a method on the proxy. This triggers the creation of a method request, which maintains the argument bindings to the method as well as any other bindings required to execute the method and return its result. The proxy then passes the method request to its scheduler, which enqueues it on the activation list. If the method is defined as a *two-way* invocation [OMG98a], a future is returned to the client. No future is returned if a method is a *one-way*, which means it has no return values.

- *Method request execution.* The active object's scheduler runs continuously in a different thread than its clients. The scheduler monitors its activation list and determines which method request(s) have become runnable by calling their guard method. When a method request becomes runnable the scheduler removes it, binds the request to its servant, and dispatches the appropriate method on the servant. When this method is called, it can access and update the state of its servant and create its result if it is a two-way method invocation.

- *Completion*. In this phase the result, if any, is stored in the future and the active object's scheduler returns to monitor the activation list for runnable method requests. After a two-way method completes, clients can retrieve its result via the future. In general, any clients that rendezvous with the future can obtain its result. The method request and future can be deleted explicitly or garbage collected when they are no longer referenced.

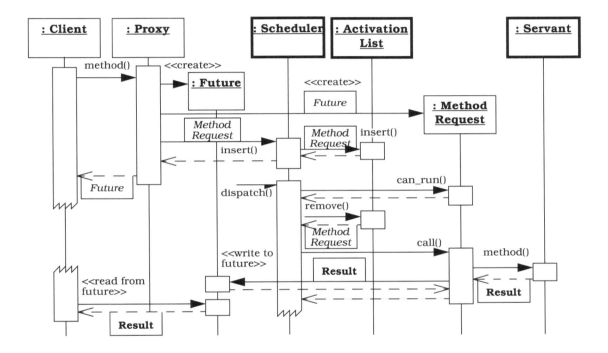

Implementation   Five activities show how to implement the Active Object pattern.

1 *Implement the servant*. A servant defines the behavior and state being modeled as an active object. In addition, a servant may contain *predicate* methods used to determine when to execute method requests.

    ➥   For each remote consumer in our gateway example there is a consumer handler containing a TCP connection to a consumer process running on a remote machine. Each consumer handler contains a message queue modeled as an active object and implemented with an MQ_Servant. This active object stores messages passed from suppliers to the gateway while they are waiting to be sent to the remote consumer.[2] The following C++ class illustrates the MQ_Servant class:

```
class MQ_Servant {
public:
    // Constructor and destructor.
    MQ_Servant (size_t mq_size);
    ~MQ_Servant ();

    // Message queue implementation operations.
    void put (const Message &msg);
    Message get ();

    // Predicates.
    bool empty () const;
    bool full () const;
private:
    // Internal queue representation, e.g., a circular
    // array or a linked list, that does not use any
    // internal synchronization mechanism.
};
```

The put() and get() methods implement the message insertion and removal operations on the queue, respectively. The servant defines two *predicates*, empty() and full(), that distinguish three internal states: empty, full, and neither empty nor full. These predicates are used to determine when put() and get() methods can be called on the servant.   ❑

In general, the synchronization mechanisms that protect a servant's critical sections from concurrent access should not be tightly coupled with the servant, which should just implement application functionality. Instead, the synchronization mechanisms should be associated with the method requests. This design avoids the *inheritance anomaly* problem [MWY91], which inhibits the reuse of servant implementations if subclasses require different synchronization policies than base classes. Thus, a change to the synchronization constraints of the active object need not affect its servant implementation.

➡   The MQ_Servant class is designed to omit synchronization mechanisms from a servant. The method implementations in the

2. The active object message queue in this example is an implementation mechanism that buffers messages to avoid blocking the gateway when flow control occurs on TCP connections. It is *not* related to the activation list, which is an Active Object pattern participant that stores method requests pending execution. See the *Example Resolved* section and the Monitor Object pattern (399) for further discussion of the example.

MQ_Servant class, which are omitted for brevity, therefore need not contain any synchronization mechanisms.   ❏

2 *Implement the invocation infrastructure.* In this activity, we describe the infrastructure necessary for clients to invoke methods on an active object. This infrastructure consists of a *proxy* that creates *method requests*, which can be implemented via two sub-activities.

2.1 *Implement the proxy.* The proxy provides clients with an interface to the servant's methods. For each method invocation by a client, the proxy creates a concrete method request. Each method request is an abstraction for the method's context, which is also called the *closure* of the method. Typically, this context includes the method parameters, a binding to the servant the method will be applied to, a future for the result, and the code that executes the method request.

➥ In our gateway the MQ_Proxy provides the following interface to the MQ_Servant defined in implementation activity 1 (375):

```
class MQ_Proxy {
public:
    // Bound the message queue size.
    enum { MQ_MAX_SIZE = /* ... */ };
    MQ_Proxy (size_t size = MQ_MAX_SIZE):
        scheduler_ (size), servant_ (size) { }

    // Schedule <put> to execute on the active object.
    void put (const Message &msg) {
        Method_Request *mr = new Put (servant_, msg);
        scheduler_.insert (mr);
    }

    // Return a <Message_Future> as the "future" result of
    // an asynchronous <get> method on the active object.
    Message_Future get () {
        Message_Future result;
        Method_Request *mr = new Get (servant_, result);
        scheduler_.insert (mr);
        return result;
    }

    // empty() and full() predicate implementations ...
private:
    // The servant that implements the active object
    // methods and a scheduler for the message queue.
    MQ_Servant servant_;
    MQ_Scheduler scheduler_;
};
```

The MP_Proxy is a factory [GoF95] that constructs instances of method requests and passes them to a scheduler, which queues them for subsequent execution in a separate thread.   ❑

Multiple client threads in a process can share the same proxy. A proxy method need not be serialized because it does not change state after it is created. Its scheduler and activation list are responsible for any necessary internal serialization.

➥ Our gateway example contains many supplier handlers that receive and route messages to peers via many consumer handlers. Several supplier handlers can invoke methods using the proxy that belongs to a single consumer handler without the need for any explicit synchronization.   ❑

2.2   *Implement the method requests.* Method requests can be considered as command objects [GoF95]. A method request class declares an interface used by all concrete method requests. It provides schedulers with a uniform interface that allows them to be decoupled from specific knowledge about how to evaluate synchronization constraints or trigger the execution of concrete method requests. Typically, this interface declares a can_run() method that defines a hook method guard that checks when it is possible to execute the method request. It also declares a call() method that defines a hook for executing a method request on the servant.

The methods in a method request class must be defined by subclasses. There should be one concrete method request class for each method defined in the proxy. The can_run() method is often implemented with the help of the servant's predicates.

➥ In our gateway example a Method_Request base class defines two virtual hook methods, which we call can_run() and call():

```
class Method_Request {
public:
    // Evaluate the synchronization constraint.
    virtual bool can_run () const = 0

    // Execute the method.
    virtual void call () = 0;
};
```

We then define two subclasses of Method_Request: class Put corresponds to the put() method call on a proxy and class Get corresponds to the get() method call. Both classes contain a pointer to the MQ_Servant. The Get class can be implemented as follows:

```
class Get : public Method_Request {
public:
    Get (MQ_Servant *rep, const Message_Future &f)
        : servant_ (rep), result_ (f) { }

    virtual bool can_run () const {
        // Synchronization constraint: cannot call a
        // <get> method until queue is not empty.
        return !servant_->empty ();
    }

    virtual void call () {
        // Bind dequeued message to the future result.
        result_ = servant_->get ();
    }
private:
    MQ_Servant *servant_;
    Message_Future result_;
};
```

Note how the can_run() method uses the MQ_Servant's empty() predicate to allow a scheduler to determine when the Get method request can execute. When the method request does execute, the active object's scheduler invokes its call() hook method. This call() hook uses the Get method request's run-time binding to MQ_Servant to invoke the servant's get() method, which is executed in the context of that servant. It does not require any explicit serialization mechanisms, however, because the active object's scheduler enforces all the necessary synchronization constraints via the method request can_run() methods.   ❏

The proxy passes a future to the constructors of the corresponding method request classes for each of its public two-way methods in the proxy that returns a value, such as the get() method in our gateway example. This future is returned to the client thread that calls the method, as discussed in implementation activity 5 (384).

3   *Implement the activation list.* Each method request is inserted into an activation list. This list can be implemented as a synchronized bounded buffer that is shared between the client threads and the thread in which the active object's scheduler and servant run. An activation list can also provide a *robust iterator* [Kof93] [CarEl95] that allows its scheduler to traverse and remove its elements.

The activation list is often designed using concurrency control patterns, such as Monitor Object (399), that use common synchronization mechanisms like condition variables and mutexes [Ste98]. When these are used in conjunction with a timer mechanism, a scheduler thread can determine how long to wait for certain operations to complete. For example, timed waits can be used to bound the time spent trying to remove a method request from an empty activation list or to insert into a full activation list.[3] If the timeout expires, control returns to the calling thread and the method request is not executed.

➡ For our gateway example we specify a class Activation_List as follows:

```
class Activation_List {
public:
    // Block for an "infinite" amount of time waiting
    // for <insert> and <remove> methods to complete.
    enum { INFINITE = -1 };

    // Define a "trait".
    typedef Activation_List_Iterator iterator;

    // Constructor creates the list with the specified
    // high water mark that determines its capacity.
    Activation_List (size_t high_water_mark);

    // Insert <method_request> into the list, waiting up
    // to <timeout> amount of time for space to become
    // available in the queue. Throws the <System_Ex>
    // exception if <timeout> expires.
    void insert (Method_Request *method_request,
                 Time_Value *timeout = 0);

    // Remove <method_request> from the list, waiting up
    // to <timeout> amount of time for a <method_request>
    // to be inserted into the list. Throws the
    // <System_Ex> exception if <timeout> expires.
    void remove (Method_Request *&method_request,
                 Time_Value *timeout = 0);
private:
    // Synchronization mechanisms, e.g., condition
    // variables and mutexes, and the queue implemen-
    // tation, e.g., an array or a linked list, go here.
};
```

---

3. A list is considered 'full' when its current method request count equals its high-water mark.

The insert() and remove() methods provide a 'bounded-buffer' producer/consumer [Grand98] synchronization model. This design allows a scheduler thread and multiple client threads to remove and insert Method_Requests simultaneously without corrupting the internal state of an Activation_List. Client threads play the role of producers and insert Method_Requests via a proxy. A scheduler thread plays the role of a consumer. It removes Method_Requests from the Activation_List when their guards evaluate to 'true'. It then invokes their call() hooks to execute servant methods.   ❏

4   *Implement the active object's scheduler.* A scheduler is a command processor [POSA1] that manages the activation list and executes pending method requests whose synchronization constraints have been met. The public interface of a scheduler often provides one method for the proxy to insert method requests into the activation list and another method that dispatches method requests to the servant.

➡   We define the following MQ_Scheduler class for our gateway:

```
class MQ_Scheduler {
public:
    // Initialize the <Activation_List> to have
    // the specified capacity and make <MQ_Scheduler>
    // run in its own thread of control.
    MQ_Scheduler (size_t high_water_mark);

    // ... Other constructors/destructors, etc.

    // Put <Method_Request> into <Activation_List>. This
    // method runs in the thread of its client, i.e.
    // in the proxy's thread.
    void insert (Method_Request *mr) {
        act_list_.insert (mr);
    }

    // Dispatch the method requests on their servant
    // in its scheduler's thread of control.
    virtual void dispatch ();
private:
    // List of pending Method_Requests.
    Activation_List act_list_;

    // Entry point into the new thread.
    static void *svc_run (void *arg);
};
```
❏

A scheduler executes its dispatch() method in a different thread of control than its client threads. Each client thread uses a proxy to insert method requests in an active object scheduler's activation list. This scheduler monitors the activation list in its own thread, selecting a method request whose *guard* evaluates to 'true,' that is, whose synchronization constraints are met. This method request is then removed from the activation list and executed by invoking its call() hook method.

➡   In our gateway example the constructor of MQ_Scheduler initializes the Activation_List and uses the Thread_Manager wrapper facade (47) to spawn a new thread of control:

```
MQ_Scheduler::MQ_Scheduler (size_t high_water_mark):
    act_queue_ (high_water_mark) {
    // Spawn separate thread to dispatch method requests.
    Thread_Manager::instance ()->spawn (&svc_run, this);
}
```

The Thread_Manager::spawn() method is passed a pointer to a static MQ_Scheduler::svc_run() method and a pointer to the MQ_Scheduler object. The svc_run() static method is the entry point into a newly created thread of control, which runs the svc_run() method. This method is simply an adapter [GoF95] that calls the MQ_Scheduler::dispatch() method on the this parameter:

```
void *MQ_Scheduler::svc_run (void *args) {
    MQ_Scheduler *this_obj =
        static_cast<MQ_Scheduler *> (args);

    this_obj->dispatch ();
}
```

The dispatch() method determines the order in which Put and Get method requests are processed based on the underlying MQ_Servant predicates empty() and full(). These predicates reflect the state of the servant, such as whether the message queue is empty, full, or neither.

By evaluating these predicate constraints via the method request can_run() methods, a scheduler can ensure fair access to the MQ_Servant:

```
virtual void MQ_Scheduler::dispatch () {
    // Iterate continuously in a separate thread.
    for (;;) {
        Activation_List::iterator request;
        // The iterator's <begin> method blocks
        // when the <Activation_List> is empty.
        for (request = act_list_.begin ();
             request != act_list_.end ();
             ++request) {
            // Select a method request whose
            // guard evaluates to true.
            if ((*request).can_run ()) {
                // Take <request> off the list.
                act_list_.remove (*request);
                (*request).call ();
                delete *request;
            }
            // Other scheduling activities can go here,
            // e.g., to handle when no <Method_Request>s
            // in the <Activation_List> have <can_run>
            // methods that evaluate to true.
        }
    }
}
```

In our example the MQ_Scheduler::dispatch() implementation iterates continuously, executing the next method request whose can_run() method evaluates to true. Scheduler implementations can be more sophisticated, however, and may contain variables that represent the servant's synchronization state.

For example, to implement a multiple-readers/single-writer synchronization policy a prospective writer will call 'write' on the proxy, passing the data to write. Similarly, readers will call 'read' and obtain a future as their return value. The active object's scheduler maintains several counter variables that keep track of the synchronization state, such as the number of read and write requests. The scheduler also maintains knowledge about the identity of the prospective writers.

The active object's scheduler can use these synchronization state counters to determine when a single writer can proceed, that is, when the current number of readers is zero and no write request from a different writer is currently pending execution. When such a write request arrives, a scheduler may choose to dispatch the writer to ensure fairness. In contrast, when read requests arrive and the servant can satisfy them because it is not empty, its scheduler can block all writing activity and dispatch read requests first.

The synchronization state counter variable values described above are independent of the servant's state because they are only used by its scheduler to enforce the correct synchronization policy on behalf of the servant. The servant focuses solely on its task to temporarily store client-specific application data. In contrast, its scheduler focuses on coordinating multiple readers and writers. This design enhances modularity and reusability.

A scheduler can support multiple synchronization policies by using the Strategy pattern [GoF95]. Each synchronization policy is encapsulated in a separate strategy class. The scheduler, which plays the context role in the Strategy pattern, is then configured with a particular synchronization strategy it uses to execute all subsequent scheduling decisions.

5   *Determine rendezvous and return value policy.* The rendezvous policy determines how clients obtain return values from methods invoked on active objects. A rendezvous occurs when an active object servant executing in one thread passes a return value to the client that invoke the method running in another thread. Implementations of the Active Object pattern often choose from the following rendezvous and return value policies:

- *Synchronous waiting.* Block the client thread synchronously in the proxy until the scheduler dispatches the method request and the result is computed and stored in the future.

- *Synchronous timed wait.* Block for a bounded amount of time and fail if the active object's scheduler does not dispatch the method request within that time period. If the timeout is zero the client thread 'polls', that is, it returns to the caller without queueing the method request if its scheduler cannot dispatch it immediately.

- *Asynchronous.* Queue the method call and return control to the client immediately. If the method is a two-way invocation that produces a result then some form of *future* must be used to provide synchronized access to the value, or to the error status if the method call fails.

The future construct allows two-way asynchronous invocations [ARSK00] that return a value to the client. When a servant completes the method execution, it acquires a write lock on the future and updates the future with its result. Any client threads that are blocked waiting for the result are awakened and can access the result concurrently. A future can be garbage-collected after the writer and all readers threads no longer reference it. In languages like C++, which do not support garbage collection, futures can be reclaimed when they are no longer in use via idioms like Counted Pointer [POSA1].

➡ In our gateway example the get() method invoked on the MQ_Proxy ultimately results in the Get::call() method being dispatched by the MQ_Scheduler, as shown in implementation activity 2 (378). The MQ_Proxy::get() method returns a value, therefore a Message_Future is returned to the client that calls it:

```
class Message_Future {
public:
        // Binds <this> and <f> to the same <Msg._Future_Imp.>
        Message_Future (const Message_Future &f);

        // Initializes <Message_Future_Implementation> to
        // point to <message> m immediately.
        Message_Future (const Message &message);

        // Creates a <Msg._Future_Imp.>
        Message_Future ();

        // Binds <this> and <f> to the same
        // <Msg._Future_Imp.>, which is created if necessary.
        void operator= (const Message_Future &f);

        // Block upto <timeout> time waiting to obtain result
        // of an asynchronous method invocation. Throws
        // <System_Ex> exception if <timeout> expires.
        Message result (Time_Value *timeout = 0) const;
private:
        // <Message_Future_Implementation> uses the Counted
        // Pointer idiom.
        Message_Future_Implementation *future_impl_;
};
```

Not clear. Creation of a future happens before method was executed. How can result be there immediately?

The Message_Future is implemented using the Counted Pointer idiom [POSA1]. This idiom simplifies memory management for

Why the client can't be responsible for deleting the future?

dynamically allocated C++ objects by using a reference counted `Message_Future_Implementation` *body* that is accessed solely through the `Message_Future` *handle*.   ❏

In general a client may choose to evaluate the result value from a future immediately, in which case the client blocks until the scheduler executes the method request. Conversely, the evaluation of a return result from a method invocation on an active object can be deferred. In this case the client thread and the thread executing the method can both proceed asynchronously.

➥   In our gateway example a consumer handler running in a separate thread may choose to block until new messages arrive from suppliers:

```
MQ_Proxy message_queue;

// Obtain future and block thread until message arrives.
Message_Future future = message_queue.get ();
Message msg = future.result ();

// Transmit message to the consumer.
send (msg);
```

Conversely, if messages are not available immediately, a consumer handler can store the `Message_Future` return value from `message_queue` and perform other 'book-keeping' tasks, such as exchanging keep-alive messages to ensure its consumer is still active. When the consumer handler is finished with these tasks, it can block until a message arrives from suppliers:

```
// Obtain a future (does not block the client).
Message_Future future = message_queue.get ();

// Do something else here...

// Evaluate future and block if result is not available.
Message msg = future.result ();
send (msg);
```
                                                                              ❏

Example Resolved   In our gateway example, the gateway's supplier and consumer handlers are local proxies [POSA1] [GoF95] for remote suppliers and consumers, respectively. Supplier handlers receive messages from remote suppliers and inspect address fields in the messages. The address is used as a key into a routing table that identifies which remote consumer will receive the message.

The routing table maintains a map of consumer handlers, each of which is responsible for delivering messages to its remote consumer over a separate TCP connection. To handle flow control over various TCP connections, each consumer handler contains a message queue implemented using the Active Object pattern. This design decouples supplier and consumer handlers so that they can run concurrently and block independently.

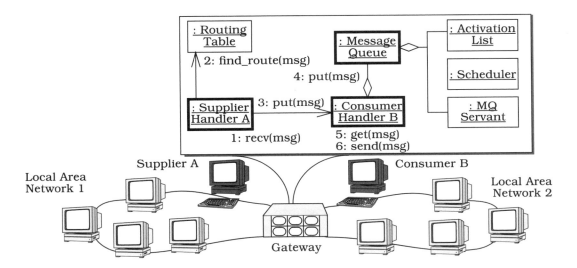

The Consumer_Handler class is defined as follows:

```
class Consumer_Handler {
public:
    // Constructor spawns the active object's thread.
    Consumer_Handler ();

    // Put the message into the queue.
    void put (const Message &msg) { msg_q_.put (msg); }
private:
    MQ_Proxy msg_q_; // Proxy to the Active Object.
    SOCK_Stream connection_; // Connection to consumer.

    // Entry point into the new thread.
    static void *svc_run (void *arg);
};
```

Supplier_Handlers running in their own threads can put messages
in the appropriate Consumer_Handler's message queue active object:

```
void Supplier_Handler::route_message (const Message &msg)
{
    // Locate the appropriate consumer based on the
    // address information in <Message>.
    Consumer_Handler *consumer_handler =
        routing_table_.find (msg.address ());

    // Put the Message into the Consumer Handler's queue.
    consumer_handler->put (msg);
}
```

To process the messages inserted into its queue, each Consumer_
Handler uses the Thread_Manager wrapper facade (47) to spawn a
separate thread of control in its constructor:

```
Consumer_Handler::Consumer_Handler () {
    // Spawn a separate thread to get messages from the
    // message queue and send them to the consumer.
    Thread_Manager::instance ()->spawn (&svc_run, this);
    // ...
}
```

This new thread executes the svc_run() method entry point, which
gets the messages placed into the queue by supplier handler threads,
and sends them to the consumer over the TCP connection:

```
void *Consumer_Handler::svc_run (void *args) {
    Consumer_Handler *this_obj =
        static_cast<Consumer_Handler *> (args);
    for (;;) {
        // Block thread until a <Message> is available.
        Message msg = this_obj->msg_q_.get ().result ();
        // Transmit <Message> to the consumer over the
        // TCP connection.
        this_obj->connection_.send (msg, msg.length ());
    }
}
```

Every Consumer_Handler object uses the message queue that is implemented as an active object and runs in its own thread. Therefore
its send() operation can block without affecting the quality of service
of other Consumer_Handler objects.

Variants   *Multiple Roles.* If an active object implements multiple roles, each
used by particular types of client, a separate proxy can be introduced
for each role. By using the Extension Interface pattern (141), clients
can obtain the proxies they need. This design helps separate
concerns because a client only sees the particular methods of an
active object it needs for its own operation, which further simplifies
an active object's evolution. For example, new services can be added
to the active object by providing new extension interface proxies
without changing existing ones. Clients that do not need access to the
new services are unaffected by the extension and need not even be recompiled.

Integrated Scheduler. To reduce the number of components needed to
implement the Active Object pattern, the roles of the proxy and
servant can be integrated into its scheduler component. Likewise, the
transformation of a method call on a proxy into a method request can
also be integrated into the scheduler. However, servants still execute
in a different thread than proxies.

➥   Here is an implementation of the message queue using an
integrated scheduler:

```cpp
class MQ_Scheduler {
public:
    MQ_Scheduler (size_t size)
        : servant_ (size), act_list_ (size) { }
    // ... other constructors/destructors, etc.

    void put (const Message m) {
        Method_Request *mr = new Put (&servant_, m);
        act_list_.insert (mr);
    }

    Message_Future get () {
        Message_Future result;
        Method_Request *mr = new Get (&servant_, result);
        act_list_.insert (mr);
        return result;
    }

    // Other methods ...
private:
    MQ_Servant servant_;
    Activation_List act_list_;
    // ...
};
```

By centralizing the point at which method requests are generated, the Active Object pattern implementation can be simplified because it has fewer components. The drawback, of course, is that a scheduler must know the type of the servant and proxy, which makes it hard to reuse the same scheduler for different types of active objects.

Message Passing. A further refinement of the integrated scheduler variant is to remove the proxy and servant altogether and use direct *message passing* between the client thread and the active object's scheduler thread.

➥   For example, consider the following scheduler implementation:

```
class Scheduler {
public:
    Scheduler (size_t size): act_list_ (size) { }
    // ... other constructors/destructors, etc.

    void insert (Message_Request *message_request) {
        act_list_.insert (message_request);
    }

    virtual void dispatch () {
        for (;;) {
            Message_Request *mr;
            // Block waiting for next request to arrive.
            act_list_.remove (mr);
            // Process the message request <mr>...
        }
    }
    // ...
private:
    Activation_List act_list_;
    // ...
};
```

In this variant, there is no proxy, so clients create an appropriate type of message request directly and call insert() themselves, which enqueues the request into the activation list. Likewise, there is no servant, so the dispatch() method running in a scheduler's thread simply dequeues the next message request and processes the request according to its type.   ❏

In general it is easier to develop a message-passing mechanism than it is to develop an active object because there are fewer components. Message passing can be more tedious and error-prone, however, because application developers, not active object developers, must program the proxy and servant logic. As a result, message passing implementations are less type-safe than active object implementations because their interfaces are implicit rather than explicit. In addition, it is harder for application developers to distribute clients and servers via message passing because there is no proxy to encapsulate the marshaling and demarshaling of data.

Polymorphic Futures [LK95]. A polymorphic future allows parameterization of the eventual result type represented by the future and enforces the necessary synchronization. In particular, a polymorphic future describes a typed future that client threads can use to retrieve a method request's result. Whether a client blocks on a future depends on whether or not a result has been computed.

➡ The following class is a polymorphic future template for C++:

```
template <class TYPE>
class Future {
    // This class can be used to return results from
    // two-way asynchronous method invocations.
public:
    // Constructor and copy constructor that binds <this>
    // and <r> to the same <Future> representation.
    Future ();
    Future (const Future<TYPE> &r);

    // Destructor.
    ~Future ();

    // Assignment operator that binds <this> and <r> to
    // the same <Future> representation.
    void operator = (const Future<TYPE> &r);

    // Cancel a <Future> and reinitialize it.
    void cancel ();

    // Block upto <timeout> time waiting to obtain result
    // of an asynchronous method invocation. Throws
    // <System_Ex> exception if <timeout> expires.
    TYPE result (Time_Value *timeout = 0) const;
private:
    // ...
};
```

A client can use a polymorphic future as follows:

```
try {
        // Obtain a future (does not block the client).
        Future<Message> future = message_queue.get ();
        // Do something else here...

        // Evaluate future and block for up to 1 second
        // waiting for the result to become available.
        Time_Value timeout (1);
        Message msg = future.result (&timeout);

        // Do something with the result ...
} catch (System_Ex &ex) {
        if (ex.status () == ETIMEDOUT) /* handle timeout */
}
```

This is the main reason for using them. Identical alternative is any asynchronous invocation May be not because this way there is only one thread for execution

❑

Timed method invocations. The activation list illustrated in implementation activity 3 (379) defines a mechanism that can bound the amount of time a scheduler waits to insert or remove a method request. Although the examples we showed earlier in the pattern do not use this feature, many applications can benefit from timed method invocations. To implement this feature we can simply export the timeout mechanism via schedulers and proxies.

➥   In our gateway example, the MQ_Proxy can be modified so that its methods allow clients to bound the amount of time they are willing to wait to execute:

```
class MQ_Proxy {
public:
        // Schedule <put> to execute, but do not block longer
        // than <timeout> time. Throws <System_Ex>
        // exception if <timeout> expires.
        void put (const Message &msg,
                  Time_Value *timeout = 0);

        // Return a <Message_Future> as the "future" result of
        // an asynchronous <get> method on the active object,
        // but do not block longer than <timeout> amount of
        // time. Throws the <System_Ex> exception if
        // <timeout> expires.
        Message_Future get (Time_Value *timeout = 0);
};
```

If timeout is 0 both get() and put() will block indefinitely until Message is either removed from or inserted into the scheduler's activation list, respectively. If timeout expires, the System_Ex exception defined in the Wrapper Facade pattern (47) is thrown with a `status()` value of `ETIMEDOUT` and the client must catch it.

To complete our support for timed method invocations, we also must add timeout support to the `MQ_Scheduler`:

[handwritten margin note: It can time out if the queue stays full for too long.]

```
class MQ_Scheduler {
public:
    // Insert a method request into the <Activation_List>
    // This method runs in the thread of its client, i.e.
    // in the proxy's thread, but does not block longer
    // than <timeout> amount of time. Throws the
    // <System_Ex> exception if the <timeout> expires.
    void insert (Method_Request *method_request,
                    Time_Value *timeout) {
        act_list_.insert (method_request, timeout);
    }
}
```
❏

Distributed Active Object. In this variant a distribution boundary exists between a proxy and a scheduler, rather than just a threading boundary. This pattern variant introduces two new participants:

- A client-side proxy plays the role of a *stub*, which marshals method parameters into a method request that is sent across a network and executed by a servant in a separate server address space.

- A server-side *skeleton*, which demarshals method request parameters before they are passed to a server's servant method.

The Distributed Active Object pattern variant is therefore similar to the Broker pattern [POSA1]. The primary difference is that a Broker usually coordinates the processing of many objects, whereas a distributed active object just handles a single object.

[handwritten margin note: Similar to our report engine.]

Thread Pool Active Object. This generalization of the Active Object pattern supports multiple servant threads per active object to increase throughput and responsiveness. When not processing requests, each servant thread in a thread pool active object blocks on a single activation list. The active object scheduler assigns a new method request to an available servant thread in the pool as soon as one is ready to be executed.

[handwritten margin note: So not exactly we have separate object instances → Broker?]

A single servant implementation is shared by all the servant threads in the pool. This design cannot therefore be used if the servant methods do not protect their internal state via some type of synchronization mechanism, such as a mutex.

Additional variants of active objects can be found in [Lea99a], Chapter 5: *Concurrency Control* and Chapter 6: *Services in Threads*.

Known Uses   **ACE Framework** [Sch97]. Reusable implementations of the method request, activation list, and future components in the Active Object pattern are provided in the ACE framework. The corresponding classes in ACE are called `ACE_Method_Request`, `ACE_Activation_Queue`, and `ACE_Future`. These components have been used to implement many production concurrent and networked systems [Sch96].

Siemens MedCom. The Active Object pattern is used in the Siemens MedCom framework, which provides a black-box component-based framework for electronic medical imaging systems. MedCom employs the Active Object pattern in conjunction with the Command Processor pattern [POSA1] to simplify client windowing applications that access patient information on various medical servers [JWS98].

Siemens FlexRouting - Automatic Call Distribution [Flex98]. This call center management system uses the Thread Pool variant of the Active Object pattern. Services that a call center offers are implemented as applications of their own. For example, there may be a hot-line application, an ordering application, and a product information application, depending on the types of service offered. These applications support operator personnel that serve various customer requests. Each instance of these applications is a separate servant component. A 'FlexRouter' component, which corresponds to the scheduler, dispatches incoming customer requests automatically to operator applications that can service these requests.

Java JDK 1.3 introduced a mechanism for executing *timer-based tasks* concurrently in the classes `java.util.Timer` and `java.util.TimerTask`. Whenever the scheduled execution time of a task occurs it is executed. Specifically, `Timer` offers different scheduling functions to clients that allow them to specify when and how often a task should be executed. One-shot tasks are straightforward and recurring tasks can be scheduled at periodic intervals. The scheduling calls are executed in the client's thread, while the tasks themselves are executed in a thread owned by the `Timer` object. A `Timer` internal task queue is protected by locks because the two threads outlined above operate on it concurrently.

The task queue is implemented as a priority queue so that the next `TimerTask` to expire can be identified efficiently. The timer thread simply waits until this expiration. There are no explicit guard methods and predicates because determining when a task is 'ready for execution' simply depends on the arrival of the scheduled time.

Tasks are implemented as subclasses of `TimerTask` that override its `run()` hook method. The `TimerTask` subclasses unify the concepts behind method requests and servants by offering just one class and one interface method via `TimerTask.run()`.

The scheme described above simplifies the Active Object machinery for the purpose of timed execution. There is no proxy and clients call the scheduler—the `Timer` object—directly. Clients do not invoke an ordinary method and therefore the concurrency is not transparent. Moreover, there are no return value or future objects linked to the `run()` method. An application can employ several active objects by constructing several `Timer` objects, each with its own thread and task queue.

Chef in a restaurant. A real-life example of the Active Object pattern is found in restaurants. Waiters and waitresses drop off customer food requests with the chef and continue to service requests from other customers asynchronously while the food is being prepared. The chef keeps track of the customer food requests via some type of worklist. However, the chef may cook the food requests in a different order than they arrived to use available resources, such as stove tops, pots, or pans, most efficiently. When the food is cooked, the chef places the results on top of a counter along with the original request so the waiters and waitresses can rendezvous to pick up the food and serve their customers.

[handwritten margin note: Compared to just asynch. execut. This is a 2nd main difference (other than tying up threads)]

Consequences   The Active Object pattern provides the following **benefits**:

Enhances application concurrency and simplifies synchronization complexity. Concurrency is enhanced by allowing client threads and asynchronous method executions to run simultaneously. Synchronization complexity is simplified by using a scheduler that evaluates synchronization constraints to guarantee serialized access to servants, in accordance with their state.

Transparently leverages available parallelism. If the hardware and software platforms support multiple CPUs efficiently, this pattern can allow multiple active objects to execute in parallel, subject only to their synchronization constraints.

Method execution order can differ from method invocation order. Methods invoked asynchronously are executed according to the synchronization constraints defined by their guards and by scheduling policies. Thus, the order of method execution can differ from the order of method invocation order. This decoupling can help improve application performance and flexibility.

However, the Active Object pattern encounters several **liabilities**:

Performance overhead. Depending on how an active object's scheduler is implemented—for example in user-space versus kernel-space [SchSu95]—context switching, synchronization, and data movement overhead may occur when scheduling and executing active object method invocations. In general the Active Object pattern is most applicable for relatively coarse-grained objects. In contrast, if the objects are fine-grained, the performance overhead of active objects can be excessive, compared with related concurrency patterns, such as Monitor Object (399).

Complicated debugging. It is hard to debug programs that use the Active Object pattern due to the concurrency and non-determinism of the various active object schedulers and the underlying operating system thread scheduler. In particular, method request guards determine the order of execution. However, the behavior of these guards may be hard to understand and debug. Improperly defined guards can cause starvation, which is a condition where certain method requests never execute. In addition, program debuggers may not support multi-threaded applications adequately.

See Also   The Monitor Object pattern (399) ensures that only one method at a time executes within a thread-safe passive object, regardless of the number of threads that invoke the object's methods concurrently. In general, monitor objects are more efficient than active objects because they incur less context switching and data movement overhead. However, it is harder to add a distribution boundary between client and server threads using the Monitor Object pattern.

It is instructive to compare the Active Object pattern solution in the *Example Resolved* section with the solution presented in the Monitor Object pattern. Both solutions have similar overall application

[handwritten note in left margin: That's the problem we have.]

architectures. In particular, the `Supplier_Handler` and `Consumer_Handler` implementations are almost identical.

The primary difference is that the `Message_Queue` in the Active Object pattern supports sophisticated method request queueing and scheduling strategies. Similarly, because active objects execute in different threads than their clients, there are situations where active objects can improve overall application concurrency by executing multiple operations asynchronously. When these operations complete, clients can obtain their results via futures [Hal85] [LS88].

On the other hand, the `Message_Queue` itself is easier to program and often more efficient when implemented using the Monitor Object pattern than the Active Object pattern.

The Reactor pattern (179) is responsible for demultiplexing and dispatching multiple event handlers that are triggered when it is possible to initiate an operation without blocking. This pattern is often used in lieu of the Active Object pattern to schedule callback operations to passive objects. Active Object also can be used in conjunction with the Reactor pattern to form the Half-Sync/Half-Async pattern (423).

The Half-Sync/Half-Async pattern (423) decouples synchronous I/O from asynchronous I/O in a system to simplify concurrent programming effort without degrading execution efficiency. Variants of this pattern use the Active Object pattern to implement its synchronous task layer, the Reactor pattern (179) to implement the asynchronous task layer, and a Producer-Consumer pattern [Lea99a], such as a variant of the Pipes and Filters pattern [POSA1] or the Monitor Object pattern (399), to implement the queueing layer.

The Command Processor pattern [POSA1] separates issuing requests from their execution. A command processor, which corresponds to the Active Object pattern's scheduler, maintains pending service requests that are implemented as commands [GoF95]. Commands are executed on suppliers, which correspond to servants. The Command Processor pattern does not focus on concurrency, however. In fact, clients, the command processor, and suppliers often reside in the same thread of control. Likewise, there are no proxies that represent the servants to clients. Clients create commands and pass them directly to the command processor.

The Broker pattern [POSA1] defines many of the same components as the Active Object pattern. In particular, clients access brokers via proxies and servers implement remote objects via servants. One difference between Broker and Active Object is that there is a distribution boundary between proxies and servants in the Broker pattern, as opposed to a threading boundary between proxies and servants in the Active Object pattern. Another difference is that active objects typically have just one servant, whereas a broker can have many servants.

Credits   The genesis for documenting Active Object as a pattern originated with Greg Lavender [PLoPD2]. Ward Cunningham helped shape this version of the Active Object pattern. Bob Laferriere and Rainer Blome provided useful suggestions that improved the clarity of the pattern's *Implementation* section. Thanks to Doug Lea for providing many additional insights in [Lea99a].

Monitor Object

The *Monitor Object* design pattern synchronizes concurrent method execution to ensure that only one method at a time runs within an object. It also allows an object's methods to cooperatively schedule their execution sequences.

Also Known As Thread-safe Passive Object

Example Let us reconsider the design of the communication gateway described in the Active Object pattern (369).[4]

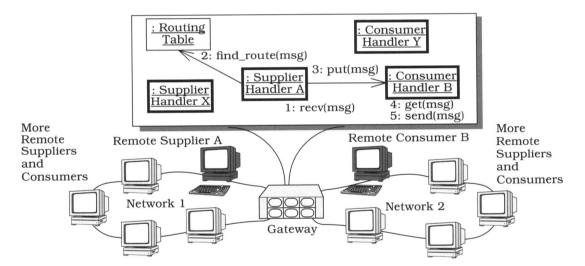

The gateway process is a mediator [GoF95] that contains multiple supplier and consumer handler objects. These objects run in separate threads and route messages from one or more remote suppliers to one or more remote consumers. When a supplier handler thread receives a message from a remote supplier, it uses an address field in the message to determine the corresponding consumer handler. The handler's thread then delivers the message to its remote consumer.

---

4. For an in-depth discussion of the gateway and its associated components, we recommend reading the Active Object pattern (369) before reading this pattern.

When suppliers and consumers reside on separate hosts, the gateway uses a connection-oriented protocol, such as TCP [Ste93], to provide reliable message delivery and end-to-end flow control. Flow control is a protocol mechanism that blocks senders when they produce messages more rapidly than receivers can process them. The entire gateway should not block while waiting for flow control to abate on outgoing TCP connections, however. In particular, incoming TCP connections should continue to be processed and messages should continue to be sent over any non-flow-controlled TCP connections.

To minimize blocking, each consumer handler can contain a thread-safe message queue. Each queue buffers new routing messages it receives from its supplier handler threads. This design decouples supplier handler threads in the gateway process from consumer handler threads, so that all threads can run concurrently and block independently when flow control occurs on various TCP connections.

One way to implement a thread-safe message queue is to apply the Active Object pattern (369) to decouple the thread used to invoke a method from the thread used to execute the method. Active Object may be inappropriate, however, if the entire infrastructure introduced by this pattern is unnecessary. For example, a message queue's enqueue and dequeue methods may not require sophisticated scheduling strategies. In this case, implementing the Active Object pattern's method request, scheduler and activation list participants incurs unnecessary performance overhead, and programming effort.

Instead, the implementation of the thread-safe message queue must be efficient to avoid degrading performance unnecessarily. To avoid tight coupling of supplier and consumer handler implementations, the mechanism should also be transparent to implementors of supplier handlers. Varying either implementation independently would otherwise become prohibitively complex.

Context   Multiple threads of control accessing the same object concurrently.

Problem   Many applications contain objects whose methods are invoked concurrently by multiple client threads. These methods often modify the state of their objects. For such concurrent applications to execute correctly, therefore, it is necessary to synchronize and schedule access to the objects.

In the presence of this problem four *forces* must be addressed:

- To separate concerns and protect object state from uncontrolled changes, object-oriented programmers are accustomed to accessing objects only through their interface methods. It is relatively straightforward to extend this object-oriented programming model to protect an object's data from uncontrolled concurrent changes, known as *race conditions*. An object's interface methods should therefore define its synchronization boundaries, and only one method at a time should be active within the same object.

- Concurrent applications are harder to program if clients must explicitly acquire and release low-level synchronization mechanisms, such as semaphores, mutexes, or condition variables [IEEE96]. Objects should therefore be responsible for ensuring that any of their methods that require synchronization are serialized transparently, without requiring explicit client intervention.

- If an object's methods must block during their execution, they should be able to relinquish their thread of control voluntarily, so that methods called from other client threads can access the object. This property helps prevent deadlock and makes it possible to take advantage of concurrency mechanisms available on hardware and software platforms.

- When a method relinquishes its thread of control voluntarily, it must leave its object in a stable state, that is, object-specific invariants must hold. Similarly, a method must resume its execution within an object only when the object is in a stable state.

Solution Synchronize the access to an object's methods so that only one method can execute at any one time.

In detail: for each object accessed concurrently by multiple client threads, define it as a *monitor object*. Clients can access the functions defined by a monitor object only through its *synchronized methods*. To prevent race conditions on its internal state, only one synchronized method at a time can run within a monitor object. To serialize concurrent access to an object's state, each monitor object contains a *monitor lock*. Synchronized methods can determine the circumstances under which they suspend and resume their execution, based on one or more *monitor conditions* associated with a monitor object.

Structure   There are four participants in the Monitor Object pattern:

A *monitor object* exports one or more methods. To protect the internal state of the monitor object from uncontrolled changes and race conditions, all clients must access the monitor object only through these methods. Each method executes in the thread of the client that invokes it, because a monitor object does not have its own thread of control.[5]

Synchronized methods implement the thread-safe functions exported by a monitor object. To prevent race conditions, only one synchronized method can execute within a monitor object at any one time. This rule applies regardless of the number of threads that invoke the object's synchronized methods concurrently, or the number of synchronized methods in the object's class.

➥   A consumer handler's message queue in the gateway application can be implemented as a monitor object by converting its put() and get() operations into synchronized methods. This design ensures that routing messages can be inserted and removed concurrently by multiple threads without corrupting the queue's internal state.   ❏

Class Monitor Object	*Collaborator* • Synchronized Methods	*Class* Synchronized Method	*Collaborator* • Monitor Lock • Monitor Condition
Responsibility • Defines the object that is accessed concurrently		*Responsibility* • Implements a publicly accessible method of a Monitor Object	

Each monitor object contains its own *monitor lock*. Synchronized methods use this lock to serialize method invocations on a per-object basis. Each synchronized method must acquire and release an object's monitor lock when entering or exiting the object. This protocol ensures the monitor lock is held whenever a synchronized method performs operations that access or modify the state of its object.

---

5. An active object, in contrast, *does* have its own thread of control.

Monitor condition. Multiple synchronized methods running in separate threads can schedule their execution sequences cooperatively by waiting for and notifying each other via monitor conditions associated with their monitor object. Synchronized methods use their monitor lock in conjunction with their monitor condition(s) to determine the circumstances under which they should suspend or resume their processing.

Class Monitor Lock	*Collaborator*
Responsibility • Ensures that only one synchronized method in a Monitor Object can execute at any given point in time	

Class Monitor Condition	*Collaborator* • Monitor Lock
Responsibility • Allows Synchronized Methods to determine the circumstances under which they should suspend or resume their processing	

➥   In the gateway application a POSIX mutex [IEEE96] can be used to implement the message queue's monitor lock. A pair of POSIX condition variables can be used to implement the message queue's *not-empty* and *not-full* monitor conditions:

• When a consumer handler thread attempts to dequeue a routing message from an empty message queue, the queue's `get()` method must atomically release the monitor lock and suspend itself on the *not-empty* monitor condition. It remains suspended until the queue is no longer empty, which happens when a supplier handler thread inserts a message into the queue.

• When a supplier handler thread attempts to enqueue a message into a full queue, the queue's `put()` method must atomically release the monitor lock and suspend itself on the *not-full* monitor condition. It remains suspended until the queue is no longer full, which happens when a consumer handler removes a message from the message queue.

Note that the *not-empty* and *not-full* monitor conditions both share the same monitor lock.   ❏

The structure of the Monitor Object pattern is illustrated in the following class diagram:

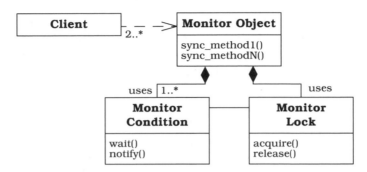

Dynamics The collaborations between participants in the Monitor Object pattern divide into four phases:

- *Synchronized method invocation and serialization.* When client thread T_1 invokes a synchronized method on a monitor object, the method must first acquire the object's monitor lock. A monitor lock cannot be acquired as long as another synchronized method in thread T_2 is executing within the monitor object. In this case, client thread T_1 will block until the synchronized method acquires the lock. Once the synchronized method called by T_1 has finished executing, the monitor lock is released so that other synchronized methods called by other threads can access the monitor object.

- *Synchronized method thread suspension.* If a synchronized method must block or cannot otherwise make immediate progress, it can *wait* on one of its monitor conditions. This causes it to 'leave' the monitor object temporarily [Hoare74]. The monitor object implementation is responsible for ensuring that it is in a stable state before switching to another thread. When a synchronized method leaves the monitor object, the client's thread is suspended on that monitor condition and the monitor lock is released atomically by the operating system's thread scheduler. Another synchronized method in another thread can now execute within the monitor object.

- *Monitor condition notification.* A synchronized method can *notify* a monitor condition. This operation awakens the thread of a synchronized method that had suspended itself on the monitor condition earlier. A synchronized method can also notify *all* other synchronized methods that suspended their threads earlier on a monitor condition. In this case all the threads are awakened and one of them at a time can acquire the monitor lock and run within the monitor object.

- *Synchronized method thread resumption.* Once a suspended synchronized method thread is notified, its execution can resume at the point where it waited on the monitor condition. The operating system thread scheduler performs this resumption implicitly. The monitor lock is reacquired atomically before the notified thread 're-enters' the monitor object and resumes its execution in the synchronized method.

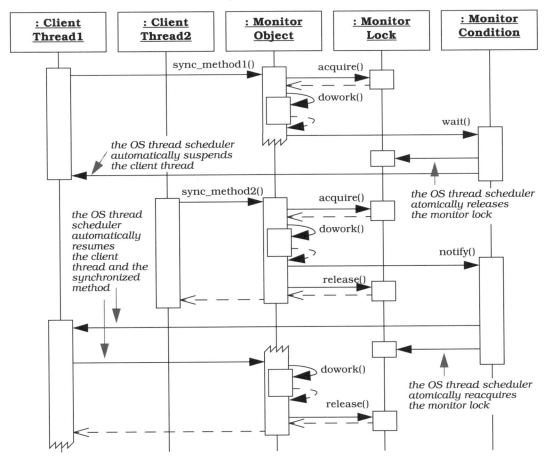

Implementation   Four activities illustrate how to implement the Monitor Object pattern.

1 *Define the monitor object's interface methods*. The interface of a monitor object exports a set of methods to clients. Interface methods are often *synchronized*, that is, only one of them at a time can be executed by a thread within a particular monitor object.

➡   In our gateway example, each consumer handler contains a message queue and a TCP connection. The message queue can be implemented as a monitor object that buffers messages it receives from supplier handler threads. This buffering helps prevent the entire gateway process from blocking whenever consumer handler threads encounter flow control on TCP connections to their remote consumers. The following C++ class defines the interface for our message queue monitor object:

```
class Message_Queue {
public:
    enum { MAX_MESSAGES = /* ... */; };

    // The constructor defines the maximum number
    // of messages in the queue. This determines
    // when the queue is 'full.'
    Message_Queue (size_t max_messages = MAX_MESSAGES);

    // Put the <Message> at the tail of the queue.
    // If the queue is full, block until the queue
    // is not full.
    /* synchronized */ void put (const Message &msg);

    // Get the <Message> from the head of the queue
    // and remove it. If the queue is empty,
    // block until the queue is not empty.
    /* synchronized */ Message get ();

    // True if the queue is empty, else false.
    /* synchronized */ bool empty () const;

    // True if the queue is full, else false.
    /* synchronized */ bool full () const;
private:
    // ... described later ...
};
```

The `Message_Queue` monitor object interface exports four synchronized methods. The `empty()` and `full()` methods are *predicates* that clients can use to distinguish three internal queue states: empty, full, and neither empty nor full. The put() and get() methods enqueue and dequeue messages into and from the queue, respectively, and will block if the queue is full or empty. ❏

2 *Define the monitor object's implementation methods.* A monitor object often contains internal implementation methods that synchronized interface methods use to perform the object's functionality. This design helps decouple the core monitor object functionality from its synchronization and scheduling logic. It also helps avoid intra-object deadlock and unnecessary locking overhead.

Two conventions, based on the Thread-Safe Interface pattern (345), can be used to structure the separation of concerns between interface and implementation methods in a monitor object:

- Interface methods only acquire and release monitor locks and wait upon or notify certain monitor conditions. They otherwise forward control to implementation methods that perform the monitor object's functionality.

- Implementation methods only perform work when called by interface methods. They do not acquire and release the monitor lock, nor do they wait upon or notify monitor conditions explicitly.

Similarly, in accordance with the Thread-Safe Interface pattern, implementation methods should not call any synchronized methods defined in the class interface. This restriction helps to avoid intra-object method deadlock or unnecessary synchronization overhead.

➡ In our gateway, the Message_Queue class defines four implementation methods: put_i(), get_i(), empty_i(), and full_ i():

```
class Message_Queue {
public:
    // ... See above ...
private:
    // Put the <Message> at the tail of the queue, and
    // get the <Message> at its head, respectively.
    void put_i (const Message &msg);
    Message get_i ();

    // True if the queue is empty, else false.
    bool empty_i () const;

    // True if the queue is full, else false.
    bool full_i () const;
};                                                    ❏
```

Implementation methods are often non-synchronized. They must be careful when invoking blocking calls, because the interface method that called the implementation method may have acquired the monitor lock. A blocking thread that owned a lock could therefore delay overall program progress indefinitely.

3   *Define the monitor object's internal state and synchronization mechanisms.* A monitor object contains data members that define its internal state. This state must be protected from corruption by race conditions resulting from unsynchronized concurrent access. A monitor object therefore contains a monitor lock that serializes the execution of its synchronized methods, as well as one or more monitor conditions used to schedule the execution of synchronized method within a monitor object. Typically there is a separate monitor condition for each of the following situations:

- Cases in which synchronized methods must suspend their processing to wait for the occurrence of some event of state change; or

- Cases in which synchronized methods must resume other threads whose synchronized methods have suspended themselves on the monitor condition.

A monitor object method implementation is responsible for ensuring that it is in a stable state before releasing its lock. Stable states can be described by invariants, such as the need for all elements in a message queue to be linked together via valid pointers. The invariant must hold whenever a monitor object method waits on the corresponding condition variable.

Similarly, when the monitor object is notified and the operating system thread scheduler decides to resume its thread, the monitor object method implementation is responsible for ensuring that the invariant is indeed satisfied before proceeding. This check is necessary because other threads may have changed the state of the object between the notification and the resumption. A a result, the monitor object must ensure that the invariant is satisfied before allowing a synchronized method to resume its execution.

A monitor lock can be implemented using a *mutex*. A mutex makes collaborating threads wait while the thread holding the mutex executes code in a critical section. Monitor conditions can be implemented using *condition variables* [IEEE96]. A condition variable can be used by a thread to make *itself* wait until a particular event occurs or an arbitrarily complex condition expression attains a particular stable state. Condition expressions typically access objects or state variables shared between threads. They can be used to implement the Guarded Suspension pattern [Lea99a].

➡ In our gateway example, the Message_Queue defines its internal state, as illustrated below:

```
class Message_Queue {
    // ... See above ....
private:
    // ... See above ...

    // Internal Queue representation omitted, could be a
    // circular array or a linked list, etc.. ...

    // Current number of <Message>s in the queue.
    size_t message_count_;

    // The maximum number <Message>s that can be
    // in a queue before it's considered `full.'
    size_t max_messages_;

    // Mutex wrapper facade that protects the queue's
    // internal state from race conditions during
    // concurrent access.
    mutable Thread_Mutex monitor_lock_;

    // Condition variable wrapper facade used in
    // conjunction with <monitor_lock_> to make
    // synchronized method threads wait until the queue
    // is no longer empty.
    Thread_Condition not_empty_;

    // Condition variable wrapper facade used in
    // conjunction with <monitor_lock_> to make
    // synchronized method threads wait until the queue
    // is no longer full.
    Thread_Condition not_full_;
};
```

A Message_Queue monitor object defines three types of internal state:

• *Queue representation data members*. These data members define the internal queue representation. This representation stores the contents of the queue in a circular array or linked list, together with book-keeping information needed to determine whether the queue is empty, full, or neither. The internal queue representation is manipulated only by the put_i(), get_i(), empty_i(), and full_i() implementation methods.

- *Monitor lock data member.* The monitor_lock_ is used by a Message_Queue's synchronized methods to serialize their access to the state of the queue's internal representation. A monitor object's lock must be held whenever its state is being changed to ensure that its invariants are satisfied. This monitor lock is implemented using the platform-independent Thread_Mutex class defined in the Wrapper Facade pattern (47).

- *Monitor condition data members.* The monitor conditions is_full_ and is_empty_ are used by the put() and get() synchronized methods to suspend and resume themselves when a Message_ Queue leaves its full and empty boundary conditions, respectively. These monitor conditions are implemented using the platform-independent Thread_Condition class defined in the Wrapper Facade pattern (47).❏

4 *Implement all the monitor object's methods and data members.* The following two sub-activities can be used to implement all the monitor object methods and internal state defined above.

4.1 *Initialize the data members.* This sub-activity initializes object-specific data members, as well as the monitor lock and any monitor conditions.

➥ The constructor of Message_Queue creates an empty queue and initializes the monitor conditions not_empty_ and not_full_:

```
Message_Queue::Message_Queue (size_t max_messages)
    :    not_full_ (monitor_lock_),
         not_empty_ (monitor_lock_),
         max_messages_ (max_messages),
         message_count_ (0) { /* ... */ }
```

In this example, both monitor conditions share the same monitor_ lock_. This design ensures that Message_Queue state, such as the message_count_, is serialized properly to prevent race conditions from violating invariants when multiple threads try to put() and get() messages on a queue simultaneously. ❏

4.2   *Apply the Thread-Safe Interface pattern.* In this sub-activity, the
      interface and implementation methods are implemented according to
      the Thread-Safe Interface pattern (345).

➡   In our `Message_Queue` implementation two pairs of interface
and implementation methods check if a queue is *empty*, which means
it contains no messages, or *full*, which means it contains
`max_messages_`. We show the interface methods first:

```
bool Message_Queue::empty () const {
    Guard<Thread_Mutex> guard (monitor_lock_);
    return empty_i ();
}

bool Message_Queue::full () const {
    Guard<Thread_Mutex> guard (monitor_lock_);
    return full_i ();
}
```

These methods illustrate a simple example of the Thread-Safe
Interface pattern (345). They use the Scoped Locking idiom (325) to
acquire and release the monitor lock, then forward immediately to
their corresponding implementation methods:

```
bool Message_Queue::empty_i () const {
    return message_count_ == 0;
}

bool Message_Queue::full_i () const {
    return message_count_ == max_messages_;
}
```

In accordance with the Thread-Safe Interface pattern, these
implementation methods assume the `monitor_lock_` is held, so they
just check for the boundary conditions in the queue.

The `put()` method inserts a new `Message`, which is a class defined in
the Active Object pattern (369), at the tail of a queue. It is a
synchronized method that illustrates a more sophisticated use of the
Thread-Safe Interface pattern (345):

```
void Message_Queue::put (const Message &msg) {
    // Use the Scoped Locking idiom to
    // acquire/release the <monitor_lock_> upon
    // entry/exit to the synchronized method.
    Guard<Thread_Mutex> guard (monitor_lock_);
```

```
    // Wait while the queue is full.
    while (full_i ()) {
        // Release <monitor_lock_> and suspend the
        // calling thread waiting for space in the queue.
        // The <monitor_lock_> is reacquired
        // automatically when <wait> returns.
        not_full_.wait ();
    }

    // Enqueue the <Message> at the tail.
    put_i (msg);

    // Notify any thread waiting in <get> that
    // the queue has at least one <Message>.
    not_empty_.notify ();

} // Destructor of <guard> releases <monitor_lock_>.
```

Note how this public synchronized put() method only performs the synchronization and scheduling logic needed to serialize access to the monitor object and wait while the queue is full. Once there is room in the queue, put() forwards to the put_i() implementation method. This inserts the message into the queue and updates its book-keeping information. Moreover, the put_i() is not synchronized because the put() method never calls it without first acquiring the monitor_lock_. Likewise, the put_i() method need not check to see if the queue is full because it is not called as long as full_i() returns true.

The get() method removes the message at the front of the queue and returns it to the caller:

```
Message Message_Queue::get () {
    // Use the Scoped Locking idiom to
    // acquire/release the <monitor_lock_> upon
    // entry/exit to the synchronized method.
    Guard<Thread_Mutex> guard (monitor_lock_);

    // Wait while the queue is empty.
    while (empty_i ()) {
        // Release <monitor_lock_> and suspend the
        // calling thread waiting for a new <Message> to
        // be put into the queue. The <monitor_lock_> is
        // reacquired automatically when <wait> returns.
        not_empty_.wait ();
    }

    // Dequeue the first <Message> in the queue
    // and update the <message_count_>.
    Message m = get_i ();
```

```
                    // Notify any thread waiting in <put> that the
                    // queue has room for at least one <Message>.
                    not_full_.notify ();
                    return m;

                    // Destructor of <guard> releases <monitor_lock_>.
              }
```

As before, note how the synchronized get() interface method performs the synchronization and scheduling logic, while forwarding the
dequeueing functionality to the get_i() implementation method. ❏

Internally, our gateway contains instances of two classes, Supplier_
Handler and Consumer_Handler. These act as local proxies [GoF95]
[POSA1] for remote suppliers and consumers, respectively. Each
Consumer_Handler contains a thread-safe Message_Queue object
implemented using the Monitor Object pattern. This design decouples
supplier handler and consumer handler threads so that they run concurrently and block independently. Moreover, by embedding and
automating synchronization inside message queue monitor objects,
we can protect their internal state from corruption, maintain invariants, and shield clients from low-level synchronization concerns.

The Consumer_Handler is defined below:

```
              class Consumer_Handler {
              public:
                    // Constructor spawns a thread and calls <svc_run>.
                    Consumer_Handler ();

                    // Put <Message> into the queue monitor object,
                    // blocking until there's room in the queue.
                    void put (const Message &msg) {
                        message_queue_.put (msg);
                    }
              private:
                    // Message queue implemented as a monitor object.
                    Message_Queue message_queue_;

                    // Connection to the remote consumer.
                    SOCK_Stream connection_;

                    // Entry point to a distinct consumer handler thread.
                    static void *svc_run (void *arg);
              };
```

Each Supplier_Handler runs in its own thread, receives messages
from its remote supplier and routes the messages to the designated

remote consumers. Routing is performed by inspecting an address field in each message, which is used as a key into a routing table that maps keys to Consumer_Handlers.

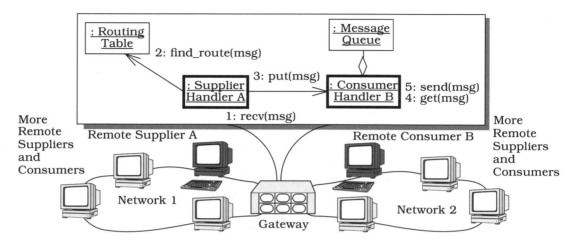

Each Consumer_Handler is responsible for receiving messages from suppliers via its put() method and storing each message in its Message_Queue monitor object:

```
void Supplier_Handler::route_message (const Message &msg)
{
    // Locate the appropriate <Consumer_Handler> based
    // on address information in the <Message>.
    Consumer_Handler *consumer_handler =
        routing_table_.find (msg.address ());

    // Put <Message> into the <Consumer Handler>, which
    // stores it in its <Message Queue> monitor object.
    consumer_handler->put (msg);
}
```

To process the messages placed into its message queue by Supplier_ Handlers, each Consumer_Handler spawns a separate thread of control in its constructor using the Thread_Manager class defined in the Wrapper Facade pattern (47), as follows:

```
Consumer_Handler::Consumer_Handler () {
    // Spawn a separate thread to get messages from the
    // message queue and send them to the remote consumer.
    Thread_Manager::instance ()->spawn (&svc_run, this);
}
```

This new `Consumer_Handler` thread executes the `svc_run()` entry point. This is a static method that retrieves routing messages placed into its message queue by `Supplier_Handler` threads and sends them over its TCP connection to the remote consumer:

```
void *Consumer_Handler::svc_run (void *args) {
    Consumer_Handler *this_obj =
        static_cast<Consumer_Handler *> (args);
    for (;;) {
        // Blocks on <get> until next <Message> arrives.
        Message msg = this_obj->message_queue_.get ();
        // Transmit message to the consumer.
        this_obj->connection_.send (msg, msg.length ());
    }
}
```

The `SOCK_Stream`'s `send()` method can block in a `Consumer_Handler` thread. It will not affect the quality of service of other `Consumer_Handler` or `Supplier_Handler` threads, because it does not share any data with the other threads. Similarly, `Message_Queue::get()` can block without affecting the quality of service of other threads, because the `Message_Queue` is a monitor object. `Supplier_Handlers` can thus insert new messages into the `Consumer_Handler`'s `Message_Queue` via its `put()` method without blocking indefinitely.

Variants   *Timed Synchronized Method Invocations.* Certain applications require 'timed' synchronized method invocations. This feature allows them to set bounds on the time they are willing to wait for a synchronized method to enter its monitor object's critical section. The Balking pattern described in [Lea99a] can be implemented using timed synchronized method invocations.

➡   The `Message_Queue` monitor object interface defined earlier can be modified to support timed synchronized method invocations:

```
class Message_Queue {
public:
    // Wait up to the <timeout> period to put <Message>
    // at the tail of the queue.
    void put
        (const Message &msg, Time_Value *timeout =0);

    // Wait up to the <timeout> period to get <Message>
    // from the head of the queue.
    Message get (Time_Value *timeout = 0);
};
```

If timeout is 0 then both get() and put() will block indefinitely until a message is either inserted into or removed from a Message_Queue monitor object. If the time-out period is non-zero and it expires, the Timedout exception is thrown. The client must be prepared to handle this exception.

The following illustrates how the put() method can be implemented using the timed wait feature of the Thread_Condition condition variable wrapper outlined in implementation activity 3 (408):

```
void Message_Queue::put
    (const Message &msg, Time_Value *timeout)
        /* throw (Timedout) */ {
    // ... Same as before ...
    while (full_i ())
        not_full_.wait (timeout);
    // ... Same as before ...
}
```

While the queue is full this 'timed' put() method releases monitor_lock_ and suspends the calling thread, to wait for space to become available in the queue or for the timeout period to elapse. The monitor_lock_ will be re-acquired automatically when wait() returns, regardless of whether a time-out occurred or not. ❑

Strategized Locking. The Strategized Locking pattern (333) can be applied to make a monitor object implementation more flexible, efficient, reusable, and robust. Strategized Locking can be used, for example, to configure a monitor object with various types of monitor locks and monitor conditions.

➥ The following template class uses *generic programming* techniques [Aus98] to parameterize the synchronization aspects of a Message_Queue:

```
template <class SYNCH_STRATEGY> class Message_Queue {
private:
    typename SYNCH_STRATEGY::Mutex monitor_lock_;
    typename SYNCH_STRATEGY::Condition not_empty_;
    typename SYNCH_STRATEGY::Condition not_full_;
    // ...
};
```

Each synchronized method is then modified as shown by the following empty() method:

```
template <class SYNCH_STRATEGY>
bool Message_Queue<SYNCH_STRATEGY>::empty () const {
    Guard<SYNCH_STRATEGY::Mutex> guard (monitor_lock_);
    return empty_i ();
}
```

To parameterize the synchronization aspects associated with a Message_Queue, we can define a pair of classes, MT_Synch and NULL_SYNCH that typedef the appropriate C++ traits:

```
class MT_Synch {
public:
    // Synchronization traits.
    typedef Thread_Mutex Mutex;
    typedef Thread_Condition Condition;
};

class Null_Synch {
public:
    // Synchronization traits.
    typedef Null_Mutex Mutex;
    typedef Null_Thread_Condition Condition;
};
```

To define a thread-safe Message_Queue, therefore, we simply parameterize it with the MT_Synch strategy:

```
Message_Queue<MT_Synch> message_queue;
```

Similarly, to create a non-thread-safe Message_Queue, we can parameterize it with the following Null_Synch strategy:

```
Message_Queue<Null_Synch> message_queue;                ❏
```

Note that when using the Strategized Locking pattern in C++ it may not be possible for a generic component class to know what type of synchronization strategy will be configured for a particular application. It is important therefore to apply the Thread-Safe Interface pattern (345) as described in implementation activity 4.2 (411), to ensure that intra-object method calls, such as put() calling full_i(), and put_i(), avoid self-deadlock and minimize locking overhead.

Multiple Roles. If a monitor object implements multiple roles, each of which is used by different types of clients, an interface can be introduced for each role. Applying the Extension Interface pattern (141) allows clients to obtain the interface they need. This design helps separate concerns, because a client only sees the particular methods of a monitor object it needs for its own operation. This design further simplifies a monitor object's evolution. For example, new services can be added to the active object by providing new extension interface without changing existing ones. Clients that do not need access to the new services are thus unaffected by the extension.

Known Uses **Dijkstra and Hoare-style Monitors**. Dijkstra [Dij68] and Hoare [Hoare74] defined programming language features called *monitors* that encapsulate functions and their internal variables into thread-safe modules. To prevent race conditions a monitor contains a lock that allows only one function at a time to be active within the monitor. Functions that want to leave the monitor temporarily can block on a condition variable. It is the responsibility of the programming language compiler to generate run-time code that implements and manages a monitor's lock and its condition variables.

Java Objects. The main synchronization mechanism in Java is based on Dijkstra/Hoare-style monitors. Each Java object can be a monitor object containing a monitor lock and a single monitor condition. Java's monitors are simple to use for common use cases, because they allow threads to serialize their execution implicitly via method-call interfaces and to coordinate their activities via calls to wait(), notify(), and notifyAll() methods defined on all objects.

For more complex use cases, however, the simplicity of the Java language constructs may mislead developers into thinking that concurrency is easier to program than it actually is in practice. In particular, heavy use of inter-dependent Java threads can yield complicated inter-relationships, starvation, deadlock, and overhead. [Lea99a] describes many patterns for handling simple and complex concurrency use cases in Java.

The Java language synchronization constructs outlined above can be implemented in several ways inside a compliant Java virtual machine (JVM). JVM implementors must choose between two implementation decisions:

• *Implement Java threads internally in the JVM*. If threads are implemented internally, the JVM appears as one monolithic task to the operating system. In this case, the JVM is free to decide when to suspend and resume threads and how to implement thread scheduling, as long as it stays within the bounds of the Java language specification.

• *Map Java threads them to native operating system threads*. In this case Java monitors can take advantage of synchronization primitives and scheduling behavior of the underlying platform.

The advantage of an internal threads implementation is its platform-independence. However, one of its disadvantages is its inability to take advantage of parallelism in the hardware. As a result, an increasing number of JVMs are implemented by mapping Java threads to native operating system threads.

ACE Gateway. The example from the *Example Resolved* section is based on a communication gateway application contained in the ACE framework [Sch96], which uses monitor objects to simplify concurrent programming and improve performance on multi-processors. Unlike the Dijkstra/Hoare and Java monitors, which are programming language features, the `Message_Queues` used by `Consumer_Handlers` in the gateway are reusable ACE C++ components implemented using the Monitor Object pattern. Although C++ does not support monitor objects directly as a language feature, ACE implements the Monitor Object pattern by applying other patterns and idioms, such as the Guarded Suspension pattern [Lea99a] and the Scoped Locking (325) idiom, as described in the *Implementation* section.

Fast food restaurant. A real-life example of the Monitor Object pattern occurs when ordering a meal at a busy fast food restaurant. Customers are the clients who wait to place their order with a cashier. Only one customer at a time interacts with a cashier. If the order cannot be serviced immediately, a customer temporarily steps aside so that other customers can place their orders. When the order is ready the customer re-enters at the front of the line and can pick up the meal from the cashier.

Consequences   The Monitor Object pattern provides two **benefits**:

Simplification of concurrency control. The Monitor Object pattern presents a concise programming model for sharing an object among cooperating threads. For example, object synchronization corresponds to method invocations. Similarly clients need not be concerned with concurrency control when invoking methods on a monitor object. It is relatively straightforward to create a monitor object out of most so-called passive objects, which are objects that borrow the thread of control of its caller to execute its methods.

Simplification of scheduling method execution. Synchronized methods use their monitor conditions to determine the circumstances under which they should suspend or resume their execution and that of collaborating monitor objects. For example, methods can suspend themselves and wait to be notified when arbitrarily complex conditions occur, without using inefficient polling. This feature makes it possible for monitor objects to schedule their methods cooperatively in separate threads.

The Monitor Object pattern has the following four **liabilities**:

The use of a single monitor lock can *limit scalability* due to increased contention when multiple threads serialize on a monitor object.

Complicated extensibility semantics resulting from the coupling between a monitor object's functionality and its synchronization mechanisms. It is relatively straightforward to decouple an active object's (369) functionality from its synchronization policies via its separate scheduler participant. However, a monitor object's synchronization and scheduling logic is often tightly coupled with its methods' functionality. This coupling often makes monitor objects more efficient than active objects. Yet it also makes it hard to change their synchronization policies or mechanisms without modifying the monitor object's method implementations.

It is also hard to inherit from a monitor object transparently, due to the *inheritance anomaly* problem [MWY91]. This problem inhibits reuse of synchronized method implementations when subclasses require different synchronization mechanisms. One way to reduce the coupling of synchronization and functionality in monitor objects is to use Aspect-Oriented Programming [KLM+97] or the Strategized Locking (333) and Thread-Safe Interface (345) patterns, as shown in the *Implementation* and *Variants* section.

Nested monitor lockout. This problem is similar to the preceding liability. It can occur when a monitor object is nested within another monitor object.

Consider the following two Java classes:

```
class Inner {
    protected boolean cond_ = false;

    public synchronized void awaitCondition () {
        while (!cond)
            try { wait (); }
            catch (InterruptedException e) { }
            // Any other code.
    }

    public synchronized void notifyCondition (boolean c){
        cond_ = c;
        notifyAll ();
    }
}

class Outer {
    protected Inner inner_ = new Inner ();

    public synchronized void process () {
        inner_.awaitCondition ();
    }
    public synchronized void set (boolean c) {
        inner_.notifyCondition (c);
    }
}
```

This code illustrates the canonical form of the nested monitor lockout problem in Java [JS97a]. When a Java thread blocks in the monitor's wait queue, all its locks are held *except* the lock of the object placed in the queue.

Consider what would happen if thread T_1 made a call to Outer.process() and as a result blocked in the wait() call in Inner.awaitCondition(). In Java, the Inner and Outer classes do not share their monitor locks. The wait() statement in waitCondition() call would therefore release the Inner monitor while retaining the Outer monitor. Another thread T_2 cannot then acquire the Outer monitor, because it is locked by the synchronized process() method. As a result Outer.set cannot set Inner.cond_ to true and T_1 will continue to block in wait() forever.

Nested monitor lockout can be avoided by sharing a monitor lock between multiple monitor conditions. This is straightforward in Monitor Object pattern implementations based on POSIX condition variables [IEEE96]. It is surprisingly hard in Java due to its simple concurrency and synchronization model, which tightly couples a monitor lock with each monitor object. Java idioms for avoiding nested monitor lockout in Java are described in [Lea99a] [JS97a].

See Also The Monitor Object pattern is an object-oriented analog of the Code Locking pattern [McK95], which ensures that a region of code is serialized. In the Monitor Object pattern, the region of code is the synchronized method implementation.

The Monitor Object pattern has several properties in common with the Active Object pattern (369). Both patterns can synchronize and schedule methods invoked concurrently on objects, for example. There are two key differences, however:

- An active object executes its methods in a different thread than its client(s), whereas a monitor object executes its methods in its client threads. As a result, active objects can perform more sophisticated, albeit more expensive, scheduling to rearrange the order in which their methods execute.

- Monitor objects often couple their synchronization logic more closely to their methods' functionality. In contrast, it is easier to decouple an active object's functionality from its synchronization policies, because it has a separate scheduler.

It is instructive to compare the Monitor Object pattern solution in the *Example Resolved* section with the solution presented in the Active Object pattern. Both solutions have similar overall application architectures. In particular, the `Supplier_Handler` and `Consumer_Handler` implementations are almost identical. The primary difference is that the `Message_Queue` itself is easier to program and often more efficient when implemented using the Monitor Object pattern than the Active Object pattern.

If a more sophisticated queueing strategy is necessary, however, the Active Object pattern may be more appropriate. Similarly, because active objects execute in different threads than their clients, there are situations where active objects can improve overall application concurrency by executing multiple operations asynchronously. When these operations complete, clients can obtain their results via futures [Hal85] [LS88].

Half-Sync/Half-Async

The *Half-Sync/Half-Async* architectural pattern decouples asynchronous and synchronous service processing in concurrent systems, to simplify programming without unduly reducing performance. The pattern introduces two intercommunicating layers, one for asynchronous and one for synchronous service processing.

Example Performance-sensitive concurrent applications, such as telecommunications switching systems and avionics mission computers, perform a mixture of synchronous and asynchronous processing to coordinate different types of applications, system services, and hardware. Similar characteristics hold for system-level software, such as operating systems.

The BSD UNIX operating system [MBKQ96] [Ste98] is an example of a concurrent system that coordinates the communication between standard Internet application services, such as FTP, INETD, DNS, TEL-NET, SMTP, and HTTPD, and hardware I/O devices, such as network interfaces, disk controllers, end-user terminals, and printers.

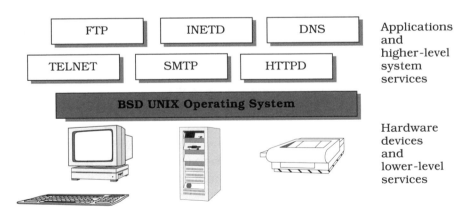

The BSD UNIX operating system processes certain services asynchronously to maximize performance. Protocol processing within the BSD UNIX kernel, for example, runs asynchronously, because I/O devices are driven by interrupts triggered by network interface hardware. If the kernel does not handle these asynchronous interrupts immediately, hardware devices may malfunction and drop packets or corrupt memory buffers.

Although the BSD operating system kernel is driven by asynchronous interrupts, it is hard to develop applications and higher-level system services using asynchrony mechanisms, such as interrupts or signals. In particular, the effort required to program, validate, debug, and maintain asynchronous programs can be prohibitive. For example, asynchrony can cause subtle timing problems and race conditions when an interrupt preempts a running computation unexpectedly.

To avoid the complexities of asynchronous programming, higher-level services in BSD UNIX run synchronously in multiple processes. For example, FTP or TELNET Internet services that use synchronous read() and write() system calls can block awaiting the completion of I/O operations. Blocking I/O, in turn, enables developers to maintain state information and execution history implicitly in the run-time stacks of their threads, rather than in separate data structures that must be managed explicitly by developers.

Within the context of an operating system, however, synchronous and asynchronous processing is not wholly independent. In particular, application-level Internet services that execute synchronously within BSD UNIX must cooperate with kernel-level protocol processing that runs asynchronously. For example, the synchronous read() system call invoked by an HTTP server cooperates indirectly with the asynchronous reception and protocol processing of data arriving on the Ethernet network interface.

A key challenge in the development of BSD UNIX was the structuring of asynchronous and synchronous processing, to enhance both programming simplicity and system performance. In particular, developers of synchronous application programs must be shielded from the complex details of asynchronous programming. Yet, the overall performance of the system must not be degraded by using inefficient synchronous processing mechanisms in the BSD UNIX kernel.

Context   A concurrent system that performs both asynchronous and synchronous processing services that must intercommunicate.

Problem   Concurrent systems often contain a mixture of asynchronous and synchronous processing services. There is a strong incentive for system programmers to use asynchrony to improve performance. Asynchronous programs are generally more efficient, because services can be mapped directly onto asynchrony mechanisms, such as hardware interrupt handlers or software signal handlers.

Conversely, there is a strong incentive for application developers to use synchronous processing to simplify their programming effort. Synchronous programs are usually less complex, because certain services can be constrained to run at well-defined points in the processing sequence.

Two *forces* must therefore be resolved when specifying a software architecture that executes services both synchronously and asynchronously:

- The architecture should be designed so that application developers who want the simplicity of synchronous processing need not address the complexities of asynchrony. Similarly, system developers who must maximize performance should not need to address the inefficiencies of synchronous processing.

- The architecture should enable the synchronous and asynchronous processing services to communicate without complicating their programming model or unduly degrading their performance.

Although the need for both programming simplicity *and* high performance may seem contradictory, it is essential that both these forces be resolved in certain types of concurrent systems, particularly large-scale or complex ones.

Solution   Decompose the services in the system into two layers [POSA1], *synchronous* and *asynchronous*, and add a *queueing* layer between them to mediate the communication between services in the asynchronous and synchronous layers.

In detail: process higher-layer services, such as long-duration database queries or file transfers, *synchronously* in separate threads or processes, to simplify concurrent programming. Conversely, process lower-layer services, such as short-lived protocol handlers driven by interrupts from network interface hardware, *asynchronously* to enhance performance. If services residing in separate synchronous and asynchronous layers must communicate or synchronize their processing, allow them to pass messages to each other via a queueing layer.

Structure   The structure of the Half-Sync/Half-Async pattern follows the Layers pattern [POSA1] and includes four participants:

The *synchronous service layer* performs high-level processing services. Services in the synchronous layer run in separate threads or processes that can block while performing operations.

➡   The Internet services in our operating system example run in separate application processes. These processes invoke `read()` and `write()` operations to perform I/O synchronously on behalf of their Internet services.   ❑

The *asynchronous service layer* performs lower-level processing services, which typically emanate from one or more external event sources. Services in the asynchronous layer cannot block while performing operations without unduly degrading the performance of other services.

➡   The processing of I/O devices and protocols in the BSD UNIX operating system kernel is performed asynchronously in interrupt handlers. These handlers run to completion, that is, they do not block or synchronize their execution with other threads until they are finished.   ❑

Class	*Collaborator*	*Class*	*Collaborator*
Synchronous Service Layer	• Queueing Layer	Asynchronous Service Layer	• Queueing Layer • External Event Source
Responsibility		*Responsibility*	
• Executes high-level processing services synchronously		• Executes low-level processing services asynchronously	

The *queueing layer* provides the mechanism for communicating between services in the synchronous and asynchronous layers. For example, messages containing data and control information are produced by asynchronous services, then buffered at the queueing layer for subsequent retrieval by synchronous services, and vice versa. The queueing layer is responsible for notifying services in one layer when messages are passed to them from the other layer. The queueing layer therefore enables the asynchronous and synchronous layers to interact in a 'producer/consumer' manner, similar to the structure defined by the Pipes and Filters pattern [POSA1].

➡ The BSD UNIX operating system provides a Socket layer [Ste98]. This layer serves as the buffering and notification point between the synchronous Internet service application processes and the asynchronous, interrupt-driven I/O hardware services in the BSD UNIX kernel. ❏

External event sources generate events that are received and processed by the asynchronous service layer. Common sources of external events for operating systems include network interfaces, disk controllers, and end-user terminals.

Class	*Collaborator*
Queueing Layer	• Asynchronous Service Layer
Responsibility	• Synchronous Service Layer
• Provides a buffering between the synchronous service layer and the asynchronous service layer	

Class	*Collaborator*
External Event Source	• Asynchronous Service Layer
Responsibility	
• Generates events received and processed by the asynchronous service layer	

The following class diagram illustrates the structure and relationships between these participants:

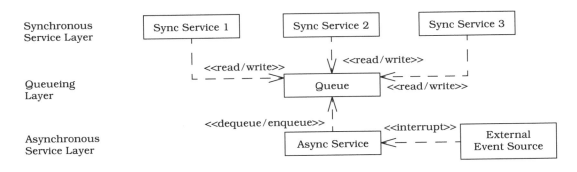

Dynamics   Asynchronous and synchronous layers in the Half-Sync/Half-Async pattern interact by passing messages via a queueing layer. We describe three phases of interactions that occur when input arrives 'bottom-up' from external event sources:

- *Asynchronous phase.* In this phase external sources of input interact with the asynchronous service layer via an asynchronous event notification, such as an interrupt or signal. When asynchronous services have finished processing the input, they can communicate their results to the designated services in the synchronous layer via the queueing layer.

- *Queueing phase.* In this phase the queueing layer buffers input passed from the asynchronous layer to the synchronous layer and notifies the synchronous layer that input is available.

- *Synchronous phase.* In this phase the appropriate service(s) in the synchronous layer retrieve and process the input placed into the queueing layer by service(s) in the asynchronous layer.

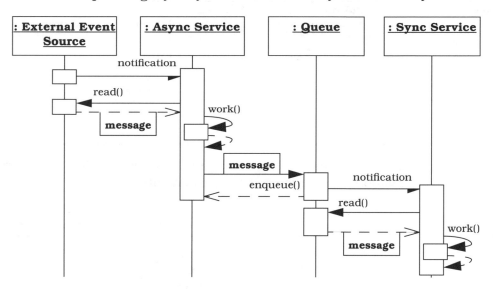

The interactions between layers and pattern participants is reversed to form a 'top-down' sequence when output arrives from services running in the synchronous layer.

Implementation This section describes the activities used to implement the Half-Sync/Half-Async pattern and apply it to structure the concurrency architecture of higher-level applications, such as Web servers [Sch97] and database servers, as well as to lower-level systems, such as the BSD UNIX operating system. We therefore present examples from several different domains.

1 *Decompose the overall system into three layers*: synchronous, asynchronous, and queueing. Three sub-activities can be used to determine how to decompose a system architecture designed in accordance with the Half-Sync/Half-Async pattern.

1.1 *Identify higher-level and/or long-duration services and configure them into the synchronous layer*. Many services in a concurrent system are easier to implement when they are programmed using synchronous processing. These services often perform relatively high-level or long-duration application processing, such as transferring large streams of content in a Web server or performing complex queries in a database. Services in the synchronous layer should therefore run in separate processes or threads. If data is not available the services can block at the queueing layer awaiting responses, under the control of peer-to-peer application communication protocols.

➡ Each Internet service shown in our BSD UNIX operating system example runs in a separate application process. Each application process communicates with its clients using the protocol associated with the Internet service it implements. I/O operations within these processes can be performed by blocking synchronously on TCP Sockets and waiting for the BSD UNIX kernel to complete the I/O operations asynchronously. ❑

1.2 *Identify lower-level and/or short-duration services and configure them into the asynchronous layer*. Certain services in a system cannot block for prolonged amounts of time. Such services typically perform lower-level or short-duration system processing that interacts with external sources of events, such as end-user terminals or interrupt-driven hardware network interfaces. To maximize responsiveness and efficiency, these sources of events must be handled rapidly and must not block the thread that services them. Their services should be triggered by asynchronous notifications or interrupts from external event sources and run to completion, at which point they can insert messages containing their results into the queueing layer.

➥   In our operating system example, processing of I/O device drivers and communication protocols in the BSD UNIX kernel occurs in response to asynchronous hardware interrupts. Each asynchronous operation in the kernel runs to completion, inserting messages containing data and/or control information into the Socket layer if it must communicate with an application process running an Internet service in the synchronous layer.   ❑

1.3   *Identify inter-layer communication strategies and configure them into the queueing layer.* The queueing layer is a mediator [GoF95] that decouples the communication between services in the asynchronous and synchronous layers. Thus these services do not access each other directly, but only via the queueing layer. The communication-related strategies performed by the queueing layer involve (de)multiplexing, buffering, notification, and flow control. Services in the asynchronous and synchronous layers use these queueing strategies to implement protocols for passing messages between the synchronous and asynchronous layers [SC96].

➥   In our BSD UNIX operating system example, the Sockets mechanism [Ste98] defines the queueing layer between the synchronous Internet service application processes and the asynchronous operating system kernel. Each Internet service uses one or more Sockets, which are queues maintained by BSD UNIX to buffer messages exchanged between application processes, and the TCP/IP protocol stack and networking hardware devices in the kernel.   ❑

2   *Implement the services in the synchronous layer.* High-level and/or long-duration services in the synchronous layer are often implemented using either multi-threading or multi-processing. Compared to a thread, a process maintains more state information and requires more overhead to spawn, synchronize, schedule, and inter-communicate. Implementing synchronous services in separate threads, rather than separate processes, can therefore yield simpler and more efficient applications.

Multi-threading can reduce application robustness, however, because separate threads within a process are not protected from one another. For instance, one faulty thread can corrupt data shared with other threads in the process, which may produce incorrect results, crash the process, or cause the process to hang indefinitely. To increase robustness, therefore, application services can be implemented in separate processes.

➡   The Internet services in our BSD UNIX example are implemented in separate processes. This design increases their robustness and prevents unauthorized access to certain resources, such as files owned by other users.   ❑

3   *Implement the services in the asynchronous layer.* Lower-level and/or shorter-duration services in the asynchronous layer often do not have their own dedicated thread of control. Instead, they must borrow a thread from elsewhere, such as the operating system kernel's 'idle thread' or a separate interrupt stack. To ensure adequate response time for other system services, such as high-priority hardware interrupts, these services must run asynchronously and cannot block for long periods of time.

The following are two strategies that can be used to trigger the execution of asynchronous services:

- *Asynchronous interrupts.* This strategy is often used when developing asynchronous services that are triggered directly by hardware interrupts from external event sources, such as network interfaces or disk controllers. In this strategy, when an event occurs on an external event source, an interrupt notifies the handler associated with the event, which then processes the event to completion.

  In complex concurrent systems, it may be necessary to define a *hierarchy* of interrupts to allow less critical handlers to be preempted by higher-priority ones. To prevent interrupt handlers from corrupting shared state while they are being accessed, data structures used by the asynchronous layer must be protected, for example by raising the interrupt priority [WS95].

  ➡   The BSD UNIX kernel uses a two-level interrupt scheme to handle network packet processing [MBKQ96]. Time-critical processing is done at a high priority and less critical software processing is done at a lower priority. This two-level interrupt scheme prevents the overhead of software protocol processing from delaying the servicing of high-priority hardware interrupts.   ❑

- *Proactive I/O.* This strategy is often used when developing asynchronous services based on higher-level operating system

APIs, such as the Windows NT overlapped I/O and I/O completion ports [Sol98] or the POSIX `aio_*` family of asynchronous I/O system calls [POSIX95]. In this strategy, I/O operations are executed by an asynchronous operation processor. When an asynchronous operation finishes, the asynchronous operation processor generates a completion event. This event is then dispatched to the handler associated with the event, which processes the event to completion.

➡ For example, the Web server in the Proactor pattern (215) illustrates an application that uses the proactive I/O mechanisms defined by the Windows NT system call API. This example underscores the fact that asynchronous processing and the Half-Sync/Half-Async pattern can be used for higher-level applications that do not access hardware devices directly.   ❏

Both of these asynchronous processing strategies share the constraint that a handler cannot block for a long period of time without disrupting the processing of events from other external event sources.

4   *Implement the queueing layer.* After services in the asynchronous layer finish processing input arriving from external event sources, they typically insert the resulting messages into the queueing layer. The appropriate service in the synchronous layer will subsequently remove these messages from the queueing layer and process them. These roles are reversed for output processing. Two communication-related strategies must be defined when implementing the queueing layer:

4.1   *Implement the buffering strategy.* Services in the asynchronous and synchronous layers do not access each other's memory directly—instead, they exchange messages via a queueing layer. This queueing layer buffers messages so that synchronous and asynchronous services can run concurrently, rather than running in lockstep via a 'stop-and-wait' flow control protocol. The buffering strategy must therefore implement an ordering, serialization, notification, and flow-control strategy. Note that the Strategy pattern [GoF95] can be applied to simplify the configuration of alternative strategies.

• *Implement the ordering strategy.* Simple queueing layers store their messages in the order they arrive, that is, 'first-in, first-out' (FIFO). The first message that was placed in the queue by a service in one layer is thus the first message to be removed by a service in the other layer. FIFO ordering is easy to implement, but may result in priority inversions [SMFG00] if high-priority messages are queued behind lower-priority messages. Therefore, more sophisticated queueing strategies can be used to store and retrieve messages in 'priority' order.

* *Implement the serialization strategy.* Services in the asynchronous and synchronous layer can execute concurrently. A queue must therefore be serialized to avoid race conditions when messages are inserted and removed concurrently. This serialization is often implemented using lightweight synchronization mechanisms, such as mutexes [Lew95]. Such mechanisms ensure that messages can be inserted into and removed from the queueing layer's message buffers without corrupting its internal data structures.

* *Implement the notification strategy.* It may be necessary to notify a service in one layer when messages addressed to it arrive from another layer. The notification strategy provided by the queueing layer is often implemented using more sophisticated and heavyweight synchronization mechanisms, such as semaphores or condition variables [Lew95]. These synchronization mechanisms can notify the appropriate services in the synchronous or asynchronous layers when data arrives for them in the queueing layer. The *Variations* section outlines several other notification strategies based on asynchronous signals and interrupts.

* *Implement the flow-control strategy.* Systems cannot devote an unlimited amount of resource to buffer messages in the queueing layer. It may therefore be necessary to regulate the amount of data passed between the synchronous and asynchronous layers. Flow control is a technique that prevents synchronous services from flooding the asynchronous layer at a rate greater than that at which messages can be transmitted and queued on network interfaces [SchSu93].

Services in the synchronous layer can block. A common flow control policy simply puts a synchronous service to sleep if it produces and queues more than a certain number of messages. After the asynchronous service layer empties the queue to below a certain level, the queueing layer can awaken the synchronous service to continue its processing.

In contrast, services in the asynchronous layer cannot block. If they can produce an excessive number of messages, a common flow-control policy allows the queueing layer to discard messages until the synchronous service layer finishes processing the messages in its queue. If the messages are associated with a reliable connection-oriented transport protocol, such as TCP [Ste93], senders will time-out eventually and retransmit discarded messages.

4.2 *Implement the (de)multiplexing mechanism.* In simple implementations of the Half-Sync/Half-Async pattern, such as the OLTP servers described in the *Example* section of the Leader/Followers pattern (447), there is only one queue in the queueing layer. This queue is shared by all services in the asynchronous and synchronous layers and any service can process any request. This configuration alleviates the need for a sophisticated (de)multiplexing mechanism. In this case, a common implementation is to define a singleton [GoF95] queue that all services use to insert and remove messages.

In more complex implementations of the Half-Sync/Half-Async pattern, services in one layer may need to send and receive certain messages to particular services in another layer. A queueing layer may therefore need multiple queues, for example one queue per service. With multiple queues, more sophisticated demultiplexing mechanism are needed to ensure messages exchanged between services in different layers are placed in the appropriate queue. A common implementation is to use some type of (de)multiplexing mechanism, such as a hash table [HMPT89] [MD91], to place messages into the appropriate queue(s).

➥ The `Message_Queue` components defined in the Monitor Object (399) and Active Object (369) patterns illustrate various strategies for implementing a queueing layer:

- The Monitor Object pattern ensures that only one method at a time executes within a queue, regardless of the number of threads that invoke the queue's methods concurrently, by using mutexes and condition variables. The queue executes its methods in its client threads, that is, in the threads that run the synchronous and asynchronous services.

- The Active Object pattern decouples method invocations on the queue from method execution. Multiple synchronous and asynchronous services can therefore invoke methods on the queue concurrently. Methods are executed in a different thread than the threads that run the synchronous and asynchronous services.

The *See Also* sections of the Active Object (369) and Monitor Object (399) patterns discuss the pros and cons of using these patterns to implement a queueing layer.   ❏

Example Resolved   Chapter 1, *Concurrent and Networked Objects*, and other patterns in this book, such as Proactor (215), Scoped Locking (325), Strategized Locking (333), and Thread-Safe Interface (345), illustrate various aspects of the design of a Web server application. In this section, we explore the broader system context in which Web servers execute, by outlining how the BSD UNIX operating system [MBKQ96] [Ste93] applies the Half-Sync/Half-Async pattern to receive an HTTP GET request via its TCP/IP protocol stack over Ethernet.

BSD UNIX is an example of an operating system that does not support asynchronous I/O efficiently. It is therefore not feasible to implement the Web server using the Proactor pattern (215). We instead outline how BSD UNIX coordinates the services and communication between synchronous application processes and the asynchronous operating system kernel.

In particular, we describe:[6]

- The synchronous invocation of a `read()` system call by a Web server application (the HTTPD process).

- The asynchronous reception and protocol processing of data arriving on the Ethernet network interface.

- The synchronous completion of the `read()` call, which returns control and the GET request data back to the HTTPD process.

---

6. An in-depth code walk-through showing how the Half-Sync/Half-Async pattern is applied in the BSD UNIX networking and file systems is described in [PLoPD2].

These steps are shown in the following figure:

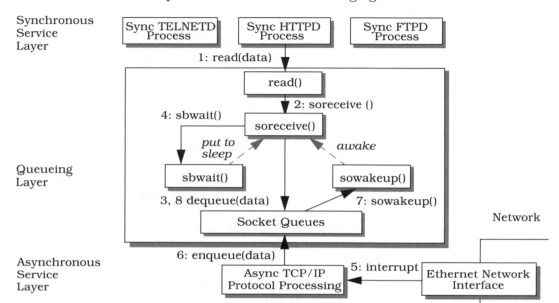

As shown in this figure, the HTTPD process invokes a `read()` system call on a connected socket handle to receive an HTTP GET request encapsulated in a TCP packet. From the perspective of the HTTPD process, the `read()` system call is synchronous, because the process invokes `read()` and blocks until the GET request data is returned. If data is not available immediately, however, the BSD UNIX kernel puts the HTTPD process to sleep until the data arrives from the network.

Many asynchronous steps occur to implement the synchronous `read()` system call, however. Although the HTTPD process can sleep while waiting for data, the BSD UNIX kernel cannot sleep, because other application processes, such as the FTP and TELNET services and I/O devices in the kernel, require its services to run concurrently and efficiently.

After the `read()` system call is issued the application process switches to 'kernel mode' and starts running privileged instructions, which direct it synchronously into the BSD UNIX networking subsystem. Ultimately, the thread of control from the application process ends in the kernel's `soreceive()` function. This function processes input for various types of sockets, such as datagram sockets and stream sockets, by transferring data from the socket queue to the application process. The `soreceive()` function thus defines the boundary between the synchronous application process layer and the asynchronous kernel layer for outgoing packets.

There are two ways in which the HTTPD process's `read()` system call can be handled by `soreceive()`, depending on the characteristics of the Socket and the amount of data in the socket queue:

- *Completely synchronous*. If the data requested by the HTTPD process is in the socket queue, the `soreceive()` function can copy it immediately and the `read()` system call will complete synchronously.

- *Half-synchronous and half-asynchronous*. If the data requested by the HTTPD process is not yet available, the kernel calls the `sbwait()` function to put the process to sleep until the requested data arrives.

After `sbwait()` puts the process to sleep, the BSD UNIX scheduler will switch to another process context that is ready to run. From the perspective of the HTTPD process, however, the `read()` system call appears to execute synchronously. When packet(s) containing the requested data arrive, the kernel will process them asynchronously, as described below. When enough data has been placed in the socket queue to satisfy the HTTPD process' request, the kernel will wake this process and complete its `read()` system call. This call then returns synchronously so that the HTTPD process can parse and execute the GET request.

To maximize performance within the BSD UNIX kernel, all protocol processing is executed *asynchronously*, because I/O devices are driven by hardware interrupts. For example, packets arriving at the Ethernet network interface are delivered to the kernel via interrupt handlers initiated asynchronously by the Ethernet hardware. These handlers receive packets from devices and trigger subsequent asynchronous processing of higher-layer protocols, such as IP and TCP. Ultimately, valid packets containing application data are queued at the Socket layer, where the BSD UNIX kernel schedules and dispatches the waiting HTTPD process to consume this data synchronously.

For example, the 'half-async' processing associated with an HTTPD process's `read()` system call starts when a packet arrives at an

Ethernet network interface, which triggers an asynchronous hardware interrupt. All incoming packet processing is performed in the context of an interrupt handler. During an interrupt, the BSD UNIX kernel cannot sleep or block, because there is no application process context and no dedicated thread of control. The Ethernet interrupt handler therefore 'borrows' the kernel's thread of control. Similarly, the BSD UNIX kernel borrows the threads of control of application processes when they invoke system calls.

If the packet is destined for an application process, it is passed up to the transport layer, which performs additional protocol processing, such as TCP segment reassembly and acknowledgments. Eventually, the transport layer appends the data to the receive socket queue and calls sbwakeup(), which represents the boundary between the asynchronous and synchronous layers for incoming packets. This call wakes up the HTTPD process that was sleeping in soreceive() waiting for data on that socket queue. If all the data requested by the HTTPD process has arrived, soreceive() will copy it to the buffer supplied by HTTPD, allowing the system call to return control to the Web server. The read() call thus appears to be synchronous from the perspective of the HTTPD process, even though asynchronous processing and context switching were performed while this process was asleep.

Variants *Asynchronous Control with Synchronous Data I/O.* The HTTPD Web server described in the *Implementation* section 'pulls' messages synchronously from the queueing layer at its discretion, thereby combining control and data activities. On some operating system platforms, however, it is possible to decouple control and data so that services in the synchronous layer can be notified *asynchronously* when messages are inserted into the queueing layer. The primary benefit of this variant is that higher-level 'synchronous' services may be more responsive, because they can be notified asynchronously.

➡   The UNIX signal-driven I/O mechanism [Ste98] implements this variant of the Half-Sync/Half-Async pattern. The UNIX kernel uses the SIGIO signal to 'push' control to a higher-level application process when data arrives on one of its Sockets. When a process receives this control notification asynchronously, it can then 'pull' the data synchronously from socket queueing layer via read().   ❏

The disadvantage of using asynchronous control, of course, is that developers of higher-level services must now face many of the asynchrony complexities outlined in the *Problem* section.

Half-Async/Half-Async. This variant extends the previous variant by propagating asynchronous control notifications and data operations all the way up to higher-level services in the 'synchronous' layer. These higher-level services may therefore be able to take advantage of the efficiency of the lower-level asynchrony mechanisms.

➥ For example, the real-time signal interface defined in the POSIX real-time programming specification [POSIX95] supports this variant. In particular, a buffer pointer can be passed to the signal handler function dispatched by the operating system when a real-time signal occurs. Windows NT supports a similar mechanism using overlapped I/O and I/O completion ports [Sol98]. In this case, when an asynchronous operation completes, its associated overlapped I/O structure indicates which operation has completed and passes any data along. The Proactor pattern (215) and Asynchronous Completion Token pattern (261) describe how to structure applications to take advantage of asynchronous operations and overlapped I/O. ❑

The disadvantage of this variant is similar to that of the previous variant. If most or all services can be driven by asynchronous operations, the design may be modeled better by applying the Proactor pattern (215) rather than the Half-Sync/Half-Async pattern.

Half-Sync/Half-Sync. This variant provides synchronous processing to lower-level services. If the asynchronous layer is multi-threaded, its services can run autonomously and use the queueing layer to pass messages to the synchronous service layer. The benefits of this variant are that services in the asynchronous layer may be simplified, because they can block without affecting other services in this layer.

➥ Microkernel operating systems, such as Mach [Bl90] or Amoeba [Tan95], typically use this variant. The microkernel runs as a separate multi-threaded 'process' that exchanges messages with application processes. Similarly, multi-threaded operating system macrokernels, such as Solaris [EKBF+92], can support multiple synchronous I/O operations in the kernel. ❑

Multi-threading the kernel can be used to implement polled interrupts, which reduce the amount of context switching for high-performance continuous media systems by dedicating a kernel thread to poll a field in shared memory at regular intervals [CP95]. In contrast, single-threaded operating system kernels, such as BSD UNIX, restrict lower-level kernel services to use asynchronous I/O and only support synchronous multi-programming for higher-level application processes.

The drawback to providing synchronous processing to lower-level services, of course, is that it may increase overhead, thereby degrading overall system performance significantly.

Half-Sync/Half-Reactive. In object-oriented applications, the Half-Sync/Half-Async pattern can be implemented as a composite architectural pattern that combines the Reactor pattern (179) with the Thread Pool variant of the Active Object pattern (369). In this common variant, the reactor's event handlers constitute the services in the 'asynchronous' layer[7] and the queueing layer can be implemented by an active object's activation list. The servants dispatched by the scheduler in the active object's thread pool constitute the services in the synchronous layer. The primary benefit of this variant is the simplification it affords. This simplicity is achieved by performing event demultiplexing and dispatching in a single-threaded reactor that is decoupled from the concurrent processing of events in the active object's thread pool.

➡ The OLTP servers described in the *Example* section of the Leader/Followers pattern (447) apply this variant. The 'asynchronous' service layer uses the Reactor pattern (179) to demultiplex transaction requests from multiple clients and dispatch event handlers. The handlers insert requests into the queueing layer, which is an activation list implemented using the Monitor Object pattern (399). Similarly, the synchronous service layer uses the thread pool variant of the Active Object pattern (369) to disseminate requests from the activation list to a pool of worker threads that service transaction requests from clients. Each thread in the active object's thread pool can block synchronously because it has its own run-time stack.   ❑

---

7. Although this reactive layer is not truly asynchronous, it shares key properties with asynchronous services. In particular, event handlers dispatched by a reactor cannot block for long without starving other sources of events.

The drawback with this variant is that the queueing layer incurs additional context switching, synchronization, data allocation, and data copying overhead that may be unnecessary for certain applications. In such cases the Leader/Followers pattern (447) may be a more efficient, predictable, and scalable way to structure a concurrent application than the Half-Sync/Half-Async pattern.

Known Uses   **UNIX Networking Subsystems**. The BSD UNIX networking subsystem [MBKQ96] and the UNIX STREAMS communication framework [Ris98] use the Half-Sync/Half-Async pattern to structure the concurrent I/O architecture of application processes and the operating system kernel. I/O in these kernels is asynchronous and triggered by interrupts. The queueing layer is implemented by the Socket layer in BSD UNIX [Ste98] and by Stream Heads in UNIX STREAMS [Rago93]. I/O for application processes is synchronous.

Most UNIX network daemons, such as TELNETD and FTPD, are developed as application processes that invoke read() and write() system calls synchronously [Ste98]. This design shields application developers from the complexity of asynchronous I/O processed by the kernel. However, there are hybrid mechanisms, such as the UNIX SIGIO signal, that can be used to trigger synchronous I/O processing via asynchronous control notifications.

CORBA ORBs. MT-Orbix [Bak97] uses a variation of the Half-Sync/ Half-Async pattern to dispatch CORBA remote operations in a concurrent server. In MT-Orbix's ORB Core a separate thread is associated with each socket handle that is connected to a client. Each thread blocks synchronously, reading CORBA requests from the client. When a request is received it is demultiplexed and inserted into the queueing layer. An active object thread in the synchronous layer then wakes up, dequeues the request, and processes it to completion by performing an *upcall* to the CORBA servant.

ACE. The ACE framework [Sch97] applies the 'Half-Sync/Half-Reactive' variant of the Half-Sync/Half-Async pattern in an application-level gateway that routes messages between peers in a distributed system [Sch96]. The ACE_Reactor is the ACE implementation of the Reactor pattern (179) that demultiplexes indication events to their associated event handlers in the 'asynchronous' layer. The ACE Message_Queue class implements the queueing layer, while the ACE `Task` class implements the thread pool variant of the Active Object pattern (369) in the synchronous service layer.

Conduit. The Conduit communication framework [Zweig90] from the Choices operating system project [CIRM93] implements an object-oriented version of the Half-Sync/Half-Async pattern. Application processes are synchronous active objects, an Adapter Conduit serves as the queueing layer, and the Conduit micro-kernel operates asynchronously, communicating with hardware devices via interrupts.

Restaurants. Many restaurants use a variant of the Half-Sync/Half-Async pattern. For example, restaurants often employ a host or hostess who is responsible for greeting patrons and keeping track of the order in which they will be seated if the restaurant is busy and it is necessary to queue them waiting for an available table. The host or hostess is 'shared' by all the patrons and thus cannot spend much time with any given party. After patrons are seated at a table, a waiter or waitress is dedicated to service that table.

Consequences The Half-Sync/Half-Async pattern has the following **benefits**:

Simplification and performance. The programming of higher-level synchronous processing services are simplified without degrading the performance of lower-level system services. Concurrent systems often have a greater number and variety of high-level processing services than lower-level services. Decoupling higher-level synchronous services from lower-level asynchronous processing services can simplify application programming, because complex concurrency control, interrupt handling, and timing services can be localized within the asynchronous service layer. The asynchronous layer can also handle low-level details that may be hard for application developers to program robustly, such as interrupt handling. In addition, the asynchronous layer can manage the interaction with hardware-specific components, such as DMA, memory management, and I/O device registers.

The use of synchronous I/O can also simplify programming, and may improve performance on multi-processor platforms. For example, long-duration data transfers, such as downloading a large medical image from a hierarchical storage management system [PHS96], can be simplified and performed efficiently using synchronous I/O. In particular, one processor can be dedicated to the thread that is transferring the data. This enables the instruction and data cache of that CPU to be associated with the entire image transfer operation.

Separation of concerns. Synchronization policies in each layer are decoupled. Each layer therefore need not use the same concurrency control strategies. In the single-threaded BSD UNIX kernel, for example, the asynchronous service layer implements synchronization via low-level mechanisms, such as raising and lowering CPU interrupt levels. In contrast, application processes in the synchronous service layer implement synchronization via higher-level mechanisms, such as monitor objects (399) and synchronized message queues.

➡   Legacy libraries, such as X Windows and older RPC toolkits, are often not re-entrant. Multiple threads of control cannot therefore invoke these library functions concurrently within incurring race conditions. To improve performance or to take advantage of multiple CPUs, however, it may be necessary to perform bulk data transfers or database queries in separate threads. In this case, the Half-Sync/Half-Reactive variant of the Half-Sync/Half-Async pattern can be applied to decouple the single-threaded portions of an application from its multi-threaded portions.

For example, an application's X Windows GUI processing could run under the control of a reactor. Similarly, long data transfers could run under the control of an active object thread pool. By decoupling the synchronization policies in each layer of the application via the Half-Sync/Half-Async pattern, non-re-entrant functions can continue to work correctly without requiring changes to existing code.   ❏

Centralization of inter-layer communication. Inter-layer communication is centralized at a single access point, because all interaction is mediated by the queueing layer. The queueing layer buffers messages passed between the other two layers. This eliminates the complexities of locking and serialization that would otherwise be necessary if the synchronous and asynchronous service layers accessed objects in each other's memory directly.

The Half-Sync/Half-Async pattern also has the following **liabilities**:

A boundary-crossing penalty may be incurred from context switching, synchronization, and data copying overhead when data is transferred between the synchronous and asynchronous service layers via the queueing layer. For example, most operating systems implement the Half-Sync/Half-Async pattern by placing the queueing layer at the boundary between the user-level and kernel-level protection domains. A significant performance penalty can be incurred when crossing this boundary [HP91].

One way of reducing this overhead is to share a region of memory between the synchronous service layer and the asynchronous service layer [DP93]. This 'zero-copy' design allows the two layers to exchange data directly, without copying data into and out of the queueing layer.

➡ [CP95] presents a set of extensions to the BSD UNIX I/O subsystem that minimizes boundary-crossing penalties by using polled interrupts to improve the handling of continuous media I/O streams. This approach defines a buffer management system that allows efficient page re-mapping and shared memory mechanisms to be used between application processes, the kernel, and its devices.❏

Higher-level application services may not benefit from the efficiency of asynchronous I/O. Depending on the design of operating system or application framework interfaces, it may not be possible for higher-level services to use low-level asynchronous I/O devices effectively. The BSD UNIX operating system, for example, prevents applications from using certain types of hardware efficiently, even if external sources of I/O support asynchronous overlapping of computation and communication.

Complexity of debugging and testing. Applications written using the Half-Sync/Half-Async pattern can incur the same debugging and testing challenges described in *Consequences* sections of the Proactor (215) and Reactor (179) patterns.

See Also The Proactor pattern (215) can be viewed as an extension of the Half-Sync/Half-Async pattern that propagates asynchronous control and data operations all the way up to higher-level services. In general, the Proactor pattern should be applied if an operating system platform supports asynchronous I/O efficiently and application developers are comfortable with the asynchronous I/O programming model.

The Reactor pattern (179) can be used in conjunction with the Active Object pattern (369) to implement the Half-Sync/Half-Reactive variant of the Half-Sync/Half-Async pattern. Similarly, the Leader/ Followers (447) pattern can be used in lieu of the Half-Sync/Half-

Async pattern if there is no need for a queueing layer between the asynchronous and synchronous layers.

The Pipes and Filters pattern [POSA1] describes several general principles for implementing producer-consumer communication between components in a software system. Certain configurations of the Half-Sync/Half-Async pattern can therefore be viewed as instances of the Pipes and Filters pattern, where filters contain entire layers of many finer-grained services. Moreover, a filter could contain active objects, which could yield the Half-Sync/Half-Reactive or Half-Sync/Half-Sync variants.

The Layers [POSA1] pattern describes the general principle of separating services into separate layers. The Half-Sync/Half-Async pattern can thus be seen as a specialization of the Layers pattern whose purpose is to separate synchronous processing from asynchronous processing in a concurrent system by introducing two designated layers for each type of service.

Credits   Chuck Cranor was the co-author of the original version of this pattern [PLoPD2]. We would also like to thank Lorrie Cranor and Paul McKenney for comments and suggestions for improving the pattern.

Leader/Followers

The *Leader/Followers* architectural pattern provides an efficient concurrency model where multiple threads take turns sharing a set of event sources in order to detect, demultiplex, dispatch, and process service requests that occur on the event sources.

Example   Consider the design of a multi-tier, high-volume, on-line transaction processing (OLTP) system [GR93]. In this design, front-end communication servers route transaction requests from remote clients, such as travel agents, claims processing centers, or point-of-sales terminals, to back-end database servers that process the requests transactionally. After a transaction commits, the database server returns its results to the associated communication server, which then forwards the results back to the originating remote client. This multi-tier architecture is used to improve overall system throughput and reliability via load balancing and redundancy, respectively. It also relieves back-end servers from the burden of managing different communication protocols with remote clients.

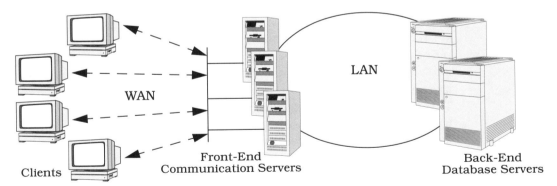

Clients   Front-End
Communication Servers   Back-End
Database Servers

LAN

WAN

One way to implement OLTP servers is to use a single-threaded event processing model based on the Reactor pattern (179). However, this model serializes event processing, which degrades the overall server performance when handling long-running or blocking client request events. Likewise, single-threaded servers cannot benefit transparently from multi-processor platforms.

A common strategy for improving OLTP server performance is to use a multi-threaded concurrency model that processes requests from different clients and corresponding results simultaneously [HPS99]. For example, we could multi-thread an OLTP back-end server by creating a thread pool based on the *Half-Sync/Half-Reactive* variant of the Half-Sync/Half-Async pattern (423). In this design, the OLTP back-end server contains a dedicated *network I/O* thread that uses the `select()` [Ste98] event demultiplexer to wait for events to occur on a set of socket handles connected to front-end communication servers.

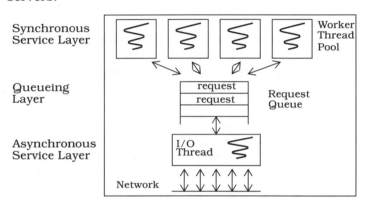

When activity occurs on handles in the set, `select()` returns control to the network I/O thread and indicates which socket handles in the set have events pending. The I/O thread then reads the transaction requests from the socket handles, stores them into dynamically allocated requests, and inserts these requests into a synchronized message queue implemented using the Monitor Object pattern (399). This message queue is serviced by a pool of *worker threads*. When a worker thread in the pool is available, it removes a request from the queue, performs the designated transaction, and then returns a response to the front-end communication server.

Although the threading model described above is used in many concurrent applications, it can incur excessive overhead when used for high-volume servers, such as those in our OLTP example. For instance, even with a light workload, the Half-Sync/Half-Reactive thread pool design will incur a dynamic memory allocation, multiple synchronization operations, and a context switch to pass a request message between the network I/O thread and a worker thread. These overheads make even the best-case latency unnecessarily high [PRS+99]. Moreover, if the OLTP back-end server is run on a multi-processor, significant overhead can occur from processor cache coherency protocols required to transfer requests between threads [SKT96].

If the OLTP back-end servers run on an operating system platform that supports asynchronous I/O efficiently, the Half-Sync/Half-Reactive thread pool can be replaced with a purely asynchronous thread pool based on the Proactor pattern (215). This alternative will reduce much of the synchronization, context switching, and cache coherency overhead outlined above by eliminating the network I/O thread. Unfortunately, many operating systems do not support asynchronous I/O and those that do often support it inefficiently.[8] Yet, it is essential that high-volume OLTP servers demultiplex requests efficiently to threads that can process the results concurrently.

Context An event-driven application where multiple service requests arriving on a set of event sources must be processed efficiently by multiple threads that share the event sources.

Problem Multi-threading is a common technique to implement applications that process multiple events concurrently. However, it is hard to implement *high-performance* multi-threaded server applications. These applications often process a high volume of multiple types of events, such as CONNECT, READ, and WRITE events in our OLTP example, that arrive simultaneously. To address this problem effectively, three *forces* must be resolved:

- Service requests can arrive from multiple event sources, such as multiple TCP/IP socket handles [Ste98], that are allocated for each connected client. A key design force, therefore, is determining *efficient demultiplexing associations* between threads and event sources. In particular, associating a thread for each event source may be infeasible due to the scalability limitations of applications or the underlying operating system and network platforms.

---

8. For instance, some operating systems support asynchronous I/O by spawning a thread for each asynchronous operation, thereby defeating the potential performance benefits of asynchrony.

➡ For our OLTP server applications, it may not be practical to associate a separate thread with each socket handle. In particular, as the number of connections increase significantly, this design may not scale efficiently on many operating system platforms.   ❑

- To maximize performance, key sources of *concurrency-related overhead*, such as context switching, synchronization, and cache coherency management, must be minimized. In particular, concurrency models that allocate memory dynamically for each request passed between multiple threads will incur significant overhead on conventional multi-processor operating systems [SchSu95].

➡ Implementing our OLTP servers using the *Half-Sync/Half-Reactive* thread pool variant (423) outlined in the *Example* section requires memory to be allocated dynamically in the network I/O thread to store incoming transaction requests into the message queue. This design incurs numerous synchronizations and context switches to insert the request into, or remove the request from, the message queue, as illustrated in the Monitor Object pattern (399).   ❑

- Multiple threads that demultiplex events on a shared set of event sources must coordinate to prevent *race conditions*. Race conditions can occur if multiple threads try to access or modify certain types of event sources simultaneously.

➡ For instance, a pool of threads cannot use `select()` concurrently to demultiplex a set of socket handles because the operating system will erroneously notify more than one thread calling `select()` when I/O events are pending on the same set of socket handles [Ste98]. Moreover, for bytestream-oriented protocols, such as TCP, having multiple threads invoking `read()` or `write()` on the same socket handle will corrupt or lose data. ❑

Solution   Structure a pool of threads to share a set of event sources efficiently by *taking turns* demultiplexing events that arrive on these event sources and synchronously dispatching the events to application services that process them.

In detail: design a *thread pool* mechanism that allows multiple threads to coordinate themselves and protect critical sections while detecting, demultiplexing, dispatching, and processing events. In this mechanism, allow one thread at a time—the *leader*—to wait for an event to occur on a *set of event sources*. Meanwhile, other threads— the *followers*—can queue up waiting their turn to become the leader. After the current leader thread detects an event from the event source set, it first promotes a follower thread to become the new leader. It then plays the role of a *processing* thread, which demultiplexes and dispatches the event to a designated *event handler* that performs application-specific event handling in the processing thread. Multiple processing threads can handle events concurrently while the current leader thread waits for new events on the set of event sources shared by the threads. After handling its event, a processing thread reverts to a follower role and waits to become the leader thread again.

Structure   There are four key participants in the Leader/Followers pattern:

Handles are provided by operating systems to identify event sources, such as network connections or open files, that can generate and queue events. Events can originate from external sources, such as CONNECT events or READ events sent to a service from clients, or internal sources, such as time-outs. A *handle set* is a collection of handles that can be used to wait for one or more events to occur on handles in the set. A handle set returns to its caller when it is possible to initiate an operation on a handle in the set without the operation blocking.

➡   OLTP servers are interested in two types of events—CONNECT events and READ events—which represent incoming connections and transaction requests, respectively. Both front-end and back-end servers maintain a separate connection for each client, where clients of front-end servers are the so-called 'remote' clients and front-end servers themselves are clients of back-end servers. Each connection is a source of events that is represented in a server by a separate socket handle. Our OLTP servers use the select() event demultiplexer, which identifies handles whose event sources have pending events, so that applications can invoke I/O operations on these handles without blocking the calling threads.   ❏

Class	Collaborator
Handle and Handle Set	
Responsibility	
• A handle identifies a source of events in an operating system • A handle can queue up events • A handle set is a collection of handles	

An *event handler* specifies an interface consisting of one or more hook methods [Pree95] [GoF95]. These methods represent the set of operations available to process application-specific events that occur on handle(s) serviced by an event handler.

Concrete event handlers specialize the event handler and implement a specific service that the application offers. In particular, concrete event handlers implement the hook method(s) responsible for processing events received from a handle.

Class	Collaborator	Class	Collaborator
Event Handler	• Handle	Concrete Event Handler	• Handle
Responsibility		**Responsibility**	
• Defines an interface for processing events that occur on a handle		• Defines an application service • Processes events received on a handle in an application-specific manner • Runs in a processing thread	

➡   For example, concrete event handlers in OLTP front-end communication servers receive and validate remote client requests, and then forward requests to back-end database servers. Likewise, concrete event handlers in back-end database servers receive transaction requests from front-end servers, read/write the appropriate database records to perform the transactions, and return the results to the front-end servers. All network I/O operations are performed via socket handles, which identify various sources of events.   ❏

At the heart of the Leader/Followers pattern is a *thread pool*, which is a group of threads that share a synchronizer, such as a semaphore or condition variable, and implement a protocol for coordinating their transition between various roles. One or more threads play the *follower* role and queue up on the thread pool synchronizer waiting to play the *leader* role. One of these threads is selected to be the leader, which waits for an event to occur on any handle in its handle set. When an event occurs, the current leader thread promotes a follower thread to become the new leader. The original leader then concurrently plays the role of a *processing* thread, which demultiplexes that event from the handle set to an appropriate event handler and dispatches the handler's hook method to handle the event. After a processing thread is finished handling an event, it returns to playing the role of a follower thread and waits on the thread pool synchronizer for its turn to become the leader thread again.

Class	Collaborator
Thread Pool	• Handle Set
	• Handle
Responsibility	• Event Handlers
• Threads that take turns playing three roles: in the leader role they await events, in the processing role they process events, in the follower role they queue up waiting to become the leader	
• Contains a synchronizer	

➡ Each OLTP server designed using the Leader/Followers pattern can have a pool of threads waiting to process transaction requests that arrive on event sources identified by a handle set. At any point in time, multiple threads in the pool can be processing transaction requests and sending results back to their clients. One thread in the pool is the current leader, which waits for a new CONNECT or READ event to arrive on the handle set shared by the threads. When this occurs, the leader thread becomes a processing thread and handles the event, while one of the follower threads in the pool is promoted to become the new leader.   ❏

The following class diagram illustrates the structure of participants in the Leader/Followers pattern. In this structure, multiple threads share the same instances of thread pool, event handler, and handle set participants. The thread pool ensures the correct and efficient coordination of the threads:

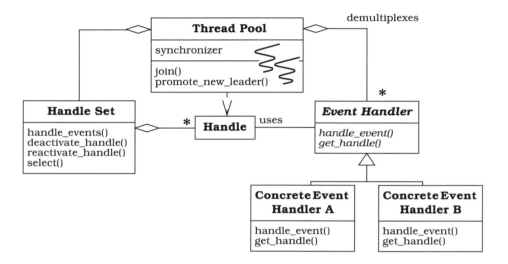

Dynamics   The collaborations in the Leader/Followers pattern divide into four phases:

- *Leader thread demultiplexing.* The leader thread waits for an event to occur on any handle in the handle set. If there is no current leader thread, for example, due to events arriving faster than the available threads can service them, the underlying operating system can queue events internally until a leader thread is available.

- *Follower thread promotion.* After the leader thread has detected a new event, it uses the thread pool to choose a follower thread to become the new leader.

- *Event handler demultiplexing and event processing.* After helping to promote a follower thread to become the new leader, the former leader thread then plays the role of a processing thread. This thread concurrently demultiplexes the event it detected to the event's associated handler and then dispatches the handler's hook method to process the event. A processing thread can execute concurrently with the leader thread and any other threads that are in the processing state.

- *Rejoining the thread pool.* After the processing thread has run its event handling to completion, it can rejoin the thread pool and wait to process another event. A processing thread can become the leader immediately if there is no current leader thread. Otherwise, the processing thread returns to playing the role of a follower thread and waits on the thread pool synchronizer until it is promoted by a leader thread.

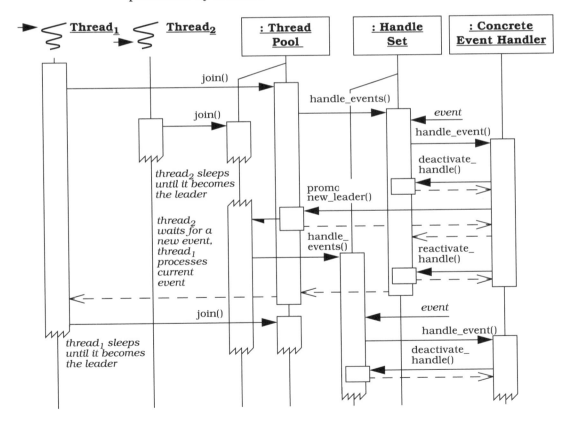

A thread's transitions between states can be visualized in the following diagram:

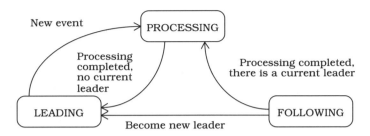

Implementation   Six activities can be used to implement the Leader/Followers pattern:

1   *Choose the handle and handle set mechanisms.* A handle set is a collection of handles that a leader thread can use to wait for an event to occur on a set of event sources. Developers often choose the handles and handle set mechanisms provided by the underlying operating system, rather than implementing them from scratch. Four sub-activities help with choosing the handle and handle set mechanisms:

1.1   *Determine the type of handles.* There are two general types of handles:

• *Concurrent handles.* This type allows multiple threads to access a handle to an event source *concurrently* without incurring race conditions that can corrupt, lose, or scramble the data [Ste98]. For instance, the Socket API for record-oriented protocols, such as UDP, allows multiple threads to invoke `read()` or `write()` operations on the same handle concurrently.

• *Iterative handles.* This type requires multiple threads to access a handle to an event source *iteratively* because concurrent access will incur race conditions. For instance, the Socket API for bytestream-oriented protocols, such as TCP, does not guarantee that `read()` or `write()` operations respect application-level message boundaries. Thus, corrupted or lost data can result if I/O operations on the Socket are not serialized properly.

1.2   *Determine the type of handle set.* There are two general types of handle sets:

- *Concurrent handle set.* This type can be acted upon concurrently, for example, by a pool of threads. Each time it becomes possible to initiate an operation on a handle in the set without blocking the operation, a concurrent handle set returns that handle to one of its calling threads. For example, the Win32 `WaitForMultipleObjects()` function [Sol98] supports concurrent handle sets by allowing a pool of threads to wait on the same set of handles simultaneously.

- *Iterative handle set.* This type returns to its caller when it is possible to initiate an operation on *one or more* handles in the set without the operation(s) blocking. Although an iterative handle set can return multiple handles in a single call, it can only be called by one thread at a time. For example, the `select()` [Ste98] and `poll()` [Rago93] functions support iterative handle sets. Thus, a pool of threads cannot use `select()` or `poll()` to demultiplex events on the same handle set concurrently because multiple threads can be notified that the same I/O events are pending, which elicits erroneous behavior.

The following table summarizes representative examples for each combination of concurrent and iterative handles and handle sets:

Handles / Handle Sets	Concurrent Handles	Iterative Handles
Concurrent Handle Sets	UDP Sockets + `WaitForMultipleObjects()`	TCP Sockets + `WaitForMultipleObjects()`
Iterative Handle Sets	UDP Sockets + `select()`, `poll()`	TCP Sockets + `select()`, `poll()`

1.3   *Determine the consequences of selecting certain handle and handle set mechanisms.* In general, the Leader/Followers pattern is used to prevent multiple threads from corrupting or losing data erroneously, such as invoking read operations on a shared TCP bytestream socket handle concurrently or invoking `select()` on a shared handle set concurrently. However, some applications need not guard against these problems. In particular, if the handle and handle set mechanisms are both concurrent, many of the subsequent implementation activities can be skipped.

As discussed in implementation activities 1.1 (456) and 1.2 (457), the semantics of certain combinations of protocols and network programming APIs support concurrent multiple I/O operations on a shared handle. For example, UDP support in the Socket API ensures a complete message is always read or written by one thread or another, without the risk of a partial read() or of data corruption from an interleaved write(). Likewise, certain handle set mechanisms, such as the Win32 WaitForMultipleObjects() function [Sol98], return a single handle per call, which allows them to be called concurrently by a pool of threads.[9]

In these situations, it may be possible to implement the Leader/ Followers pattern by simply using the operating system's thread scheduler to (de)multiplex threads, handle sets, and handles robustly, in which case, implementation activities 2 through 6 can be skipped.

1.4   *Implement an event handler demultiplexing mechanism.* In addition to calling an event demultiplexer to wait for one or more events to occur on its handle set, such as select(), a Leader/Followers pattern implementation must demultiplex events to event handlers and dispatch their hook methods to process the events. In general, two alternative strategies can be used to implement this mechanism:

- *Program to a low-level operating system event demultiplexing mechanism.* In this strategy, the handle set demultiplexing mechanisms provided by the operating system are used directly. Thus, a Leader/Followers implementation must maintain a demultiplexing table that is a manager [Som97] containing a set of *<handle, event handler, event types>* tuples. Each handle serves as a 'key' that associates handles with event handlers in its demultiplexing table, which also stores the type of event(s), such as CONNECT and READ, that each event handler will process. The

---

9. However, WaitForMultipleObjects() does not by itself address the problem of notifying a particular thread when an event is available, which is necessary to support the bound thread/handle association discussed in the *Variants* section.

contents of this table are converted into handle sets passed to the native event demultiplexing mechanism, such as `select()` [Ste98] or `WaitForMultipleObjects()` [Sol98].

➡   Implementation activity 3.3 of the Reactor pattern (179) illustrates how to implement a demultiplexing table.   ❏

- *Program to a higher-level event demultiplexing pattern.* In this strategy, developers leverage higher-level patterns, such as Reactor (179), Proactor (215), and Wrapper Facade (47). These patterns help to simplify the Leader/Followers implementation and reduce the effort needed to address the accidental complexities of programming to native operating system handle set demultiplexing mechanisms directly. Moreover, applying higher-level patterns makes it easier to decouple the I/O and demultiplexing aspects of a system from its concurrency model, thereby reducing code duplication and maintenance effort.

➡   In our OLTP server example, an event must be demultiplexed to the concrete event handler associated with the socket handle that received the event. The Reactor pattern (179) supports this activity, therefore it can be applied to simplify the implementation of the Leader/Followers pattern. In the context of the Leader/Followers pattern, however, a reactor demultiplexes just *one* handle at a time to its associated concrete event handler, regardless of how many handles have events pending on them. Demultiplexing only one handle at a time can maximize the concurrency among a pool of threads and simplify a Leader/Followers pattern implementation by alleviating its need to manage a separate queue of pending events.   ❏

2   *Implement a protocol for temporarily (de)activating handles in a handle set.* When an event arrives, the leader thread performs three steps:

- It deactivates the handle from consideration in the handle set temporarily

- It promotes a follower thread to become the new leader and

- It continues to process the event.

Deactivating the handle from the handle set avoids race conditions that could occur between the time when a new leader is selected and the event is processed. If the new leader waits on the same handle in the handle set during this interval, it could demultiplex the event a second time, which is erroneous because the dispatch is already in progress. After the event is processed, the handle is reactivated in the handle set, which allows the leader thread to wait for an event to occur on it or any other activated handles in the set.

➥   In our OLTP example, a handle deactivation and reactivation protocol can be provided by extending the `Reactor` interface defined in implementation activity 2 of the Reactor pattern (179):

```
class Reactor {
public:
    // Temporarily deactivate the <HANDLE>
    // from the internal handle set.
    void deactivate_handle (HANDLE, Event_Type);

    // Reactivate a previously deactivated
    // <Event_Handler> to the internal handle set.
    void reactivate_handle (HANDLE, Event_Type);
    // ...
};                                                                                    ❏
```

3   *Implement the thread pool.* To promote a follower thread to the leader role, as well as to determine which thread is the current leader, an implementation of the Leader/Followers pattern must manage a pool of threads. A straightforward way to implement this is to have all the follower threads in the set simply wait on a single synchronizer, such as a semaphore or condition variable. In this design, it does not matter which thread processes an event, as long as all threads in the pool that share the handle set are serialized.

➥   For example, the `LF_Thread_Pool` class shown below can be used for the back-end database servers in our OLTP example:

```
class LF_Thread_Pool {
public:
    // Constructor.
    LF_Thread_Pool (Reactor *r): reactor_ (r) { }

    // Threads call <join> to wait on a handle set and
    // demultiplex events to their event handlers.
    void join (Time_Value *timeout = 0);

    // Promote a follower thread to become the
    // leader thread.
    void promote_new_leader ();
```

```
        // Support the <HANDLE> (de)activation protocol.
        void deactivate_handle (HANDLE, Event_Type et);
        void reactivate_handle (HANDLE, Event_Type et);
    private:
        // Pointer to the event demultiplexer/dispatcher.
        Reactor *reactor_;

        // The thread id of the leader thread, which is
        // set to NO_CURRENT_LEADER if there is no leader.
        Thread_Id leader_thread_;

        // Follower threads wait on this condition
        // variable until they are promoted to leader.
        Thread_Condition followers_condition_;

        // Serialize access to our internal state.
        Thread_Mutex mutex_;
    };
```

The constructor of LF_Thread_Pool caches the reactor passed to it. By default, this reactor implementation uses select(), which supports iterative handle sets. Therefore, LF_Thread_Pool is responsible for serializing multiple threads that take turns calling select() on the reactor's handle set.

Application threads invoke join() to wait on a handle set and demultiplex new events to their associated event handlers. As shown in implementation activity 4 (462), this method does not return to its caller until the application terminates or join() times out. The promote_new_leader() method promotes one of the follower threads in the set to become the new leader, as shown in implementation activity 5.2 (464).

The deactivate_handle() method and the reactivate_handle() method deactivate and reactivate handles within a reactor's handle set. The implementations of these methods simply forward to the same methods defined in the Reactor interface shown in implementation activity 2 (459).

Note that a single condition variable synchronizer followers_condition_ is shared by all threads in this thread pool. As shown in implementation activities 4 (462) and 5 (463), the implementation of LF_Thread_Pool uses the Monitor Object pattern (399). ❏

4 *Implement a protocol to allow threads to initially join (and later rejoin) the thread pool.*

This protocol is used in the following two cases:

- After the initial creation of a pool of threads that retrieve and process events; and

- After a processing thread completes and is available to handle another event.

If no leader thread is available, a processing thread can become the leader immediately. If a leader thread is already available, a thread can become a follower by waiting on the thread pool's synchronizer.

➥   Our back-end database servers can implement the following join() method of the LF_Thread_Pool to wait on a handle set and demultiplex new events to their associated event handlers:

```
void LF_Thread_Pool::join (Time_Value *timeout) {
    // Use Scoped Locking idiom to acquire mutex
    // automatically in the constructor.
    Guard<Thread_Mutex> guard (mutex_);

    for (;;) {
        while (leader_thread_ != NO_CURRENT_LEADER)
            // Sleep and release <mutex> atomically.
            followers_condition_.wait (timeout);

        // Assume the leader role.
        leader_thread_ = Thread::self ();

        // Leave monitor temporarily to allow other
        // follower threads to join the pool.
        guard.release ();

        // After becoming the leader, the thread uses
        // the reactor to wait for an event.
        reactor_->handle_events ()'

        // Reenter monitor to serialize the test
        // for <leader_thread_> in the while loop.
        guard.acquire ();
    }
}
```

Within the for loop, the calling thread alternates between its role as a leader, processing, and follower thread. In the first part of this loop, the thread waits until it can be a leader, at which point it uses the reactor to wait for an event on the shared handle set. When the reactor detects an event on a handle, it will demultiplex the event to its associated event handler and dispatch its `handle_event()` method to promote a new leader and process the event. After the reactor demultiplexes one event, the thread re-assumes its follower role. These steps continue looping until the application terminates or a timeout occurs.   ❏

5 *Implement the follower promotion protocol.* Immediately after a leader thread detects an event, but before it demultiplexes the event to its event handler and processes the event, it must promote a follower thread to become the new leader. Two sub-activities can be used to implement this protocol:

5.1 *Implement the handle set synchronization protocol.* If the handle set is iterative and we blindly promote a new leader thread, it is possible that the new leader thread will attempt to handle the same event that was detected by the previous leader thread that is in the midst of processing the event. To avoid this race condition, we must remove the handle from consideration in the handle set before promoting a follower to new leader and dispatching the event to its concrete event handler. The handle must be reactivated in the handle set after the event has been dispatched and processed.

➥   An application can implement concrete event handlers that subclass from the `Event_Handler` class defined in implementation activity 1.2 of the Reactor pattern (179). Likewise, the Leader/Followers implementation can use the Decorator pattern [GoF95] to create an `LF_Event_Handler` class that decorates `Event_Handler`. This decorator promotes a new leader thread and activates/deactivates the handler in the reactor's handle set transparently to the concrete event handlers.

```
class LF_Event_Handler : public Event_Handler {
public:
    LF_Event_Handler (Event_Handler *eh,
                      LF_Thread_Pool *tp)
        : concrete_event_handler_ (eh),
          thread_pool_ (tp) { }

    virtual void handle_event (HANDLE h, Event_Type et) {
        // Temporarily deactivate the handler in the
        // reactor to prevent race conditions.
        thread_pool_->deactivate_handle (h, et);
```

```
                    // Promote a follower thread to become leader.
                    thread_pool_->promote_new_leader ();

                    // Dispatch application-specific event
                    // processing code.
                    concrete_event_handler_->handle_event (h, et);

                    // Reactivate the handle in the reactor.
                    thread_pool_->reactivate_handle (h, et);
             }
        private:
                    // This use of <Event_Handler> plays the
                    // <ConcreteComponent> role in the Decorator
                    // pattern, which is used to implement
                    // the application-specific functionality.
                    Event_Handler *concrete_event_handler_;

                    // Instance of an <LF_Thread_Pool>.
                    LF_Thread_Pool *thread_pool_;
        };                                                              ❑
```

5.2   *Determine the promotion protocol ordering.* Several ordering strategies
      can be used to determine which follower thread to promote:

- *LIFO order.* In many applications, it does not matter which of the
  follower threads is promoted next because all threads are
  equivalent peers. In this case, the leader thread can promote
  follower threads in *last-in, first-out* (LIFO) order. The LIFO protocol
  maximizes CPU cache affinity [SKT96] [MB91] by ensuring that the
  thread waiting the *shortest* time is promoted first [Sol98], which is
  an example of the Fresh Work Before Stale pattern [Mes96].

  Cache affinity can improve system performance if the thread that
  blocked most recently executes essentially the same code and data
  when it is scheduled to run again. Implementing a LIFO promotion
  protocol requires an additional data structure, however, such as a
  stack of waiting threads, rather than just using a native operating
  system synchronization object, such as a semaphore.

- *Priority order.* In some applications, particularly real-time
  applications, threads may run at different priorities. In this case,
  therefore, it may be necessary to promote follower threads
  according to their priority. This protocol can be implemented using
  some type of priority queue, such as a heap [BaLee98]. Although
  this protocol is more complex than the LIFO protocol, it may be

necessary to promote follower threads according to their priorities in order to minimize priority inversion [SMFG00].

* *Implementation-defined order.* This ordering is most common when implementing handle sets using operating system synchronizers, such as semaphores or condition variables, which often dispatch waiting threads in an implementation-defined order. The advantage of this protocol is that it maps onto native operating system synchronizers efficiently.

➨ Our OLTP back-end database servers could use the following simple protocol to promote follower thread in whatever order they are queued by a native operating system condition variable:

```
void LF_Thread_Pool::promote_new_leader () {
    // Use Scoped Locking idiom to acquire mutex
    // automatically in the constructor.
    Guard<Thread_Mutex> guard (mutex_);

    if (leader_thread_ != Thread::self ())
        throw /* ...only leader thread can promote... */;

    // Indicate that we are no longer the leader
    // and notify a <join> method to promote
    // the next follower.
    leader_thread_ = NO_CURRENT_LEADER;
    followers_condition_.notify ();

    // Release mutex automatically in destructor.
}
```

As shown in implementation activity 5.1 (463), the promote_new_leader() method is invoked by a LF_Event_Handler decorator before it forwards to the concrete event handler that processes an event. ❏

6   *Implement the event handlers.* Application developers must decide what actions to perform when the hook method of a concrete event handler is invoked by a processing thread in the Leader/Followers pattern implementation. Implementation activity 5 in the Reactor pattern (179) describes various issues associated with implementing concrete event handlers.

The OLTP back-end database servers described in the *Example* section can use the Leader/Followers pattern to implement a thread pool that demultiplexes I/O events from socket handles to their event handlers efficiently. In this design, there is no designated network I/O thread. Instead, a pool of threads is pre-allocated during database server initialization:

```
const int MAX_THREADS = /* ... */;

// Forward declaration.
void *worker_thread (void *);

int main () {
    LF_Thread_Pool thread_pool (Reactor::instance ());
    // Code to set up a passive-mode Acceptor omitted.
    for (int i = 0; i < MAX_THREADS - 1; ++i)
        Thread_Manager::instance ()->spawn
            (worker_thread, &thread_pool);

    // The main thread participates in the thread pool.
    thread_pool.join ();
};
```

These threads are not bound to any particular socket handle. Thus, all threads in this pool take turns playing the role of a network I/O thread by invoking the LF_Thread_Pool::join() method:

```
void *worker_thread (void *arg) {
    LF_Thread_Pool *thread_pool =
        static_cast <LF_Thread_Pool *> (arg);

    // Each worker thread participates in the thread pool.
    thread_pool->join ();
};
```

As shown in implementation activity 4 (462), the join() method allows only the leader thread to use the Reactor singleton to select() on a shared handle set of Sockets connected to OLTP front-end communication servers. If requests arrive when all threads are busy, they will be queued in socket handles until threads in the pool are available to execute the requests.

When a request event arrives, the leader thread deactivates the socket handle temporarily from consideration in select()'s handle set, promotes a follower thread to become the new leader, and continues to handle the request event as a processing thread. This processing thread then reads the request into a buffer that resides in the run-time stack or is allocated using the Thread-Specific Storage pattern (475).[10] All OLTP activities occur in the processing thread. Thus, no further context switching, synchronization, or data movement is necessary until the processing completes. When it finishes handling a request, the processing thread returns to playing the role of a follower and waits on the synchronizer in the thread pool. Moreover, the socket handle it was processing is reactivated in the `Reactor` singleton's handle set so that `select()` can wait for I/O events to occur on it, along with other Sockets in the handle set.

Variants   *Bound Handle/Thread Associations.* The earlier sections in this pattern describe *unbound* handle/thread associations, where there is no fixed association between threads and handles. Thus, any thread can process any event that occurs on any handle in a handle set. Unbound associations are often used when a pool of worker threads take turns demultiplexing a shared handle set.

A variant of the Leader/Followers pattern uses *bound* handle/thread associations. In this variant, each thread is bound to its own handle, which it uses to process particular events. Bound associations are often used in the client-side of an application when a thread waits on a socket handle for a response to a two-way request it sent to a server. In this case, the client application thread expects to process the response event on this handle in the same thread that sent the original request.

In the bound handle/thread association variant, therefore, the leader thread in the thread pool may need to hand-off an event to a follower thread if the leader does not have the necessary context to process the event. After the leader detects a new event, it checks the handle associated with the event to determine which thread is responsible for processing it. If the leader thread discovers that it is responsible for the event, it promotes a follower thread to become the new leader Conversely, if the event is intended for another thread, the leader must hand-off the event to the designated follower thread. This follower thread can then temporally disable the handle and process

---

10. In contrast, the Half-Sync/Half-Reactive thread pool described in the *Example* section must allocate each request dynamically from a shared heap because the request is passed between threads.

the event. Meanwhile, the current leader thread continues to wait for another event to occur on the handle set.

The following diagram illustrates the additional transition between the following state and the processing state:

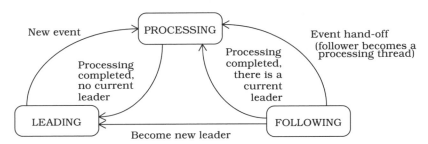

The leader/follower thread pool can be maintained implicitly, for example, using a synchronizer, such as a semaphore or condition variable, or explicitly, using a container and the Manager pattern [Som97]. The choice depends largely on whether the leader thread must notify a specific follower thread explicitly to perform event hand-offs.

A detailed discussion of the bounded handle/thread association variant and its implementation appears in [SRPKB00].

Relaxing Serialization Constraints. There are operating systems where multiple leader threads can wait on a handle set simultaneously. For example, the Win32 function `WaitForMultipleObjects()` [Sol98] supports concurrent handle sets that allow a pool of threads to wait on the same set of handles concurrently. Thus, a thread pool designed using this function can take advantage of multi-processor hardware to handle multiple events concurrently while other threads wait for events.

Two variations of the Leader/Followers pattern can be applied to allow multiple leader threads to be active simultaneously:

- *Leader/followers per multiple handle sets.* This variation applies the conventional Leader/Followers implementation to multiple handle sets separately. For instance, each thread is assigned a designated handle set. This variation is particularly useful in applications where multiple handle sets are available. However, this variant limits a thread to use a specific handle set.

- *Multiple leaders and multiple followers.* In this variation, the pattern is extended to support multiple simultaneous leader threads, where any of the leader threads can wait on any handle set. When a thread re-joins the thread pool it checks if a leader is associated with every handle set already. If there is a handle set without a leader, the re-joining thread can become the leader of that handle set immediately.

Hybrid Thread Associations. Some applications use hybrid designs that implement both bound and unbound handle/thread associations simultaneously. Likewise, some handles in an application may have dedicated threads to handle certain events, whereas other handles can be processed by any thread. Thus, one variant of the Leader/Follower pattern uses its event hand-off mechanism to notify certain subsets of threads, according to the handle on which event activity occurs.

➥   For example, the OLTP front-end communication server may have multiple threads using the Leader/Followers pattern to wait for new request events from clients. Likewise, it may also have threads waiting for responses to requests they invoked on back-end servers. In fact, threads play both roles over their lifetime, starting as threads that dispatch new incoming requests, then issuing requests to the back-end servers to satisfy the client application requirements, and finally waiting for responses to arrive from the back-end server.   ❏

Hybrid Client/Servers. In complex systems, where peer applications play both client and server roles, it is important that the communication infrastructure processes incoming requests while waiting for one or more replies. Otherwise, the system can deadlock because one client dedicates all its threads to block waiting for responses.

In this variant, the binding of threads and handles changes dynamically. For example, a thread may be unbound initially, yet while processing an incoming request the application discovers it requires a service provided by another peer in the distributed system. In this case, the unbound thread dispatches a new request while executing application code, effectively binding itself to the handle used to send the request. Later, when the response arrives and the thread completes the original request, it becomes unbound again.

Alternative Event Sources and Sinks. Consider a system where events are obtained not only through handles but also from other sources, such as shared memory or message queues. For example, in UNIX there are no event demultiplexing functions that can wait for I/O events, semaphore events, and/or message queue events simultaneously. However, a thread can either block waiting for one type of event at the same time. Thus, the Leader/Followers pattern can be extended to wait for more than one type of events simultaneously:

- A leader thread is assigned to each source of events—as opposed to a single leader thread for the complete system.

- After the event is received, but before processing the event, a leader thread can select any follower thread to wait on this event source.

A drawback with this variant, however, is that the number of participating threads must always be greater than the number of event sources. Therefore, this approach may not scale well as the number of event sources grows.

Known Uses **ACE Thread Pool Reactor framework** [Sch97]. The ACE framework provides an object-oriented framework implementation of the Leader/ Followers pattern called the 'thread pool reactor' (`ACE_TP_Reactor`) that demultiplexes events to event handlers within a pool of threads. When using a thread pool reactor, an application pre-spawns a *fixed* number of threads. When these threads invoke the `ACE_TP_ Reactor`'s `handle_events()` method, one thread will become the leader and wait for an event. Threads are considered unbound by the ACE thread pool reactor framework. Thus, after the leader thread detects the event, it promotes an arbitrary thread to become the next leader and then demultiplexes the event to its associated event handler.

CORBA ORBs and Web servers. Many CORBA implementations, including Chorus COOL ORB [SMFG00] and TAO [SC99], use the Leader/Followers pattern for both their client-side connection model and the server-side concurrency model. In addition, The JAWS Web server [HPS99] uses the Leader/Followers thread pool model for operating system platforms that do not allow multiple threads to simultaneously call `accept()` on a passive-mode socket handle.

Transaction monitors. Popular transaction monitors, such as Tuxedo, operate traditionally on a per-process basis, for example, transactions are always associated with a process. Contemporary OLTP systems demand high-performance and scalability, however, and performing transactions on a per-process basis may fail to meet these requirements. Therefore, next-generation transaction services, such as implementations of the CORBA Transaction Service [OMG97b], employ bound Leader/Followers associations between threads and transactions.

Taxi stands. The Leader/Followers pattern is used in everyday life to organize many airport taxi stands. In this use case, taxi cabs play the role of the 'threads,' with the first taxi cab in line being the *leader* and the remaining taxi cabs being the *followers*. Likewise, passengers arriving at the taxi stand constitute the events that must be demultiplexed to the cabs, typically in FIFO order. In general, if any taxi cab can service any passenger, this scenario is equivalent to the *unbound* handle/thread association described in the main *Implementation* section. However, if only certain cabs can service certain passengers, this scenario is equivalent to the *bound* handle/thread association described in the *Variants* section.

Consequences   The Leader/Followers pattern provides several **benefits**:

Performance enhancements. Compared with the Half-Sync/Half-Reactive thread pool approach described in the *Example* section, the Leader/Followers pattern can improve performance as follows:

- It enhances CPU cache affinity and eliminates the need for dynamic memory allocation and data buffer sharing between threads. For example, a processing thread can read the request into buffer space allocated on its run-time stack or by using the Thread-Specific Storage pattern (475) to allocate memory.

- It minimizes locking overhead by not exchanging data between threads, thereby reducing thread synchronization. In bound handle/thread associations, the leader thread demultiplexes the event to its event handler based on the value of the handle. The request event is then read from the handle by the follower thread processing the event. In unbound associations, the leader thread itself reads the request event from the handle and processes it.

- It can minimize priority inversion because no extra queueing is introduced in the server. When combined with real-time I/O subsystems [KSL99], the Leader/Followers thread pool model can reduce sources of non-determinism in server request processing significantly.

- It does not require a context switch to handle each event, reducing the event dispatching latency. Note that promoting a follower thread to fulfill the leader role *does* require a context switch. If two events arrive simultaneously this increases the dispatching latency for the second event, but the performance is no worse than Half-Sync/Half-Reactive thread pool implementations.

Programming simplicity. The Leader/Follower pattern simplifies the programming of concurrency models where multiple threads can receive requests, process responses, and demultiplex connections using a shared handle set.

However, the Leader/Followers pattern has the following **liabilities**:

Implementation complexity. The advanced variants of the Leader/Followers pattern are harder to implement than Half-Sync/Half-Reactive thread pools. In particular, when used as a multi-threaded connection multiplexer, the Leader/Followers pattern must maintain a pool of follower threads waiting to process requests. This set must be updated when a follower thread is promoted to a leader and when a thread rejoins the pool of follower threads. All these operations can happen concurrently, in an unpredictable order. Thus, the Leader/Follower pattern implementation must be efficient, while ensuring operation atomicity.

Lack of flexibility. Thread pool models based on the Half-Sync/Half-Reactive variant of the Half-Sync/Half-Async pattern (423) allow events in the queueing layer to be discarded or re-prioritized. Similarly, the system can maintain multiple separate queues serviced by threads at different priorities to reduce contention and priority inversion between events at different priorities. In the Leader/Followers model, however, it is harder to discard or reorder events because there is no explicit queue. One way to provide this functionality is to offer different levels of service by using multiple Leader/Followers groups in the application, each one serviced by threads at different priorities.

Network I/O bottlenecks. The Leader/Followers pattern, as described in the *Implementation* section, serializes processing by allowing only a single thread at a time to wait on the handle set. In some environments, this design could become a bottleneck because only one thread at a time can demultiplex I/O events. In practice, however, this may not be a problem because most of the I/O-intensive processing is performed by the operating system kernel. Thus, application-level I/O operations can be performed rapidly.

See Also The Reactor pattern (179) often forms the core of Leader/Followers pattern implementations. However, the Reactor pattern can be used in lieu of the Leader/Followers pattern when each event only requires a short amount of time to process. In this case, the additional scheduling complexity of the Leader/Followers pattern is unnecessary.

The Proactor pattern (215) defines another model for demultiplexing asynchronous event completions concurrently. It can be used instead of the Leader/Followers pattern:

* When an operating system supports asynchronous I/O efficiently and

* When programmers are comfortable with the asynchronous inversion of control associated with the Proactor pattern

The Half-Sync/Half-Async (423) and Active Object (369) patterns are two other alternatives to the Leader/Followers pattern. These patterns may be a more appropriate choice than the Leader/Followers pattern:

* When there are additional synchronization or ordering constraints that must be addressed by reordering requests in a queue before they can be processed by threads in the pool and/or

* When event sources cannot be waited for by a single event demultiplexer efficiently

The Controlled Reactor pattern [DeFe99] includes a performance manager that controls the use of threads for event handlers according to a user's specification and may be an alternative when controlled performance is an important objective.

Credits   Michael Kircher, Carlos O'Ryan, and Irfan Pyarali are the co-authors of the original version of the Leader/Followers pattern. Thanks to Ed Fernandez for his comments that helped improve this version of the pattern.

Thread-Specific Storage

The *Thread-Specific Storage* design pattern allows multiple threads to use one 'logically global' access point to retrieve an object that is local to a thread, without incurring locking overhead on each object access.

Also Known As Thread-Local Storage

Example Consider the design of a multi-threaded network logging server that remote client applications use to record information about their status centrally within a distributed system. Unlike the logging server shown in the Reactor pattern example (179), which demultiplexed all client connections iteratively within a single thread, this logging server uses a thread-per-connection [Sch97] concurrency model to process requests concurrently.

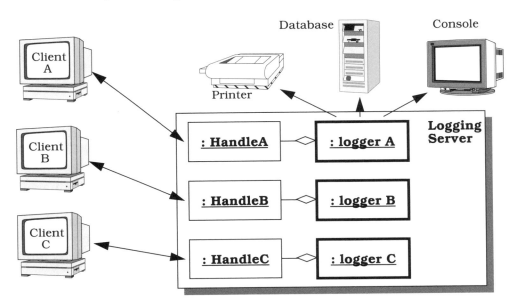

In the thread-per-connection model a separate thread is created for each client connection. Each thread reads logging records from its associated TCP Socket, processes these records and writes them to the appropriate output device, such as a log file or a printer.

Each logging server thread is also responsible for detecting and reporting any low-level network conditions or system errors that occur when performing I/O. Many operating systems, such as UNIX and Windows NT, report this low-level information to applications via a global access point, called errno. When an error or unusual condition occurs during system calls, such as read() or write(), the operating system sets errno to indicate what has happened and returns a specific status value, such as –1. Applications must test for these return values and then check errno to determine what type of error or unusual condition occurred.

Consider the following C code fragment that receives client logging records from a TCP socket handle set to non-blocking mode [Ste98].

```
// One global <errno> per-process.
extern int errno;

void *logger (HANDLE socket) {
    // Read logging records until connection is closed.
    for (;;) {
        char log_record[MAXREC];
        if (recv (socket, log_record, MAXREC, 0) == -1) {
            // Check to see why <recv> failed.
            if (errno == EWOULDBLOCK)
                sleep (1); // Try getting data later.
            else // Display error result.
                cerr << "recv failed, errno=" << errno;
        } else // Normal case ...
    }
}
```

If recv() returns –1 the logging server logger code checks errno to determine what happened and decide how to proceed.

Although implementing errno at global scope works reasonably well for single-threaded applications, it can incur subtle problems for multi-threaded applications. In particular, race conditions in preemptive multi-threaded systems can cause an errno value set in one thread to be interpreted erroneously in other threads. If multiple threads execute the logger() function simultaneously erroneous interactions may occur.

For example, assume that thread T_1 invokes a non-blocking recv() call that returns –1 and sets errno to EWOULDBLOCK, which indicates that no data is currently queued on the Socket. Before T_1 can check for this case, however, it is preempted and thread T_2 starts running.

Assuming that T_2 is then interrupted by an asynchronous signal, such as SIGALRM, it sets errno to EINTR. If T_2 is preempted immediately because its time-slice is finished, T_1 will falsely assume its recv() call was interrupted and perform the wrong action:

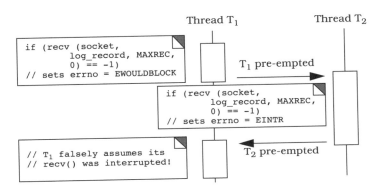

One apparent solution to this problem is to apply the Wrapper Facade pattern (47) to encapsulate errno with an object wrapper that contains a lock. The Scoped Locking idiom (325) can then be used to acquire the lock before setting or checking errno and to release it afterwards. Unfortunately, this design will not solve the race condition problem, because setting and checking the global errno value is not atomic. Instead, it involves the following two activities:

1 The recv() call sets errno.

2 The application checks errno to determine what action to take.

A more robust way to prevent race conditions is to improve the errno locking protocol. For example, the recv() system call could acquire a global errno_lock before it sets errno. Subsequently, when recv() returns, the application releases the errno_lock after it tests the value of errno. This solution is error-prone, however, because applications may forget to release errno_lock, causing starvation and deadlock. Also, because applications may need to check the status of errno frequently, the extra locking overhead will degrade performance significantly, particularly when an application happens to run in a single-threaded configuration.

What is needed therefore is mechanism that *transparently* gives each thread its own local copy of 'logically global' objects, such as errno.

Context   Multi-threaded applications that frequently access data or objects that are *logically global* but whose state should be *physically local* to each thread.

Problem   Multi-threaded applications can be hard to program due to the complex concurrency control protocols needed to avoid race conditions, starvation and deadlocks [Lea99a]. Due to locking overhead, multi-threaded applications also often perform no better than single-threaded applications. In fact, they may perform worse, particularly on multi-processor platforms [SchSu95]. Two *forces* can arise in concurrent programs:

- Multi-threaded applications should be both easy to program and efficient. In particular, access to data that is logically global but physically local to a thread should be atomic *without* incurring locking overhead for each access.[11]

  ➥   As described in the *Example* section, operating systems often implement errno as a 'logically global' variable that developers program as if it were an actual global variable. To avoid race conditions, however, the memory used to store errno is allocated locally, once per thread.   ❑

- Many legacy libraries and applications were written originally assuming a single thread of control. They therefore often pass data implicitly between methods via global objects, such as errno, rather than passing parameters explicitly. When retrofitting such code to run in multiple threads it is often not feasible to change existing interfaces and code in legacy applications.

  ➥   Operating systems that return error status codes implicitly in errno cannot be changed easily to return these error codes explicitly without causing existing applications and library components to break.   ❑

Solution   Introduce a global access point for each thread-specific object, but maintain the 'real' object in storage that is local to each thread. Let

11. Note that this use case contrasts with the situation in which multiple threads collaborate on a single task using global or shared data. In that case, the data is not thread-specific and each thread's access to it must be controlled via a synchronization mechanism, such as a mutex or semaphore.

applications manipulate these thread-specific objects only through their global access points.

Structure The Thread-Specific Storage pattern is composed of six participants.

A *thread-specific object* is an instance of an object that can be accessed only by a particular thread.

➡   For example, in operating systems that support multi-threaded processes, `errno` is an `int` that has a different instance in each thread.   ❏

Class	Collaborator
Thread-Specific Object	
Responsibility	
• Provides a service or data that is only accessible via a particular thread.	

A thread identifies a thread-specific object using a *key* that is allocated by a *key factory.* Keys generated by the key factory are assigned from a single range of values to ensure that each thread-specific object is 'logically' global.

➡   For example, a multi-threaded operating system implements errno by creating a globally-unique key. Each thread uses this key to access its own local instance of `errno` implicitly.   ❏

Class	Collaborator		Class	Collaborator
Key			Key Factory	
Responsibility			**Responsibility**	
• Identifies a Thread-Specific Object.			• Creates Keys	

A *thread-specific object set* contains the collection of thread-specific objects that are associated with a particular thread. Each thread has its own thread-specific object set. Internally, this thread-specific object set defines a pair of methods, which we call `set()` and `get()`, to map the globally-managed set of keys to the thread-specific objects stored in the set. Clients of a thread-specific object set can obtain a pointer to a particular thread-specific object by passing a key that identifies the object as a parameter to get(). The client can inspect or modify the object via the pointer returned by the get() method. Similarly, clients can add a pointer to a thread-specific object into the object set by passing the pointer to the object and its associated key as parameters to set().

➥   An operating system's threads library typically implements the thread-specific object set. This set contains the errno data, among other thread-specific objects.   ❑

Class	*Collaborator*
Thread-Specific Object Set	• Thread-Specific Object
Responsibility	
• Maintains Thread-Specific Objects	

A *thread-specific object proxy* [GoF95] [POSA1] can be defined to enable clients to access a specific type of thread-specific object as if it were an ordinary object. If proxies are not used, clients must access thread-specific object sets directly and use keys explicitly, which is tedious and error-prone. Each proxy instance stores a key that identifies the thread-specific object uniquely. Thus, there is one thread-specific object per-key, per-thread.

A thread-specific object proxy exposes the same interface as its associated thread-specific object. Internally, the interface methods of the proxy first use the set() and get() methods provided by its thread-specific object set to obtain a pointer to the thread-specific object designated by the key stored in the proxy. After a pointer to the appropriate thread-specific object has been obtained, the proxy then delegates the original method call to it.

➥   For example, errno is implemented as a preprocessor macro that plays the role of the proxy and shields applications from thread-specific operations.   ❑

Application threads are clients that use thread-specific object proxies to access particular thread-specific objects that reside in thread-specific storage. To an application thread, the method appears to be invoked on an ordinary object, when in fact it is invoked on a thread-specific object. Multiple application threads can use the same thread-specific object proxy to access their unique thread-specific objects. A proxy uses the identifier of the application thread that calls its interface methods to differentiate between the thread-specific objects it encapsulates.

➥   For example, the thread that runs the `logger` function in the *Example* section is an application thread.   ❏

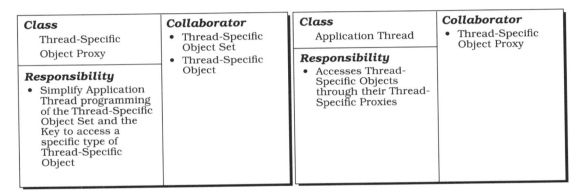

The following class diagram illustrates the general structure of the Thread-Specific Storage pattern:

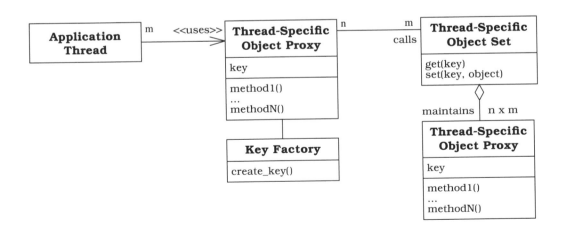

The participants in the Thread-Specific Storage pattern can be modeled conceptually as a two-dimensional matrix that has one row per key and one column per thread. The matrix entry at row k and column t yields a pointer to the corresponding thread-specific object. Creating a key is analogous to adding a row to the matrix; creating a new thread is analogous to adding a column.

A thread-specific object proxy works in conjunction with the thread-specific object set to provide application threads with a type-safe mechanism to access a particular object located at row k and column t. The key factory maintains a count of how many keys have been used. A thread-specific object set contains the entries in one column.

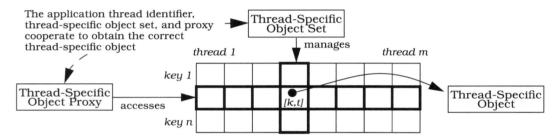

Note that the model above is only an analogy. In practice, implementations of the Thread-Specific Storage pattern do not use two-dimensional matrices, because keys are not necessarily consecutive integers. The entries in the thread-specific object set may also reside in their corresponding thread, rather than in a global two-dimensional matrix. It is helpful to visualize the structure of the Thread-Specific Storage pattern as a two-dimensional matrix, however. We therefore refer to this metaphor in the following sections.

Dynamics There are two general scenarios in the Thread-Specific Storage pattern: *creating* and *accessing* a thread-specific object. **Scenario I** describes the creation of a thread-specific object:

- An application thread invokes a method defined in the interface of a thread-specific object proxy.

- If the proxy does not yet have an associated key it asks the key factory to create a new key. This key identifies the associated thread-specific object uniquely in each thread's object set. The proxy then stores the key, to optimize subsequent method invocations by application threads.

- The thread-specific object proxy creates a new object dynamically. It then uses the thread-specific object set's set() method to store a pointer to this object in the location designated by the key.

- The method that was invoked by the application thread is then executed, as shown in Scenario II.

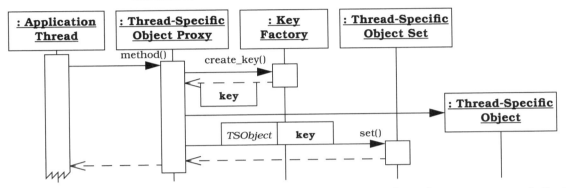

Scenario II describes how an application thread accesses an existing thread-specific object:

- An application thread invokes a method on a thread-specific object proxy.

- The thread-specific object proxy passes its stored key to the get() method of the application thread's thread-specific object set. It then retrieves a pointer to the corresponding thread-specific object.

- The proxy uses this pointer to delegate the original method call to the thread-specific object. Note that no locking is necessary, because the object is referenced through a pointer that is accessed only within the client application thread itself.

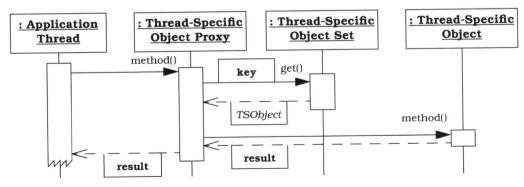

Implementation   Implementing the Thread-Specific Storage pattern centers on
implementing thread-specific object sets and thread-specific object
proxies. These two components create the mechanisms for managing
and accessing objects residing in thread-specific storage. We
therefore describe their implementation—including potential
alternatives—as two separate activities, starting with thread-specific
object sets and then covering thread-specific object proxies.

The thread-specific objects themselves, as well as the application
code that accesses them, are defined by application developers. We
therefore do not provide general implementation activities for these
pattern participants. In the *Example Resolved* section, however, we
use our multi-threaded logging server example to illustrate how
applications can program the Thread-Specific Storage pattern
effectively.

1   *Implement the thread-specific object sets.* This activity is divided into
six sub-activities:

1.1   *Determine the type of the thread-specific objects.* In terms of our two-
dimensional matrix analogy, a thread-specific object is an entry in the
matrix that has the following properties:

• Its row number corresponds to the key that uniquely identifies the
'logically global' object.

• Its column number corresponds to a particular application thread
identifier.

To make implementations of the Thread-Specific Storage pattern
more generic, a pointer to a thread-specific object is stored rather
than storing the object itself. These pointers are often 'loosely typed',
such as C/C++ void *'s, so that they can point to any type of object.
Although loosely typed void *'s are highly flexible, they are hard to
program correctly. Implementation activity 2 (491) therefore
describes several strategies to encapsulate void *'s with less error-
prone, strongly-typed proxy classes.

1.2   *Determine where to store the thread-specific object sets.* In terms of
our two-dimensional matrix analogy, the thread-specific object sets
correspond to matrix columns, which are allocated one per
application thread. Each application thread identifier therefore
designates one column in our conceptual two-dimensional matrix.

Each thread-specific object set can be stored either *externally* to all threads or *internally* to its own thread:

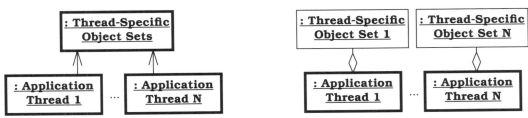

Thread-external Thread-Specific Object Set   Thread-internal Thread-Specific Object Set

There are pros and cons for each strategy:

- *External to all threads.* This strategy maps each application thread's identifier to a global table of thread-specific object sets that are stored externally to all threads. Note that an application thread can obtain its own thread identifier by calling an API in the threading library. Implementations of external thread-specific object sets can therefore readily determine which thread-specific object set is associated with a particular application thread.

  Depending on the implementation of the external table strategy, threads can access thread-specific object sets in other threads. At first, this design may appear to defeat the whole point of the Thread-Specific Storage pattern, because the objects and pointers themselves do not reside in thread-specific storage. It may be useful, however, if the thread-specific storage implementation can recycle keys when they are no longer needed, for example if an application no longer needs to access a global object, such as errno, for some reason.

  A global table facilitates access to all thread-specific object sets from one 'clean-up' thread, to remove the entries corresponding to the recycled key. Recycling keys is particularly useful for Thread-Specific Storage pattern implementations that support only a limited number of keys. For example, Windows NT has a limit of 64 keys per process. Real-time operating systems often support even fewer keys.

  One drawback of storing thread-specific object sets in a global table external to all threads is the increased overhead for accessing each thread-specific object. This overhead stems from the synchronization mechanisms needed to avoid race conditions every time the global table containing all the thread-specific object sets is modified. In particular, serialization is necessary when the key factory creates a new key, because other application threads may be creating keys concurrently. After the appropriate thread-specific object set is identified, however, the application thread need not perform any more locking operations to access a thread-specific object in the set.

- *Internal to each thread.* This strategy requires each thread to store a thread-specific object set with its other internal state, such as its run-time thread stack, program counter, general-purpose registers, and thread identifier. When a thread accesses a thread-specific object, the object is retrieved by using its associated key as an index into the thread's internal thread-specific object set. Unlike the external strategy described above, no serialization is required when the thread-specific object set is stored internally to each thread. In this case all accesses to a thread's internal state occurs within the thread itself.

  Storing the thread-specific object set locally in each thread requires more state per-thread, however, though not necessarily more total memory consumption. As long as the growth in size does not increase the cost of thread creation, context switching or destruction significantly, the internal thread-specific object strategy can be more efficient than the external strategy.

If an operating system provides an adequate thread-specific storage mechanism, thread-specific object sets can be implemented internally to each thread via the native operating system mechanism. If not, thread-specific object sets can be implemented externally using a two-level mapping strategy. In this strategy, one key in the native thread-specific storage mechanism is dedicated to point to a thread-specific object set implemented externally to each thread.

1.3 *Define a data structure to map application thread identifiers to thread-specific object sets.* In terms of the two-dimensional matrix analogy, application thread identifiers map to the columns in the matrix that represent thread-specific object sets.

Application thread identifiers can range in value from very small to very large. A large range in values presents no problem for object sets that reside internally to each thread. In this case the thread identifier is associated implicitly with the corresponding thread-specific object set contained within the thread's state. Thus, there is no need to implement a separate data structure to map application thread identifiers to thread-specific object sets.

For thread-specific object sets residing externally to all threads, however, it may be impractical to have a fixed-size array with an entry for every possible thread identifier value. This is one reason why the two-dimensional matrix analogy is just a conceptual model rather than a realistic implementation strategy. In this case it may be more space efficient to use a dynamic data structure that maps thread identifiers to thread-specific object sets.

For example, a common strategy is to compute a hash function using the thread identifier to obtain an offset to a hash table. The entry at this offset contains a chain of tuples that map thread identifiers to their corresponding thread-specific object sets.

1.4   *Define the data structure that maps keys to thread-specific objects within a thread-specific object set.* In terms of the two-dimensional matrix analogy, this mapping identifies a particular matrix entry (the thread-specific object) according to its row (the key) at a particular column (the thread-specific object set associated with a particular application thread identifier). For both the external and internal thread-specific object set implementations, we must select either a fixed-sized or a variable-sized data structure for this mapping.

The thread-specific object set can be stored in a fixed-size array if the range of thread-specific key values is relatively small and contiguous. The POSIX Pthreads standard [IEEE96], for example, defines a standard macro, `_POSIX_THREAD_KEYS_MAX`, that sets the maximum number of keys supported by a Pthreads implementation. If the size defined by this macro is small and fixed, for example 64 keys, the lookup time can be $O(1)$ by indexing into the thread-specific object set array directly using the key that identifies a thread-specific object.

Some thread-specific storage implementations provide a range of thread-specific keys that is large and nearly unbounded, however. Solaris threads, for example, have no predefined limit on the number of thread-specific storage keys in an application process. Solaris therefore uses a variable-sized data structure, such as a hash table to map keys to thread-specific objects. Although this data structure is more flexible than a fixed-size array, it can increase the overhead of managing the thread-specific object set when a many keys are allocated.

➡   The following code shows how thread-specific object sets can be implemented internally within each thread using a fixed-sized array of thread-specific objects that are stored as void *'s. Using this internal design means that it is not necessary to map application thread identifiers to thread-specific object sets. Instead, we need only provide a data structure that maps keys to thread-specific objects within a thread-specific object set.

All the C code examples shown in this *Implementation* section are adapted from a publicly available user-level library implementation [Mue93] of POSIX Pthreads [IEEE96]. For example, the object_set_ data structure corresponding to implementation activity 1.4 (487) is contained within the following thread_state struct. This struct is used by the Pthreads library implementation to store the state of each thread:

```
struct thread_state {
    // Thread-specific 'object' set implemented via
    // void *'s.
    void *object_set_[_POSIX_THREAD_KEYS_MAX];
    // ... Other thread state.
};
```

In addition to keeping track of the array of pointers to thread-specific storage objects, an instance of thread_state also includes other thread state. This includes a pointer to the thread's stack and space to store thread-specific registers that are saved and restored during a context switch. Our Pthreads implementation also defines several macros to simplify its internal programming:

```
// Note that <errno>'s key number is 0, i.e.,
// it is in first slot of array object_set_.
#define ERRNO_KEY 0
// Define a macro that's used internally to the Pthreads
// implementation to set and get <errno> values.
#define INTERNAL_ERRNO \
        (pthread_self ()->object_set_[ERRNO_KEY])
```

The pthread_self() function used by the INTERNAL_ERRNO macro is an internal implementation subroutine that returns a pointer to the context of the currently active thread.   ❑

1.5 *Define the key factory.* In our two-dimensional matrix analogy, keys correspond to rows in the matrix. The key factory creates a new key that identifies a 'logically global' object (row) uniquely. The state of this object will physically reside in storage that is local to each thread.

For a particular object that is logically global yet physically local to each thread, the same key value k is used by all threads to access their corresponding thread-specific object. The count of the number of keys currently in use can therefore be stored globally to all threads.

➥ The code below illustrates our Pthreads library implementation of the pthread_key_create() key factory. Keys are represented by integer values:

```
typedef int pthread_key_t;
```

A static variable keeps track of the current key count within the thread-specific storage implementation:

```
// All threads share the same key counter.
static pthread_key_t total_keys_ = 0;
```

The total_keys_ variable is incremented automatically every time a new thread-specific key is required, which is equivalent to adding a new row to our conceptual two-dimensional matrix. Next, we define the key factory itself:

```
int pthread_key_create (pthread_key_t *key,
                        void (*thread_exit_hook)(void *)) {
    if (total_keys_ >= _POSIX_THREAD_KEYS_MAX) {
        // Use our internal <errno> macro.
        INTERNAL_ERRNO = ENOMEM;
        return -1;
    }
    thread_exit_hook_[total_keys_] = thread_exit_hook;
    *key = total_keys_++;
    return 0;
}
```

The pthread_key_create() function is a key factory. It allocates a new key that identifies a thread-specific data object uniquely. This function requires no internal synchronization, because it *must* be called with an external lock held, as shown by the TS_Proxy in implementation activity 2.1 (492).

When a key is created, the pthread_key_create() function allows the calling thread to associate a thread_exit_hook with the new key. This hook is a pointer to a function that will be used to delete any dynamically allocated thread-specific objects that are associated with the key. When a thread exits, the Pthreads library calls this function pointer automatically for each key that has registered an exit hook.

To implement this feature, an array of function pointers to 'thread exit hooks' can be stored as a static global variable in the Pthreads library:

```
// Array of exit hook function pointers that can be used
// to deallocate thread-specific data objects.
static void
(*thread_exit_hook_[_POSIX_THREAD_KEYS_MAX]) (void *);
```

The pthread_exit() function shows how exit hook functions are called back just before a thread exits:

```
// Terminate the thread and call thread exit hooks.
void pthread_exit (void *status) {
    // ...
    for (i = 0; i < total_keys_; ++i)
        if (pthread_self ()->object_set_[i]
            && thread_exit_hook_[i])
            // Indirect pointer to function call.
            (*thread_exit_hook_[i])
                (pthread_self ()->object_set_[i]);
    // Terminate the thread and clean up internal
    // resources...
}
```

For each key, an application can either register the same function pointer, a different function pointer, or any combination of function pointers. When each thread exits, the Pthreads implementation calls the same function that was registered when each key was created. Applications often implement thread exit hooks as follows because deleting dynamically allocated thread-specific objects is common:

```
void cleanup_tss_object (void *ptr) {
    // This cast is necessary to invoke the
    // appropriate destructor (if one exists).
    delete (Object_Foo *) ptr;
}                                                        ❏
```

1.6 *Define methods to store and retrieve thread-specific objects from a thread-specific object set.* In terms of the matrix analogy, these two methods set and get the value of matrix entries. The set() method stores a void* at matrix entry [k,t], whereas the get() method retrieves a void* at matrix entry [k,t]. In thread-specific storage implementations, k is passed as a key argument and t is the implicit thread identifier returned by a call to pthread_self().

➥ The pthread_setspecific() function is a set() method that stores a void* using the key passed by the client application thread that calls it:

```
int pthread_setspecific (pthread_key_t key, void *value) {
    if (key < 0 || key >= total_keys) {
        // Use our internal <errno> macro.
        INTERNAL_ERRNO = EINVAL;
        return -1;
    }
    // Store value into appropriate slot in the thread-
    // specific object set.
    pthread_self ()->object_set_[key] = value;
    return 0;
}
```

Similarly, the pthread_getspecific() function retrieves a void* using the key passed by the client application thread:

```
int pthread_getspecific (pthread_key_t key, void **value){
    if (key < 0 || key >= total_keys) {
        // Use our internal <errno> macro.
        INTERNAL_ERRNO = EINVAL;
        return -1;
    }
    *value = pthread_self ()->object_set_[key];
    return 0;
}
```

In this implementation, neither function requires any locks to access its thread-specific object set, because the set resides internally within the state of each thread.   ❏

2   *Implement thread-specific object proxies.* In theory, the thread-specific object sets written in C above are sufficient to implement the Thread-Specific Storage pattern. In practice, however, it is undesirable to rely on such low-level C function APIs for two reasons:

   • Although the thread-specific storage APIs of popular threading libraries, such as POSIX Pthreads, Solaris threads, and Win32 threads, are similar, their semantics differ subtly. For example, Win32 threads, unlike POSIX Pthreads and Solaris threads, do not provide a reliable way to deallocate objects allocated in thread-specific storage when a thread exits. In Solaris threads, conversely, there is no API to delete a key. These diverse semantics make it hard to write code that runs portably on all three platforms.

- The POSIX Pthreads, Solaris, and Win32 thread-specific storage APIs store pointers to thread-specific objects as void*'s. Although this approach provides maximal flexibility, it is error-prone because void*'s eliminate type-safety.

To overcome these limitations the Thread-Specific Storage pattern defines a thread-specific object proxy. Each proxy applies the Proxy pattern [GoF95] [POSA1] to define an object that acts as a 'surrogate' for a thread-specific object. Application threads that invoke methods on a proxy appear to access an ordinary object, when in fact the proxy forwards the methods to a thread-specific object. This design shields applications from knowing when or how thread-specific storage is being used. It also allows applications to use higher-level, type-safe, and platform-independent wrapper facades (47) to access thread-specific objects managed by lower-level C function APIs.

The implementation of thread-specific object proxies can be divided into three sub-activities:

2.1 *Define the thread-specific object proxy interfaces.* For the thread-specific object there are two strategies for designing a proxy interface, *polymorphism* or *parameterized types*:

- *Polymorphism.* In this strategy an abstract proxy class declares and implements the data structures and methods that every proxy supports. Examples include the key that the thread-specific object set associates with a particular 'logically global' object, or the lock needed to avoid race conditions when creating this key.

  Access to the concrete methods offered by thread-specific objects is provided by subclasses of the general proxy, with one class for each type of thread-specific object. Before forwarding client application requests to the corresponding methods in the thread-specific object, a proxy first retrieves an object pointer from the thread-specific object set via the key stored in the proxy.

  Using polymorphism to implement a proxy is a common strategy [POSA1]. It can incur overhead, however, due to the extra level of indirection caused by dynamic binding.

- *Parameterized types.* In this strategy the proxy can be parameterized by the types of objects that will reside in thread-specific storage. As with the polymorphism strategy described above, the proxy mechanism only declares and implements the data structures and methods every proxy supports. It also performs all necessary operations on the thread-specific object set before invoking the designated method on the thread-specific object. Parameterization can remove the indirection associated with polymorphism, which can improve the proxy's performance.

A key design problem that arises when using the parameterized type strategy is selecting a convenient mechanism to access the methods of thread-specific objects encapsulated by a proxy. In particular, different types of thread-specific objects have different interfaces. The mechanism for accessing these objects cannot therefore define any concrete service methods. This differs from the polymorphism strategy described above.

One way to address this problem is to use *smart pointers* [Mey95], such as operator->, also known as the C++ arrow operator [Str97]. This operator allow client application threads to access the proxy as if they were accessing the thread-specific object directly. The operator-> method receives special treatment from the C++ compiler. It first obtains a pointer to the appropriate type of thread-specific object, then delegates the original method invoked on it.

Another generic way to access the methods of thread-specific objects is to apply the Extension Interface pattern (141). This solution introduces a generic method for the proxy that allows clients to retrieve the concrete interfaces supported by the configured thread-specific object.

➡   In our example we use C++ parameterized types to define a type-safe template that applications can use to instantiate thread-specific object proxies with concrete thread-specific objects:

```
template <class TYPE>
class TS_Proxy {
public:
    // Constructor and destructor.
    TS_Proxy ();
    ~TS_Proxy ();

    // Define the C++ '->' and '*' operators to access
    // the thread-specific <TYPE> object.
    TYPE *operator-> () const;
    TYPE &operator* () const;
private:
    // Key that uniquely identifies the 'logically
    // global' object that 'physically' resides locally
    // in thread-specific storage.
    mutable pthread_key_t key_;

    // "First time in" flag.
    mutable bool once_;

    // Avoid race conditions during initialization.
    mutable Thread_Mutex keylock_;

    // A static cleanup hook method that deletes
    // dynamically allocated memory.
    static void cleanup_hook (void *ptr);
};
```

This thread-specific proxy template is parameterized by the type of object that will be accessed via thread-specific storage. In addition, it defines the C++ smart pointer operator-> to access a thread-specific object of type TYPE.   ❏

2.2 *Implement the creation and destruction of the thread-specific object proxy.* Regardless of whether we apply the polymorphism or parameterized type strategy to define the thread-specific object proxy, we must manage the creation and destruction of thread-specific object proxies.

➡ The constructor for our thread-specific object proxy template class is minimal, it simply initializes the object's data members:

```
template <class TYPE>
TS_Proxy<TYPE>::TS_Proxy (): once_ (false), key_ (0) { }
```

In general, a proxy's constructor does not allocate the key or a new thread-specific object instance in the constructor for two reasons:

- *Thread-specific storage semantics.* A thread-specific object proxy is often created by a thread, for example the application's main thread, that is different from thread(s) that use the proxy. Thus, there is no benefit from pre-initializing a new thread-specific object in its constructor because this instance will only be accessible by the thread that created it.

- *Deferred creation.* On some operating systems, keys are limited resources and should not be allocated until absolutely necessary. Their creation should therefore be deferred until the first time a method of the proxy is invoked. In our example implementation this point of time occurs in the operator-> method.

The destructor for the thread-specific object proxy presents us with several tricky design issues. The 'obvious' solution is to release the key that was allocated by the key factory. There are several problems with this approach, however:

- *Non-portability.* It is hard to write a proxy destructor that releases keys *portably*. For example, Solaris threads, unlike Win32 and POSIX Pthreads, lacks an API to release keys that are not needed.

- *Race conditions.* One reason that Solaris threads do not provide an API to release keys is that it hard to implement efficiently and correctly. The problem is that each thread maintains independent copies of the objects referenced by a key. Only after all threads have exited and the memory reclaimed can a key be released safely.

As a result of these problems the proxy's destructor is generally a 'no-op'. This means that we do not recycle keys in this implementation. In lieu of a destructor, therefore, we implement a thread-exit hook function, as discussed in implementation activity 1.5 (489). This hook is dispatched automatically by the thread-specific storage implementation when a thread exits. It deletes the thread-specific object, thereby ensuring that the destructor of the object is invoked.

➡   The destructor of our `TS_Proxy` class is a 'no-op':

```
template <class TYPE>
TS_Proxy<TYPE>::~TS_Proxy () { }
```

To ensure the right destructor is called, the thread-exit hook casts its `ptr` argument to a pointer to the appropriate `TYPE` before deleting it:

```
template <class TYPE>
void TS_Proxy<TYPE>::cleanup_hook (void *ptr) {
    // This cast invokes the destructor (if one exists).
    delete (TYPE *) ptr;
}
```

Note that the `cleanup_hook()` is defined as a `static` method in the `TS_Proxy` class. By defining this method as `static`, it can be passed as a pointer-to-function thread exit hook to `pthread_key_create()`.   ❑

2.3   *Implement the access to the thread-specific object.* As we discussed earlier, there are two general strategies—*polymorphism* and *parameterized types*—for accessing the methods of a thread-specific object that is represented by a proxy.

When using the polymorphism strategy, the interface of each concrete proxy must include all methods offered by the thread-specific object that is represented by this class. Method implementations in a concrete proxy generally perform four steps:

- Create a new key, if no such thread-specific object has been created yet. We must avoid race conditions by preventing multiple threads from creating a new key for the same `TYPE` of thread-specific object simultaneously. We can resolve this problem by applying the Double-Checked Locking Optimization pattern (365).

- The method must next use the key stored by the proxy to get the thread-specific object via its thread-specific object set.

- If the object does not yet exist, it is created 'on-demand'.

- The requested operation is forwarded to the thread-specific object. Any operation results are returned to the client application thread.

To avoid repeating this code within each proxy method, we recommend introducing a helper method in the thread-specific object proxy base class that implements these general steps.

When using parameterized types to instantiate a generic proxy, the smart pointer and Extension Interface pattern (365) strategies described in implementation activity 2.1 (492) can be applied to implement a general access mechanism for any thread-specific object's methods. Analogously to the polymorphism strategy, the general access mechanism must follow the implementation steps described above.

➡ By using the parameterized type strategy and overloading the C++ arrow operator, operator->, applications can invoke methods on instances of TS_Proxy as if they were invoking a method on an instance of the TYPE parameter. The C++ arrow operator controls all access to the thread-specific object of class TYPE. It performs most of the work, as follows:

```
template <class TYPE>
TYPE *TS_Proxy<TYPE>::operator->() const {
    TYPE *tss_data = 0;
    // Use the Double-Checked Locking Optimization
    // pattern to avoid excessive locking.
    if (!once_) {
        // Use Scoped Locking idiom to ensure <keylock_>
        // is acquired to serialize critical section.
        Guard <Thread_Mutex> guard (keylock_);
        if (!once_) {
            pthread_key_create (&key_,
                                &cleanup_hook);
            // Must come last so that other threads
            // don't use the key until it's created.
            once_ = true;
        }
        // <Guard> destructor releases the lock.
    }
    // Get data from thread-specific storage. Note that no
    // locks are required, because this thread's own copy
    // of the thread-specific object will be accessed.
    pthread_getspecific (key_, (void **) &tss_data);

    // Check if it's the first time in for this thread.
    if (tss_data == 0) {
        // Allocate memory dynamically off the heap,
        tss_data = new TYPE;
        // Store pointer in thread-specific storage.
        pthread_setspecific (key_, (void *) tss_data);
    }
    return tss_data;
}
```

The `TS_Proxy` template is a proxy that transforms ordinary C++ classes into type-safe classes whose instances reside in thread-specific storage. It combines the `operator->` method with C++ features, such as templates, inlining, and overloading. In addition, it uses common concurrency control patterns and idioms, such as Double-Checked Locking Optimization (353), Scoped Locking (325), and Strategized Locking (333).

The Double-Checked Locking Optimization pattern is used in `operator->` to test the `once_` flag twice. Although multiple threads could access the same instance of `TS_Proxy` simultaneously, only one thread can validly create a key via the `pthread_key_create()` method. All threads then use this key to access their associated thread-specific object of the parameterized class `TYPE`. The `operator->` method therefore uses a `keylock_` of type `Thread_Mutex` to ensure that only one thread at a time executes `pthread_key_create()`.

After `key_` is created, no other locking is needed to access thread-specific objects, because the `pthread_getspecific()` and `pthread_setspecific()` functions both retrieve the thread-specific object of class `TYPE` from the state of the client application thread, which is independent from other threads. In addition to reducing locking overhead, the implementation of class `TS_Proxy` shown above shields application code from the fact that objects are local to the calling thread.   ❏

The implementation of the extension interface and polymorphic proxy are similar to the generic smart pointer approach shown above. The polymorphic proxy approach simply forwards to a method of the thread-specific object and returns the result. Similarly, the extension interface approach returns an extension interface from the thread-specific object and passes this back to the client.

Example Resolved   The following application is similar to our original logging server from the *Example* section. The `logger()` function shown below is the entry point to each thread that has its own unique connection to a remote client application. The main difference is that the `logger()` function uses the `TS_Proxy` template class defined in implementation activity 2.3 (496) to access the `errno` value.

This template is instantiated by the following Error_Logger class:

```
class Error_Logger { // Define a simple logging API.
public:
    // Return the most recent error residing in thread-
    // specific storage.
    int last_error ();

    // Format and display a logging message.
    void log (const char *format, ...);
    // ...
};
```

The Error_Logger class defines the type of the 'logically' global, but 'physically' thread-specific, logger object, which is created via the following TS_Proxy thread-specific object proxy template:

```
static TS_Proxy<Error_Logger> my_logger;
```

The logger() function is called by each connection handling thread in the logging server. We use the SOCK_Stream class described in the Wrapper Facade pattern (47) to read data from the network connection, instead of accessing the lower-level C Socket API directly:

```
static void *logger (void *arg) {
    // Network connection stream.
    SOCK_Stream *stream =
        static_cast <SOCK_Stream *> arg;

    // Read a logging record from the network connection
    // until the connection is closed.
    for (;;) {
        char log_record[MAXREC];

        // Check to see if the <recv> call failed, which
        // is signified by a return value of -1.
        if (stream->recv (log_record, MAXREC) == -1) {
            if (my_logger->last_error () == EWOULDBLOCK)
                // Sleep a bit and try again.
                sleep (1);
            else // Record error result.
                my_logger->log
                    ("recv failed, errno = %d",
                     my_logger->last_error ());
        } else // Other processing.
    }
}
```

Consider the call to the my_logger->last_error() method above. The C++ compiler generates code that replaces this call with two method calls. The first is a call to the TS_Proxy::operator->, which returns the appropriate `Error_Logger` instance residing in thread-specific storage. The compiler then generates a second method call to the `last_error()` method of the `Error_Logger` object returned by the previous call. In this case, `TS_Proxy` behaves as a proxy that allows an application to access and manipulate the thread-specific error value as if it were an ordinary C++ object.

Variants   Starting with JDK 1.2, Java supports the Thread-Specific Storage pattern via class `java.lang.ThreadLocal`. An object of class `java.lang.ThreadLocal` is a thread-specific object proxy, which corresponds to one row in our two-dimensional matrix analogy. `ThreadLocal` objects are often created as static variables in a central location so that they are broadly visible. A `ThreadLocal` internal hash table maintains the entries for the thread-specific objects, one per-thread. These entries are of type `Object`, which means that the hash table does not know the concrete type of the objects it holds. Applications must therefore maintain that knowledge and perform the necessary downcasting, which has the pros and cons discussed in implementation activities 1.1 (484) and 2 (491).

A Java application thread can set the value of a `ThreadLocal` object `foo` by calling `foo.set(newValue)`. The `foo` object of type `ThreadLocal` uses the thread identifier to return the thread's current object entry from the hash table. The hash table is a normal data structure, but by calling `Collections.synchronizedMap(hashtable)` wraps a thread-safe layer around `hashtable`. This feature combines the Decorator [GoF95] and Thread-Safe Interface patterns (345) to ensure that an existing Java collection will be serialized correctly.

The class `java.lang.InheritableThreadLocal` is an extension of the `ThreadLocal` class. This subclass allows a child thread to inherit all thread-specific objects from its parent thread, with values preset to its current parent's values.

Known Uses   Widely-used examples of the Thread-Specific Storage pattern are **operating system platforms**, such as Win32 and Solaris, that support the `errno` mechanism. The following definition of `errno` is defined by Solaris in `<errno.h>`:

```
#define errno (*(___errno()))
```

The ___errno() function invoked by this macro can be implemented as follows, based upon the low-level C thread-specific storage functions we described in implementation activity 1 (484):

```
int *___errno () {
    // Solaris ensures that static synchronization
    // objects are always initialized properly.
    static pthread_mutex_t keylock;
    static pthread_key_t key;
    static int once;
    int *error_number = 0;

    if (once) {
        // Apply Double-Checked Locking Optimization.
        pthread_mutex_lock (&keylock);
        if (once) {
            // Note that we pass in the <free> function
            // so the <error_number> memory will be
            // deallocated when this thread exits!
            pthread_key_create (&key, free);
            once = 1;
        }
        pthread_mutex_unlock (&keylock);
    }
    // Use <key> to retrieve <error_number> from the
    // thread-specific object set.
    pthread_getspecific (key, &error_number);
    if (error_number == 0) {
        // If we get here, then <error_number> has not
        // been created in this thread yet. Thus, we'll
        // create it and store it into the appropriate
        // location in the thread-specific object set.
        error_number = (int *) malloc (sizeof (int));
        pthread_setspecific (key, error_number);
    }
    return error_number;
}
```

The Win32 GetLastError() and SetLastError() functions implement the Thread-Specific Storage pattern in a similar manner.

In the **Win32** operating system API, windows are owned by threads [Pet95]. Each thread that owns a window has a private message queue where the operating system enqueues user interface events. Event processing API calls then dequeue the next message on the calling thread's message queue residing in thread-specific storage.

The **Active Template Library** from COM uses the Extension Interface approach to implement the Thread-Specific Storage pattern.

OpenGL [NDW93] is a C API for rendering three-dimensional graphics. The program renders graphics in terms of polygons that are described by making repeated calls to the glVertex() function to pass each vertex of the polygon to the library. State variables set before the vertices are passed to the library determine precisely what OpenGL draws as it receives the vertices. This state is stored as encapsulated global variables within the OpenGL library or on the graphics card itself. On the Win32 platform, the OpenGL library maintains a unique set of state variables in thread-specific storage for each thread using the library.

Thread-specific storage is used within the **ACE** framework [Sch97] to implement its error handling scheme, which is similar to the approach described in the *Example Resolved* section. In addition, ACE implements the type-safe thread-specific object proxy using C++ templates, as described in implementation activity 2 (491). The ACE thread-specific storage template class is called ACE_TSS.

Local telephone directory services. A real-life example of the Thread-Specific Storage pattern is found in telephone directory services. For example, in the United States, the 'logically global' number 411 can be used to connect with the local directory assistance operator for a particular area code or region.

Consequences   There are four **benefits** of using the Thread-Specific Storage pattern:

Efficiency. The Thread-Specific Storage pattern can be implemented so that no locking is necessary to access thread-specific data. For example, by placing errno into thread-specific storage, each thread can reliably and efficiently set and test the completion status of methods called within that thread, without using complex synchronization protocols. This design eliminates locking overhead for data shared within a thread, which is faster than acquiring and releasing a mutex [EKBF+92].

Reusability. Applying the Wrapper Facade pattern (47) and decoupling the reusable the Thread-Specific Storage pattern code from application-specific classes can shield developers from subtle and non-portable thread-specific key creation and allocation logic. For example, the Double-Checked Locking Optimization pattern (365) can be integrated into a reusable thread-specific object proxy component to prevent race conditions automatically.

Ease of use. When encapsulated with wrapper facades, thread-specific storage is relatively straightforward for application programmers to use. For example, thread-specific storage can be hidden completely at the source-code level by abstractions, such as the thread-specific object proxy templates, or macros, such as `errno`. Changing a class to or from a thread-specific class therefore simply requires changing the way in which an object of the class is defined.

Portability. Thread-specific storage is available on most multi-threaded operating systems platforms. It can be implemented conveniently on platforms that lack it, such as VxWorks or pSoS. Furthermore, thread-specific object proxies can encapsulate platform-dependent operations behind a uniform and portable interface. Porting an application to another thread library, such as the TLS interfaces in Win32, therefore only requires changing the `TS_Proxy` class, rather than application code that uses the class.

However, the following are **liabilities** of using the Thread-Specific Storage pattern:

It encourages the use of (thread-specific) global objects. Many applications do not require multiple threads to access thread-specific data via a common access point. In this case, data should be stored so that only the thread owning the data can access it.

➡ Consider our logging server that uses a pool of threads to handle incoming logging records from clients. In addition to writing the logging records to persistent storage, each thread can log the number and type of services it performs. This logging mechanism could be accessed as a global `Error_Logger` object via thread-specific storage. However, a simpler approach, though potentially less efficient and more obtrusive, is to represent each logger thread as an active object (369), with an instance of the `Error_Logger` stored as a data member rather than in thread-specific storage. In this case, the `Error_Logger` can be accessed as a data member by active object methods or passed as a parameter to all external methods or functions called by the active object. ❏

It obscures the structure of the system. The use of thread-specific storage potentially makes an application harder to understand, by obscuring the relationships between its components. For example, it is not obvious from examining the source code of our logging server that each thread has its own instance of Error_Logger, because my_logger resembles an ordinary global object. In some cases it may be possible to eliminate the need for thread-specific storage, by representing relationships between components explicitly via containment or aggregation relationships.

It restricts implementation options. Not all languages support parameterized types or smart pointers, and not all application classes offer Extension Interfaces (141). 'Elegant' implementation solutions for the thread-specific object proxy therefore cannot be applied for all systems. When this occurs, less elegant and less efficient solutions, such as polymorphism or low-level functions, must be used to implement the Thread-Specific Storage pattern.

See Also   Thread-specific objects such as errno are often used as per-thread singletons [GoF95]. Not all uses of thread-specific storage are singletons, however, because a thread can have multiple instances of a type allocated from thread-specific storage. For example, each instance of an active object (369) implemented via an ACE_Task [Sch97] stores a thread-specific cleanup hook.

The Thread-Specific Storage pattern is related to the Data Ownership pattern [McK95], where a thread mediates client access to an object.

Credits   Tim Harrison and Nat Pryce were co-authors of the original version of the Thread-Specific Storage pattern. Thanks to Tom Cargill for comments on the original version of this pattern.

6 Weaving the Patterns Together

*"The limits of my language
are the limits of my world."*

Ludwig Wittgenstein

*"No pattern is an island, entire of itself; every pattern is
a piece of the continent, a part of the main."*

Paraphrase of John Donne's 'Devotions'

The patterns in this book can be applied individually, each helping to resolve a particular set of forces related to concurrency and networking. However, just using these patterns in a stand-alone way limits their power unnecessarily, because real-world software systems cannot be developed effectively by resolving problems in isolation.

To increase the power of this book, this chapter shows how the patterns presented in Chapter 2 connect, complement, and complete each other to form the basis of a pattern language for building high-quality distributed object computing middleware, and concurrent and networked applications. In addition, we outline how many of these patterns can be applied outside the context of concurrency and networking.

6.1   From Individual Patterns to Pattern Languages

The patterns presented in Chapter 2 are described in a self-contained manner, as are the patterns in [POSA1]. For example, the patterns' contexts are expressed as generally as possible, to avoid limiting their applicability to a particular configuration of other problems, patterns, or designs. The patterns can therefore be applied whenever a problem arises that they address. Moreover, neither the patterns' solution descriptions nor their implementation guidelines focus on the solutions of similar problems described by other patterns. Each pattern references only those patterns that help implement its own solution structure and dynamics.

No Pattern is an Island

Unfortunately, focusing on individual patterns does not support the construction of real-world software systems effectively. For example, many inter-related design problems and forces must be resolved when developing concurrent and networked systems, as shown in the Web server example described in Chapter 1, *Concurrent and Networked Objects*. These relationships must be considered when addressing key design and implementation issues. Regardless of their individual utility, therefore, stand-alone patterns can only resolve small problems in isolation, as they do not consider the larger context in which they apply.

Even if stand-alone patterns were somehow connected, giving them the potential to solve larger problems, it might be hard to extract these relationships from their descriptions. For example, if two pattern descriptions reference each other, it may not be obvious when one pattern should be applied before the other. When developing software applications and systems with patterns, however, the order in which the patterns are applied may be crucial for their successful integration [Bus00a].

The importance of proper ordering is particularly relevant for *architectural patterns*, which introduce a structure that defines the base-line architecture for an entire software system. Each component in such a structure is 'complex' by itself, and often these components can be implemented using other design patterns. It is therefore crucial to express the precise relationships between such patterns to determine which pattern to apply first and which later.

For example, the Reactor architectural pattern (179) introduces a participant—event handler—whose concrete implementations may define their own concurrency model. The discussion of an event handler's implementation in the *Variants* section of the Reactor pattern therefore references applicable concurrency patterns, including Active Object (369) and Monitor Object (399).

Similarly, to illustrate which particular types of event handlers are useful for networked applications, the Reactor's implementation guidelines reference the Acceptor-Connector pattern (285). In turn, this pattern introduces a participant—the service handler—whose concrete implementations may also define their own concurrency model. The implementation guidelines for service handlers thus reference the Active Object and Monitor Object patterns again. This somewhat convoluted set of inter-relationships among the various patterns participants is illustrated in the figure below:

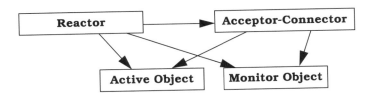

When reading the Reactor pattern description in isolation, however, it is not obvious how to apply Active Object or Monitor Object effectively in the presence of Acceptor-Connector, which may also use these patterns. For example, the Reactor pattern does not specify whether or not a Reactor should apply Active Object to implement a particular type of event handler. Nor does it specify whether an Acceptor-Connector that uses the Reactor should use Monitor Object to implement its acceptors, connectors, and service handlers.

In general, not all possible combinations of these four patterns are useful. However, because each pattern description is self-contained and independent of the others, it is hard to extract the useful combinations from the individual pattern descriptions.

Towards Pattern Languages

To support the development a particular family of software systems or application frameworks [POSA1], a broader viewpoint should be applied to the set of available patterns. In particular, patterns should not be considered solely as islands. They should instead be woven into networks of interrelated patterns that define a process for resolving software development problems systematically [Cope96] [Gab96] [Cope97]. We call these *pattern languages*.

Pattern languages are not formal languages, although they do provide a vocabulary for talking about particular problems [SFJ96]. Together, patterns and pattern languages help developers communicate architectural knowledge, learn a new design paradigm or architectural style, and elude traps and pitfalls that have been avoided traditionally only through costly experience [PLoPD1].

One or more patterns define the 'entry point' of a pattern language and address the coarsest-grained problems that must be resolved when developing a particular type of application or part of an application. When reading this book, you may identify the *architectural* patterns as those addressing coarse-grained problems in software architecture. Each entry point pattern specifies which other patterns should be used to resolve sub-problems of the original problem, as well as the order in which to apply these other patterns.

The referenced patterns therefore complete these 'larger' patterns, which in turn specify useful combinations of the 'smaller' patterns in the presence of a particular problem. In software architecture, these smaller patterns often correspond to *design* patterns. The smaller patterns may then define how to apply other patterns in their own solutions to resolve additional sub-problems. This iterative decomposition of larger into smaller patterns continues until all problems in a given domain are addressed by a designated pattern.

As pattern writers become more familiar with their domain, therefore, they should strive to connect patterns that can complement and 'complete' each other [AIS77]. By applying one pattern at a time [Ale79] [Bus00b] and following the relationships between the patterns, it becomes possible to generate high-quality software architectures and designs. The resulting pattern language is 'synergistic', that is, it is more than the sum of its constituent patterns. For example, the connected patterns help to produce better system architectures by resolving groups of problems that arise during software development. Each solution builds upon the solutions of related problems that are addressed by patterns in the language.

To illustrate this iterative decomposition process, the patterns from the Reactor (179) example shown earlier in this chapter can be integrated to form a mini pattern language. Rather than suggesting the Acceptor-Connector pattern (285) as an option to implement a Reactor's event handlers, we could *require* that it be applied. In a Reactor's architectural structure there could therefore be three types of event handlers—acceptors, connectors and service handlers—where the latter can be implemented using a concurrency model, such as Active Object (369) and Monitor Object (399):

Refactoring the relationships between these four patterns in this manner has two effects on a Reactor implementation:

- It ensures that implementors of the Reactor pattern specify the 'right' types of event handlers—acceptors, connectors, and service handlers—associated with the Acceptor-Connector pattern. Relating the Active Object and Monitor Object patterns with Acceptor-Connector also clarifies which type of event handler—the service handlers—is most useful for introducing concurrency.

- The references to the concurrency patterns can be removed from the Reactor pattern and need only appear in the Acceptor-Connector pattern. This simplifies the relationships between the four patterns and emphasizes the important ones.

This mini pattern language we have created with the Reactor, Acceptor-Connector, Active Object, and Monitor Object patterns helps to generate good software architectures, because common implementation mistakes that might occur if the Reactor or one of the other patterns was applied in isolation can be avoided. Refactoring the patterns' relationships also helps to improve our collective understanding of how the four patterns connect to a broader pattern language that can generate larger architectural structures.

6.2   A Pattern Language for Middleware and Applications

In this section we want to explore the relationships that exist between the patterns described in this book. Our goal is to define the foundation of a pattern language that supports the development of concurrent and networked software systems more effectively than by merely applying the patterns in isolation.

We apply a two-step process to connect the patterns in this book into a pattern language:

- *Identify pattern relationships*. Firstly we examine the self-contained descriptions of each pattern to determine which relationships listed in the patterns should be kept and which should be ignored. In particular, we only consider the 'uses' relationship among the patterns and ignore all others, such as the 'is used by' and transitive relationships. We also include all optional uses of other patterns into our set of relationships.

- *Define pattern ordering*. Secondly, based on the remaining relationships, we then define the order of the patterns in the language, that is, which patterns are entry points, which patterns follow, and which patterns are leafs. In our language, we define the patterns with the broadest scope—the architectural patterns—as its entry points. The 'uses' relationships then define the ordering between the patterns.

The Pattern Language in Detail

By following the strategy outlined above, we connect the patterns described in this book to a pattern language. This language is summarized in the following diagram. We recommend that you refer back to this diagram as you are reading the pattern language entries.

If a pattern uses another pattern in its implementation, it points to the pattern with an arrow. 'Duplicate' entries for patterns that are frequently referenced by other patterns avoid having too many crossed relationships. Architectural patterns are shaded to indicate where the language 'begins'.

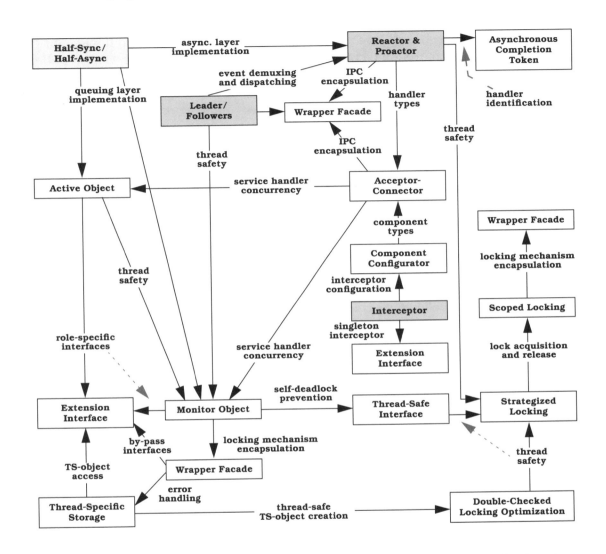

Half-Sync/   The *Half-Sync/Half-Async* architectural pattern (423) structures
Half-Async   concurrent systems that can be implemented using a mixture of
                  asynchronous and synchronous service processing.

                  The pattern introduces two designated layers for asynchronous and
                  synchronous service processing, plus a queuing layer that allows
                  services to exchange messages and data between the other two layers.

If the operating system supports sophisticated asynchronous I/O operations, the *Proactor* pattern (215) can be used to implement the asynchronous service processing layer. The *Active Object* pattern (369) and *Monitor Object* pattern (399) can help implement the queueing layer. The Half-Sync/Half-Reactive variant of the Half-Sync/Half-Async pattern can be implemented by combining the *Reactor* pattern (179) with the *Active Object* pattern (369).

Leader/
Followers
The *Leader/Followers* architectural pattern (447) provides a concurrency model that allows multiple threads to take turns sharing a set of event sources, to detect, demultiplex, dispatch, and process service requests that occur on the event sources.

At the heart of this pattern is a thread pool mechanism. It allows multiple threads to coordinate themselves and protects critical sections involved with detecting, demultiplexing, dispatching, and processing events. One thread at a time—the *leader*—is allowed to wait for an event to occur on a set of event sources. Meanwhile other threads—the *followers*—can queue awaiting their turn to become the leader.

When the current leader thread detects an event from the event source set, it first promotes a follower thread to become the new leader. Then it plays the role of a processing thread, demultiplexing and dispatching the event to a designated event handler. The event handler in turn performs the required application-specific event processing. Multiple processing threads can run concurrently while the leader thread waits for new events on the set of event sources shared by the threads. After handling its event, a processing thread reverts to a follower role and waits to become the leader thread again.

The *Monitor Object* pattern (399) can be used to implement the thread pool mechanism that allows multiple threads to coordinate themselves. The *Reactor* (179) or *Proactor* (215) patterns can be used to demultiplex and dispatch events from the set of event sources to their designated event handlers.

Reactor
The *Reactor* architectural pattern (179) structures event-driven applications, particularly servers, that receive requests from multiple clients concurrently but process them iteratively.

The pattern introduces two co-operating components, a reactor and a synchronous event demultiplexer. These demultiplex and dispatch incoming requests to a set of event handlers, which define the application's services that process these requests. Requests from clients are received and responses are sent through handles, which encapsulate transport endpoints in a networked system.

In general there are three types of event handlers—acceptors, connectors, and service handlers—as specified by the *Acceptor-Connector* pattern (285). The handles that encapsulate the IPC mechanisms are often implemented according to the *Wrapper Facade* design pattern (47). A thread-safe reactor can be implemented using the *Strategized Locking* pattern (333). The timer queue mechanism of the Reactor pattern can use the *Asynchronous Completion Token* pattern (261) to identify which event handler has expired.

Proactor   The *Proactor* architectural pattern (215) structures event-driven applications, particularly servers, that receive and process requests from multiple clients concurrently.

Application services are split into two parts:

- Operations that execute asynchronously, for example to receive client requests.

- Corresponding completion handlers that process the results of these asynchronous operations, for example a particular client request.

Asynchronous operations are executed by an asynchronous operation processor, which inserts the results of these asynchronous operations—the completion events—into a completion event queue. A proactor then removes the completion events from the completion event queue using an asynchronous event demultiplexer, then dispatches them on the appropriate completion handler to finish processing the service. Requests from clients are received and responses are sent via handles, which encapsulate transport endpoints in a networked system.

To support an effective demultiplexing and dispatching of completion events from asynchronous operation to their designated completion handler, the asynchronous operation processor and the proactor can both use the *Asynchronous Completion Token* pattern (261) to identify which asynchronous operation has finished and which completion handler should process its results. As with the Reactor pattern, there are three general types of completion handlers—acceptors, connectors, and service handlers—as specified by the *Acceptor-Connector* pattern (285). The asynchronous operation processor, as well as the handles that encapsulate the IPC mechanisms, can be implemented according to the *Wrapper Facade* pattern (47). A thread-safe proactor can be implemented using the *Strategized Locking* pattern (333).

Interceptor   The *Interceptor* architectural pattern (109) allows functionality to be added to an application framework transparently. This functionality is invoked automatically when framework-internal events occur.

The Interceptor pattern specifies and exposes an interceptor interface callback for selected event types internal to a framework. Applications can derive concrete interceptors from this interface to implement out-of-band functionality that processes occurrences of the corresponding event type in an application-specific manner. A dispatcher is provided for every interceptor, so that applications can register their concrete interceptors with the framework. The framework calls back the concrete interceptors via their associated dispatchers whenever the designated event occurs. Concrete interceptors that must modify framework behavior during their event processing can leverage context objects, which provide controlled access to the framework's internal state. Context objects are passed to concrete interceptors when they are dispatched by the framework.

The *Extension Interface* pattern (141) can be used to help avoid implementing multiple concrete interceptors. Instead, a single interceptor implements multiple interfaces, each corresponding to a particular concrete interceptor. Similarly, the *Component Configurator* pattern (75) can be used to link concrete interceptors into a concrete framework dynamically at run-time.

Acceptor-   The *Acceptor-Connector* design pattern (285) decouples connection
Connector   establishment and service initialization from service processing in a networked system.

This pattern introduces three types of components:

*   Service handlers define one half of an end-to-end service in a networked system and process requests from their connected remote peer.

- Acceptors perform passive connection establishment, accept connection requests from remote peers, and initialize a service handler to process subsequent service requests from these peers.

- Connectors perform active connection establishment and initiate a connection to a remote component on behalf of a service handler. This then communicates with the remote component once the connection is established.

Acceptors, connectors, and service handlers send and receive requests from peers via handles, which encapsulate transport endpoints in a networked system.

To process multiple service requests simultaneously, service handlers can be implemented using the concurrency models defined by the *Active Object* (369) and *Monitor Object* (399) patterns. The handles used to access the underlying operating system IPC mechanisms can be implemented via the *Wrapper Facade* pattern (47).

Component Configurator The *Component Configurator* design pattern (75) allows a system to link and unlink its component implementations at run-time without having to modify, recompile, or statically relink the application. It also supports the reconfiguration of components into different processes without having to shut down and re-start running processes.

In this pattern a component defines a uniform interface for configuring and controlling a particular type of application service or functionality that it provides. Concrete components implement the interface in an application-specific manner. Applications or administrators can use component interfaces to initialize, suspend, resume, and terminate their concrete components dynamically, as well as to obtain run-time information about each configured concrete component. Concrete components are packaged into a suitable unit of configuration, such as a dynamically linked library (DLL) or shared library, that can be linked and unlinked in and out of an application dynamically under control of a component configurator. This uses a component repository to keep track of all concrete components configured into an application.

Components configured into a networked system using Component Configurator can be acceptors, connectors, and service handlers as defined by the *Acceptor-Connector* pattern (285), or interceptors, as defined by the *Interceptor* pattern (109).

Active Object   The *Active Object* design pattern (369) decouples method execution from method invocation to enhance concurrency and simplify synchronized access to objects that reside in their own threads of control.

A proxy represents the interface of an active object and a servant provides the object's implementation. Both the proxy and the servant run in separate threads, so that method invocations and method executions can run concurrently. At run-time the proxy transforms the client's method invocations into method requests, which are stored in an activation list by a scheduler. The scheduler's event loop runs continuously in the same thread as the servant, dequeueing method requests from the activation list and dispatching them on the servant. Clients can obtain the result of a method's execution via a future returned by the proxy when the method was invoked.

The *Extension Interface* pattern (141) helps provide role-specific proxies, so that clients access only those services of an active object that they require. The *Monitor Object* pattern (399) can be used to implement a thread-safe activation list.

Monitor Object   The *Monitor Object* design pattern (399) synchronizes concurrent method execution to ensure that only one method at a time runs within an object. It also allows an object's methods to schedule their execution sequences cooperatively.

Clients can only access the functions defined by a monitor object via its synchronized methods. To prevent race conditions involving monitor object state, just one synchronized method at a time can run within a monitor object. Each monitored object contains a monitor lock that synchronized methods use to serialize their access to an object's behavior and state. In addition, synchronized methods can determine the circumstances under which they suspend and resume their execution, based on one or more monitor conditions associated with a monitor object.

The *Extension Interface* pattern (141) helps export role-specific views on a monitor object, so that clients only access those services that they require. The *Thread-Safe Interface* pattern (345) helps prevent self-deadlock when a synchronized method of a monitor object calls another synchronized method on the same monitor object.

Wrapper Facade

The *Wrapper Facade* design pattern (47) encapsulates the functions and data provided by existing non-object-oriented APIs within more concise, robust, portable, maintainable, and cohesive object-oriented class interfaces.

The *Extension Interface* pattern (141) can be used to allow clients to access certain implementation-related aspects of a wrapper facade. The *Thread-Specific Storage* pattern (475) may be useful when implementing the error-handling mechanism of a wrapper facade on platforms that do not support exception handling efficiently or portably.

Extension Interface

The *Extension Interface* design pattern (141) prevents bloating of interfaces and breaking of client code when developers extend or modify the functionality of components. Multiple extension interfaces can be attached to the same component, each defining a contract between the component and its clients.

Using the Extension Interface pattern, a component's functionality is exported only via extension interfaces, one for each role it implements. Clients therefore access interfaces but never access component implementations directly. An associated factory is responsible for creating component instances and returning an initial interface reference to clients. Clients can use this interface to retrieve other extension interfaces.

Implementations of the extension interface functionality within components can use the *Active Object* (369) and *Monitor Object* (399) patterns to run in their own thread of control.

Asynchronous Completion Token

The *Asynchronous Completion Token* design pattern (261) allows clients to invoke operations on services asynchronously and to dispatch their subsequent processing actions efficiently when the operations complete and return their results.

For every asynchronous operation that a client invokes on a service, the client creates an asynchronous completion token (ACT) that identifies the actions and state necessary to process the operation's completion. The client passes the ACT to the service together with the operation. When the service replies to the client, its response must include the ACT that was sent originally. The client then uses the ACT to identify the completion handler that processes the results of the asynchronous operation.

Thread-Specific Storage

The *Thread-Specific Storage* design pattern (475) allows multiple threads to use one 'logically global' access point to retrieve an object that is local to a thread—called a 'thread-specific object'—without incurring locking overhead for each access to the object.

The thread-specific objects of a particular thread are maintained using a thread-specific object set. The global access point to a particular thread-specific object can be implemented by a thread-specific object proxy. This hides the details of the creation of the thread-specific object and retrieves it from the thread-specific object set when accessing its methods.

An alternative to accessing the methods of a thread-specific object via the proxy is to use the *Extension Interface* pattern (141), in which the proxy returns an interface that the thread-specific object implements. The *Double-Checked Locking Optimization* pattern (353) is often used to create a thread-specific object correctly and transparently in multi-threaded applications.

Thread-Safe Interface

The *Thread-Safe Interface* design pattern (345) minimizes locking overhead and ensures that intra-component method calls do not incur 'self-deadlock' by trying to reacquire a lock that a component already holds. By using this pattern, a component's methods are divided into two categories, *implementation* and *interface* methods:

- Implementation methods, which are internal to the component and cannot be called by its clients, implement the component's functionality, if necessary by calling other implementation methods. Implementation methods 'trust' that they are called correctly and thus do not acquire/release locks.

- In contrast, interface methods export the component's functionality to clients. These methods first 'check' by acquiring a lock, delegating the method's execution to an appropriate implementation method, and finally releasing the lock when the implementation method finishes executing. Interface methods never call other interface methods on the same component.

The *Strategized Locking* pattern (333) can be used to implement the acquisition and release of locks, as well as to parameterize the type of lock being used.

Double-Checked Locking Optimization

The *Double-Checked Locking Optimization* design pattern (353) reduces contention and synchronization overhead whenever critical sections of code must acquire locks in a thread-safe manner only once during program execution.

The pattern uses a flag to indicate whether it is necessary to execute a critical section before acquiring the lock that guards it. If the critical section code has already been initialized, it need not be executed again, thereby avoiding unnecessary locking overhead.

The *Strategized Locking* pattern (333) is used to implement the acquisition and release of locks, as well as to parameterize the type of lock being used.

Strategized Locking

The *Strategized Locking* design pattern (333) parameterizes synchronization mechanisms in a component that protect its critical sections from concurrent access. This allows a component's synchronization mechanisms to be implemented as 'pluggable' types. Each type objectifies a particular synchronization strategy, such as a mutex, readers/writer lock, or semaphore. Instances of these pluggable types can be defined as objects contained within a component, which can use these objects to synchronize its method implementations efficiently.

The *Scoped Locking* idiom (325) can be used to acquire and release a particular type of lock that is parameterized into a component via the Strategized Locking pattern. Moreover, Strategized Locking can templatize guard classes that apply the *Scoped Locking* idiom, so that synchronization mechanisms can be parameterized transparently.

Scoped Locking

The *Scoped Locking* C++ idiom (325) ensures that a lock is acquired when control enters a scope and released automatically when control leaves the scope, regardless of the return path from the scope.

The pattern defines a guard class whose constructor acquires a lock automatically when control enters a scope and whose destructor releases the lock automatically when control leaves the scope. Instances of the guard class are created to acquire and release locks in method or block scopes that define critical sections.

A Discussion of the Pattern Language

The condensed description of the patterns and the pattern relationship diagram above reveal how most of the patterns complement and complete each other in multiple ways to form a pattern language:

- Although each pattern is useful in isolation, the pattern language is even more powerful, because it integrates solutions to particular problems in important problem areas, such as event handling, connection management and service access, concurrency models, and synchronization strategies. Each problem in these problem areas must be resolved coherently and consistently when developing concurrent and networked systems.

- The pattern language also exposes the interdependencies of these general problem areas. For example, when selecting a particular event-handling pattern for a networked application, not all potentially-available concurrency patterns can be applied usefully.

These two points become clear only when connecting patterns into a pattern language, because each pattern in isolation only focuses on itself. This makes it harder to recognize pattern inter-relationships and solve more complex system architecture problems effectively. In contrast, a pattern-based design can fulfill a software system's requirements more successfully by integrating the patterns consistently and synergistically.

Our pattern language has been applied to many real-world applications, in particular, but not only to systems that are built using the ACE framework [Sch97]. This language is therefore an important tool for specifying and implementing middleware and applications. Note, however, that the pattern language is incomplete, providing the foundation for a larger language for developing distributed object computing middleware, and concurrent and networked applications.

Fortunately our pattern language can be completed by applying other patterns defined in the pattern literature. For example, the Interceptor pattern (109) is orthogonal to most other patterns presented in this book. The Broker architectural pattern [POSA1], however, defines a fundamental structure for distributed software systems that often uses the Interceptor pattern to support out-of-band extensions [NMM99] [HS99a], and the Half-Sync/Half-Async architectural pattern (423) or its Half-Sync/Half-Reactive variant [Sch98b] to structure its broker component. The Broker pattern therefore connects the Interceptor pattern with the other patterns in our pattern language and clarifies their inter-relationships explicitly.

Other patterns from the literature help refine the patterns in our language. For example, peer service handlers defined by the Acceptor-Connector pattern (285) can be implemented using the Half Object plus Protocol pattern [Mes95] and/or the Abstract Session pattern [Pry99]. Similarly, the Remote Proxy variant of the Proxy pattern [GoF95] [POSA1] can be used to implement a particular Interceptor (109) variant. Other examples exist: the Forwarder-Receiver pattern [POSA1] helps implement the Half-Sync/Half-Reactive variant of the Half-Sync/Half-Async pattern (423). Similarly, the Broker [POSA1] and Object Synchronizer [SPM99] patterns can be used to implement variants of the Active Object pattern (369).

Our pattern language can also integrate patterns motivated originally by examples from domains other than concurrency and networking. For example, the patterns described in this book reference many well-known general-purpose patterns, including Abstract Factory, Adapter, Bridge, Command, Decorator, Facade, Factory Method, Iterator, Mediator, Memento, Observer, Singleton, Strategy, and Template Method from [GoF95], Command Processor, Layers, Pipes and Filters, and Reflection from [POSA1], Manager and Null Object from [PLoPD3], and Hook Method from [Pree95].

The integration of all these connected patterns forms a broader pattern language for developing distributed object computing middleware, and concurrent and networked applications. This language can undoubtedly be extended with yet other published patterns or those that remain to be discovered and documented. With each extension the pattern language will become more powerful, complete, and expressive. In this way we can improve the integration of patterns for concurrent and networked software systems.

6.3   Beyond Concurrency and Networking

In the preceding sections we show how the patterns described in this book, together with patterns from other sources, define the basis of a pattern language for developing distributed object computing middleware, and concurrent and networked applications. While this pattern language accentuates the use of these patterns in this particular domain, many of the patterns also apply outside of it.

Analyzing the *Problem* sections and *Known Uses* sections of the patterns reveals that the scope of many of them is broader than the focus of this book implies. Some patterns, for example Wrapper Facade (47), are generally applicable to any domain where it is necessary to encapsulate existing stand-alone functions and data with object-oriented class interfaces. Other patterns apply to particular types of problems that arise in many systems. Extension Interface (141), for example, addresses how to design extensible access to functionality provided by a multi-role component.

In this section, therefore, we outline domains beyond concurrency and networking in which the patterns in this book can be applied.

Graphical User Interfaces

Several of the patterns we describe have been used to design and implement a wide variety of graphical user interfaces:

- The Wrapper Facade pattern (47) is often used to encapsulate details of a particular GUI library to conceal its implementation details from application developers. Two prominent known uses of the pattern in the GUI library context are the Microsoft Foundation Classes (MFC) [Pro99] and the Java Swing library [RBV99].

- Variants of the Reactor (179) pattern have been applied to organize event handling in systems with graphical user interfaces. For example, the Reactor pattern is implemented by the Interviews Dispatcher framework where it is used to define an application's main event loop and manage connections to one or more physical GUI displays [LC87]. The Reactor pattern is also used in the Xt toolkit from the X Windows distribution.

Components

Several patterns apply in the context of components and component-based development:

- The Wrapper Facade pattern (47) specifies how to implement collections of cohesive low-level components and apply them in various contexts, such as components for threading and interprocess communication [Sch97].

- The Component Configurator pattern (75) supports the dynamic configuration and reconfiguration of component implementations. In addition to being used as the basis for installing operating system device drivers dynamically [Rago93], this pattern is also the basis for downloading and configuring Java applets dynamically [JS97b].

- The Interceptor pattern (109) introduces a mechanism for building extensible components and applications. Its *Known Uses* section lists contemporary component models that apply this pattern, such as Microsoft's Component Object Model (COM) [Box97], Enterprise JavaBeans (EJB) [MaHa99], and the CORBA Component Model (CCM) [OMG99a].

- The Extension Interface pattern (141) defines a general mechanism for designing components and allowing clients access to their services. All contemporary component standards, such as COM, EJB, and CCM, implement variants of this pattern.

General Programming

Some patterns or idioms in this book can be applied to programming in general:

- Scoped Locking (325) is a specialization of a general C++ programming technique for safe resource acquisition and release. This technique, described in a more general context by Bjarne Stroustrup in [Str97], is known as 'Object-Construction-is-Resource-Acquisition'.

- Double-Checked Locking Optimization (353) can be used to protect code that should be executed just once, particularly initialization code.

In summary, the seven distinct patterns and idioms discussed above—Wrapper Facade, Reactor, Component Configurator, Interceptor, Extension Interface, Scoped Locking, and Double-Checked Locking Optimization—are clearly applicable beyond the scope of concurrency and networking. If you analyze well-designed software systems you will probably discover other domains in which these or other POSA2 patterns apply. Although this book has presented the patterns primarily in the context of developing concurrent and networked systems, it is important to recognize these patterns can help resolve recurring problems in other domains.

6.4   Pattern Languages versus Pattern Systems

The previous sections explore the pattern language aspects of the patterns presented in this book. In addition to defining the foundation of a pattern language for building distributed object computing middleware, and concurrent and networked applications, however, we can also organize the patterns in this book into a *pattern system* [POSA1]. For example, we can extend the pattern system defined in [POSA1] with the problem areas covered by patterns in this book: service access and configuration, event handling, synchronization, and concurrency. We can then reclassify the patterns accordingly.

This classification scheme presents an interesting conceptual exercise for taxonomizing the pattern space. Each pattern can classified and assigned to a cell in a multi-dimensional matrix, with the dimension of each matrix denoting a particular pattern property. If isolated problems must be resolved, this taxonomy can enable rapid access to potentially useful pattern-based solutions. The following table shows one way to organize the patterns from this book, together with selected patterns from [GoF95] [POSA1] [PLoPD1] [PLoPD2] [PLoPD3] [PLoPD4], into a pattern system for concurrency and networking.[1]

---

1. Patterns described in this book are in **bold**, patterns from [POSA1] are in *italics*, and other patterns from the literature are in regular font.

	Architectural Pattern	Design Pattern	Idiom
Base-line Architecture	*Broker* *Layers* *Microkernel*		
Communication	*Pipes and Filters*	Abstract Session [Pry99] *Command Processor* *Forwarder-Receiver* Observer [GoF95] Remote Operation [KTB98] Serializer [RSB+97]	
Initialization		Activator [Stal00] *Client-Dispatcher-Server* Evictor [HV99] Locator [JK00] Object Lifetime Manager [LGS99]	
Service Access and Configuration	**Interceptor**	**Component Configurator** **Extension Interface** Half Object plus Protocol [Mes95] Manager-Agent [KTB98] *Proxy* **Wrapper Facade**	
Event Handling	**Proactor** **Reactor**	**Acceptor-Connector** **Asynchronous Completion Token** Event Notification [Rie96] Observer [GoF95] *Publisher-Subscriber*	
Synchronization	Object Synchronizer [SPM99]	Balking [Lea99a] Code Locking [McK95] Data Locking [McK95] Guarded Suspension [Lea99a] **Double-Checked Locking Optimization** Reader/Writer Locking [McK95] Specific Notification [Lea99a] **Strategized Locking** **Thread-Safe Interface**	**Scoped Locking**
Concurrency	**Half-Sync/Half-Async** **Leader/Followers**	**Active Object** *Master-Slave* **Monitor Object** Producer-Consumer [Grand98] Scheduler [Lea99a] Two-phase Termination [Grand98] **Thread-Specific Storage**	

Categorizing patterns according to certain specific areas or properties fails to capture the relationships and interdependencies that exist between a particular set of patterns to some extent, however. These relationships and interdependencies influence a pattern's applicability in the presence of other patterns, because not every pattern can be combined with ever other in a meaningful way.

For example, Thread-Specific Storage (475) may be inappropriate for use with a Leader/Followers (447) thread pool design, because there may not be a fixed association between threads in the pool and events that are processed over time. In general, therefore, it is important to identify the 'right' pattern combinations when building real-world systems, because these systems exhibit dependencies between many problems that must be resolved.

Large pattern systems also tend to be complex, because the more problem areas a pattern system includes, the more likely a pattern is to be assigned to multiple categories. The Wrapper Facade pattern (47) is a good example of this phenomenon, because it can be used to build concurrent and networked systems, graphical user interfaces and components, as discussed in Section 6.3, *Beyond Concurrency and Networking*. It would appear at least three times in a pattern system that covered all these systems as a result. As the number of patterns increases, a pattern system may become bloated by these repeated pattern entries, making it hard to learn and use.

One way to resolve this problem is to specify a number of smaller pattern systems for particular domains, rather than to specify a universal pattern system. Examples are our pattern system for concurrency and networking described earlier, or a pattern system for component construction. If you apply this approach to the patterns presented in this book, however, you will notice that the pattern system is structurally similar to the pattern language whose foundations we specified in Section 6.2, *A Pattern Language for Middleware and Applications*.

Moreover, the resulting pattern system would not emphasize the relationships between the patterns as well as the pattern language we described, however. The patterns would instead remain as islands, and the pattern system would be less useful for a pattern-based development of complete software systems for concurrent and networked middleware and applications as a result.

It has been our experience that organizing the patterns presented in this book as a pattern language is more effective than classifying them in a pattern system. Much research remains to be done, however, to identify, document and integrate all patterns that are necessary to complete this pattern language.

7 The Past, Present, and Future of Patterns

"Prediction is hard, especially about the future."
Yogi Berra, Philosopher in the Baseball Hall of Fame

Philosopher of science James Burke is fond of noting that history rarely happens in the right order or at the right time, but the job of a historian is to make it appear as if it did. One benefit of writing a series of *Pattern-Oriented Software Architecture* (POSA) books is we have the opportunity to revisit our earlier predictions, summarize what actually occurred, and examine why it occurred the way it did.

This chapter revisits our 1996 forecasts on 'where patterns will go' that appeared in the first volume of the POSA series, *A System of Patterns* [POSA1]. We discuss the directions that patterns actually took during the past four years, analyze where patterns are now, and revise our vision about their future given the benefit of hindsight.

7.1 What Has Happened in the Past Four Years

In *A System of Patterns* [POSA1] we predicted how we thought patterns would evolve. Four years later we iterate through the same parts of the corresponding chapter in this book and summarize what actually transpired. We reference much of the relevant work during this period, although our list is not exhaustive. Additional references are available at `http://hillside.net/patterns/`.

Patterns

In 1996 we predicted that many patterns for many software development domains would be (re)discovered and documented during the next several years. We expected that these patterns would fill many gaps in the pattern literature. That part of our forecast has certainly come true, although gaps remain in the literature, particularly in distributed, fault-tolerant, transactional, real-time, and embedded systems, middleware, and applications.

The body of pattern literature has grown significantly during the past four years. For example, the PLoP and EuroPLoP pattern conferences in the USA and Europe have prospered and expanded to several new venues, including ChiliPLoP in the USA and KoalaPLoP in Australia. These conferences are based on a 'writers workshop' format [POSA1] [CW99]. In a writers workshop authors read each others' patterns and pattern languages and discuss their pros and cons to help improve content and style.

In the past fours years books have appeared containing patterns on a wide range of subjects, including:

- Edited collections of patterns from many areas of software development [PLoPD3] [PLoPD4] [Ris98] [Ris00a] [Ris00b].

- A seminal book on analysis patterns for the health care and corporate finance domains from Martin Fowler [Fow97a].

- This book—*Patterns for Concurrent and Networked Objects*—which focuses on the architecture and design patterns for concurrent and networked middleware frameworks and application software.

- Software development process patterns [Amb99a] [Amb99b] and patterns for configuration management [BMT99].

- Patterns for particular programming languages, such as Smalltalk [Beck97] and Java [Grand98] [Grand99], or specific to particular middleware, such as CORBA [MM97].

- So-called 'anti-patterns' [BMBMM98] [BMT99], which present common 'solutions' to software development problems that seem reasonable, but that fail to work for various reasons.

It is important for us to note that these books differ in their focus and their quality. However, it is beyond the scope of this chapter to critique and review all these publications—we leave this to your judgement and on-line book reviews, such as those at amazon.com. Nevertheless, the volume of publications during the past four years reveals a growing interest in patterns in the software research and development communities

Many of the most widely-applied patterns are derived from or used to document frameworks [GoF95] [POSA1] [Sch96] [RKSOP00]. These patterns can be viewed as abstract descriptions of frameworks that help developers reuse their software architectures [JML92]. Frameworks can be regarded from another perspective as reifications of patterns that enable direct design and code reuse [HJE95] [HS98]. Experience has shown that mature frameworks exhibit high pattern density [RBGM00].

Pattern Systems and Pattern Languages

As the awareness of patterns has grown in the software community, an increasing amount of work has focused on pattern languages [Cope96] [Gab96] [Cope97]. As early as 1995 leading authors in the pattern community began documenting collections of patterns for specific software development domains [PLoPD1], particularly telecommunications [DeBr95] [Mes96] [ACGH+96] [HS99b]. These patterns were more closely related than the stand-alone patterns published earlier. In fact, some patterns were so closely related that they did not exist in isolation. The patterns were organized into pattern languages in which each pattern built upon and wove together other patterns in the language.

Many of the published pattern languages appear in [Beck97] [PLoPD2] [PLoPD3] [PLoPD4]. As we demonstrate in Section 6.2, *A Pattern Language for Middleware and Applications*, the patterns in this book also form a pattern language, or more precisely the core of a pattern language, for developing distributed object computing middleware, applications, and services. Our prediction that work on pattern languages would expand has therefore also come true. Again, however, significant gaps remain in the literature, due in large part to the effort required to write comprehensive pattern languages.

There has been work on classifying patterns and organizing them into categories [Tichy98], pattern systems [POSA1], and the comprehensive *Pattern Almanac* appearing in [Ris00a]. In general, however, pattern languages have become more popular than pattern systems and pattern catalogs during the past four years. The patterns community has found pattern languages to be the most promising way to document sets of closely-related patterns. Section 6.4, *Pattern Languages versus Pattern Systems* provides further justification and motivation for the gradual transition from pattern catalogs and systems to pattern languages.

Methods and Tools

In 1996 we predicted that work on methods and tools for using patterns effectively would expand, despite the scepticism of some experienced developers [POSA1]. The software research community has worked steadily on this topic, yielding methods for identifying patterns in existing systems [SMB96], as well as many tools for applying patterns to forward [BFVY96] [FMW97] [SRZ99] and reverse engineer software [Ban98] [PK98] [Mic00] [PC00] [PSJ00].

Research on automating software tools for patterns has not yet impacted the software tools community significantly, however, though there has been some recent progress. For example, notations for documenting patterns have been integrated into UML [BRJ98]. Similarly, tools are emerging that generate code automatically from patterns described via meta-models [AONIX99] [MTOOL99].

Algorithms and Data Structures

We predicted a growing interest in the application of patterns to the analysis of the relationships between algorithms, data structures, and patterns. We expected that this effort would be followed by the documentation of algorithms and data structures as patterns, using a specialized pattern form.

To date there have been several papers [Nuy96] and textbooks [FF97] [Preiss98] that integrate patterns from [GoF95] into undergraduate algorithms and data structures courses. In general, however, the focus of this work has been on undergraduate education, rather than a direct contribution to the body of literature from the pattern research community.

Formalizing Patterns

Over the past four years, much research has been conducted to formalize patterns [LBG97] [MK97] [LS98] [Mik98] [BGJ99] [EGHY99]. This work has not yet impacted the pattern community or software practitioners directly, however.

One reason for the lack of impact is that a pattern is a schema for solving a set of related problems, so it can be implemented repeatedly without necessarily being exactly the same each time. In contrast, formalisms aim to capture a particular concept as precisely as possible. Consequently, to capture the inherent variation in patterns, the formalisms used to specify patterns are often large and complex, which makes them hard to understand and use. Unfortunately this defeats many of the benefits of patterns, which are most effective when they enhance—rather than impede—communication among software development team members.

7.2 Where Patterns are Now

Today the pattern community has advanced significantly compared to where it was four years ago. In particular, the body of documented concrete patterns and pattern languages is larger and more diverse than it was four years ago—and it is still growing.

However, different groups in the community prefer different pattern paradigms, including:

- The top-down theoretically-oriented approach inspired by Christopher Alexander's view of patterns [Ale79] and pattern languages [AIS77] [Cope96] [Cope97].

- The more bottom-up engineering-oriented approach pioneered by the Gang-of-Four [GoF95] and POSA work [POSA1].

- The approach advocated by authors of 'special-purpose' patterns, such as anti-patterns [BMBMM98].

In addition to a better understanding of what patterns are in theory, the patterns community now has a better understanding of how patterns work in practice [Vlis98a] [Bus00b]. By 1996 patterns had been applied opportunistically by isolated pockets of researchers and developers [GR96] [HJE95] [John92] [Cope95] [McK95] [SchSt95] [Maf96] [Sch96] [KCC+96]. In the intervening years patterns have been applied more systematically to production systems throughout a wide range of topics and domains in the software industry, including:

- Application frameworks [FS97] [BGHS98] [FJS99a] [FJS99b] [FJ99].

- Real-time CORBA middleware [SC99] [PRS00], high-performance Web servers [Sch97], network management [KTB98], concurrency control, and synchronization [SPM99].

- Input and output processing [Har97] [HS99b] [Tow99].

- Performance measurement [NLN+99] [GP97] and optimization [PRS+99].

- Security [YB99] and dependability [Maf96] [SPM98] [ACGH+96].

- Empirical studies that evaluate the pros and cons of applying patterns [PUPT97].

- The Java programming language [AG98] [GJS96], its standard libraries [Sun00a] [FHA99] and third-party frameworks [IBM98], its virtual machine specification [LY99] and implementation [Sun00b], and its development community [GG99].

Further evidence of the growing impact of patterns is the extent to which developers today not only use them in their designs implicitly—which they did long before patterns were described in books—but how they now apply patterns explicitly in their daily work. Patterns provide a common vocabulary that researchers and developers now use to exchange ideas concisely in design reviews, problem resolutions, training on system-specific features, and documentation of software architectures.

Naturally, it is important to guard against over-enthusiasm, where developers apply patterns blindly wherever possible. While patterns can improve design flexibility and (re-)usability, they may also incur additional costs. Implementing certain patterns may, for example, require more initial programming or design effort, or may yield more code to maintain. Some pattern implementations involve extra indirection that can yield performance overhead on certain platforms. Developers and managers must therefore always evaluate the benefits and liabilities of patterns carefully before using them, particularly if a simple class or function is sufficient to meet the requirements!

7.3   Where Patterns are Going

In the future we expect interest in patterns to grow substantially, as researchers and mainstream software projects continue adopting pattern-oriented paradigms, methods, and processes. This section describes our vision for each major topic area reviewed above, and outlines the key issues we foresee in future research. We also add several new categories—software development processes and education—to reflect promising directions in the patterns community not covered in [POSA1].

Patterns

The patterns literature with the most impact in the past four years has focused on concrete patterns and pattern languages, often derived from object-oriented application frameworks [John97]. Looking ahead, we expect that future work in the pattern community will expand upon this tradition. For example, the next generation of object-oriented applications and frameworks will embody patterns explicitly. Patterns will also continue to be used to document the form and content of frameworks [SFJ96]. Other key topics and domains that will benefit from concrete pattern mining include the following:

- *Distributed objects.* Many patterns associated with middleware and applications for concurrent and networked objects have been documented during the past decade [SC99] [Lea99a], including those in this book. A key next step is to document the patterns for *distributed* objects, extending earlier work to focus on distribution topics, such as remote service location [JK00] and partitioning, naming and directory services, load balancing, dependability, and security.

  An increasing number of distributed object computing systems, for example, must provide high levels of dependability to client programs and end-users. With the adoption of the CORBA Fault Tolerance specification [OMG99g] and ORBs that implement this specification, developers will have more opportunities to capture their experience in the form of patterns for fault-tolerant distributed object computing, than they had in the past [IM96] [ACGH+96] [NMM00].

- *Real-time and embedded systems.* An increasing number of computing systems are embedded, including automotive control systems and car-based applications, control software for factory automation equipment [BGHS98], avionics mission computing [HLS97], and hand-held computing devices. Many of these systems are subject to stringent computing resource limitations, particularly memory footprint and time-constraints.

  Developing high-quality real-time and embedded systems is hard and remains somewhat of a 'black art'. Relatively few patterns have been published in this area as a result [NW98] [Bus98] [Lan98] [Lea94]. We expect the body of patterns for real-time and embedded systems to grow in the future. A driving force will be the maturation of object technology, together with the development tools, methods, and techniques that make it successful (including patterns), that will be applied increasingly in these domains.

- *Mobile systems*. Wireless networks are becoming pervasive and embedded computing devices are become smaller, lighter, and more capable. Thus, mobile systems will soon support many consumer communication and computing needs. Application areas for mobile systems include ubiquitous computing, mobile agents, personal assistants, position-dependent information provision, remote medical diagnostics and teleradiology, and home and office automation. In addition, Internet services, ranging from Web browsing to on-line banking, will be accessed from mobile systems.

  Mobile systems present many challenges, such as managing low and variable bandwidth and power, adapting to frequent disruptions in connectivity and service quality, diverging protocols, and maintaining cache consistency across disconnected network nodes. We expect that experienced mobile systems developers will document their expertise in pattern form to help meet the growing demand for best software development practices in this area.

- *Business transaction and e-commerce systems*. Many business in-formation systems, such as accounting, payroll, inventory, and billing systems, are based on transactions. The rules for processing transactions are complex and must be flexible to reflect new busi-ness practices and mergers. Business systems must also handle increasingly large volumes of transactions on-line, as discussed in the *Example* section of the Leader/Followers pattern (447).

  The advent of e-commerce on the Web is exposing many business-to-business systems directly to consumers. Despite the importance of these systems, relatively little has been written about their analysis, architecture, or design patterns. We expect the body of patterns on transactions and e-commerce to grow, based on the preliminary work of [John96] [Fow97a] [KC97].

- *Quality of service for commercial-off-the-shelf (COTS)-based distributed systems*. Distributed systems, such as streaming video, Internet telephony, and large-scale interactive simulation systems [BHG00] [FJS99b], have increasingly stringent quality of service

(QoS) requirements. Key QoS requirements include network bandwidth and latency, CPU speed, memory access time, and power levels. To reduce development cycle-time and cost, such distributed systems are increasingly being developed using multiple layers of COTS hardware, operating systems, and middleware components.

Historically, however, it has been hard to configure COTS-based systems that can simultaneously satisfy *multiple* QoS properties, such as security, timeliness, *and* fault tolerance. As developers and integrators continue to master the complexities of providing end-to-end QoS guarantees, it is essential that they document the successful patterns to help others configure, monitor, and control COTS-based distributed systems that possess a range of interdependent QoS properties [ZBS97].

- *Reflective middleware.* This term describes a collection of technologies designed to manage and control system resources in autonomous or semi-autonomous distributed application and systems. Reflective middleware techniques enable dynamic changes in application behavior by adapting core software and hardware protocols, policies, and mechanisms with or without the knowledge of applications or end-users [KRL+00]. As with distributed system QoS, patterns will play a key role in documenting best practices that can help to ensure the effective application of reflective middleware-based applications.

- *Optimization principle patterns.* Much of the existing patterns literature has focused on software quality factors other than performance. Although this may be acceptable in domains where non-functional requirements, such as usability or extensibility, are paramount, other domains—particularly distributed and embedded real-time systems—value efficiency, scalability, predictability, and dependability above many other software qualities.

In these domains, therefore, we expect to see an increasing focus on optimization principle patterns that document rules for optimizing complex software systems [NLN+99] [PRS+99]. Yet there is some debate in the patterns community whether optimization principle patterns are really patterns, or just principles [Bus00b].

In addition to the pattern mining activities described above, we expect to see increased publication of edited collections of concrete patterns related to particular application domains. For example, Linda Rising has edited a special issue of the IEEE Communication Magazine [IEEE99] and an edited book collection [Ris00b] that focus on the patterns and pattern languages in the telecommunication domain.

Pattern Languages

In addition to documenting stand-alone patterns, we expect to see continued codification of patterns into full-fledged pattern languages. We also expect to see existing stand-alone patterns [GoF95] [POSA1] and compound patterns [Vlis98c] *integrated* into current or new pattern languages, as discussed in Section 6.2, *A Pattern Language for Middleware and Applications*.

Conversely, as more experience is gained implementing larger architectural patterns, such as Reactor (179) and Proactor (215), we expect that smaller patterns, such as 'Event Demultiplexor' or 'Continuation-passing Event-driven System', will emerge. These patterns can help to improve the concrete realization of the larger architectural patterns by 'decomposing' them into smaller patterns. This decomposition process is yet another way to define pattern languages for the types of systems that follow the structure defined by architectural patterns that are being decomposed.

The trend towards pattern languages stems from the confluence of two forces:

- As more patterns are documented, the coverage of patterns in certain domains is gradually becoming more complete.

- As the patterns in a domain become complete it is more likely that other patterns in these domains can build upon or expose relationships to existing patterns [Ris00a].

This synergism occurs because as new patterns are documented in a domain they often address issues or sub-problems related to existing patterns' problems. As these relationships become explicit, many patterns in a domain can be connected to form pattern languages.

The transition from patterns to pattern languages is ambitious and non-trivial [Vlis98b]. A key impediment to the growth of pattern languages is the effort required to document them. Pattern languages are easier to read and apply than they are to write because their authors must both:

- Be experts on the technical topics in a particular domain and

- Devote considerable time to documenting their expertise in a comprehensible form that identifies all patterns in the language and integrates each individual pattern into the overall language

Fortunately, individual patterns and compound patterns [Vlis98c] are increasingly being documented by the patterns community, based largely on abstractions from common frameworks [Rie97]. As a result, more material is becoming available to weave into pattern languages, alleviating the need to write everything from scratch.

New generations of authors are also gradually emerging from the writers workshops held at venues, such as the PLoP family of conferences. Over time we hope that these authors will help fill key gaps in the existing pattern language literature.

Experience Reports, Methods, and Tools

As noted in Section 7.2, *Where Patterns are Now*, many reports on experiences using patterns for industrial software development have now been published. We expect the number of such reports still to grow, in particular in domains where no such reports are available today, including electronic medical imaging, real-time aerospace control systems, and global Internet e-commerce systems.

This accumulation of documented experience will then allow researchers and developers to identify general, domain-independent core principles for using patterns effectively. Many of these principles have only been understood and applied *implicitly* in earlier projects. With a sufficient number of experience reports available, we expect the pattern community will distill and document these common core principles *explicitly* to help increase developers' potential for applying patterns successfully.

We also expect these core principles will be woven together to form a 'method' or set of principles for pattern-based software development [Bus00a]. This method or set of principles will complement and complete existing software development methods, such as the Unified

Software Development Process [JBR99], and documentation 'methods', such as UML [BRJ98]. The UML models of today largely denote the *what* and *when* of software designs. The pattern-oriented methods and principles of tomorrow will also help to justify *why* certain models are suitable for resolving key challenges in a particular domain.

We believe the most successful pattern-oriented methods and principles will be created 'bottom-up', by generalizing from the collective experience of expert pattern users and software architects. This inductive process has a better chance of success than approaches that try to define pattern-oriented methods and principles 'top-down'. Similarly, when experience-based methods and principles for pattern-based software development become available, we expect that they will be codified into software development tools. Such tools should see wider adoption than at present, because they will automate good practices that are derived from experience.

Pattern Documentation

We expect books will remain the primary media for disseminating concrete information on patterns. However, we anticipate increased use of the Web, and Web-based protocols and tools, such as HTML and XML, to make it easier to document patterns and connect them into pattern languages. Prior efforts have had some success within isolated contexts, such as the Portland Pattern Repository in Ward Cunningham's WikiWikiWeb [PPR]. The state-of-the-practice in this area may advance as a result of three trends:

- The growing ubiquity of Web access
- The advent of low-cost and high-quality electronic book viewers
- More effective e-commerce methods to remunerate authors

Formalizing Patterns and Pattern Languages

Research on formalizing the concept of patterns will certainly continue, and be extended by formalisms to capture more comprehensive pattern languages. It is unclear, however, whether such work will have greater impact in the future than it does currently. We do expect that useful work on formalizing particular instances of patterns in a given system or context will occur to document *specific* pattern implementations.

Certain formal techniques, such as design-by-contract [Mey97], can help to prevent improper use of a pattern implementation within a particular application. Focusing on formalizing instances of patterns therefore can be of practical use in production software development, to help improve system design and implementation quality.

Software Development Processes and Organizations

Much work on pattern languages has focused on improving software development processes and organizations [Cope95] [Cock97] [Ris98] [Har96]. Some software development teams have applied these patterns to help improve the quality of their workplace [Gab96] and their productivity. This work is also beginning to influence the academic software process research community. We expect to see more integration between patterns and software development processes and organizations over the next few years.

Patterns appear to be particularly useful for documenting 'lightweight' software development processes, such as open-source [OS99] and eXtreme Programming (XP) [Beck99] [KiLe00] processes. In addition, processes based on refactoring [Opd92] [FBBOR99] have been applying patterns successfully to help restructure existing software and enhance its modularity, maintainability, and reusability.

Education

In 1996 we did not foresee the significant effort that has arisen to document so-called 'pedagogical patterns' [PPP00] [Bir00]. Pedagogical patterns aim at capturing the principles of educating people effectively. Moreover, patterns are now widely used to teach software design and programming in undergraduate curricula [Lea99b] [Sch99] [LG00] [TM00] [Wal00]. They are also used to train and retrain software professionals [Ant96].

In the short term we expect that many undergraduate courses will apply and teach patterns to convey key points of good practice and sound principles of software architecture and design [Ken98].

Patterns are now commonplace in many professional software development organizations. Substantial experience has therefore accrued on how to apply patterns successfully. Academic institutions will hopefully codify this experience to help educate the next generation of software development professionals in patterns and their effective documentation and application. When these students graduate and start their professional careers, patterns will become even more pervasive than they are today.

Our Long-Term Vision

Looking much further ahead, we believe that knowledge of patterns, pattern languages, and framework components will ultimately progress to the point where software developers will possess methods and tools similar to those of biologists. After centuries of experimentation and modeling, biologists have totally or partially deciphered the genetic code of some organisms. Guided by this knowledge, biologists are now beginning to understand those basic elements within DNA sequences that are shared between organisms, as well as those that make each one unique.

Biologists are applying this information to develop new techniques for manipulating DNA, to provide cures for hereditary conditions, such as the desease Cystic Fibrosis. In this context scientists are both:

- Discovering core properties of DNA sequences and

- Inventing new techniques for manipulating these sequences safely and ethically

Both biological systems and software systems are highly complex. When decomposed into their basic components, such as DNA sequences and genes or patterns and pattern languages, however, they can be understood and controlled more readily. We believe that as core software patterns and pattern languages are understood and reified in the form of reusable components and frameworks, larger-scale complex software systems can be developed more predictably.

We expect that contemporary research and development on patterns and pattern languages will ultimately yield breakthrough discoveries of core software properties. In turn, these 'software DNA' discoveries will spur the invention of new processes, methods, tools, components, frameworks, architectures, and languages. These artifacts will enable us to engineer the complexity of large-scale software more effectively than is possible with the current state-of-the-art.

7.4   A Parting Thought on Predicting the Future

As the Baseball Hall of Fame's resident philosopher Yogi Berra so eloquently stated: 'prediction is hard, especially about the future'. Not all of the predictions we made in 1996 became true, particularly our forecast that use of pattern-oriented software tools would become widespread. Our revised predictions of the future in this chapter include a healthy dose of uncertainty. In particular, our current forecasts are based upon:

- Our knowledge of the pattern community

- Its ongoing and planned interests and research activities—insofar as we are aware of them and

- The future research directions we are guiding or that we consider fruitful

We expect many of our predictions to come true. The future of patterns and pattern languages may take directions however, such as pattern-based model checking, that we have not imagined today. Consider the forecasts in this chapter as one possible vision among many in the ongoing dialogue on patterns and their future, and not as the prophesies of infallible oracles.

When the next book in the POSA series is published in several years, we will revisit these forecasts, as we have revisited our 1996 forecasts from *A System of Patterns* [POSA1]. We will then know what *really* happened and will hopefully have the benefit of hindsight to explain why!

Credits   Thanks to the external reviewers who gave us comments on this section, including Joe Bergin, Bob Hanmer, Neil Harrison, Doug Lea, Ossama Othman, Carlos O'Ryan, Dirk Riehle, Linda Rising, John Vlissides, and Roger Whitney.

8 Concluding Remarks

Writing is an adventure.
To begin with, it is a toy and an amusement.
Then it becomes a mistress, then it becomes a master,
then it becomes a tyrant. The last phase is that just as
you are about to be reconciled to your servitude,
you kill the monster and fling him to the public.

Winston Churchill

This chapter calls on you, the reader, to snatch the baton from us and run the next leg in the race to create a more comprehensive pattern language for concurrent and networked object-oriented applications and middleware.

In this book we have documented the insights and patterns gained during dozens of years of developing and deploying these types of software systems. The resulting book represents much more than a catalog of our own experiences—it articulates the collective experience of the hundreds of researchers and developers we have worked with during the past two decades. Moreover, the patterns we present have been applied successfully in many systems we have not worked on directly, demonstrated by the extensive list of known uses presented throughout the book.

Even so, as we discussed in Section 6.2, *A Pattern Language for Middleware and Applications*, the patterns in this book capture only the foundation of a pattern language that will ultimately encompass all aspects of concurrency and networking. As with all pattern literature, the patterns presented here are perennially 'works in progress'. We could only document the knowledge we possessed collectively when we wrote the book, working always within the limitations of a 'linear' literary form, maximum page counts, publishing deadlines, and occupational and familial commitments. There are undoubtedly topics that we did not address in certain patterns, or implementation activities, consequences, or known uses that we failed to include.

We consider the current edition of this book to be an incremental step on our life-long journey to explore and map the fascinating realm of software development and capture the essence of 'software DNA'. Over the next decade we will continue to improve, complete, and complement the patterns and pattern language contained in POSA2 to form a related collection of books in the POSA series.

In parting, we entreat you to join us in this activity so together we can shape and polish the patterns documented here. Only with your contribution can we ensure that these pattern descriptions codify the best practices and experience from the real world. In turn, this will help us all gain a broader and deeper understanding of solutions to the inherent and accidental complexities found in concurrent and networked software.

Glossary

This glossary defines many of the terms that we use frequently throughout the book. All terms are related to various aspects of concurrent and networked software. When a definition consists of other terms in the glossary we italicize these terms.

We have omitted terminology used in only one context, for example the network management terms from the Extension Interface and Asynchronous Completion Token patterns. Where such terms need a definition, we present them in context rather than including them here. For completeness, we have also included common terms, such as 'pattern', 'software architecture', and 'idiom', that were explained in depth in various sections of [POSA1].

Abstract Class A *class* that does not implement all the methods defined in its *interface*. An abstract class defines a common abstraction for its *subclasses*.

Abstract Component A *component* that specifies an *interface* for other components. An abstract component can either be explicit, such as an *abstract class*, or implicit, such as a class parameter of a C++ *template* function. Abstract components form the basis for exploiting polymorphism and implementing flexible *systems*. This term is used in the same way as abstract class, to avoid restricting the *pattern* to object-oriented languages.

Abstract Method The declaration of an operation of a *class* that must be defined by a *subclass*.

Active Connection Establishment The connection role played by a peer application that initiates a connection to a remote peer. (Compare with *Passive Connection Establishment*).

Active Object An *object* that executes its *methods* in a different *thread* than the *clients* that invoke its methods. (Compare with *passive object*).

API Application programming *interface*. The external interface of a software *platform*, such as an operating system, that is used by *systems* or *applications* built on top of it.

Application A program or collection of programs that fulfills a customer or user's requirements.

Application Framework An integrated set of *components* that collaborate to provide a reusable *software architecture* for a family of related *applications*. In an object-oriented environment an application framework consists of *abstract* and *concrete classes*. *Instantiation* of such a framework consists of composing and *subclassing* from existing classes.

Architectural Pattern An architectural *pattern* expresses a fundamental structural organization schema for software *systems*. It provides a set of predefined *subsystems*, specifies their responsibilities, and includes rules and guidelines for organizing the relationships between them.

Associative Array An array indexed via arbitrary key values, such as strings, rather than integers. Hash tables are a common way to implement associative arrays.

Asynchronous I/O A mechanism for sending or receiving data in which an I/O operation is initiated but the caller does not block waiting for the operation to complete.

Backus Naur Form (BNF) A standard technique for describing the syntax of a language.

Bandwidth The capacity of a communication media, such as a *network* or *bus*.

Bus A high-speed communication channel that links computing *devices*, such as *CPUs*, disks, and *network interfaces*.

Busy Wait A technique used by a *thread* to wait for a *lock* by executing a tight loop and polling to see if the lock is available on each iteration, in contrast to waiting for the lock to be released by sleeping and allowing other threads to run.

Cache Affinity A *thread scheduling* optimization that gives preference to dispatching a thread on the *CPU* on which it most recently ran to maximize the probability of its state being present in the CPU's *instruction and data caches*.

Class
A fundamental building block in object-oriented languages. A class specifies an *interface* and encapsulates its internal data structure as well as the functionality of its *instances* or *objects*. A class can extend on one or more other classes via *inheritance*.

Client
In our descriptions *client* denotes a *role, component*, or *subsystem* that invokes or uses the functionality offered by other components.

Closure
See *Method Closure*.

Collaborator
A *component* that cooperates with another component. An element of a *CRC card*.

Collocation
The activities associated with placing an *object* into the same *process* or *host* with the *clients* that access it. Collocation is often applied to improve locality of reference. (Compare with *Distribution*).

Completion Event
A *event* containing response information related to a *request event* initiated by a *client*.

Component
An encapsulated part of a software *system* that implements a specific service or set of services. A component has one or more *interfaces* that provide access to its services. Components serve as building blocks for the structure of a system. On a programming language level components may be represented as *modules, classes, objects*, or a set of related functions. A component that does not implement all the elements of its interface is called an *abstract component*.

Concrete Class
A *class* from which objects can be *instantiated*. In contrast to *abstract classes*, all methods are implemented in a concrete class. The term is used to distinguish concrete *subclasses* from their abstract *superclass*.

Concrete Component
A *component* that implements all elements defined in its *interfaces*. Used to distinguish components from the *abstract component* that defines their interface, in the same way that a *concrete class* is distinguished from an *abstract class*.

Concurrency
The ability of an *object, component*, or *system* to execute operations that are 'logically simultaneous'. (Compare with *parallelism*).

Condition Variable
A condition variable [IEEE96] is a *synchronization* mechanism used by collaborating *threads* to suspend themselves temporarily until

condition expressions involving data shared between the threads attain desired states. A condition variable is always used in conjunction with a *mutex*, which the thread must acquire before evaluating the condition expression. If the condition expression is false the thread atomically suspends itself on the condition variable and releases the mutex, so that other threads can change the shared data. When a cooperating thread changes this data, it can notify the condition variable, which atomically resumes a thread that had previously suspended on the condition variable and acquires its mutex again.

Connection A *full association* that is used by *peers* to exchange data between *endpoints* of a *network application*.

Container A common name for data structures that hold a collection of elements. Examples of containers are lists, sets, and *associative arrays*. In addition, *component* models, such as EJB [MaHa99] and ActiveX Controls, define containers that provide a run-time environment that shields components from the details of their underlying infrastructure, such as an *operating system*.

Continuation A continuation is a language feature that allows a program's run-time system to transfer the control of a method closure from one part of the program to another [DBRD91].

CORBA The Common *Object Request Broker* Architecture (CORBA), a distributed object computing *middleware* standard defined by the Object Management Group (OMG).

CPU Central processing unit. A hardware component that executes binary program instructions.

CRC Card Class-Responsibility-Collaborator card. A design tool and notation for describing the responsibilities and collaborators of *classes* in a *software architecture*. In this book, we also use CRC cards to describe *components* that are not *classes*.

Critical Section Code that should not execute *concurrently* in an *object* or *subsystem* can be *synchronized* by a critical section. A critical section is a sequence of instructions that obeys the following *invariant*: while one *thread* or *process* is executing in the critical section, no other thread or process can execute in the critical section [Tan95]. (Compare with *Read-side* and *Write-side Critical Section*).

Deadlock   A deadlock is a *concurrency* hazard that occurs when multiple *threads* attempt to acquire multiple *locks* and become blocked indefinitely in a circular wait state.

Daemon   A *server process* that runs continuously as in the background performing various *services* for *clients*.

Data-Mode Socket   See *Socket*.

Demarshaling   The conversion of a *marshaled message* from a *host*-independent format into a host-specific format.

Demultiplexing   A mechanism that routes incoming *events* from an input *port* to its intended receivers. There is a 1:N relationship between input port and receivers. Demultiplexing is commonly applied to incoming events and data streams. The reverse operation is known as 'multiplexing'.

Design   The activities performed by software developers that results in the *software architecture* of a *system*. Often the term 'design' is also used as a name for the result of these activities.

Design Pattern   A design *pattern* provides a scheme for refining *components* of a software *system* or the relationships between them. It describes a commonly-recurring structure of communicating components that solves a general design problem within a particular context [GoF95].

Device   A hardware *component* that provides a service in a computing and/or communication *system*.

Device Driver   A software *component* in an *operating system kernel* that is responsible for controlling a hardware *device* attached to the computer, or a software device, such as a ram disc.

Distribution   The activities associated with placing an *object* into a different *process* or *host* than the *clients* that access it. Distribution is often applied to improve fault tolerance or to access remote resources. (Compare with *Collocation*).

Domain   Denotes concepts, knowledge and other items that are related to a particular problem area. Often used in 'application domain' to denote the problem area addressed by an application. On the *Internet*, a domain is a logical addressing entity, such as uci.edu or siemens.de.

Dynamic Binding	A mechanism that defers the association of an operation name (a *message*) to the corresponding code (a *method*) until run-time. Used to implement *polymorphism* in object-oriented languages.
Dynamically Linked Library (DLL)	A library that can be shared by multiple *processes* and linked into and out of a process' address space dynamically in order to improve application flexibility and extensibility at run-time.
Endpoint	The termination point of a *connection*.
Exception-Safe	A *component* is exception-safe if an exception raised in the component or propagated from a component called by the component does not cause resource leaks or an unstable state.
Event	A message that conveys the occurrence of a significant activity, together with any data associated with the activity.
Factory	A *method* or *function* that creates and assembles the resources needed to instantiate and initialize an *object* or *component* instance.
Flow Control	A communication *protocol* mechanism that prevents a fast sender from overrunning the buffering and computing resources of a slow receiver.
Framework	See *Application Framework*.
Full Association	The five-tuple in the *Internet* protocol domain that identifies a *TCP connection*. It consists of the protocol type, the local address and *port number*, and the remote address and port number.
Function	A closed sub-routine that is passed zero or more *parameters* and that may return a value to its caller. Functions are typically 'stand-alone', as opposed to *methods*, which are associated with a *class*.
Functional Property	A particular aspect of a *system*'s functionality, usually related to a specified functional requirement. A functional property may be either made directly visible to users of an *application* by means of a particular *function*, or it may represent aspects of its implementation, such as the algorithm used to compute the function.
Future	A future [Hal85] [LS88] allows a *client* to obtain the result of *method* invocations after the invoked method finishes executing. The future reserves space for the invoked method to store its result. When a

client wants to obtain this result it can rendezvous with the future, either blocking or polling until the result is computed and stored in the future.

Gateway   A gateway decouples co-operating components in a *network* and allows them to interact without having direct dependencies among each other.

GUI   Graphical user *interface*.

Handle   A handle identifies resources that are managed by an *operating system kernel*. These resources commonly include, among others, network *connections*, open files, timers, and *synchronization* objects.

Hardwiring   Writing inflexible programs, for example by using a literal number or string instead of a variable. Such literals are also known as 'magic numbers' because the number itself provides no clue to the understanding of its origin or purpose.

Host   An addressable computer attached to a *network*.

HTTP   The Hyper Text Transport Protocol, which is a simple *protocol layered* on top of *TCP* and used by *clients* to download content from a Web *server* via GET requests.

Idempotent Initialization   *Object* initialization is idempotent if an object can be reinitialized multiple times without harmful side-effects.

Idiom   An idiom is a low-level *pattern* specific to a programming language. An idiom describes how to implement particular aspects of *components* or the relationships between them using the features of the given language.

Indication Event   A *event* containing request information sent from a *client* to a *service* provider.

Inheritance   A feature of object-oriented languages that allows new *classes* to be derived from existing ones. Inheritance defines implementation reuse, a subtype relationship, or both. Depending on the programming language, single or multiple inheritance is possible.

Inlining   Code expansion at compile-time that inserts the code of a *function* or *method* body instead of the code used to call the function/method.

Inlining long function/method bodies can lead to code 'bloat', with negative effects on storage consumption and paging effects.

Instance An *object* originated from a specific *class*. Often used as a synonym for object in an object-oriented environment. This term may also be used in other contexts (see *Instantiation*).

Instantiation A mechanism that creates a new *instance* from a template. The term is used in several contexts. *Objects* are instantiated from *classes*. C++ *templates* are instantiated to create new classes or functions. An *application framework* is instantiated to create an *application*. The phrase 'instantiating a pattern' is sometimes used to refer to taking the pattern as described and filling in the necessary details to implement it in the context of a specific application.

Instruction and Data Caches Special high-speed memory collocated with a *CPU* that can improve overall system performance.

Interface A publically accessible portion of a *class*, *component*, or *subsystem*.

Internet A world-wide 'network of networks' that is based on the *Internet Protocol* (IP). Widely considered to be the most important human invention since fire and MTV.

Internet Protocol (IP) A *network layer protocol* that performs segmentation, reassembly, and routing of *packets*.

Intranet A *network* of computers within a company or other organization. Such a network may be secured from outside access and provide a *platform* for company-wide information exchange, co-operative work, and work flow, using *Internet* technologies for communication.

Introspection The examination of selected aspects of the structure, behavior, or state of a *system* by the system itself.

Interprocess Communication (IPC) Communication between processes residing in separate address spaces. Examples of IPC mechanisms include *shared memory*, UNIX pipes, message queues, and *socket* communication.

Invariant A property of the state of an *object*, *component*, or *module* that always holds at a specific point in time or space. For example: 'the invariant a < b holds whenever control passes line 50 of method foo( )'.

Jitter The standard deviation of the *latency* for a series of operations.

Late Binding Synonym for *Dynamic Binding*.

Latency The delay experienced by operations.

Layer A level of abstraction that defines a particular set of *services* in a hierarchy. Layer$_n$ is a consumer of services at layer$_{n-1}$ and a supplier of services to layer$_{n+1}$.

Load Balancing A technique used to distribute *client* workloads among various *processes* and *hosts* in a *network*.

Lock A mechanism used to implement some type of a *critical section*. A lock that can be acquired and released serially, such as a static *mutex*, may be added to a *class*. If multiple *threads* attempt to acquire the lock simultaneously, only one thread will succeed and the others will block until the lock is available [Tan92]. Other locking mechanisms, such as *semaphores* or *readers/writer* locks, define different *synchronization* semantics.

Loopback Device A software *device* that appears like a *network interface* to *applications*, but instead simply redirects *messages* passed to it back to another *process* or *thread* on the same *host*.

Marshaling The conversion of an unmarshaled *message* from a *host*-specific format into a host-independent format.

Message Messages are used to communicate between *objects*, *threads*, or *processes*. In an object-oriented *system* the term message is used to describe the selection and activation of an operation or the *method* of an object. This kind of message is synchronous, which means that the sender waits until the receiver finishes the activated operation. Threads and processes often communicate asynchronously, in which the sender continues its execution without waiting for the receiver to reply. Remote procedure calls (RPC) are a means of synchronous *IPC* over a *network*. While messages in *IPC* communication protocols consist of a *protocol*-defined structure and are generally not visible to higher *layers*, Message Queueing systems, such as IBM MQSeries or Microsoft MSMQ messages, define a user-defined body where higher layers can implicitly transmit user data.

Message Passing An *IPC* mechanism that exchanges *messages* between *threads* or *processes*. (Compare with *shared memory*).

Method A *function* performed by an *object*. A method is specified within a *class*. The term is also used in 'software development method', which consists of a set of rules, guidelines, and notations to be used by engineers during the process of developing software.

Method Closure An object that contains the context of a method, which can include the method's parameters, a binding to the servant or completion handler that will process the method, and potentially a *future* for the method's result.

Mix-In A 'small' *class* that defines an additional *interface* or functionality to be added to classes by multiple *inheritance*. Mix-in also denotes the mechanism for adding such functionality by *inheriting* from classes.

Middleware A set of *layers* and *components* that provides reusable common *services* and *network* programming mechanisms. Middleware resides on top of an *operating system* and its *protocol stacks* but below the structure and functionality of any particular *application*.

Module A syntactical or conceptual entity of a software *system* that is often used synonymously for *component* or *subsystem*. Sometimes 'modules' also denote compilation units or files. We use the term in its former sense. Other writers use the term as an equivalent to 'package' when referring to a code body with its own name space.

Monitor A monitor encapsulates *functions* and their internal variables into *thread*-safe modules. To prevent *race conditions*, a monitor contains a *lock* that allows only one thread at a time to be active within the monitor. Threads that want to leave the monitor temporarily can block on a *condition variable*.

Moore's Law A surprisingly accurate heuristic that states the pace of change in microchip technology is such that the amount of data storage a microchip can hold doubles every year, or at least every eighteen months. When preparing a lecture in 1965, Gordon Moore noticed that up to that time microchip capacity seemed to double each year. As the pace of change has slowed a little over the past few years, the definition has changed—with Gordon Moore's approval—to reflect the fact that the doubling occurs only every eighteen months.

Multiple Inheritance	*Inheritance* in which a *class* can have more than one *superclass*.
Multicast	A communication *protocol* that allows a *client* to transmit *messages* to multiple *servers*. A broadcast is a special form of multicast, where messages are transmitted to all servers in a particular domain.
Mutex	A mutex is a 'mutual exclusion' *locking* mechanism that ensures only one *thread* at a time is active *concurrently* within a *critical section* in order to prevent *race conditions*.
Network	A communication medium that enables *hosts* and other *devices* to exchange *messages*.
Network Interface	A hardware *device* that connects a *network* with a *host*.
Non-functional Property	A feature of a *system* not covered by its *functional* description. A non-functional property typically addresses aspects related to the reliability, compatibility, efficiency, cost, ease of use, maintenance, or enhancement of a system.
Object	An identifiable entity in an object-oriented *system*. Objects respond to *messages* by performing a *method* (operation). An object may contain data values and references to other objects, which together define the state of the object. An object therefore has state, behavior, and identity.
Object Request Broker	A *middleware layer* that allows *clients* to invoke *methods* on distributed *objects* without concern for object location, programming language, *operating system platform*, communication *protocols*, or hardware.
On-the-wire Protocol	An 'on-the-wire *protocol*' defines how higher-level communication *middleware*, such as DCE, *CORBA*, or Java RMI, or other communication protocols, such as HTTP, transform *messages* or *objects* into buffers that can be passed 'across the wire' (*network*). The term 'wire' encompasses a range of transmission media, such as microwave, fiber-optics, and radio waveforms.
One-way Method Invocation	A call to a *method* that passes *parameters* to a *server object* but does not receive any results from the server. (Compare with *Two-way Method Invocation*).

Operating System	A collection of *services* and *APIs* that manage hardware and software resources on behalf of *applications* and end-users.
Operating System Kernel	A collection of core *operating system services*, such as *process* and *thread* management, *virtual memory*, and *interprocess communication (IPC)*.
Out-of-Band	A *protocol* or mechanism that occurs outside the normal 'in-band' processing sequence.
Packet	A *message* used to convey header and data information in the *TCP/IP protocols*.
Parallelism	The ability of an *object*, *component*, or *system* to execute operations that are 'physically simultaneous'. (Compare with *concurrency*).
Parameter	An instance of a data type or *object* passed to a *function*, *method*, or *parameterized type*.
Parameterized Type	A programming language feature that allows *classes* to be parameterized by various other types. (Compare with *template*.)
Passive-Mode Socket	See *Socket*.
Passive Connection Establishment	The connection role played by a peer application that accepts a connection from a remote peer. (Compare with *Active Connection Establishment*).
Passive Object	An *object* that borrows the *thread* of its caller to execute its methods. (Compare with *active object*).
Pattern	A pattern describes a particular recurring design problem that arises in specific design contexts and presents a well-proven solution for the problem. The solution is specified by describing its constituent participants, their responsibilities and relationships, and the ways in which they collaborate.
Pattern Language	A family of interrelated patterns that define a process for resolving software development problems systematically.
Peer-to-peer	In a distributed *system* peers are processes that communicate with each other. In contrast to *components* in client-server architectures,

peers may act as *clients*, as *servers*, or as both, and may change these *roles* dynamically.

Platform   The combination of hardware and/or software that a *system* uses for its implementation. Software platforms include *operating systems*, libraries, and *frameworks*. A platform implements a *virtual machine* with *applications* running on top of it.

Polymorphism   A concept in which a single name may denote different things. For example, a *function* name may be bound over time to several different operations, or a variable may be bound to objects of different types. This concept makes it possible to implement flexible *systems* based on abstractions. In object-oriented languages polymorphism is implemented by the *dynamic binding* mechanism of operations. This implies that a fixed portion of code may behave differently depending on its collaborating objects.

Port   An *endpoint* of communication.

Port Number   A 16 bit number used to identify an *endpoint* of communication in the *TCP protocol*.

Priority Inversion   A scheduling hazard that occurs when a lower-priority thread or request blocks the execution of a higher-priority thread or request.

Process   A process provides certain resources, such as *virtual memory*, and protection capabilities, such as user/group identifiers and a hardware-protected address space, that can be used by one or more *threads* in the process. Compared with a thread, however, a process maintains more state information, requires more overhead to spawn, *synchronize*, and *schedule*, and often communicates with other processes via *message passing* or *shared memory*.

Protocol   A set of rules that describe how *messages* are exchanged between communicating *peers*, as well as the syntax and semantics of these messages.

Protocol Stack   A group of hierarchically-*layered protocols*.

Quality of Service   A collection of policies and mechanisms designed to control and enhance communication properties, such as *bandwidth*, *latency*, and *jitter*.

Race Condition   A race condition is a *concurrency* hazard that can occur when multiple *threads* simultaneously execute within a *critical section* that is not properly *serialized*.

Read-side Critical Section   A set of sequences of instructions that obeys the following *invariant*: while one or more *threads* or *processes* are executing in the read-side *critical section*, no thread or process can execute in a corresponding write-side critical section. (Compare with *Write-side Critical Section*).

Readers/Writer Lock   A *lock* that allows multiple *threads* to access a resource *concurrently*, but allows only one thread at a time to modify the resource and further prevents concurrent access and modifications.

Reification   The act of creating a concrete instance of an abstraction. For example, a concrete reactor implementation is a reification of the Reactor *pattern* (179) and an object reifies a class.

Request Event   A *event* sent by a *client* to a *service* provider asking it to perform some processing on the client's behalf.

Response Event   A *event* sent by a *service* provider containing the reply to a *client*'s *request event*.

Recursive Mutex   A *lock* that can be re-acquired by the *thread* that owns the mutex without incurring self-*deadlock* on the thread.

Refactoring   An incremental activity that abstracts general-purpose behavior from existing software to enhance the structure and reusability of *components* and *frameworks*.

Relationship   An association between *components*. A relationship may be static or dynamic. Static relationships show directly in source code. They deal with the placement of components within an architecture. Dynamic relationships deal with the interaction between components. They may not be easily visible from source code or diagrams.

Responsibility   The functionality of an *object* or a *component* in a specific context. A responsibility is typically specified by a set of semantically-related operations. The responsibility section is an element of a *CRC card*.

Role   The *responsibility* of a *component* within a context of related components. For example, an object-oriented *class* defines a single role that all its instances support. Another example is an *interface* that defines a role that all implementations support. If a component supports a given role it must provide an implementation of the interface defining the role. Components expose different roles by implementing different interfaces. Different components may expose the same role by implementing the same interface, which allows clients to treat them polymorphically with respect to that particular role. An implemented component may take different roles, even within a single pattern.

Scheduler A mechanism that determines the order in which *threads* or *request events* are executed.

Semaphore A *locking* mechanism that maintains a count. As long as the count is greater than zero a *thread* can acquire the semaphore without blocking. After the count becomes zero, however, threads block on the semaphore until its count become greater than zero as a result of another thread releasing the semaphore, which increments the count.

SEP Somebody Else's Problem, Software Engineering Process, or Software Engineering with Patterns, whichever you prefer.

Serialization A mechanism for ensuring that only one *thread* at a time executes within a *critical section* in order to prevent *race conditions*.

Servant A *component* triggered by *client* requests. When a client request arrives the servant attempts to fulfill it, either by itself or by delegating subtasks to other components.

Server Servers denote applications that provide *services* such as *middleware* functionality, database access, or Web page access, to *clients*. In distributed object computing middleware these services are typically implemented by *servants* that represent distributed *objects*.

Service A set of functionality offered by a service provider or *server* to its *clients*.

Shared Memory An *operating system* mechanism that allows multiple *processes* on a computer to share a common memory segment. (Compare with *message passing*).

Single Inheritance *Inheritance* in which a *class* can have at most one direct *superclass*.

Socket   A family of terms related to network programming. A socket is an *endpoint* of communication that identifies a particular network address and port number. The Socket API is a set of *function* calls supported by most *operating systems* and used by *network applications* to establish *connections* and communicate via socket endpoints. A *data-mode socket* can be used to exchanged data between connected *peers*. A *passive-mode socket* is a *factory* that returns a *handle* to a connected data-mode socket.

Software Architecture   A software architecture is a description of the *subsystems* and *components* of a software system and the *relationships* between them. Subsystems and components are often specified via different *views* to show the relevant *functional* and *non-functional properties* of a software system. The software architecture of a system is an artifact that results from software *design* activities.

Starvation   A *scheduling* hazard that occurs when one or more *threads* are continually pre-empted by higher-priority threads and never execute.

Subclass   A *class* that inherits from a *superclass*.

Subsystem   A set of collaborating *components* that perform a given *service* or services. A subsystem is considered a separate entity within a *software architecture*. It performs its designated service(s) by interacting with other subsystems and components.

Superclass   A *class* from which another class inherits.

Synchronization   A *locking* mechanism that coordinates the order in which *threads* execute.

Synchronous I/O   A mechanism for sending or receiving data in which an I/O operation is initiated and the caller blocks waiting for the operation to complete.

System   A collection of software and/or hardware performing one or several *services*. A system can be a *platform*, an *application*, or both.

System Family   A set of related *systems* solving similar *services*. Systems in a system family share much of their *software architecture* and implementation, often because every system is derived from the same *framework*. When a single system evolves over time, its delivered releases also build a system family.

Template   A C++ programming language feature that enables *classes* and *functions* to be parameterized by various types, constants, or pointers to functions. A template is often called a *generic* or *parameterized type*.

Thread   An independent sequence of instructions that executes within an address space that can be shared with other threads. Each thread has its own run-time stack and registers, which enables it to perform synchronous I/O without blocking other threads that are executing concurrently. Compared to *processes*, threads maintain minimal state information, require relatively little overhead to spawn, *synchronize* and *schedule*, and usually communicate with other threads via objects in global memory, rather than *shared memory*.

Thread-per-Connection   A *concurrency* model that associates a separate *thread* for each *network connection*. This model handles each *client* that connects with a *server* in a separate thread for the duration of the connection. It is useful for servers that must support long-duration sessions with multiple clients. It is not useful for clients, such as *HTTP* 1.0 Web browsers, that associate a single request with each connection, which is effectively a *thread-per-request* model.

Thread-per-Request   A *concurrency* model that spawns a new *thread* for each request. This model is useful for *servers* that must handle long-duration *request events* from multiple *clients*, such as database queries. It is less useful for short-duration requests, due to the overhead of creating a new thread for each request. It can also consume a large number of *operating system* resources if many clients send requests simultaneously.

Thread Pool   A *concurrency* model that allocates a pool of *threads* that can execute *request events* simultaneously. This model is a variant of *thread-per-request* that amortizes thread creation costs by pre-spawning a pool of threads. It is useful for *servers* that want to bound the number of *operating system* resources they consume. *Client* requests can be executed concurrently until the number of simultaneous requests exceeds the number of threads in the pool. At this point, additional requests must be queued until a thread becomes available.

Transmission Control Protocol (TCP)   A *connection*-oriented transport *protocol* that reliably exchanges byte-streams of data in-order and un-duplicated between a local and remote *process*.

Transport Endpoint	An *endpoint* that connects *peer applications* at the *transport layer*.
Transport Layer	The *layer* in a *protocol stack* that is responsible for end-to-end data transfer and *connection* management.
Transport Layer Interface (TLI)	TLI is a set of *function* calls provided in System V UNIX and used by *network applications* to establish *connections* and communicate via connected *transport endpoints*.
Two-way Method Invocation	A call to a *method* that passes *parameters* to a *server object* and receives results back from the server. (Compare with *One-way Method Invocation*).
Unicode	A standard for character representation using 16-bit coding. Unicode includes characters for most written languages as well as representations for punctuation, mathematical notations, and other symbols.
Upcall	A callback that is invoked from a lower layer of a software architecture to a higher layer [Cla85].
User Datagram Protocol (UDP)	An unreliable, connectionless transport *protocol* that exchanges datagram *messages* between local and remote *processes*.
View	A view presents a partial aspect of a *software architecture* that emphasizes specific properties of a software system.
Virtual Machine	An abstraction *layer* that offers a set of *services* to higher-level *applications* or other virtual machines.
Virtual Memory	An *operating system* mechanism that permits developers to program *applications* whose address space is larger than the amount of physical memory on the computer.
Write-side Critical Section	A set of sequences of instructions that obeys the following *invariant*: at most one *thread* or *process* may be executing in the write-side *critical section*, and while a thread or process is executing in this write-site critical section, no thread or process can execute in a corresponding read-side critical section. (Compare with *Read-side Critical Section*).

Notations

Class-Responsibility-Collaborator Cards

Class-Responsibility-Collaborators (CRC) cards [BeCu89] help to identify and specify objects or the components of an application in an informal way, especially in the early phases of software development.

Class	Collaborators
Name	• Partner
	• Components
Responsibility	
• Operations may go across several lines.	

A CRC-card describes a component, an object, or a class of objects. The card consists of three fields that describe the name of the component, its responsibilities, and the names of other collaborating components. The use of the term 'class' is historical [Ree92]—we also use CRC cards for other types of components or even single objects.

UML Class Diagrams

The Unified Modeling Language (UML) [BRJ98] is a widely-used object-oriented analysis and design method. An important type of diagram within UML is the class diagram. A class diagram describes the types of objects in a system and the various types of static relationships that exist among them.

As an extension to the standard UML notation we introduce a symbol to indicate that instances of a class run in separate threads.

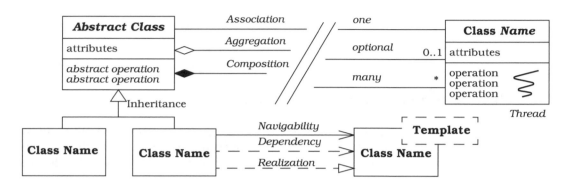

Class. A rectangular box, denoting the name of the class and optionally its attributes and operations. Abstract classes names are labeled in *italics* along with their corresponding abstract methods.

Operation. Operation names are written in the class boxes. They denote the methods of classes. Abstract operations, that is, those that only provide the interface for polymorphism, are denoted by *italics*.

Attributes. Attribute names are written in the class boxes. They denote the instance variables of a class.

Association. A line that connects classes. Associations can be optional or multiple. A number at the end of an association denotes its cardinality. Association of classes is used to show any type of class relationship except aggregation, composition and inheritance.

Aggregation. A hollow diamond shape at the termination of an association line denotes that the class(es) at the other end of the association are *used* by the class.

Composition. A solid diamond shape at the termination of an association line denotes that the class(es) at the other end of the association are *part* of the class and have the same life-time.

Navigability. Navigability denotes a directed association.

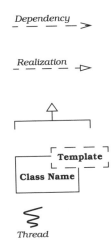

Dependency. A dependency indicates that a class uses the interface of another class for some purpose.

Realization. A realization represents the relationship between a specification and its implementation.

Inheritance. Inheritance is denoted by a triangle at the top of an association line. The apex of the triangle points to the superclass.

Templates. Parameterized classes are declared by attaching a dashed rectangular box to a class box, which includes the class' template parameters.

Thread. A wavy line attached to a class indicates that instances of this class run in separate threads. The thread symbol is an extension to the UML class diagram notation, which lacks an effective way to denote multi-threading.

UML Sequence Diagrams

UML sequence diagrams describe how groups of objects collaborate in some behavior [BRJ98]. The notation is based on the Object Message Sequencing Chart (OMSC) notation defined in [POSA1].

In addition to the standard UML notation, however, we also use the notation for illustrating parameter-passing that we specified in our original OMSC definition. This allows us to indicate when the responsibility for an object is passed from one object to another or when an object obtains a reference to another object. As a second extension to standard UML we introduce a special symbol that allows us to label activities initiated by a thread of control rather than a particular UML active object.

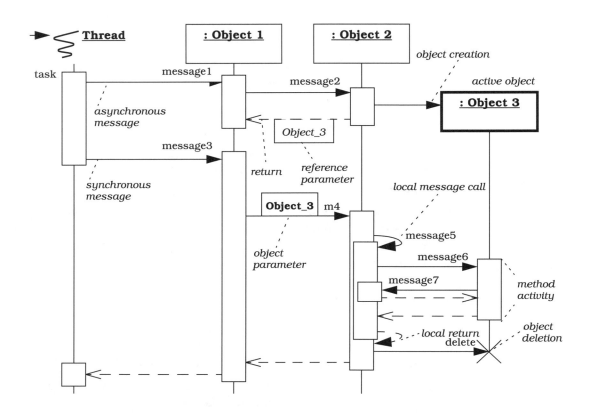

Object. An object or component in a sequence diagram is drawn as a rectangular box. The box is labeled with the underlined name of the component in the pattern. An object that sends or receives messages in the sequence diagram has a vertical bar attached to the bottom of the box. Active objects are denoted by thicker lines for the rectangular box.

Time. Time flows from top to bottom. The time axis is not scaled.

Messages. Messages between objects are denoted by arrows. These arrows are labeled with the method name at the head, if applicable. Synchronous messages are indicated by solid full-arrowheads, asynchronous messages by solid half-arrowheads. Returns are indicated by dashed arrows with open arrowheads.

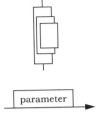

Object Activity. To denote the activity of objects that perform a specific function, procedure or method, rectangular boxes are placed on the vertical bar attached to the object. An object may also send messages to itself to activate other methods. This situation is represented by nested boxes offset slightly to the right.

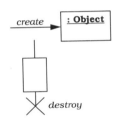

Parameter. Parameters are only noted explicitly when they are necessary to understand a sequence diagram. Parameters of a message are shown as a box on top of the arrow and return parameters below the returning arrow. If responsibility for a parameter object is passed along the arrow the name of the object is shown in **boldface**. If only a reference to the object is passed as a parameter, its name is shown in *italics*. This notation is an extension to UML sequence diagram.

Object Lifecycle. In most cases we assume that all relevant objects already exist, so the corresponding boxes are drawn at the top of the sequence diagram. If a sequence diagram shows object creation, this is denoted by an arrow to a box placed within the sequence diagram. If an object ceases to exist, this is denoted by a cross that terminates the vertical bar. This notation corresponds to constructor and destructor calls in C++.

Thread. A wavy line attached to a time line indicates a thread of control that sends or receives messages. A thread is labeled with the underlined identifier of the thread. The thread symbol is an extension to the UML sequence diagram notation, which allows us to denote activities initiated by *any* object running in a designated thread of control rather than by a *specific* active object.

UML Statechart Diagrams

UML statechart diagrams specify the sequences of states that an object or an interaction goes through in response to events during its life, together with its responsive actions [BRJ98]. This book only uses basic state diagram notations.

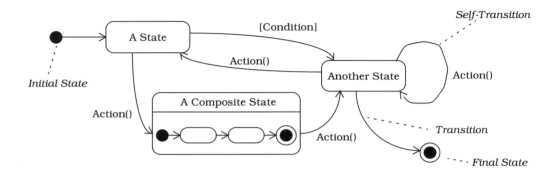

State. A condition or situation in the life of an object during which it satisfies some condition, performs some activity, or waits for some event. States are denoted by rounded rectangular boxes, labeled with their names. There are two additional states: the *initial* state, denoted by a black circle, which indicates the entry point into a state machine and the *final* state, denoted by a hollow circle with a black circle enclosed, which indicates the completion of the state machine.

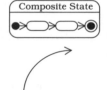

Composite State. A state that consists itself of a sequence of disjoint substates.

Transition. A relationship within a state machine between two states. A transition indicates that an object in the first state will enter the second state when a specified event such as an action occurs or a condition evaluates to true. If the source and target state are the same the transition is called a 'self-transition'.

Action. An executable computation, such as a method, that is conceptually atomic with respect to changing the current state.

Condition. A condition is a guard that triggers a transition if it evaluates to true.

References

[ABLL92] T.E. Anderson, B.N. Bershad, E.D. Lazowska, H.M. Levy: *Scheduler Activation: Effective Kernel Support for the User-Level Management of Parallelism*, ACM Transactions on Computer Systems, pp. 53–79, February 1992

[ACGH+96] M. Adams, J. Coplien, R. Gamoke, R. Hanmer, F. Keeve, K. Nicodemus: *Fault-Tolerant Telecommunication System Patterns*, in [PLoPD2], 1996

[Ada79] D. Adams: *The Hitchhiker's Guide to the Galaxy*, Pan Books Ltd., London, 1979

[AG98] K. Arnold, J. Gosling: *The Java Programming Language (Java Series)*, 2nd edition, Addison-Wesley, 1998

[Agha86] G. Agha: *A Model of Concurrent Computation in Distributed Systems*, MIT Press, 1986

[AIS77] C. Alexander, S. Ishikawa, M. Silverstein with M. Jacobson, I. Fiksdahl-King, S. Angel: *A Pattern Language – Towns·Buildings·Construction*, Oxford University Press, 1977

[Ale79] C. Alexander: *The Timeless Way of Building*, Oxford University Press, 1979

[Amb99a] S.W. Ambler: *Process Patterns: Building Large-Scale Systems Using Object Technology*, Cambridge University Press, 1999

[Amb99b] S.W. Ambler: *More Process Patterns: Delivering Large-Scale Systems Using Object Technology*, Cambridge University Press, 1999

[Ant96] D.L.G. Anthony: *Patterns for Classroom Education*, in [PLoPD2], 1996

[AONIX99] Aonix: Software Through Pictures, Aonix, http://www.aonix.com/, 1999

[ARSK00] A.B. Arulanthu, C. O'Ryan, D.C. Schmidt, M. Kircher: *The Design and Performance of a Scalable ORB Architecture for CORBA Asynchronous Messaging*, in J. Sventek, G. Coulson (eds.): Middleware 2000, Proceedings of the IFIP/ACM International Conference on Distributed Systems Platforms,

Springer, 2000, ACM/IFIP, Lecture Notes in Computer Science, Springer, 2000

[Aus98]   M.H. Austern: *Generic Programming and the STL : Using and Extending the C++ Standard*, Addison-Wesley, 1998

[Bak97]   S. Baker: *CORBA Distributed Objects using Orbix*, Addison-Wesley, 1997

[BaLee98]   R.E. Barkley, T.P.Lee: *A Heap-Based Callout Implementation to Meet Real-Time Needs*, Proceedings of the USENIX Summer Conference, USENIX Association, pp. 213–222, June 1998

[BaMo98]   G. Banga, J.C. Mogul: *Scalable Kernel Performance for Internet Servers Under Realistic Loads*, Proceedings of the USENIX 1998 Annual Technical Conference, USENIX, New Orleans, Louisiana, June 1998

[Ban98]   J. Bansiya: *Automating Design-Pattern Identification*, Dr. Dobb's Journal, June 1998

[Bat97]   G. Bateson: *Mind and Nature: A Necessary Unity*, Bantam Books, 1997

[BBC94]   G. Blaine, M. Boyd, S. Crider: *Project Spectrum: Scalable Bandwidth for the BJC Health System*, HIMSS, Health Care Communications, pp. 71–81, 1994

[Beck97]   K. Beck: *Smalltalk Best Practice Patterns*, Prentice Hall, 1997

[Beck99]   K. Beck: *Extreme Programming Explained: Embrace Change*, Addison-Wesley, 1999

[BeCu89]   K. Beck, W. Cunningham: *A Laboratory For Teaching Object-Oriented Thinking*, Proceedings of OOPSLA '89, N. Meyrowitz (ed.), special issue of SIGPLAN Notices, vol. 24, no. 10, pp. 1–6, October1989

[Ben90]   M. Ben-Ari: *Principles of Concurrent and Distributed Programming*, Prentice Hall, 1990

[Ber95]   S. Berczuk: *A Pattern for Separating Assembly and Processing*, in [PLoPD1], 1995

[BGHS98]   F. Buschmann, A. Geisler, T. Heimke, C. Schuderer: *Framework-Based Software Architectures for Process Automation Systems*, Proceedings of the 9th IFAC Symposium on Automation in Mining, Mineral and Metal Processing (MMM '98), Cologne, Germany, 1998

[BGJ99]   A. Berner, M. Glinz, S. Joos: *A Classification of Stereotypes for Object-Oriented Modeling Languages*, Proceedings of <<UML>>'99 – The Unified Modeling

Language, (eds.) R. France, B. Rumpe, Lecture Notes in Computer Science, 1723, Springer, 1999

[BFF96] T. Berners-Lee, R. T. Fielding, H. Frystyk: *Hypertext Transfer Protocol – HTTP/1.0*, Network Working Group, RFC 1945, May 1996

[BFVY96] F.J. Budinsky, M.A. Finnie, J.M. Vlissides, P.S. Yu: *Automatic code generation from design patterns*, IBM Systems Journal, vol. 35, no. 2, 1996

[BHG00] H. Berndt, T. Hamada, P. Graubmann: *TINA: Its Achievements and Future Directions*, IEEE Communication Surveys, on-line publication, `http://www.comsoc.org/pubs/surveys`, 2000

[Bir91] A.D. Birrell: *An Introduction to Programming with Threads*, Systems Programming with Modula-3, Greg Nelson (ed.), Prentice Hall, 1991

[Bir00] J. Birgin: *Fourteen Pedagogical Patterns*, `http://csis.pace.edu/~bergin/PedPat1.3.html`, 2000

[Bl90] D.L. Black: *Scheduling Support for Concurrency Parallelism in the Mach Operating System*, IEEE Computer, vol. 23, pp. 23–33, May 1990

[Bl91] U.D. Black: *OSI: A Model for Computer Communications Standards*, Prentice Hall, 1991

[BMBMM98] W.J. Brown, R.C. Malveau, W.H. Brown, H.W. McCormick, T.J. Mowbray: *Antipatterns: Refactoring Software, Architecture, and Projects in Crisis*, John Wiley & Sons, 1998

[BMT99] W.J. Brown, H.W. McCormick, S.W. Thomas: *Anti-Patterns and Patterns in Configuration Management*, John Wiley & Sons, 1999

[Boe81] B.W. Boehm: *Software Engineering Economics*, Prentice Hall, 1991

[Boo94] G. Booch: *Object-Oriented Analysis and Design With Applications*, Second Edition, Benjamin/Cummings, Redwood City, California, 1994

[Box97] D. Box: *Essential COM*, Addison-Wesley, 1997

[BR94] K. Birman, R. van Renesse: *Reliable Distributed Computing with the Isis Toolkit*, IEEE Computer Society Press, 1994

[BRJ98] G. Booch, J. Rumbaugh, I. Jacobsen: *The Unified Modeling Language User Guide*, Addison-Wesley, 1998

[Broo87]   F.P. Brooks: *No Silver Bullet: Essence and Accidents of Software Engineering*, IEEE Computer, vol. 20, no. 4, pp. 10–19, April 1987

[Bus98]   F. Buschmann: *Real-Time Constraints as Strategies*, http://www.posa.uci.edu/, 1998

[Bus00a]   F. Buschmann: *Applying Patterns*, http://www.posa.uci.edu/, 2000

[Bus00b]   F. Buschmann: *Inside Patterns*, http://www.posa.uci.edu/, 2000

[BV93]   G. Booch, M. Vilot: *Simplifying the Booch Components*, C++ Report, vol. 5, June 1993

[CarEl95]   M.D. Carroll, M.A. Ellis (Contributor): *Designing and Coding Reusable C++*, Addison Wesley ,1995

[CFFT97]   T. Chaney, A. Fingerhut, M. Flucke, J. S. Turner: *Design of a Gigabit ATM Switch*, IEEE INFOCOM '97, IEEE Computer Society Press, Kobe, Japan, April 1997

[CIRM93]   R. Campbell, N. Islam, D. Raila, P. Madany: *Designing and Implementing Choices: an Object-Oriented System in C++*, Communications of the ACM, vol. 36, pp. 117–126, September 1993

[Cla85]   D.D. Clark: *The Structuring of Systems Using Upcalls*, Proceedings of the 10th Symposium on Operating System Principles, 1985

[CMP95]   S. Crane, J. Magee, N. Pryce: *Design Patterns for Binding in Distributed Systems*, OOPSLA '95 workshop on Design Patterns for Concurrent, Parallel, and Distributed Object-Oriented Systems, ACM, October 1995

[Cock96]   A. Cockburn: *Prioritizing Forces in Software Design*, in [PLoPD2], 1996

[Cock97]   A. Cockburn: *Surviving Object-Oriented Projects: A Manager's Guide*, Addison Wesley Object Technology Series, Addison-Wesley, 1997

[Cope92]   J.O. Coplien: *Advanced C++ – Programming Styles and Idioms*, Addison-Wesley, 1992

[Cope95]   J.O. Coplien: *A Development Process Generative Pattern Language*, in [PLoPD1], 1995

[Cope96]   J.O. Coplien: *Software Patterns*, SIGS Books, New York, New York, 1996

[Cope97]   J.O. Coplien: *The Column Without a Name: Pattern Languages*, C++ Report, vol. 9, no. 1, pp. 15–21, January 1997

[Cope98]   J.O. Coplien: *Multi-Paradigm Design with C++*, Addison-Wesley, 1998

[CoSte91]   D.E. Comer, D.L. Stevens: *Internetworking with TCP/IP Volume II: Design, Implementation, and Internals*, Prentice Hall, 1991

[CoSte92]   D.E. Comer, D.L. Stevens: *Internetworking with TCP/IP Volume III: Client-Server Programming and Applications*, Prentice Hall, 1992

[CP95]   C. Cranor, G. Parulkar: *Design of Universal Continuous Media I/O*, Proceedings of the 5th International Workshop on Network and Operating Systems Support for Digital Audio and Video (NOSSDAV '95), pp. 83–86, April 1995

[Cris89]   F. Cristian: *Probabilistic Clock Synchronization*, Distributed Computing, vol. 3, pp 146–158, 1989

[CRSS+98]   M. Cukier, J. Ren, C. Sabnis, W.H. Sanders, D.E. Bakken, M.E. Berman, D.A. Karr, R.E. Schantz: *AQuA: An Adaptive Architecture that provides Dependable Distributed Objects*, IEEE Symposium on Reliable and Distributed Systems (SRDS), West Lafayette, IN, October 1998

[CW99]   J.O. Coplien with B. Woolf: *A Pattern Language for Writers' Workshops*, in [PLoPD4], 1999

[CY91]   P. Coad, E. Yourdon: *Object-Oriented Analysis*, Prentice Hall, second edition, 1991

[DBRD91]   R.P. Draves, B.N. Bershad, R.F. Rashid, R.W. Dean: *Using Continuations to Implement Thread Management and Communication in Operating Systems*, Proceedings of the 13th Symposium on Operating System Principles (SOSP), October 1991

[DeBr95]   D. DeBruler: *A Generative Pattern Language for Distributed Processing*, in [PLoPD1], 1995

[DeFe99]   A. Delarue and E.B. Fernandez: *Extension and Java implementation of the Reactor-Acceptor-Connector pattern combination*, Proceedings of the 1999 Conference on Pattern Languages of Programming, 1999

[Dij68]   E.W. Dijkstra: *Cooperating Sequential Processes*, in Programming Languages (F. Genuys, ed.), Academic Press, 1968

[DLF93]   D. de Champeaux, D. Lea, P. Faure: *Object-Oriented System Development*, Addison-Wesley, 1993

[Doble96]   J. Doble: Shopper, in [PLoPD2], 1996

[DP93]   P. Druschel, and L.L. Peterson: *Fbufs: A High-Bandwidth Cross-Domain Transfer Facility*, Proceedings of the 14th Symposium on Operating System Principles (SOSP), December 1993

[ECOOP95]   W. Olthoff (ed.): *ECOOP '95 – Object-Oriented Programming*, Proceedings of 9th European Conference on Object-Oriented Programming, Åarhus, Denmark, August 1995, Lecture Notes in Computer Science 952, Springer-Verlag, Berlin Heidelberg New York, 1995

[ECOOP97]   M. Aksit, S. Matsuoka (eds.): *ECOOP '97 – Object-Oriented Programming*, Proceedings of 11th European Conference on Object-Oriented Programming, Jyväskylä, Finland, June 1997, Lecture Notes in Computer Science 1241, Springer-Verlag, Berlin Heidelberg New York, 1997

[ECOOP98]   E. Jul (ed.): *ECOOP '98 – Object-Oriented Programming*, Proceedings of the 12th European Conference on Object-Oriented Programming, Brussels, Belgium, July 1998, Lecture Notes in Computer Science 1445, Springer-Verlag, Berlin Heidelberg New York, 1998

[EGHY99]   A. H. Eden, J. Gil, Y. Hirshfeld, A. Yehudai: *Motifs in Object Oriented Architecture*, IEEE Transactions on Software Engineering, 1999

[EKBF+92]   J. Eykholt, S. Kleiman, S. Barton, R. Faulkner, A. Shivalingiah, M. Smith, D. Stein, J. Voll, M. Wecks, D. Williams: *Beyond Multiprocessing... Multithreading the SunOS Kernel*, Proceedings of the Summer USENIX Conference, San Antonio, TX, June 1992

[Eng99]   J. Engel: *Programming for the Java Virtual Machine*, Addison-Wesley, 1999

[ENTERA00]   Entera: *Internet Content Delivery Techniques*, Entera Inc., http://www.entera.com/, 2000

[FoYo99]   B. Foote, J. Yoder: *Big Ball of Mud*, in [PLoPD4], 1999

[FBBOR99]   M. Fowler, K. Beck, J. Brant, W. Opdyke, D. Roberts: *Refactoring: Improving the Design of Existing Code*, Addison-Wesley, 1999

[FF97]   M. Felleisen, D.P. Friedman: *A Little Java, A Few Patterns*, MIT Press, 1997

[FGMFB97]   R. Fielding, J. Gettys, J. Mogul, H. Frystyk, T. Berners-Lee: *Hypertext Transfer Protocol – HTTP/1.1*, Network Working Group, RFC 2068, January 1997

[FGS98]   P. Felber, R. Guerraoui, A. Schiper: *The Implementation of a CORBA Object Group Service*, Theory and Practice of Object Systems (TAPOS), vol. 4, no. 2, pp. 93–105, February 1998

[FHA99]   E. Freeman, S. Hupfer, K. Arnold: *JavaSpaces Principles, Patterns and Practice*, Addison-Wesley, 1999

[FJ99]   M. Fayad, R. Johnson (eds.): *Domain-Specific Application Frameworks: Frameworks Experience by Industry*, John Wiley & Sons, New York, NY, 1999

[FJS99a]   M. Fayad, R. Johnson, D.C. Schmidt (eds.): *Object-Oriented Application Frameworks: Problems & Perspectives*, John Wiley & Sons, New York, NY, 1999

[FJS99b]   M. Fayad, R. Johnson, D.C. Schmidt (eds.): *Object-Oriented Application Frameworks: Applications & Experiences*, John Wiley & Sons, New York, NY, 1999

[Flex98]   Siemens AG, Geschäftsbereich Private Netze: *FlexRouting und BusinessView Produkte*, Folien zur Akquisitionsunterstützung, Siemens AG, 1998

[FMW97]   G. Florijn, M. Meijers, P. van Winsen: *Tool support for object-oriented patterns*, in [ECOOP97], 1997

[Fow97a]   M. Fowler: *Analysis Patterns*, Addison-Wesley, 1997

[Fow97b]   M. Fowler: *UML Distilled*, Addison-Wesley, 1997

[FS97]   M. Fayad, R. Johnson, D.C. Schmidt (eds.): *Special Issue on Object-Oriented Application Frameworks*, Communications of the ACM, vol. 40, no. 10, October 1997

[Gab96]   R.P. Gabriel: *Patterns of Software*, Oxford University Press, 1996

[GG99]   R.P. Gabriel, R. Goldman: *Jini Community Pattern Language*, Proceedings of the 1999 conference on Pattern Languages of Programming, 1999, http://jerry.cs.uiuc.edu/~plop/plop99/proceedings/

[GJS96]   J. Gosling, B. Joy, G. Steele: *The Java Language Specification*, Addison-Wesley, 1996

[GLDW87]   R. Gingell, M. Lee, X. Dang, M. Weeks: *Shared Libraries in SunOS*, Proceedings of the Summer 19987 USENIX Technical Conference, 1987

[GoF95]   E. Gamma, R. Helm, R. Johnson, J. Vlissides: *Design Patterns – Elements of Reusable Object-Oriented Software*, Addison-Wesley, 1995

[GP97]   G. Somadder, D.C. Petri: *A Pattern Language for Improving the Capacity of Layered Client/Server Systems with Multi-Threaded Servers*, Proceedings of the 2nd European Conference on Pattern Languages of Programming (EuroPLoP'97), pp. 179–189, Irsee, Germany, 1997

[GR93]   J. Gray, A. Reuter: *Transaction Processing: Concepts and Techniques*, Morgan Kaufman, 1993

[Grand98]   M. Grand: *Patterns in Java*, Volume 1, John Wiley & Sons, 1998

[Grand99]   M. Grand: *Patterns in Java*, Volume 2, John Wiley & Sons, 1999

[GR96]   B. Goldfedder, L. Rising: *A Training Experience with Patterns*, Communications of the ACM, vol. 39, no. 10, 1996

[GS96]   A. Gokhale, D.C. Schmidt: *Measuring the Performance of Communication Middleware on High-Speed Networks*, Proceedings of SIGCOMM '96, Stanford, CA, ACM, pp. 306–317, August 1996

[GS97]   R. Guerraoui, A. Schiper: *Software-Based Replication for Fault Tolerance*, IEEE Computer, vol 30. no. 4, pp. 68–74, April 1997

[GS98]   A. Gokhale, D.C. Schmidt: *Optimizing a CORBA IIOP Protocol Engine for Minimal Footprint Multimedia Systems*, Journal on Selected Areas in Communications, special issue on Service Enabling Platforms for Networked Multimedia Systems, vol. 17, no. 9, September 1999

[GZ89]   R. Gusella, S. Zatti: *The Accuracy of the Clock Synchronization Achieved by TEMPO in Berkeley UNIX 4.3 BSD*, IEEE Transactions on Software Engineering, vol. 15, pp. 847–853, July 1989

[Hal85]   R.H. Halstead, Jr.: *Multilisp: A Language for Concurrent Symbolic Computation*, ACM Transactions on Programming Languages and Systems, vol. 7, pp. 501–538, October 1985

[Har96]   N.B. Harrison: *Organizational Patterns for Teams*, in [PLoPD2], 1996

[Har97]   N.B. Harrison: *Patterns for Logging Diagnostic Messages*, in [PLoPD3], 1997

[Hen98]   M. Henning: *Binding, Migration and Scalability in CORBA*, in Communications of the ACM, special issue on CORBA, ed. K. Seetharaman, vol. 41, no. 10, ACM, October 1998

[Hen00]   K. Henney: *Executing Around Sequences*, Proceedings of the 5th European conference on Pattern Languages of Programming, EuroPLoP 2000, Irsee, July 2000

[HJE95]   H. Hüni, R. Johnson, R. Engel: *A Framework for Network Protocol Software*, Proceedings of OOPSLA '95, ACM, Austin, TX, October 15–19, 1995

[HK93]   Y. Huang, C. Kintala: *Software Implemented Fault Tolerance: Technologies and Experience*, Proceedings of the 23rd International Symposium on Fault-tolerance Computing (FTCS), pp. 2–10, Toulouse, France, June 1993

[HLS97]   T. Harrison, D. Levine, D.C. Schmidt: *The Design and Performance of a Real-Time CORBA Event Service*, Proceedings of OOPSLA '97, ACM, Atlanta, GA, October 6–7, 1997.

[HMPT89]   N.C. Hutchinson, S. Mishra, L.L. Peterson, V.T. Thomas: Tools for Implementing Network Protocols, Software Practice and Experience, vol. 19, no. 9, 1989

[HMS98]   J. Hu, S. Mungee, Douglas C. Schmidt: *Principles for Developing and Measuring High-performance Web Servers over ATM*, Proceedings of INFOCOM '98, 1998

[Hoare74]   C.A.R. Hoare: *Monitors: An Operating System Structuring Mechanism*, Communications of the ACM, vol. 17, October 1974

[HP91]   N.C. Hutchinson, L.L. Peterson: *The x-kernel: An Architecture for Implementing Network Protocols*, IEEE Transactions on Software Engineering, vol. 17, pp. 64–76, January 1991

[HPS99]   J.C. Hu, I. Pyarali, D.C. Schmidt: *The Object-Oriented Design and Performance of JAWS: A High-performance Web Server Optimized for High-speed Networks*, Parallel and Distributed Computing Practices Journal, special issue on Distributed Object-Oriented Systems, 1999

[HS98]   J.C. Hu, D.C. Schmidt: JAWS: *A Framework for High-performance Web Servers*, in [FJ99], 1999

[HS99a]   G.C. Hunt, M.L. Scott: *Intercepting and Instrumenting COM Application*, Proceedings of the 5th Conference on Object-Oriented Technologies and Systems, USENIX, San Diego, CA, May 1999

[HS99b]   R. Hanmer, G. Stymfal: *An Input and Output Pattern Language: Lessons from Telecommunications*, in [PLoPD4], 1999

[HSGH99]   T. Howes, M.C. Smith, G.S. Good, T.A. Howes: *Understanding and Deploying Ldap Directory Services*, Macmillan Network Architecture and Development Series), Macmillan Technical Publishing, 1999

[HV99]   M. Henning, S. Vinoski: *Advanced CORBA Programming with C++*, Addison-Wesley, 1999

[IBM98]   IBM Corporation: *San Francisco Patterns*,
              `http://www-4.ibm.com/software/ad/sanfrancisco/concepts/`
              `ibmsf.sf.SFConceptsAndFacilitiesPatterns.html`, 1998

[IEEE95]   IEEE: *Scheduling and Load Balancing in Parallel and Distributed Systems*,
              (eds.) B.A. Shirazi, A.R. Hurson, K.M. Kavi, IEEE Computer Society, 1995

[IEEE96]   IEEE: *Threads Extension for Portable Operating Systems*, (Draft 10), February
              1996

[IEEE99]   IEEE: *Design Patterns in Communications Software Architecture*, L. Rising
              (ed.), special issue of IEEE Communications Magazine, vol. 37, no. 4, April
              1999

[IM96]   N. Islam, M.V. Devarakonda: *An Essential Design Pattern for Fault-Tolerant
              Distributed State Sharing*, Communications of the ACM (CACM), vol. 39, no.
              10, pp. 55–74, 1996

[ITUT92]   ITU-T: *Principles for a Telecommunications Management Network*, (Recom-
              mendation M.3010), 1992

[JACE99]   DOC Group at Washington University in St. Louis: *Java ACE, An Object-
              Oriented Network Programming Toolkit in Java*, Washington University, St.
              Louis, USA, 1999, `http://www.cs.wustl.edu/~schmidt/JACE.html`

[JBR99]   I. Jacobson, G. Booch, J. Rumbaugh: *Unified Software Development Process*,
              Addison-Wesley, 1999

[JH98]   G. James, D. Hillard: *The TAO Of Programming, Book 3 – Design*,
              `http://www.gnomehome.demon.nl/uddf/pages/zzztao.htm`, 1998

[JK00]   P. Jain, M. Kircher: *The Lookup Design Pattern*, Proceedings of the 5th
              European Conference on Pattern Languages of Programming, EuroPLoP
              2000, July 2000

[JML92]   R. Johnson, C. McConnell, J.M. Lake: *The RTL System: A Framework for Code
              Optimization*, in R. Giegerich, S. Graham (eds.): Code Generation – Concepts,
              Tools, Techniques, pp. 255–274, Springer-Verlag, London, 1991

[John92]   R. Johnson: *Documenting Frameworks Using Patterns*, in Proceedings of the
              1992 Conference on Object-Oriented Programming Systems, Languages and
              Applications (OOPSLA '92), pp. 63–76, ACM Press, 1992

[John96]   R. Johnson: *Transactions and Accounts*, in [PLoPD2], 1996

[John97]   R. Johnson: *Frameworks = Patterns + Components*, Communications of the ACM, M. Fayad and D. C. Schmidt (eds.), vol. 40, no. 10, October 1997

[JS97a]   P. Jain, D.C. Schmidt: *Experiences Converting a C++ Communication Software Framework to Java*, C++ Report, vol. 9, Issue 1, January 1997

[JS97b]   P. Jain, D.C. Schmidt: *Service Configurator: A Pattern for Dynamic Configuration of Services*, Proceedings of the 3rd Conference on Object-Oriented Technologies and Systems, USENIX, June 1997

[JSR51]   *New I/O APIs for the Java Platform*, http://java.sun.com/aboutJava/communityprocess/jsr/jsr_051_ioapis.html

[JWS98]   P. Jain, S. Widoff, D.C. Schmidt: *The Design and Performance of MedJava – Experience Developing Performance-Sensitive Distributed Applications with Java*, IEE/BCS Distributed Systems Engineering Journal, 1998

[Kan92]   S. Khanna: *Real-Time Scheduling in SunOS 5.0*, in Proceedings of the 1992 USENIX Winter Conference, USENIX Association, pp. 375–390, 1992

[Kar95]   E-A. Karlsson (Ed.): *Software Reuse – A Holistic Approach*, John Wiley & Sons, 1995

[KC97]   W. Keller, J. Coldewey: *Accessing Relational Databases*, in [PLoPD3], 1997

[KCC+96]   K. Beck, R. Crocker, J.O. Coplien, L. Dominick, G. Meszaros, F. Paulisch, J. Vlissides: *Industrial Experience with Design Patterns*, Proceedings of the International Conference on Software Engineering 1996 (ICSE '96), Berlin, March 1996, also available in [Ris98]

[Ken98]   E. Kendall: *Utilizing Patterns and Pattern Languages in Software Engineering Education*, Annals of Software Engineering, vol. 6, Software Engineering Education, 1998

[Kic92]   G. Kiczales: *Towards a New Model of Abstraction in Software Engineering*, in A. Yonezawa, B.C. Smith (eds.): Proceedings of the International Workshop on New Models for Software Architecture '92 – Reflection and Meta-Level Architecture, Tokyo, Japan, 1992

[KiLe00]   M. Kircher and D.L. Levine: *The XP of TAO – eXtreme Programming of Large, Open-source Frameworks*, in Proceedings of the 1st International Conference on eXtreme Programming and Flexible Processes in Software Engineering, Cagliari, Italy, June 2000

[KLM+97]   G. Kiczales. J. Lamping, A. Mendhekar, C. Maeda, C. Lopes, J-M. Loingtier, J. Irwin: *Aspect-Oriented Programming*, in [ECOOP97], 1997

[KML92]   D. Kafura, M. Mukherji, G. Lavender: *ACT++: A Class Library for Concurrent Programming in C++ using Actors*, Journal of Object-Oriented Programming, pp. 47–56, October 1992

[Kof93]   T. Kofler: *Robust Iterators for {ET++}*, Structured Programming, vol. 14, no. 2, pp. 62–85, 1993

[KRL+00]   F. Kon, M. Román, P. Liu, J. Mao, T. Yamane, L.C. Magalhães, R.H. Campbell: *Monitoring, Security, and Dynamic Configuration with the dynamicTAO Reflective ORB*, in J. Sventek, G. Coulson (ed.): Middleware 2000, Proceedings of the IFIP/ACM International Conference on Distributed Systems Platforms, 2000, ACM/IFIP, Lecture Notes in Computer Science, Springer, 2000

[KSL99]   F. Kuhns, D.C. Schmidt, D.L. Levine: *The Design and Performance of a Real-Time I/O Subsystem*, Proceedings of the IEEE Real-Time Technology and Applications Symposium, IEEE, Vancouver, British Columbia, Canada, pp. 154–163, June 1999

[KTB98]   R.K. Keller, J. Tessier, G. von Bochmann: *A Pattern System for Network Management Interfaces*, Communications of the ACM, vol. 41, no. 9. pp. 86–93, September 1998

[Lak95]   J. Lakos: *Large-Scale Software Development with C++*, Addison-Wesley, 1995

[Lan98]   M. Lange: *Time Patterns*, Proceedings of the 1998 European Conference on Pattern Languages of Programming, July 1998

[LBG97]   K. Lano, J. Bicarregui, and S Goldsack: *Formalising Design Patterns*, in 1st BCS-FACS Northern Formal Methods Workshop, Electronic Workshops in Computer Science, Springer-Verlag, 1997

[LC87]   M.A. Linton, P.R. Calder: *The Design and Implementation of InterViews*, Proceedings of the USENIX C++ Workshop, November 1987

[Lea94]   Doug Lea: *Design Patterns for Avionics Control Systems*, DSSA ADAGE Technical Report ADAGE-OSW-94-01, Loral Federal Systems, 1994

[Lea99a]   D. Lea: *Concurrent Programming in Java, Design Principles and Patterns*, 2nd edition, Addison-Wesley, 1999

[Lea99b]   D. Lea: *Software Design*, State University Of New York at Oswego, class no. CSC 480, State University Of New York at Oswego, Oswego, 1999

[Lew95]   B. Lewis: *Threads Primer: A Guide to Multithreaded Programming*, Prentice Hall, 1995

[LGS99]   D.L. Levine, C.D. Gill, D.C. Schmidt: *Object Lifetime Manager – A Complementary Pattern for Controlling Object Creation and Destruction*, C++ Report, vol. 12, Number 1, January 2000,
`http://www.cs.wustl.edu/~levine/research/ObjMan.ps.gz`

[LG00]   D.L. Levine, C.D. Gill: *Object-Oriented Software Development Laboratory*, Washington University in St. Louis, Class no. CS E61 342S, Washington University, St. Louis, 2000,
`http://www.cs.wustl.edu/~levine/courses/cs342`

[LK95]   R.G. Lavender, D.G. Kafura: *A Polymorphic Future and First-Class Function Type for Concurrent Object-Oriented Programming in C++*,
`http://www.cs.utexas.edu/users/lavender/papers/future.ps`, 1995

[LS88]   B. Liskov, L. Shrira: *Promises: Linguistic Support for Efficient Asynchronous Procedure Calls in Distributed Systems*, Proceedings of the SIGPLAN '88 Conference on Programming Language Design and Implementation, pp. 260–267, June 1988

[LS98]   A. Lauder, S. Kent: *Precise Visual Specification of Design Patterns*, in [ECOOP98], 1998

[LT93]   D.L. Levine, R.N. Taylor: *Metric-Driven Re-engineering for Static Concurrency Analysis*, Proceedings of the ACM SIGSOFT International Symposium on Software Testing and Analysis (ISSTA '93), ACM press, 1993

[LY99]   T. Lindholm, F. Yellin: *The Java Virtual Machine Specification*, 2nd Edition, Addison-Wesley, 1999

[Maf96]   S. Maffeis: *The Object Group Design Pattern*, Proceedings of the 1996 USENIX Conference on Object-Oriented Technologies, USENIX, Toronto, Canada, June 1996

[MaHa99]   V. Matena, M Hapner: *Enterprise JavaBeans*, Version 1.1, Sun Microsystems, 1999

[Mar95]   R.C. Martin: *Designing Object-Oriented C++ Applications Using the Booch Method*, Prentice Hall, 1995

[MB91]   J.C. Mogul, A. Borg: *The Effects of Context Switches on Cache Performance*, Proceedings of the 4th International Conference on Architectural Support for

Programming Languages and Operating Systems (ASPLOS), ACM, Santa Clara, CA, April 1991

[MBKQ96]   M.K. McKusick, K. Bostic, M.J. Karels, J.S. Quarterman: *The Design and Implementation of the 4.4 BSD Operating System*, Addison-Wesley 1996

[MD91]   P.E. McKenney, K.F. Dove: *Efficient Demultiplexing of Incoming TCP Packets*, Sequent Computer Systems, Inc., SQN TR92-01, December 1991

[McK95]   P.E. McKenney: *Selecting Locking Designs for Parallel Programs*, in [PLoPD2], 1996

[MDS96]   *Microsoft Developers Studio, Version 4.2 – Software Development Kit*, 1996

[Mey95]   S. Meyers: *More Effective C++ – 35 New Ways to Improve Your Programs and Designs*, Addison-Wesley, 1995

[Mey97]   B. Meyer: *Object-Oriented Software Construction*, 2nd Edition, Prentice Hall, Englewood Cliffs, NJ, 1997

[Mey98]   S. Meyers: *Effective C++*, 2nd edition, Addison-Wesley,1998

[Mes95]   G. Meszaros: *Half Object plus Protocol*, in [PLoPD1], 1995

[Mes96]   G. Meszaros: *A Pattern Language for Improving the Capacity of Reactive Systems*, in [PLoPD2], 1996

[MGG00]   P. Merle, C. Gransart, J.M. Geib: *Using and Implementing CORBA Objects with CorbaScript*, in J.P. Bashoun, T. Baba, J.P. Briot, A. Yonezawa (eds.): Object-Oriented Parallel and Distributed Programming, Editions Hermes, Paris, France, January 2000

[Mic00]   A. Michail: *Data Mining Library Reuse Patterns using Generalized Association Rules*, Proceedings of the 22nd International Conference on Software Engineering, 2000

[Mik98]   T. Mikkonen: *Formalizing Design Patterns*, Proceedings of the 1998 International Conference on Software Engineering, pp. 115–124, IEEE Computer Society Press, 1998

[Mil88]   D. Mills: *The Network Time Protocol*, University of Delaware, Network, 1988

[MK97]   A. Mester, H. Krumm: *Formal behavioural patterns for the tool-assisted design of distributed applications*, IFIP WG 6.1 International Working Conference on Distributed Applications and Interoperable Systems (DAIS 97), Cottbus, Germany, Sep/Oct 1997, Chapman & Hall, 1997

[MM97]   R.C. Malveau, T.J. Mowbray: *CORBA Design Patterns*, John Wiley & Sons, 1997

[MMN99]   L.E. Moser, P.M. Melliar-Smith, P. Narasimhan: *A Fault Tolerance Framework for CORBA*, International Symposium on Fault Tolerant Computing, Madison, WI, June 1999

[Mog95]   J.C. Mogul: *The Case for Persistent-connection HTTP*, Proceedings of the ACM SIGCOMM'95 Conference in Computer Communication Review, ACM press, pp. 299–314, 1995

[MWY91]   S. Matsuoka, K. Wakita, A. Yonezawa: *Analysis of Inheritance Anomaly in Concurrent Object-Oriented Languages*, OOPS Messenger, 1991

[Mue93]   F. Mueller: *A Library Implementation of POSIX Threads Under UNIX*, Proceedings of the Winter USENIX Conference, San Diego, CA, USA, 1993

[Mue96]   H. Mueller: *Patterns for Handling Exception Handling Successfully*, C++ Report vol. 8, January 1996

[Naka00]   T. Nakajima: *Dynamic Transport Protocol Selection in a CORBA System*, The 3rd IEEE International Symposium on Object-Oriented Real-Time Distributed Computing, Newport Beach, California, USA, March 15–17 2000

[NDW93]   J. Neider, T. Davis, M. Woo: *OpenGL Programming Guide: The Official Guide to Learning OpenGL, Release 1*, Addison-Wesley, 1993

[NLN+99]   S. Nimmagadda, C. Liyanaarchchi, D. Niehaus, A. Gopinath, A. Kaushal: *Performance Patterns: Automated Scenario Based ORB Performance Evaluation*, Proceedings of the 5th Conference on Object-Oriented Technologies and Systems, USENIX, San Diego, CA, May 1999

[NMM99]   P. Narasimhan, L.E. Moser, P.M. Melliar-Smith: *Using Interceptors to Enhance CORBA*, IEEE Computer, vol. 32, no. 7, pp. 64–68, July 1999

[NMM00]   P. Narasimhan, L.E. Moser, P.M. Melliar-Smith: *Patterns for Building Transparent Reliable Middleware*, Theory and Practice of Object Systems, vol. 6, 2000

[Nuy96]   D. Nguyen: *Design Patterns for Data Structures*, http://csis.pace.edu/~bergin/papers/nguyen/ DesPat4DatStruct.html, 1996

[NW98]   J. Noble, C. Weir: *Proceedings of the Memory Preservation Society*, Proceedings of the 1998 European Conference on Pattern Languages of Programming, July 1998

[MTOOL99]   microTOOL: *objectiF – For the Development of Object-Oriented and Component-Based Software Systems*, microTOOL GmbH, http://www.microtool.de, 1999

[OHE96]   R. Orfali, D. Harkey, J. Edwards: *The Essential Distributed Objects Survival Guide*, Wiley & Sons, 1996

[OMG97a]   Object Management Group: *CORBA Services – Naming Service*, TC Document formal/97-07-12, July 1997

[OMG97b]   Object Management Group: *CORBA Services – Transactions Service*, TC Document formal/97-12-17, 1997

[OMG97c]   Object Management Group: *CORBA Time Service Specification*, OMG TC Document orbos/97-12-21, December 1997

[OMG98a]   Object Management Group: *CORBA Messaging Specification*, OMG TC Document orbos/98-05-05, May 1998

[OMG98b]   Object Management Group: *CORBA Services: Common Object Services Specification Updated Version: December 1998, Chapter 16: The Trading Object Service Specification*, formal/98-07-05, 1998

[OMG98c]   Object Management Group: *The Common Object Request Broker: Architecture and Specification*, 2.3 ed., December 1998

[OMG98d]   Object Management Group: *CORBA Security Service v1.2 Specification*, OMG TC Document formal/98-12-17, December 1998

[OMG99a]   Object Management Group: *CORBA Components Final Submission*, OMG TC Document orbos/99-02-05, February 1999

[OMG99b]   Object Management Group: *Real-Time CORBA Joint Revised Submission*, OMG TC Document orbos/99-02-12, February 1999

[OMG99c]   Object Management Group: *Notification Service Specification*, OMG TC Document telecom/99-07-01, July 1999

[OMG99d]   Object Management Group: *minimumCORBA Joint Revised Submission*, OMG TC Document orbos/98-08-04, August1999

[OMG99e]   Object Management Group: *Persistent State Service 2.0 Joint Revised Submission*, orbos/99-07-07, August 1999

[OMG99f]   Object Management Group: *Portable Interceptors*, OMG TC Document orbos/99-12-02, December 1999

[OMG99g]   Object Management Group: *Fault Tolerant CORBA Joint Revised Submission*, OMG TC Document orbos/99-12-08, December 1999

[Opd92]   W.F. Opdyke: *Refactoring Object-Oriented Frameworks*, PhD Thesis, University of Illinois at Urbana Champaign, 1992

[OS99]   O'Reilly On-line Book: *Open Sources: Voices from the Open Source Revolution*, http://www.oreilly.com/catalog/opensources/book/toc.html, O'Reilly, 1999

[OSSL00]   OpenSSL: *An Open Source toolkit implementing the Secure Sockets Layer (SSL v2/v3) and Transport Layer Security (TLS v1)*, http://www.openssl.org/, 2000

[PC00]   M.P. Plezbert, R.K. Cytron: *Recognition and Verification of Design Patterns*, Technical Report WUCS-00-01, Washington University in St. Louis, January 2000

[Pet95]   C. Petzold: *Programming Windows 95*, Microsoft Press, 1995

[PHS96]   I. Pyarali, T.H. Harrison, D.C. Schmidt: *Design and Performance of an Object-Oriented Framework for High-Performance Electronic Medical Imaging*, USENIX Computing Systems, vol. 9, November/December 1996

[PK98]   L. Prechelt, C. Krämer: *Functionality versus Practicality: Employing Existing Tools for Recovering Structural Design Patterns*, Journal of Universal Computer Science, vol. 4, no. 12, pp. 866–882, December 1998

[PLoPD1]   J.O. Coplien, D.C. Schmidt (eds.): *Pattern Languages of Program Design*, Addison-Wesley, 1995 (a book publishing the reviewed Proceedings of the First International Conference on Pattern Languages of Programming, Monticello, Illinois, 1994)

[PLoPD2]   J.O. Coplien, N. Kerth, J. Vlissides (eds.): *Pattern Languages of Program Design 2*, Addison-Wesley, 1996 (a book publishing the reviewed Proceedings of the Second International Conference on Pattern Languages of Programming, Monticello, Illinois, 1995)

[PLoPD3]   R.C. Martin, D. Riehle, F. Buschmann (eds.): *Pattern Languages of Program Design 3*, Addison-Wesley, 1997 (a book publishing selected papers from the Third International Conference on Pattern Languages of Programming, Monticello, Illinois, USA, 1996, the First European Conference on Pattern Languages of Programming, Irsee, Bavaria, Germany, 1996, and the Telecommunication Pattern Workshop at OOPSLA '96, San Jose, California, USA, 1996)

[PLoPD4]   N. Harrison, B. Foote, H. Rohnert (eds.): *Pattern Languages of Program Design 4*, Addison-Wesley, 1999 (a book publishing selected papers from the Fourth and Fifth International Conference on Pattern Languages of Programming, Monticello, Illinois, USA, 1997 and 1998, and the Second and Third European Conference on Pattern Languages of Programming, Irsee, Bavaria, Germany, 1997 and 1998)

[POSA1]   F. Buschmann, R. Meunier, H. Rohnert, P. Sommerlad, M. Stal: *Pattern-Oriented Software Architecture – A System of Patterns*, John Wiley & Sons, 1996

[POSIX95]   *Information Technology – Portable Operating System Interface (POSIX) – Part 1: System Application: Program Interface (API) [C Language]*, 1995

[PPP00]   *The Pedagogical Patterns Project*, http://www-lifia.info.unlp.edu.ar/ppp/, 2000

[PPR]   *The Portland Pattern Repository*, http://www.c2.com

[PR90]   D.L. Presotto, D.M. Ritchie: *Interprocess Communication in the Ninth Edition UNIX System*, UNIX Research System Papers, Tenth Edition, vol. 2, no. 8, pp. 523–530, 1990

[PQ00]   V. N. Padmanabhan, L. Qiu: *The Content and Access Dynamics of A Busy Web Site: Findings and Interpretations*, Proceedings of the ACM SIGCOMM Conference, Stockholm, Sweden, August/September, 2000

[Pree95]   W. Pree: *Design Patterns for Object-Oriented Software Development*, Addison-Wesley, 1995

[Preiss98]   B.R. Preiss: *Data Structures and Algorithms with Object-Oriented Design Patterns in C++*, John Wiley & Sons, 1998

[Pro99]   J. Prosise: *Programming Windows With MFC*, 2nd edition, Microsoft Press, 1999

[PRS+99]   I. Pyarali, C. O'Ryan, D.C. Schmidt, N. Wang, V. Kachroo, A. Gokhale: *Applying Optimization Patterns to the Design of Real-Time ORBs*, Proceedings of the 5th conference on Object-Oriented Technologies and Systems, San Diego, CA, USENIX, 1999

[PRS00]   I. Pyarali, C. O'Ryan, D.C. Schmidt: *A Pattern Language for Efficient, Predictable, Scalable, and Flexible Dispatching Mechanisms for Distributed Object Computing Middleware*, Proceedings of the International Symposium on Object-Oriented Real-Time Distributed Computing (ISORC), IEEE/IFIP Newport Beach, CA, March 2000

[Pry99]   N. Pryce: *Abstract Session*, in [PLoPD4], 1999

[PSJ00]   D.C. Petriu, C. Shousha, A. Jalnapurkar: *Architecture-Based Performance Analysis Applied to a Telecommunication System*, accepted for publication in IEEE Transactions on Software Engineering, special issue on Software and Performance, 2000

[PSK+97]   G. Parulkar, D.C. Schmidt, E. Kraemer, J. Turner, A. Kantawala: *An Architecture for Monitoring, Visualizing and Control of Gigabit Networks*, IEEE Network vol. 11, Sept. 1997

[PUPT97]   L. Prechelt, B. Unger, M. Philippsen, W.F. Tichy: *Two Controlled Experiments Assessing the Usefulness of Design Pattern Information During Program Maintenance*, Empirical Software Engineering – An International Journal, December 1997

[Rago93]   S. Rago: *UNIX System V Network Programming*, Addison-Wesley, 1993

[RBGM00]   D. Riehle, R. Brudermann, T. Gross, K.U. Mätzel: *Pattern Density and Role Modeling of an Object Transport Service*, ACM Computing Surveys, March 2000.

[RBPEL91]   J. Rumbaugh, M. Blaha, W. Premerlani, F. Eddy, W. Lorensen: *Object-Oriented Modeling and Design*, Prentice Hall, 1991

[RBV99]   M. Robinson, K. Brown, P.A. Vorobiev: *Swing*, Manning Publications Company, 1999

[Ree92]   T. Reenskaug: *Intermediate Smalltalk, Practical Design and Implementation*, Tutorial, TOOLS Europe '92, Dortmund, 1992

[RG98]   D. Riehle, T. Gross: *Role Model Based Framework Design and Integration*, Proceedings of the 1998 Conference on Object-Oriented Programming Systems, Languages and Applications (OOPSLA '98), pp. 117–133, ACM Press, 1998

[Ric97]   J. Richter: *Advanced Windows*, 3rd edition, Microsoft Press, 1997

[Rie96]   D. Riehle: *The Event Notification Pattern – Integrating Implicit Invocation with Object-Orientation*, Theory and Practice of Object Systems vol. 2, no. 1, pp. 43–52, John Wiley & Sons, 1996

[Rie97]   D. Riehle: *Composite Design Patterns*, Proceedings of the 1997 Conference on Object-Oriented Programming Systems, Languages and Applications (OOPSLA '97). ACM Press, 1997

[Ris98]   L. Rising (ed.): *The Patterns Handbook*, SIGS Publications, Cambridge University Press, 1998

[Ris00a]   L. Rising: *The Pattern Almanac 2000*, Addison-Wesley, 2000

[Ris00b]   L. Rising: *Design Patterns in Communications Software*, Cambridge University Press, 2000

[Rit84]   D. Ritchie: *A Stream Input-Output System*, AT&T Bell Labs Technical Journal, vol 63 pp. 311–324, October 1984

[RKF92]   W. Rosenberry, D. Kenney, G. Fischer: *Understanding DCE*, O'Reilly and Associates, Inc., 1992

[RKSOP00]   C. O'Ryan, F. Kuhns, Douglas C. Schmidt, O. Othman, J. Parsons: *The Design and Performance of a Pluggable Protocols Framework for Real-Time Distributed Object Computing Middleware*, J. Sventek, G. Coulson (eds.): Middleware 2000, Proceedings of the IFIP/ACM International Conference on Distributed Systems Platforms, 2000, ACM/IFIP, Lecture Notes in Computer Science, Springer, 2000

[RSB+97]   D. Riehle, W. Siberski, B. Bäumer, D. Megert, B. Fletcher: *Serializer*, in [PLoPD3], 1997

[San98]   R.E. Sanders: *ODBC 3.5 Developer's Guide*, McGraw-Hill Series on Data Warehousing and Data, 1998

[SC96]   A. Sane, R. Campbell: *Resource Exchanger: A Behavioral Pattern for Low-Overhead Concurrent Resource Management*, in [PLoPD2], 1996

[SC99]   D.C. Schmidt, C. Cleeland: *Applying Patterns to Develop Extensible ORB Middleware*, IEEE Communications Magazine, special issue on Design Patterns, April 1999

[Sch92]   D.C. Schmidt: *IPC_SAP: An Object-Oriented Interface to Interprocess Communication Services*, C++ Report vol. 4, November/December 1992

[Sch94]   D.C. Schmidt: *A Domain Analysis of Network Daemon Design Dimensions*, C++ Report, SIGS, vol. 6, no. 3, pp. 1–12, March/April 1994

[Sch95]   D.C. Schmidt: *An OO Encapsulation of Lightweight OS Concurrency Mechanisms in the ACE Toolkit*, Technical Report WUCS-95-31, Washington Univer-

sity, St. Louis, September 1995,
http://www.cs.wustl.edu/~schmidt/Concurrency.ps.gz

[Sch96] D.C. Schmidt: *A Family of Design Patterns for Application-level Gateways*, The Theory and Practice of Object Systems, special issue on Patterns and Pattern Languages, vol. 2, no. 1, 1996

[Sch97] D.C. Schmidt: *Applying Design Patterns and Frameworks to Develop Object-Oriented Communication Software*, Handbook of Programming Languages, Peter Salus (ed.), MacMillan Computer Publishing, 1997

[Sch98a] D.C. Schmidt: *GPERF: A Perfect Hash Function Generator*, C++ Report, vol. 10, no. 10, November/December 1998

[Sch98b] D.C. Schmidt: *Evaluating Architectures for Multi-threaded CORBA Object Request Brokers*, Communications of the ACM, special issue on CORBA, Krishnan Seetharaman (ed.), vol 41., no. 10, ACM, October 1998

[Sch99] D.C. Schmidt: *Developing Object-Oriented Software with Patterns and Frameworks*, Washington University in St. Louis, Class no. CS 242, Washington University, St. Louis, 1999,
http://www.cs.wustl.edu/~schmidt/courses.html

[SchSt95] D.C. Schmidt, P. Stephenson: *Experiences Using Design Patterns to Evolve System Software Across Diverse OS Platforms*, in [ECOOP95], 1995

[SchSu93] D.C. Schmidt, T. Suda: *Transport System Architecture Services for High-Performance Communications Systems*, IEEE Journal on Selected Areas in Communication, vol. 11, no. 4, pp. 489–506, IEEE, May 1993

[SchSu94] D.C. Schmidt, T. Suda: *An Object-Oriented Framework for Dynamically Configuring Extensible Distributed Communication Systems*, IEE/BCS Distributed Systems Engineering Journal, vol. 2, pp. 280–293, December 1994

[SchSu95] D.C. Schmidt, T. Suda: *Measuring the Performance of Parallel Message-Based Process Architectures*, Proceedings of the Conference on Computer Communications (INFOCOM), pp. 624–633, IEEE, April 1995

[SeSch70] A. Seidelmann, A. Schwarzenegger: *Hercules in New York*, RAF Industries, 1970

[SFJ96] D.C. Schmidt, M. Fayad. R.E. Johnson: *Software Patterns*, Communications of the ACM (CACM), vol. 39, no. 10, pp. 36–39, 1996

[SG96] M. Shaw, D. Garlan: *Software Architecture – Perspectives of an Emerging Discipline*, Prentice Hall, 1996

[SGWSM94] B. Selic, G.Gullekson, P.T. Ward, B. Selic, J. McGee: *Real-Time Object-Oriented Modeling*, John Wiley & Sons, 1994

[Shap93] M. Shapiro: *Flexible Bindings for Fine-Grain, Distributed Objects*, INRIA, Rapport de Recherche INRIA 2007, August 1993

[SHS95] D.C. Schmidt, T.H. Harrison, E. Al-Shaer, *Object-Oriented Components for High-Speed Networking Programming*, Proceedings of the 1st Conference on Object Technologies and Systems, USENIX, Monterey, CA, June 1995

[SKT96] J.D. Salehi, J.F. Kurose, D. Towsley: *The Effectiveness of Affinity-Based Scheduling in Multiprocessor Networks*, IEEE INFOCOM, IEEE Computer Society Press, March, 1996

[SM88] S. Shlaer, S.J. Mellor: *Object-Oriented Systems Analysis – Modeling the World In Data*, Yourdon Press, Prentice Hall, 1988

[SMB96] F. Shull, W. Melo, V. Basili: *An Inductive Method for Discovering Design Patterns from Object-Oriented Software Systems*, University of Maryland CS-TR-3597, 1996

[SLM98] D.C. Schmidt, D.L. Levine, S. Mungee: *The Design and Performance of Real-Time Object Request Brokers*, Computer Communications, vol. 21, no. 4, pp. 294–324, Elsevier, April 1998

[SMFG00] D.C. Schmidt, S. Mungee, S. Flores-Gaitan, A. Gokhale: *Software Architectures for Reducing Priority Inversion and Non-Determinism in Real-Time Object Request Brokers*, Journal of Real-Time Systems, special issue on Real-Time Computing in the Age of the Web and the Internet, Ed.: A. Stoyen, Kluwer, 2000

[Sol98] D.A. Solomon: *Inside Windows NT*, 2nd Edition, Microsoft Press, 1998

[Som97] P. Sommerlad: *Manager*, in [PLoPD3], 1997

[SPM98] A.R Silva, J.D. Pereira, J.A. Marques: *Object Recovery*, in [PLoPD3], 1998

[SPM99] A.R Silva, J.D. Pereira, J.A. Marques: *Object Synchronizer*, in [PLoPD4], 1998

[SRPKB00] D.C. Schmidt, C. O'Ryan, I. Pyarali, M. Kircher, and F. Buschmann, *Leader/Followers: A Design Pattern for Efficient Multi-Threaded Event Demultiplexing and Dispatching*, Proceedings of the 7th Pattern Language of Programming Conference, PLoP, Allerton Park, Illinois, USA, August 2000

[SRZ99]   M. Schütze, J.P. Riegel, G. Zimmermann: *PSiGene – A Pattern-Based Component Generator for Building Simulation*, Theory and Practice of Object Systems (TAPOS), vol. 5, no. 2, 1999

[SS99]   D. Sheresh, B. Sheresh: *Understanding Directory Services*, New Riders Publishing, 1999

[Stal00]   M. Stal: *The Activator Design Pattern*, http://www.posa.uci.edu/, 2000

[Ste93]   W.R. Stevens: *TCP/IP Illustrated, Volume 1*, Addison-Wesley, 1993

[Ste96]   W.R. Stevens: *TCP/IP Illustrated, Volume 3*, Addison-Wesley, 1996

[Ste98]   W.R. Stevens: *Unix Network Programming, Volume 1: Networking APIs: Sockets and XTI, Second Edition*, Prentice Hall, 1998

[Ste99]   W.R. Stevens: *Unix Network Programming, Volume 2: Interprocess Communications*, 2nd Edition, Prentice Hall, 1999

[Str97]   B. Stroustrup: *The C++ Programming Language*, 3rd Edition, Addison-Wesley 1997

[Sun88]   Sun Microsystems: *Remote Procedure Call Protocol Specification*, Sun Microsystems, Inc., RFC-1057, June 1988

[Sun99a]   Sun Microsystems: *The Jini Architecture Specification (AR)*, Version 1.0.1, http://www.sun.com/jini/specs/jini101.html, November 1999

[Sun99b]   Sun Microsystems: *The Jini Distributed Event Specification (EV)*, Version 1.0.1, http://www.sun.com/jini/specs/event101.html, November 1999

[Sun00a]   Sun Microsystems: *Java 2 Platform, Standard Edition Documentation*, http://java.sun.com/products/jdk/1.3/docs/index.html, May 2000

[Sun00b]   Sun Microsystems: *Java 2 Platform, Sun Community Source Licensing*, http://www.sun.com/software/communitysource/java2/, May 2000

[SV96a]   D.C. Schmidt, S. Vinoski: *Comparing Alternative Programming Techniques for Multi-Threaded CORBA Servers: Thread-per-Request*, C++ Report, vol. 8, no. 2, February 1996

[SV96b]   D.C. Schmidt, S. Vinoski: *Comparing Alternative Programming Techniques for Multi-Threaded CORBA Servers: Thread Pool*, C++ Report, vol. 8, no. 4, February 1996

[SV96c]   D.C. Schmidt, S. Vinoski: *Comparing Alternative Programming Techniques for Multi-Threaded CORBA Servers: Thread-per-Object*, C++ Report, vol. 8, no. 7, July 1996

[SV98a]   D.C. Schmidt, S. Vinoski: *Using the Portable Object Adapter for Transient and Persistent CORBA Objects*, C++ Report, vol. 10, no. 4, April 1998

[SV98b]   D.C. Schmidt, S. Vinoski: *Introduction to CORBA Messaging*, C++ Report, vol. 10, November/December 1998

[SW94]   W.R. Stevens, G Wright: *TCP/IP Illustrated, Volume 2*, Addison-Wesley, 1994

[Tan92]   A.S. Tanenbaum: *Modern Operating Systems*, Prentice Hall, 1992

[Tan95]   A.S. Tanenbaum: *Distributed Operating Systems*, Prentice Hall, 1995

[Tichy98]   W.F. Tichy: *A Catalogue of General-Purpose Design Patterns*, Proceedings of the 23rd conference on the Technology of Object-Oriented Languages and Systems (TOOLS 23), IEEE Computer Society, 1998

[TM00]   W.F Tichy, M. Müller: *Ausgewählte Kapitel der Softwaretechnik*, Universität Karlsruhe, LV no. 24646, Universität Karlsruhe, 2000

[ToSi89]   C. Tomlinson, V. Singh: *Inheritance and Synchronization with Enabled-Sets*, OOPSLA '89 Conference Proceedings, pp. 103–112, October 1998

[Tow99]   D. Towell: *Display Maintenance: A Pattern Language*, in [PLoPD4], 1999

[U2]   U2: *even BETTER than the REAL THING*, Island Records Ltd., 1991

[VaLa97]   G. Varghese, T. Lauck: *Hashed and Hierarchical Timing Wheels: Data Structures for the Efficient Implementation of a Timer Facility*, IEEE Transactions on Networking, December 1997

[Vin98]   S. Vinoski: *New Features for CORBA 3.0*, Communications of the ACM, vol. 41, no. 10, pp. 44–52, October 1998

[Vlis98a]   J. Vlissides: *Pattern Hatching – Design Patterns Applied*, Addison-Wesley, 1998

[Vlis98b]   J. Vlissides: *Composite Design Patterns (They Aren't What You Think)*, C++ Report, June 1998

[Vlis98c]   J. Vlissides: *Pluggable Factory, Pt. 1*, C++ Report, November/December 1998

[Wal00]   E. Wallingford: *The Elementary Patterns Home Page*, http://www.cs.uni.edu/~wallingf/patterns/elementary/, 2000

[WHO91]   W. Wilson Ho, R.A. Olsson: *An Approach to Genuine Dynamic Linking*, Software: Practice and Experience, vol. 21, no. 4, pp. 375–390, April 1991

[WRW96]   A. Wollrath, R. Riggs, and J. Waldo: *A Distributed Object Model for the Java System*, in Proceedings of the 1996 USENIX Conference on Object-Oriented Technologies (COOTS), Toronto, Canada, 1996

[WS95]   G.W Wright, W.R. Stevens: *TCP/IP Illustrated, Volume 2*, Addison-Wesley, 1995

[WSV99]   N. Wang, D.C. Schmidt, S, Vinoski: *Collocation Optimizations for CORBA*, C++ Report, vol. 11, no. 9, October 1999

[W3C98]   W3C HTTP-NG Working Group: *W3C HTTP-NG Protocol*, www.w3.org/ Protocols/HTTP-NG, 1998

[YB99]   J. Yoder, J. Barcalow: *Architectural Patterns for Enabling Application Security*, in [PLoPD4], 1999

[ZBS97]   J. A. Zinky, D.E. Bakken, R. Schantz: *Architectural Support for Quality of Service for CORBA Objects*, Theory and Practice of Object Systems, vol. 3, no. 1, John Wiley & Sons, 1997

[Zweig90]   J.M. Zweig: *The Conduit: a Communication Abstraction in C++*, Proceedings of the 2nd USENIC C++ Conference, pp. 191–203, USENIX Association, April 1990

Index of Patterns

Index

Index of Names